The State of the Art
in Intrusion Prevention
and Detection

The State of the Art in Intrusion Prevention and Detection

Edited by
Al-Sakib Khan Pathan

CRC Press
Taylor & Francis Group
Boca Raton   London   New York

CRC Press is an imprint of the
Taylor & Francis Group, an **informa** business
AN AUERBACH BOOK

CRC Press
Taylor & Francis Group
6000 Broken Sound Parkway NW, Suite 300
Boca Raton, FL 33487-2742

First issued in paperback 2016

© 2014 by Taylor & Francis Group, LLC
CRC Press is an imprint of Taylor & Francis Group, an Informa business

No claim to original U.S. Government works

Version Date: 20131114

ISBN 13: 978-1-138-03398-6 (pbk)
ISBN 13: 978-1-4822-0351-6 (hbk)

Library of Congress Cataloging-in-Publication Data

The state of the art in intrusion prevention and detection / edited by Al-Sakib Khan Pathan.
       pages cm
    Includes bibliographical references and index.
    ISBN 978-1-4822-0351-6 (hbk. : alk. paper)
      1. Computer security. 2. Computers--Access control. 3. Computer networks--Security measures.
    I. Pathan, Al-Sakib Khan.

    QA76.9.A25 S7354
    005.8--dc23   2013030986

Visit the Taylor & Francis Web site at
http://www.taylorandfrancis.com

and the CRC Press Web site at
http://www.crcpress.com

Dedicated to

_____

"All the seekers of knowledge and the truth"

Al-Sakib Khan Pathan

Contents

SECTION I   Network Traffic Analysis and Management for IDS

SECTION II   IDS Issues for Different Infrastructures

SECTION III   Artificial Intelligence Techniques for IDS

SECTION IV   IDS for Wireless Systems

Preface

INTRODUCTION

Most of the security threats in various communications networks are posed by the illegitimate entities that enter or intrude within the network perimeter, which could commonly be termed as *intruders*. Sometimes a legitimate entity in a system could also be compromised in some way so that an *attacker-intended* task could be performed for breaching the security of the system. To tackle intrusions of various kinds, we commonly hear about intrusion detection systems (IDSs) and intrusion prevention systems (IPSs) or a combination of both called IDPS (intrusion detection and prevention systems). The main task of an IDS is to defend a computer system or computer network by detecting an attack and possibly repelling it. Successful detection of hostile attacks depends on the number and type of appropriate actions. On the other hand, intrusion prevention requires a well-selected combination of *baiting and trapping* aimed at the investigations of threats. Diverting the intruder's attention from protected resources is another task. Both the real system and a possible trap system are constantly monitored. Various tasks and functionalities can be thought of under intrusion-related topics in computer, communications, or networking fields:

- Regular checking of the data in computers and systems
- Monitoring and analyzing network traffic
- Analyzing network configuration and vulnerabilities
- Assessing network and data integrity
- Ability to recognize patterns typical to attacks
- Tracking the network policy violations
- Analysis of abnormal activities
- Outside influence and its impact on a system's security

OBJECTIVE OF THE BOOK

This book compiles the latest trends and issues in intrusion tackling in computer networks and systems, especially in communications networks. It is written for graduate students in universities, researchers, academics, and industry practitioners working in the areas of wired or wireless networking or computer systems, who want to improve their understanding of the interrelated topics.

ABOUT TARGET AUDIENCE AND CONTENT

The target audience of this book is composed of students, professionals, and researchers working in the field of computer and network security especially. Moreover, the book includes some chapters written in a tutorial style so that general readers can be able to easily grasp some of the ideas in the relevant areas. There are a total of four sections of the book with a total of 19 chapters. These chapters have been contributed by authors from 12 countries.

Section I: Network Traffic Analysis and Management for IDS

- Chapter 1 - Outlier Detection
- Chapter 2 - Network Traffic Monitoring and Analysis

Section II: IDS Issues for Different Infrastructures

Section III: Artificial Intelligence Techniques for IDS

Section IV: IDS for Wireless Systems

The first section contains four chapters, which deal with traffic analysis and management for intrusion detection systems. Concepts such as honeypots, honeynets, network traffic analysis, and the basics of outlier detection are discussed in these chapters. The second section has six chapters that discuss different kinds of IDSs for different infrastructures. The chapters in this section also cover new and emerging technologies and systems such as smart grids, cyber physical systems (CPSs), cloud computing, hardware techniques for high performance intrusion detection, and so on. The third section, with three chapters, is dedicated to artificial intelligence (AI)–related intrusion detection techniques. The fourth section covers intrusion tackling mechanisms for various wireless systems and networks such as wireless sensor networks (WSNs), WiFi (wireless-fidelity), wireless automation systems, and other wireless systems. This section contains six chapters.

MATLAB® is a registered trademark of The MathWorks, Inc. For product information, please contact:

The MathWorks, Inc.
3 Apple Hill Drive
Natick, MA 01760-2098 USA
Tel: (508) 647-7000
Fax: (508) 647-7001
E-mail: info@mathworks.com
Web: http://www.mathworks.com

Acknowledgments

I am very much grateful to the Almighty Allah to allow me the time to complete another work of such kind. The entire process has been lengthy, needing non-stop work, interaction with several people in various ways, and firm determination. I am thankful to all the authors, reviewers, and critics who helped me shape the book in a better way. My hearty thanks should go to my loving wife, Labiba Mahmud, who has supported me all throughout the process. Last but not least, I thank the publisher and publication staff for giving me this opportunity and assisting me to work on this book project.

Best wishes,

Al-Sakib Khan Pathan, PhD
Department of Computer Science
International Islamic University Malaysia, Malaysia

Editor

Al-Sakib Khan Pathan received a PhD degree in computer engineering in 2009 from Kyung Hee University, South Korea. He received a BSc degree in computer science and information technology from Islamic University of Technology (IUT), Bangladesh, in 2003. He is currently an assistant professor in the computer science department at International Islamic University Malaysia (IIUM), Malaysia. Until June 2010, he served as an assistant professor in the computer science and engineering department in BRAC University, Bangladesh. Prior to holding this position, he worked as a researcher at Networking Lab, Kyung Hee University, South Korea, until August 2009. His research interests include wireless sensor networks, network security, and e-services technologies. He is a recipient of several awards/best paper awards and has several publications in these areas. He has served as a chair, organizing committee member, and technical program committee member in numerous international conferences or workshops such as GreenCom, HPCS, ICA3PP, IWCMC, VTC, HPCC, IDCS, etc. He is currently serving as the editor-in-chief of *IJIDS*, an area editor of *IJCNIS*, editor of *IJCSE, Interscience*, associate editor of *IASTED/ACTA Press IJCA and CCS*, guest editor of some special issues of top-ranked journals, and editor/author of nine books. He also serves as a referee of some renowned journals. He is a member of the Institute of Electrical and Electronics Engineers (IEEE), USA; IEEE Communications Society, USA; IEEE ComSoc Bangladesh Chapter, and several other international professional organizations.

FULL CONTACT DETAILS

Al-Sakib Khan Pathan, PhD
Assistant Professor
Department of Computer Science, KICT
International Islamic University Malaysia (IIUM)
Jalan Gombak, 53100, Kuala Lumpur, Malaysia
Tel: +603-61964000 Ext. 5653, Cell: +60163910754
E-Mail: spathan@ieee.org, sakib@iium.edu.my, sakib.pathan@gmail.com
Personal URL: http://staff.iium.edu.my/sakib/
NDC Lab URL: http://staff.iium.edu.my/sakib/ndclab/

Contributors

Mohiuddin Ahmed
School of Engineering and Information
  Technology
The University of New South Wales
Canberra, Australia

Tarem Ahmed
Department of Computer Science
International Islamic University Malaysia (IIUM)
Kuala Lumpur, Malaysia

Adnan Anwar
School of Engineering and Information
  Technology
The University of New South Wales
Canberra, Australia

Alaa Atassi
Department of Electrical and Computer
  Engineering
American University of Beirut
Beirut, Lebanon

Mohamed Azab
The City of Scientific Research and
  Technological Applications
Alexandria, Egypt

and

Virginia Polytechnic Institute and State
  University
Blacksburg, Virginia

Ali Chehab
Department of Electrical and Computer
  Engineering
American University of Beirut
Beirut, Lebanon

Imad H. Elhajj
Department of Electrical and Computer
  Engineering
American University of Beirut
Beirut, Lebanon

Mohamed Eltoweissy
Pacific Northwest National Laboratory
Richland, Washington

and

Virginia Polytechnic Institute and State
  University
Blacksburg, Virginia

Amrita Ghosal
Department of Computer Science and
  Engineering
Dr. B. C. Roy Engineering College
Durgapur, India

Subir Halder
Department of Computer Science and
  Engineering
Dr. B. C. Roy Engineering College
Durgapur, India

Jiankun Hu
School of Engineering and Information
  Technology
The University of New South Wales
Canberra, Australia

Zahra Jadidi
School of Information and Communication
  Technology
Griffith University
Queensland, Australia

Weirong Jiang
Xilinx Research Labs
San Jose, California

Ayman Kayssi
Department of Electrical and Computer
  Engineering
American University of Beirut
Beirut, Lebanon

Zbigniew Kotulski
Faculty of Electronics and Information
    Technology
Warsaw University of Technology
Warsaw, Poland

Jana Krimmling
System Design Department
Innovations for High Performance
    Microelectronics
Frankfurt, Germany

Przemysław Kukiełka
Research and Development Department
Polish Telecom
Warsaw, Poland

Lam-For Kwok
Department of Computer Science
City University of Hong Kong
Hong Kong, SAR, China

Peter Langendörfer
System Design Department
Innovations for High Performance
    Microelectronics
Frankfurt, Germany

Lee Luan Ling
School of Electrical and Computer Engineering
State University of Campinas
Campinas, Brazil

Abdun Naser Mahmood
School of Engineering and Information
    Technology
The University of New South Wales
Canberra, Australia

Mohammad Saiful Islam Mamun
School of Information Science
Japan Advanced Institute of Science and
    Technology
Nomi, Japan

Kieran McLaughlin
Institute of Electronics, Communications and
    Information Technology
Queen's University Belfast
Belfast, United Kingdom

Yuxin Meng
Department of Computer Science
City University of Hong Kong
Hong Kong, SAR, China

Jonny Milliken
The Institute of Electronics, Communications
    and Information Technology
Queen's University Belfast
Belfast, United Kingdom

Mohssen Mohammed
College of Computer and Information Sciences
Al-Imam Muhammad ibn Saud Islamic
    University
Riyadh, Saudi Arabia

Asit More
ABV-Indian Institute of Information
    Technology and Management
Gwalior, India

Vallipuram Muthukkumarasamy
School of Information and Communication
    Technology
Griffith University
Queensland, Australia

Al-Sakib Khan Pathan
Department of Computer Science
International Islamic University Malaysia
Kuala Lumpur, Malaysia

Bernardi Pranggono
Department of Computer, Communications and
    Interactive Systems
Glasgow Caledonian University
Glasgow, United Kingdom

Viktor K. Prasanna
University of Southern California
Los Angeles, California

Sakir Sezer
Institute of Electronics, Communications and
    Information Technology
Queen's University Belfast
Belfast, United Kingdom

Elankayer Sithirasenan
School of Information and Communication
    Technology
Griffith University
Queensland, Australia

Jeferson Wilian de Godoy Stênico
School of Electrical and Computer Engineering
State University of Campinas
Campinas, Brazil

Shashikala Tapaswi
ABV-Indian Institute of Information
    Technology and Management
Gwalior, India

Yang Xiang
School of Information Technology
Deakin University
Melbourne, Australia

Yi Yang
Institute of Electronics, Communications and
    Information Technology
Queen's University Belfast
Belfast, United Kingdom

Steven Zittrower
Department of Electrical Engineering and
    Computer Science
University of Central Florida
Orlando, Florida

Cliff C. Zou
Department of Electrical Engineering and
    Computer Science
University of Central Florida
Orlando, Florida

Section I

Network Traffic Analysis and
Management for IDS

1 Outlier Detection

Mohiuddin Ahmed, Abdun Naser Mahmood, and Jiankun Hu

CONTENTS

1.1   INTRODUCTION

Outlier detection is an important data analysis task. It is used in many domains to identify interesting and emerging patterns, trends, and anomalies from data. Outlier detection is used to detect anomalies in many different domains, including computer network intrusion; gene expression analysis; disease onset identification, including cancer detection; financial fraud detection; and human behavioral analysis. Among the four primary tasks of data mining, outlier detection is the closest to the motivation of data mining as discovering interesting patterns and modeling relationships are the main aims of data mining research. Outlier detection, also known as anomaly detection, deviation detection, novelty detection, and exception mining, has been widely studied in data mining as well as in statistics and machine learning.

An outlier is a special event or object that is not similar to the rest of the data. Outliers are considered to be important because they may represent significant information that often requires critical actions to be taken in a wide range of application domains. For example, an outlier in a MRI image may indicate the presence of a malignant tumor. Abnormal behaviors in credit card transactions could indicate forgery, and an unusual traffic pattern in a network could mean that a computer is hacked and it is transmitting classified data to an unauthorized destination.

Computer intrusion includes hacking and spreading of viruses and worms across networks to infiltrate a local or remote machine or to cause damage using distributed denial of service (DDoS) attacks. However, an intrusion constitutes only a small percentage of the total network and computer usage that is considered normal usage. This small number of intrusion activities is very different from normal or regular user activities and hence can easily be detected using outlier detection techniques. Outlier detection can be used to identify malicious activities of programs as well as hackers from network traffic data and computer activities.

In this chapter, outlier detection has been introduced along with case studies and explanations of different outlier detection techniques. Existing outlier detection techniques based on various application domains have been discussed. This chapter intends to be a comprehensive reference in the field of intrusion detection and prevention. It can be used as a reference for academicians and also as a suitable textbook for final-year undergraduate and postgraduate students.

We begin in Section 1.2 with the basics of outlier detection. We provide definitions of "outlier" widely adapted in the field. Then we discuss the relationship with anomaly detection, data types, outlier types, evaluation methods, and research challenges.

In Section 1.3, we highlight the data labels and how outlier detection techniques are classified based on data labels. We also mention the output of outlier detection.

Section 1.4 includes the application domain of outlier detection. We discuss few important domains and have included one case study for intrusion detection.

In Section 1.5, we discuss clustering-based outlier detection methodologies. These techniques are classified into two groups based on their output. These are scoring-based and binary-based approaches. We also discuss the merits and demerits of these techniques.

In Section 1.6, statistical-based approaches for outlier detection are discussed in two broad categories, including their advantages and disadvantages. Finally, we conclude the chapter in Section 1.7 followed by necessary references.

1.2   BASICS OF OUTLIER DETECTION

1.2.1   DEFINITION

Out of four primary tasks of data mining, outlier detection is the closest to the motivation of data mining for discovering interesting patterns. Outlier detection has been widely researched from not only the data mining perspective, but also in statistics and machine learning [1]. One widely accepted definition of "outlier" is given by Hawkins [2]. According to him, "An outlier is an observation which deviates so much from other observations as to arouse suspicions that it was generated by a different mechanism." Barnett and Lewis [3] defined outlier: "An outlier is an observation or subset of observations which appears to be inconsistent with the remainder of data." Outlier detection is also defined specifically for different methods such as the following:

Clustering-based outlier: Outliers are the points that do not belong to clusters of a data set or as clusters that are significantly smaller than other clusters [4,5].

Depth-based outlier: Outliers are the points in the shallow convex hull layers with the lowest depth [6].

Graph-based outlier: Outliers are the points that are present in particular positions in the graph [7].

Density-based outliers: Outliers are the points that lie in the lower local density with respect to the density of its local neighborhood [8].

Neural network–based outlier: Points that are not reproduced well at the output layer with high reconstruction error are considered as outliers [9].

Support vector machine–based outlier: Points that are distant from most other points or points that are present in relatively sparse regions of the feature space are considered as outliers [10].

Spatial outlier: A spatial outlier is a spatially referenced point whose non-spatial attribute values are significantly different from those of other spatially referenced points in its spatial neighborhood [11].

1.2.2 RELATIONSHIP WITH ANOMALY DETECTION

Outlier detection is also named as anomaly detection, deviation detection, novelty detection, exception mining, etc. Outlier detection and anomaly detection are almost the same, but outliers are more focused on data and follow strict rules, for example, in normally distributed data, $\mu + 3\sigma$ is considered as an outlier. Anomalous events have no objection to fall under rules. For example, one goes to play lawn tennis every afternoon in a month, but if the same person plays table tennis one afternoon instead of lawn tennis, that can be considered as an anomalous event. If we consider this event in a data set, then this can be detected as an outlier. So, anomalies and outliers are related to each other and hence can be researched together.

1.2.3 DATA TYPES

One important issue of outlier detection is the nature of data. In outlier detection, perspective data is also regarded as a point, object, record, vector, sample, observation, etc. Each data instance can be explained with a group of features or attributes. Basically, the attributes form a data instance and its characteristics. Attributes can be binary, continuous, or categorical. Each data instance can be comprised of different types of attributes. Generally, there are two types of data, simple and complex.

1.2.3.1 Simple Data

Simple data are the most commonly used data with low dimensionality and real-valued attributes. Almost all outlier detection techniques can be applied to simple data.

1.2.3.2 Complex Data

Complex data creates significant challenges for outlier detection techniques due to their nature. Complex data has a mixture of different types of attributes with high dimensions. Sequence data, spatial data, streaming data, and spatio-temporal data are generally considered to be complex.

1.2.4   TYPES OF OUTLIERS

Based on data and detection techniques, outliers can be categorized into the following groups:

1.2.4.1   Point Outliers

When a particular data instance does not follow the rest of the data, it can be considered as a point outlier. For a realistic example, we can consider expenditure on car fuel. If usual fuel consumption per day is five liters and one day it becomes 50 liters, then obviously it is a point outlier. Figure 1.1 elucidates the point outlier concept.

1.2.4.2   Contextual Outliers

When a data instance is behaving anomalously in a particular context and not otherwise, then it is termed as a contextual outlier, which can also be referred to as a conditional outlier. For example, the expenditure on a credit card during a festive period is not like at a regular time of the year. If the regular expenditure every month is $500, which is normal, then an expenditure of $2000 during a nonfestive period is considered abnormal and hence is a contextual outlier (Figure 1.2).

1.2.4.3   Collective Outliers

When a collection of similar data instances are behaving anomalously, then with respect to the entire data set that collection is termed a collective outlier. It might happen that the individual data instance is not an outlier by itself, but due to its presence in a collection, it is becoming an outlier.

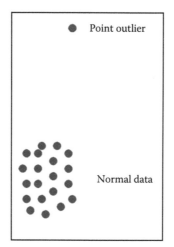

FIGURE 1.1   Point outlier.

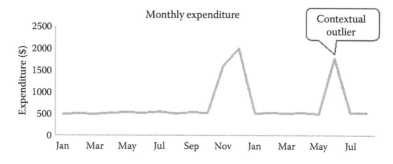

FIGURE 1.2   Contextual outlier.

For example, in a human electrocardiogram output, the existence of a low value for a long period of time indicates an outlying phenomenon corresponding to abnormal premature contraction [12]. But one low value itself is not an outlier.

1.2.5 EVALUATION METHODS

Outlier detection techniques are evaluated mainly in the following ways:

1.2.5.1 ROC Curve

A receiver operating characteristic (ROC) curve [13] is a 2-D graph used to show detection rates and false alarm rates. Detection rate defines the correctly identified outliers whereas a false alarm rate is the opposite. Figure 1.3 represents an ideal ROC curve in which the detection rate is high, and the false alarm rate is very low.

1.2.5.2 Computational Complexity

Efficiency of outlier detection methods can be also computed by computational cost, which seems to be a universal method. An efficient technique is reflected on its time and space complexity regardless of type of data. Moreover, efficient techniques should have the ability to handle large and high dimensional data with a lower computational burden.

1.2.5.3 User-Defined Parameters

Existing outlier detection techniques require user-defined parameters, which are very critical for effectiveness and efficiency. The optimal parameter choice is not always easy and requires extensive testing. Therefore, the minimal use of user-defined parameters is more applicable for outlier detection methods.

1.2.6 RESEARCH CHALLENGES

Although outlier detection seems to be very straightforward as we just have to find the data that do not follow the normal behavioral pattern. But there are still some research challenges regardless of so many techniques available. Research challenges are as follows:

a) No universal outlier detection technique is available. One technique in a domain is not suitable for others. For example, in the medical domain, outliers are very subtle whereas in image processing it might be considered as a normal phenomenon.
b) Data contains noise, which tends to be anomalous and hence difficult to segregate.
c) Labeled data for training of models used by many techniques are hardly available.

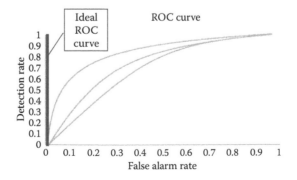

FIGURE 1.3 ROC curves.

d) Normal behaviors keep evolving; hence normal behavior once is not normal forever. Thus current outlier detection techniques might be of no use in the future.
e) When outliers are caused by fraudulent activities, the malicious adversaries try to make abnormal activities appear normal; thus such behaviors are difficult to detect.

For these above-mentioned challenges, outlier detection is not an easy problem to solve. Most of the existing techniques are based on application domain and the nature of data. Researchers from diversified disciplines have adopted miscellaneous concepts to solve these problems.

1.3 DATA LABELS

Data labels associated with each data instance specify the status of the data, i.e., normal or abnormal. We discussed in Section 1.6 about the challenges, and we mentioned it is very expensive to obtain labeled data. Data labeling is handled by human experts or analysts, and hence it becomes a difficult job to get prelabeled data for outlier detection. Moreover, some outliers cannot be labeled because of dynamic characteristics. Based on labeling, outlier detection is categorized into three of the following categories:

1.3.1 SUPERVISED OUTLIER DETECTION

These approaches require the learning of normal and outlying models from the knowledge of prelabeled data. According to this learning, supervised techniques detect a new data instance as normal or outlying. Actually it is tested with the normal and outlying models and checks where it is fitted. Supervised approaches are basically used in intrusion detection, but gaining access to prelabeled data is the main challenge of these approaches.

1.3.2 UNSUPERVISED OUTLIER DETECTION

These approaches do not require any prelabeled data to detect outliers. For example, in normally distributed data, we use the three-sigma rule to detect outliers. Some methodologies use distance to detect outliers without any prelabeled data. Compared with supervised approaches, unsupervised approaches are more applicable in various real life domains.

1.3.3 SEMISUPERVISED OUTLIER DETECTION

These approaches require prelabeled data but only normal class. These approaches do not require the outlying class data to be labeled beforehand, thus these approaches can be widely applicable and more usable than supervised techniques. There are many situations in which outlying scenarios are difficult to model, like in spacecraft fault detection [14] in which accidents are outlying events, which are difficult to model. So, semisupervised approaches detect outliers by comparing new data points with the prelabeled normal class.

1.3.4 OUTPUT OF OUTLIER DETECTION

One important issue in outlier detection is how the outliers are represented as output. Generally, there are these two following categories:

Scores: Scoring-based outlier detection techniques assign an outlier score to each of the data instances. Then the scores are ranked, and an analyst uses them to decide the outliers or use a threshold to select outliers.
Binary: According to these techniques, outputs are considered in a binary fashion, i.e., either outlier or nonoutlier.

Techniques that provide binary labels are computationally efficient because each of the data instances do not have to provide an outlier score.

1.4 APPLICATION DOMAINS

Outlier detection has been widely applied in various application domains. We highlight a few important domains here.

1.4.1 INTRUSION DETECTION

Computer intrusion includes hacking and spreading of viruses and worms across networks to infiltrate a local or remote machine or cause damage using distributed denial of service (DDoS) attacks. However, intrusions constitute only a small percentage of the total network and computer usage. Outlier detection can be used to identify malicious activities of programs as well as hackers [15] from network traffic data and computer activities. Outlier detection techniques need to be computationally efficient to handle large-sized input data, which also causes a false alarm rate. The data that come in a streaming fashion requires online analysis. IDS are classified into two groups. These are host based and network based. The major differences between them are in the nature of outliers, profiling, and data analysis.

1.4.1.1 Case Study: Haystack

The Haystack prototype [16] was developed for intrusion detection in a multiuser US Air Force computer system. It was a Unisys 1100/60 mainframe computer with an OS/1100 operating system. Haystack was designed to identify six different types of intrusions:

a) Malicious use: Sundry attacks like deletion of files, resource misuse, etc.
b) Denial of service: Keeping the resource unavailable to other users.
c) Penetration of security control systems: Attempts to handle the security characteristics of the system by a user.
d) Leakage: Transferring important data from the system.
e) Masquerade attacks: When an unauthorized user attempts to assume the identity of another user.
f) Attempted break-ins: When an unauthorized user wants to access the computer illegally.

To detect these six types of intrusions, the system uses outlier detection techniques. For Haystack, it is supervised outlier detection as the past behaviors are modeled using prelabeled data.

1.4.2 FRAUD DETECTION

Fraud detection considers the criminal activities in commercial organizations. The most vulnerable areas of fraudulent activities are credit cards, cell phones, insurance claims, and insider trading. Stolen credit cards are used in a more unusual way than the normal pattern. The usage behavior of the stolen credit card is not like that of the regular user. The identification of such activities helps prevent thieves and reduces the monetary loss of the individual [17]. To prevent the misuse of a mobile phone account, it is necessary to detect the unusual usage pattern. The basic function is to monitor the calling behavior of each account and issue an alarm when an account appears to be misused. Automobile insurance fraud is a very common crime. Criminal rings of illegal claimants and providers manipulate the claim processing system for unauthorized claims. Tracking such activities helps the company to avoid financial losses. Neural network–based techniques are applied to detect such activities [18,19]. In recent times, the stock market business attracted enough mass people. Insider trading is a criminal activity in business, in which profit is made by inside information before it is made public [20].

1.4.3 Medical and Public Health

Anomalous records can be generated due to patient condition or instrumental error or recording errors. A wrong test report might have serious repercussions. On the other hand, outlier detection in this domain is a very important tool that can potentially save human lives [21] by detecting a problem early from test results and images. The most challenging aspect of the outlier detection problem is that the cost of classifying an outlier as normal can be very high. Outlier detection in this domain requires maximum accuracy. The data consists of different attributes of a patient, such as age, blood pressure, weight, and height. Most of the techniques use a semisupervised approach. Collective anomaly detection techniques have been used to detect anomalies in time series data, such as electrocardiograms (ECGs) and electroencephalograms (EEGs).

1.4.4 Sensor Networks

A sensor network might comprise a multiple number of sensors in which each sensor collects different types of data. The collected data often contains noise and missing values due to limitations created by environmental and communication channels. Outlier detection in a sensor network has several real-life applications, such as environmental monitoring, habitat monitoring, industrial monitoring, target tracking, surveillance monitoring, etc. Conventional outlier detection techniques might not be suitable for handling sensor data for the following reasons: resource constraints, high communication costs, distributed streaming, dynamic network topology, large-scale deployment, etc. [22].

1.4.5 Image Processing

This domain includes satellite imagery [23], digit recognition [24], and mammographic image analysis [25]. The outliers are generated by motion or instrumental faults. The data has spatial as well as temporal characteristics. Each data point has continuous attributes like color, lightness, texture, etc. Interesting outliers are supposed to be anomalous points or a particular region of the image. The main challenge of this domain is to deal with large-size input data.

   The above-mentioned domains are not the end. Outlier detection is also applied to several other domains like astronomical data [26], biological data [27], speech recognition [28], robot behavior [29], and many more.

1.5 CLUSTERING-BASED OUTLIER DETECTION TECHNIQUES

Clustering is a way of grouping similar objects in a group. Using clustering techniques, many outlier detection techniques have been proposed by various researchers. Here in this section, we classify these techniques based on output.

1.5.1 Binary Output

Knorr and Ng et al. [30] presented the algorithms to detect distance-based outliers. They consider a data point O in a data set T, a $DB(p;D)$ outlier, if at least a fraction p of the data points in T lies greater than distance D from O. Their index-based algorithm executes a range search with radius D for each data point. If the number of data points in its D neighborhood exceeds a threshold, the search stops, and that data point is declared as a nonoutlier; otherwise, it is an outlier. In their cell-based approach, they quantize the complete data space and assign the data points to the cells. By pruning away a large number of red cells that contain too many data points and their immediate neighbors, their approach avoids testing unnecessary cells and speeds up outlier detection. Their experiments show that their cell-based algorithm is the most efficient when the number of dimensions is less than or equal to four. However, for a higher number of dimensions (>5), the number of cells grows exponentially, and the nested loop that they provided in the same paper outperforms the cell-based algorithm.

Yang et al. [31] attempted to automatically detect novel events from a temporally ordered stream of news stories, either retrospectively or as the stories arrive. The objective is to identify stories in several continuous news streams that belong to previously unidentified events. This can be done in an online fashion, i.e., as the events occur or as an accumulated collection. In retrospective event detection, stories are grouped together, and each cluster uniquely identifies an event. In online event detection, each document is labeled, and a single pass algorithm (INCR) generates a nonhierarchical partition of the input collection. The former is appropriate for retrospective event detection whereas the latter can be used for both. A story is represented using a vector of weighted terms. The normalized vector sum of documents in a cluster is used to represent the cluster, and it is called a prototype or centroid. The standard cosine similarity measure is used to describe the similarity of a cluster centroid and a document. GAC is an agglomerative algorithm that maximizes the average similarity between document pairs in the resulting clusters. At each iteration, it divides the current set of clusters into buckets and does local clustering within each bucket. The process is repeated and generates clusters at higher and higher levels until a predefined number of clusters are obtained. The input to the algorithm is a set of documents, and the output is a forest of cluster trees with the number of trees specified by the user. Clusters are produced by growing a binary tree using the bottom-up approach. Novelty detection is used in the case of single-pass clustering. The algorithm sequentially processes the input documents, one at a time, and grows clusters incrementally. A new document is classified to its most similar cluster if the similarity exceeds a predefined threshold; otherwise, it becomes the seed for a new cluster. By adjusting the threshold, one can obtain clusters at different levels of granularity.

David et al. [32] proposed clustering based on multivariate outlier detection by using Mahalanobis distance. At first, calculate the Mahalanobis distance for n observations on P variables. Then determine the observations that are above the upper control limit (UCL) of the T-square statistic [33] and consider those observations to be outlier cluster 1. Repeat the same procedure until the nature of the variance-covariance matrix for the variables in the last cluster achieves singularity. Their experimental data was comprised of 19 different attributes about a two-wheeler company in India, and data was collected from 275 two-wheeler users.

$$(\text{Mahalanobis distance})_i = \sqrt{(X_i - X_{mean})^T S^{-1}(X_i - X_{mean})} \tag{1.1}$$

$$T_i^2 = (X_i - X_{mean})^T S^{-1}(X_i - X_{mean}) \tag{1.2}$$

Zoubi et al. [34] proposed fuzzy clustering-based outlier detection. At first they execute a fuzzy clustering algorithm [35] to produce a set of k clusters and objective function and calculate a threshold from the average distances between each point in the cluster. Then they determine the small cluster and consider them as outliers. For the rest of the data, they remove a point and recalculate the objective function. If the change in objective function is greater than the threshold, then the point is considered as an outlier. They worked with iris data and bupa data from a UCI machine-learning repository [36]. Their approach of calculating the threshold from average has no significant explanation and hence might result in poor performance in large-scale high-dimensional data sets. The objective function for FCM is

$$J(U, c_1, \ldots c_c) = \sum_{i=1}^{c} J_i = \sum_{i=j}^{c} \sum_{j}^{n} u_{ij}^m d_{ij}^2 \tag{1.3}$$

Another clustering-based approach by Zoubi et al. [39] used partition around medoid (PAM), a data order–independent algorithm, to provide a set of clusters and a set of medoids (cluster center). Small clusters are then determined as outliers. The definition of a small cluster includes the clusters with fewer points than half of the average number of points in k clusters. There is no justification of the calculation or any proof for this small cluster determination. Then, to detect outliers in the rest of the data, a threshold value is calculated from the average of absolute distances between medoid and each point of each cluster. If a particular distance is greater than the threshold, it is considered as an outlier. Their experimental data was iris data and bupa data [36].

Yoon et al. [37] used k-means clustering on the complete data set, and to find the proper value of k, used cubic clustering criterion (CCC). CCC is a technique used to estimate the number of clusters evaluated by the Monte Carlo method. Once the clustering is done, the domain expert searches for external and internal outliers in the clustering results. External outliers are the data points positioned at a greater distance than other clusters, and internal outliers are the data points distantly positioned inside a cluster. If the removal of outliers creates meaningful clusters, then the procedure halts. Their approach has been applied only for software measurement data, and a domain expert is required for interpretation.

Loureior et al. [38] used hierarchical clustering to detect outliers. Their key idea is to use the size of resulting clusters as indicators of the presence of outliers. As their methodology is tested on the problem cleaning official statistics data and the goal is to detect erroneous foreign trade transaction in data collected by the Portuguese Institute of Statistics (INE), the outliers are the unusual values that are distant from the normal and more frequent observations and that, therefore, will be isolated in smaller clusters.

Jiang et al. [5] presented a two-phase clustering technique to detect outliers. First, they used a modified k-means algorithm to create clusters. If the points in the same cluster are not close enough, the cluster can be split into two smaller clusters and merged when a given threshold is exceeded. In the second step, they construct a minimum spanning tree with cluster centers and remove the longest edge. The smaller subtrees are considered as outliers. Their technique considers an entire cluster as an outlier, which may not be applicable for many data sets and increase the false positive rate.

Yu et al. [4] presented an approach, FindOut. Using the multi-resolution property of wavelet transforms, FindOut can successfully identify various percentages of outliers from large data sets. It can also detect the outliers for complicated data patterns with various densities. Furthermore, FindOut can handle high-dimensional data sets, which have not been addressed by most existing approaches.

Given a linear space system LSw and density function φ, a data point in a cell c is an outlier if $\hat{\varphi} w (c) < \tau$, where τ is given. For a data set, it defines a density function φ. Kernel function g is defined as follows:

$$G(c_i) = \begin{cases} 1 & \text{if } D(c_i, \overrightarrow{0}) \leq \epsilon \\ 0 & \text{otherwise} \end{cases} \tag{1.4}$$

where $\overrightarrow{0}$ is the origin in the data space, and D is a distance function. A linear system LSg is defined based on g. A data point oi in LSg is an outlier if $\hat{\varphi} g (oi) < p \times N$, where N is the size of the data points.

1.5.2 SCORING OUTPUT

He et al. [18] proposed another definition for cluster-based local outliers. According to their definition, all the data points in a certain cluster are considered as outliers rather than a single point as shown in Figure 1.4. The smaller clusters C1 and C3 are considered as outliers. They used some numeric

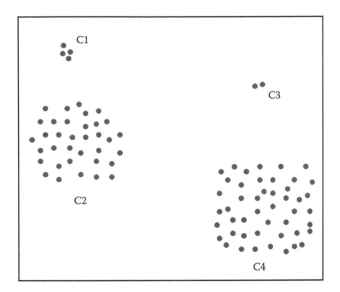

FIGURE 1.4 Cluster-based outlier. (From He, Z. et al., *Pattern Recognition Letters, 24*, 9–10, 1641, 2003.)

parameters, i.e., a and b, to identify small clusters (SC) and large clusters (LC). The clustering technique depends on these parameters, but it is not clear how the values can be set for various data sets. They used the SQUEEZER algorithm to cluster data as it achieves both a high quality of clustering and can handle high-dimensional data. Then, the FindCBLOF algorithm determines the outlier factor of each individual record in the data set. CBLOF(t) for each record t is calculated as follows:

$$\text{CBLOF}(t) = \begin{cases} |C_i| * \min\left(d(t, C_j)\right) \text{where } t \in C_i, C_i \in SC \text{ and } C_j \in LC \text{ for } j = 1 \text{ to } b \\ |C_i| * \left(d(t, C_i)\right) \text{where } t \in C_i \text{ and } C_i \in LC \end{cases} \quad (1.5)$$

Svetlona et al. [40] presented an outlier removal clustering (ORC) algorithm that provides outlier detection and data clustering simultaneously. Their proposed algorithm has two stages. At first the *k-means* clustering is applied and then an *outlyingness factor*, o_i, for each of the data points is calculated by taking the ratio of a point's distance to the centroid and the maximum distance from centroid to any other point. A threshold T is set less than one to check for outliers. If the outlying factor for any point is greater than the threshold, then it is considered as an outlier and removed from the data set. Their experimental data includes synthetic data and some map images. Mean absolute error (MAE) is used to evaluate algorithm performance. The parameter T value is dependent on the data set, which may cause poor performance in heterogeneous large-scale data sets.

$$o_i = \frac{x_i - C_{pi}}{d_{max}} \quad (1.6)$$

Ren et al. [41] proposed a vertical outlier detection algorithm with clusters as a byproduct. Their approach doesn't require beforehand clustering of the data; rather it is a one-time process. Outliers are measured by a local connective factor (LCF), which indicates how significantly the point connects with other points in a data set. LCF is calculated by a vertical data representation P tree. Outliers are the points that are not connected with clusters. They defined a neighborhood density factor to calculate the LCF of each point in the data set. Their experimental analysis was based on run times and scalability to data size and compared with two-phase clustering [5] and a cluster-based local outlier [18].

The LCF of the point P, denoted as LCF(P,r) is the ratio of $DF_{nbr}(P,r)$ over $DF_{cluster}(P,R)$.

$$LCF(P,r) = \frac{DF_{nbr}(P,r)}{DF_{cluster}(P,R)} \tag{1.7}$$

$Ol_{factor} = N(Nbr(P,r))*DF_{nbr}(P,r)$, where r is the radius of neighborhood of P.
The outlier set is denoted as

$$Ols(X, t) = \{x \in X \,|\, Ol_{factor}(x) < t\} \tag{1.8}$$

Fan et al. [42] introduced a nonparametric outlier detection technique for efficiently discovering top-n outliers from engineering data (2-D and 3-D synthetic data). Their algorithm generates reasonable outlier results by taking both local and global features of a data set into consideration. They proposed a resolution-based outlier factor (ROF) as

$$ROF(O) = \sum_{i=1}^{R} \frac{ClusterSize(O,r_{i-1}) - 1}{ClusterSize(O,r_i)} \tag{1.9}$$

where $r_0,.....,r_R$ is the resolution at each step. A resolution-based outlier mining algorithm works in two steps. At first, the RB-CLUSTER algorithm is used to cluster and label all the objects. Then the RB-MINE algorithm ranks the ROF values in an increasing order and obtains top-N outliers. The RB-outlier measures an object against its degree of outlyingness by taking both "global" and "local" features into account.

Breunig et al. [8] proposed an idea to assign each object a degree of being an outlier. This degree is called the local outlier factor (LOF). LOF depends on how isolated the object is with respect to the surrounding neighborhood. The local outlier factor of an object p is

$$LOF_{MinPts}^{(p)} = \frac{\sum_{o \in N_{MinPts}^{(p)}} \frac{lrd_{MinPts}(o)}{lrd_{MinPts}(p)}}{\left| N_{MinPts}(p) \right|} \tag{1.10}$$

This outlier factor of object p calculates the degree to which p can be called as an outlier. The outlier factor is the average of the ratio of the local reachability density of p and those of ps MinPts–nearest neighbors. The author also described mathematically the LOF for objects deep in a cluster along with general bounds (upper, lower, and tight). The impact of MinPts to calculate LOF is also elaborated with necessary examples. Their approach can intelligently choose the range of k; the LOF approach has a lower computational complexity than the depth-based approaches for large dimensionality.

Jin et al. [43] proposed an approach for mining only top-n local outliers because the LOF [45] values for every data object require a large number of k–nearest neighbor searches and can be very much computationally expensive. They proposed an efficient microcluster-based local outlier mining algorithm to find the top-n local outliers in a large database. A microcluster MC (n, c, and r) is a summarized representation of a group of data $p_1,...,p_n$, which are so close together that they are likely to belong to the same cluster. Here, $c = \frac{\sum_{i=1}^{n} p_i}{n}$, is the mean center while $r =$ max$\{d(p_i,c)\}$, $i = 1,...,n$, is the radius. Data are compressed into small clusters, and small clusters are represented using some statistical information as microclusters. Three different algorithms are used to find top-n local outliers. At first, k-distance bounds for each microcluster are computed. Then using these k-distance bounds, the LOF bound is calculated. Finally given an upper bound and a lower bound for the LOF of each microcluster, top-n local outliers are ranked.

Ramaswamy et al. [44] provided outlier definition based on the distance of a point from its kth nearest neighbor. They provided a ranking of top-n outliers by the measure of the outlierness of the points. According to them, top-n points with the maximum distance to their own kth nearest neighbor are considered as outliers. They also exploited index-based and nested-loop algorithms to detect outliers. Furthermore, they proposed a partition-based algorithm to prune and process the partitioned groups to improve efficiency for outlier detection. Their algorithm reduces the cost of computation in large, multidimensional data sets.

He et al. [45] introduced a new definition for outlier, the semantic outlier. A semantic outlier is a data point that behaves differently from the other data points in the same class. A measure for identifying the degree of each object being an outlier is presented, which is called the semantic outlier factor (SOF). To mine semantic outliers, an algorithm is also proposed. They used a SQUEEZER algorithm, which is used to produce good clusters for categorical data sets and then used their algorithm to calculate the SOF value for each of the objects. Their proposed outlier definition works by identifying the similarity between a specific set and a record. Given a set of records R and a record t, the similarity between R and t is defined as follows:

$$\mathrm{Sim}(t,R) = \frac{\sum_{i=1}^{|R|} similarity(t,T_i)}{|R|} \quad \text{where } \forall\ T_i \in R \quad (1.11)$$

The semantic outlier factor of a record t is defined as:

$$\mathrm{SOF}(t) = \frac{\Pr(cl_i|C_k) * sim(t,R)}{\Pr(cl_i|D)} \quad (1.12)$$

Spiros et al. [46] introduced local correlation integral (LOCI) for evaluating outlierness, which is very efficient in detecting outliers and groups of outliers. The main advantage of this approach is an automatic data-dictated cut-off to determine whether a point is an outlier. They introduced the multigranularity deviation factor (MDEF), which at radius r for a point p_i is the relative deviation of its local neighborhood density from the average local neighborhood density in its neighborhood.

$$\mathrm{MDEF}(p_i,r,\alpha) = 1 - \frac{n(p_i,\alpha r)}{\hat{n}(p_i,\alpha,r)} \quad (1.13)$$

A point is flagged as an outlier if for any $r \in [r_{\min}, r_{\max}]$ its MDEF is sufficiently large, i.e.,

$$\mathrm{MDEF}(p_i, r, \alpha) > k_\sigma \sigma_{MDEF}(p_i, r, \alpha) \quad (1.14)$$

Zhange et al. [47] proposed a new outlier detection definition, local distance-based outlier factor (LDOF), which is sensitive to outliers in scattered data sets. LDOF uses the relative distances from an object to its neighborhood to measure how much objects deviate from their scattered neighborhood. The higher the violation degree an object has, the more likely the object is an outlier. The local distance-based outlier factor of x_p is defined as

$$\mathrm{LDOF}_k(x_p) = \frac{\overline{d}_{x_p}}{\overline{D}_{x_p}} \quad (1.15)$$

where $\overline{d}_{x_p}$ the k-nearest neighbors are the distance of object x_p and $\overline{D}_{x_p}$ is the k-nearest neighbor's inner distance of x_p (Figure 1.5).

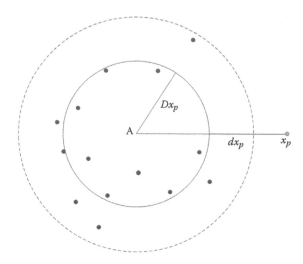

FIGURE 1.5 The explicit outlierness of object x_p with the help of LDOF definition. A is the center of the neighborhood system of x_p. The dashed circle includes all neighbors of x_p. The solid circle is x_p's "reformed" neighborhood region. (From Zhang, K. et al., In *Proc. PAKDD*, 2009.)

Kriegel et al. [48] formulated a local density-based outlier detection method providing an outlier "score" in the range of [0, 1] that is directly interpretable as a probability of a data object for being an outlier. The probabilistic local outlier factor (PLOF) of an object $o \in D$ w.r.t. a significance, a context set $S(o)$, can be defined as follows:

$$PLOF_{\lambda,S}(o) = \frac{pdist(\lambda, o, S(o))}{E_{s \in S(o)}[pdist(\lambda, s, S(s))]} - 1.$$ (1.16)

To achieve a normalization making the scaling of PLOF independent of the particular data distribution, the aggregate value nPLOF is obtained during PLOF computation.

$$nPLOF = \lambda . \sqrt{E[(PLOF)^2]}$$ (1.17)

Local outlier probability (LoOP), indicating the probability that a point $o \in D$ is an outlier:

$$LoOP_s(o) = \max \left\{ 0, erf \left(\frac{PLOF_{\lambda,s}(o)}{nPLOF . \sqrt{2}} \right) \right\}$$ (1.18)

1.5.3 ADVANTAGES AND DISADVANTAGES

The techniques used to detect outliers in binary fashion are computationally efficient irrespective of the clustering algorithm because each object in a data set is not required to assign an outlying factor as with scoring-based output. The top-N outlier concept is absent in these techniques and hence is unsupervised. The main drawback of these techniques is the accuracy of detecting all the rare class instances; because all the data objects are not taken into consideration for being outliers, many of them might be missing, and normal instances may be detected as outliers.

The scoring-based techniques have the maximum efficiency in detecting outlier accurately because all the objects are under consideration as candidate outliers. But the loophole of these techniques is computational cost because all the objects are taken under consideration to assign the outlyingness factor. Top-N outliers must have to be specified by a data analyst, and thus the approach becomes supervised.

1.6 STATISTICAL-BASED APPROACHES

These approaches are the first-generation techniques for outlier detection. Actually, these techniques are called model-based techniques. Models are based on probability distribution of the data, and outliers are detected as to how well the data fit into the model. Statistically based approaches are categorized into two groups, depending on probability distribution, as follows:

1.6.1 PARAMETRIC APPROACHES

In these approaches, the probability distribution of the data is known. Then, using the distribution parameters, outliers are detected. A point is an outlier if it deviates significantly from the data model; however, in many situations, a prior knowledge of distribution is not possible to attain.

Wu et al. [49] proposed two algorithms for outlying sensors and event boundary detection. The basic idea of outlying sensor detection is as such, each sensor first computes the difference between its reading and the median reading from the neighboring reading. Each sensor then collects all differences from its neighborhood and standardizes them. A sensor is an outlier if the absolute value of its standardized difference is sufficiently large. The algorithm for event boundary detection is based on an outlying sensor detection algorithm. For an event sensor, there often exist two regions, with each containing the sensor, such that the absolute value of the difference between the reading of the sensor and the median reading from all other sensors in one region is much larger than that in another region. These approaches are not efficient because they do not consider the temporal correlation of sensor readings.

Bettencourt et al. [50] proposed an outlier detection technique to identify anomalous events and errors in ecological applications of distributed sensor networks. This method uses spatio-temporal correlation of sensor data to distinguish erroneous measurements and events. A measurement is considered to be an outlier when its value in the statistical significance test is less than the user-specified threshold. The drawback of this approach is dependence on the user-specified threshold.

Jun et al. [51] presents a statistically based approach, which uses alpha-stable distribution. The proposed algorithm consists of collaborative time-series estimation, variogram application, and principle component analysis (PCA). Each node detects any temporally abnormal data and transmits the verified data to a local cluster-head, which detects any survived spatial outlier and determines the faulty sensors accordingly. Their approach achieves 94% accuracy when the noise level is alpha = 0.9 although alpha-stable distribution might be considered for real sensor data and a cluster-based structure may be susceptible to dynamic changes of network topology.

1.6.2 NONPARAMETRIC APPROACHES

These approaches have no knowledge about the underlying data distribution. They typically define a distance measure to identify outliers. Outliers are those points that are distant from their own neighborhood in a data set. Various detection techniques are available with a wide range of parameters. Parametric methods are not flexible enough like nonparametric methods, but due to dimensionality and computational complexity, the efficiency might deteriorate in some cases. Two widely used approaches in this category are discussed as follows:

1.6.2.1 Histogramming

It is a model that involves counting the frequency of occurrence of different data instances and then compares the test instance with each of the histogram categories to test whether it belongs to any of them.

Sheng et al. [52] proposed a histogram-based technique for outlier detection to reduce the communication cost for data collection applications of sensor networks. Rather than collecting all the data in one location for centralized processing, they propose collecting hints about the data distribution and using the hints to filter out unnecessary data and identify potential outliers. The main drawbacks of this technique are communication overhead and one-dimensional data.

1.6.2.2 Kernel Function

This function is used to estimate the probability distribution function (pdf) of the normal instances. Data instances that lie in the low probability area of the pdf are declared as outliers.

Palapans et al. [53] proposed a technique for online deviation detection in streaming data. They discussed how their technique can be operated efficiently in the distributed environment of a sensor network. In the sensor data, a value is considered as an outlier if the number of values in its neighborhood is less than a user-specified threshold. This technique can also be implemented for identification of an outlier in a more global perspective. The main problem of this technique is the user-defined threshold.

1.6.3 Strength and Weakness

Statistical approaches are holding a strong mathematical background to detect outliers. But parametric approaches are not feasible when the prior knowledge of the data distribution is not available and hence quite useless in many aspects. But nonparametric methods are quite useful compared to parametric methods because the data distribution knowledge is not required. However, these methods might have high computational complexity due to high-dimensional data sets. Also user-defined parameters are not easy to set.

1.7 CONCLUSION

Outlier detection is an interesting arena of computer and network security. It is also applied in various application domains. It is regarded as one of the fundamental problems of data mining as well. In this chapter, we have summarized outlier detection techniques along with various research direction and application domains. We have described existing approaches for outlier detection techniques and believe that our contribution will help the reader to easily understand the particular research focus in this chapter.

AUTHORS' BIOGRAPHIES

Mohiuddin Ahmed is working in the arena of data mining and network security toward his PhD degree at the University of New South Wales, Canberra. He received his bachelor of science degree in computer science and information technology from Islamic University of Technology, Bangladesh, in 2011.

Abdun Naser Mahmood received the BSc degree in applied physics and electronics and the MSc degree in computer science from the University of Dhaka, Bangladesh, in 1997 and 1999, respectively. He completed his PhD degree from the University of Melbourne in 2008. He joined the University of Dhaka as a lecturer in 2000 and as assistant professor in 2003, when he took a leave of absence for his PhD studies. Currently, he is working as a lecturer at the University of New South Wales, Canberra, with the School of Engineering and Information Technology. His research interests include data mining techniques for network monitoring and algorithm design for adaptive sorting and sampling.

Jiankun Hu obtained his masters degree from the Department of Computer Science and Software Engineering at Monash University, Australia and his PhD degree in control engineering at Harbin Institute of Technology, China. He has been awarded the German Alexander von Humboldt Fellowship working at Ruhr University, Germany. He is currently a professor of cyber security at the School of Engineering and Information Technology, UNSW Canberra. Dr. Hu's current research interests are in network security with an emphasis on biometric security, mobile template protection, and anomaly intrusion detection. These research activities have been funded by three Australia Research Council (ARC) Grants. His research work has been published in top international journals.

REFERENCES

1. V. J. Hodge and J. Austin (2003). A survey of outlier detection methodologies. *Artificial Intelligence Review*, vol. 22, pp. 85–126.
2. D. Hawkins (1980). *Identification of Outliers*. London: Chapman and Hall.
3. V. Barnett and T. Lewis (1994). *Outliers in Statistical Data*. New York: John Wiley Sons.
4. D. Yu, G. Sheikholeslami, and A. Zhang (2002). Findout: Finding outliers in very large datasets. *Journal of Knowledge and Information Systems*, vol. 4, no. 3, pp. 387–412.
5. M. F. Jiang, S. S. Tseng, and C. M. Su (2001). Two-phase clustering process for outliers detection. *Pattern Recognition Letters*, vol. 22, no. 6–7, pp. 691–700.
6. P. J. Rousseeuw and A. M. Leroy (1996). *Robust Regression and Outlier Detection*. John Wiley and Sons.
7. J. Laurikkala, M. Juhola, and E. Kentala (2000). Informal identification of outliers in medical data. In *Proceedings of IDAMAP*.
8. M. M. Breunig, H.-P. Kriegel, R. T. Ng, and J. Sander (2000). LOF: Identifying density-based local outliers. In *Proceedings of ACM SIGMOD*, pp. 93–104.
9. S. Harkins, H. He, G. J. Willams, and R. A. Baster (2002). Outlier detection using replicator neural networks. In *Proceedings of DaWaK*, pp. 170–180.
10. B. Schlkopf, J. Platt, J. Shawe-Taylor, A. J. Smola, and R. C. Williamson (2001). Estimating the support of a high dimensional distribution. *Neural Computation*, vol. 13, no. 7, pp. 1443–1471.
11. S. Shekhar, C.-T. Lu, and P. Zhang (2001). A unified approach to spatial outliers detection. *GeoInformatica*, vol. 7, no. 2, pp. 139–166.
12. A. L. Goldberger, L. A. N. Amaral, L. Glass, J. M. Hausdorff, P. C. Ivanov, R. G. Mark, J. E. Mietus, G. B. Moody, C.-K. Peng, and H. E. Stanley (2000). Physio Bank, Physio Toolkit, and Physio Net: Components of a new research resource for complex physiologic signals. *Circulation*, vol. 101, no. 23, pp. 215–220, http://circ.ahajournals.org/cgi/content/full/101/23/e215.
13. A. Lazarevic, A. Ozgur, L. Ertoz, J. Srivastava, and V. Kumar (2003). A comparative study of anomaly detection schemes in network intrusion detection. In *Proceedings of SIAM*.
14. R. Fujimaki, T. Yairi, and K. Machida (2005). An approach to spacecraft anomaly detection problem using kernel feature space. In *Proceedings of the Eleventh ACM SIGKDD International Conference on Knowledge Discovery in Data Mining*. New York: ACM Press, pp. 401–410.
15. D. J. Marchette (2001). *Computer Intrusion Detection and Network Monitoring: A Statistical Viewpoint*. New York: Springer.

16. S. E. Smaha (1988). Haystack: An intrusion detection system. In *Proceedings of the IEEE Fourth Aerospace Computer Security Applications Conference*, Orlando, FL, USA, December 1988. Los Alamitos, CA: IEEE Computer Society Press.

17. R. J. Bolton, and D. J. Hand (2001). Unsupervised profiling methods for fraud detection. In *Proceedings of CSCC*.

18. Z. He, X. Xu, and S. Deng (2003). Discovering cluster-based local outliers. *Pattern Recognition Letters*, vol. 24, no. 9–10, p. 1641.

19. P. L. Brockett, X. Xia, and R. A. Derrig (1998). Using Kohonen's self-organizing feature map to uncover automobile bodily injury claims fraud. *Journal of Risk and Insurance*, vol. 65, no. 2 (June), pp. 245–274.

20. A. Arning, R. Agrawal, and P. Raghavan (1996). A linear method for deviation detection in large databases. In *Proceedings of 2nd International Conference of Knowledge Discovery and Data Mining*, pp. 164–169.

21. J. Lin, A. E. Fu, and H. V. Herle (2005). Approximations to magic: Finding unusual medical time series. In *Proceedings of Symposium on Computer-Based Medical Systems*, Washington, DC, USA, pp. 329–334.

22. V. Chatzigiannakis, S. Papavassiliou, M. Grammatikou, and B. Maglaris (2006). Hierarchical anomaly detection in distributed large-scale sensor networks. In *ISCC '06: Proceedings of the 11th IEEE Symposium on Computers and Communications*. Washington, DC: IEEE Computer Society, pp. 761–767.

23. M. Augusteijn and B. Folkert (2002). Neural network classification and novelty detection. *International Journal on Remote Sensing*, vol. 23, no. 14, pp. 2891–2902.

24. Y. L. Cun, B. Boser, J. S. Denker, R. E. Howard, W. Habbard, L. D. Jackel, and D. Henderson (1990). Handwritten digit recognition with a back-propagation network. *Advances in Neural Information Processing Systems*, vol. 396, p. 404.

25. C. Spence, L. Parra, and P. Sajda (2001). Detection, synthesis and compression in mammographic image analysis with a hierarchical image probability model. In *Proceedings of the IEEE Workshop on Mathematical Methods in Biomedical Image Analysis*. Washington, DC: IEEE Computer Society, p. 3.

26. H. Dutta, C. Giannella, K. Borne, and H. Kargupta (2007). Distributed top-k outlier detection in astronomy catalogs using the demac system. In *Proceedings of 7th SIAM International Conference on Data Mining*.

27. K. Kadota, D. Tominaga, Y. Akiyama, and K. Takahashi (2003). Detecting outlying samples in microarray data: A critical assessment of the effect of outliers on sample classification. *Chem-Bio Informatics*, vol. 3, no. 1, pp. 30–45.

28. S. Albrecht, J. Busch, M. Kloppenburg, F. Metze, and P. Tavan (2000). Generalized radial basis function networks for classification and novelty detection: Self-organization of optional Bayesian decision. *Neural Networks*, vol. 13, no. 10, pp. 1075–1093.

29. P. Crook and G. Hayes (2001). A robot implementation of a biologically inspired method for novelty detection. In *Proceedings of Towards Intelligent Mobile Robots Conference*. Manchester, UK.

30. E. M. Knorr and R. T. Ng (1998). Algorithms for mining distance-based outliers in large datasets. *Proceedings of the VLDB Conference*, New York, USA, pp. 392–403.

31. Y. Yang, T. Pierce, and J. Carbonell (1998). A study on retrospective and on-line event detection, *Proceedings of the ACM SIGIR Conference on Research and Development in Information Retrieval*, Melbourne, Australia, pp. 28–36.

32. G. S. David Sam Jayakumar and B. John Thomas (2013). A new procedure of clustering based on multivariate outlier detection. *Journal of Data Science*, vol. 11, pp. 69–84.

33. H. Hotelling (1951). A generalized T test and measure of multivariate dispersion. In *Proceedings of the Second Berkeley Symposium on Mathematical Statistics and Probability* (Edited by J. Neyman), Berkeley, CA: University of California Press, pp. 23–41.

34. M. Belal Al-Zoubi, A. Al-Dahoud Ali, and A. Abdelfatah Yahya (2010). Fuzzy clustering-based approach for outlier detection, *Proceedings of the 9th WSEAS International Conference on Applications of Computer Engineering*.

35. D. Pham (2001). Spatial models for fuzzy clustering, *Computer Vision and Image Understanding*, vol. 84, no. 2, pp. 285–297.

36. C. L. Blake and C. J. Merz (1998). UCI repository of machine learning databases, http://www.ics. uci.edu/mlearn/MLRepository.html, Department of Information and Computer Sciences. Irvine, CA: University of California.

37. K. Yoon, O. Kwon, and D. Bae (2007). An approach to outlier detection of software measurement data using the K-means clustering method, *First International Symposium on Empirical Software Engineering and Measurement (ESEM 2007)*, Madrid, pp. 443–445.

38. A. Loureiro, L. Torgo, and C. Soares (2004). Outlier detection using clustering methods: A data cleaning application. In *Proceedings of KDNet Symposium on Knowledge-Based Systems for the Public Sector*. Bonn, Germany.

39. M. Belal Al-Zoubi, A. Al-Dahoud, and A. Abdelfatah Yahya (2010). New outlier detection method based on fuzzy clustering. *WSEAS Transaction on Information Science and Application*, vol. 7, no. 5, May.

40. V. Hautamäki, S. Cherednichenko, I. Kärkkäinen, T. Kinnunen, and P. Fränti (2005). Improving k-means by outlier removal, in *Proc. 14th Scandinavian Conference on Image Analysis (SCIA '05)*, pp. 978–987.

41. D. Ren, I. Rahal, and W. Perrizo (2004). A vertical outlier detection algorithm with clusters as by-product. In *Proceedings of ICTAI*.

42. H. Fan, O. Zaïane, A. Foss, and J. Wu (2006). Nonparametric outlier detection for efficiently discovering top-*n* outliers from engineering data. In *Proc. Pacific-Asia Conf. on Knowledge Discovery and Data Mining (PAKDD)*, Singapore.

43. W. Jin, A. Tung, and J. Han (2001). Mining top-*n* local outliers in large databases. In *Proc. ACM SIGKDD Int. Conf. on Knowledge Discovery and Data Mining (SIGKDD)*, San Francisco, CA.

44. S. Ramaswamy, R. Rastogi, and K. Shim (2000). Efficient algorithms for mining outliers from large data sets. In *Proc. ACM SIGMOD Int. Conf. on Management of Data (SIGMOD)*, Dallas, TX.

45. H. Zengyou, D. Shengchun, and X. Xiaofei (2002). Outlier detection integrating semantic knowledge. *Advances in Web-Age Information, Management*, Lecture Notes in Computer Science, vol. 2419, pp. 126–131.

46. S. Papadimitriou, H. Kitagawa, P. Gibbons, and C. Faloutsos (2003). LOCI: Fast outlier detection using the local correlation integral. In *Proc. ICDE*.

47. K. Zhang, M. Hutter, and H. Jin (2009). A new local distance based outlier detection approach for scattered real world data. In *Proc. PAKDD*.

48. H.-P. Kriegel, P. Kroger, E. Schubert, and A. Zimek (2009). Loop: Local outlier probabilities. In *Proceedings of the 18th ACM Conference on Information and Knowledge Management, CIKM '09*, New York, USA, pp. 1649–1652.

49. W. Wu, X. Cheng, M. Ding, K. Xing, F. Liu, and P. Deng (2007). Localized outlying and boundary data detection in sensor networks, *IEEE Trans. Knowl. Data Eng.*, vol. 19, no. 8, pp. 1145–1157.

50. L. A. Bettencourt, A. Hagberg, and L. Larkey (2007). Separating the wheat from the chaff: Practical anomaly detection schemes in ecological applications of distributed sensor networks, *Proc. IEEE International Conference on Distributed Computing in Sensor Systems*.

51. M. C. Jun, H. Jeong, and C. C. J. Kuo (2006). Distributed spatio-temporal outlier detection in sensor networks, *Proc. SPIE*.

52. B. Sheng, Q. Li, W. Mao, and W. Jin (2007). Outlier detection in sensor networks, Proc. MobiHoc.

53. T. Palpanas, D. Papadopoulos, V. Kalogeraki, and D. Gunopulos (2003). Distributed deviation detection in sensor networks, *ACM Special Interest Group on Management of Data*, pp. 77–82.

2 Network Traffic Monitoring and Analysis

Jeferson Wilian de Godoy Stênico and Lee Luan Ling

CONTENTS

2.1   INTRODUCTION

At their very first stage, computer networks were invented in order to be able to share documents and devices. With significant advances in electronics and signal processing technologies during past decades, accessing, searching, and sharing information via communication networks (e.g., the Internet) have become a part of our everyday life. Because frequently a great part of this information is confidential or has restricted access only for authorized persons, preventing unauthorized use and accessing this information and detecting intruders have become an indispensable mechanism for all information systems and communication networks. Efficient prevention mechanisms require a combination of the expertise of security technicians and powerful hardware and software tools in order to be able to achieve high levels of security management, especially for today's modern computing systems. An intrusion detection system (IDS), by its turn, is one of these security tools for this end.

An intrusion detection system is used to monitor the security status of networks by detection of external invasions and abnormal operations of servers, whether contaminated or not. The information provided by an IDS is crucial for the guarantee and protection of integrity, privacy, and authenticity of the flowing data in networks. Another major function of an IDS is attack prevention by learning. From a real attacking experience, the data should be carefully analyzed, the origin of the attack should be determined, and the level of hazards and malicious penetration should be measured in order to improve the security system's ability to prevent any future attacks.

2.1.1   EVOLUTION OF INTRUSION DETECTION SYSTEMS

A very first research work on intrusion detection (ID), titled *Computer Security Threat Monitoring and Surveillance* [1], appeared in 1980, in which the concept of an *audit trail* was presented. *Audit trails* provide valuable information that can be used for tracking misuses of information systems and understanding user's behavior. This research work had established the foundation for the later design and development of intrusion detection systems (IDS).

Dorothy E. Denning, of SRI International,* in 1983, participated in a project that resulted in significant advances in IDS development. She examined the records of government mainframes and created users' profiles according to their activities.

In 1984, Denning collaborated with the construction of the first intrusion detection system, the *Intrusion Detection Expert System* (IDES) [2]. IDES can be viewed as the first functional IDS. During the same year, SRI International presented a method to analyze information used for user authentication on the records of ARPANET (the precursor of Internet).

Later, in 1987, based on her wide experience in IDS research and development, Denning published an article called "An Intrusion Detection Model" [3], which had served as an important guidance for new IDS development. In spite of all these research efforts, the real and significant advances in intrusion detection were demonstrated by the Haystack project in 1988 [4]. This project improved the conventional IDS by incorporating a new approach, resulting in the so-called distributed intrusion detection system (DIDS) [5]. The DIDS introduced techniques for data pattern detection, which consisted of a comparison of the input data with predefined standard data patterns. Later, in 1989, a trade company named Haystack Labs, composed of some researchers of the Haystack project, released the latest generation of the IDS technology, called Stalker. Stalker was a host-based intrusion detection system (HIDS) having robust capabilities of information searching on record systems (manually or automatically via the methodology of questions). In summary, the Stalker technology and the methodologies developed by SRI International and Dorothy E. Denning constituted the major advances in the technology of host-based IDS (HIDSs) in the 1980s.

In the early 1990s, Heberlein et al. suggested the concept of network-based intrusion detection systems (NIDS) [6]. In fact, they were the major inventors of network security monitor (NSM), the

---

* http://www.sri.com/

first NIDS implemented and used by important government organizations. NSM was designed to extract information through network traffic analysis. NSM had motivated significant increasing interest in intrusion detection inside the research community as well as in the investments in NIDS production. Later, the group of Heberlein and some staff of Haystack jointly went beyond their initial objectives of the NIDS project, extending to and producing the hybrid intrusion detection systems (HIDSs/NIDSs).

Still in early 1990s, several companies started to release their commercialized IDS versions. Among them, the Haystack Labs was the first company marketing its IDS tools, more specifically, the host-market based Stalker. The Science Applications International Corporation (SAIC)* had developed a host-based detection system called the computer misuse detection system (CMDS) [7]. Simultaneously, the US Air Force's Cryptologic Support Center developed the automated security measurement system (ASIM) to monitor network traffic on the US Air Force's communication network [8]. ASIM was probably the very first IDS that had achieved considerable breakthrough in terms of scalability and portability, the main issues that had plagued NID products since the beginning. Moreover, ASIM was considered as the first IDS capable of incorporating both hardware and software solutions into network intrusion detection systems.

However, the commercialization of IDS products became significant in the market only in the middle of 1997. During that year, Internet Security Systems (ISS) was the market leader among most commercially available products because of its outstanding and distinguished NIDS solution, called RealSecure. A year later, Cisco acquired Wheel Group in order to be able to compete with ISS. Centrax Corporation, a new company formed by some previous Haystack Labs' researchers and SAIC's CMDS team had also succeeded with its HIDS solution. From then on, many new companies marketing IDSs have emerged by corporation merging and acquisition.

According to reported statistics [9], currently the IDSs are one of the most used security devices. In fact, IDS technologies occupy the seventh position in terms of number of usages for network security purposes (see Figure 2.1).

Moreover, the employment of IDS technology has remarkably increased in comparison with other security technology types. As illustrated by Figure 2.1, there was almost a 25% increase in IDS usage from 1998 to 2002.

This chapter aims to provide a comprehensible description of intrusion detection systems and their evolution, implementation, and operation inside communication network environments. Precisely, the description will be carried out in the context of network monitoring and network traffic analysis. For easy understanding of all addressed issues, we make use of currently widely employed security tools as examples to illustrate the details of host-based intrusion detection systems (HIDSs) and network-based intrusion detection system (NIDSs) (Figure 2.2).

2.1.2 Classification of Intrusion Detection Systems

As mentioned previously, intrusion detection systems aim to provide plausible traces of information systems being invaded. Figure 2.3 shows a complete characterization and classification of intrusion detection systems.

2.1.2.1 Intrusion Detection Categories

2.1.2.1.1 Misuse Intrusion Detection Systems

Misuse intrusion detection systems are designed to search for already known patterns of attacks and intrusions. The systems are also named as signature-based intrusion detection systems or knowledge-based intrusion detection systems. Some interesting features of these kinds of intrusion detection systems are that (a) the characteristics of the attacks are well known and (b) the attack patterns can

---

* www.saic.com

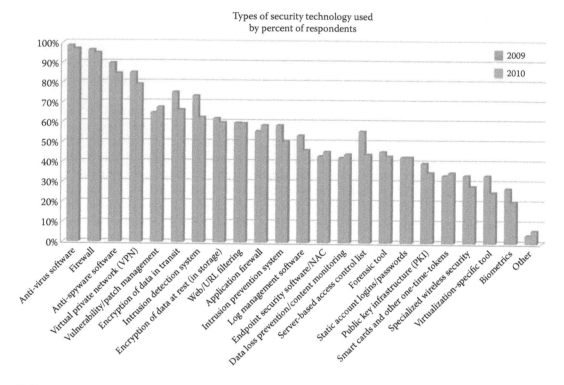

FIGURE 2.1 Statistics of usages of security technologies. (From 15th Annual Computer Crime and Security Survey, CSI/FBI, 2010/2011: https://cours.etsmtl.ca/log619/documents/divers/CSIsurvey2010.pdf.)

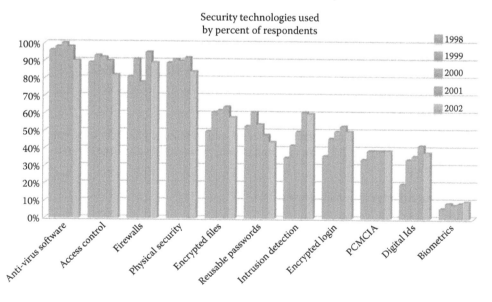

FIGURE 2.2 Evolution of usages of security technologies from 1998 to 2002. (From Computer Crime and Security Survey, CSI/FBI, VIII, 1, Spring 2002. http://diogenesllc.com/2002cybercrimesurvey.pdf.)

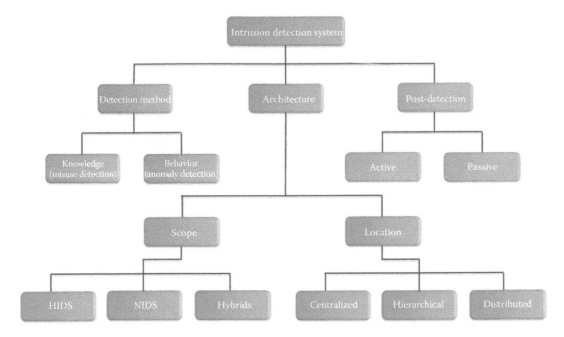

FIGURE 2.3 Characterization and classification of intrusion detection systems.

be easily encoded into an expert system. In other words, this detection system category usually holds a database of known attack signatures that need to be updated whenever new attack types are identified.

A well-known encoded instruction (or rule) in a misuse IDS for detecting a denial of service attack is called the "Ping of Death," which is one of the oldest network attack types [11]. This kind of attack is mainly characterized by sending a very large ICMP echo request packet, intending to provoke an unavailability of network services among connected multiple operating systems by generating bugs or causing programming errors in vulnerable software. An "ICMP echo request" packet thus is considered as an attack when its size is superior to 65.535 bytes. Notice that this encoded rule simultaneously belongs to misuse-based and network-based IDSs.

When an encoded instruction focuses on events related to any specific isolated information system or computer, it is specified as an instruction of the host-based intrusion detection system (HIDS). Examples of this kind are (a) alerts caused by excessive processor occupancy time when a particular sequence of calls to operating system functions occurs and (b) certain critical files are changed.

IDSs also detect intrusions based on knowledge. In other words, intrusions are interpreted in terms of knowledge, which defines system states according to actions performed by the system. Pairs of attributes-values are used to represent the possible system. The transition of state is provoked by some actions. Figure 2.4 illustrates the identification of intrusion by the knowledge-based IDS.

Independent of the focus of an IDS (network or host based), a misuse IDS requires the incorporation of human expert knowledge into the IDS in order to be able to operate adequately. A main disadvantage of a misuse intrusion detection system is its inability to detect new attack types because novel attack information has not been added to the standard database yet. As a result, this

FIGURE 2.4 Sequence of changing states in knowledge-based ID systems.

fact has motivated the flourish of research and development of anomaly-based intrusion detection approaches.

2.1.2.1.2 Anomaly-Based Intrusion Detection

Security systems for anomaly intrusion detection, also called behavior-based intrusion detection systems, seek to determine or create models that represent the normal or expected behavior of computational systems or communication networks. An alert will be raised whenever deviations from the expected behavior are found. It is presumed that involved system intrusion or attack activities are parts of the subset composed of anomalous activities. Ideally, it is desirable that the set of all malicious activities is exactly equal to the set of all anomalous activities. Under this idealized situation, the system will generate zero false-positive and false-negative errors. However, in practice, all four possible situations occur with nonzero probabilities:

- *Intrusive activity but normally declared:* This situation, also known as false-negative, is extremely dangerous because the system fails to detect an attack or intrusion.
- *Nonintrusive and normal activity:* Also called the positive-negative condition. Because it consists of a normal and nonintrusive activity, the monitoring system will not be activated.
- *Nonintrusive and abnormal activity:* Also called the false-positive condition. The system alerts, indicating the detection of an intrusion which has not actually occurred.
- *Intrusive and abnormal activity:* An ideal situation in which the system correctly detects an attack or intrusion.

Figure 2.5 illustrates all four possible situations through one-dimensional probability distributions (probability distributions of normal and abnormal activities).

2.1.2.2 Intrusion Detection System Architecture

The architecture of intrusion detection systems should be elaborated, taking into account several relevant issues: (a) what source of information is being monitored ("network," "host computer," or "hybrid" entities), (b) how tasks are being distributed, and (c) what kinds of processing modules comprise the IDS. Through a classic example, Figure 2.6 illustrates several aspects commonly encountered in elaborating solutions for intrusion detection in practice. The given example shows a LAN (possibly representing networks of corporations or universities) connected to the Internet by a "firewall." The firewall is a security device that separates different networks; however, all are connected to a distinct network that provides Internet service and forms a so-called

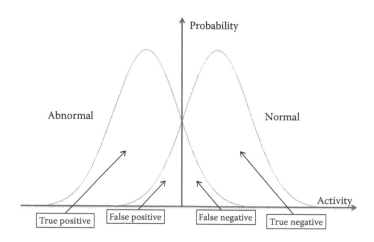

FIGURE 2.5 Four situations defined by probability distributions of normal and abnormal activities.

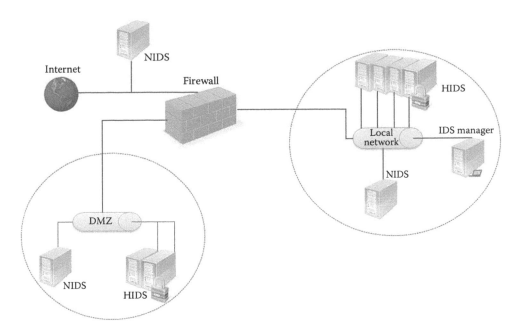

FIGURE 2.6 Example of classic intrusion detection solution.

DMZ ("demilitarized zone"). Each segment of this connected network, (local network, DMZ, and Internet) holds a network-based intrusion detection system (NIDS) monitoring the corresponding network segment. In addition, those servers that are considered critical may have a host-based intrusion detection system (HIDS) implemented and used to monitor some specific events possibly happening on these servers. Finally, there is a management tool of IDS at LAN used to collect and organize the information received from various connected modules.

2.1.2.2.1 Scopes of IDSs

In terms of the analyzed and monitored source of information, an IDS can be classified into the group of host-based intrusion detection systems, network-based intrusion detection systems, or hybrid intrusion detection systems. Each kind of IDS has its peculiar approach for problem formulation and solution elaboration. In this section, we describe the problems and solutions encountered as well as the advantages and disadvantages of each IDS category.

2.1.2.2.1.1 Host-Based Intrusion Detection Systems (HIDS) A host-based intrusion detection system is used to monitor the behavior or dynamic states of a machine. To this end, it consults its log analysis files or data from the audit agents and thus detects and assesses changes in the file system, user access control, behavior of system processes, and use of resources among others. HIDS can also perform simple and concise inspections of packets arriving from the network on which the machine is connected. A typical example that involves HIDSs is record systems. Figure 2.7 shows the architecture of a recording system, in which a HIDS uses recorded information as a standard pattern.

Another feature found in many HIDS is the hash of the file system. HIDS creates an initial database with hash values of files that are considered important. To identify any violation of recorded data, the hash value is recalculated and compared with the correct one previously saved in the database. If any discrepancy between two hash values appears, it implies some changes have occurred. This hash number verification mechanism is very effective for the following actions: detection of rootkit installation,* inclusion of new users, or setting changes. Once any suspicious activity is

---

* A rootkit is a specific type of malware that runs actions to intercept the operational system and change the results.

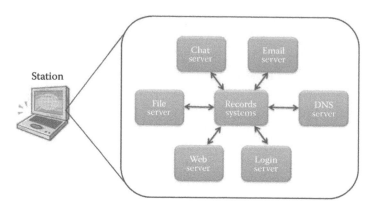

FIGURE 2.7 Architecture of a recording system.

detected after performing hash data comparison and analysis, the HIDS can either generate an alert or place in the logs the encountered suspicious activity.

Among many benefits from using a HIDS, we can highlight the following [12]:

- Establishing a strong association between programs and users: identifying the author and the time at which applications or commands were executed.
- Because of being one of the potential targets of attack, HIDS is capable of collecting considerable and valuable information during the attack.
- Confronting coming threats directed only to the machine where the HIDS resides without the necessity of capturing whole network traffic.
- Direct access to the system with priority and without any dependence on other means to access data.
- No need for additional hardware.

Among the disadvantages of using a HIDS, we can cite the following [13]:

- High complexity in management and scalability of HIDS (because of the necessity of configuration and constant observation on all hosts, impacting scalability).
- Operational system dependent.
- Susceptible to attacks, resulting in corrupted data or data deletion. This is due to the fact of its priority in direct access and belonging to or being part of the host environment.
- Possibly becoming correlated with attack data and requiring some additional performance data correlation analysis on data from all involved network hosts.
- Deep data analysis and very detailed information collection can affect negatively the performance of host monitoring.

2.1.2.2.1.2 Network-Based Intrusion Detection Systems (NIDS)   The NIDS can monitor data collected from its own network segment or from multiple network hosts. Currently, there are many commercially available NIDS tools, for example, NADIR [14] and DIDS [15]. Many of these tools have implemented data collecting facilities. Although the architecture of NIDS may vary among these tools, according to Hofmeyr et al. [16], basically, it is composed of three units: a data collector, a manager, and a communication module responsible for transmission and receiving of data and analysis results.

The collector usually has a set of sensors, possibly distributed over the network, and is responsible for the data capture and formatting as well as network traffic analysis. The collector can be viewed as a NIDS component responsible for data preprocessing and preliminary network traffic analysis. On the collector, the collected input information is processed and normalized so that it becomes prepared and eventually used to compare with the standard anomaly profiles. After having entry data standardized, the classification mechanism implemented on the manager will attribute (classify) the input information into one of two possible events with intrusive behavior or normally behaved. Notice that the event classification mechanism has distinguished implementation according to IDS types, i.e., misuse-based detection and anomaly-based detection. The manager itself is also responsible for two important tasks: the integrated management of sensors and the specification of response patterns for each network behavior type. Finally, the most basic module—the communicator—executes the tasks of transmitting and receiving data and analysis results according to the policies set by administrators.

For anomaly detection, the IDS captures packets, analyzes their headers, and compares them with known patterns or signatures. The NIDS found efficiency against several different types of attack and can block some of them in real time.

For misuse-based detection, the classification mechanism compares the input data with instructions and other behavior descriptors. On the other hand, for anomaly-based detection, the comparison is usually based on the statistical profiles of the user's or the system's historical behaviors. For this end, a default behavior of each user is outlined and used as the standard pattern for comparison with captured data [17].

Among some remarking benefits of using the NIDS we point out the following [12,13]:

- No impact on network performance.
- Attacks can be identified in real time, thus enabling the administrator to respond to the attacks quickly.
- Able to capture suspicious attacks that have not yet been identified.
- Operational system independent.
- Possibly being invisible to attackers. NIDS does not leave any trace of its network monitoring actions whereas a HIDS certainly leaves its proper vestiges in the system where it is installed.
- Having wide areas of applications and requiring simple and concise infrastructures.

Among some negative views of the NIDS, we outline the following [12,13]:

- May require highly complex protocols for specific applications
- Inability to monitor encrypted traffic
- Restricted applications on fragmented networks, especially those with switches
- Inability to perform traffic analysis when the volume of network traffic traces exceeds the system's collecting capacity
- Need of large recording capacity for data storage (for instance, monitoring the states of TCP connections with large network flows)

2.1.2.2.1.3 Hybrids The conception of the hybrid IDSs were based on the possibility of maximizing the strengths of both HIDS and NIDS. In practice, a hybrid IDS operates as a NIDS, collecting and processing network traffic in order to detect attacks. On the other hand, as a HIDS, the hybrid system focuses on each host, only processing the packets addressed to its own system. The hybrid system can resolve the low performance problem of NIDS but still leave the scalability as an open problem (IDS is required to be installed on equipment).

One author [18] argues that both NIDS and HIDS can be characterized by two distinct methods (knowledge-based detection or misuse detection and behavior-based detection or anomaly detection), and a hybrid IDS is viewed as an IDS that combines these two detection methods. In general the pattern-based strategy provides a low false alarm rate but fails to identify unpublished attacks. On the other hand, a behavior-based approach can provoke a large number of alerts, and not all of

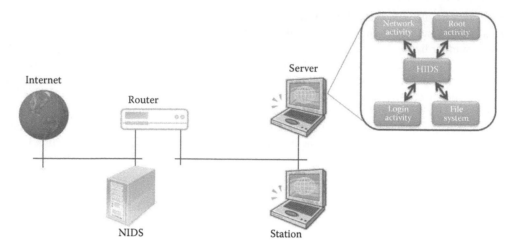

FIGURE 2.8   An example configuration of hybrid intrusion detection systems.

them are indeed attack attempts. An interesting aspect of behavior-based approach is its ability to detect new attack types.

Another important feature of a hybrid IDS is its centralized management; i.e., the IDS can locate sensors in various network segments and other host-based IDSs used in machines. The management center can control the rules or instructions for both IDS types, thus forming a hybrid IDS [19]. Figure 2.8 shows a widely employed configuration of a hybrid IDS in which a NIDS belongs to a local network and HIDS run on their corresponding master servers.

2.1.2.2.2   Location and Distribution of IDSs

Practical implementation of an intrusion detection system means a functional and operational combination of monitoring agents (network sensors or hosts equipped with data processing modules), detection modules, and management tools. Figure 2.9 shows how these processing and operational modules are organized and functionally related in the IDS. According to the network architecture

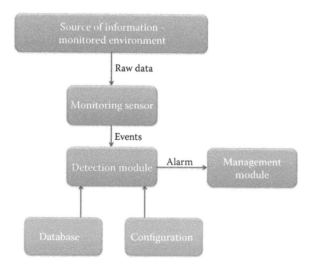

FIGURE 2.9   Elements and a functional diagram of intrusion detection systems.

and location of these modules, an IDS can be classified into one of the following categories: centralized, hierarchical, and distributed.

2.1.2.2.2.1 Centralized IDS A centralized IDS, in principle, has only one manager responsible for the event analysis, detection, classification, and system action. One or more monitoring modules (also called agents) can be employed, responsible for data collecting and transmission to the central module (manager). Under this IDS architecture model, the central module also is known as the agent-manager.

2.1.2.2.2.2 Hierarchical IDS Both hierarchical and centralized ID systems belong to the agent-manager model category. However, the former ones allow some variation of system configuration on several different subordination levels. In a centralized IDS, all monitoring agents are subordinated (sending information and reporting results) to the same central module or manager. The hierarchical system model permits distinct subordinations. Agents that collect information regarding the network (NIDS) can be subordinated to the network manager module. Agents that monitor specific computers (HIDS) can be subordinated to the host manager module.

2.1.2.2.2.3 Distributed IDS A distributed intrusion detection system permits data processing and analysis and event detection being partially or fully executed by the collecting modules (agents). This task distribution strategy implies that the system intelligence is distributed among the manager modules and agents that make up the ID system.

2.1.2.3 Actions of Post-Detection

Once having detected an intrusion, the IDS initiates certain actions of post-detection in responding to the detected intrusions. The actions of post-detection can be classified into two classes: active and passive actions.

2.1.2.3.1 Active Actions

With the declaration of detected intrusion, the IDS may react actively to protect the threatened entity against the attack. This kind of ID system class has been the subject of recent research works and, due to its importance, has earned a specific name: intrusion prevention systems (IPS). For example, during a TCP connection, an active and network-based IDS may send some specific purposed packets (TCP packets with FIN and RST flags) to the source entity of traffic flows to interrupt the connection (which is considered as an intrusion). In addition, the IPS can interact with edge routers (routers located at the perimeter between the local networks of an organization and external networks to the Internet) or firewalls and establish rules to filter certain packet flows originating from some specific source addresses.

2.1.2.3.2 Passive Actions

A passive classified IDS only generates and sends notifications to the system operator or administrator through the expert management console, after having detected attack patterns. These notifications or alerts can be generated and transmitted via various standard protocols, e.g., email, SNMP alerts, etc. The intrusion detection exchange format [21], a working group belonging to the IETF (Internet Engineering Task Force) [20], was created to standardize the communication mechanisms as well as the communication language between ID systems, also between agents and detection management modules. The RFC (request for comments) documents, released by this working group for the standardization of exchanged information between modules of IDS or between several different IDSs, deal with the following issues:

- Intrusion detection message exchange requirements
- Intrusion detection message exchange format
- Intrusion detection exchange protocol (IDXP)

2.2   NETWORK MONITORING

Network monitoring is an extremely important task in combating system intrusion. The monitoring procedure consists of collecting and recording data from the affected network elements in operation. The tasks performed by these network elements vary greatly in their nature, including statistical information collecting, traffic analysis, and problem diagnosis, among others.

Network monitoring can be performed at defined instances or continuously depending on pre-established objectives and tasks. That is, expected information and results require adequate data collecting methods. For example, if one wishes to obtain the information about monthly network availability, it is necessary to monitor the network continuously for at least a month and to register the periods in which the networks were out of function. Another typical example is monitoring networks to extract some information about the periods of peak usage. The procedure for this end may consist of recording traffic continuously for long periods (several days) and counting and comparing amounts of bytes of traffic flows for each short time segment that composes the whole periods. The tasks of network traffic monitoring can be executed using the SNMP (simple network management protocol) [22]. However, this protocol cannot identify which networks or hosts (both internal and external ones) were more demanded.

Two mechanisms can be applied for network monitoring: active and passive. Through an active method, it is necessary to generate testing traffic flows and transmit them in a controlled manner along one or more network paths (routers). During the transmission, the quality of traffic flows as well as the network performances are monitored.

Notice that there are two factors needed to be considered if the active approach is adopted: network performance can be affected by using testing traffic flows and adopting dynamic routing; performance measures can be altered (becoming better or worse) depending on the selected routing paths.

Through the passive method, real traffic flows (or their statistics) are captured at one or more network points and then analyzed [23].

2.2.1   NETWORK MONITORING SYSTEMS

A "network monitoring system" is created software to facilitate network monitoring tasks. This computing program tool is an improved programming version of currently existing network analysis algorithms that automate network data collection and analysis.

One of the key features of a monitoring system is the storage of collected data for historical database compilation and system training. The information acquired from past network activities makes network planning (for either short, medium, or long time periods) easier, aiming to ensure acceptable qualities of offered network services. The recorded data have also demonstrated their utility in helping networks operating appropriately according to the preestablished criteria, e.g., SLAs* (service level agreements). It is important that those network service providers monitor networks constantly in order to guarantee the contracted traffic rates and quality of services.

2.2.2   NETWORK MONITORING TECHNOLOGIES

There are many published research works and implemented computational tools available on the subject of traffic monitoring technology. Cottrell [24] gives an extensive list of these computational tools. Computational tools operating on the packet level, such as "tcpdump" [25] and "Wireshark" [26], are quite popular and widely used by network administrators. Although these tools can capture traffic packets easily, they are not allowed to make any arbitrary query over the captured traffic. Furthermore, these tools typically are directed to process traffic flows originating from a single data source.

---

* An SLA is a part of a service contract in which a service is formally defined.

Authors [27] present a computational tool solution that allows query. The proposed solution consists of distributed collectors capable of receiving data in the NetFlow format and exporting them in the pcap format so that "Wireshark" is able to execute necessary analysis. However, the authors remarked that the amount of information can be huge and recommend that each collector filters (selects) the data of its own interest.

The network monitoring tool called "ntop" [28] is one capable of operating on both packet and flow levels. The capture of traffic information can be done through a plug via Netflow. Although this monitoring tool is capable of release reports in varying formats, it is not allowed to make arbitrary queries elaborated by the network administrator.

Among the monitoring tools operating with Netflow, the "cflowd" [29] was one of the first ones distributed with open source and later gave rise to "flowscan" [30]. Authors [31] claim that monitoring systems operating on the packet level do not scale in high-speed networks. In fact, network-based intrusion detection systems set their focus on packet-level inspection in stub networks. In addition, the authors suggest a framework for real-time backbone monitoring and attack detection based on NetFlow. The given framework operates under centralized administration and requires users to write plugins for each task to be performed.

A traffic monitoring system [32] based on NetFlow has information stored in an Oracle database. The use of the database greatly increases the flexibility in information consultations. However, such an approach still requires storage of information for later processing as well as centralized management.

The authors of the monitoring tool "SMART" [33] argue that the traditional monitoring tools, operating with NetFlow and storing information on disk for later processing, prevent the efficient handling of large traffic volumes. "SMART," in turn, uses flash memories for data storage and processing. According to experimental investigation, "SMART" is capable of processing 30,000 records per second.

The "Gigascope" monitoring system [34,35] can be viewed as a DSMS dedicated for high-speed network monitoring. The tool has been considered the most efficient monitoring system based on its practical results provided by AT&T. Notice that "Gigascope" is a commercial tool under the closed source condition.

Motivated by investigation on the usage of open source DSMS for traffic monitoring, authors [36] made a case study on the "TelegraphCQ" DSMS. Although only a moderate amount of traffic data was analyzed, the study work has provided additional motivation for further investigation and elaboration of open source tools. A good example is "Paquet" [37].

The monitoring tool "Paquet" uses the data stream management system called "Borealis" operating on the packet level and allows that the network administrator makes arbitrary queries on captured traffic by network interfaces or on data files in pcap format.

An alternative to NetFlow is SFlow, which is a traffic monitoring technology defined by RFC 3176 [38]. The RFC document defines a packet sampling mechanism for SFlow agents, a MIB and a data format used for communication between an agent and a SFlow collector. Because it is not required that a SFlow agent keeps any flow information, the implementation of agents is highly simplified. Moreover, the system specifications require precise monitoring of interfaces up to Gigabits speed rates and possibly more. The data collection of the SFlow is based on a statistical packet sampling method. However, as the collector that receives the samples knows the sampling rate, it is possible to accurately reconstruct the sampled traffic [38–40].

2.3   INTRUSION DETECTION ANALYSIS

As mentioned before, there are two categories of network data traffic analysis, namely misuse detection and anomaly detection. The former one consists of a comparative approach searching for one among a group of preestablished attack patterns (signatures), most matching with the coming network traffic flow, which is known as a pattern matching method. For the anomaly detection technique, also known as behavior-based detection, the IDS learns from past network data to establish normal system behavior patterns (without attacks) and sets boundaries for this pattern. Any deviation beyond these boundaries is treated as an attack.

2.3.1 Pattern Matching Method

It is a methodology used by intrusion detection devices to detect attacks based on signature matching. This method is the simplest and most widely employed approach for attack detection although it has limitations on application generalization. The basic idea of this method is to compare the captured packet with a sequence of data on text or under binary format, i.e., searching for and identifying known attack signatures. Intrusion detection systems employing signature detection methods are required to continuously update the signature database with appeared novelties.

Constant and continuous research work is needed to create new signature patterns in order to maintain IDS in terms of efficiency against any change of and/or new attack schemes and strategies. Notice that a simple change in an attack scheme could be enough to "fool" an IDS, making signatures no longer effective.

Although a task of pattern matching can be quickly executed for attack detection, this may not be fully true with the evolution of networks in terms of size, speed, and complexity, which turns signatures-based IDS very complex. Definitely, a higher processing capacity will be needed to accommodate growing traffic volumes, network expansion, and even sophisticated attack strategies.

The mechanics of a pattern matching technique is of a reactive type, similar to actions carried out against viruses. When criminals create and spread viruses to attack information systems, antivirus companies learn the viruses (attacks) and create the vaccine (antivirus software) to protect information systems.

2.3.2 Protocol Analysis

In general, intrusion detection systems analyze essentially the header contents of protocols (e.g., IP, TCP, UDP, and ICMP). However, a more advanced intrusion detection system can go further, performing the so-called "protocol analysis." The protocol analysis here introduced implies that the ID system has full knowledge about all related communication protocols and is capable of detecting abnormal or suspicious activities on the network through traffic data analysis. In other words, through traffic patterns supported by those protocols, the IDS can detect the violation of the standards established by the protocols. Notice that the protocol analysis facilitates the detection of both known and unknown attack types, based on the principle of protocol violation in terms of traffic abnormalities, rather than focusing on signature pattern verification.

In protocol detection, despite the need to develop specific signatures by protocol, it is classified as a "behavioral" technique, thus any anomaly differentiation in the use of the protocol will be perceived by the sensing device and generate an alert on change.

2.3.3 Statistical and Probabilistic Approach Based ID

The probabilistic approach of ID provides a powerful complement to the signature-based approach. Most developers of intrusion prevention systems rely on Bayesian strategy to implement probabilistic-based detection modules, i.e., learning situations through conditional probability relationships instead of rules or signatures. With this additional knowledge acquired from these probabilistic studies, signature-based IDSs become more sensitive with and oriented to situations, and simultaneously, anomaly-based IDSs are still able to retain their detection capabilities.

The engineering of this probabilistic technique is as follows. First of all, network data are collected and studied. The study work consists of building a Bayesian statistical model using both real attack samples and false positive samples. Notice that a Bayesian system will be robust only if the number of samples is big enough for system training.

The statistical analysis carried out here shows what traffic patterns are most probable to be false positive and those being actually malicious attacks. Then, these learned patterns can be incorporated into and used by IDSs to provide more precise distinction between false positives and malicious traffic and consequently to reduce significantly false positive identification rates. It is important to highlight that IDSs may require a long time period initially for system model learning what may let information systems be vulnerable to attacks during this period.

2.3.4 Neural Network Based ID

Intrusion detection systems based on neural networks, through adaptive learning procedures, have been used to recognize abnormal behaviors found in network traffic. This is an interesting approach due to the fact that neural networks do not take into account user defined parameters.

The neural network must first be trained with clean traffic data, i.e., traffic flows without malicious activity contents. The training should be constantly executed in order to permit that the neural networks learn constant changes of traffic behaviors. Because of their inherited learning ability, neural networks have been considered as the most appropriate tools for abnormality detection. In spite of their plausible quality, neural networks lack the ability to determine the cause of the abnormality. In other words, neural networks can only determine if there is a breach of security, but not its cause. The effort adopted to circumvent this problem is the development of dedicated neural networks that specialize in a specific type of attack. This makes its use extremely efficient for intrusion detection; however, currently, this technology is still restricted to research labs, and no commercial solution has been implemented in corporate environments as yet.

The anomaly detection techniques, despite still being in their early stages, have already become a reality for business solutions. In fact the technologies of intrusion detection still have much to evolve, despite having been investigated and receiving mass investments from the security industry. Currently, publications of new works with a variety of proposals for development of new approaches and algorithms for intrusion detection occur frequently. This fact clearly demonstrates the need for improvement and investment in the both hardware and software technologies of intrusion detection.

Next we present some examples of these propositions:

a) Strict Anomalies Detection

This detection technique is based on either heuristics or rules (rather than on pattern or signatures matching) and attempts to detect any type of misuse that falls out of normal system operations. This is opposed to signature-based approaches, which can only detect attacks through related signatures previously created.

One of the most interesting points of this ID technique is that the IDS does not generate false positive (false alarm) events. As a consequence, the employment of such an IDS (based on the model of strict anomaly detection) may be widely accepted due to the fact that this IDS type is more suitable for network environments in which network resources can be, or have already been, well defined.

b) Holistic Analysis

The holistic approach is seen as the opposite of the conventional view of security [41]. The conventional analysis is also called reductionist analysis.

Holism is based on the belief that the whole is greater than the sum of its parts, i.e., the whole is indivisible and inseparable. Translating this concept in safety approach means that it is possible to infer the existence of an attack when a group of observations (apparently not correlated) are related to a structure that represents the knowledge of a method that employs an attack at a high level. In other words, the reductionist methods generate an assumption of truth based on observation of a particular action (a bottom-up approach).

Holistic methods have their reverse engineering, i.e., the method starts from a general knowledge to infer a specific observation (a top-down approach). There are several ways to implement holistic analysis. One possible implementation consists of a path or track build-ing over a network, in which the main node of the network acts as a final barrier that an attacker needs to overcome in order to reach his final goal.

Another implementation option would be as follows: performing wide and global analy-ses of possible tactics that an attacker may use and using observed facts to deduce the next tactic that could be used in attack. Note that the holistic model is based on data collected in an environment using reductionist methods; therefore, it is method dependent and needs to be used in conjunction with the reductionist method.

c) Genetic Algorithms

The creation and implementation of genetic algorithms was inspired by the evolutionary theory of Darwin when associated with genetic engineering [42]. Genetic algorithms have been used to solve many problems with very distinct natures. The genetic algorithms seek a solution that is "good enough" instead of "the best" solution.

The basic idea of genetic algorithms seeks to transform any solution of a problem into a "genetic code" that will be scored by an evaluation function, and when that score is not enough, the code is rejected. Explicitly, it is necessary to have a minimum number of gen-erated genetic code solutions. This set of "genetic codes" is called a "population" and is used to evaluate against the problem. The expectation is that some of these codes are good enough for solving the problem. If not, some of the best codes are selected and recombined with the existing ones. The recombination here mentioned means performing an exchange of the scores of codes (depending on the type of solution), applying mutation (through a randomizing algorithm), and then reevaluating the new set of codes.

For IDS, these genetic algorithms may, for example, be used to acquire some knowl-edge of the examined rule-based system. The major difficulty encountered in using this approach lies in finding the right way to translate the solution into a genetic blueprint and defining the best evaluation function.

d) Biotechnology Algorithm

Biotechnology algorithms are used to detect masked attacks [43]. Masked attacks occur when the attacker succeeds in stealing a legitimate TCP session. The sequence alignment is a procedure used to determine the similarity between two DNA or protein sequences. The procedure can be executed globally, semiglobally, or locally by aligning the nucleo-tides or amino acids in each sequence and then producing a score indicating how well two sequences are aligned and, consequently, how similar they are.

The accuracy of DNA comparison and the flexibility provided by these algorithms have motivated their use in different applications. Particularly, the method has become attrac-tive for solving intrusion detection problems because of conceptual equivalences between biotechnical matching and traffic pattern matching. For instance, the replacement of nucle-otide sequences in biotechnology means the change of collections of user commands in intrusion detection prevention.

Although this method cannot offer the best system performance for intrusion detection in general, it particularly outperforms many other approaches when masked attacking is under discussion.

e) Fuzzy Logic Algorithms

Fuzzy logic is a computational methodology based on "degrees of truth" rather than the usual "true or false" (1 or 0) Boolean logic on which the modern computer logics are based. The fuzzy reasoning is based on rules and has enjoyed considerable successes dealing with problems in automation, control, data classification, decision analysis, and expert systems, among others. Based on the well-established fuzzy theory, the model for intrusion detection uses fuzzy logic to describe uncertainties and imprecisions of an intrusion attempt. This concept of uncertainty and imprecision is well accepted for the case because security itself is relatively defined, so it can be uncertain and vague, thus fuzzy. The use of fuzzy logic algorithms in dealing with intrusion detection can increase the degree of reliability [44].

2.4 COMPUTATIONAL IDS TOOLS

To find out if a computer or a network has been violated is not a trivial or simple task. Sometimes, it is necessary to verify several pieces of information located at distinct units or processes inside an information system, such as the following:

- Log records (records of events)
- Unauthorized processes
- User accounts
- File systems change
- Others

Notice that the investigation of the related events and pieces of information definitely cannot be manually performed by an information system security manager. Instead, the verification and analysis should be carried out by appropriate and powerful computational tools. For network security, intrusion detection systems (IDS) are the desired and dedicated computational tools.

Under this context, the IDS can be described as an expert tool capable of reading and interpreting the contents of log files from routers, firewalls, servers, and other network devices, issuing a warning about a possible attack and identifying the hacker.

In this section, we will describe some IDS tools being widely used today. Most of these tools are based on the principle of signature matching.

2.4.1 HOST-BASED INTRUSION DETECTION SYSTEMS (HIDS)

2.4.1.1 OSSEC (Open Source Security)

OSSEC [45] is an open source, host-based intrusion detection system developed by the Brazilian Daniel Cid with the following main functions:

- Logs analysis
- System integrity
- Rootkit detection
- Alerts and active responses (performed by firewalls or TCP wrappers)

OSSEC supports a large variety of logs, such as Unix pan, sshd (Open SSH), Unix telnetd, Samba, Su, Sudo, Proftpd, Pure-ftpd, vsftpd, Solaris ftpd, Imapd, and pop3d. Horde It can analyze protocols, search for specific content, and can also be used to detect a variety of attacks and probes, such as buffer overflows, portscans, CGI attacks, attempts to identify the operating system, among others. imp, Named (bind), Postfix, Sendmail, Iptables firewall, Solaisip filter firewall, AIX, ipsec/firewall, Netscreen firewall, Snort IDS, Apache web server (access log and error log), IIS web server, Squid proxy, Windows event logs, Generic unix authentication (adduser, logins, etc.). This HIDS offers the following operational modes:

- Local IDS: Monitoring and analyzing only the host on which OSSEC is installed
- Server: Monitoring and analyzing the logs sent by agents
- Agent: Working as a client and sending all information to the server for processing and analysis

OSSEC can work in conjunction with Snort [46] (a network-based intrusion detection system) under a hybrid detection environment, under which it analyzes the logs and alerts generated by Snort and classifies them according to the generated signatures and alerts the administrator whenever necessary.

2.4.1.2 Osiris

Osiris [47] is a host integrity monitoring system. It verifies any change occurring on network hosts as well as that on the file system and reports to the administrator. Osiris takes periodic snapshots of the file system and stores them in a database. This database, as well as the settings and logs, are stored on a central management server. When changes are detected, Osiris will record these events in the system log and optionally send an email to the administrator.

In addition to file monitoring, Osiris has the ability to monitor other system information, including user lists, group lists, and kernel modules or extensions.

Osiris runs on any Windows and UNIX system, including BSD, Linux, Mac OS X and Darwin, AIX, IRIX, and Windows NT/2K/XP. Such flexibility allows Osiris to manage any platform supported under a Windows or UNIX environment. Another facility that Osiris possesses is its modular interface. This unit allows developers to easily extend the monitoring functionality of scanning agents.

2.4.1.3 Tripwire

Tripwire [48] is a tool for evaluating the integrity of files, which is extremely useful for intrusion detection. Tripwire creates a database based on some information provided by system critical files, including file size and a cryptographic checking code. It compares the current information with that previously generated and detects the change. Then, it is the user's responsibility to decide whether this change was due to an attack or not.

In order to have reliable judgments, the database of Tripwire should be protected against forgery and invasion attempts. This can be done by keeping the database disconnected from the network or using a storage read-only mechanism. The configuration of Tripwire can be very complex for large multi-user systems. It is necessary to associate each file with its corresponding service or application and detect occurred changes.

2.4.1.4 HP-UX HIDS

HP-UX HIDS (Hewlett-Packard Development Company) [49] is a HIDS solution provided by Hewlett-Packard that performs monitoring and generation of an alert in the event of intrusion. The intrusion detection is based on areas of vulnerability, that is, when one area is investigated, audit data are correlated to determine which of them was exploited in near real time.

2.4.1.5 CACIC

CACIC is the first public IDS developed in Brazil [50] (from Portuguese – Configurador Automático e Coletor de Informações Computacionais). CACIC is able to provide an accurate diagnosis of the computational park and display information, such as the number of devices and their distribution in various units, the types of used and licensed software, and hardware configurations, among others. It can also provide standard information and the physical location of attached equipment devices, thus extending the control of the park computational and network security.

2.4.1.6 Nagios

Nagios [51] is open source software, created originally by Ethan Galstad and called Netsaint in the 1990s. Currently, there is a large community of programmers based around developing Nagios-based IDS tools. It is a popular network monitoring application with a distributed open source under the GPL license. It can monitor both hosts and services, alerting the user when problems occur and when problems are resolved.

2.4.1.7 Radmind

The Radmind [52] consists of a set of UNIX commands and a designed manager to execute evaluation on several other client machines. Radmind has Tripwire as its core and implements an additional tool enabling the recovery of the machine after having being changed.

2.4.1.8 Other HIDS Tools

In this section will be listed other examples of host-based intrusion detection system tools as well as their link to where it is possible to obtain more information.

- Advanced Intrusion Detection Environment (AIDE)
  http://sourceforge.net/projects/aide
- Another File Integrity Checker (AFICK)
  http://afick.sourceforge.net/
- AuditGUARD
  http://www.s4software.com/ag.htm
- Event Monitoring Enabling Responses to Anomalous Live Disturbances (EMERALD's eXpert-BSM)
  http://www.sdl.sri.com/projects/emerald/releases/eXpert-BSM/index.html
- System iNtrusion Analysis and Reporting Environment (SNARE)
  http://sourceforge.net/projects/snare/
- Enterasys Dragon Host Sensor
  http://www.enterasys.com/ids/
- GrSecurity – PaX
  http://www.grsecurity.net/
- LIDS
  http://www.lids.org/
- Logsurfer
  http://www.dfn-cert.de/eng/logsurf/
- McAfee Host Intrusion Prevention
  http://www.mcafee.com/us/enterprise/products/host_intrusion_prevention/index.html
- Samhain
  http://www.la-samhna.de/samhain/
- Sentry Tools
  http://sourceforge.net/projects/sentrytools/

2.4.2 Network-Based Intrusion Detection Systems (HIDS)

2.4.2.1 Snort

The Snort [46] is an open source network-based intrusion detection system, capable of performing traffic analysis and packet capture in real time on networks using the IP protocol. Snort has three operational modes, namely, the following:

- Packet capturing
- Network traffic analysis (Sniffer)
- Complete network system intrusion detection

Snort performs its detection based on signatures using a flexible rules language to analyze collected traffic data. These signatures/rules are updated daily by its development/management team as well as by enthusiasts and volunteers. The updating information and results can be acquired directly from the Internet, normally through some automated procedures.

Besides its established rules, Snort also interacts with those preprocessors located at network devices. These preprocessors are designated to perform some specific functions, which are crucial for Snort being efficient. Some well-known functionalities include portscans detection, complex attack pattern detection, and reassembling mechanisms of fragmented packet sequences.

Snort also interacts with Firewalls. The integrated mechanisms transform Snort into a reactive IDS model. Some important integrated mechanisms are SnortSam and Snort-Inline. SnortSam allows that SNORT interacts directly with many different network firewalls currently available in the market, ranging from simple and basic IPChains/IPTiptables to highly advanced Cisco firewalls.

Snort-Inline is a compiled version of SNORT. This integrated mechanism offers alternatives for dealing with input traffic packets. Instead of recording and alert generation in a suspicious connection, one may "drop" (delete) packets.

2.4.2.2 Internet Security System (ISS)

An Internet security system [53] is a real time IDS. Its architecture consists of three parts: a recognition mechanism based on the network (HIDS), a mechanism-based machine, and an administrator module.

The mechanism of network recognition is implemented on dedicated stations, each responsible for a network segment. This mechanism seeks to identify packets having attack characteristics. When an intrusion activity is detected, some action will be executed, for example, termination of the network connection, sending an alert, recording the session, reconfiguring the firewall, and sending an alert to the administrator module, among others. Mechanism-based machines compare input patterns with those recorded in order to identify attacks. The administrator module receives data from both detection mechanisms (recognition mechanism based on the network and mechanism-based machines). The presence of this module enables centralized configuration and system administration.

2.4.2.3 Kismet

Kismet [54] is a network analyzer (a sniffer) and an intrusion detection system for 802.11 wireless networks. When Kismet is implemented on wireless cards operating in the monitoring mode, the cards can capture network packets under different protocols, i.e., 802.11a, 802.11b, and 802.11g. Kismet also can run under the following operational systems: Linux, FreeBSD, NetBSD, OpenBSD, and Mac OS X.

2.4.2.4 Cisco Secure IPS

The Cisco Secure IPS [55] is a commercial IDS. This IDS actually is an updated version of NetRanger, one of the very first intrusion detection systems. The Cisco Secure IPS is a powerful IDS, capable of combining and executing different network security facilities and also acting as a prevention system against intruders.

2.4.2.5 Prelude IDS

The Prelude Hybrid [56] is an open source network-based intrusion detection system similar to Snort. The Prelude Hybrid is used to manage security information security and can be integrated with other network tools, including even more system intrusion detectors (sensors).

2.4.2.6 Bro Intrusion Detection System

The Bro Intrusion Detection System [57] is a system that performs passive monitoring of network traffic and analyzes the events with suspicious activities through semantic analysis, i.e., from the acquired knowledge, the IDS becomes enabled to investigate attacks.

2.4.2.7 Other Examples of NIDS Tools

In this section will be listed other examples of network-based intrusion detection systems tools as well as their link to where it is possible to obtain more information.

- Cyclpops IDS
  http://www.e-cop.net/cyclops-intrusion-detection-system.html
- Enterasys Dragon IDS
  http://www.enterasys.com/products/advanced-securityapps/dragon-intrusion-detection-protection.aspx
- Firestorm NIDS
  http://www.scaramanga.co.uk/firestorm/
- GFI LANguard
  http://www.gfi.com/lannetscan/?adv=62&loc=22&adclickid=14257624
- RealSecure Network
  http://www-935.ibm.com/services/us/en/it-services/gts-it-service-home-page-1.html
- SecureMetrics
  http://www.securitymetrics.com/securitymetricsappliance.adp
- Shoki
  http://shoki.sourceforge.net/
- SNIPS
  http://www.navya.com/software/snips/
- McAfee IntruShield Network IPS Solution
  http://www.mcafee.com/us/business-home.aspx
- SnorbySpsa
  http://bailey.st/blog/snorby-spsa/

2.5 CONCLUSION

The intrusion detection systems (IDS) have evolved considerably since the 1980s and are now indispensable in today's communication networks.

Modern intrusion detection systems are based almost exclusively on signature detection strategies due to their remarkable successes in detection of most already known attacks. However, the appearance of new and sophisticated attacking methods is constantly and quickly making network systems again vulnerable even though they are supposedly protected by the well-established signature detection systems. Although the new approach of anomaly detection has been invented to overcome this drawback, up until now, the reported performances are still far from satisfactory, precisely because of its high false alarm rates. Definitely further research on anomaly detection is needed.

As described in this chapter, many different IDS methodologies and tools have been proposed, implemented, and used by network systems. Unfortunately, individually they have their own weak points, which make them vulnerable. Fighting against those malicious attempts, which vary and are becoming more sophisticated day by day, requires more complex and intelligent IDS. A promising tendency toward this end currently focuses on new approaches that intelligently combine these methodologies.

Characterization of "normal" behaviors has also become one of the main stimuli in the field of intrusion detection systems. One expects that, based on some standardized behaviors, it is possible to easily detect anomaly behaviors. Unfortunately normal behaviors are environmentally dependent. In other words, optimization of anomaly detectors is not a trivial task due to environmental influences. Under this context, a possible challenge for new intrusion detection systems based on anomaly detection could be development of adequate theory for intrusive behavior in order to help detection system designing.

It is also noteworthy to observe that intrusion detection systems alone cannot offer all security purposes; the use of other types of protection mechanisms will always be necessary.

AUTHORS' BIOGRAPHIES

Jeferson Wilian de Godoy Stênico received a BS in mathematics from the Universidade Estadual Paulista Júlio de Mesquita Filho (UNESP, São Paulo State University), Brazil (2006) and a MSc in electrical engineering from State University of Campinas – Unicamp, Brazil (2009). He is currently a PhD student in electrical engineering from the State University of Campinas – Unicamp. His current research interests include network traffic modeling, network design, performance analysis, and communications systems.

Lee Luan Ling received BS and MSc degrees in electrical engineering from the University of São Paulo (1980) and the State University of Campinas (1984), respectively, in São Paulo, Brazil. In 1991, he received a PhD degree in electrical engineering from Cornell University, Ithaca, United States. In 1984, he became a faculty member at the School of Electrical and Computer Engineering, State University of Campinas where currently he is a full professor. Dr. Lee has published more than 150 technical papers and also serves as a reviewer for many journals and international conferences. His current research interests include pattern recognition, handwriting recognition, biometrics, image processing, artificial intelligence, video monitoring and surveillances, network traffic modeling, and network design and performance analysis. Dr. Lee is the recipient of several awards, including the 1997 academically outstanding young Chinese in Brazil and Honorable Mention Award in the 1993 National Invention Competition (São Paulo, Brazil).

REFERENCES

1. Anderson, J. P. *Computer Security Threat Monitoring and Surveillance*, Fort Washington, 1980.
2. Denning, D. E. and Neumann, P. G. *Requirements and Model for IDES—A Real-Time Intrusion Detection Expert System*, SRI International, 1985.
3. Denning, D. E. An intrusion-detection model, *IEEE Transactions on Software Engineering*, Volume SE-13, Issue 2, Feb. 1987, pp. 222–232; also in *Proceedings of the 1986 Symposium on Security and Privacy, IEEE Computer Society*, April 1986, pp. 118–131.
4. Smaha, S. E. Haystack: An intrusion detection system, *IEEE Fourth Aerospace Computer Security Applications Conference*. TracorAppl Sci. Inc., Austin, TX, pp. 37–44, 1988.
5. Distributed Intrusion Detection System (DIDS), http://seclab.cs.ucdavis.edu.
6. Heberlein, L. T., Dias, G. V., Levitt, K. N., Mukherjee, B., Wood, J., and Wolber, D. A network security model, In *Proceedings of the Symposium on Research in Security and Privacy*, Oakland, CA, pp. 296–304, 1990.
7. Proctor, P. Audit reduction and misuse detection in heterogeneous environments: Framework and application. In *Proceedings of the Tenth Annual Computer Security Applications Conference*, pp. 117–125, Orlando, FL, 1994.
8. Automated Security Measurement System (ASIM), http://www.access.gpo.gov.
9. 15th Annual Computer Crime and Security Survey, CSI/FBI, 2010/2011, https://cours.etsmtl.ca/log619/documents/divers/CSIsurvey2010.pdf.
10. Computer Crime and Security Survey, CSI/FBI, vol. VIII, no. 1, Spring 2002. http://diogenesllc.com/2002cybercrimesurvey.pdf.
11. IBM Emergency Response Service Security Vulnerability Alert ERS-SVA-E01-1996:006.1 Newly available patches for IBM AIX(r) address "SYN flood" and "ping of death" vulnerabilities, http://www.nmr.mgh.harvard.edu/MGH-UNIX/sec_advisories/CIAC:H-12.html.
12. Ranum, M. J. *Coverage in Intrusion Detection Systems*. NFRSecurity, Inc. Technical Publications, pp. 1–9, June 2001.
13. Shah, B. How to choose introduction detection solution. Whitepaper, SANS Institute, InfoSec Reading Room, July 2001.
14. Hochberg, J., Jackson, K., Stallings, C., McClary, J. F., DuBois, D., and Ford, J. Nadir: An automated system for detecting network intrusion and misuse. *Journal Computers and Security*, vol. 12, no. 3, pp. 235–248, May 1993.

15. Heberlein, L. T., Mukherjee, B., and Levitt, K. N. Internet security monitor: An intrusion detection system for large-scale networks. In *Proceedings of the 15th National Computer Security Conference*, Baltimore, MD, vol. 12, no. 3, pp. 235–248, 1993.
16. Hofmeyr, S. A., Forrest, S., and Somayaji, A. Intrusion detection using sequences of system calls. *Journal of Computer Security*, vol. 6, pp. 151–180, 1998.
17. Schupp, S. Limitations of network intrusion detection. SANS Institute, December 2000, http://www.sans.org.
18. Wang, Y. A hybrid intrusion detection system. PhD Thesis, Iowa State University, Ames, IA, 2004.
19. Nakamura, E. T., and Geus, P. L. *Segurança de Redes em Ambientes Cooperativos*. Novatec, 2007.
20. IETF, Internet Engineering Task Force, http://www.ietf.org.
21. IETF Intrusion Detection Exchange Format Working Group, http://www.ietf.org/html.charters/idwg-charter.html.
22. SNMP, http://en.wikipedia.org/wiki/Simple_Network_Management_Protocol.
23. Park, J. A. Survey on flow-based internet traffic measurement technologies. Asian Info-Communications Council, Electronics and Telecommunications Research Institute (ETRI), Korea, 2005.
24. Cottrell, L. Network monitoring tools. Last updated: 2013, http://www.slac.stanford.edu/xorg/nmtf/nmtf-tools.html.
25. Jacobson, V., Leres, C., and MacCanne, S. Tcpdump. Last updated: August 2009, http://ftp.ee.lbl.gov.
26. Combs, G. Wireshark. http://www.wireshark.org.
27. Munz, G. and Carle, G. Distributed network analysis using TOPAS and Wireshark. *IEEE Network Operations and Management Symposium Workshops*, pp. 161–164, April 2008.
28. Deri, L., and Suin, S. Effective traffic measurement using ntop. *IEEE Communications Magazine*, vol. 38, no. 5, pp. 138–143, May 2000.
29. CAIDA, cflowd Tools 1998, http://www.caida.org/tools/measurement/cflowd.
30. Plonka, D. Flowscan, http://www.caida.org/tools/utilities/flowscan/.
31. Dubendorfer, T., Wagner, A., and Plattner, B. A framework for real-time worm attack detection and backbone monitoring. In *Proceedings of the First IEEE International Workshop on Critical Infrastructure Protection*, November 2005.
32. Bin, L., Chuang, L., Jian, Q., Jianping, H., and Ungsunan, P. A NetFlow based flow analysis and monitoring system in enterprise networks. *Computer Networks*, vol. 52, Issue 5, pp. 1074–1092, April 2008.
33. Zhou, A., Yan, Y., Gong, X., Chang, J., and Dai, D. SMART: A system for online monitoring large volumes of network traffic. In *IEEE 24th International Conference on Data Engineering*. ICDE 2008, pp. 1576–1579, April 2008.
34. Cranor, C., Gao, Y., Johnson, T., Shkapenyuk, V., and Spatscheck, O. Gigascope: High performance network monitoring with a SQL interface. In *SIGMOD '02: Proceedings of the 2002 ACM SIGMOD International Conference on Management of Data*, pp. 623–627, 2002.
35. Cranor, C., Johnson, T., and Spataschek, O. Gigascope: A stream database for network applications. In *SIGMOD '03: Proceedings of the 2003 ACM SIGMOD International Conference on Management of Data*, pp. 647–651, 2003.
36. Plagemann, T., Goebel, V., Bergamini, A., Tolu, G., Urvoy-Keller, G., and Biersack, E. W. Using data stream management systems for traffic analysis—A case study. *Proceedings of the 5th International Workshop on Passive and Active Network Measurement (PAM '04)*, pp. 215–226, 2004.
37. Ligocki, N., Gomes, C. L., and Hara, C. A flexible network monitoring tool based on a data stream management system. In *Proceedings of the IEEE Symposium on Computers and Communications (ISCC 2008)*, pp. 800–805, July 2008.
38. Phaal, P., Panchen, S., and McKee, N. RFC 3176: InMon Corporation's sFlow: A method for monitoring traffic in switched and routed networks, September 2001. http://tools.ietf.org/html//rfc3176.
39. Phaal, P. and Panchen, S. Packet sampling basics [Online]. Available at http://www.sflow.org/packetSamplingBasics.
40. Duffield, N., Lund, C., and Thorup, M. Properties and prediction of flow statistics from sampled packet streams. In *Proceedings of the 2nd ACM SIGCOMM Workshop on Internet Measurement*, Marseille, France, pp. 159–171, 2002.
41. Sasha-Phrack Inc. Holistic approaches to attack detection. Volume 0x0b, Issue 0x39, Phile #0x11 of 0x12, 2003, http://www.phrack.com/issues.html?issue=57&id=11#article.
42. Li, W. Using genetic algorithm for network intrusion detection. In *Proceedings of the United States Department of Energy Cyber Security Group 2004 Training Conference*, pp. 24–27, 2004.
43. Coull, S. E., Branch, J. W., Szymanski, B. K., and Breimer, E. Intrusion detection: A bioinformatics approach, In *Proceedings of the 19th Annual Computer Security Applications Conference*, pp. 34–33, 2003.

44. Dhopte, S., and Tarapore, N. Z. Design of intrusion detection system using fuzzy class-association rule mining based on genetic algorithm. *International Journal of Computer Applications*, vol. 53, no. 14, 2012.
45. OSSEC, http://www.ossec.net.
46. SNORT, http://www.snort.org.
47. OSIRIS, http://osiris.shmoo.com/.
48. Tripwire, http://www.tripwire.com.
49. HP-UX HIDS, http://h20338.www2.hp.com/hpux11i/cache/324806-0-0-0-121.html.
50. CACIC, http://www.softwarepublico.gov.br/spb/ver-comunidade?community_id=3585.
51. Nagios, http://www.nagios.org/.
52. Craig, W. D., and McNeal, P. M. Radmind: The integration of filesystem integrity checking with filesystem management. In *LISA '03: Proceedings of the 17th USENIX Conference on System Administration*, pp. 181–196, 2003.
53. IBM Internet Security Systems, http://www.iss.net.
54. Kismet, http://www.kismetwireless.net/.
55. Cisco Intrusion Detection, http://www.cisco.com/warp/public/cc/pd/sqsw/sqidsz/index.shtml.
56. Prelude IDS, https://www.prelude-ids.org/.
57. Bro Intrusion Detection System, http://bro-ids.org/.

3 Using Routers and Honeypots in Combination for Collecting Internet Worm Attacks

Mohssen Mohammed and Al-Sakib Khan Pathan

CONTENTS

3.1   DEFINITION AND HISTORY OF HONEYPOTS

3.1.1   HONEYPOT AND ITS WORKING PRINCIPLE

The best way to first define *honeypot* would be to talk about its history, which we understand as an appropriate sequence of reading and understanding relevant critical information.

There are many definitions of honeypot [1]. In other words, there is no clearly standardized definition of honeypot. Different researchers may have their own definitions of what a honeypot is. This fact has created a great deal of confusion and miscommunication. Some think that it is a tool for deception whereas others consider it as a weapon to lure hackers, and still there are others who believe that it is simply another intrusion detection tool. Some believe a honeypot should emulate vulnerabilities. Others see it simply as a *jail*! There are also some who view honeypots as controlled production systems that attackers can break into. These various viewpoints have caused a lot of misunderstanding about what a honeypot is and thus have caused barriers to realizing their true value.

The formal definition of honeypot given by Lance Spitzner [1] is "A honeypot is a security resource whose value lies in being probed, attacked, or compromised."

Before proceeding further, a series of questions will be asked for exploring the definition of honeypot. First of all, why do we need to create a honeypot? The answer is to do the following:

- To collect information about who is trying to compromise our system. How? The honeypot has tools that can keep traces of the sources and destinations.
- A honeypot can provide us with the information about which tools and tactics have been used by the attacker(s) to compromise our system. Such information can be found in the techniques that have been used inside a honeypot, such as firewall logs, intrusion detection systems (IDSs), and system logs. By getting this information, we can avoid such attacks in the future. How? By improving our system against these known attacks. This point (i.e., collecting information about tools and tactics) is considered as the most important goal of a honeypot. This is because anyone likes to make his system as complex as possible so that it becomes more difficult for the attackers to compromise the system (of course, keeping one's own ease of using it).
- By using a honeypot, we can get zero-day attacks (unknown or unrecorded attacks). We should mention that most of the honeypot users are researchers because a honeypot provides them with extensive information about various attacks and their patterns. There are other people as well who make honeypots for other goals, such as finding a solution for the attack in a company or simply as a test or for a demonstration of the concept and so on.

An interesting fact about a honeypot is that there is no value of a honeypot if it is not attacked by the attacker! This is because in order to capture information about the attacker the honeypot must be compromised. Otherwise, it has no utility as it cannot provide the required information. This point explains why we need a honeypot. Then, we can ask another question, which is, *"How can we apply a honeypot to get attacked?"* There are several ways:

1. First, we should put a honeypot in our real network as real machines or as software in a device.
2. We should separate the honeypot from other machines in the network using firewalls, routers, or other defense mechanisms. Why should we make such a separation between the honeypot and other machines? To safeguard other machines from the attackers and also to add fake values to it so that an attacker may be interested in breaking through its security barriers.
3. If we need to improve our defense systems, then in the honeypot we should use the same defense systems that we are using in other protected machines. Using the same defense systems in the honeypot helps us know how the attackers can compromise these defense systems, so we can improve them. For example, if we want to discover zero-day attacks, we should use an updated IDPS and antivirus and add supporting defense mechanisms because these defense systems can filter out the known attacks and then only unknown attack(s) will compromise our honeypot (which is our expectation). Therefore, we can reduce the heavy loads for our honeypot.
4. Based on need, we can use weak defense systems in the honeypot, or we may not use any defense system at all if we would like to trace an attacker and get information about how it causes damage. For example, if a government of a country wants to trace who will try to compromise their systems, then they can use a honeypot with weak defense systems or no defensive mechanism at all. Therefore, the attacker will be lured and can easily compromise the government systems. Then, the authority can trace this attacker. We should note that in this case, the attacker can at least guess it to be a honeypot because if a device with weak defense systems is set up, especially in a government institution, it is highly likely that it is a honeypot. The attackers are very clever. Hence, such a trap may not always work to entice the attackers when it comes to a government institution's machines and computers.
5. We should inform all the people in an organization when we set up a honeypot so that they do not try to access it. Therefore, anything going out or coming in to the honeypot should be considered as an attack. After a considerable amount of time, we can go to the honeypot and check what it has captured. Also, in real time, we can see what exactly is happening in the honeypot.

As should be apparent from these descriptions, honeypots are different than most security tools. Most of the security technologies in use today are designed to address specific problems. For example, a firewall is a technology that protects your organization by controlling what traffic can flow where. They are used as an access control tool. Firewalls are most commonly deployed around an organization's perimeter to block unauthorized activity. Network intrusion detection systems are designed to detect attacks by monitoring either system or network activity. Honeypots are different because they are not limited to solving a single, specific problem. Instead, a honeypot is a highly flexible tool that can be applied to a variety of different situations. This is why the definition of honeypot may at first seem vague as they can be used to achieve so many different goals and can come in a variety of different forms. For example, honeypots can be used to deter attacks, a goal shared with firewalls. Honeypots also can be used to detect attacks, similar to the functionality of an intrusion detection system (IDS). Honeypots can be used to capture and analyze automated attacks, such as worms, or act as early indications and warning sensors. Honeypots also have the capability to analyze the activities of the black hat community (i.e., hackers, crackers, attackers), capturing the keystrokes or conversations of attackers. How you use honeypots is up to you. It depends on what you are trying to achieve. However, all the possible manifestations share one common feature: Their value lies in being probed, attacked, or compromised.

It is important to note that honeypots do not contain valuable data. Instead, they contain some kind of fake data. Therefore, honeypots are the security resources that have no production value; no person or resource should be communicating with them. As such, any activity sent their way is *suspect* by nature. Any traffic sent to the honeypot is most likely a probe, scan, or attack. Any traffic initiated by the honeypot means the system has most likely been compromised, and the attacker is making outbound connections.

Let us give a practical example to complete the understanding of the definition of honeypot. Let us consider that there is a house with three rooms. We assume that this house is targeted by the attackers. The house's owner needs to know who the attacker is and how he compromises the house defense systems (i.e., door locks, money storage, window grills, etc.). The house owner has put all his valuable things in the first two rooms, and he has set inside the third room, a camera (hidden) with another camera (hidden) in the front of the room to monitor the attacker(s). The other defense systems used for the third room are the same as the defense systems used in the first two rooms, but the third room does not contain any valuable thing. In this scenario, when an attacker breaks in or comes to the third room, the camera would capture all the attacker's activities. So, in this case, the third room is working in the same way as a honeypot does because this room gives a free movement option for the attacker but records all his moves (how he approaches to search something within the room).

3.1.2 History of Honeypots

In this section, we present a brief history of honeypots [1].

- 1990–1991—First public works documenting honeypot concepts: Clifford Stoll's *The Cuckoo's Egg* and Bill Cheswick's "An Evening with Berferd."
- 1997—Version 0.1 of Fred Cohen's Deception Toolkit was released, one of the first honeypot solutions available to the security community [2,3].
- 1998—Development began on CyberCop Sting, one of the first commercial honeypots sold to the public. CyberCop Sting introduces the concept of multiple, virtual systems bound to a single honeypot.
- 1998—Marty Roesch and GTE Internetworking begin development on a honeypot solution that eventually becomes NetFacade. This work also begins the concept of Snort [1,5].
- 1998—BackOfficer Friendly is released: a free, simple-to-use Windows-based honeypot.
- 1999—Formation of the Honeynet Project and publication of the *Know Your Enemy* series of papers. This work helped increase awareness and validated the value of honeypots and honeypot technologies [1,6].
- 2000–2001—Use of honeypots to capture and study worm activity. More organizations are adopting honeypots for both detecting attacks and for doing research on new threats.
- 2002—A honeypot is used to detect and capture in the wild a new and unknown attack, specifically the *Solaris dtspcd* exploit.

3.1.2.1 Early Publications

Very few written or recorded materials can be found before 1990 about honeypot concepts. The first visible resource was a book written by Clifford Stoll titled *The Cuckoo's Egg* [2]. The second is the white paper "An Evening with Berferd in Which a Cracker Is Lured, Endured, and Studied" [3] by the security icon Bill Cheswick. This does not mean that honeypots were not invented until 1990; they were undoubtedly developed and used by a variety of organizations well before that time.

A great deal of research and deployment occurred within military, government, and commercial organizations, but very little of it was public knowledge before 1990.

In *The Cuckoo's Egg*, Clifford Stoll discusses a series of true events that occurred over a 10-month period in 1986 and 1987. Stoll was an astronomer at Lawrence Berkeley Lab who worked with and helped administer a variety of computer systems used by the astronomer community. A 75-cent accounting error led him to discover that an attacker, code named "Hunter," had infiltrated one of his systems. Instead of disabling the attacker's accounts and locking him out of the system, Stoll decided to allow the attacker to stay on his system. His motives were to learn more about the attacker and hunt him down. Over the following months he attempted to discover the attacker's identity while at the same time protecting the various government and military computers the attacker was targeting. Stoll's computers were not honeypots; they were production systems used by the academic and research communities. However, he used the compromised systems to track the attacker in a manner very similar to the concept of honeypots and honeypot technologies. Stoll's book is not technical; it reads more like some kind of spy novel. What makes the book unique and important in the history of honeypots are the concepts Stoll discusses in it.

The most fascinating thing in the book is Stoll's approach to gaining information without the attacker realizing it. For example, he creates a bogus directory on the compromised system called SDINET, for Strategic Defense Initiative Network. He wanted to create material that would attract the attention of the attacker. He then filled the directory with a variety of interesting-sounding files. The goal was to waste the attacker's time by compelling him to look through a lot of files. The more time he spent on the system, the more time authorities had to track down the attacker. Stoll also included documents with different values. By observing which particular documents the attacker copied, he could identify the attacker's motives. For example, Stoll provided documents that included those that appeared to have financial value and those that had government secrets. The attacker bypassed the financial documents and focused on materials about national security. This indicated that the attacker's motives were not financial gain but access to highly secret documents.

Bill Cheswick's paper, "An Evening with Berferd in Which a Cracker Is Lured, Endured, and Studied," was released in 1990. This paper is more technical than *The Cuckoo's Egg*. It was written by security professionals for the security community. Like *The Cuckoo's Egg*, everything in Cheswick's paper is nonfiction. However, unlike the book, Cheswick builds a system that he wants to be compromised—which should be the first documented case of a true honeypot. In the paper, he discusses not only how the honeypot was built and used, but how a Dutch hacker was studied as he attacked and compromised a variety of systems.

Cheswick initially built a system with several vulnerabilities (including Sendmail) to determine what threats existed and how they operated. His goal was not to capture someone specific, but rather to learn what threatening activity was happening on his networks and systems.

Cheswick's paper explains not only the different methodologies he used in building his system (he never called it a honeypot), but also how these methodologies were used. In addition to a variety of services that appeared vulnerable, he created a controlled environment called a *jail*, which contained the activities of the attacker. He takes us step by step through how an intruder (called Berferd) attempts to infiltrate the system and what Cheswick was able to learn from the attacker. We see how Berferd infiltrated a system using a Sendmail vulnerability and then gained control of the system. Cheswick describes the advantages and disadvantages of his approach.

Both Stoll's book and Cheswick's paper are good-read documents. However, none of the resources describes how to design and deploy honeypots in detail. And neither provides a precise definition of honeypots or explores the value of honeypot technologies.

3.1.2.2 Early Products

The first public honeypot solution, called Deception Toolkit (DTK) [4], was developed by Fred Cohen. Version 0.1 was released in November 1997, seven years after *The Cuckoo's Egg* and "An Evening with Berferd." DTK is one of the first free honeypot solutions one could download, install, and try out on one's own. It is a collection of PERL scripts and C code that is compiled and installed on a Unix system. DTK is similar to Bill Cheswick's Berferd system in that it emulates a variety of known Unix vulnerabilities. When attacked, these emulated vulnerabilities log the attacker's behavior and actions and reveal information about the attacker. The goal of DTK is not only to gain information but also to deceive the attacker and psychologically confuse him. DTK introduced honeypot solutions to the security community.

Following DTK, in 1998, development began on the first commercial honeypot product, CyberCop Sting. Originally developed by Alfred Huger at Secure Networks, Inc., it was purchased by NAI in 1998. This honeypot had several features different from DTK. First, it ran on Windows NT systems and not Unix. Second, it could emulate different systems at the same time, specifically a Cisco router, a Solaris server, and an NT system.

Thus, CyberCop Sting could emulate an entire network with each system having its own unique services devoted to the operating system it was emulating. It would be possible for an attacker to scan a network and find a variety of Cisco, Solaris, and NT systems. The attacker could then Telnet to the Cisco router and get a banner saying the system was Cisco, FTP to the Solaris server and get a banner saying the system was Solaris, or make an HTTP connection to the NT server. Even the emulated IP stacks were modified to replicate the proper OS. This way, if active fingerprinting measures were used, such as Nmap [7], the detected OS would reflect the services for that IP address. The multiple honeypot images created by a single CyberCop Sting installation greatly increased the chances of the honeypots being found and attacked. This improved detection of and alerting to the attacker's activity.

For its time and development, CyberCop Sting was a cutting-edge and advanced honeypot. Also, it was easy to install, configure, and maintain, making it accessible to a large part of the security community. However, as a commercial product, it never really took off and has now been discontinued. Since its demise, several excellent commercial honeypot products have been released, including NetSec's Specter [8] and Recourse's Mantrap [9].

In 1998, Marty Roesch, while working at GTE Internetworking, began working on a honeypot solution for a large government client. Roesch and his colleagues developed a honeypot system that would simulate an entire class C network, up to 254 systems, using a single host to create the entire network. Up to seven different types of operating systems could be emulated with a variety of services. Although the resulting commercial product, NetFacade [5], has seen little public exposure, an important side benefit of this honeypot solution is that Roesch also developed a network-based debugging tool, which eventually led to his OpenSource IDS, Snort [10].

The year 1998 also saw the release of BackOfficer Friendly (BOF), a Windows- and Unix-based honeypot developed by Marcus Ranum and released by Network Flight Recorder. What made BOF unique is that it was free, extremely easy to use, and could run on any Windows-based desktop system. All you had to do was download the tool, install it on your system, and you instantly had your own personal honeypot. Though limited in its capabilities, BOF was many people's first introduction to the concepts of honeypot technologies.

In 1999, the Honeynet Project was undertaken [11]. As a nonprofit research group of 30 security professionals, this group is dedicated to researching the black hat community and sharing what they learned. Their primary tool for learning is the "Honeynet," an advanced type of honeypot. Over several years, the Honeynet Project demonstrated the capabilities and value of honeypots, specifically Honeynets, for detecting and learning about attacks and the attackers themselves. All of the group's research methods, specifically how they designed and deployed honeypots, were publicly documented and released for the security community in a series of papers known as "Know Your Enemy." In 2001, they released the book *Know Your Enemy* [6] that documented their research works and findings. This helped develop the awareness, credibility, and value of honeypots.

3.1.2.3   Recent History: Honeypots in Action

During 2000 and 2001, there was a sudden growth in both Unix-based and Windows-based worms. These worms proved to be extremely effective. Their ability to exponentially spread across the

Internet astounded the Internet community. One of the challenges that various security organizations faced was obtaining a copy of the worm for analysis and understanding how it worked. Obtaining copies of the worm from compromised production systems was difficult because of data pollution or, as in the case of the CodeRed worm [12], because the worms only resided in the system's memory. Honeypots proved themselves to be a powerful solution in quickly capturing these worms, once again proving their value to the security community.

One example was the capture and analysis of the Leaves worm by Incidents.org. On June 19, 2001, a sudden rise of scans for the Sub7 Trojan was detected. Sub7 was a Trojan that took over Windows systems, giving an attacker total remote control of the system. The Trojan listened on the default port 27374. The attacker controlled the compromised system by connecting to this port with special client software. A team of security experts from Incidents.org attempted to find the reason for the activity.

On June 21, Johannes Ullrich of the SANS Institute deployed a honeypot that he had developed to emulate a Windows system infected with the Sub7 Trojan. Within minutes, this honeypot captured an attack, giving the Incidents team the ability to analyze it. They discovered that a worm was pretending to be a Sub7 client and attempting to infect systems already infected by the Sub7 Trojan. This saved the attacker from the trouble of hacking into systems because the systems were already attacked and compromised. Matt Fearnow and the Incidents.org team were able to do a full analysis of the worm, which was eventually identified as the W32/Leaves worm, and forward the critical information to the National Infrastructure Protection Center (NIPC). Other organizations also began using honeypots for capturing worms for analysis, such as Ryan Russel at SecurityFocus. com for analysis of the CodeRed II worm. These incidents again helped develop awareness of the value of honeypots within the security community and security research areas.

The first recorded instance involving honeypot technologies in capturing an unknown exploit occurred on January 8, 2002. A Solaris honeypot captured a *dtspcd* exploit, an attack never seen before. On November 12, 2001, the CERT Coordination Center, a security research organization, released an advisory for the CDE Subprocess Control Service [13], or, more specifically, *dtspcd*. The security community was aware that the service was vulnerable. An attacker could theoretically remotely attack and gain access to any Unix system running the *dtspcd* service. However, no actual exploit was known, and it was believed that there was no exploit being used in the wild. When a honeypot was used to detect and capture a *dtspcd* attack, it confirmed that the exploit code did exist and was being used by the black hat community. CERT was able to release an advisory [14] based on this information, warning the security community that the vulnerability was now being actively attacked and exploited. This demonstrated the value of honeypots not only in capturing known attacks, such as the worm, but also in detecting and capturing unknown attacks.

3.1.3 TYPES OF HONEYPOTS

There are mainly two types of honeypots:

- Production honeypots
- Research honeypots

The concept of such *types* comes from Marty Roesch, the developer of Snort. It evolved during his work and research at GTE Internetworking. Production honeypots protect an organization, and research honeypots are used to learn.

Production honeypots are easy to use, capture only limited information, and are used primarily by companies or corporations. These honeypots are placed inside the production network with other production servers by an organization to improve their overall state of security. They add value to the security of a specific organization and help mitigate risk. Normally, production honeypots give less information about the attacks or attackers than research honeypots do.

As we have mentioned above, production honeypots usually are easier to build and deploy than research honeypots because they require less functionality. Production honeypots are relatively simple and generally have less risk. One of the disadvantages of the production honeypots is that they generally give us less information about the attacks or the attackers than research honeypots do. We may learn about which systems the attackers are coming from or what exploits they launch, but we will most likely not learn how they communicate among each other or how they develop their tools.

Research honeypots are often very complex to deploy. The main goals of the research honeypots are to gather extensive information about the motives and tactics of the black hat community targeting different networks. It should be mentioned that the research honeypots do not add direct value to a specific organization; instead, they are used to analyze the threats that the organizations face and to learn how to better protect against those threats. Research honeypots are complex to deploy and maintain, capture extensive information, and are used primarily by research, military, or government organizations.

To get extensive information about the attackers, we need to use research honeypots; there is no other alternative. These honeypots give attackers real operating systems and applications with which to interact. This helps us to potentially learn who the attackers are, how they communicate, or how they develop or acquire their tools, but we should mention that the research honeypots have great risks as well and require more time and effort to administer. In fact, research honeypots could potentially reduce the security of an organization because they require extensive resources and maintenance efforts.

3.2   TYPES OF THREATS

A honeypot is a kind of security solution. Therefore, it is better to discuss what the problem is, e.g., the attacker. By understanding who our threat is and how he operates, we can easily understand the solution better, which is the concept of the honeypot.

3.2.1   SCRIPT KIDDIES AND ADVANCED BLACK HAT ATTACKS

There are two types of attackers, which are script kiddies and advanced black hat. It does not matter if these threats are coming from the outside, such as the Internet, or from inside, such as a disgruntled employee. Most threats tend to fall into one of these two categories.

Script kiddies: These types of attackers usually depend on scripted attacks. Sometimes these attackers have certain requirements, such as hacking systems with a fast connection to the Internet or a large hard drive for storing files. In general, however, all they care about are numbers. They tend to be less sophisticated, but they are far more numerous, representing the vast majority of probes, scans, and attacks you see today.

To compromise a device using script kiddies is very simple, and the attacker only needs to follow a number of steps to reach its intended goal. Without script kiddies, the task is much more complicated and may only be performed by experts. For example, steps would be the following:

- First, an attacker has to identify a vulnerability within an operating system (OS) or application. This is not an easy task. It requires extensive knowledge of how operating systems work, such as memory management, kernel mechanisms, and file systems' functionality. To identify vulnerabilities in an application, an attacker would have to learn how an application operated and interacted with both the input and output of information. It could take days, weeks, even months, to identify vulnerabilities.
- However, after a vulnerability is identified, an attacker would have to develop a tool to exploit it. This requires extensive coding skills, potentially in several different computer programming languages.

- After the exploit is developed, the attacker has to find vulnerable systems. Often one scanning tool is used to find systems that are accessible on the Internet, using such functionality as an ICMP ping or a full TCP connection. These tools are used to develop a database of systems that are accessible. Then the attacker has to determine what services existed on the reachable systems—that is, what was actually running on the targets. Furthermore, the attacker has to determine if any of these services was vulnerable.
- The next step would be launching the exploit against the victim, hacking into and gaining control of the system. Finally, various other tools (often called rootkits) should be used to take over and maintain control of a compromised system.

Each of these steps just described requires the development of a unique tool, and using all those tools takes a lot of time and resources. Once the attack is launched, the tools are often manually operated, requiring a great deal of work from an experienced attacker.

The above mentioned steps are too difficult and need a great deal of experience from the attackers; that means there could be only a few people who could do these successfully. Unfortunately, today, the story is too different. With almost no technical skills or knowledge, anyone can simply download tools from the Internet that can do all the work for them. Sometimes, these tools combine all of the activities that we have just described into a fully automated weapon that only needs to be pointed at certain systems or even at an entire network. This is as simple as just clicking a button or pressing a key on the keyboard! An attacker simply downloads these tools, follows the instructions, launches the attacks, and happily hacks his way into hundreds or even thousands of systems. These tools are rapidly spreading across the Internet, giving access to thousands of attackers who may do such tasks just for fun. What used to be a highly complex development process is now extremely simple!

Attackers can download the automated tools from a variety of resources or exchange them with their friends. IRC (Internet relay chat) and the World Wide Web (www) enabled black hats to instantly share new attack tools around the world. Then, they simply learn the command line syntax for the tool. For attackers who are unfamiliar with command line syntax, a variety of tools have been designed for Windows with point-and-click capabilities. Some of the exploits even come with well-written, step-by-step instructions.

Advanced black hat: These types of attackers focus on targets of choice and may want to compromise a specific system or systems of high value. These individuals are most likely highly experienced and knowledgeable attackers. Their attack is usually financially or nationally motivated, such as with *state-sponsored terrorism*. They have a specific target they want to compromise, and they focus only on that one. Though less common and fewer in number, these attackers are far more dangerous due to their advanced skill level. Not only can they penetrate highly secured systems, their actions are difficult to detect and trace. Advanced black hats make little "noise" while attacking systems, and they excel at covering their tracks. Even if you have been successfully attacked by such a skilled black hat, you may never even be aware of it.

While script kiddies and automated attacks represent the largest percentage of attackers, the smaller, more dangerous percentage of attackers are the skilled ones that do not want anyone to know about their existence. These advanced black hats do not release their tools. They only attack and compromise systems of high value (i.e., systems of choice). When these attackers are successful, they do not tell the world about it. Instead, they silently infiltrate organizations, collecting information, users' accounts, and access to critical resources. Often organizations have no idea that they have been compromised. Advanced attackers can spend months, even years, within a compromised organization without anyone finding out.

These attackers are interested in a variety of targets. It could be an online banking system, in which the attacker is after the database containing millions of peoples' credit card information. It could be a case of corporate espionage, in which the attacker is attempting to infiltrate a car manufacturer and obtain research designs of future cars. Or it can be as sinister as a foreign government attempting to access highly confidential government secrets, potentially compromising the security of a country.

These individuals are highly trained and experienced, and they are far more difficult to detect than script kiddies. Even after they have successfully penetrated an organization, they will take advanced steps to ensure that their presence or activity cannot be detected. Very little is known about these attackers. Unlike unskilled attackers, advanced black hats do not share the same tools or techniques. Each one tends to develop his own skills, methods, and tool sets specialized for specific activities. As such, when the tools and methods of one advanced attacker are discovered, the information gained may not apply to other advanced black hats.

We should mention that every computer connected to the Internet is exposed to a great danger. This danger may cost you all your life; for example, what would happen if an attacker uses your hard drive to store all of the stolen credit card information that he has collected? If the competent authorities for credit cards prosecute thieves, track the attacker traces, and find that the credit card information is in your computer, what will you do? It may happen that the amount of money that was stolen from the credit cards is too much. In such an embarrassing case, how can you deny the charge against you? Therefore, everyone should take care about this great issue and try to make his computer as secure as possible.

3.2.2 Motivations of the Attackers

Understanding the motivation of the attackers will help us understand threats better. The following attacks will help for understanding why an attacker would target and attempt to compromise a system.

3.2.2.1 Denial of Service (DoS) Attack

DoS attacks are those designed to take out the computer systems or networks of a victim. This is commonly done by flooding the intended target (such as a Web server) with a barrage of network traffic. The more traffic that is thrown at a victim, the more effective the attack is. Attackers will often compromise hundreds, if not thousands, of systems to be used for attacks. The more computers they own, the more traffic they can launch at a target. Many black hats use DoS attacks to take out other black hats. One example is IRC wars, in which one individual attempts to knock out another individual from an IRC channel, using DoS attacks [15].

3.2.2.2 BOTs

BOTs (the word *bot* has been derived from *robot*) are automated robots that act on behalf of an individual in a preprogrammed fashion. They are most commonly used to maintain control of IRC. The more computers one hacks into, the more BOTs one can launch, and the more one can control specific IRC channels. Using many BOTs protects individuals from losing control of an IRC from denial of service attacks.

3.2.2.3 Phishing

Phishing is a way of attempting to acquire information (and sometimes, indirectly, money) such as usernames, passwords, and credit card details by masquerading as a trustworthy entity in an electronic communication. Communications purporting to be from popular social websites, auction sites, online payment processors, or IT (information technology) administrators are commonly used to lure the unsuspecting public. Phishing is typically carried out by email spoofing or instant messaging, and it often directs users to enter details at a fake website whose look and feel are almost identical to the legitimate one. Phishing is an example of social engineering techniques used to deceive users and exploit the poor usability of current web security technologies. Attempts to deal with the growing number of reported phishing incidents include legislation, user training, public awareness, and technical security measures [16].

3.3   THE VALUE OF HONEYPOTS

We know now from all the above discussions that there is no specific definition of what a honeypot is. Therefore, the value of a honeypot depends on what your problem is or why you need to build honeypots. The answers to these questions will highlight the value of honeypots. Therefore, the value of honeypots basically depends on your goals.

There are advantages and disadvantages of the honeypots, which affect their value. In this section, we show the advantages and disadvantages of them. Moreover, we will present the differences between production and research honeypots and their respective roles.

3.3.1   ADVANTAGES OF HONEYPOTS

There are many advantages of using honeypots, but in this section we will focus on only some of those [1].

- *Data value:* One of the challenges that the security community faces is gaining value from data. Organizations collect vast amounts of data every day, including firewall logs, system logs, and intrusion detection alerts. The sheer amount of information can be overwhelming, making it extremely difficult to derive any value from the data. Honeypots, on the other hand, collect very little data, but what they do collect is normally of high value. The honeypot concept of no expected production activity dramatically reduces the noise level. Instead of logging gigabytes of data every day, most honeypots collect several megabytes of data per day, if even that much. Any data that is logged is most likely a scan, probe, or attack—information of high value.

  Honeypots can give you the precise information you need in a quick and easy-to-understand format. This makes analysis much easier and reaction time much quicker. For example, the Honeynet Project, a group researching honeypots, collects, on average, less than 1 MB of data per day. Even though this is a very small amount of data, it contains primarily malicious activities. These data can then be used for statistical modeling, trend analysis, detecting attacks, or even analyzing attackers. This is similar to a microscope effect. Whatever data you capture is placed under a microscope for detailed scrutiny.

- *Resources:* Another challenge most security mechanisms face is resource limitations or even resource exhaustion. Resource exhaustion is when a security resource can no longer continue to function because its resources are overwhelmed. For example, a firewall may fail because its connections table is full, it has run out of resources, or it can no longer monitor connections. This forces the firewall to block all connections instead of just blocking unauthorized activity. An intrusion detection system may have too much network activity to monitor, perhaps hundreds of megabytes of data per second. When this happens, the IDS sensor's buffers become full, and it begins dropping packets. Its resources have been exhausted, and it can no longer effectively monitor network activity, potentially missing attacks. Another example is centralized log servers. They may not be able to collect all the events from remote systems, potentially dropping and failing to log critical events.

  Because they capture and monitor little activity, honeypots typically do not have problems of resource exhaustion. As a point of contrast, most IDS sensors have difficulty monitoring networks that have gigabits speed. The speed and volume of the traffic are simply too great for the sensor to analyze every packet. As a result, traffic is dropped and potential attacks are missed. A honeypot deployed on the same network does not share this problem. It only captures activities directed to it; so the system is not overwhelmed by the traffic. Where the IDS sensor may fail because of resource exhaustion, the honeypot is not likely to have a problem. A side benefit of the limited resource requirements of a honeypot is that you do not have to invest a great deal of money in hardware for it. Honeypots, in contrast to many security mechanisms, such as firewalls or IDS sensors, do not require the latest cutting-edge technology, vast amounts of RAM or chip speed, or large disk drives. You can use leftover computers found in your organization or that old laptop your boss no longer wants. This means that not only can a honeypot be deployed on your gigabit network, but also it can be a relatively cheap computer.

- *Simplicity:* Simplicity is the biggest single advantage of honeypots. There are no fancy algorithms to develop, no signature databases to maintain, no rule-bases to misconfigure. You just take the honeypot, drop it somewhere in your organization, and sit back and wait. While some honeypots, especially research honeypots, can be more complex, they all operate on the same simple premise: If somebody or someone connects to the honeypot, check it out. As experienced security professionals will tell you, the simpler the concept is, the more reliable it is. With complexity comes misconfiguration, breakdowns, and failures.

- *Fewer false positives:* We mentioned earlier that any interaction with the honeypots will be considered as suspicious. Moreover, when all people in an organization are informed that there is a honeypot set up in the organization (i.e., some devices are acting as honeypots), nobody will try to access those.

- *Do not require known attack signatures, unlike IDS:* Honeypots do not require known attack signatures to detect suspicious activities. All activities in honeypots will be stored as suspicious.

3.3.2 DISADVANTAGES OF HONEYPOTS

While it is true that the honeypots have great advantages, they also have several disadvantages [1]. A critical point to remember is that honeypots do not replace any security mechanisms; they only work with and enhance your overall security architecture. Let us see now some of the significant disadvantages:

- *Only monitor interactions made directly with the Honeypot:* This is considered as the greatest disadvantage of honeypots. They only see what activity is directed against them. If an attacker breaks into your network and attacks a variety of systems, your honeypot will be unaware of the activity unless it is attacked directly. If the attacker has identified your honeypot as what it is, he can avoid that system and infiltrate your organization with the honeypot never knowing something bad happened! As noted earlier, honeypots have a microscope effect on the value of the data you collect, enabling you to focus closely on data of known value. However, like a microscope, the honeypot's very limited field of view can exclude events happening all around it.

- *Risk:* Honeypots can be used by expert attackers to attack other systems. Therefore, they can be even greater threats for your network.

- *Fingerprinting:* Another disadvantage found especially in many commercial versions is fingerprinting. Fingerprinting is when an attacker can identify the true identity of a honeypot because it has certain expected characteristics or behaviors. For example, a honeypot may emulate a Web server. Whenever an attacker connects to this specific type of honeypot, the Web server responds by sending a common error message using standard HTML. This is the exact response we would expect from any Web server. However, for instance, if the honeypot has a weakness in it and misspells one of the HTML commands, such as spelling the word *length* as *legnht*, then this misspelling becomes a fingerprint for the honeypot. This is because any attacker can quickly identify such types of mistakes in the Web server emulation. Also, an incorrectly implemented honeypot can identify itself. For example, a honeypot may be designed to emulate an NT IIS Web server, but it also has certain characteristics that identify it as a Unix Solaris server. These contradictory identities can act as a signature for a Honeypot. There are a variety of other methods to fingerprint a Honeypot that we discuss in other parts of this book.

If a black hat identifies an organization using a honeypot on its internal networks, he could spoof the identity of other production systems and attack the honeypot. The honeypot would detect these spoofed attacks and falsely alert administrators that a production system is attacking it, sending the organization on a wild goose chase! Meanwhile, in the midst of all the confusion, an attacker could focus on real attacks.

Fingerprinting is an even greater risk for research honeypots. A system designed to gain intelligence can be devastated if detected. An attacker can feed bad/wrong information to a research honeypot as opposed to avoiding detection. This wrong information would then lead the security community to make incorrect conclusions about the black hat community.

Although these disadvantages seem to be diminishing the value of honeypots, some organizations might want to use them positively to scare away or confuse attackers. Once a honeypot is attacked, it can identify itself and then warn the attacker in hopes of scaring him off. However, in most situations, organizations do not want their honeypots to be detected.

3.3.3 ROLES OF HONEYPOTS IN NETWORK SECURITY

We have discussed the advantages and disadvantages of the honeypots. So to see what the greatest value of the honeypots could be, we must apply them to security. We may analyze how they add value to security and reduce an organization's overall risk.

The security is broken into three categories by Bruce Schneier in *Secrets and Lies* [17]. These are prevention, detection, and response. Here, we will discuss how honeypots can or cannot add value to each one of them.

3.3.3.1 Prevention

In network security, prevention means keeping the bad guy out (i.e., preventing the bad guy from entering your network). Honeypots add a little value to prevention. Moreover, we know that honeypots can be used by the attackers to attack other systems in your organizations. The good news is that there are many methods that can be used by the honeypots to prevent the attackers from entering your organization. When attackers know that an organization has applied honeypots, they will worry about being detected, and also they will waste time and resources attacking the honeypots. This method that we discussed earlier is known as prevention by deception or deterrence. The deception concept is to make attackers waste time and resources attacking honeypots as opposed to attacking production systems. The deterrence concept is that if attackers know there are honeypots in an organization, they may be scared off. Perhaps they will not want to be detected or they will not want to waste their time or resources.

We should mention that deception and deterrence fail to prevent the most common of the attacks, especially targets of opportunity. This is because *targets-of-opportunity* attackers use automated tools to compromise as many systems as possible. These attackers do not spend time analyzing the systems they target. Deception or deterrence will not prevent these attacks because there is no conscious individual to deter or deceive. Finally, we can say that there is no real prevention done by honeypots or a limited prevention can be provided by them.

3.3.3.2 Detection

Detection means the act of monitoring, identifying, and alerting unauthorized activity. While prevention means to block unauthorized activities from entering your organization, detection means that unauthorized activities can enter your organization, and the system then sends an alert in real time to the administrators. Consequently, the administrators would check whether these activities are really authorized or not. If those are confirmed as unauthorized, the administrators would deny those or purge those out.

The security community has designed several technologies for doing detection tasks; one of those is an intrusion detection system (IDS), for example. An IDS is a security solution that is designed to detect unauthorized activities in the network or on an individual machine.

After these descriptions about detection, one question comes forward, that is, do honeypots add value in detecting unauthorized or suspicious activity? The answer is yes! Honeypots add a great value in detection, which we will explore now.

There are mainly three common challenges of the detection environment:

- False positives
- False negatives
- Data aggregation

False positives happen when the IDS falsely alerts suspicious or malicious activity, typically because of flawed traffic modeling or weak rules/signatures/anomalies specified. False negatives are when the system fails to detect an attack. The third challenge is data aggregation, centrally collecting all the data used for detection and then corroborating that data into valuable information.

A single false positive is not a problem. The problem occurs when a system sends too many false positives (i.e., hundreds or even thousands of times a day). So too many false positives are a big problem because the administrator should take care of all these false positives to check whether those are truly false positives or not. This adds to the burden of tasks of an administrator as we know that a person in that role has too many tasks to perform each day including taking care of the IDS. If an IDS has a huge number of false positives, an administrator is supposed to give most of his time for this issue and ignore all the other issues. Often some people say that an IDS is good if it has a few false positives, and they seem not to care about the danger of false negatives. Our view on this matter is that both false positives and false negatives are equally crucial for an organization because a successful false negative will make a big problem in an organization, such as information theft, network delay, system down, and so on. Again, false positives are considered to be big trouble as these can occupy an administrator's working hours and drain him out.

It is well understood that there is not a single manmade system in the world that is 100% perfect. But usually our goal is to design and develop any system as flawless as we can to the best of our abilities. A perfect system needs Godly inputs and supports, which would be free from any error, which is not applicable for human beings. So a very good IDS also should have a few false positives and false negatives.

The third challenge is data aggregation as mentioned before. Modern technology is extremely effective at capturing extensive amounts of data. NIDS, system logs, application logs—all of these resources are very good at capturing and generating gigabytes of data. The challenge is how to aggregate all these data so that they have value in detecting and confirming an attack. New technologies are constantly being devised to pull all these data together to create value to potentially detect attacks. At the same time, new technologies are being developed that can generate more new forms of data. So here the problem is that the technology is advancing too rapidly, and the solutions for aggregating data cannot cope with the pace of data production.

To make a good environment for detection, we must address the above three challenges. The honeypots can address these challenges in style! Let us find out how:

- *False positives:* Most honeypots have no production traffic nor will it run any legitimate production services. So there is little activity to generate false positives.
- *False negatives:* Honeypots address false negatives because they are not easily evaded or defeated by new exploits. Moreover, as we know that there is little or no production activity within the honeypots, they reduce false negatives by capturing absolutely everything that enters and leaves the system. This means that all the activities that are captured are most likely the suspects.
- *Data aggregation:* Honeypots address this issue by capturing high-value data. They usually generate only several megabytes of data a day, most of which are of high value. Also, honeypots can capture zero-day attacks (i.e., unknown attacks), which are not detected by other security tools. This makes them extremely handy for use in network systems.

One example of using a honeypot for detection would be its deployment within a DMZ, often called the demilitarized zone. This is a network of untrusted systems normally used to provide services to the Internet, such as email or Web servers. These are usually the systems at great risk because anyone on the Internet can initiate a connection to them, so they are highly likely to be attacked and potentially compromised. Detection of such activity is critical. The problem is that such attacks are difficult to detect because there are so many production activities going on. All of this traffic can generate a significant amount of false positives. Administrators may quickly ignore alerts generated by traffic within the DMZ. Also, because of the large amount of traffic generated, data aggregation becomes a challenge. However, we do not want to miss any attacks, specifically false negatives. Hence, such implementation is often welcome.

3.3.3.3   Response

Once an attack is detected, we need the ability to respond to this attack. A honeypot can help protect an organization in response to such an event. One of the greatest challenges that the organizations face today is how to respond to an attack. There is often little information about the attacker(s), how they got in, or how much damage they have already done. In an attack situation, detailed information about the attacker's activities is critical. The main problem to attack response is that often the compromised system is a production system and is running essential services. Hence, it is difficult to shut it down or take it offline. Even if the system is taken offline, the logs and data entries are so much that it can be difficult to determine what normal day-to-day activities are and what the attacker's activities are.

Honeypots can help address both problems. Honeypots make an excellent incident response tool as they can quickly and easily be taken offline for a full forensic analysis without impacting day-to-day production operations. Also, the only activity a honeypot captures is unauthorized or malicious activity (as already mentioned). This makes hacked honeypots much easier to analyze than hacked production systems as any data we retrieve from a honeypot are most likely related to the attacker. The precious gift they (i.e., honeypots) provide here is quickly giving organizations some kind of in-depth information that the organizations need to respond to an attack effectively. Generally, high-interaction honeypots make the best solutions for response. We will soon talk about this in this chapter.

3.4   HONEYPOT TYPES BASED ON INTERACTION LEVEL

The level of interaction gives us a scale with which we could measure and compare honeypots. The more a honeypot can do and the more an attacker can do to a honeypot, the greater the information that can be derived from it. However, by the same token, the more an attacker can do to the honeypot, the more potential damage an attacker can incur. Based on interaction levels, honeypots fall into three categories [1], which are low-interaction honeypots, mid-interaction honeypots, and high-interaction honeypots.

3.4.1   Low-Interaction Honeypots

Low-interaction honeypots are the simplest in terms of implementation and typically are the easiest to install, configure, deploy, and maintain because of their simple design and basic functionality. These honeypots merely emulate a variety of services. So the attacker is limited to interacting with these predesignated services. For example, a low-interaction honeypot could emulate a standard Unix server with several running services, such as Telnet and FTP. An attacker could Telnet to the honeypot, get a banner that states the operating system, and perhaps obtain a login prompt. The attacker can then attempt to log in by brute force or by guessing the passwords. The honeypot would capture and collect these attempts, but we should mention that there is no real operating system for the attacker to log in to. So, the attacker's interaction is limited to login attempts!

In fact, the main function of the low-interaction honeypots is detection, specifically of unauthorized scans or unauthorized connection attempts. As we mentioned above, low-interaction honeypots offer a limited functionality; most of this can be emulated by a program. The program is simply installed on a host system and configured to offer whatever services the admin wants, and the honeypot is ready. This makes both deployment and maintenance of the honeypot easy. All that the administrator has to do is to maintain patch levels of the program and monitor any alerting mechanisms.

Low-interaction honeypots have the lowest risk because there is no real operating system for the attacker to interact with (i.e., all of the services are emulated, not real). So these honeypots cannot be used to harm or monitor other systems. Low-interaction honeypots log only limited information and are designed to capture known activities. An attacker can detect a low-interaction honeypot by executing a command that the emulation does not support.

One of the advantages of this approach is that the activities of the attacker are naturally *sandboxed* within the boundaries of the software running on a host operating system. The honeypot can pretend to be, for example, a Solaris server, with the TCP/IP stack characteristics of a Solaris system emulated to fool OS fingerprinting and services that one would expect to see on such a server running Solaris. However, because these services are incompletely implemented, exploits written to compromise a Solaris server will, at best, result in a simulated compromise of the honeypot. That is, if the exploit is known and handled by the honeypot, the actual host operating system is not compromised. At the worst case, the exploit will fail because the exploit is unknown, or the vulnerability is not implemented in the honeypot.

Another advantage of the low-interaction honeypot is that the attacker is also restricted from attacking other hosts from the honeypot system. This is again because the compromise of the server is emulated.

Using low-interaction honeypots has also some disadvantages, which come from the advantages! By definition, no low-interaction emulation of an operating system and its services will be complete. The responses an attacker would expect for known vulnerabilities and exploits are emulated, so a low-interaction honeypot will not respond accurately to exploits we have not included in the emulated responses. The so called zero-day exploits would fall into this category. These exploits are kept private by the attackers, and it is, therefore, difficult to prepare your honeypot for these kinds of exploits [18].

3.4.2   HIGH-INTERACTION HONEYPOTS

The high-interaction honeypots are so different from low-interaction honeypots in terms of implementation and collecting information. High-interaction honeypots utilize actual operating systems rather than emulations. As actual operating systems are used in the high-interaction honeypots, the attacker gets a more realistic experience, and we can be able to gather more information about intended attacks. This makes high-interaction honeypots very useful in situations in which one wishes to capture details of vulnerabilities or exploits that are not yet known to the public. These vulnerabilities or exploits are being used only by a small number of attackers who discovered the vulnerability and wrote an exploit for it. Such exploits are known as *zero-day* exploits. It is very important to find and publicize these vulnerabilities quickly so that the system administrators can filter or work around these problems. Also vendors can develop and release software patches to fix these vulnerabilities [18].

The high-interaction honeypots can be sometimes very dangerous because the attackers can use these systems to harm other systems. So, most often, high-interaction honeypots are placed within a controlled environment, such as behind a firewall. The ability to control the attacker comes not only from the honeypot itself but also from the network access control device—in many cases the firewall. The firewall allows the attacker to compromise one of the honeypots sitting behind the firewall, but it does not let the attacker use the honeypot to launch attacks back out. Such architecture is very complex to deploy and maintain (and it also may be expensive), especially if you do not want the attacker to realize that he is being monitored and controlled. A great amount of work goes into building a firewall with proper rule bases.

As we have mentioned above, the high-interaction honeypots need extensive control mechanisms; these can be extremely difficult and time consuming to install and configure. To implement high-interaction honeypots, a variety of different technologies should be combined, such as firewall and intrusion detection systems. All of the technologies have to be properly customized for the high-interaction honeypot. Maintenance is also time consuming because we must update firewall rule bases and IDS signature databases and monitor the honeypot activity around the clock. Because of these complexities, the high-interaction honeypots have high risk. The more interaction we allow the attacker, the more that can go wrong. However, once implemented correctly, a high-interaction honeypot can give valuable insights about attackers that no other honeypot can do.

3.4.3 MEDIUM-INTERACTION HONEYPOTS

Medium-interaction honeypots [19] try to combine the benefits of both approaches (low interaction and high interaction) in regards to botnet detection and malware collection while removing their shortcomings.

The key feature of medium-interaction honeypots is application layer virtualization. The medium-interaction honeypots do not aim at fully simulating a full operational system environment, nor do they implement all details of an application protocol. What these honeypots do is to provide sufficient responses that known exploits wait on certain ports that will trick them into sending their payloads.

Once the payload has been received, the shellcode is extracted and analyzed somehow. The medium-interaction honeypot then emulates the actions the shellcode would perform to download the malware. Therefore, the honeypot has to provide some virtual file system as well as virtual standard Windows download utilities. The honeypot can then download the malware from the serving location and store it locally or submit it somewhere else for analysis.

3.5 NOTABLE HONEYPOTS

In this section, we present an overview of five notable honeypots [1]. These examples can give the readers some idea about what honeypot products are available (the open source products and the commercial versions).

3.5.1 BACKOFFICER FRIENDLY

BackOfficer Friendly, or BOF, was developed by Marcus Ranum and the folks at Network Flight Recorder. The BackOfficer Friendly is commonly called a simple, free honeypot solution. BOF is considered a low-interaction honeypot designed to run on almost any Windows system.

BOF is very simple so that anyone can install it on his system; also it is easy to configure and requires low maintenance tasks. Because of the fact that it is simple, its capabilities are also severely limited. It has a small set of services that simply listen to ports with notably limited emulation capabilities.

3.5.2 SPECTER

Specter is developed and sold by the folks at NetSec, and it is considered to be a commercially supported honeypot. Specter is also considered as a low-interaction honeypot like BOF, but it has more functionality and capabilities than BOF has. In fact, Specter is not just the emulated services; it has the ability to emulate different operating systems and vulnerabilities. It also has extensive alerting and logging capabilities. Moreover, Specter is easy to deploy, simple to maintain, and is of low risk because it only emulates services with limited interaction. However, compared to medium- and high-interaction honeypots, it is limited in the amount of information that it can gather. Specter is primarily a production honeypot.

3.5.3 HONEYD

Honeyd is considered as an open source, low-interaction honeypot. The main functions of Honeyd are to do the following:

- Detect
- Capture
- Alert to suspicious activity

Honeyd was developed by Niels Provos in April 2002. It introduces several new concepts for honeypots. First, it does not monitor a single IP address for activity; instead it monitors networks of millions of systems. When it detects probes against a system that does not exist, it dynamically assumes the identity of the victim and then interacts with the attacker, exponentially increasing the honeypot's ability to detect and capture attacks. It can emulate hundreds of operating systems at both the application and IP stack levels. As an open source solution, Honeyd is a free technology, giving you full access to the source code. You can customize your own solutions or use those developed by other members of the security community. Designed for the Unix platform, Honeyd is relatively easy to install and configure, relying primarily on a command line interface.

3.5.4 MANTRAP

ManTrap is considered to be a medium- to high-interaction honeypot, and it is a commercial honeypot. ManTrap does not emulate any services like BOF, Spector, and Honeyd. Instead, it takes an operating system and creates up to four virtual operating systems. This gives the administrator extensive control and data-capturing capabilities over the virtual operating systems. Organizations can even install production applications that they want to test, such as DNS, Web servers, or even a database. These virtual operating systems have almost the exact same interaction and functionality as standard production systems. Thus, a great deal can be learned from the attacker.

ManTrap is fairly easy to deploy and maintain as a commercial product. It can also capture an incredible amount of information. Not only does ManTrap detect scans and unauthorized connections, but also it can capture unknown attacks, black hat conversations, or new vulnerabilities. However, its versatility comes at the cost of increased risk. As the honeypot has a full operating system for the attacker to work with, the honeypot can be used to attack other systems and execute unauthorized activity.

One limitation of ManTrap is that it may not work on all operating systems. As technology moves forward at great speed, the readers are suggested to seek out the latest product version (and which operating systems it may support). ManTrap has the flexibility to be used as either a production or research honeypot although it is most commonly used for production purposes.

3.5.5 HONEYNETS

Honeynets are high-interaction honeypots. In fact, it is difficult to envisage any other honeypot solution that can offer a greater level of interaction than honeynets do. The concept of a honeynet is simple: building a network of standard production systems, just as we would find in most organizations today; putting this network of systems behind some type of access control device (such as a firewall); and watching what happens. Attackers can probe, attack, and exploit any system within the honeynet, giving them full operating systems and applications to interact with. No services are emulated, and no caged environments are created. The systems within a honeynet can be anything: a Solaris server running an Oracle database, a Windows XP server running an IIS Web server, a Cisco router, etc. In short, the systems within a honeynet are true production systems [1].

The complexity of a honeynet is not in the building of the honeypots themselves (they can easily be nothing more than default installations) but rather in building the controlled network that both controls and captures all the activities that are happening to and from the honeypots. As such, honeynets are some of the most difficult honeypots to both deploy and maintain. This complexity makes a honeynet the highest-risk honeypot solution. One of the most important advantages of honeynets is that they can also capture the greatest level of information on almost any platform that may exist. Honeynets are primarily used for research purposes. Because of the incredible amount of work involved, they have little value as production honeypots.

3.5.5.1   Virtual Honeynets

A virtual honeynet is a solution that allows you to run everything you need on a single computer. We use the term *virtual* because different operating systems have the *appearance* to be running on their own independent computers, which are not real machines. These solutions are possible because of virtualization software that allows running multiple operating systems at the same time on the same hardware. Virtual honeynets are not a radically new technology; these simply take the concept of honeynet technologies and implement that into a single system. This implementation has its unique advantages and disadvantages over traditional honeynets [20].

The advantages of a virtual honeynet include reduced cost and easier management as everything is combined in a single system. Instead of taking many computers to deploy as with a full honeynet, you can do it with only one computer. However, this simplicity comes at a cost. First, you are restricted to choose what types of operating systems you can deploy by the hardware and virtualization software. For example, most virtual honeynets are based on the Intel X86 chip, so you are restricted to operating systems based on that architecture. You most likely cannot deploy an Alteon switch, VAX, or Cray computer within a virtual honeynet. Secondly, virtual honeynets come with a risk. Specifically, an attacker may be able to compromise the virtualization software and take over the entire honeynet, giving them control over all the systems. Finally, there is the risk of fingerprinting. Once the bad guys have hacked the systems within your virtual honeynet, they may be able to determine what systems are running in a virtual environment.

We have broken virtual honeynets into two categories: self-contained and hybrid. Of the two, self-contained is the more common. We will first define these two different types and then cover the different ways that virtual honeynets can be deployed.

Self-Contained Virtual Honeynet: A self-contained virtual honeynet is an entire honeynet network condensed onto a single computer. The entire network is virtually contained on a single, physical system. A honeynet network typically consists of a firewall gateway for data control and data capture and the honeypots within the honeynet. Some advantages of this type of virtual honeynet(s) are the following:

- *Portable:* Virtual honeynets can be placed on a laptop and taken anywhere.
- *Plug and catch:* You can take the one box and just plug it in to any network, and it can be ready to catch the black hats. This makes deployment much easier as you are physically deploying and connecting only one system.
- *Cheap in terms of money and space:* You only need one computer, so it cuts down on your hardware expenses. It also has a small footprint and only takes one outlet and one port! For those of us with very limited space and power, this is a life saver.

There are some disadvantages as well:

- *Single point of failure:* If something goes wrong with the hardware, the entire honeynet could be out of order.
- *High quality computer:* Even though a self-contained honeynet only requires one computer, it will have to be a powerful system. Depending on your setup, you may need a great deal of memory and processing power.

- *Security:* Because everything might be sharing the same hardware, there is a danger of an attacker getting at other parts of the system. Much of this depends on the virtualization software, which will be discussed later.
- *Limited software:* Because everything has to run on one box, you are limited to the software you can use. For instance, it is difficult to run Cisco IOS on an Intel chip.

Hybrid Virtual Honeynet: A hybrid virtual honeynet is a combination of the classic honeynet and virtualization software. Data capture, such as firewalls, and data control, such as IDS sensors and logging, are on a separate, isolated system. This isolation reduces the risk of compromise. However, all the Honeypots are virtually run on a single box. The advantages to this setup are the following:

- *Secure:* As we saw with the self-contained virtual honeynets, there is a danger of an attacker getting to the other parts of the honeynet (like the firewall). With hybrid virtual honeynets, the only danger would be that the attacker has access to the other honeypots.
- *Flexible:* You are able to use a wide variety of software and hardware for the data control and data capture elements of the hybrid network. An example would be that you can use the OpenSnort sensor on the network or a Cisco pix appliance. You can also run any kind of honeypot you want because you can just drop another computer on the network (in addition to your virtual honeypot's box).

Some disadvantages are the following:

- *Not portable:* Because the honeynet network will consist of more than one box, it makes it more difficult to move.
- *Expensive in terms of time and space:* You will have to spend more in terms of power, space, and possibly money because there is more than one computer in the network.

3.5.5.2 Virtualization Software

Hybrid virtual honeynets can allow you to leverage the flexibility of classic honeynets and let you increase the amount of honeypots by using virtualization software. Now that we have defined the two general categories of virtual honeynets, let us highlight some of the possible ways to implement a virtual honeynet. Here, we outline three different technologies that will allow you to deploy your own. Undoubtedly, there are other options, such as Bochs; however, the Honeynet Project has used and tested all three methods. No one solution is better than the other. Instead, each of them has its own unique advantages and disadvantages; it is up to you to decide which solution works the best. The three options we will now cover are VMware Workstation, VMware GSX Server, and User Mode Linux [6].

- VMware Workstation

VMware Workstation is a long used and established virtualization option. It is designed for the desktop user and is available for Linux and Windows platforms. Advantages to using VMware Workstation as a virtual honeynet are the following:

1. *Wide range of operating system support:* You are able to run a variety of operating systems within the virtual environment (called GuestOSs), including Linux, Solaris, Windows, and FreeBSD honeypots.
2. *Networking options:* VMware Workstation provides two ways to handle networking. The first is Bridged, which is useful for hybrid virtual honeynet networks because it lets a honeypot use the computer's card and appear to be any other host on the honeynet network.

The second option is host-only networking; this is good for self-contained virtual honeynets because you are able to better control traffic with a firewall.

3. *VMware Workstation creates an image of each guest operating system:* These images are simply a file, making them highly portable. This means that you can transfer them to other computers. To restore a honeypot to its original condition, you can just copy a backup into its place.

4. *Ability to mount VMware virtual disk images:* You are able to mount a VMware image just like you would mount a drive using vmware-mount.pl.

5. *Easy to use:* VMware Workstation comes with a graphical interface (both Windows and Linux) that makes installing, configuring, and running the operating systems very simple.

6. *As a commercial product:* VMware Workstation comes with support, upgrades, and patches.

Some disadvantages are the following:

1. *Cost:* VMware Workstation costs around $300 per license (price may vary over time). This might be a bit expensive for the hobbyist or the unemployed student.

2. *Resource requirements:* VMware Workstation must run under an X environment, and each virtual machine will need its own window. So on top of the memory you allocate for the GuestOSs, you have the overhead of the X system.

3. *Limited amount of GuestOSs:* With VMware Workstation, you can only run a small number of virtual machines (~1–4). This might make for a limited honeynet.

4. *Closed source:* Because VMware Workstation is closed source, you can't really make any custom adjustments.

5. *Fingerprinting:* It may be possible to fingerprint the VMware Workstation software on a honeypot, especially if the "VMware tools" are installed on the systems. This could give the honeypots away to the black hat. However, VMware Workstation does have options that can make fingerprinting more difficult, such as the ability to set the MAC address for virtual interfaces.

VMware products also have some nice features, like the ability to suspend a virtual machine (VM). You are able to *pause* the VM, and when you take it out of suspension, all the processes go on like nothing happened! An interesting use of VMware, and other virtualization software too, is the ease and speed of bringing up VMs. Once a honeynet is compromised, and we learned as much as we can from it, we want to start over. With a virtual honeynet, all we have to do is copy files or use the undoable disk or non-persistent disk feature in VMware Workstation to discard any changes made. Another feature of VMware Workstation is the ability to run several networks behind the host OS. So if you only have one box, you can have your honeynet and personal computers all on the one box without worrying about data pollution on either side.

- VMware GSX Server

The VMware GSX Server is a heavy-duty version of VMware Workstation. It is meant for running many higher-end servers. As we will see, this is perfect for use as a honeynet. GSX Server currently runs on Linux and Windows as a host OS.

Advantages of using GSX Server include the following:

1. *Wide range of operating system support:* GSX Server supports Windows (including '95, '98, NT, 2000, XP, and .NET server), various Linux distributions, and potentially BSD and Solaris (not officially supported).

2. *Networking:* It includes all of the options that Workstation has.

3. *No X means more GuestOSs:* GSX Server does not need X running in order to have VMware running. This allows you to run many more GuestOSs at the same time. However, it does require that some of the X libraries be installed if the host is running Linux.
4. *Web interface:* GSX Server can be managed through a web page interface. GuestOSs can be started, paused, stopped, and created via the web page.
5. *Remote terminal:* This is one of the best features of GSX Server. Through the web page and with some VMware software, you can remotely access the GuestOSs as if you were sitting at the console. You are able to do things like remote installs and checking out the system without generating traffic on the honeynet.
6. *Ability to mount:* VMware virtual disk images, just like in Workstation.
7. *VMware GSX Server supports more host memory (up to 8 GB):* more CPUs (up to eight) and more memory per virtual machine (2 BG) than VMware Workstation.
8. Includes a Perl API to manage GuestOSs.
9. *Similar to Workstation:* GSX Server is a supported product, including patches and upgrades.

Some disadvantages are the following:

1. *Cost:* A GSX Server license will run around $3500 (again, cost may vary over time, please check for the latest).
2. *Limited types of GuestOSs:* Operating systems like Solaris X86 and FreeBSD are not officially supported (however you may be able to install them). This can limit the diversity of your honeynet.
3. *Memory hog:* GSX Server recommends greater than 256 MB just to run the GSX Server software. GUI–based operating systems, such as Windows XP, require another 256 MB for each instance.
4. *Closed source:* Just like Workstation.
5. *Fingerprinting:* It may be possible to fingerprint the VMware software on a honeypot, especially if the "VMware tools" are installed on the systems. This could give the honeypots away to the black hat. However, like Workstation there are configuration options that can reduce that risk.

VMware also makes a VMware ESX server. Instead of being just a software solution, ESX Server runs in the hardware of the interface. ESX Server provides its own virtual machine OS monitor that takes over the host hardware. This allows more granular control of resources allocated to virtual machines, such as CPU shares, network bandwidth shares, and disk bandwidth shares, and it allows those resources to be changed dynamically. This product is even higher end than GSX Server. Some of its features are that it can support multiple processors, more concurrent virtual machines (up to 64 VMs), more host memory (up to 64 GB), and more memory per virtual machine (up to 3.6 GB) than GSX Server.

• User Mode Linux

User Mode Linux is a special kernel module that allows one to run many virtual versions of Linux at the same time. Developed by Jeff Dike, UML gives you the ability to have multiple instances of Linux running on the same system at the same time. It is a relatively new tool with great amounts of potential. Some advantages to using User Mode Linux are the following:

1. Free and open source; you have access to the source code.
2. Small footprint and fewer resource requirements. User Mode Linux does not need to use X. It can also run an extensive number of systems with little memory.

3. Ability to create several virtual networks and even create virtual routers all inside the original virtual network.

4. Supports both bridging and networking, similar to VMware.

5. UML has the ability to log keystrokes through the GuestOS kernel. The keystrokes are logged right on the host OS, so there are no issues with how to get the keystrokes off the honeypot in a stealth way.

6. UML comes with preconfigured and downloadable file systems, making it fast and easy to populate your honeynet with honeypots. Like VMware, these file system images are mountable.

7. You can access UML consoles in a wide variety of ways, including through pseudotermi-nals, xterms, and portals on the host, which you can Telnet to. And there's always screen. Run UML inside screen, detach it, and you can log in to the host from anywhere and attach it back.

Some disadvantages are the following:

1. Mainly supports Linux virtual machines (please check for the latest information available on the Web); however a port to Windows is under development.

2. There are still some bugs, documentation, and security issues.

3. There is no GUI interface; currently all configurations and implementations are done at the command line. Has a steeper learning curve.

4. As an Open Source tool, there is no official or commercial support.

5. Similar to VMware, it may be possible to fingerprint a UML honeynet due to the virtual-ization software.

3.6 HONEYPOT IMPLEMENTATION STEPS

All the concepts of honeypots discussed above are very important to understand so that you can select the most suitable honeypot for your organization. We should mention that selecting the cor-rect honeypot will lead you to what you need to achieve from it. Selecting an incorrect honeypot will lead your organization to high risk. So the most important question that comes is, "How can someone select the correct honeypot?" To answer this question, we need to ask you another question, which is, "Why do you want to apply honeypot?" If your answer is to protect your organization from unauthorized access through the deception or deterrence method, it means your honeypot is a production honeypot. If your answer is to collect more information about the attackers to know the new vulnerabilities in your systems and to make a defense from these new vulnerabilities, it means you should select a research honeypot. Another question is "Do you want to protect your organization or do you want to learn about new vulnerabilities?" If your answer is the first one, it means it's preferable for you to select the production honeypot; otherwise, choose a research honeypot.

After you have selected a correct honeypot type for your organization (i.e., a production or research honeypot), the next step is to plan more about your selected honeypot. For example, if you have selected a production honeypot to protect your organization, the question is "What types of protections do you need?" As we have discussed before, the primary purpose of a production honeypot is to help protect your environment. This functionality (i.e., protection) falls into three cat-egories: prevention, detection, and reaction. So you should determine which of these three primary purposes is needed from your honeypot. For more explanation, if you want to deceive attackers, potentially confusing them or slowing them down, it means you want a honeypot for prevention. If you want to detect attackers that access your organization, it means you want a honeypot for detection. If you want to improve your current reaction system, it means you want a honeypot for *incident-response*, which is reaction. We should mention that a production honeypot adds value to all of the above mentioned three categories (prevention, detection, and reaction), but we should be more specific about the primary production honeypot's goal.

Let us give an example. We have noted before that the BackOfficer Friendly is a low-interaction honeypot, and it excels at detecting attacks, but it gives a little value for incident response because it can only tell you what source systems probed what port and when (note that as being a low-interaction honeypot, it does not offer real operating systems and applications for attackers to interact with). Let us take into consideration the ManTrap honeypot, which is a high-interaction honeypot. ManTrap can collect extensive information about the attackers, potentially including the attacker's tools, modifications made to the system, and even what other systems were compromised. From the above mentioned honeypots (the BackOfficer Friendly and ManTrap honeypots), if you want to apply a production honeypot for incident response, which one can you select? For sure, you would select the ManTrap honeypot. Why? Because the ManTrap honeypot can capture a great deal of information on the attacker's actions, and this helps you respond to the attackers. Finally, if you intend to implement a production honeypot, then define its primary role: prevention, detection, or reaction. This is crucial to implementing the correct honeypot technologies based on demand and the situation at hand.

Let us talk about the research honeypot's case. For the research honeypot, you should determine what do you want to learn? For example, do you want to capture automated malicious code? Or do you want to develop forensic analysis skills? Or do you want to learn about attacker tools? Or do you want to learn about the new vulnerabilities? From these questions, you can identify your research honeypot's goal. We should keep in mind that a honeypot that captures malicious payloads of automated attacks is the easiest to deploy with the lowest level of risk.

To get a perfect honeypot solution for your organization, you are recommended to be as specific as possible in your requirements analysis. For instance, if you have selected a production honeypot to prevent your organization from attackers, you need to be more specific about what types of information you are looking for when your honeypot is detecting attacks. Do you need to capture only the source IP address? Or do you want to capture the actual attack itself? This will help determine the level of interaction of your honeypot. After you have clearly defined your goals for deploying or utilizing the honeypot, the next step is selecting a honeypot solution.

3.6.1 Steps of Selecting a Honeypot Solution

After going through all the steps as mentioned in the previous section, this step of selecting a honeypot solution is more crucial. In fact, failing in this step will incur very high risk to your organization. So let us analyze what we should consider when selecting a honeypot solution. There are mainly three issues you must take care of (as adopted from [1]):

1. *Level of interaction:* How can you select the level of interaction? As we discussed earlier, this depends on how much functionality you need to provide to attackers for your honeypot to perform. The greater interaction level that it offers, the better chance you have to learn, but as at the same time it increases your organization's risk, what can you do? You must consider each risk coming from the high level and fix them as much as possible before deploying it. Also reducing the level of interaction will reduce the risk to your organization. We should recommend that if you need a high level of interaction, you must select it because if you select a low level of interaction, you will not achieve the intended goals from the honeypot.

2. *Commercial versus homemade:* Which one is better? A commercial or homemade honeypot? Let us analyze. Commercial honeypots have the following advantages:

    a. They are relatively easier to configure, manage, and support.

    b. They are supported by graphical user interface (GUI), which allows all people to understand and use it in easier way.

    c. Commercial honeypots are supported by their manufacturers, which gives individuals a resource to go to for direct question or help.

    d. Commercial honeypot manufacturers update their product by adding extra functionality or fixing old problems.

The main disadvantage of commercial honeypots is that often these are not customizable as per the requirements. Also you should pay for commercial honeypots; some of those may be expensive or beyond your budget.

Homemade honeypots have the following advantages:

    a. Homemade honeypots are customizable.

    b. Homemade honeypots are cheaper than commercial honeypots, but it will take more time for configurations and more resources than its commercial counterpart.

    c. The main disadvantage of homemade honeypots is their complex command line interfaces (CLI) that can be difficult to use. For example, you need to edit configuration files, making them much more difficult to configure and deploy. Any additional functionality, such as *alerting*, has to be developed.

    d. We should mention that homemade honeypots require a great level of skill and knowledge for customization. Also, there is no real official support for such solutions.

3. *Platform:* The last issue is the platform. What operating system (OS) or platform do you need for your honeypot to run on? There are honeypots that are based on Windows OS, and also there are honeypots based on Unix OS. The Windows solutions are relatively easier to install, configure, and manage. The Unix solutions are often very difficult to implement, but they have greater flexibility than that of Windows solutions. So the most important question here is: "How can you select your operating system?" This, of course, depends on what operating system your organization is experienced with and what your organization could afford to buy or use. Some organizations may have many general computer-skilled workers who would simply prefer Windows over Unix. Hence, that organization may have to pay for only Windows OS.

3.6.2 Determining the Number of Honeypots

After you have successfully determined your goals and selected the correct honeypot for your organization, the next step is to determine how many honeypots you need to deploy. The most important question that arises is, how can you determine the number of honeypots suitable for your organization? To answer this question, once again check the goals which you specified earlier; these goals will help you determine the number of honeypots.

If you have selected the research honeypot, then you can use just one or two honeypots deployed in different locations. Why? Because with a research honeypot, if you have deployed several honeypots at the same level (i.e., for example, the network level), you will collect the same information from all the honeypots that you have deployed. So to reduce the cost, you can just deploy two honeypots, one on the network level and the second one on the host level. In contrast, if you have selected the production honeypot and you have a large organization with multiple networks, you need to deploy several of them. This is because different networks may require different honeypots to help secure the environment.

To illustrate more, if the goals of the production honeypots for an organization are to prevent attacks, if we have N networks in this organization, and we have deployed $N - 1$ honeypots, that means there is one network of this organization that has no honeypot; eventually, it means this network (i.e., the network without the honeypot) has a low level of prevention from the rest of the networks, so it may get attacked. We should also mention that more honeypots deployed means more cost is needed; the cost is not only of the honeypots themselves but also of time, resources, and infrastructure to maintain those. Also, there is another important issue in determining the number of honeypots, which is that you need to know how many you can manage. If you have too many honeypots, you may not be able to manage all of them, so you should deploy as many as you can manage. At the same time, the honeypots that you have deployed should meet your intended goals. Another critical point is that you cannot only depend on the honeypots to secure your organization, but rather you should use other security technologies to support the systems, such as intrusion detection systems (IDSs), intrusion prevention systems (IPSs), firewalls, or the like. Overall, it means that the honeypots are for use in more secured environments.

3.6.3 SELECTING LOCATION FOR HONEYPOT DEPLOYMENT

The next step is to determine where you should deploy your honeypots. As usual, the goals of your honeypots can be used to help decide this.

- If you have selected a production honeypot and your goal is to detect attackers who have penetrated your perimeter, the best place for your honeypots is within your internal network behind the perimeter firewalls.
- If you have selected a research honeypot, and your goal is to research how many attack attempts are made against your organization each day, the best place of installing it is outside the perimeter firewall because this place will help the honeypot detect all the activities to which your organization is vulnerable.

Generally, most of the production honeypots are placed behind an organization's security perimeter because the main role of the security perimeter is to keep the bad guys out while the honeypot's role is to interact with anything that has passed through the perimeter security [1].

3.6.4 DATA CAPTURE IMPLEMENTATION

One of functions of any honeypot is to capture information regardless of whether it is a production or research honeypot. However, we know by now that the research honeypots focus on capturing as much information as possible, and the production honeypots do not have the same ability (i.e., less information is enough for production honeypots).

Let us now talk about which types of data the production and/or research honeypots collect. For a simple production honeypot, the following information is captured [1]:

- IP address of the attacking system
- Time and date of the attack
- The service attacked

For advanced research honeypots, more extensive information is captured; for example, everything from new toolkits to the attacker's keystrokes, the packet's payload, and the like. We should mention here that how much data you would capture depends also on the place of deployment of your honeypot.

As production honeypots have limitations in data capturing, if you want to increase the ability of capturing more data for some other purpose, you can do that by using a network sniffer (packet analyzer) tool to actually capture every single packet and the packet's payload. Figure 3.1 shows how you could use a sniffer to increase your data capturing ability for your honeypot.

In addition, you can use another source for data capturing, such as firewalls or router logs. Any logged connection in the firewall going to or from the honeypot would represent an additional layer. This information should be easy to extract because we know the IP address of our honeypot.

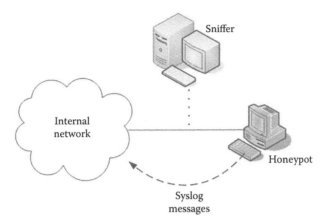

FIGURE 3.1   Using a sniffer to increase data capturing ability for a honeypot.

3.6.5 Data Management Planning

Data management issues in the honeypots are considered very important because from the collected data, we will get our goals from building a honeypot. So, let us explain what we mean by *data management planning* for honeypots. Let us consider two scenarios to discuss this issue:

a. *Organizations that deploy only one or two honeypots*

Some organizations just deploy one or two honeypots. For such organizations, the data collection and management from these two honeypots are not a great challenge. Data can simply be logged onto the local system and retrieved from there!

b. *Organizations that deploy multiple honeypots*

Some organizations deploy multiple honeypots in a variety of networks, and these honeypots may be located in different geographical places. In such cases, we need a centralized architecture to aggregate and manage all of the information that we could collect from these honeypots. Now, a question arises, "Why do we need to centrally manage the honeypots?" Because, the main goal of centrally managing the honeypots is that the management process would be very easy as all of the collected data would be in one place! Also, there are other advantages from the central management of the honeypots:

- You have just one point to retrieve the data.
- One point for backups, archiving, and one point for data maintenance.
- Another good reason is that combining all data in one point can increase the value of data. Why? The data that are collected could be used for data mining, statistical modeling, and trends analysis.

A better method to manage the centralized data is to create a separate honeypot management and logging network, especially for low-interaction honeypots. That means any deployed honeypot should have two interfaces; one interface is for the administrator of that honeypot, and the second interface is to manage and log the centralized data architecture. However, here is a potential problem. This second interface can cause great trouble to our internal network if an attacker compromises this interface and uses it to compromise our internal network devices. So we should be careful enough to ensure that the attacker cannot use the honeypot management network to attack internal honeypots.

One challenge for the centralized data collection is that you may have different honeypots with different data capture capabilities in different formats. So you need a method of collecting such divergent types of data. One of the best ways to approach this is a database system.

A great advantage of a database system is that it has a variety of tables that can handle different data and logging types, such as the ability to store logs generated by *syslogd*, commercial honeypots, and firewall logs. A question may arise here, how can we implement a database system in our organization to solve the collection of these divergent data types? This depends on your organization, requirements, and data types. There are several open source and commercially produced solutions for such cases. Here, we mention two examples of the open source solutions: ACID [21] and Demarc [22]. One example of commercial solution is NetForensics [23]. Whatever you choose as your solution, you should make sure that you get flexibility to work with different data types and could query the collected data.

In the above section, we have discussed how we can implement centralized data architecture, and we have explained its advantages. In addition, to capture more data (i.e., which can increase the data value even more) for a honeypot, we can use the network address translation (NAT). Below, we will talk about how we can use the NAT for a honeypot.

3.6.6 USING THE NETWORK ADDRESS TRANSLATION (NAT) IN A HONEYPOT

What is NAT? Let us explore a bit.

First, let us revisit the public IP addressing and private IP addressing issues.

* Public IP Addressing

An IP address is considered *public*, if the IP number is valid and falls outside any of the IP address ranges reserved for private uses by Internet standards groups. Public IP addresses are used by Internet servers (including those for websites and DNS [domain name system] servers), network routers, or any computer directly connected to the Internet via a modem.

Each public IP is assigned to a range or block of addresses. The Internet Assigned Numbers Authority (IANA) controls ownership of these IP ranges and assigns each block to organizations such as Internet service providers (ISPs), who, in turn, allocate individual IP addresses to customers.

* Private IP Addressing

Many organizations use an internal addressing scheme known as private addressing (described in RFC [request for comments] 1918). This addressing scheme uses IP addresses that are not publicly routed on the Internet. That means once you have seen an IP address, you can identify whether it is public or private.

RFC 1918 defines a pool of IP addresses that anyone can use on her internal networks but that are not intended to be publicly routed on the Internet. Specifically, the private IP addresses are [1] the following:

- 10.0.0.0 through 10.255.255.255
- 72.16.0.0 through 172.31.255.255
- 192.168.0.0 through 192.168.255.255

The systems with these private IP addresses cannot communicate directly with the Internet because these are not publicly routed. That means these systems can communicate with the Internet indirectly using a channel, such as a firewall. The firewall is considered as a channel between the internal systems that use private IP addresses and the Internet. The firewall does this task by using a tool to translate the private IP addresses to public IP addresses; this tool is called network address translation (NAT).

The network address translation (NAT) most commonly works by translating the private addresses of outbound packets from the internal systems to the same public IP address as the external interface of the firewall (or router) has. By using this method, the packets can reach others systems on the Internet. The Internet systems would respond to the IP address on the firewall (or router) and not to the internal system. The question here is, if the firewall receives a return packet, to which device in the internal network would the firewall forward this packet? The answer is the firewall maintains a database of who is sending what packet where. Therefore, when the firewall receives a return packet, it reverses the translation process and forwards the packet to the proper system in the internal network, using its RFC 1918 IP address. This is commonly called hide or one-to-many address translation. Within an organization, multiple systems using RFC 1918 private addressing need only one public IP address to communicate with the Internet—the IP address of the external interface on the firewall.

There is another way called one-to-one or static translation. With static translation, a single RFC 1918 IP address is mapped to a single public IP address, so every system is given a unique public and private IP address matching. The purpose of this is such that the systems on the Internet can initiate a connection to an internal system using address translation. Static translation is often done for organizations' Internet servers, such as DNS, Web server, or mail server. Once again, the firewall does the translation for the systems.

We can summarize the above discussions like this: Let us assume that we have an organization that needs to communicate with the outside world, i.e., with the Internet. This origination has just one public IP address, and the internal network contains several devices (internal systems). The organization may use RFC 1918 IP schemes to populate its internal systems with IP addresses and use a firewall (or router) to translate the internal system's request to the public IP so that the system requests can communicate with the Internet system. When a return response reaches to the firewall, it should translate it to the appropriate system in the internal network. One question arises here, that is, why do we need to use private IP addressing (i.e., why are the public IP addresses not enough for internal devices)? The answer is the following:

- First, you should pay for each public IP address. Hence, if you have too many internal devices, it is not suitable to buy a public IP address for each one. Also, it is not feasible to have only one public IP address for a very large organization (i.e., an organization with numerous internal systems and devices) because this will delay the internal system's requests. So we should make a balance between the number of internal systems/devices and the number of the public IP addresses that are needed.
- Using the private IP addressing scheme with the network address translation (NAT) is good in terms of management because you will know what is the outbound connection and inbound connection in one point (firewall or router).
- Using the private IP addressing with NAT will enhance your internal network security by limiting the access of external computers (i.e., the Internet) into the internal IP network.

After having these discussions, let us now look into the role of network address translation (NAT) with the honeypots.

3.6.6.1 NAT Roles with the Honeypots

There are many roles of NAT in the honeypots. Here, we will present two examples: (i) *translate unused IP addresses* and (ii) *port forwarding*.

3.6.6.1.1 Translate Unused IP Addresses

As an example, if the IP address space of your LAN is 212.0.50.0/24 with one public Web server, the server's IP address is 212.0.50.19. If an attacker outside the network launches a worm attack against 212.0.50.0/24, the worm scans the IP address space of the victims. It is highly probable that an unused IP address, e.g., 212.0.50.10 will be attempted before 212.0.50.19. Therefore, we would like the router to translate such attackers that try to see the unused IP addresses to a honeypot so that we can collect and learn about the attacker's motivation, tactics, and tools that they use. To explain more, we will give a real example for unused IP address translation. This example is called a double honeynet system worked out by Mohammed et al. [24–26]. These works show how you could collect zero-day polymorphic worms using the unused IP address translation and a double honeynet. Before presenting the necessary details, we would like to mention a brief summary about the zero-day polymorphic worms so that the readers can well-understand the double honeynet method.

A computer worm is defined as a standalone malware computer program that replicates itself in order to spread to other computers without requiring any human intervention by sending copies of the code in network packets and ensuring the code is executed by the computers that receive it. Often worms use a computer network to spread themselves. This is due to security shortcomings on the target computer. Unlike a computer virus, a worm does not need to attach itself to an existing program. Worms almost always cause at least some harm to the network even if it is only by consuming bandwidth whereas viruses almost always corrupt or modify files on a targeted computer. When computers become infected, they spread further copies of the worm and possibly perform other malicious activities. A polymorphic worm is a computer worm that changes its appearance in every infection attempt; polymorphic worms use this method (changes its appearance in every infection attempt) to avoid the security detection methods. Zero-day polymorphic worms, which means the unknown worms (i.e., the polymorphic worms that are not yet detected and are not yet put in a database signature of a security method).

Let us now know about the double honeynet system. This system contains several components, but we will discuss one component in detail, which is the *local router component*. With this component, we will learn how the local router uses the network address translation (NAT) to translate the unused IP addresses to the double honeynet system. The example mentioned here has two parts: The first part will discuss the double honeynet system design, and the second part will discuss the implementation (configurations) of this system.

3.6.6.1.1.1   Double Honeynet System

Motivation of double honeynet system: Unknown Internet worms pose a major threat to Internet infrastructure security, and often, their destruction causes losses of millions of dollars. Security experts, in many cases, manually generate the IDS (intrusion detection system) signatures by studying the network traces after a new worm has been released. Unfortunately, this job takes a lot of time. We propose a double honeynet system that could automatically detect unknown worms without any human intervention. In our system, interaction between the two honeynets works by forming a loop, which allows us to collect all polymorphic worm instances that enables the system to produce accurate worm signatures. The double honeynet system is a hybrid system with both network-based and host-based mechanisms. This allows us to collect polymorphic worm instances at the network-level and host-level, which reduces the false positives and false negatives dramatically.

Double honeynet architecture: The purpose of a double honeynet system is to detect unknown (i.e., previously unreported) worms automatically. A key contribution of this system is the ability of distinguishing worm activities from normal activities without any involvement of experts in the field.

Figure 3.2 shows the main components of the double honeynet system. First, the incoming traffic goes through the local router, which samples the unwanted inbound connections and redirects the samples' connections to honeynet 1. As the redirected packets pass through the local router, packet capture (PCAP) library is used to capture the packets and then to analyze their payloads to contribute to the signature generation process.

The local router is configured with publicly accessible addresses, which represent wanted services. Connections made to other addresses are considered unwanted and redirected to honeynet 1 through the internal router. Once honeynet 1 is compromised, the worm will attempt to make outbound connections to attack another network. The internal router is implemented to separate the double honeynet from the local area network (LAN). This router intercepts all outbound connections from honeynet 1 and redirects those to honeynet 2, which does the same task forming a

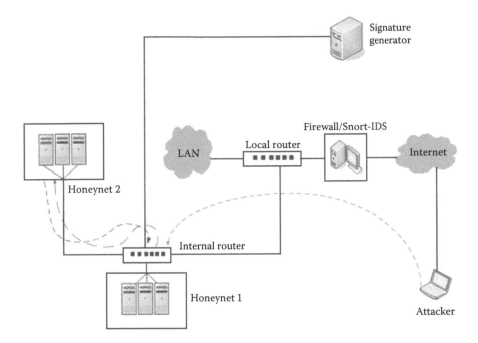

FIGURE 3.2   Double honeynet system.

loop. The looping mechanism allows us to capture different instances of the polymorphic worm as it mutates on each loop-iteration.

We stop the loop after a considerable amount of time in order to collect polymorphic worms. Only those packets that make outbound connections are considered as polymorphic worms, and hence, the double honeynet system forwards only the packets that make outbound connections. This policy is in place due to the fact that benign users do not try to make outbound connections if they are faced with nonexisting addresses. In fact, our system collects other malicious activities, which do not intend to propagate themselves but to attack targeted machines only. Such malicious attack is out of our work scope.

When enough instances of worm payloads are collected by honeynet 1 and honeynet 2, they are forwarded to the signature generator component, which generates signatures automatically using specific algorithms. To learn about these algorithms, readers are suggested to look into Mohammed and Pathan [27].

For example, as shown in Figure 3.2, if the local router suspects packet 1 (P_1), packet 2 (P_2), and packet 3 (P_3) as malicious, it redirects them to the honeynet 1 through the internal router. Among these three packets, P_1 and P_2 make outbound connections, and the internal router redirects these outbound connections to honeynet 2. In honeynet 2, P_1 and P_2 change their payloads and become $P1'$ and $P2'$, respectively (i.e., $P1'$ and $P2'$ are the instances of P_1 and P_2). Therefore, in this case, $P1'$ and $P2'$ make outbound connections, and the internal router redirects these connections to honeynet 1. In honeynet 1, $P1'$ and $P2'$ change their payloads and become $P1''$ and $P2''$, respectively (i.e., $P1''$ and $P2''$ are also other instances of P_1 and P_2).

Now, P_1 and P_2 are found malicious because of the outbound connections. Therefore, honeynet 1 forwards P_1, $P1''$, P_2, and $P2''$ to the signature generator for the signature generation process. Similarly, honeynet 2 forwards $P1'$ and $P2'$ to the signature generator for signature generation process.

In this scenario, P_3 does not make any outbound connection when it gets to honeynet 1. Therefore, P_2 is not considered malicious.

3.6.6.1.1.2 *Double Honeynet Implementation (i.e., Configurations)*

This part will discuss the double honeynet system architecture, and configurations of how the local router can use the network address translation (NAT) to translate the unused IP addresses to the double honeynet.

Double honeynet system architecture: Figure 3.3 shows the architecture of the double honeynet system, implemented using VMware Workstation version 7 on PC Intel Pentium 4, 3.19-GHZ CPU, 8 GB RAM, and the PC running on Windows XP 64-bit. The operating system of the personal computer is referred to as the host operating system in Figure 3.3. The host machine is connected to our home router, and it accesses the Internet through it.

We used a virtual machine to deploy the double honeynet system due to the lack of resources and to keep the establishment low cost. One personal computer (PC) was used, and VMware Workstation was installed on it. The VMware Workstation is a software package that gives its users the opportunity to create virtual machines that constitute virtual networks interconnected with each other. Thus, we created the double honeynet system as a virtual network seen from the outside world as an independent network. Attackers could locate the honeypot and attack it. The honeypot was transparently connected to the Internet through the honeywall, which, in turn, intercepted all outbound and inbound traffic. Therefore, malicious traffic targeting the honeypot (inbound) or malicious traffic generated by the compromised honeypot (outbound) were available to us from the honeywall for further analysis and investigation. Honeynet 1 and honeynet 2 were configured to deliver unlimited outbound connections. The internal router was used to protect our local network by redirecting all outbound connections from honeynet 1 to honeynet 2 and vice versa.

Double honeynet configuration: Our double-honeynet system contains six components, which are the local router, the internal router, LAN, honeynet 1, honeynet 2, and the signature generator. The subnet mask for each subnet (whether local router, internal router, LAN, honeynet 1, honeynet 2, and signature generator) is consequently 255.255.255.0. The following subsequent sections will discuss the configuration of the local router component.

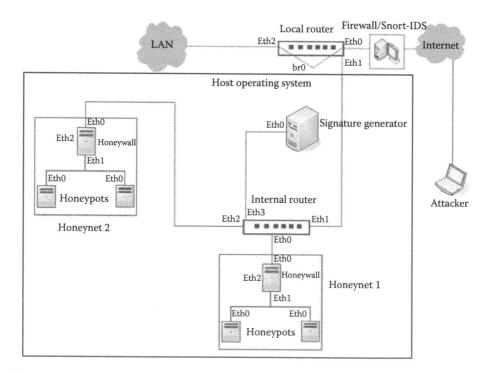

FIGURE 3.3   Double honeynet architecture.

Local router configuration: A local router's function is to pass unwanted traffic to the honeynet 1 through the internal router. For example, if the IP address space of our LAN is 212.0.50.0/24 with one public Web server, the server's IP address is 212.0.50.19. If an attacker outside the network launches a worm attack against 212.0.50.0/24, the worm scans the IP address space of the victims. It is highly probable that an unused IP address, e.g., 212.0.50.10, will be attempted before 212.0.50.19. Therefore, the local router will redirect the packet to honeynet 1 through the internal router. After the worm compromises honeynet 1, the worm will try to make an outbound connection to harm another network. We configured the internal router to protect the LAN from worms' outbound connections. The internal router intercepts all outbound connections from honeynet 1 and redirects those to honeynet 2, which performs the same task done by the honeynet 1 forming loop connections. Below, we mention the details of local router machine properties and IPtables configuration.

3.6.6.1.1.3   Machine Properties of the Local Router
- Operating System: Ubuntu Linux 9.10
- Number of Network Cards:
  Three network cards (Eth0, Eth1, and Eth2).
  Eth0 and Eth2 are bridged LAN port.
  The Eth1 function is to connect the local router with honeynet 1 through the internal router.
- IP Addresses:
  - Eth1: 192.168.50.20
- Prior to the IPtables setting, we enabled IP forwarding in the local router.
  -Edit /etc/sysctl.conf file as follows:
  Net.ipv4.ip_frowrd = 1
- IPtables configuration

The settings of the network address translator (NAT) in the kernel using IPtables are as follows:

1. Do not translate packets going to the real public server:
   # iptables -t nat -A PREROUTING -m physdev— physdev-in eth0 -d 212.0.50.19 -j RETURN
2. Translate all other packets going to the public LAN to the internal router:
   # iptables -t nat -A PREROUTING -m physdev— physdev-in eth0 -d 212.0.50.0/24 -j DNAT— to 192.168.50.22

3.6.6.1.2   Port Forwarding
In the previous section, we showed how the NAT can be used to translate the unused IP addresses. It should be mentioned that we not only can translate the IP addresses but also can translate the ports! To illustrate more, let us consider that we have a production Web server on the DMZ (demilitarized zone), which is using static IP address translation. Just to clarify here for the general readers, in computer security, a DMZ is a physical or logical subnetwork that contains and exposes an organization's external-facing services to a larger untrusted network, usually the Internet (i.e., roughly it is the perimeter network). Okay, let's focus on our example. Because this is a Web server that we are talking about, it should only receive connections to port 80, HTTP (hypertext transfer protocol). So if attackers attempt to launch connections for other ports, these connections would be blocked by the firewall. Rather than blocking such connections (i.e., connections for other ports), we can use the network address translation (NAT) and port forwarding to benefit from such connections. How? We can get extensive information about such attackers by these translated and forwarded connections to a honeypot. Figure 3.4 shows how a firewall uses the port address translation to separate the HTTP packets from non-HTTP packets (adopted from [1]).

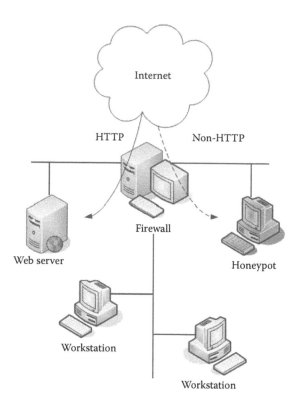

FIGURE 3.4   Firewall using port address translation.

3.6.7 How to Mitigate the Risk

In the previous sections, we have discussed how you can implement honeypots. The goal of the honeypots should be positive to your organization and not negative. There is basically no security system that can guarantee security 100%. This is the nature of this world and any of its systems unless it is divinely perfected! So to develop a good security system, you should focus on reducing the risks as much as possible. Implementing honeypots properly would add value to your organization; otherwise, i.e., implementing honeypots incorrectly would be negative for your organization.

The levels of interaction play a main role in reducing the risks. As we mentioned before, the greater the level of interaction is, the greater is the complexity and risk of something going wrong. Therefore, to reduce the risk, you should select as little interaction as necessary for their intended value. By reducing the level of interaction, both complexity and risk could be reduced. Let us now talk about how you can reduce the risk for high-interaction and low-interaction honeypots [1].

High-interaction honeypots: Let us consider that you have selected building a honeynet environment for your organization and that is a high-interaction honeypot. To get good security for your internal network, you should build the honeynet in a separate network (i.e., separate from your internal networks). Then, you should use a router (or firewall) between these networks. The main goal of this router (or firewall) is to allow inbound connections to go to your honeynet and deny the outbound connections from the honeynet to your internal networks. By applying such a method, you can protect your internal networks from being harmed by the honeynet's outbound connections.

Low-interaction honeypots: The low-interaction honeypots, in reality, offer a little risk because they just emulate the operating systems and services; that means there are no real operating systems and services. The issue here is not in the level of interaction but in the base of the operating system. That means the risk here is not coming from the honeypots, but from the base of the operating system (on which the honeypot is installed). Therefore, if your base operating system is vulnerable, it can easily be compromised. To solve this problem, you should follow best practices for a secure operating system before installing the honeypot. To illustrate a bit more, you should turn off any service that you do not need and patch any service that you do. Each operating system has unique security requirements. It is highly recommended that you review and understand these requirements before deploying any low-interaction honeypot.

There is another way to reduce the risk, which is a testing mechanism. For example, you have implemented a honeypot to detect authorized activities in your network. So you are recommended to test your honeypot before deploying. You can do that testing by launching authorized activities against your honeypot and seeing whether your honeypot detects what you have launched or not. Also, to see the strength of your honeypot against the authorized activities, you can launch authorized activities against your honeypot and then count how much (percentage) it has detected. If the percentage is high, that means your honeypot is strong and will add a value to your organization. If you got a low percentage, it means your honeypot will be negative to your organization. To solve this problem, you must look again at your honeypot's implementation steps and detect where the mistake might have had happened.

3.6.8 Fingerprinting Mitigation

The goal of a honeypot is to add value to a network in which it is deployed. The most critical *value-adding* factor is fingerprinting. Fingerprinting means when an attacker is in a honeypot, he is identified. For many organizations, mitigating signature detection is important because they want to collect and trace the attackers. For some other organizations, mitigating signature detection is not important because when an attacker is identified to be in a honeypot, he will avoid attacking this organization, and the organization wants no one to attack its systems (i.e., that means the organization's goal for deploying the honeypot will be easily detected by the attackers so that they would avoid interacting with the systems). So mitigating signature detection is needed according to the organization's goals. Now, let us we assume that an organization has deployed a honeypot and wants to mitigate signature detection. How can the organization mitigate signature detection? There are three most effective measures for reducing detection [1], which are (i) modifying honeypot behavior, (ii) blending with the environment, and (iii) developing realism.

3.6.8.1 Modifying Honeypot Behavior

Modifying honeypot behavior applies mainly to commercial or repackaged honeypot solutions. Why? Because such a honeypot has the potential for signatures. If you have downloaded or purchased a honeypot for your organization, you must know that such solutions may have standard configurations or specific behaviors that can be identified. So once the attackers recognize these signatures, your honeypot is exposed. For example, a default installation of a honeypot may come with 10 emulated services. An attacker can identify these 10 services and use them as a signature.

How can you avoid such type of detection? The answer is to modify the functionality of the honeypot. How? The answer is, after installing the honeypot, you should modify the default setting, disable some services that you do not need, and modify services that you allow to run. The goal of these modifications is to make your honeypot very hard to be detected by the attackers. We should mention that homemade honeypots do not have this problem because each is unique.

3.6.8.2 Blending with the Environment

If your organization exclusively uses a specific type of operating system, such as Windows-based operating systems, then, it is better for your honeypots to be on Windows-based operating systems, or you could emulate Windows-based operating systems.

3.6.8.3 Developing Realism

The last method to mitigating signature detection is the realism. We should mention that honeypots can be easily detected if they do not apply real systems. This is especially true for the honeypots that emulate the operating systems. For example, your honeypot can easily emulate a Solaris operating system (OS), but the real operating system of your honeypot is Windows. Attackers can detect just such a trick! How? If the attacker uses advanced operating system detection techniques, such as analyzing the IP stack of the honeypot, the attacker may identify the system as a Windows-based OS! Honeypots that run real operating systems, such as a honeynet, can reduce such problems.

3.6.9 MAINTAINING A HONEYPOT

Now, we have deployed our honeypot. There still remains another important step, which is maintaining the honeypot. Implementation is only half of any honeypot system. Maintenance is the other half. To build a robust honeypot system, we should carefully emphasize this step. There are mainly four areas of maintaining honeypots, which are Alert detection, response, data analysis, and updates. Let us talk about these a bit.

- Alert detection
    Alert detection is considered to be the most important because it will send you an alert once an attacker has compromised your system. Sometimes you need to stop some attacks to protect your internal systems. So if you do not have an alert detection method, your internal system may be compromised.
- Response
    The second method is the response; assume that you have received an alert message, so what can you do in term of response to this attack? You may have two options according to your honeypot goals. If your honeypot goal is to collect as much information as possible, you can let the attacker proceed to collect information. You can only respond to some attacks if you think that these attacks would compromise your internal systems. If your honeypot goal is to prevent your organizations from attacks, you should respond to the attack immediately. You can quickly react, attempting to track down the black hat. You can immediately shut the guy out at the firewall, protecting your resources.
- Data analysis
    As we mentioned before, one of the goals is to collect data about the attackers. So what is the next step after collecting such data? The answer is, analysis of all the collected data and turning those into useful information. For example, let us consider that your honeypot's goal is to collect zero-day polymorphic worms' payloads. If you have successfully collected these payloads, the next step is to analyze these payloads using a method, and the result of your analysis will be used for avoiding such polymorphic worms in future attempts.
- Updates
    To ensure that your honeypots do provide enough security to your organization, you should keep up the underlying operating system and the honeypot software with the latest updates. One of the most important reasons for updates is managing risk. Attackers are constantly identifying new vulnerabilities and releasing new exploits to take advantage of them, exposing your honeypot to high risk. So by keeping updates and installing updates, you can ensure more security to your organization.

In fact, maintaining a honeypot is very crucial for any honeypot's success. You may deploy the greatest honeypot solution in your organization, but if you do not care about maintaining that properly, you will not achieve your goals for implementing this technology.

3.7 CONCLUSION

Before concluding this chapter, it should be clarified that honeypots do not perform the same functions as an intrusion detection system (IDS) does. Yes, they have some similarities, but from an operational point of view, they are fairly different. For example, if we would like to devise a good IDS for a network, we must collect valuable data about attacks then analyze these attacks to generate signatures for them; then we have to use these signatures in the IDS. Honeypots, on the other hand, are good tools to collect valuable data, but they are set up for being attacked by the potential attackers. A honeypot is not a usual defense mechanism meant for protecting a system, but an IDS is a core part of the defense system or strategy. Honeypots are often deployed for collecting valuable information about the attackers that could be analyzed and used for developing appropriate countermeasures, and an IDS simply implements a set of rules based on whether it detects if there is any rogue entity that enters into the network and then it asks for purging it out.

AUTHORS' BIOGRAPHIES

Mohssen Mohammed received his BSc (honors) degree in computer science from Computer Man College for Computer Studies (Future University), Khartoum, Sudan, in 2003. In 2006, he received the MSc degree in computer science from the Faculty of Mathematical Sciences, University of Khartoum, Sudan. In 2012, he received a PhD degree in electrical engineering from Cape Town University, South Africa. He published several papers at top international conferences, such as GLOBECOM and MILCOM. He has served as a technical program committee member in numerous international conferences, such as ICSEA 2010, and ICNS 2011. He received the University of Cape Town prize for International Scholarship for Academic Merit (years 2007, 2008, and 2009). From 2005 to 2012, he has been working as a permanent academic staff member at the University of Juba, South of Sudan. Now he is working as an assistant professor in the College of Computer and Information Sciences, Al-Imam Muhammad bin Saud Islamic University, Riyadh, Saudi Arabia. His research interests include network security, especially intrusion detection and prevention systems, honeypots, firewalls, and malware detection methods.

Al-Sakib Khan Pathan received a PhD degree in computer engineering in 2009 from Kyung Hee University, South Korea. He received a BSc degree in computer science and information technology from Islamic University of Technology (IUT), Bangladesh, in 2003. He is currently an assistant professor in the computer science department in International Islamic University Malaysia (IIUM), Malaysia. Until June 2010, he served as an assistant professor in the computer science and engineering department at BRAC University, Bangladesh. Prior to holding this position, he worked as a researcher at the networking lab, Kyung Hee University, South Korea, until August 2009. His research interests include wireless sensor networks, network security, and e-services technologies. He is a recipient of several awards and best paper awards and has several publications in these areas. He has served as a chair, organizing committee member, and technical program committee member in numerous international conferences and workshops, such as HPCS, ICA3PP, IWCMC, VTC, HPCC, IDCS, etc. He is currently serving as the editor-in-chief of IJIDS, an area editor of IJCNIS, editor of IJCSE, Interscience, associate editor of IASTED/ACTA Press IJCA and CCS, guest editor of some special issues of top-ranked journals, and editor/author of nine books. He also serves as a referee of some renowned journals. He is a member of Institute of Electrical and Electronics Engineers (IEEE), USA; IEEE Communications Society, USA; IEEE ComSoc Bangladesh Chapter, and several other international professional organizations.

REFERENCES

1. Spitzner, L. *Honeypots: Tracking Hackers*. Addison-Wesley Professional, Boston, MA, September 20, 2002.
2. Stoll, C. *The Cuckoo's Egg: Tracking a Spy Through the Maze of Computer Espionage*. Gallery Books, September 13, 2005.
3. Cheswick, B. An evening with Berferd in which a cracker is lured, endured, and studied, *Proceedings of the Winter 1992 USENIX Technical Conference*. USENIX Association: San Francisco, CA, January 20–24, 1992.

4. Deception Toolkit. http://www.all.net/dtk/index.html (last accessed August 11, 2012).
5. NetFacade Honeypot. http://www22.verizon.com/fns/solutions/netsec/netsec_netfacade.html (last accessed March 7, 2013).
6. The Honeynet Project. 2001. *Know Your Enemy.* Addison-Wesley: Boston, MA. http://project.honeynet.org/book/ (last accessed March 7, 2013).
7. Nmap, port scanning tool developed by Fyodor. http://www.insecure.org/nmap (last accessed March 7, 2013).
8. Specter Honeypot. http://www.specter.com (last accessed March 7, 2013).
9. Mantrap Honeypot. http://www.mantrap.com (last accessed March 7, 2013).
10. Snort, OpenSource Intrusion Detection System. http://www.snort.org (last accessed March 7, 2013).
11. The Honeynet Project. http://project.honeynet.org (last accessed March 7, 2013).
12. CERT Advisory CA-2001-18 Multiple vulnerabilities in several implementations of the lightweight directory access protocol (LDAP). http://www.cert.org/advisories/CA-2001-18.html (last accessed March 7, 2013).
13. CERT Advisory CA-2001-31 Buffer overflow in CDE subprocess control service. http://www.cert.org/advisories/CA-2001-31.html (last accessed March 7, 2013).
14. CERT Advisory CA-2002-01 Exploitation of vulnerability in CDE subprocess control service. http://www.cert.org/advisories/CA-2002-01.html (last accessed March 7, 2013).
15. DDoS and Security Reports. http://ddos.arbornetworks.com/ (last accessed March 7, 2013).
16. Tan, K.Y. Phishing and spamming via IM (SPIM). Available at: http://isc.sans.org/diary.php?storyid=1905 (last accessed March 7, 2013).
17. Schneier, B. *Secrets and Lies: Digital Security in a Networked World.* Wiley, New York, 1st ed., January 30, 2004.
18. Pasman, D.N. Catching hackers using a virtual honeynet: A case study, 6th Twente. Conference on IT, Enschede, University of Twente, February 2, 2007.
19. Wicherski, G. Medium interaction honeypots. April 2006. http://citeseerx.ist.psu.edu/viewdoc/summary?doi=10.1.1.133.9431 (last accessed March 7, 2013).
20. Honeynet Project. http://www.honeynet.org/ (last accessed August 11, 2012).
21. ACID (Analysis Console for Intrusion Databases). OpenSource solution for managing logs. http://www.cert.org/kb/acid/ (last accessed March 7, 2013).
22. Demarc. Solution for centralized logging and management. http://www.demarc.org (last accessed March 7, 2013).
23. Commercial solution for centralized logging. http://www.netforensics.com (last accessed March 7, 2013).
24. Mohammed, M.M.Z.E., Chan, H.A., Ventura, N., Hashim, M., and Amin, I. A modified Knuth-Morris-Pratt algorithm for zero-day polymorphic worms detection, *Proceedings of the 2009 International Conference on Security & Management (SAM 2009)*, July 13–16, 2009, Las Vegas, Nevada, USA, 2 Volumes, CSREA Press, 2009, pp. 652–657.
25. Mohammed, M.M.Z.E., and Chan, H.A. Honeycyber: Automated signature generation for zero-day polymorphic worms, *Proceedings of the IEEE Military Communications Conference (MILCOM)*, San Diego, USA, November 17–19, 2008, pp. 1–6.
26. Mohssen, M.Z.E.M., Chan, H.A., Ventura, N., Hashim, M., and Amin, I. Accurate signature generation for polymorphic worms using principal component analysis, *Proceedings of IEEE Globecom 2010 Workshop on Web and Pervasive Security (WPS 2010)*, Miami, Florida, USA, December 6–10, 2010, pp. 1555–1560.
27. Mohammed, M. and Pathan, A.-S.K. *Automatic Defense against Zero-day Polymorphic Worms in Communication Networks.* CRC Press, Taylor & Francis Group, Boca Raton, FL, 2013.

4 Attack Severity–Based Honeynet Management Framework

Asit More and Shashikala Tapaswi

CONTENTS

4.1   INTRODUCTION

The past two decades have been marked by an immense growth in the use of the Internet and its capabilities. This immense growth has brought a wealth of valuable information to the fingertips of its users. But on the darker side, it has also laid a number of gateways for the hackers and attackers to get into a network or capture the confidential information of the users. These attacks not only lead to monetary losses, but also are a cause of concern for the security and integrity of nations as the use of information technology has also expanded to the defense and administrative services of a nation. Recent attacks on high-profile companies such as Foxconn, Facebook, PayPal, and the Sun grid (Shankalan 2006; Pauli 2010) are an indication of the changing trends followed by the attacker and have raised the issue of a need for an intrusion detection scheme that can detect new attacks in contrast to the signature-based techniques commonly used. A recent attack on the websites of the US government (McMillan 2009) also indicates that none of the systems can be totally secure, and thus a considerable amount of work needs to be done in the development of a model that is efficient in capturing the trends followed by the attackers and ways to predict attacks based on these trends. Such a prediction based on trends is only possible if we can capture all the activities performed by the attackers. This task of capturing the activities of the attacker can be efficiently done with the help of honeypots.

Honeypots have evolved as a security tool. The basic motive behind a honeypot is to lure the attacker away from the production network and its valuable resources, such as file servers, web servers, administrator hosts, etc. Over the years, honeypots have evolved as a powerful tool for recording malicious behavior inside the host. On the other hand, honeynets are the special arrangement of honeypots inside the network, and they have the capacity to record various activities over the network. Honeypots are predominantly used for analysis of viruses and worms on a specific host, and honeynets are designed to record and analyze network-based attacks.

Recent years have witnessed the use of honeypots and honeynets in the detection, analysis, and examination of worms, viruses, and various network-based attacks. Honeypot technology has helped researchers to distinguish between various types of attacks, developing their countermeasures and learning the behavior of attacks under a controlled environment. Honeypots also provide a good way of filtering information related to attacks as they process no production data and capture all activities performed by the attacker along with all the traffic directed toward or away from it. Thus, the tracked activities can be of great value for network security personnel in developing methods for detecting zero day attacks.*

Hence honeynet installations provide the ability to analyze signatures of malwares, viruses, and various attacks happening on a production network. Research in the past decade shows the proposal of various techniques and architectures for implementation of honeypots inside a honeynet. Their goal was to maximize the attack surface exposure and to record every possible attack. Our contribution through this framework is concluded as below:

- The probabilistic algorithm is introduced for traffic filtering, roaming the honeypots, and ensuring the safety of the production network.
- The framework developed by this method could be applied to a load balance between high-interaction and low-interaction honeypots or hybrid honeynets.
- A well-guided example of how this framework can be used in conjunction with a honeynet to increase the efficiency of the network attack analysis.

Our manuscript is organized as follows: The requirement of this framework and the thorough problem description is given in Section 4.2. A detailed literature survey with an introduction to similar frameworks is in Section 4.3. The basic knowledge required to understand the framework and some related work is defined in Section 4.4. The mathematical background and related terms are elaborated through Section 4.5. Structural details and a general idea of the overall working of our framework can be found in Section 4.6. A brief explanation of our algorithm and a mathematical explanation of how probabilities are calculated are given in Section 4.7. A detailed explanation of facilities provided by our framework and its procedure of use, limitations, and configuration are given in Section 4.8. Transparency, compatibility, and related issues with the use of this framework are discussed in Section 4.9. Possible security risks and countermeasures are compiled in Section 4.10. Future work and scopes are given in Section 4.11. The appendix contains configuration files for case studies.

4.2 PROBLEM DESCRIPTION

As stated earlier, researchers have always contributed toward maximizing the exposure of honeypots toward attacks. Researchers have always tried to determine the honeypot location such that it should entertain a maximum number of attacks. We can find various techniques for a similar purpose. There are multiple reasons to expose a honeypot to the maximum possible attacks. Initially, honeypot installation is very expensive in terms of resource consumption. A typical high-end, third-generation, or even advanced honeypot requires virtualization support and a huge amount of storage for logging attacker activities. In short, the hardware and software requirements for a honeypot, its working environment, are very expensive. It is also true that the cost incurred in maintaining honeypots is very high. It needs expert assistance to ensure its smooth working. Our research is driven by the above mentioned problems. In short, we are restricted by the number of honeypots to be placed, and we have to utilize them to maximum benefit.

In general, when honeynets are concerned, they are nothing but an arrangement of various types of honeypots inside a network where a reverse firewall is placed. The role of the reverse firewall

---

* Zero day attack: An attack that exploits an unknown vulnerability and has no countermeasure or remedy available.

is to monitor and limit the traffic going outside the network (which is nothing but the honeynet). Honeypots are placed as fake entities against production servers, hosts, or critical resources. Cases such as monitoring of attacks taking place on a particular network give rise to the need for a honeynet. In case of a conventional honeynet, a similar type of resources from the production network is mapped to a particular honeypot inside the honeynet. This honeypot is configured to pretend to be that type of resource. Sometimes honeynets are the subnets allocated for research and analysis purposes by organizations where we can find different types of honeypots configured between the address range of that specific subnet.

Our scenario has been derived for the above mentioned cases. We have the following design goals:

1. To provide the technique such that the need of putting the honeypot against every production host gets reduced.
2. To provide an efficient way to redirect malicious traffic from production network resources to honeypots.
3. To provide a dynamic load-balancing scheme for honeynets based on the attack severity, the current number of attacks, and the future probability of attacks.
4. To filter legitimate traffic from being entertained by honeypots. (This will help in reducing the honeypot load.)
5. To provide a security system for a production network using honeynets. This should ensure that malicious traffic gets redirected to the honeynet, and legitimate traffic for hosts of the production network should never get hampered.
6. To provide a roaming scheme based on attack scenarios and run time attack development. We call it "reactive roaming."

4.3   RELATED WORK

Lance Spitzner (2002) has summarized the development of honeypots and honeynets in his book *Honeypots: Tracking Hackers*. The book introduces readers to the available honeypots through their generations. The author has included almost all possible types of honeypots in his literature. Honeypots are no longer the magic word for security researchers. Another paper (Spitzner 2003a) summarizes honeypots and definitions related to honeypots in brief. The general idea about tracking attackers is given in Splitzner (2003b). Thorough hands-on tutorials and case studies of tracking attackers and intrusion detection are available in Provos and Holz (2007).

Details about planning, building, and maintaining first and second generation, virtual, and distributed honeynets can be found in Project (2004). It also reveals about capturing and analyzing data through a honeynet, including the latest on reverse engineering and forensics for Windows, UNIX, and networks. Use of honeypot roaming for countering different types of network-based attacks is explained in various publications (Khattab et al. 2004, 2006), in which use of a honeypot as a security tool is revealed. Honeypots have been found useful to detect wireless network attacks (Prathapani et al. 2009). A self network defense strategy using roaming honeypots was introduced for the first time by Zenggang and Xue-min in 2010. However their strategy has no room for managing honeynets.

A comparatively new concept in honeynets is the double honeynet. It is used in the detection of polymorphic worms (Mohammed et al. 2010). Another scheme based on the same concept discusses automatic signature generation for polymorphic worms (Mohammed and Chan 2008). As stated earlier, many frameworks have been suggested to expose a honeypot to a maximum attack surface (Jain and Sardana 2011; Chin 2009).

There are solutions that are effective and equipped to distribute incoming traffic for a given network on a predefined set of honeypots. Honeybrid (Berthier 2008) is an example of such a system. It is developed to address the same problem with a static decision about packet filtering. Honeybrid relies upon a packet header to decide the fate of that packet, and according to predefined rules, it redirects that packet to the expected honeypot. Honeybrid is worthy up to some extent to redirect available traffic between honeypots. Still, there is no strong base for the decision of roaming. It never considers the attacker behavior, its past history, or even a current attack's severity, but Honeybrid successfully transfers active TCP sessions between honeypots.

None of the above mentioned systems provides all features collectively. Also, their decision to distribute traffic is based purely upon network load. These techniques provide static decisions for traffic roaming. However our framework will decide the fate of attacker traffic based on the severity of the attack, its past history of attack, and the load on a given honeypot. Also, this framework could be used to safeguard the production network.

4.4 FORMAL FOUNDATION

4.4.1 HONEYPOTS

A honeypot is a tool that is used to track an attacker's activities. It lures the attacker to attack the system. Honeypots have no production value; in fact, their value lies in being probed, attacked, or compromised. The main goal of deploying a honeypot is to get it attacked. An important point about honeypots is that they are not a solution to network attack, but they are a tool to analyze network traffic so that data can be captured about various types of attacks, including zero-day attacks.

Honeypots can be classified based on the type of working, the nature of deployment, and the level of interaction with attackers. The classification is as follows:

1. Research honeypots
2. Production honeypots

4.4.1.1 Research Honeypots

Research honeypots are the honeypots used to their maximum capacity to record the tactics and moves of an attacker. These honeypots are responsible for analyzing possible threats over an installed network. They can be further classified into the following subcategories:

4.4.1.1.1 Low-Interaction Honeypots

Basically they are the simulations of particular operating systems (OS) or devices such as routers, etc. They provide very limited replies, either prerecorded or preconfigured by the administrator. They try to simulate the legitimate behavior of the system that they are pretending to be. Still, the responses of such honeypots are limited.

4.4.1.1.2 High-Interaction Honeypots

High-interaction honeypots offer a complete system to the attacker. This type of system tries to imitate almost all features of a given operating system. The system deployed as a high-interaction honeypot can emulate any services, base operating system, or any other functionality. Advantages of such a system include that they have the capability of providing almost every possible option available on a legitimate system. This makes them look like legitimate systems. This, in turn, enables researchers to analyze possible loopholes in the system. Also, they get a chance to find out possible attacker behavior on the same OS in ordinary working conditions. Although these honeypots reveal complete details about the attacker activities, implementing them requires a high operational cost. Implementation of such a system is resource consuming and costly. Many of the high-interaction honeypot architectures make use of virtualization as their implementation platform. This approach gives an opportunity to learn about the tools, tactics used, and also the motives behind attacks.

4.4.1.1.3 Pure Honeypots

They are the full-fledged implementation of any operating system over the production network. They are monitored for incoming traffic by putting a tap or by monitoring a gateway associated to it. Such systems have no external software installed on them and work as a legitimate system would work. In a later section, we will demonstrate the working of such a system, which is developed by us based on a virtualization framework.

4.4.1.2 Production Honeypots

They are easy to use commercial versions of research honeypots. They provide limited support to a particular service, application, etc. They are part of the production network and placed along with production machines to strengthen the security of the organizational network. Overall deployment, management, and working of such honeypot are simpler than research counterparts.

4.4.2 Honeynets

A honeynet is a network of honeypots placed behind a reverse firewall. The reverse firewall is used to capture all inbound and outbound traffic from the honeypot network. The reverse firewall also limits the amount of inbound and outbound traffic flowing through the honeypots so that the systems may not be able to infect other systems on the network. A different operating system is used for implementing the honeypots on the host system, giving the appearance of independent computers. Virtual honeynets provide advantages of reduced cost and easier management. Implementing honeypots on a single computer may provide complete control of the virtualization software to the attacker and may lead to a compromise of the entire honeynet.

4.4.3 Honeyfarm

Sometimes a research union needs different types of honeypots to be installed over the network to perform various tasks. High-interaction, low-interaction, production, etc., types of honeypots have various roles and unique characteristic properties. There are dedicated honeypots, which are expert in analysis of a particular type of service. To research and analyze worm behavior network attacks, it is advisable to have different types of analysis tools available over the network. Honeyfarm is a type of arrangement in which various types of honeypots are installed over the network in multiple numbers.

4.4.4 Roaming Honeypots

A major problem with attackers is that they lose their interest in a host system once they detect that a given system is a honeypot. There are many tools and tricks available in the market which can detect honeypot installations on a given system. So to confuse attackers and to let them reveal maximum tricks, it's necessary to hold them in the honeypot network. This can be achieved using roaming concepts. The idea is to shift the attacker onto different hosts having different configurations. This, in turn, becomes a challenge for the attacker to determine the exact behavior of the system he is attacking. It has also been observed many times that once an attacker comes to know about a honeypot at some IP address, the attacker stops attacking on such a system. In our system, the attacker will never come to know the location of the honeypot. Also, every legitimate system will get secured by our architecture.

Honeypot roaming is something also related to advertising different honeypot configurations on the same IP address. For the same, we are using an innovative approach. We are using a software router, which is updated with its routing tables according to our decision algorithm. The router will redirect packets from the previous honeypot to a new honeypot address. As our honeypots are on an internal network, when traffic for the original IP address is forwarded to the honeypot IP address, an intruder will get a feeling that he or she is working on a particular honeypot. This will also assure that honeypot implementation on that particular IP will remain hidden from the attacker, and we will get all his moves recorded. This technique provides us with two benefits. The legitimate traffic to a particular host will never get blocked or diverted as it is from a different IP address than the attacker's IP. Another benefit is that the attacker will never come to know he has been roamed to a honeypot.

4.4.5 Click Router

A click router is used to divert the packets destined for a particular system to any other system. It is a software-based modular router. A click can supersede the in-built routing mechanism of the Linux kernel, thereby providing the user with a huge degree of flexibility and customization. We have used Click to perform a simple NAT (network address translation) using some of the in-built modules of Click. A click router also enables us to redirect the traffic from a particular source to an expected destination honeypot. In our model, if we have to roam a particular honeypot, then we simply divert its packets to any other location, thereby shifting the honeypot. This scheme is implemented for the high-interaction honeypot.

4.4.6 IP Tables

IP tables is a packet filtering utility developed by Netfilter (McHardy, n.d.) for UNIX kernel 2.4 onward. It provides various capabilities to its user, including network address translation (NAT). IP tables provide a unique command line interface and set of rules to configure packet handling. They are widely used as Linux firewalls, software routers, and in packet-handling utilities. Due to the simplicity of defining rules, IP tables have become a great success for such type of applications.

IP tables work with the concept of a chains of rules. It provides unique facilities of stateless or state-full firewalls. IP tables also provide additional administrative choices to log, accept, drop (reject), or continue (no external modification) to every packet it encounters. This feature gives enough reliance to the network administrator for defining tailor rules for his network.

Using IP tables at the gateway, we can mold almost every incoming packet according to our requirements and decide its fate inside our network (honeynet or production network). On the contrary, we can also modify every outgoing packet from our network and pretend that it is legitimate for the outside world.

4.4.7 Double Honeynets

A double honeynet is very similar terminology introduced to tackle some of the design issues mentioned in Section 4.2. It is used to detect and monitor network worms. In the case of a double honeynet, an extra protection layer called a "gate translator" is used to distinguish between legitimate and malicious traffic. It is seen that cases in which honeypots are installed inside a production network, there are possibilities that a genuine user may get accidentally directed to a honeypot rather than the production network servers, which are meant to provide various services. To avoid such encounters, the gate translator is put at a network gateway. The classification is done basically based upon the destination addresses of packets. Generally, organizations advertise only their public address to the rest of the world, and it is used by genuine users. Also if a server is limited to providing basic http, mail, etc. services, then all requests to other than the mentioned ports would be malicious. So based on such distinctions, the gate translator classifies the traffic. It redirects legitimate traffic to production servers and the rest to the honeynet.

A multiple number of honeynets (at least two) can be deployed with such a setup. The goal is to trace and analyze polymorphic worms. When malicious traffic is initially redirected to honeynet 1, worms may spread their net inside that honeynet. The general tendency of a polymorphic worm is to attack neighboring networks once it infects a majority of hosts in a given network. Outbound traffic from such a honeynet is monitored. Intelligently, another internal translator does that work. Polymorphic worms keep on changing their payloads with successive attacks. An internal translator maps such outgoing requests to another honeynet. This helps in analyzing variations in worm signatures.

However, classifying malicious traffic based upon IP headers is vulnerable. An advanced attacker could initialize the connection with a production server pretending to be a normal service-seeking user and use this host as his "attack cannon" to reach the rest of the network. Our framework is a lot more mature, and a possible attack detection method is a combination of IDS results and our own predictions.

4.5 MATHEMATICAL BACKGROUND

The working of our attack prediction suite is based upon some mathematical terminologies. We have used data analysis and forecasting methodologies to predict incoming attacks on each host of the network. We have implemented a time series analysis for trend estimation of an attacker. The accuracy of our prediction is strongly based upon the following data analysis methods.

4.5.1 TIME SERIES ANALYSIS

A time series is a data point sequence, spaced at uniform time intervals and measured typically at successive points in time. Time series forecasting is nothing but predicting future values based on values previously observed. Time series data have natural temporal ordering.

Modeling time series data for future estimation has various possible available models. The selection of any such model solely depends upon its application. We have summarized these models below:

4.5.1.1 Auto-Aggressive Model

This model is used to represent events in the real natural world that are truly random and have no common pattern. This model has widespread usage, ranging from speech recognition to radar and sonar applications.

4.5.1.2 Moving Average Model (MA)

It is a type of finite impulse response filter used to analyze a set of data points by creating a series of averages of different subsets of the full data set. Given a series of numbers and a fixed subset size, the first element of the MA is obtained by taking the average of the initial fixed subset of the number series. Then the subset is modified by "shifting forward"; it is done by excluding the first number of the series and including the next number following the original subset in the series. This creates a new subset of numbers, which is averaged. This process is repeated over the entire data series. The MA method is refined for accuracy using some other markers. Such type of moving average model is the exponential weighted moving average.

In case of EWMA, more weight is assigned to the latest values. In our scenario, the recent past of the attacker plays a very vital role in the determination of its future moves. If an attacker has shown a very intense attack profile in the last few observations, then the chances of such an attacker attacking again are very high. Similarly, an attacker that was active a long while back but was not active in the recent past has less of a chance of attacking immediately. Hence, the EWMA model suits very well in our case. We put maximum weight to the most recently recorded value and keep on exponentially decreasing weight associated with past values. Hence, the last observed value gets the least weight. On the other hand, this arrangement makes sure that recent readings about attacks will dominate in the decision process heavily.

The general formula for EWMA–based time series evaluation is given by the following equation:

$$Z_i = \lambda Y_i + (1 - \lambda)Z_{i-1} \quad 0 < \lambda \le 1 \tag{4.1}$$

In above Equation 4.1, Y_i are the sequentially recorded observations, which can be individually observed values from the process. Z_i is the result obtained at instance i at any given time. The value of Z_o is always estimated, and the procedure depends upon the application.

4.5.2 kNN

kNN or k-nearest neighborhood is a method used for pattern recognition based upon the similarity of examples in a featured space. It is basically a machine learning algorithm. It is developed as a way to recognize patterns of data without requiring an exact match to any stored patterns or cases. The concept behind it is that similar cases are nearer to each other, and dissimilar cases are farther. Here in this algorithm, "k" is the neighborhood count. It is user-defined, and in our case, it is equal to the square root of the number of hosts available in the production network. The algorithm consists of various phases. They are explained as follows:

1. Training Phase:
   It consists of calculating distances between the various points inside the feature set. Here in our case, it calculates the similarity between the hosts based upon the attack patterns observed by every host. This step is resource intensive and needs to calculate the distance between every possible pair.
2. Statistics:
   General statistics could be found from training results, which can detect correction percentage, error rates, etc.
3. Scoring:
   Classification of each case is carried out in this phase. Scores are evaluated, and top "k" neighbors are determined for each point. This detects the similarity between the available observation points. In the case of this framework, hosts that have encountered a similar attack pattern are identified by this method.

4.5.3 Pearson Similarity

Similar to the kNN algorithm, which is used to find out similarity between different points, the Pearson similarity finds out a correlation between any two given points. It is basically a metric, which measures how highly correlated two variables are. The range is measured from −1 to +1. We have made use of the Pearson similarity as input to the kNN measure.

4.6 FRAMEWORK DETAILS

The general overview of our framework and its cooperating modules is given in Figure 4.1.

4.6.1 Initialization

There have always been efforts to make this framework easy to use and configure. Configuration of the entire framework is possible using a single file named "honeyframe.config." This file provides the administrator with the following configuration options:

1. Specification of the types of honeypots. (i.e., low interaction, high interaction, etc.)
2. Specification of honeypot details such as IP address, host name, type, etc.
3. Specification of subnet or list of host IPs to be monitored
4. Specification of roaming strategies
5. Selection of honeygroup load-sharing methods
6. Determining thresholds for roaming

Our framework groups various same types of honeypots together. For example, all low-interaction honeypots can be grouped into a single group. There is no upper bound on such honeypot groups. Each group can contain one to as many as possible available honeypots. This makes the work of

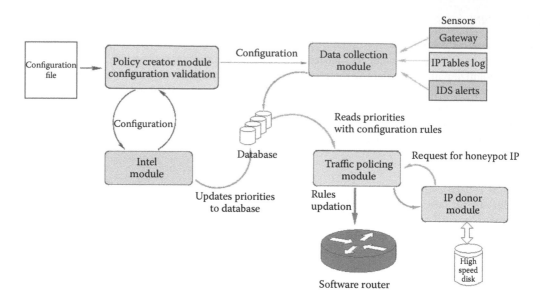

FIGURE 4.1 Architectural diagram for framework.

the administrator easier. The administrator has to define the group ID of the honeypots to redirect specific traffic. We call each such group a "honeygroup."

4.6.2 ROAMING DECISIONS

The decision of roaming is based on many markers. There are two types of hosts inside the network. They are honeypots and hosts of the production network. Each host requires different criteria for roaming inbound traffic coming toward that host.

The following options can be set for any host of a production network:

1. Opt to take part in malicious traffic roaming or not.
2. If opted, then set a threshold for attacks after which traffic should be titled as harmful.
3. An initial roaming point after crossing the "harmful" threshold (honeygroup).

Here in this case, when any production network host opts to take part in the roaming decision process, our algorithm starts monitoring possible traffic destined for that host. Based on the observations, a database is maintained to predict the future attacks on that particular system. When this prediction crosses the harmful threshold set for that host, our framework roams malicious traffic to a specified honeygroup. Note that the type of honeygroup for roaming can be set for the initial purpose only. It could be possible that our honeynet may contain a bunch of the same type of honeypots. The decision of roaming to a particular honeypot inside that honeygroup is solely based on load and the decision of the administration module "IP donor."

For every honeygroup, the following options can be set as follows:

1. For each honeygroup, upper and lower thresholds are set. They determine the range of attack probabilities a given honeygroup will handle.
2. Action to be taken on crossing thresholds. (Roam to other honeygroup, roam to original location, and don't roam.)
3. Next destination honeygroup ID on crossing thresholds.

The basic task of the framework is to redirect incoming traffic between the honeygroups based upon the current and future severity of attacks. The administrator has to set the lower bound and upper bound of probability for such movement. If, for some attacker, the probability of attack shoots up above the upper bound, the framework redirects its traffic from the current honeygroup to the next mentioned honeygroup. On the contrary, if the attack probability reduces below the lower bound, then it is shifted to the honeygroup having a lower level.

4.6.3 Development of Rules and Working

Our framework is divided into four major modules. They are listed below with their short descriptions:

4.6.3.1 Data Collection Module

This module is responsible for scanning the configuration file to determine hosts, honeypots, and network arrangements. From the configuration file, it reads the number of cycles required as a training window. The basic work of this module is to collect attack information, traffic details, and every other piece of information required by our Intel module. IDS logs are parsed to get attacker details, host details, and attack severity information. The extracted knowledge is stored in MySQL database. This database, in turn, helps to generate the training data for a given timing window cycle. This training data is required in the next phase to perform attack prediction for every next cycle. The alert parsing method runs on a periodic basis, and after knowledge discovery, it triggers to the training database generation method. This method keeps track of the database. It removes all the entries past the time window and appends the new entries at the end of each cycle. It ensures that the training database always remains up to date.

4.6.3.2 The Intel Module

Our Intel module has the key role to play in our framework. It operates based upon the algorithm defined in Section 4.7. The role of this module begins with the data collection module, and it produces results that play an important role in the roaming decision. With the available record of attacks for every host, the probability is calculated using algorithm 1 for each pair of host and attacker. This module, in turn, generates intelligence for the roaming decision and helps to load balance and distribute traffic according to the administrator's choice.

4.6.3.3 Policy Creator Module

Every honeynet installation is different, and every administrator has a different situation to implement. For maintaining the scenario as per the requirements of a given network, a framework has made the work of the administrator easier, using the single "honeyframe.config" configuration file. The exact implementation and structure of this file is explained in Section 4.8. The role of this module is to validate the configuration file and then to update the Intel module and other corresponding modules with necessary information.

4.6.3.4 Traffic Policing Module

The traffic policing module (TPM) is responsible for managing all incoming traffic of the network with the help of a network gateway. This module, in coordination with the Intel module, is responsible to handle the incoming feed of malicious and legitimate traffic. Based on the calculations of the Intel module and the roaming rules defined by the policy creator module, it generates traffic routing rules. This module has a responsibility to run the entire show of load balancing and roaming actually.

The working of a conventional gateway is a bit complex. Initially, it has to read every incoming packet of the network for its source and destination address. In the next step, it tries to match that packet with the rules defined by the TPM module. If it matches with any one of the rules, the corresponding action associated with that rule is taken. The action could range from redirection to some host or no redirection to dropping the packet.

The majority of the work done by the TPM module could be implemented by the access control lists (ACLs) of any network gateway. Software routers have inbound robustness and correctness features. Our framework provides two options for software routers. There is absolutely no difference in the working of both routing schemes. They are as follows:

a. By use of IP tables–based routing
b. By use of a click modular router

Based on the selection of the configuration file, this module generates rules for any one of the routers. Please note that based on the interval these rules need either to be updated or to be flushed from the router memory.

4.7 ALGORITHM IMPLEMENTATION

Our framework is driven by an estimation-based algorithm, which is responsible for load sharing between the honeypots. The implementation of software system modules is as shown in Figure 4.2. The working of the algorithm can be explained as below.

4.7.1 PHASE 1

There are three phases involved in the roaming decision. During the first phase, attacks on the entire network are detected and logged using an intrusion detection system (IDS). In the current implementation, network monitoring is done using SNORT IDS. It is working in inline mode at the network gateway. The SNORT is running at the gateway continuously. Attack logs are extracted from the SNORT logging utility on a fixed periodic basis. This work is exclusively handled by the data collection module.

4.7.2 PHASE 2

Phase 2 solely deals with predicting the possible attackers and their probability of attack for the next cycle $(t + 1)$ on each host of the network. The facility is provided to monitor and predict the attackers for select hosts only on requirement. This phase provides the probabilistic analysis for every possible host and possible attacker on it with their respective probabilities of attack. This phase uses three methods to predict the future attackers. They are time series analysis, the kNN nearest neighbor victim similarity measure, and the cross association algorithm. As mentioned, this technique has proved very efficient at predicting attackers. In case of attack, prediction problem ratings may vary widely over time as they represent the number of attacks (logs) reported between different time slots.

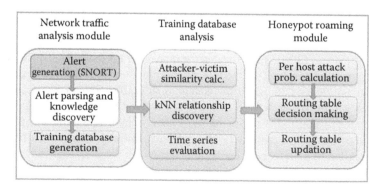

FIGURE 4.2 Algorithm implementation.

In case of time series analysis, the future activity strongly depends on the recent past. Motivated by this, the exponential weighted moving average model is used. Every rating $num_{a,v}(t)$ describes the number of attacks at the mentioned hour t by an attack IP a on the host v. The $TS_{a,v}(t+1)$ indicates the forecast for $num_{a,v}(t+1)$ given the past observations $num_{a,v}(t')$ at time $t' \leq t$. $TS_{a,v}(t+1)$. It can be interpreted as a measure of how likely an attacker is to attack again given its past history. The estimation is given as

$$TS_{a,v}(t+1) = \sum_{t'=1}^{t} \alpha(1-\alpha)^{t-t'} num_{a,v}(t') \qquad (4.2)$$

A prediction based solely on time will fail to capture the correlation between different attackers and different victims in the network. For the same victim, the neighborhood (kNN) approach is used, which is built on the idea that a prediction can be made by trusting similar hosts. In this work, a variation of the Pearson similarity has been used to account for the time the attacks were performed. For every pair of victims x, y, their similarity $s_{x,y}$ is defined as

$$sim_{x,y} = \sum_{t_1 \leq t_2 \in T_{train}} e^{-|t_2 - t_1|} \frac{\sum_{a \in A} num_{a,x}(t_1) num_{a,y}(t_2)}{\|num_x(t_1)\|_2 \|num_y(t_2)\|_2} \qquad (4.3)$$

where

$$\|num_x(t_1)\|_2 = \sqrt{\sum_{a \in A} num_{a,x}^2(t_1)}$$

The idea of a kNN model is to model missing ratings as a weighted average of a known rating given to the same item by similar users:

$$kNN_{a,y}(t) = \frac{\sum_{x \in N^k(y;a)} s_{x,v} TS_{a,x}(t)}{\sum_{x \in N^k(y;a)} s_{xy}}, \quad \forall t \in T_{test} \qquad (4.4)$$

where $kNN_{a,y}(t)$ is the prediction provided by the kNN model, and $N^k(y; a)$ represents the neighborhood of top k similar victims to y according to the similarity measure, sim, for which $TS_{a,x}(t)$ is known.

In addition to the victim neighborhood explored by the kNN model, the joint neighborhood of attackers and victims is given by a cross association (CA) algorithm. The intuition is that if an attacker shows up in a neighborhood of a victim persistently he is more likely to attack the victim than other attackers. The probability is given by

$$CA_{a,v}(t+1) = \sum_{t'=1}^{t} \alpha(1-\alpha)^{t-t'} \gamma_{a,v}(t') \qquad (4.5)$$

where $\gamma_{a,v}(t') \in [0,1]$ is the density of the attack, i.e., it represents 1 if the attacker has performed the attack at time t on host v. We have calculated $\gamma_{a,v}(t')$ as follows:

$$\gamma_{a,v}(t') = \frac{num_{a,v}(t')}{\sum_{t'=1}^{t} num_{a,v}(t')} \qquad (4.6)$$

The results obtained by all three methods mentioned above are combined to get a collective attack probability. The time series prediction used as a base predictor and neighborhood models are weighted proportionally to their accuracy. The weights for both the models are defined as follows:

$$w_{a,v}^{kNN} = \frac{\sum\limits_{u \in N(v;a)} sim_{uv}}{\sum\limits_{u \in N(v;a)} sim_{uv} + \beta_1} \tag{4.7}$$

$$w_{a,v}^{CA} = \frac{\sum\limits_{t \in T_{train}} \gamma_{a,v}(t)}{\sum\limits_{t \in T_{train}} \gamma_{a,v}(t) + \beta_2} \tag{4.8}$$

where in above equations β_1 and β_2 are parameters, which are estimated. The idea is that by this weighting we can rely more on kNN when v has a strong neighborhood of similar victims. On the other hand, $w_{a,v}^{CA} \cong 1$ for the pair of (a,v) that belong to a dense attack. The combined rating is given for every host and its corresponding attacker as

$$\widehat{fin}_{a,v}(t) = TS_{a,v}(t) + w_{a,v}^{kNN} * kNN_{a,v}(t) + w_{a,v}^{CA} * CA_{a,v}(t) \tag{4.9}$$

where $\widehat{fin}_{a,v}(t)$ is the estimated value of probability of attack at time $(t + 1)$ by an attacker a on host v.

4.7.3   PHASE 3

The third phase exclusively deals with updating the database for traffic redirection. From Phase 2, we get separate lists generated ($List_h$) for each host h inside the network and under monitoring. The list for each host contains attacker IPs "a" and their respective probabilities of attack for a given host v, i.e., $\widehat{fin}_{a,v}(t)$. Note that these lists for each host contain entry for every possible attacker. However, we are only interested in redirecting the traffic sourced from attackers having a probability more than the thresholds we have defined. The traffic redirection scheme is illustrated with the help of the rules below.

For every legitimate host (h) on the network:

a. Select only those attackers (attacker IPs) from the list ($List_h$) for which attack probability is > threshold. Name that selection as AL_h (attacker list for host h).
b. For each $A_{ip} \in AL_h$, select its traffic forward destination, i.e., the honeypot IP (HP_{IP}) according to the attack probability associated with it. (Note that there could be different honeygroups associated for different probability ranges. Our framework selects an appropriate honeygroup according to database entry.)
c. Create a traffic forward rule such that all traffic coming from A_{ip} and destined for host h should be redirected to the honeypot IP (HP_{IP}).

For every honeypot (HP) on the network:

a. Here in this case h of ($List_h$) is $h = HP$.
b. Select only those attackers (attack IPs) from the list ($List_h$) for which the attack probability is above the threshold. Name the list AL_{ha} (attacker list for honeypot host h).
c. Select only those attackers (attack IPs) from the list ($List_h$) for which the attack probability is below the threshold. Name the list AL_{hb} (attacker list for honeypot host h).

d. If for *HP*, the prediction is below the threshold, forward traffic from attacker IP $\in AL_{hb}$ to the *HP* of the previous honeygroup.

e. If for *HP*, the prediction is above the threshold, forward traffic from attacker IP $\in AL_{ha}$ to the *HP* of the previous honeygroup.

The above rules ensure that legitimate hosts will always receive filtered traffic, and severe attack cases will be handled by the most capable honeypots without getting overloaded by casual requests.

4.7.4 IP DONOR

Note that the actual implementation of redirecting traffic to a new honeypot of a defined honeygroup is a little complex. Traffic redirection needs to be done from one IP address to another IP address belonging to a honeypot from the new honeygroup. The same is achieved using an exclusive method, which is called "IP donation." This method ensures even distribution of incoming traffic between all honeypots in the given honeygroup. It keeps track of live and active incoming connections to honeypots inside every honeygroup. It delivers a unique IP address of a honeypot from that honeygroup. There are two modes associated with the working of this framework. They are explained in Section 4.8. This module provides an option to select between available roaming strategies. These strategies are listed below:

4.7.4.1 Strict Load Sharing

For achieving load balancing inside a honeygroup, the IP donor module performs round robin allocation. With each incoming request for a honeypot, the next available honeypot IP is provided. An algorithm similar to round robin is used to assign honeypots from a given honeygroup. This is the default option of working and can be opted by putting unique code 00 in the field "ip_donor_opt."

4.7.4.2 Fixed Load Sharing

This option assigns a fixed number of requests to every honeypot. An administrator has to define the number of assignments to be done for every honeypot. This mode has a mandatory condition that there should be at least two honeypots available in a given honeygroup. Note that if *n* is the total number of honeypots in any given honeygroup, then only *n* − 1 honeypots can be assigned to a fixed number of allocations. One honeypot is to be intentionally left behind for handling the situation, in which in all the rest of the honeypots have reached their limit. This mode has unique code 01.

4.7.5 ALGORITHM 1

```
INPUTS: List_h
for Each host h do
        if h! = HP_IP then
        Select List_h = list for h
                for each attacker IP attk_IP in list List_h do
                        if Probability of attack > up_threshold then
                                Create rule
                                    Redirect traffic coming from attk_IP for Host_IP to HP_IP
                            else if Probability of attack < low_threshold then
                                Create Rule
                                    Redirect traffic coming from attk_IP for Host_IP to HP_IP
                        end if
                end for
        end if
end for
Flush all existing rules
Load new rule set
```

4.8 CASE STUDY

The actual working of our framework can explain it in a more elaborated way. Our framework has the capability of working in two different modes. They are as follows:

1. Production Hosts Modes
2. Honeygroups Only Mode

This flexibility is provided for two purposes. There will be some cases in which an organization may want to apply our framework with its existing setup. This is possible only when they will need minimum changes to their existing network. The first case provides the flexibility of adopting this framework without modification to a production network and the hosts inside it. Changing production server configurations and adopting a new system is very cumbersome. It makes sure that the organization will never need to make any major changes in its existing setup. The second mode is an exclusive mode. This mode is beneficial to researchers and organizations that want to manage their honeynets in more sophisticated ways. This mode will satisfy all needs of the honeynet administrator to manage honeynets.

4.8.1 CASE I: WITH PRODUCTION HOSTS

As we said, this mode is a provision to make the proposed framework applicable to existing setups. The case discusses the scenario, which an administrator may deploy using our framework. A production network may contain multiple servers and some hosts that need direct external access. Although the only address known to the external world is of a server enabling various services, there still are very few steps required to get knowledge of other hosts present inside the production network. This, in turn, becomes an overhead for the network administrator, and he usually is interested in knowing about attacks taking place not only on servers but also on such hosts. Sometimes it has been observed that attackers would never attack directly on a production server but will first ensure access to such hosts and through them will launch a final attack on the servers. In short, there are scenarios in which it is necessary to monitor an entire production network and also to safeguard it.

4.8.1.1 Scenario

The following Figure 4.3 shows such a network in which there is a production server with some hosts for which the administrator wants to have a honeynet. He also needs to know that once an attacker is detected he should be redirected to the honeynet. Again, inside the honeynet, he wants the attacker having a strong probability of a severe attack to be monitored by a honeygroup of high-interaction honeypots. For other attacks that are comparatively less severe, he wants them to be handled by a honeygroup of low-interaction honeypots. Figure 4.3 below will explain the architecture under consideration.

4.8.1.2 Solution

Keeping the above scenario in mind, the administrator has to customize the "honeyframe.config" file. The generated configuration file is given in appendix A. This file contains three sections as follows:

i. Setup
ii. Hosts
iii. Honeygroup

Note that the order of these sections should be strictly followed inside the configuration file. The setup section contains all the generic information required for the working of the framework. This

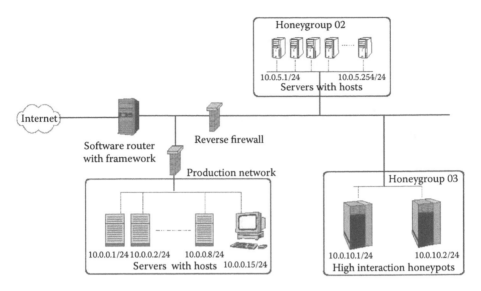

FIGURE 4.3 Case study 1 architecture.

section initially asks for "mode," which in this case is set as 0. In mode 0, the policy creator module checks for two more sections in the configuration file. We will explain the meaning of each field of each section as follows. Note that for this case the actual values of each field are given in parentheses.

4.8.1.2.1 Setup Section
- mode: Mode of working (0).
- ids_log: Location from where IDS logs are to be accessed. Sometimes the administrator may want to provide a separate copy of such logs (File Path).
- period: It defines the time period between two consecutive observations considered by the Intel module. If set X min, then all attacks for X min are considered as one instance (5 min).
- time_window: Number of such observations to be considered for attack prediction. If Y is selected as the time window, Y numbers of periods of each X min are taken into consideration for predicting the next X min window (10).
- hgroup_no: Total number of honeygroups available (2).

Note that here the period taken is 5 min. It means that the data collection module will update its database with the latest information every 5 min. It will take cumulative results of the last 5 min. each time. On the other hand, a *time_window* of 10 observations is taken. This means for predicting attack probability for the next 5 min., the history of 5 * 10 = 50 min. will be considered. It will cover the last 10 observations taken on a periodical basis of 5 min. each.

4.8.1.2.2 Hosts Section
This section is exclusively used when mode = 0, i.e., in this type of scenario. It generally provides details about the production network.

- host_no: Total number of hosts present inside the production network (3).
- file: location of the file containing the IP addresses of all hosts. File can contain a subnet address if the entire subnet is present. IP addresses should be delimited by a single white space (file address).
- threshold: It is the upper bound probability up to which traffic coming for the hosts inside the production network will not be diverted to the mentioned honeygroup (30).

4.8.1.2.3   Honeygroup Section

This section defines the honeygroups. A honeygroup is a conceptual grouping of the same type of honeypots. They possess similar properties.

- hgroup_id: User-defined honeygroup ID. User can select any two-digit unique ID for honeygroup except 00 and 01. ID 01 is by default treated for no traffic redirection even if the threshold has been satisfied. 00 is reserved to specify, sustain current redirection irrespective of the threshold.
- hpot_no: This number represents the number of honeypots present inside a given honeygroup.
- file: This file contains the IP addresses or subnet address of the honeypots, separated by white space.
- ip_donor_opt: As explained in Section 4.7.4 (00).
- low_threshold: This field is optional. When the framework predicts probability lesser than what was predicted by it in earlier runs, then the administrator can again free the slot of the high-end honeygroup and allocate this attacker to another honeygroup. But this option is hazardous in the sense that the attacker may become less active once he will break inside the high-interaction honeypot. Eventually, after setting the backdoor, it will start listening to events taking place upon that honeypot; however, at that instance, looking at its current behavior and roaming it to another honeypot may not be recommended.
- low_t_location: Honeygroup ID to which a given attacker must be moved. This field is considered only if *low_threshold* is set.
- up_threshold: This field provides an upper bound up to which a given honeygroup will handle attacker traffic. If set 00, then no further roaming will be done to any other honeygroup.
- up_t_location: This field is active if *up_threshold* is not equal to 00. It provides the ID of the next honeygroup to which traffic should be redirected on crossing *up_threshold*.

4.8.2   Honeynets Only Mode

This mode exclusively serves all requirements to manage honeynets. The primary goal of this mode is to handle honeynets so that the traffic load on the honeypots will get distributed according to the severity of the attacks. This mode enables the administrator to create a ladder of honeygroups according to their efficiency and capacity to handle attacks. For example, an administrator can configure a scenario such that it assigns a very serious attack situation to the highest capable honeypot while, at same time, assigning general attacks to a series of other honeypots that belong to another honeygroup. This mode provides various optional schemes for assigning honeypots inside a honeygroup. This internal honeypot allocation scheme selection is available only with this mode. In case of mode 0, i.e., the production host mode, assignment of honeypots is carried out by the IP donor module in linear fashion as explained in Section 4.7.4. All possible options of honeypot assignment are summarized below. Note that actual IP assignments are performed by the IP donor module itself.

The above options are helpful for the administrator when honeypots are resource constrained. The following scenario discusses a situation in which honeynets-only mode can prove useful.

4.8.2.1   Scenario

Consider a scenario in which the research team has set up a honeynet consisting of various types of honeypots. Honeypots range from a number of low-interaction honeypots to a few high-interaction honeypots. The team wants to distribute traffic coming from various feeds to this honeynet. They want to utilize their setup thoroughly. And the only necessary condition they have is that high-interaction honeypots should handle rich attacks only. Because they have

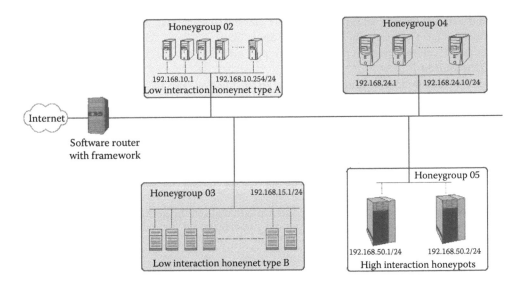

FIGURE 4.4 Case study 2 architecture.

only two high-interaction honeypots, they want them to be consumed appropriately. They are also having some medium-interaction honeypots, which they want to handle some of the above-average traffic. The group owns four public IP addresses and wants all incoming traffic to these four addresses to be delivered by default to two available low-interaction honeynets. The scenario is shown in Figure 4.4.

4.8.2.2 Solution
Figure 4.4 shows the arrangement of honeypots according to our scheme. Appendix B shows the configuration file for such a scenario. This file contains three sections with a few additional parameters than mode 0. These additional parameters and their significance are explained in this section. The remaining parameters have the same meaning as mode 0. The configuration file has three sections. They are as follows:

  i. Setup
  ii. Mappings
  iii. Honeygroup

As stated, there exists a new section, "mappings," instead of "hosts." The working is explained as follows:

4.8.2.3 Setup
The setup section is identical in both working modes.

4.8.2.4 Mappings
This section contains the initial mappings of public addresses to the corresponding honeygroups. These mappings are represented using a unique rule format. A freelance is given to a user of the system to distribute traffic coming from public IP addresses between the honeypots based upon parameters such as destination IP address, destination port, and protocol. The administrator has to mention only the honeygroup ID and has not to worry about individual honeypot allocation. The IP donor module at run time will assign traffic to a particular honeypot based upon the distribution

strategy of that honeygroup. Fields of each rule are comma (,) separated, and each rule is terminated with a semicolon (;). The format of the rule is given below:

Destination IP address (required), destination port address (optional), protocol (optional), honeygroup ID (required).

The user can distribute incoming traffic between the honeygroups based on protocol details and the destination port address.

4.8.2.5   Honeygroup

This section contains information related to honeypots in the honeygroup. It also contains the information or roaming thresholds, the next possible honeygroups, etc. This section is similar to the section in mode 0 except for the addition of one field.

- ip_donor_opt: This field directs the IP donor module about the option to be used for traffic allocation to honeypots inside a given honeygroup (00/01).

4.9   RESULTS AND COMPARISONS

We have compared our framework qualitatively with the other available options providing similar services. The detailed comparison is given in Table 4.1 below.

From Table 4.1, it can be concluded that our framework has taken care of almost every possible requirement. Modular implementation and room for expansion are key benefits of it. Also production network support is an exclusive feature, which helps to solve both problems, i.e., security and analysis.

4.10   TRANSPARENCY

4.10.1   In Terms of IDS

The framework makes use of IDS alerts in prediction of future attacks. The framework is open for any type of IDS. Currently, it is configured to use SNORT as a default IDS. There are very few changes required in the IDS rule parser module to incorporate other types of IDS. However, for the

TABLE 4.1
Framework Comparison

Features	Honeybrid	Honeynet Framework	Double Honeynet
Dynamic traffic roaming	N	Y	N
Provision of honeypot grouping	N	Y	N
Honeynet wise load sharing	N	Y	N
Inter honeypot communication monitoring and control	N	Y	Limited between honeynets
Outgoing packet modification	Limited	Possible	Limited
Customization according to network	Through configuration file	Possible	N
Ability to configure custom load sharing strategy for each honeygroup	N	Y	N
Production network support	N	Y	N
Security against accidental honeypot roaming	Possible	N	N
Production network security	N	Y	N
Independent honeynet and honeynet–production n/w modes	N	Y	N

current version to work with other IDS systems, the user can format given IDS alerts in the SNORT alert log format and then feed them to this framework. The flexibility to choose IDS alert file is provided by provisioning the file location parameter in a configuration file. This enables the user to specify an alerts file of his or her own choice. For better predictions, one can think of using two different IDS systems together.

4.10.2 IN TERMS OF SOFTWARE ROUTER

It is not possible to have the same software router/gateway in every scenario. The main objective of such a gateway is to distribute and route traffic to the correct host. The framework is tested with two different types of routing mechanisms: Click router and IP tables–based software router. The Intel module of the framework generates prediction results in an internal understandable format. It is the task of the traffic policing module to communicate with the router software and apply the rules according to its defined format. To comply with any available router, the TPM needs to be updated such that it should generate access control rules (ACL) in a specific router format.

4.10.3 IN TERMS OF DATABASE

This framework needs to store lots of data for various reasons. The major contribution in the database is through the data collection module, which periodically updates network attacks, IDS logs, and other related information. For a better prediction, it is always preferable to have precise and enough samples. Currently, database support is provided with MySQL. It is possible to migrate the database to any other database engine without any hassle.

4.11 SECURITY MEASURES

4.11.1 HONEYPOT DETECTION

Today, there are many ways available in the market to detect honeypot setups. They are based upon the type of honeypot and its configuration. The design goal of this framework was to develop a mechanism that will help in detecting network attacks and will again help to redirect those attacks to the appropriate honeypot of choice. Many times, some sequence of commands used with some expertise along with past experience could help in detecting the honeypot setup. There are prewritten scripts available that are able to detect some popular honeypot setups such as Sebek. Generally, low-interaction honeypots are victims of such detection methods due to the limitation of responses they provide with every command. Use of IDS rules to match the packet signatures that are identical to such detection routines may help in preventing such attacks. It is possible in such cases to generate a high-priority IDS alert, which, in turn, will help this framework in redirecting honeypot traffic to a more capable honeypot. This may help to protect honeypot detection to some extent. The idea is to fortify IDS with such script signatures. When a match is found, such traffic is redirected to the honeypot that is not vulnerable to that detection method.

4.11.2 IP SPOOFING

No doubt that our framework depends upon an attacker's IP address for entire calculations. IP spoofing on the Internet requires heavy support of a series of routers such as Tor (The Tor Project). As we said, this framework is meant for load sharing and distributing attacks over a range of honeypots. Practically, a framework needs an IP address and IDS alerts for that address. Based on these and some other parameters, its destination is fixed. Unless an attacker is using a different IP address for every other request he makes, we can predict its future. Our cross association module tries to find out the correlation between different attackers. This helps in improving results and evades spoofing attacks to some extent. Generally, frameworks like Tor have a fixed IP address range, so the administrator can opt to block traffic from such blocks of IPs.

4.12   FUTURE WORK

4.12.1   FRAMEWORK UPDATE

This framework is currently undergoing evolution, and it is in its early stage. Some additional capabilities will surely improve its application over a much wider range of problem areas. It is not necessary that a honeynet will always be implemented at the same location or with a continuous series of IP addresses. Many of the honeynets have been deployed over geographically widespread areas or over different networks. To connect them using this framework and distribute traffic among them, it needs to have some special support. Tunneling can help in such cases. Also tunneling provides help to communicate using different protocols. We hope to add GRE tunneling to this framework very soon.

Route cloning is another method used to determine the route to distant hosts. It allows creating a route for every host to be communicated with. This feature is supported by CISCO routers and has to be equipped with our framework. A virtual private network (VPN) provides the ability to extend a private network across the public network with security. This feature may prove helpful to connecting different honeynets. VPN support will be provided soon.

4.12.2   FUTURE DIRECTIONS FOR RESEARCH

Honeypots and honeynets have evolved over the years as malware catchers and attack scenario recording tools. Use of honeypots in computer science has been found to be realistic and beneficial for malware analyzers and forensics investigators. It is well accepted that to analyze any type of attack, there is no other effective way possible than providing a realistic environment like a honeypot does. High-interaction honeypots have always demanded heavy resource arrangements, which restricted their use in environments that are resource sensitive. However, the concept of honeypots could be applied to detect and record attacks on low-powered devices such as mobile phones. With the existing rate of adoption of such devices, there exists a strong need to analyze attacks, post-attack effects, and responses from such devices.

Efforts have been taken by a few like Matthias Wählisch (2012) to implement honeypots for mobile devices. Authors have implemented a mobile honeypot, which is capable of analyzing attacks over a mobile telephony network. Implementing a honeypot setup over such devices is critical. Rather a reverse approach of implementing the mobile device environment over resourceful computer systems is viable. With the help of emulation tools such as QEMU and the help of virtualization technology, it is possible to emulate mobile and low-power devices on capable systems. Some of the existing honeypots in the market are capable of running a router and other network device OSs and providing emulated environments for network devices.

On similar grounds, mobile devices could be emulated on real computer systems, and these systems could be configured to record and analyze various activities over such devices. It has another advantage in that there are no hardware and resource limitations such as database support, network bandwidth, and battery life, etc. The implementer of such a system can even go further to introduce concepts such as virtual machine introspection (VMI). VMI is a brand new approach to introspect virtual machine (VM) activities from out of the VM. This ensures the almost real emulated environment on that VM and that no entity from inside the VM could detect any monitoring activity taking place. With honeypots that were used to have their data logging agents inside VM, they always had a risk of getting detected by malware or an attacker due to the existence of such agents. VMI theoretically nullifies such risk as the entire monitoring will be done from outside VM. Such techniques need to be implemented for attack analysis and honeypot deployment over low-power devices.

4.13 CONCLUSION

This framework has been developed keeping various goals in mind. Existing honeynet management systems had some serious flaws. Also practical limitations and issues related to honeynet management were considered for development. With this framework, the limitations associated with existing similar technologies have also been addressed.

This framework is capable of distinguishing groups of honeypots according to the administrator's choice. The primary and niche task of traffic load distribution among honeynets has been effectively addressed by use of artificial intelligence. While distributing the load among the honeynets, various parameters were considered such as attack severity, attack possibility, and the future fate of an attacker. The administrator has been geared up with full liberty to configure it according to his strategy. All updates and configurations are possible using a single configuration file. A special mode has also been introduced for the sake of the existing honeypot-only networks. This enables such users to adopt the framework easily. Loosely coupled modules of the framework enable it to be cooperated with various IDS systems and routing software. This is one of the major achievements that provide flexibility to its users.

ACKNOWLEDGMENTS

The authors would like to acknowledge the Department of Electronics and Information Technology (Deity), the Government of India, and the ABV-Indian Institute of Information Technology & Management, Gwalior, for their support for the project "Development of Reactive Roaming Scheme for Honeypots."

AUTHORS' BIOGRAPHIES

Asit More is a MTech research scholar in information security at the Indian Institute of Information Technology and Management (IIITM), Gwalior, India. He received his BE (computer engineering) from the University of Pune, India, in 2009. He has worked as an ETL developer in Data Warehousing for Cognizant Technology Solutions. His research interests include honeypots, virtualization security, and cloud and mobile security.

Shashikala Tapaswi is a professor at ABV Indian Institute of Information Technology and Management, Gwalior, India. She received her PhD (computer engineering) from the Indian Institute of Technology (IIT), Roorkee, India, in 2002; her MTech (computer science) from the University of Delhi, India, in 1993; and her BE (electronics engineering) from Jiwaji University, Gwalior, India, in 1986. Her primary research areas of interest are artificial intelligence, neural network, fuzzy logic, digital image processing, computer networks, and mobile networks.

APPENDIX

A. Configuration File for Case Study 1

```
# There are two or three sections depending upon mode of operation
setup{
        #Mode of working (0: With Production Hosts, 1: Honeynet)
        mode = 0
        #IDS log file location
        ids_log =/var/usr/snort/logs
        #Periodic data updation time (Duration between two observations to
be considered)
        period = 5
```

```
        #Time window for prediction (Total number of such instances to be
considered)
        time_window = 10
        #Number of honeygroups
        hgroup_no = 2
}
hosts{
        #Number of hosts in production network
        host_no = 3
        #location of list of IP address of each host (text file with space
delimited IPs)
        file =/usr/home/hosts.txt
        #threshold for redirection (must be two digit number. 00: for
every suspicious packet redirection)
        threshold = 30
}
honeygroup{
hgroup{
        #honeygroup id (any two digit unique number except 00 and 01)
        hgroup_id = 02
        #number of honeypots
        hpot_no = 3
        #location of list of IP address of each honeypot of honeygroup
        file =/usr/home/honeygroup2.txt
        #IP donor module Mode Selection (Optional)
        #ip_donor_opt = 00
        #lowerbound of threshold to roam traffic to any honeygroup
(Optional)
        low_threshold = 31
        #honeygroup ID for lower bound threshold redirection (00 for no
change, 01 for original host, Optional)
        low_t_location = 01
        #upperbound of threshold to roam traffic to any honeygroup (00 if
no upper bound)
        up_threshold = 60
        #honeygroup ID for upper bound threshold redirection (comment if
not req.)
        up_t_location = 03
}
hgroup{
        #honeygroup id (any two digit unique number except 00 and 01)
        hgroup_id = 03
        #number of honeypots
        hpot_no = 2
        #location of list of IP address of each honeypot of honeygroup
        file =/usr/home/honeygroup3.txt
#IP donor module Mode Selection (Optional)
        ip_donor_opt = 00
        #lower bound of threshold to roam traffic to any honeygroup
        low_threshold = 61
        #honeygroup ID for lower bound threshold redirection (00: for no
change, 01: for original host)
        low_t_location = 02
        #upper bound of threshold to roam traffic to any honeygroup (00 if
no upper bound)
        up_threshold = 00
```

```
        #honeygroup ID for upper bound threshold redirection (comment if
not req.)
        #up_t_location = 03
}
}
```

B. Configuration File for Case Study 2

```
# There are two or three sections depending upon mode of operation
setup{
        #Mode of working (0: With Production Hosts, 1: Honeynet)
        mode = 1
        #IDS log file location
        ids_log =/var/usr/snort/logs
        #Periodic data updation time (Duration between two observations to
be considered)
        period = 10
        #Time window for prediction (Total number of such instances to be
considered)
        time_window = 15
        #Number of honeygroups
        hgroup_no = 4
}
mappings{
        #specifies default traffic mapping rules.
        #original destination-address:port, redirected honeygroup-
address:port, protocol(any,tcp,udp);
        59.90.169.113,02,any;
        59.90.169.70:80,03:80,any;
        59.90.169.111,02,any;
        59.90.169.120,03,tcp;
}
honeygroup{
hgroup{
        #honeygroup id (any two digit unique number except 00 and 01)
        hgroup_id = 02
        #number of honeypots
        hpot_no = 254
        #location of list of IP address of each honeypot of honeygroup
        file =/usr/home/honeygroup2.txt
#IP donor module Mode Selection (Optional)
        ip_donor_opt = 00
        #honeypot assignment method type
        assign_type = 00
        #lower bound of threshold to roam traffic to any honeygroup
(Optional)
        low_threshold = 10
        #honeygroup ID for lower bound threshold redirection (00 for no
change, 01 for original host, Optional)
        low_t_location = 01
        #upper bound of threshold to roam traffic to any honeygroup (00 if
no upper bound)
        up_threshold = 40
        #honeygroup ID for upper bound threshold redirection (comment if
not req.)
        up_t_location = 04
```

```
}
hgroup{
        #honeygroup id (any two digit unique number except 00 and 01)
        hgroup_id = 03
        #number of honeypots
        hpot_no = 254
        #location of list of ip address of each honeypot of honeygroup
        file =/usr/home/honeygroup3.txt
#IP donor module Mode Selection (Optional)
        ip_donor_opt = 01
        #honeypot assignment method type
        assign_type = 01
        #lower bound of threshold to roam traffic to any honeygroup
(Optional)
        low_threshold = 10
        #honeygroup ID for lower bound threshold redirection (00 for no
change, 01 for original host, Optional)
        low_t_location = 01
        #upperbound of threshold to roam traffic to any honeygroup (00 if
no upper bound)
        up_threshold = 40
        #honeygroup ID for upper bound threshold redirection (comment if
not req.)
        up_t_location = 04
}
hgroup{
        #honeygroup id (any two digit unique number except 00 and 01)
        hgroup_id = 04
        #number of honeypots
        hpot_no = 10
        #location of list of ip address of each honeypot of honeygroup
        file =/usr/home/honeygroup4.txt
#IP donor module Mode Selection (Optional)
        ip_donor_opt = 00
        #honeypot assignment method type
        assign_type = 00
        #lower bound of threshold to roam traffic to any honeygroup
(Optional)
        low_threshold = 40
        #honeygroup ID for lower bound threshold redirection (00 for no
change, 01 for original host, Optional)
        low_t_location = 03
        #upper bound of threshold to roam traffic to any honeygroup (00 if
no upper bound)
        up_threshold = 60
        #honeygroup ID for upper bound threshold redirection (comment if
not req.)
        up_t_location = 05
}
hgroup{
        #honeygroup id (any two digit unique number except 00 and 01)
        hgroup_id = 05
        #number of honeypots
        hpot_no = 02
        #location of list of ip address of each honeypot of honeygroup
        file =/usr/home/honeygroup5.txt
```

```
#IP donor module Mode Selection (Optional)
    ip_donor_opt = 00
    #honeypot assignment method type
    assign_type = 00
    #lower bound of threshold to roam traffic to any honeygroup (Optional)
    low_threshold = 60
    #honeygroup ID for lower bound threshold redirection (00 for no
change, 01 for original host, Optional)
    low_t_location = 00
    #upper bound of threshold to roam traffic to any honeygroup (00 if
no upper bound)
    up_threshold = 00
    #honeygroup ID for upper bound threshold redirection (comment if
not req.)
    #up_t_location = 05
}
}
```

NOMENCLATURES

a	An attacker
ACL	Access control list
EWMA	Exponential weighted moving average
IDS	Intrusion detection system
kNN	k nearest neighborhood
$num_{a,v}(t)$	Number of attacks by attacker a on victim v at time period t
TPM	Traffic policing module
v	Victim host being attacked
VM	Virtual machine
VMI	Virtual machine introspection

REFERENCES

Berthier, R. (2008). Honeybrid: Hybrid honeypot famework, Software framework, 2008.

Chin, W. Y. (2009). HoneyLab: Large-scale honeypot deployment and resource sharing. Network and System Security, 2009. NSS '09. Third International Conference.

Jain, P. and Sardana, A. (2011). A hybrid honeyfarm based technique for defense against worm attacks. Information and Communication Technologies (WICT), 2011 World Congress.

Khattab, S., Melhem, R., Mosse, D., and Znati, T. (2006). Honeypot back-propagation for mitigating spoofing distributed denial-of-service attacks. Parallel and Distributed Processing Symposium, 2006. IPDPS 2006. 20th International.

Khattab, S., Sangpachatanaruk, C., Mosse, D., Melhem, R., and Znati, T. (2004). Roaming honeypots for mitigating service-level denial-of-service attacks. Distributed Computing Systems, 2004. Proceedings. 24th International Conference.

Matthias Wählisch, S. T. (2012). First insights from a mobile honeypot. *Proceedings of the ACM SIGCOMM 2012 Conference on Applications, Technologies, Architectures, and Protocols for Computer Communication (SIGCOMM '12)*, (pp. 305–306). ACM, New York.

McHardy, P. (n.d.). IP Tables.

McMillan, R. (2009, July 7). Online attack hits US government. Retrieved from http://www.computerworld.com/s/article/9135274.

Mohammed, M. and Chan, H. (2008). Fast automated signature generation for polymorphic worms using double-honeynet. Broadband Communications, Information Technology Biomedical Applications, 2008 Third International Conference.

Mohammed, M., Chan, H., Ventura, N., Hashim, M., and Bashier, E. (2010). Fast and accurate detection for polymorphic worms. Internet Technology and Secured Transactions (ICITST), 2010 International Conference.

Pauli, D. (2010, December 6). Paypal hit by DDOS attack after dropping Wikileaks.

Prathapani, A., Santhanam, L., and Agrawal, D. (2009). Intelligent honeypot agent for blackhole attack detection in wireless mesh networks. *Mobile Adhoc and Sensor Systems, 2009. MASS '09*. IEEE 6th International Conference.

Project, T. H. (2004, May 27). *Know Your Enemy: Learning about Security Threats* (2nd Edition). Addison-Wesley Professional, Boston, MA.

Provos, N. and Holz, T. (2007, July 26). *Virtual Honeypots: From Botnet Tracking to Intrusion Detection*. Addison-Wesley Professional, Boston, MA.

Shankalan, S. (2006, August 6). Micro-blogging service Twitter and social networking site Facebook have been severely disrupted by hackers. Retrieved from http://news.bbc.co.uk/2/hi/8188201.stm.

Spitzner, L. (2003a, May 29). Honeypots: Definitions and value of honeypots. Retrieved March 26, 2013, from http://www.spitzner.net/honeypots.html.

Spitzner, L. (2003b, April 30). Honeypots: Simple, cost-effective detection. Retrieved March 26, 2013, from http://www.symantec.com: http://www.symantec.com/connect/articles/honeypots-simple-cost-effective-detection.

Spitzner, L. (2002, September 20). *Honeypots: Tracking Hackers*. Addison-Wesley Professional, Boston, MA.

The Tor Project. (n.d.).

Zeng-gang, X. and Xue-min, Z. (2010). Design and implementation of a new roaming honeypots defense strategy. Computer and Automation Engineering (ICCAE), 2010, The 2nd International Conference.

Section II

IDS Issues for Different Infrastructures

5 Intrusion Detection Systems for Critical Infrastructure

Bernardi Pranggono, Kieran McLaughlin,
Yi Yang, and Sakir Sezer

CONTENTS

The art of war teaches us to rely not on the likelihood of the enemy's not coming, but on our own readiness to receive him; not on the chance of his not attacking, but rather on the fact that we have made our position unassailable.

—The Art of War, **Sun Tzu**

5.1 INTRODUCTION

According to Bace and Mell [1], the intrusion is an attempt to compromise computer security policies, i.e., confidentiality, integrity, and availability (CIA), or to bypass the security mechanisms of a computer or network. Accurate intrusion detection and prevention requires a holistic and comprehensive approach. For instance, we need reliable, precise, and complete information about the system that we want to protect. Here, we are facing a major problem as obtaining reliable, precise, and complete information is expensive and time consuming. Therefore, it is important to carefully choose what information to monitor and collect and where from is very important.

In essence, critical infrastructure (CI) is automated physical processes controlled by a group of devoted networked computers. These devoted networked computers are commonly known as industrial controlled systems (ICSs). ICSs are used as the general term for more specific systems, such as the most familiar supervisory control and data acquisition (SCADA) system, distributed control systems (DCS), and other control system configurations, such as skid-mounted programmable logic controllers (PLC), that are often found in the industrial control sectors. Critical national infrastructures refer to specific systems whose incapacity or destruction would have a devastating impact on multiple aspects of the security of one nation. Some examples of critical national infrastructures include utilities (water, electricity, gas, and telecommunications), transportation (public transport, traffic management), waste management, etc. For the purpose of this chapter, the terms ICS and SCADA are used somewhat loosely and interchangeably.

In modern days, information and communication technologies (ICT) are being combined with critical infrastructure control systems to create increasingly complex interconnected systems. Consequently, new vulnerabilities are emerging in critical infrastructure systems that threaten their operation. Such threats come not only from conventional external sources, such as terrorists, hackers, industrial espionage, etc., but also from internal sources, such as disgruntled employees, third-party contractors, or as a result of inadvertent user error, negligence, equipment failure, etc.

As a result of the complex nature of the threats described above, it is possible for attacks to occur that are previously unknown to the system. This means it is not possible to provide comprehensive cyber security solely by means of traditional IT security measures, such as firewalls and intrusion detection and prevention systems (IDPS), which predominantly react to already known attacks.

A multi-layered or defense-in-depth (DiD) approach [2] (see Figure 5.1) is therefore necessary, in which a first layer of conventional IT security tools that aim at preventing attacks is supported with a second layer of advanced monitoring tools that aim at detecting and reacting to attacks that are able to breach the first layer. A defense-in-depth model that was originally inspired by ancient castle defense has been proposed for information insurance, computer antivirus, antispam, database security, etc. Bass and Robichaux [3] exhibited that a DiD model is able to scale to large and complex network operations.

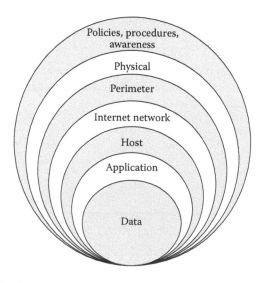

FIGURE 5.1　Defense-in-depth model.

As shown in Figure 5.1, the layers of defensive positions in a DiD model are as follows:

- Data: an attacker's ultimate target, including main databases, active directory service information, documents, etc.
- Application: the software that manipulates the data that is the ultimate target of the attack
- Host: the computers that are running the applications
- Internal network: the network in the corporate IT infrastructure
- Perimeter: the network that connects the corporate IT infrastructure to another network, such as to external users or the Internet
- Physical: the physical aspects in computing, such as the server computers, PCs, hard disks, network switches, routers, power, etc.
- Policies, procedures, awareness: the overall central principles of the security strategy of any organization

In this chapter, the authors survey the methodologies, applications, and tools to conduct studies on IDPS for critical infrastructure through a literature review and classification of the international journal articles, reports, and standards that appeared during the period from 1980 to early 2013. It presents a review about the evolution of IDPS over the past two decades. This chapter also seeks to compile and to enrich scientific knowledge associated with critical infrastructure protection. To the best of our knowledge, a study on intrusion detection and prevention systems with an emphasis on the critical infrastructure system is not widely available.

The remaining parts of this chapter are organized as follows: Section II introduces a general background on cyber security for critical infrastructure. Section III discusses intrusion detection and prevention systems in general, which include concepts, evolution, trends, and tools. Section IV describes intrusion detection and prevention systems for critical infrastructure in detail, including SCADA–specific IDSs. Open issues and challenges are discussed in Section V. Finally, the chapter is summarized in Section VI.

5.2 BACKGROUND AND MOTIVATION

Cyber security for critical infrastructure is a very concerning issue because of emerging cyber threats and security incidents targeting critical infrastructures all over the world. Cyber security must address not only deliberate attacks, for example, from disgruntled employees, industrial espionage, and terrorists, but also accidental compromises of the cyber infrastructure due to user neglect, user errors, equipment failure, and natural disasters. Vulnerabilities may allow an attacker to penetrate a system, get access to a control center, and modify load conditions to destabilize a critical infrastructure in unpredictable ways leading to serious results or disaster, for example, a brownout or even catastrophic blackout [4]. In addition, cyber security issues may also result in a breach of customer privacy and unpredicted economic losses in the electricity market. In the United States, it is interesting to note that approximately 90% of the critical infrastructures are privately owned and operated [5].

Both malicious and unintended cyber security incidents have happened from time to time; several representations of these incidents are as follows:

In 2000, millions of liters of raw sewage were spilled out into local parks and rivers due to a series of actions from a disgruntled employee in Queensland, Australia, by gaining unauthorized access into a computerized management system. The access had been made possible by installing company software on the employee's personal laptop and infiltrating the company's network at least 46 times to take control of the waste management system [6].

In 2003, the safety parameter display system and the plant process computer system at Davis-Besse nuclear power plant in Ohio, in the United States, was successfully attacked and paralyzed by the Slammer worm. The responsible managers considered the plant to be "secure" because its outside network connection was protected by a corporate firewall. The worm entered the plant network by a contractor's infected computer that was connected via telephone dial-up directly to the plant network, thus bypassing the firewall [6].

In 2010, the Stuxnet worm attacked the Siemens SIMATIC WinCC supervisory control and data acquisition (SCADA) system, using at least four vulnerabilities of the Microsoft Windows operating system [7]. It was the first malicious code attack that damaged the industrial infrastructures directly. According to Symantec's statistics, about 45,000 networks around the world have been infected with the worm so far, and 60% of the victim hosts are in Iran [8]. The Iranian government has confirmed that the country's Bushehr nuclear power plant has been attacked by Stuxnet. Stuxnet has become the first worm crossing both the cyber and physical world by manipulating the control system of the critical infrastructure.

In 2012, Flame [9] infiltrated and transferred data from thousands of computers in the Middle East including the biggest oil and gas company by counterfeiting an official Microsoft security certificate in the form of a Microsoft update. Flame is more complex and more sophisticated compared to Stuxnet. Although Flame is designed for spying, not for destruction, the damage it caused is comparable or more. The high flexibility of Flame also possesses a great possibility to deploy it as a cyber-attack tool for critical infrastructure.

Stuxnet, Flame, and Duqu [10] malwares indicate the development tendency of cyber wars and terrorism in the future. It also means that cyber security must be inherently embedded into any critical infrastructure network as a foundation of next-generation critical infrastructure. Stuxnet showed us that the security-by-obscurity concept has serious loopholes, which can be exploited.

From published cyber security incidents involving critical infrastructure, it is apparent that the critical infrastructure, such as the electricity power grid, water distribution, oil and gas, nuclear power plant, etc., has been and is susceptible to potential cyber security threats [11]. In addition, once installed and configured, the industrial control systems tend to stay in operation for a relatively long time (decades) [12]. Therefore, timely research on cyber security issues for the critical infrastructure is a highly relevant, immediate, and a particularly significant engineering task.

A typical cyber attack practice involves three phases: reconnaissance, vulnerability identification, and penetration. An attacker must first know precisely the attack target before determining the subsequent correct steps. Reconnaissance will include analysis of an application's functionality, data in the form of information stored in and used by the application as well as input data fields presented to the client, and design and architectural aspects. The task of identifying vulnerabilities and weaknesses and then creating a successful exploit becomes easier as more useful information is obtained.

An attempt to break or misuse a system is called "intrusion" or "penetration." An intrusion normally exploits a specific vulnerability found in the previous step. Intrusion must be detected as quickly as possible to minimize the risk to the critical infrastructure. An intrusion detection system is a system for detecting such intrusions. Intrusion detection systems are notable components in network security infrastructure. They examine system or network activity to find possible intrusions or attacks and trigger security alerts for the malicious activities. They are generally categorized as signature-based and anomaly-based detection systems. Other categories are network-based and host-based intrusion detection systems.

5.3   INTRUSION DETECTION AND PREVENTION SYSTEMS (IDPS)

In order to protect ICS more effectively, we need to determine what needs to be protected. We need to know the structure and components of typical ICS. Generally there are eight major control components in ICS [5]:

- Control server: hosts the DCS or PLC supervisory control software that communicates with lower-level control devices.
- SCADA server or master terminal unit (MTU): the device that acts as the master in a SCADA system.

- Human-machine interface (HMI): software/hardware that provide information to security administrators on the state of a process under control and, if necessary, to override automatic control operations in the event of an emergency.
- Data historian: a central database for recording all process information within an ICS.
- Remote terminal unit (RTU): a special purpose data acquisition and control unit designed to support SCADA remote stations.
- Programmable logic controller (PLC): a small industrial computer originally designed to perform the logic functions executed by electrical hardware (relays, switches, and mechanical timer or counters).
- Intelligent electronic devices (IED): a "smart" sensor or actuator containing the intelligence required to acquire data, communicate to other devices, and perform local processing and control.
- Input/output (IO) server: a control component responsible for collecting, buffering, and providing access to process information from control subcomponents, such as PLCs, RTUs, and IEDs. An IO server can reside on the control server or on a separate computer platform. IO servers are also used for interfacing third-party control components, such as an HMI and a control server.

5.3.1 IDPS DEFINITIONS

An intrusion detection system (IDS) has as its objective to detect attacks against computer systems and networks or against information systems in general. A network-based IDS (NIDS) is designed to passively monitor traffic in a network environment by analyzing packets for signs of possible incidents, which may be attacks or unauthorized activity. The main objective is to detect malicious behavior that can compromise the security and trust of a network. A NIDS provides an additional layer of defense, which monitors network traffic for predefined activity or patterns and alerts security administrators when potential cyber attacks are detected. Such systems log information about each incident and report them to security administrators. On the other hand, a host-based IDS (HIDS) detects attacks against a specific host by analyzing audit data produced by the host operating systems. An intrusion prevention system (IPS) performs intrusion detection and at the same time tries to stop detected incidents in real time. Typically, an intrusion detection and prevention systems (IDPS) utilizes anomaly detection, stateful protocol analysis (also known as deep packet inspection), signature matching, or a combination of the three techniques (hybrid) to analyze incoming cyber attacks. Today, an IDPS along with a firewall are the two essential components in any secure industrial control network (see Figure 5.2). In this chapter, the term IDPS is loosely used to represent both IDSs and IPSs in general.

Since it was first proposed by Anderson in his paper "Computer Security Threat Monitoring and Surveillance" in 1980 [13] and then developed further by Denning in 1987 with his seminal paper, "An Intrusion Detection Model," [14], IDS and its extension IPS in the IT domain have become relatively established technologies. Denning provided a methodological framework that stimulated many research projects and set up the foundation for commercial products in intrusion

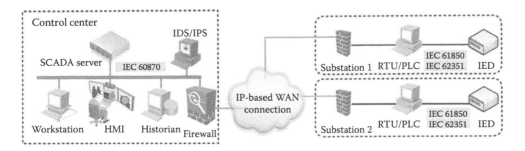

FIGURE 5.2 Typical industrial control network.

detection. Numerous intrusion detection methods have been presented [15] and some of them have been applied into SCADA systems [16–21]. However, research in a cross-disciplinary context, especially for critical infrastructure system network operation, is still at an early stage and immature.

Early IDS models were limited in capability and designed to monitor a single host only. However, more recent models accommodate the monitoring of a number of hosts interconnected by a network. Another main issue is on the difficulty of developing IDS rules for recognizing attacks. It is not a trivial task as it requires knowledge of the vulnerabilities in the various protocols. This knowledge comes at the cost of extensive vulnerability assessments of SCADA protocols.

In brief, we can conclude that a fundamental difference between the IT and ICS industry is in the order of priorities. The IT security industry views the CIA concept (confidentiality, integrity, availability) as the most important security goals, plus privacy as a fourth priority. Therefore, preventing attackers from listening to sensitive information encryption is considered a very important part. On the other hand, in the ICS industry, the SRA model (safety, reliability, availability) represents the most important priorities [22]. In the ICS industry, cyber security issues were not considered to a great extent or not at all during the designing phase of a product.

There are primarily two issues for consideration regarding the use of IDPS technology: The first is dealing with detection of issues in the TCP/IP part of the stack; the second is dealing with detection of information at the SCADA protocol (or application) level, which can also involve inspection of the packet payload.

This highlights that any IDPS focusing on the depth of the SCADA protocols (e.g., above networking L4) requires some expert knowledge and tailoring for particular critical infrastructure SCADA systems.

Protection of critical infrastructure ICT systems will require IDPS technologies that can deliver both traditional IT security measures and more specific measures tailored to the unique features of industrial control systems.

Representations of the most-used IDS/IPS tools are briefly reviewed in the following part of the chapter.

5.3.2 SNORT

Snort [23] is an open source *libpcap*-based [24] network intrusion detection and prevention system performing packet sniffing and logging and traffic analysis on IP networks. Snort was originally written by Martin Roesch [25] and is now maintained by Sourcefire. The current version of Snort employs different types of techniques, such as signature-, protocol-, and anomaly-based inspection to detect and prevent cyber attacks.

Snort is considered as the de facto standard of the IDS/IPS with millions of downloads and is the most extensively deployed IDS technique worldwide. Snort is also widely supported by an active open source community. Snort is capable of performing real-time traffic analysis and packet sniffing and logging onto IP networks. It can perform protocol analysis and content searching or matching and can be used to detect a variety of attacks and probes, such as buffer overflows, stealth port scans, SMB probes, OS fingerprinting attempts, and much more. Snort is mostly used as intrusion prevention tools by dropping attacks as they are taking place. Snort can be combined with other tools, such as OSSIM [26], Sguil, etc. to provide a visual representation of intrusion data. However, current Snort does not support multi-threading in packet processing, which has become its main drawback.

In its implementation, Snort can be operated in three different operation modes [23]:

1. Sniffer mode: In this mode, Snort reads the packet in the network and then displays them on the console continuously.
2. Packet logger mode: In this mode, Snort simply logs the packets to the disk.
3. Network intrusion detection systems (NIDS) mode: In this mode, Snort detects and analyzes network traffic.

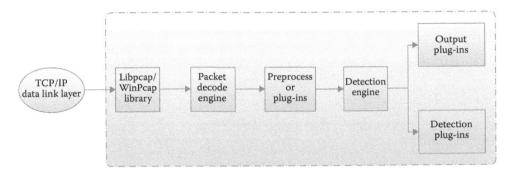

FIGURE 5.3   Snort architecture.

Snort architecture comprises the following modules [27] as illustrated in Figure 5.3:

- Packet decoder: The decoder turns the captured packets into data structures and identifies link layer protocols. Then, it takes the next step, decodes IP and then TCP or UDP depending on the case in order to get useful information such as ports and addresses. An alarm will be raised if Snort finds malformed headers, unusual length TCP options, or similar issues.
- Preprocessors: The function of the preprocessor is to take potentially dangerous packets by the detection engine trying to find known suspicious patterns.
- Detection engine: The detection engine is making use of the detection plug-ins; it matches packets against rules previously loaded into memory when the Snort system was initialized.
- Output plug-ins: These modules allow for the formatting of notifications (alerts, logs) for access by the user in many ways (console, external files, databases, etc.).
- Detection plug-ins: These modules are referenced from its definition in the rules files, and they are intended to identify patterns whenever a rule is evaluated.
- Rule files: Rule files are plain text files that contain a list of rules with a known syntax. This syntax includes protocols, addresses, output plug-ins associated, and other pertinent information. Those rule files are updated like virus definition files are.

5.3.3   BRO

Bro [28] is an open-source network traffic analyzer widely used as an intrusion detection system. Bro was originally written by Vern Paxson at Lawrence Berkeley National Laboratory and the International Computer Science Institute [29]. Bro was initially developed as a research platform for intrusion detection and traffic analysis. Bro distinguishes itself from Snort by offering high-speed network capability. In order to achieve real-time, large-volume intrusion detection, Bro utilizes two separate network interfaces (one for each direction) to capture the network traffic. Bro is divided into two engines: an "event engine" that reduces a kernel-filtered network traffic stream into a series of higher-level events and a "policy script interpreter engine" that interprets even handler written in a specialized language to express a site's security policy. Bro has gained its reputation mainly due to its stateful protocol analysis capabilities.

A built-in parser in Bro supports DNP3, a network protocol that is commonly implemented in electrical power grids. Bro first parses the network traffic and then executes event-oriented analyzers that compare the activity with patterns deemed potentially harmful. Bro uses its own policy language, which allows for tailoring Bro's operation. If something of interest is detected, a log entry or an alert can be generated.

Bro has been developed primarily as a flexible and customizable research platform for intrusion detection. Its main advantage is the separation of policies from mechanisms. Bro contains several analyzers that communicate through events. Based on scripts written in Bro's own scripting language the

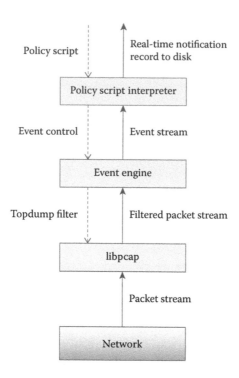

FIGURE 5.4 Structure of the Bro system. (Adapted from Paxson, V., *Comput. Netw.*, 31, 2435–2463, 1999.)

user defines event handlers to state his specific policy. The lack of the necessary user community to create, develop, and maintain a good set of signatures has become a bottleneck in the wide usage of Bro.

The internal structure of Bro is illustrated in Figure 5.4 [30]:

- Packet capture: Bro captures network traffic using *libpcap* [24]. This helps in porting Bro to different Unix variants and allows it to operate on *tcpdump* packet traces. Using *libcap* also brings another additional advantage: It isolates Bro from details of the network link technology (Ethernet, FDDI, etc.); also it allows basic packet filtering, which is very useful in environments in which only certain traffic must be analyzed.
- Event engine: In this layer, several integrity checks are performed to guarantee that the packet headers are well formed. For example, it verifies whether the IP header checksum is correct. At this point, Bro reassembles IP fragments so the network layer analyzer can accent to complete IP datagrams. It sends events to the policy layer.
- Policy script interpreter: This layer executes scripts written in a specialized Bro language [30]. These scripts specify event handlers. "For each event passed to the interpreter, it retrieves the (semi-) compiled code for the corresponding handler, binds the values of the events to the arguments of the handler, and interprets the code." [30] The event handler can execute arbitrary Bro scripting commands to generate new events, log notifications, or record data to disk.

5.3.4 Suricata

Suricata [31] is an open-source rule-based IDS/IPS that utilizes externally developed rule sets to monitor network traffic and provide alerts to the security administrators when a possible cyber attack is detected. It was developed by the Open Information Security Foundation (OISF). Suricata uses a different rule format than Snort. Suricata also differentiates itself from Snort by supporting multi-threading in a multiple-CPU environment to speed up packet processing in high-speed networks (see Figure 5.5) [32].

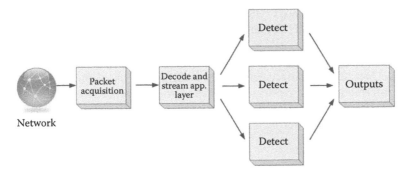

FIGURE 5.5   Suricata multi-threading architecture. (Adapted from Suricata, *Open Info Security Foundation – Suricata*, http://www.openinfosecfoundation.org, 2013.)

The high-performance Suricata IDS for computer-network monitoring has been advanced as an open-source improvement for the popular Snort system that has been available for more than a decade. Suricata has several features, which include multi-threading to improve processing speed beyond Snort. Suricata also improves on Snort in state-based analysis, which is particularly important for HTTP traffic. It is also based on signatures but incorporates revolutionary techniques. This engine embeds a HTTP normalizer and parser (HTP library) that provides very advanced processing of HTTP streams, enabling the understanding of traffic on the seventh level of the OSI model. However, performance comparison between Suricata and Snort did not show conclusive results [33] [34]. Overall, Suricata performs at least as well as Snort [34].

5.3.5   Prelude IDS

The Prelude Intrusion Detection System [35] is a hybrid IDS originally developed by Yoann Vandoorselaere and licensed under GNU public license (GPL). Prelude is a security information management (SIM) system. The product can collect alert data from other security applications or generate its own alert data using home-grown components. It includes a plug-in for importing alarms from Snort.

Prelude comes as an open source version (Prelude OSS) with reduced performance and a commercial version, Prelude Pro. As a whole, Prelude consists of sensors that generate security data. Its global architecture is shown in Figure 5.6. Sensors feed their data to the Prelude manager in intrusion detection message exchange format (IDMEF) [36]. The manager collects and normalizes IDMEF data and makes it available to output plug-ins. These output options include PostgreSQL and MySQL databases and Web-based interfaces like Prewikka.

The main components of Prelude IDS are the following:

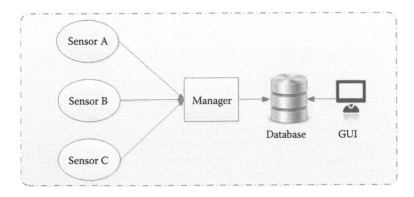

FIGURE 5.6   Prelude simple architecture. (Adapted from Prelude-IDS, http://www.prelude-ids.com/.)

- Prelude-NIDS: a network-based IDS capable of stateful inspection, fragment reassembly, protocol normalization for HTTP and RPC, polymorphic shell code detection, and ARP spoof detection.
- Libprelude: an application programming interface to facilitate integration of other data sources.
- Prelude-manager: the centralized data processor. Engineers can deploy managers as relays to collect information from clusters of sensors. The managers relay the data to a central top-level manager.
- Prelude-LML: the log monitoring Lackey, accepts syslog messages from devices that provide such information.

5.3.6 Sguil

Sguil [37] is a security information management (SIM) system like Prelude IDS. Its main component is an intuitive GUI that provides access to real-time events, session data, and raw packet captures. Sguil facilitates the practices of network security monitoring (NSM) and event-driven analysis. The Sguil client is written in tcl/tk and can be run on any operation system that supports tcl/tk (Figure 5.7).

Sguil utilizes the following tools as a sensor for the problem of collecting, analyzing, validating, and escalating NSM information [37] (Figure 5.8):

- Snort is used to monitor the link for security events and then writes them to a file on the local disk.
- *Barnyard* takes events from the Snort log file and sends them to the sensor agent, which then inserts them into a database running on the Sguil server in near real-time.
- The security analyst network connection profiler (SANCP) records TCP/IP sessions and forwards them to the database on the Sguil server.
- A separate instance of Snort collects full content of all network packets to the local disk. Because this data consists of *libpcap* trace files, Snort could be replaced by *Tcpdump* or *Ethereal*.
- The Sguil agent also listens for commands from the Sguil server.
- *MySQL* stores alert and packet data gathered from Snort.

5.3.7 OSSEC

OSSEC [38] is a cross-platform open-source host-based intrusion detection system (HIDS) that merges security log analysis, file integrity checking (Unix and Windows), registry integrity checking (Windows), time-based alerting, policy monitoring, active response, and host-based anomaly detection (for Unix–rootkit detection). It blends together all the aspects of HIDS, log monitoring and analysis, and security incident management/security information, and event management (SIM/SIEM) together in a simple and open source solution. Because of its powerful log analysis mechanism, many ISPs, universities, and data centers are implementing OSSEC HIDS to monitor and

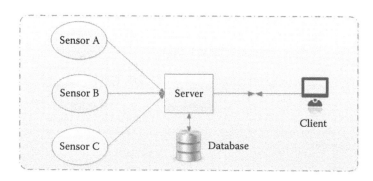

FIGURE 5.7   Sguil network architecture.

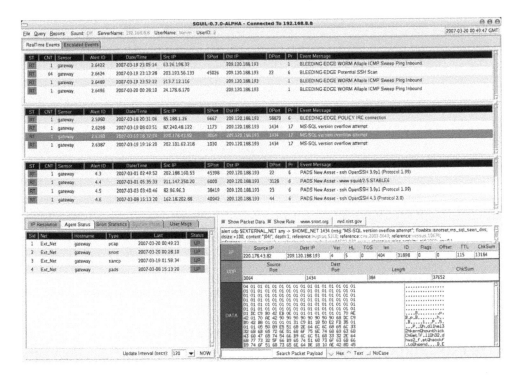

FIGURE 5.8 Sguil main screen. (Adapted from Sguil: The analyst console for network security monitoring, http://sguil.sourceforge.net/.)

analyze their firewalls, IDSs, web servers, and authentication logs. OSSEC also can be categorized as a log-based IDS (LIDS) as it uses logs as the primary source for detection.

A HIDS detects attacks against a specific host by analyzing audit data produced by the host operating systems. OSSEC HIDS are widely available to provide intrusion detection for most operating systems, including Windows, Linux, Solaris, AIX, HP-UX, OpenBSD, FreeBSD, Mac OS X, and VMWare ESX.

As OSSEC implements a centralized, cross-platform architecture, it is relatively easy to monitor and manage multiple systems with OSSEC. OSSEC's system has a central manager, which monitors everything and receives information from agents, syslog, databases, and from agentless devices. The network architecture of OSSEC is composed of a central manager, which collects information from OSSEC agents, syslog, databases, and from agentless devices and several agents or agentless devices (see Figure 5.9). When a possible cyber attack is detected, active responses can be executed, and the alerts to the security administrator are raised.

The main components of OSSEC are as follows [38]:

- Manager: The central manager is the main component of the OSSEC architecture. It stores the file integrity-checking database, the logs, events, and system auditing entries as well as rules, decoders, and major configuration options.
- Agents: The OSSEC agent is a small program installed on the system to be monitored. The agent collects information in real time and sends it to the manager for analysis and correlation. The performance of the monitored system will not be affected as the agents have a very small memory and a CPU footprint and runs inside a *chroot* jail isolated from the system.
- Agentless: OSSEC also support systems in which an agent cannot be installed by allowing file integrity monitoring without the agent installed, for example, in routers or firewalls.

Key features of OSSEC include file integrity checking, log monitoring, root detection, and active response.

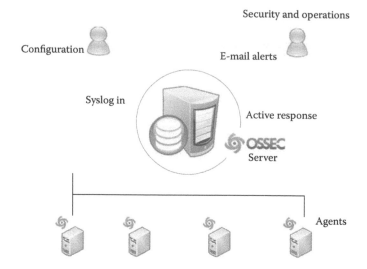

FIGURE 5.9 OSSEC architecture. (Adapted from OSSEC host-based intrusion detection system, http://www.ossec.net/.)

5.4 INTRUSION DETECTION AND PREVENTION SYSTEM FOR INDUSTRIAL CONTROL SYSTEMS

5.4.1 INDUSTRIAL CONTROL SYSTEMS VS. CONVENTIONAL IT SYSTEMS

As we understand from the previous discussion that the nature of IT systems in industrial control systems and SCADA are different from conventional IT systems. Therefore, security solutions that are applicable to IT systems might not fit perfectly into SCADA systems. The main differences between ICSs, such as SCADA and IT systems with respect to security, are summarized in Table 5.1 [5,39].

5.4.2 ICS-SPECIFIC APPROACHES

Compared to IDS in conventional IT systems, IDS in SCADA systems are rather a new area and immature. In the following section, we review recent work on IDS for SCADA systems in the research and industry community. These approaches give an overview of the landscape of SCADA-specific IDS solutions and the research direction and trend in this field.

TABLE 5.1
Industrial Control Systems vs. Conventional IT Systems

Category	Industrial Control Systems	Conventional IT Systems
Availability	24 × 7 × 365 (continuous)	Some delays are acceptable
Risk management	Human safety is paramount	Data confidentiality and integrity is paramount
Time-critical	Delays are unacceptable	Some delays are acceptable
Change management	Highly managed and complex	Regularly scheduled
Physical security	Remote/unmanned secure	Secure (server rooms, etc.)
Component lifetime	20–30 years	3–5 years
Software patches	Rare, unscheduled	Regularly scheduled
Outsourcing	Operations are often outsourced but not diverse to various providers	Common, widely used
Managed support	Single vendor	Diversified vendors

IDSs have been applied to SCADA systems using statistical approaches to classify network traffic as normal or abnormal. To build the statistical models, various modeling methods can be utilized, such as neural networks, linear methods, regression models, and Bayesian networks [40]. However, most of the statistical intrusion methods may bring a great number of false positives, which generate false alerts and false negatives, which miss real attacks.

SCADA-specific IDSs have been developed for SCADA systems using critical state, model, and rule-based methods. The primary concern of current SCADA-specific IDSs is a lack of full understanding of SCADA applications and protocols as highlighted by the Idaho National Laboratory [16]. For example, Carcano et al. [21] proposed a critical state-based IDS for SCADA based on the Modbus protocol in a power plant. However, it can only detect a limited class of attacks against PLC systems.

5.4.3 Signature-Based IDS

A signature-based or model-based IDS uses pattern-matching techniques against a frequently updated database of attack signatures. A well-crafted signature almost certainly detects the attack it represents. However, other packets may match the signature and generate false alarms. It is useful to detect already known attacks but not the new ones, such as zero-day attacks. In signature-based IDS, every signature requires an entry in the database. Each packet is to be compared with all the entries in the database, just like a typical antivirus. However, if typical antivirus software is able to detect hundreds of thousands of virus signatures, typical IDSs have signatures for only a few hundred attacks. In addition, most antivirus software has daily updates available from the web; on the other hand, IDS vendors issue updates a couple of times per year. This is mainly due to privacy and confidentiality; little analysis of real attacks is available to the public, which can be included in the signature-based IDS database. Due to these reasons, signature-based IDSs are not widely implemented to protect ICS from cyber attacks.

The model-based detection is not new in traditional IDSs, e.g., specification-based intrusion detection can be seen as model-based. Cheung et al. [19] believe that model-based monitoring to detect unknown attacks is more feasible in SCADA systems than in general enterprise networks. The expected and acceptable behavior of the system is characterized by formal models. Attacks that cause violations of the models are detected. The assumption is that SCADA systems have static topologies, regular traffic patterns, and a limited number of application and protocols running in the system, which makes it feasible to use model-based monitoring. Their work targets Modbus TCP, which is one of the most popular proprietary protocols used widely in many SCADA systems [41]. They described three model-based techniques to monitor Modbus transmission control protocol (TCP) networks, i.e., protocol-level modes, communication pattern–based detection, and learning-based approach. Unfortunately, they did not provide quantitative results and analysis in terms of experimental validation. A rule-based IDS for an intelligent electronic device (IED) based on IEC 61850 is realized by Snort [42]. The authors developed rules by using experimental data based upon simulated cyber-attacks, such as a denial of service (DoS) attack, password crack attack, and address resolution protocol (ARP) spoofing attack. The proposed blacklist approach can detect the known attacks effectively. However, blacklists are typically not effective against unknown threats, such as zero-day attacks.

Model-based IDS proposed by Cheung et al. implements three different methods to detect cyber attacks [19]:

1. Develop a protocol-level model for Modbus TCP and use Snort rules for detecting violation of the models
2. Specify a communication pattern in the SCADA network and use Snort rules for detection
3. Specify models for service usage patterns, which can heuristically learn the availability of servers and services and detect changes in server and service availability

Cheung et al. validated its IDS by developing a testbed, which showed that model-based intrusion detection is a promising approach for monitoring industrial control networks.

Oman and Phillips [43] propose automation of intrusion detection and settings retrieval for RTUs in an electrical power grid supporting widely used protocols, such as Modbus, DNP3, and RTU/ASCII protocols. The IDSs use Snort for detection and utilize XML to express the SCADA device's details, such as its IP address, telnet port, etc. The system utilizes a Perl program to parse the XML profile and creates Snort IDS signatures for legal commands on the RTU to monitor normal operations. A testbed is developed to evaluate the performance of the system. One most important contribution of their work is the creation of comprehensive intrusion detection signatures for unauthorized access to SCADA devices besides baseline-setting files for those devices.

Xiao et al. [44] implemented an IDS with the signature based in a water treatment system. The authors used a matching fault model to detect an attack to the SCADA system. Their work splits a SCADA system into two layers: a physical layer and a cyber layer and proposes a separate workflow above it. Each essential component in the physical layer should have a corresponding node in the workflow. The proposed system is evaluated by means of simulation. As typical to signature-based IDSs, this type of IDS is also only capable to detect the known attacks.

Model-based detection, at best, can only attempt to keep pace with known attacks because it relies on first capturing an attack instance and then analyzing it to determine a new signature for that instance. This has resulted in a weapons race in which attackers have employed obfuscation techniques to counter IDPS [45].

5.4.4 ANOMALY-BASED IDS

Anomaly-based techniques are necessary to protect critical infrastructure networks against unknown cyber-attacks. An anomaly-based IDS creates a model of normal behavior of the system and detects deviation from this model as a potential attack. Techniques used in detecting anomalies include data mining, clustering, and statistical signal processing. The main advantage of anomaly-based systems is the ability to detect unknown attacks or zero-day attacks. The typical disadvantages are high false-positive alarms and difficulty in identification of attack type. Moreover, because what is considered normal could be different in different environments, a distinct model of normalcy needs to be learned individually.

One of the early works in using anomaly detection techniques in IDS to protect a SCADA system was proposed by Bigham et al. [46] in 2003. The work suggests an IDS to protect a SCADA system in an electrical power grid by implementing Bayesian network algorithms with *n-gram* and invariant anomaly detectors to identify deliberate or accidental corruption of data within the SCADA system caused by attacks and faults. The work also shows that by strategically combining several different anomaly detectors, anomaly detection rates can be improved. Specifically, the authors utilized a Bayesian network to correlate their outputs with other data sources. Experiment results showed that this technique is able to reduce the false positive rate and would enable more accurate pinpointing of errors. The proposed work is studied in a real world environment by building a testbed.

Tsang and Kwong proposed the ant colony clustering model (ACCM) as an unsupervised anomaly learning model in a multi-agent SCADA system IDS [18]. Their approach uses an IDS with multiple intelligent agents and a decentralized IDS to reduce data dimensionality and increase modeling accuracy. The monitor agents monitor and capture network packets. Then, the principle component analysis (PCA) is used to extract features from the packets. The decision agents perform clustering on the preprocessed data and notify the action agents if abnormal network patterns are detected. The action agents issue responses accordingly. Instead of using real network traffic from a critical infrastructure, the KDD cup dataset [47] is used to validate the system.

Slay and Miller [48,49] adopt the DiD philosophy and use a demilitarized zone (DMZ) in order to protect and isolate the SCADA system in water distribution facilities from malicious attacks. Based on the DiD philosophy, the proposed IDS uses a multiple-layer defense, such as zoning, etc. The IDS also makes use of a combination of security mechanisms and the application of policies and procedures to create a secure SCADA environment.

In 2009, Linda et al. [50] proposed an IDS–neural network based modeling (NNM) for critical infrastructure (nuclear plan) by implementing a combination of two neural network learning algorithms (error-back propagation and Levenberg-Marquardt) for behavioral modeling. IDS–NNM consists of two main phases: the specific training set construction and the neural network training process. The IDS implements a window-based attribute extraction approach, which uses construction of a dataset using randomly generated intrusion vectors. To validate the proposal, IDS–NNM uses real network traffic data (recorded from existing critical infrastructure) in its experiment. To detect abnormal network traffic in SCADA systems, IDS–NNM uses destination addresses, port numbers, and other attributes of network packet headers. Because IDS–NNM only inspects the packet headers, the proposed IDS is not effective in detecting malicious activities hidden in the network payload.

A distributed intrusion detection system (DIDS) based on a community collaboration between multiple agents of anomaly detectors is proposed by Shosha et al. [51] in 2011. To protect a SCADA system in an electrical power grid, DIDS employs two main detection engines: general network protocol traffic (GNPT) and SCADA specific protocol traffic (SSPT). DIDS employs an events correlation engine to gather and correlate information from GNPT and SSPT. DIDS support many popular protocols in an electrical power grid, such as ICCP, Modbus, DNP3, and IEC 61850 GOOSE. A testbed is developed to validate DIDS. As SCADA systems tends to be huge in nature with millions of devices, a distributed IDS with event correlation is a necessary requirement to effectively detect coordinated and simultaneous attacks in critical infrastructure.

Specific intrusion detection for an embedded control system in critical infrastructure was proposed by Reeves et al. [52] in 2012. The study proposed an experimental host-based intrusion detection mechanism that operates within an operating system (OS) kernel to minimize overhead performance to the system. The intrusion detection system leverages its built-in tracing framework to identify control-flow anomalies. Separate virtual machines (VM) are used to capture different network traffic from different directions. One VM captures Modbus RTU/ASCII traffic from the MTU or upstream direction. The other VM captures Modbus RTU/ASCII traffic from the RTU or downstream direction.

Morris et al. [40] proposed an IDS for a SCADA system, which was running the Modbus RTU/ASCI protocol. The work uses Snort and Quickdraw [53] to detect an attack in the SCADA system. Retrofit data logger [54] is used to capture Modbus RTU and Modbus ASCII network traffic. Captured traffic is required to be converted to Modbus TCP/IP before being transmitted over a closed virtual Ethernet network to allow Snort to capture the traffic. Snort parses the captured traffic to detect rule matches. Rule matches lead to logging and or dropping of packets. The validation of Modbus RTU/ASCII Snort was through rules available from Digital Bond, Inc., in their Quickdraw software package.

The statistical IDS [40] applied to SCADA systems adopts statistical approaches, such as neural networks, linear methods, and Bayesian methods to distinguish the abnormal data from the normal traffic. However, these methods may lead to false positives and false negatives, which inevitably will result in false alarms and missed attacks. Therefore, although such techniques have some merits, when used alone, they are not sufficiently accurate. This is partly why a multi-attribute approach is preferable.

5.4.5 Hybrid-Based IDS

While most of the approaches build their IDPS systems as signature based and anomaly based, the rapid development in machine learning and data mining will boost hybrid-based systems to dominate the IDPS market for critical infrastructure in the near future. The main objectives of hybrid-based IDS are to reduce both false negative and false positive alerts by intelligently combining multiple techniques, including signature based and anomaly based.

The work of Naess et al. [55] discussed an approach for IDS implementation in the embedded middleware level, which can also be applied in SCADA systems because it is easier to make slight changes to an existing system at the middleware level. Their approach embeds interval-based and procedural-based IDS sensors and misuse-based IDS detectors in the middleware of the applications.

Valdes and Cheung develop an IDS on the supply-side of the smart grid by combining statistical anomaly and signature detection techniques deployed in both the network and host [56]. A model-based approach is adopted in which the network behavior is characterized using a model, and deviations from the model are considered as attacks. Multiple techniques are implemented for analysis: specification-based, change detection, and statistical anomaly detection. The IDS uses Snort for actual detection. The system also provides events correlation and visualization of network packets traces to help the operator in analyzing incoming attacks. The proposal was not adaptive because it used a fixed topology model based on network traffic only.

A network-based IDS (NIDS), which employs different techniques, is proposed by Fovino et al. [57,58]. The NIDS is using state-based intrusion detection, which makes use of both signature and anomaly detection techniques. The IDS is developed based on the concept of system knowledge base and system state analysis. The main goal is to detect complex attacks to SCADA systems by monitoring its state of evolution. Complex attacks, which are composed of a set of commands that, while licit when considered in isolation on a single-packet basis, can disrupt the correct behavior of the system when executed in particular operating states. The system is implemented in an electrical power grid with Modbus and DNP3 protocols and evaluated in a testbed.

In order to protect from cyber attacks in smart grid environments, Patel et al. [59] in 2012 considered a fully distributed managed collaborative smart IDPS (CSIDPS) by combining a set of autonomic, machine learning, and ontology knowledge-base (KB) interface engine and fuzzy logic risk manager functionalities. To evaluate the performance of the proposed system, 3256 attacks of various types were simulated over the network in 30 hours. After detecting abnormal activities, the CSIDPS matched them with its KB to identify the attacks and optimize the two attributes of fuzzy violation and target in self-learning procedures to generate alerts, responses, and prevention plans. Simulation results for CSIDPS showed that detection accuracy is increased and false-positive alarms are decreased compared to ordinary IDPS.

5.4.6 CYBER-PHYSICAL CORRELATION

Most critical infrastructures are managed at least in some part by a cyber-physical system (CPS). As reflected in the name, a CPS is a system that has both cyber components and physical elements in it. As described in NISTIR 7628 [60] and in the Government Accountability Office (GAO) Report 118, the critical infrastructure such as smart grid is vulnerable to coordinated cyber-physical attacks, which combine a traditional cyber attack with a physical element. Assessing the impact of coordinated cyber-physical attacks will require expertise in cyber security, physical security, and the electric infrastructure. The NIST cyber security working group (CSWG) recognizes that collaboration is critical to effective identification of cyber and physical vulnerabilities and threats.

Rrushi and Campbell suggest using probabilistic validation of attack-effect bindings to detect attacks in IEC 61850 [20]. In their work, IEC 61850 is used for communication between a nuclear power plant and substations. The authors statistically construct structural equation models estimating the causal relationship between variables of substation and power plant operation. Then they probabilistically model legitimate data flows and potential attack data flows along with characteristics of legitimate and attack data frames as well as models of substation operation models. These models are used to derive intrusion detection rules implementable in the substations. The R program is utilized to construct structural equation models estimating the causality relations. The authors also mentioned that their IDS is implementable in electrical substations, and all construction of attack-effects are based on known failure models.

SCADA-specific IDPSs are summarized in Table 5.2. Although the list of IDPS shown in Table 5.2 is not exhaustive, it does reflect most of the research being conducted in the area of critical infrastructure cyber-security protection through IDPS.

TABLE 5.2
Summary of IDS for Critical Infrastructure

Work	Year	IDS/IPS Technique	Characteristic/Algorithm/Tool	Target/Protocol	Real Traces
Bigham et al. [46]	2003	Anomaly	• Bayesian networks • Implement n-gram and invariant anomaly detectors • Sliding window	Electrical power grid, RTU	Testbed
Tsang and Kwong [18]	2005	Anomaly	• Use the ant colony clustering model (ACCM) as an unsupervised anomaly learning model in a multi-agent SCADA system IDS • Decentralized IDS • Use IDS with multiple intelligent agents	N/A	KDD cup datasets [47]
Naess et al. [55]	2005	Embedded middleware IDS, anomaly, signature	• Embed interval-based and procedural-based IDS sensors and misuse-based IDS detectors in the middleware of the applications • Application specific • Simple rule based, sliding window	N/A	Simulation
Slay and Miller [48,49]	2006	Anomaly	• Adopted the defense-in-depth philosophy • Use demilitarized zone (DMZ) to isolate SCADA system • Multiple-layer defense: zoning, etc. • Combines security mechanisms and the application of policies and procedures to create a secure SCADA environment	Water distribution	N/A
Cheung et al. [19]	2007	Signature (model-based)	• Construct models that characterize the expected/acceptable behavior of the entities • Three models: protocol-level models, communication pattern–based detection, and module for monitoring network services to detect • Implement multi-algorithm detection appliance based on EMERALD [64] detection and correlation system	Modbus TCP	Testbed
Oman and Phillips [43]	2007	Signature	• Automates intrusion detection and settings retrieval for RTUs • Use XML to express the SCADA device's details • Use Snort for detection	Electrical power grid, Modbus, DNP3, RTU/ASCII	Testbed
Xiao et al. [44]	2007	Signature	• Matching fault model • Divide a SCADA system into two layers: a physical layer and a cyber layer and propose a separate workflow layer above it • Only able to detect known attacks	Water treatment system	Simulation

(continued)

TABLE 5.2 (Continued)
Summary of IDS for Critical Infrastructure

Work	Year	IDS/IPS Technique	Characteristic/Algorithm/Tool	Target/Protocol	Real Traces
Rrushi and Campbell [20]	2008	Cyber-physical correlation, anomaly	• Use probabilistic validation of attack-effect bindings to detect attacks in IEC 61850 • Statistically construct structural equation models estimating the causal relationship between variables of substation and power plant operation • Structural equation modeling, Bayesian belief networks, Stochastic activity networks • Packet-based • Use R to construct structural equation models estimating the causality relationships	Electrical power grid, IEC 61850, DNP3	Testbed
Linda et al. [50]	2009	Anomaly (neural network based modeling, NNM)	• Use a combination of two neural network learning algorithms (error-back propagation and Levenberg-Marquardt) for behavioral modeling • Use real network data (recorded from existing critical infrastructure) • Implement window-based attribute extraction approach • Construction of dataset using randomly generated intrusion vectors • IDS–NNM consists of two main phases: the specific training set construction and the neural network training process	Nuclear plant	Testbed, real network traffic
Quickdraw [53]	2009	Anomaly	• Specific ad-hoc rules set and pre-processing modules use with Snort • Use Snort	Ethernet/IP, DNP3, Modbus	Testbed
Valdes and Cheung [56]	2009	Hybrid (signature and anomaly)	• Use multi-layer approach • Statistical anomaly and signature detection techniques deployed in both the network and host • Use Snort for detection • Use event correlation and visualization network packets for attack analysis • Not adaptive because they built a fixed topology model based on network traffic only	Modbus TCP [41], DNP3 over TCP/IP	Testbed

Reference	Year	Type	Description	Domain/Protocol	Evaluation
Fovino et al. [57,58]	2010	Hybrid (state-based: signature and anomaly)	• Aim to detect complex attacks to SCADA systems by monitoring its state evolution • Complex attacks: composed of a set of commands that, while licit when considered in isolation on a single-packet basis, can disrupt the correct behavior of the system when executed in particular operating states • Based on the concept of system knowledge base and system state analysis • NIDS	Electrical power grid, Modbus, DNP3	Testbed
Shosha et al. [51]	2011	Anomaly	• Distributed intrusion detection system (DIDS) based on community collaboration between multiple agents of anomaly detectors • Two main detection engines: general network protocol traffic (GNPT) and SCADA specific protocol traffic (SSPT)	ICCP, Modbus, DNP3, IEC 61850 GOOSE	Testbed
Carcano et al. [21]	2011	Critical state based	• Based on critical state analysis • Use multidimensional metrics for tracking the evolution of the system, indicating its proximity to the set of predefined critical states • Use PLC • The dataset is made of standard SCADA traffic reflecting normal industrial activities, plus traffic generated by simulating random malicious attacks targeting critical states	Power plant (boiling water reactor), Modbus TCP [41]	Testbed, 15 days experimental data
Reeves et al. [52]	2012	Anomaly	• Operates within the OS kernel to minimize performance overhead • Offers the flexibility to balance detection functionality with the overhead to the system • Detect specific type of control-flow alteration; looks for a certain type of pointer hijacking • Other protection measures are needed at hardware/software level	Electrical power grid	Simulation
Morris et al. [40]	2012	Anomaly (statistical)	• Proposed • Use rules from Quickdraw to validate Modbus RTU/ASCII Snort results • Use Snort and Quickdraw for attack detection	Gas pipeline distribution, Modbus RTU/ASCII	Testbed
Patel et al. [59]	2013	Hybrid (anomaly, knowledge-base and ontology)	• Intelligent collaborative IDPS for smart grid environments • Combination use of SVM, fuzzy model, ontology of network traffic and intrusion	Smart grid	Simulation

One of the common issues in deploying extensive intrusion detection in infrastructure systems is the large number of IDS alerts, many of which are false positive or indicative of low-level and failed threats.

Valdes and Skinner's work [61] is considered to be one of the early studies that implements sensor correlation in IDS. Three phases are considered in their work: event aggregation, sensor coupling, and meta-alert function. An alert correlation concept proposed by Cuppens and Miege [62] is conceived from this idea and some of the early research in the area with the main objective of creating more accurate and more succinct IDS alerts by reducing the false positive alert messages. In their work, pre- and post-conditions to model dependencies between attacks are implemented.

Unlike the IT system in typical critical infrastructure, IDS need to be reviewed, evaluated, and updated regularly to ensure its effectiveness against attacks. Signatures need to be regularly updated, rules may need to be reviewed as new threats are identified, and requirements change.

5.5   OPEN ISSUES

Mainly due to security and privacy concerns, it is very challenging to find good and adequate real traces of SCADA systems. Researchers often are forced to exploit and modify minimal data in their experiments. There are some efforts to simulate SCADA network traffic such as implementing simple network management protocol (SNMP) models [63]. The early results show that SCADA network traffic has similar characteristics with SNMP traffic. However, the simulated traffic is still far from the original SCADA network traffic, and more thorough and comprehensive research is needed in this area.

A difficulty with research in this area is the lack of an openly available test dataset to compare the performance and accuracy of proposed solutions. This is understandable from the perspective of SCADA system operators due to the sensitive nature of the data. However, for research in the community to progress, such a dataset would be valuable. In addition, because the proposed SCADA-IDS needs to be configured in the initialization stage, security engineers need to understand specific knowledge of SCADA systems, such as communication protocols, field device functions, and application environments; otherwise, the efficiency of implementation in practical scenarios will decrease, and the false positive or false negative alarms will increase.

Rapid development in network technologies, such as increasing network speed or killer applications that implement encrypted network traffic, also creates new challenges that need to be addressed.

5.6   CONCLUSION

The chapter surveys significant works in the field of intrusion detection and prevention systems for critical infrastructure in the past two decades. Motivated by a significant increase in cyber attacks to critical infrastructure, it is clear that critical infrastructure specific IDPS is essential.

Several characteristics are required for next-generation IDPS in order to effectively protect critical infrastructure. A multi-layer approach, various detection techniques, distributed in nature, smart event correlation engines, easy to configure, widely supported by large community, etc. are some of the "must have" characteristics in designing IDPS for critical infrastructure.

There is still a lot of room for further research in the field. While most of the approaches build their IDPS systems as signature based and anomaly based, the rapid development in machine learning, data mining, etc. will boost a hybrid system to dominate the IDPS market for critical infrastructure in the near future.

Furthermore, in order to enhance attack detection, it is useful to think beyond classic IT-based detection approaches that monitor very IT focused parameters. It is possible that attacks may manifest themselves in subtle changes in the operational behavior of the critical infrastructure systems while remaining undetected elsewhere.

ACKNOWLEDGMENTS

The authors would like to acknowledge all partners in the EU FP7 research project 'PRECYSE' for their contributions to this chapter.

AUTHORS' BIOGRAPHIES

Bernardi Pranggono received his BEng degree in electronics and telecommunication engineering from Waseda University, Japan; his MDigComms degree in digital communications from Monash University, Australia; and his PhD degree in electronics and electrical engineering from the University of Leeds, UK. Dr. Pranggono is currently a lecturer in network & security at Glasgow Caledonian University, UK. He has previously held research positions at Queen's University Belfast and University of Leeds. His current research interests include optical networking, network security, critical infrastructure cyber-security, big data and green ICT. He has served as a vice-chair, technical program committee member in numerous international conferences/workshops, such as HPCC, GLOBECOM, etc. He also serves as referee of some renowned journals/conferences, such as *IEEE Transactions on Power Delivery*, *IEEE Communications Magazine*, IEEE GLOBECOM, IEEE ICC, Elsevier *Optical Switching and Networking*, etc. Previously, he has held industrial positions at Accenture and Telstra.

Kieran McLaughlin is a lecturer at the Centre for Secure Information Technologies (CSIT) at Queen's University Belfast. He currently leads research at CSIT in critical infrastructure cyber-security, including smart grid and industrial control systems. His research focuses on advanced network intrusion detection and prevention technologies, protective measures against malware and advanced persistent threats, and cyber-physical anomaly detection within smart grids and industrial control systems. He obtained a MEng degree in 2003 from Queen's University of Belfast, where he was also awarded a PhD in 2006 for his work investigating high-throughput lookup architectures for network processing, and he has several years experience as a researcher and senior engineer working in the fields of digital communications, network processing technologies, and cyber-security.

Yi Yang received the BS degree in electrical engineering and automation from Chongqing University, Chongqing, China, in July 2005, and an MS degree in electrical engineering from Huazhong University of Science and Technology, Wuhan, China, in July 2007. He worked for the State Grid Corporation of China from 2007 to 2010. Currently, he is pursuing the PhD degree in electrical and electronic engineering at Queen's University Belfast, Belfast, UK. His research interests include smart grids, supervisory control and data acquisition (SCADA) systems, synchrophasor systems, communication protocols, network security, and intrusion detection systems. He is a student member of IEEE.

Sakir Sezer is a professor at the Centre for Secure Information Technologies (CSIT) at Queen's University Belfast. He graduated in 1994 with a Dipl Ing. in electrical and electronic engineering from RWTH Aachen University, Germany. In 2000 he completed his PhD at Queen's University Belfast (QUB), UK. In October 1998, Dr. Sezer joined QUB to lead research and teaching in the areas of communication and digital systems. At Queen's University Belfast, Dr. Sezer has established a research team spanning all aspects of hardware-based network processing and network security. Dr. Sezer has co-authored more than 70 publications in the field of network security, communication systems, programmable systems, VLSI and SoC, and also serves as a technical committee member for a number of prestigious international conferences, including IEEE SoCC, ICT, FPT, RAW, and ICONS. He led a number of industry and government sponsored research programs, including JIGSAW, FP7, and EPSRC.

REFERENCES

1. R. Bace and P. Mell, Intrusion detection systems, NIST Technical Report 800-31, National Institute of Standards and Technology (NIST), 2001.
2. N. S. A., Defense in depth: A practical strategy for achieving information assurance in today's highly networked environments. Available at http://www.nsa.gov/ia/_files/support/defenseindepth.pdf.
3. T. Bass and R. Robichaux, Defense-in-depth revisited: Qualitative risk analysis methodology for complex network-centric operations, in *Military Communications Conference, 2001. MILCOM 2001. Communications for Network-Centric Operations: Creating the Information Force. IEEE*, vol. 1, pp. 64–70, 2001.
4. D. V. Dollen, Report to NIST on smart grid interoperability standards roadmap, Electric Power Research Institute (EPRI), Palo Alto, CA, 2009.
5. K. Stouffer, J. Falco, and K. Kent, Guide to supervisory control and data acquisition (SCADA) and industrial control systems security—Recommendations of the National Institute of Standards and Technology (NIST), 2011.
6. A. Nicholson, S. Webber, S. Dyer, T. Patel, and H. Janicke, SCADA security in the light of cyber-warfare, *Computers & Security,* vol. 31, pp. 418–436, 2012.
7. T. M. Chen and S. Abu-Nimeh, Lessons from Stuxnet, *Computer,* vol. 44, pp. 91–93, 2011.
8. N. Falliere, L. O. Murchu, and E. Chien, W32. Stuxnet dossier. Symantec security response, 2011.
9. K. Munro, Deconstructing flame: The limitations of traditional defences, *Computer Fraud & Security,* vol. 2012, pp. 8–11, 2012.
10. B. Bencsáth, G. Pék, L. Buttyán, and M. Félegyházi, Duqu: Analysis, detection, and lessons learned, in *ACM European Workshop on System Security (EuroSec)*, 2012.
11. Y. Yang, T. Littler, S. Sezer, K. McLaughlin, and H. F. Wang, Impact of cyber-security issues on smart grid, in *2nd IEEE PES Int. Conf. and Exhibition on Innovative Smart Grid Technologies (ISGT Europe)*, Manchester, UK, pp. 1–7, 2011.
12. R. Anderson and S. Fuloria, Security economics and critical national infrastructure, *Economics of Information Security and Privacy,* pp. 55–66, 2010.
13. J. P. Anderson, Computer security threat monitoring and surveillance, James P. Anderson Co., Fort Washington, PA, 1980.
14. D. E. Denning, An intrusion-detection model, *IEEE Transactions on Software Engineering,* vol. SE-13, pp. 222–232, 1987.
15. A. A. Ghorbani, W. Lu, and M. Tavallaee, *Network Intrusion Detection and Prevention: Concepts and Techniques*. Springer, New York, 2009.
16. J. Verba and M. Milvich, Idaho National Laboratory supervisory control and data acquisition intrusion detection system (SCADA IDS), in *IEEE Conf. on Technologies for Homeland Security*, pp. 469–473, 2008.
17. M. P. Coutinho, G. Lambert-Torres, L. E. B. da Silva, H. G. Martins, H. Lazarek, and J. C. Neto, Anomaly detection in power system control center critical infrastructures using rough classification algorithm, in *3rd IEEE Int. Conf. on Digital Ecosystems and Technologies (DEST)*, pp. 733–738, 2009.
18. C.-H. Tsang and S. Kwong, Multi-agent intrusion detection system in industrial network using ant colony clustering approach and unsupervised feature extraction, in *IEEE Int. Conf. on Industrial Technology (ICIT)*, pp. 51–56, 2005.
19. S. Cheung, K. Skinner, B. Dutertre, M. Fong, U. Lindqvist, and A. Valdes, Using model-based intrusion detection for SCADA networks, in *SCADA Security Scientific Symposium (S4)*, Miami, FL, pp. 1–12, 2007.
20. J. Rrushi and R. Campbell, Detecting attacks in power plant interfacing substations through probabilistic validation of attack-effect bindings, in *Proceedings of S4: SCADA Security Scientific Symposium*, Miami, FL, 2008.
21. A. Carcano, A. Coletta, M. Guglielmi, M. Masera, I. N. Fovino, and A. Trombetta, A multidimensional critical state analysis for detecting intrusions in SCADA systems, in *Transactions on Industrial Informatics, IEEE,* vol. 7, pp. 179–186, 2011.
22. E. Egozcue, D. H. Rodriguez, J. A. Ortiz, V. F. Villar, and L. Tarrafeta, Smart grid security: Recommendation for Europe and member states, ENISA, 2012.
23. Snort, Network intrusion prevention and detection system (IDS/IPS). Available at http://www.snort.org, 2012.
24. V. Jacobson, C. Leres, and S. McCanne, libpcap, Lawrence Berkeley National Laboratory, http://www-nrg.ee.lbl.gov/, 1994.
25. M. Roesch, Snort: Lightweight intrusion detection for networks, in *Proceedings of the 13th USENIX Conference on System Administration,* Seattle, Washington, pp. 229–238, 1999.

26. L. Coppolino, S. D'Antonio, V. Formicola, and L. Romano, Integration of a system for critical infrastructure protection with the OSSIM SIEM platform: A dam case study, in *Proceedings of the 30th Int. Conf. on Computer Safety, Reliability, and Security*, Naples, Italy, pp. 199–212, 2011.

27. A. F. Arboleda and C. E. Bedón. Snort™ diagrams for developers. Universidad del Cauca, Columbia. Available at www.cs.ucdavis.edu/~wu/ecs236/snortdevdiagrams.doc, 2005.

28. Bro, The Bro network security monitor. Available at http://bro-ids.org/, 2012.

29. V. Paxson, Bro: A system for detecting network intruders in real-time, *Computer Network*, vol. 31, pp. 2435–2463, 1999.

30. V. Paxson, Bro: A system for detecting network intruders in real-time, *Computer Network*, vol. 31, pp. 2435–2463, 1999.

31. Suricata, Open Info Security Foundation—Suricata. Available at http://www.openinfosecfoundation.org, 2013.

32. Suricata, Open source IDS/IPS/NMS engine. Available at http://suricata-ids.org/, 2013.

33. D. Day and B. Burns, A performance analysis of Snort and Suricata network intrusion detection and prevention engines, in *5th Int. Conf. on Digital Society*, Gosier, Guadeloupe, pp. 187–192, 2011.

34. E. Albin and N. C. Rowe, A realistic experimental comparison of the Suricata and Snort intrusion-detection systems, in *26th IEEE Int. Conf. on Advanced Information Networking and Applications Workshops (WAINA)*, pp. 122–127, 2012.

35. Prelude-IDS, Available at http://www.prelude-ids.com/, 2013.

36. H. Debar, D. Curry, and B. Feinstein, RFC4765—The intrusion detection message exchange format (IDMEF), IETF, 2007.

37. Sguil: The analyst console for network security monitoring. Available at http://sguil.sourceforge.net/, 2013.

38. OSSEC host-based intrusion detection system. Available at http://www.ossec.net/, 2013.

39. D. Kuipers and M. Fabro, Control systems cyber security: Defense in depth strategies INL/EXT-06-11478, Idaho National Laboratory, 2006.

40. T. Morris, R. Vaughn, and Y. Dandass, A retrofit network intrusion detection system for MODBUS RTU and ASCII industrial control systems, in *45th Hawaii Int. Conf. on System Science (HICSS)*, pp. 2338–2345, 2012.

41. The Modbus organization: Modbus messaging on TCP/IP implementation guide v1.0b, http://modbus.org, 2006.

42. U. K. Premaratne, J. Samarabandu, T. S. Sidhu, R. Beresh, and T. Jian-Cheng, An intrusion detection system for IEC61850 automated substations, *IEEE Transactions on Power Delivery*, vol. 25, pp. 2376–2383, 2010.

43. P. Oman and M. Phillips, Intrusion detection and event monitoring in SCADA networks, in *Critical Infrastructure Protection*, vol. 253, E. Goetz and S. Shenoi, Eds., Springer, New York, pp. 161–173, 2007.

44. K. Xiao, N. Chen, S. Ren, L. Shen, X. Sun, K. Kwiat et al., A workflow-based non-intrusive approach for enhancing the survivability of critical infrastructures in cyber environment, in *Proceedings of the Third Int. Workshop on Software Engineering for Secure Systems (SEES)*, p. 4, 2007.

45. P. O'Kane, S. Sezer, and K. McLaughlin, Obfuscation: The hidden malware, *Security & Privacy, IEEE*, vol. 9, pp. 41–47, 2011.

46. J. Bigham, D. Gamez, and N. Lu, Safeguarding SCADA systems with anomaly detection, *Computer Network Security*, pp. 171–182, 2003.

47. UCI. Knowledge discovery in databases (KDD) cup datasets. Available at http://kdd.ics.uci.edu.

48. J. Slay and M. Miller, A security architecture for SCADA networks, in *Proceedings of the 17th Australasian Conference on Information Systems (ACIS)*, Paper 12, 2006.

49. J. Slay and M. Miller, Lessons learned from the Maroochy Water Breach critical infrastructure protection, in *IFIP International Federation for Information Processing*, vol. 253, E. Goetz and S. Shenoi, Eds., Springer, Boston, MA, pp. 73–82, 2007.

50. O. Linda, T. Vollmer, and M. Manic, Neural network based intrusion detection system for critical infrastructures, in *2009. Int. Joint Conf. on Neural Networks, 2009. IJCNN*, pp. 1827–1834, 2009.

51. A. F. Shosha, P. Gladyshev, W. Shinn-Shyan, and L. Chen-Ching, Detecting cyber intrusions in SCADA networks using multi-agent collaboration, in *2011 16th Int. Conf. on Intelligent System Application to Power Systems (ISAP)*, pp. 1–7, 2011.

52. J. Reeves, A. Ramaswamy, M. Locasto, S. Bratus, and S. Smith, Intrusion detection for resource-constrained embedded control systems in the power grid, *International Journal of Critical Infrastructure Protection*, vol. 5, pp. 74–83, 2012.

53. D. Peterson, Quickdraw: Generating security log events for legacy SCADA and control system devices, in *Conf. for Homeland Security (CATCH '09). Cybersecurity Applications & Technology*, pp. 227–229, 2009.

54. T. Morris and K. Pavurapu, A retrofit network transaction data logger and intrusion detection system for transmission and distribution substations, in *IEEE Int. Conf. on Power and Energy (PECon)*, pp. 958–963, 2010.

55. E. Naess, D. A. Frincke, A. D. McKinnon, and D. E. Bakken, Configurable middleware-level intrusion detection for embedded systems, in *Second Int. Workshop on Security in Distributed Computing Systems (SDCS) (ICDCSW '05)*, pp. 144–151, 2005.

56. A. Valdes and S. Cheung, Intrusion monitoring in process control systems, in *42nd Hawaii International Conference on System Sciences, 2009. HICSS*, pp. 1–7, 2009.

57. I. N. Fovino, A. Carcano, T. De Lacheze Murel, A. Trombetta, and M. Masera, Modbus/DNP3 state-based intrusion detection system, *in 2010 24th IEEE Int. Conf. on Advanced Information Networking and Applications (AINA)*, pp. 729–736, 2010.

58. A. Carcano, I. Fovino, M. Masera, and A. Trombetta, State-based network intrusion detection systems for SCADA protocols: A proof of concept, *Critical Information Infrastructures Security*, pp. 138–150, 2010.

59. A. Patel, J. C. Junior, and J. M. Pedersen, An intelligent collaborative intrusion detection and prevention system for smart grid environments, *Computer Standards & Interfaces*, 2013.

60. NIST, NISTIR 7628 guidelines for smart grid cyber security, National Institute of Standards and Technology, 2010.

61. A. Valdes and K. Skinner, An approach to sensor correlation, in *Int. Symposium on Recent Advances in Intrusion Detection (RAID)*, 2000.

62. F. Cuppens and A. Miege, Alert correlation in a cooperative intrusion detection framework, in *2002. Proceedings. 2002 IEEE Symposium on Security and Privacy*, pp. 202–215, 2002.

63. R. Barbosa, R. Sadre, and A. Pras, A first look into SCADA network traffic, in *Network Operations and Management Symposium (NOMS), IEEE*, pp. 518–521, 2012.

64. P. G. Neumann and P. A. Porras, Experience with EMERALD to date, in *Proceedings 1st USENIX Workshop on Intrusion Detection and Network Monitoring*, Santa Clara, California, pp. 73–80, 1999.

6 Cyber Security of Smart Grid Infrastructure

Adnan Anwar and Abdun Naser Mahmood

CONTENTS

6.1 INTRODUCTION: CYBER ATTACKS ON SMART GRID

In recent years, the power system has faced several cyber-related attacks, which have raised the question regarding the security vulnerabilities and its large-scale impact on the critical power system infrastructure. Some significant issues related to a cyber attack on the power grid are discussed in the following section.

1. In the middle of 2010, a computer worm, Stuxnet, was discovered, which spreads using Windows operating systems and targets Siemens industrial software and equipment to create unstable power system operation [1]. This type of cyber attack based on the intrusion of

a computer virus targeting an industrial power plant introduces new threats to both cyber and physical systems [2].

2. On August 14, 2003, large portions of the midwest and northeast United States and Ontario, Canada, experienced an electric power blackout, which remained for up to four days in some parts by affecting around 50 million people and 61,800 megawatts (MW) of electric load in some parts of the United States [3]. Although this historical large-scale blackout was not directly related to malicious activity of the cyber terrorists, it was caused by a failure in the software program of the cyber system [3].

3. On September 28, 2003, Italy and some parts of Switzerland faced their largest power supply disruption affecting 56 million people in total [3]. This blackout was restored after 18 hours in Italy, resulting in huge financial loss. The blackout happened because of the technical difficulties caused by human error and ineffective communication within the power grid operators.

4. Another large blackout occurred in the southwest of Europe due to human error on November 4, 2006 [3]. Insufficient communication was also an important issue behind the blackout.

5. According to the 2011 annual report of the Repository for Industrial Security Incidents (RISI), around 35% of industrial control system (ICS) security incidents were instigated through the remote access within the cyber system [4,5]. Power and utility sectors faced around 12 cyber security incidents between 2004 to 2008, which is around a 20% increase of this type of cyber incident compared with the previous four years [4]. As ICS and SCADA are playing a vital role in a smart grid infrastructure, the cyber security concern is increasing rapidly.

From the above discussion, it can be seen that some major cyber-physical vulnerabilities of the smart grid are related to the cyber issues. Therefore, smart grid infrastructure security (SGIS) must address the deliberate attacks by the cyber terrorists and industrial espionage, disgruntled employees, user errors, equipment failures, and natural disasters [6]. In order to protect the critical smart grid infrastructure, anomaly detection can play a vital role by identifying malicious data in the network.

The recent incidents related to cyber attacks in a smart grid are discussed in this section, which motivates the power system, communication and computer engineers, and researchers for future research in this challenging area. In Section 6.2, definitions and characteristics of a cyber-physical smart grid are discussed. Different aspects affecting the smart grid security are presented in Section 6.3. In Section 6.4, security requirements of an attack-resilient smart grid are discussed. Some possible smart grid anomalies are described and reviewed in Section 6.5. In Section 6.6, protection techniques of a smart grid from cyber attacks are discussed. Finally, Section 6.7 concludes with references.

6.2 SMART GRID INFRASTRUCTURES

6.2.1 DEFINITION OF A SMART GRID

The smart grid concept is evolved to make the power grid more energy efficient and intelligent. According to the US Department of Energy, a smart grid can be defined as:

> "Smart grid generally refers to a class of technology people are using to bring utility electricity delivery systems into the 21st century, using computer-based remote control and automation. These systems are made possible by two-way communication technology and computer processing that has been used for decades in other industries. They are beginning to be used on electricity networks, from the power plants and wind farms all the way to the consumers of electricity in homes and businesses. They offer many benefits to utilities and consumers—mostly seen in big improvements in energy efficiency on the electricity grid and in the energy users' homes and offices."

Traditionally, a power grid was designed to transport power from the generation plant to the end users. Therefore, the whole power flow pattern was unidirectional, and the control structure was centralized. In order to take advantage of the advanced technology to control power flow and to mitigate the ever-growing load demand, new communication techniques and distributed energy resources are being incorporated within the physical power system infrastructure. Integration of distributed generations has introduced bidirectional power flows into the grid. Moreover, energy storage devices, plug-in hybrid electric vehicles, and other advanced physical components of the power system have introduced more complexity into the grid. On the other hand, deployment of the communication network (e.g., SCADA system and advanced metering infrastructure) has provided more stability, reliability, flexibility, and efficiency in the operation and control of this complex power system. However, increasingly, the vulnerabilities of the physical system are being exposed due to malicious attacks on the cyber-physical smart grid infrastructure. Therefore, there is a need to identify the smart grid security issues related to cyber security.

6.2.2   IDEAL FUNCTIONALITIES OF A SMART GRID

A smart grid is the modernization of the traditional power grid, which should ideally have some advanced functionalities [7]:

- Self-healing
- Motivates and includes the consumer
- Resists attack
- Increases power quality
- Accommodates all generation and storage options
- Enables electrical markets
- Optimizes assets and operates efficiently

Generally, a power system is a massive and complex system and is very vulnerable in terms of physical or cyber attack. The term "self-healing" signifies the ability of the modern smart grid to recover from a situation and become stable after facing any interruption. According to the European technology platform of the smart grid, a self-healing network not only addresses automated network restoration strategies considering distributed energy resources, but also deals with high-level decentralized control methodologies to prevent blackouts [8]. Another key characteristic of a smart grid is attack resiliency due to the cyber-physical attack of the grid. A power system can be treated as one of the major key public infrastructures. Therefore, damage of any component of the grid may cause enormous loss in terms of a country's economy and social welfare. It is very important to protect the power grid infrastructure. In a smart grid environment, it is expected that the cyber-physical system would be attack-resilient, which will help to protect the country's assets and ensure national security.

6.3   SECURITY ISSUES OF A CYBER-PHYSICAL SMART GRID

In a smart grid, the physical power system and the cyber system of information and communication technologies are highly coupled, which introduces new security concerns [9]. Smart grid security issues need to address new challenges for a reliable, safe, efficient, and stable operation of the grid. It is important to note that current security approaches are either inapplicable, not viable, insufficiently scalable, incompatible, or simply inadequate, which need to be replaced by new and advanced techniques to ensure the security of the highly massive and complex dynamic smart grid environment [9].

A smart grid can be treated as the combination of physical power system components and a cyber system infrastructure, including software, hardware, and communication requirements [10]. In Figure 6.1, a typical smart grid architecture is shown in which power will flow from a bulk generation plant to the end users. On the other hand, information flow will occur in both directions, i.e., at the device level for coordination and among the operators and at the service provider level for efficient and advanced control. Therefore, in a smart grid, both cyber and physical system securities

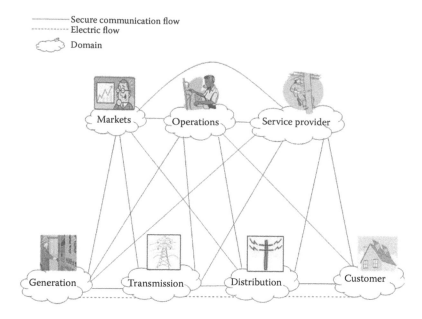

FIGURE 6.1 Typical smart grid architecture. (From The Smart Grid Interoperability Panel Cyber Security Working Group, Introduction to NISTIR7628 guidelines for smart grid cyber security, September 2010, http://csrc.nist.gov/publications/nistir/ir7628/introduction-to-nistir-7628.pdf.)

are crucial, and consideration of security issues in the cyber domain and the physical power system in isolation cannot capture the whole picture. The security issues of a cyber-physical smart grid are composed of the following issues [10]:

1. The physical components of the smart grid
2. Control centers and control applications
3. The cyber infrastructures for smart grid stable, reliable, and efficient operation and planning
4. The correlation between cyber attacks and the resulting physical system impacts
5. The protection measures to mitigate risks from cyber threats

The backbone of a smart grid is the physical power system. In recent days, many new types of load are being introduced in the grid, including plug-in hybrid electric vehicles. Therefore, power demand is increasing rapidly, and the grid is becoming more complex due to the adoption of new technologies. Moreover, green technologies are increasingly used to make the grid more sustainable. These new ideas and technologies are making the grid more complex to analyze. In such a complex cyber-physical smart grid, the resources are coordinated by the control center, which can be considered as the brain of the smart grid. These control centers are interconnected by a bidirectional cyber system, including the communication network, software, and hardware. Consequently, the introduction of new technologies in the grid is making the cyber-physical system more vulnerable to the cyber threats that can degrade the performance of the physical system and even can cause a critical cascading failure of the power grid. The potential risks associated with the cyber-physical smart grid include the following [11]:

1. Increased complexity: The interconnection of new technologies in the grid is introducing greater complexities.
2. Risk of cascading failures: In a smart grid, the cyber system and the physical system are very tightly coupled. Therefore, failure due to a random attack or a targeted attack in either domain may affect the other domain and may lead to potential cascading failures.

3. Increase in potential adversaries: As the number of network nodes increases, the entry points for attackers on the network increase which also introduces potential risks. This is considered to be one of the main reasons why malicious code and related types of attacks and intrusions are also increasing for smart grids.
4. Data privacy issues: In a smart grid, widespread use of intelligent electronic devices (IEDs) have increased the data gathering and two-way information flows extensively, which have introduced the problems related to data confidentiality and intrusions of customer privacy.

6.4 SECURITY REQUIREMENTS OF A SMART GRID

The security requirements for a smart grid are different from other critical infrastructures. The security objectives of the smart grid can be classified into three groups that are discussed below [11]:

6.4.1 DATA AVAILABILITY

This requirement of data security is very important and one of the primary objectives to ensure the reliable operation of the smart grid. Generally, availability refers to the "timely and reliable access to the use of information" [11]. However, the time latency of the availability depends on the application as shown in Table 6.1.

6.4.2 DATA INTEGRITY

Data integrity means that the source and quality of the data is known and authenticated. The modification or destruction of original data leads to a loss of data integration. Loss of data integration may occur due to the intrusion in the cyber domain by the attacker or disgruntled employees or by human error. Data integrity problems degrade the reliability of the system, and with the increased system complexity, this problem is rising rapidly.

6.4.3 DATA CONFIDENTIALITY

This security requirement is important for privacy concerns of the end users. Although it has the least impact on the smart grid reliability, importance is increasing with the deployment of advanced metering infrastructure and decentralized control within the grid.

TABLE 6.1
Time Latency for Different Smart Grid Applications

Time Requirements	Data Availability for the Specific Applications
< = 4 ms	Protective relaying
Sub seconds	Transmission wide-area situational awareness monitoring
Seconds	Substation and feeder SCADA data
Minutes	Monitoring noncritical equipment and some market pricing information
Hours	Meter reading and longer-term market pricing information
Days/weeks/months	Collecting long-term data, such as power quality information

Source: The Smart Grid Interoperability Panel Cyber Security Working Group, Introduction to NISTIR7628 guidelines for smart grid cyber security, September 2010, http://csrc.nist.gov/publications/nistir/ir7628/introduction-to-nistir-7628.pdf.

6.5 SMART GRID ANOMALIES

6.5.1 ANOMALIES IN THE STATE ESTIMATION PROGRAM

In order to fulfill the ever-growing load demand, it is important to operate the power system at its maximum capacity. For a safe and reliable operation of the power system, operators need to monitor and control the system as it progresses through its various operating states. Different intelligent electronic devices (IEDs), e.g., like the remote terminal units (RTUs) are used to monitor the system states. However, these measurement data may be corrupted by an intruder or affected by noise or may be missing due to the sensor failure. Power system operators need to have confidence about the measurement data. For this reason, state estimation is widely used by the power system operators to calculate the system states. In addition, state estimation algorithms can detect any bad data and provide high-accuracy estimation using limited measurement [12]. The concepts of state estimation for the reliable operation of a power system already exist and have been successfully applied by power companies. In recent years, the importance of the security of state estimation algorithms is increasing with the growing complexity of the smart grid interconnections. In the recent research, it has been shown that the smart grid state estimators are now highly vulnerable to the cyber attacks. From the literature of recent cyber security, analysis of the state estimation program is basically related to a false data injection attack [13–18] and load redistribution attack [19–20]. Both of these types of attacks are data integrity attacks and are discussed next.

6.5.1.1 False Data Injection Attack

During power system operation, state estimation (SE) is important for optimal power flow (OPF) operation, contingency analysis (CA), automatic generator control (AGC), etc. A simple block diagram of a power system control center is shown in Figure 6.2 in which it can be seen that SE plays a vital role for smooth operation of different energy management system (EMS) applications. Basically, OPF, CA, and AGC take the output SE data as an input to make the intelligent decision. For the processing purpose, SE receives data from the SCADA network. Due to the false data injection attack, SCADA sends the SE the wrong information and makes the smart grid vulnerable.

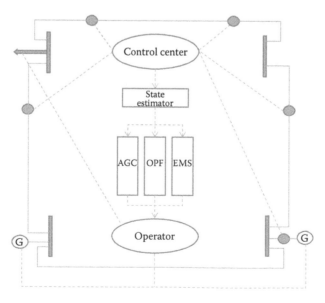

FIGURE 6.2 Energy management system (EMS) working principles. (From Huang, Y. et al., *Communications Magazine, IEEE*, 51, 27–33, 2013.)

The states in a power system are the complex voltage magnitude and the angles of each bus. If the state vector is $\mathbf{X}$, then

$$\mathbf{X} = [\delta_1 \delta_2 \delta_3 \ldots \ldots \delta_n \; V_1 V_2 V_3 \ldots \ldots V_n]^\mathrm{T}$$

Generally, the states of the system cannot be obtained directly; therefore, it is important to use the SE to infer the states from the measurement values. However, the measurement values may be noisy, which increases the probability of error. As a result, SE can be traditionally formulated as the weighted least-square criterion below [14]:

$$\min J(x) = \sum_{i=1}^{m} w_i \, (z_i - h_i(x))^2$$

where, $h(x)$ is the measurement function, which represents the measurement of z and w is the weight. Here, m is the maximum number of the measurement. If there is no error in the measurement, then

$$z_i = h_i(x)$$

otherwise,

$$z_i = h_i(x) + e_i$$

where e represents the error in the measurement. With the deployment of a smart grid, SE is now vulnerable to cyber attack. An intruder can attack on the measurement data of the SCADA system. Therefore, the control center receives the following measured data due to the malicious data attack:

$$z_i = h_i(x) + e_i + \alpha$$

where α is an attack vector. A significant amount of research is performed to prevent the false data intrusion, which can be divided into three categories as below [13].

  i. Vulnerability analysis of state estimation
 ii. Consequence analysis
iii. Development of countermeasures

The class of false data injection attack in the electric power grid is first presented [14] where the author shows that an unobservable attack can be introduced based on a limited number of meters, which can significantly degrade the performance of the results obtained from the SE [15]. Although a bad data detection technique has been well established in the classical SE algorithm, a malicious data attack is considered as the worst interacting bad data injected by an intruder [15]. A special type of stealth attack is discussed [16] in which the strategies of the defenders and the attackers are also investigated. Authors [17] focus on the economic impact due to the false data injection attack on a real-time market operation of a power grid. In order to protect the grid from the false data injection, the strategic placement of phasor measurement units (PMUs) is discussed [18]. An efficient and accurate anomaly detection technique can be employed considering a nonlinear AC state estimation model to protect the grid from the intruders.

6.5.1.2 Load Redistribution Attacks in a Power System

A load redistribution (LR) attack is a sub-class of false data injection attack. ED and OPF are heavily dependent on the output of the SE. Therefore, due to the LR attack, a wrong estimation of the states may lead to an uneconomical solution and violate the stable operating conditions. Although significant research has been done based on a false data injection attack, a few are performed considering the LR attack model. An LR attack model can be formulated as a bilevel programming problem [19]. This LR attack model has been formulated [19] as below:

$$\sum_d \Delta D_d = 0$$

$$\Delta PL = -SF.KD. \Delta D$$

$$-\tau D_d \le \Delta D_d \le \tau D_d$$

The LR attack artificially increases or decreases demand at the load buses although total change of load remains zero as shown in the first equation. SF is the shifting factor matrix, and KD is the bus-load incidence matrix. The attack magnitude of load ΔD_d is limited within an equality constraint as shown in the last equation. To solve the immediate LR attack problem, the Karush–Kuhn–Tucker (KKT)–based method is proposed [20]. Although the KKT–based method finds the global optimal solution, it is computationally very demanding. The efficiency of the proposed method is increased significantly [19] using Benders decomposition. The concept of the most damaging LR attack is discussed from the attacker's perspective throughout the research [19,20]; significant contribution is yet to come considering the power grid operator's or defender's perspective.

6.5.2 ANOMALIES IN THE POWER SYSTEM CONTROL CENTERS (PSCC)

Generally, power system control centers receive information from the sensors using the SCADA network, and it is the responsibility of the control centers to make intelligent decisions. The decision is then sent to the actuators to perform actions on the field devices. A typical power system control loop is presented in Figure 6.3. It is important to note that an adversary can easily exploit vulnerabilities along different steps of the control process of the power system [21]. The attack in the PSCC is related to the data integrity attack in which information is corrupted, denial of service (DoS) attack, de-synchronization, and timing-based attacks [22].

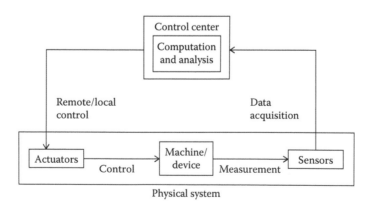

FIGURE 6.3 A typical power system control loop. (From Sridhar, S. et al., *Proceedings of the IEEE*, 100, 210–224, 2012.)

An automatic voltage regulator (AVR) control, governor control (GC), and automatic generation control (AGC) are essential in the generation side of a power system. Generally, the generation is controlled by a local controller (e.g., AVR, GC) or wide area control (e.g., AGC) schemes [21].

6.5.2.1 Attacks on the AGC

In a power system, the load is changing throughout the time. Therefore, the AGC is used to balance the power output from different generation plants [23]. System frequency is monitored to make the decision of balancing the load demand and the generation of a system. In this secondary frequency control loop, both frequency and tie-line power are measured and sent to other devices through wide area communication (e.g., IEC 61850) [21]. For control purposes, a point-to-point communication (e.g., DNP 3.0) is used [21]. As a SCADA telemetry system is used for making the decision of AGC, security issues need to be addressed to ensure a stable and reliable power grid operation.

A reachability framework is developed [24] to evaluate the impact of a two-area power system during a cyber attack. Based on the reachability framework, policy is developed that an attacker can follow to disrupt the power grid. Although the methodology of identification of an AGC attack is proposed [24], protection schemes need to be introduced for ensuring secured operation of AGC.

An approach [25] to develop threat models for control system attacks is proposed. The proposed method [25] is extended to define an attack model for a power system control center by the authors [26]. In that work, two types of attacks are considered, which are "min attack" and "max attack." The objective of these types of attacks is to manipulate the area control error (ACE) signal. Generally, the ACE is calculated from the difference of the net tie-line power flow to the deviation of frequency output [26]. To measure the actual power output and frequency, sensors are used. During the attack, sensor measured values are manipulated, which directly impacts on the system operating conditions.

6.5.2.2 Attacks on the GC

Due to load incremental change of a generator, the electric output power exceeds the mechanical input power, which leads to the speed deviation and frequency fall of the generator [27]. The reduction of generator speed is then detected by a sensor in a governor control system, and necessary control actions are taken to run the generator in a steady-state condition. The GC is highly dependent on the local measurement. However, the modern generator governors use standard communication protocols to correspond information with the operation center [21]. For example, the $800 \times A$ Governor of one leading power and automation expert company ABB makes the use of MODBUS, HART, PROFIBUS, PROFINET, DeviceNet, and IEC 61850 as a standard FieldBus and network communication protocol [28]. Therefore, an adversary can attack the GC system through any access point of the communication system. As the GC plays a vital role for the stable operation of a generator, any cyber attack can cause enormous disruption of the physical system.

6.5.3 Attacks on the FACTS Device

Flexible alternating current transmission system (FACTS) devices make the use of power electronics to stabilize and regulate power flow in a grid. Some applications of the FACTS devices are power flow control, load sharing, voltage regulation, transient stability enhancements, and power system oscillation mitigation [29]. FACTS devices help to utilize the network in a better way by increasing the capacity of the network with optimal power flow. However, optimal power flow of the network cannot be achieved by a single FACTS devise, and therefore, multiple devices need to communicate and cooperate with each other during the operation. Therefore, a communication link is important among the coordinated FACTS devices, which also increase the vulnerabilities to cyber attacks [30]. To face the new challenges, two approaches are proposed [30], which are agent-based management and improved visualization. Improved security policies and procedures need to be addressed handle the cyber attacks among the coordinated FACTS devices.

6.5.4 MALICIOUS MODIFICATION OF NETWORK DATA STORED IN A DATABASE

Both the unauthorized access and malicious code is dangerous for stable power system operation. It has been reported [31] that any of these types of attacks can disrupt the power system operation. To ensure the security of any power system control center, requirements, policies, and regulatory issues are predefined by the NERC, NIST, and DOE [32] in the United States. However, alarmingly it has been shown [31] that any adversary can manage to get access to the network data stored in a database and manipulate the stored data leading to a compromise and failure of the smart grid.

Optimal power flow (OPF) is a widely adopted power system analysis tool used in the control centers for intelligent decision making. The operation of OPF is highly dependent on the network configuration data and the measured data obtained from the SCADA system. The interruption of power system operation due to the malicious modification of the network data stored in a database is discussed [31]. A method based on principle component analysis (PCA) is proposed to detect the anomalies related to this type of attack. The method is successfully applied in IEEE benchmark test systems and has significant impact on false alarm reduction.

6.6 PROTECTING SMART GRID FROM CYBER VULNERABILITIES

In recent years, the vulnerabilities of the smart grid have increased many times due to the wide adoption of communication networks in different levels of operation and planning of a power grid. To protect the smart grid, it is important to protect the physical grid from the three broad classes of cyber attacks [33] mentioned below.

6.6.1 PROTECTION FROM COMPONENT-WISE CYBER ATTACK

To protect the smart grid at the device or component level, a security agent based framework has been proposed [32,34]. The security agents should be placed both in field devices (e.g., IEDs) and at the substation level (e.g., RTUs) as shown in Figure 6.4. Some key functions of security agents described [32] are the following:

1. Collecting network traffic patterns and traffic data analyzing
2. Maintaining data log and reporting
3. Run security patches and intrusion detection algorithms
4. Maintain end-to-end security
5. Alarm management

To protect the smart grid control system component, an anomaly detection technique has been proposed [35,36]. In this research, a rough classification algorithm has been used to detect the anomaly for improving the security of power system control centers in the electric power system critical infrastructure. During the security analysis, authors have considered two operation modes (the normal and the abnormal operation mode) of the smart grid. The rough classification algorithm is used for data reduction that enhances the performance of anomaly detection by introducing a compact set of knowledge-based rules. To protect the critical power system infrastructure, a comprehensive framework has been developed [37]. In this work, SCADA security has been investigated considering real-time monitoring, anomaly detection, impact analysis, and implementing mitigation strategies as shown in Figure 6.5. In order to protect the relay from the false data attack, a probabilistic neural network based approach has been proposed in [38].

As smart meters and PMUs are vulnerable to cyber attacks, several research studies have been undertaken to learn about the security of the smart meters and PMUs. A strategic placement method of PMU components has been developed [18]. The requirements and architectural directions of the IDS for smart meters are discussed [39] in which a specification-based IDS is used. In the case of

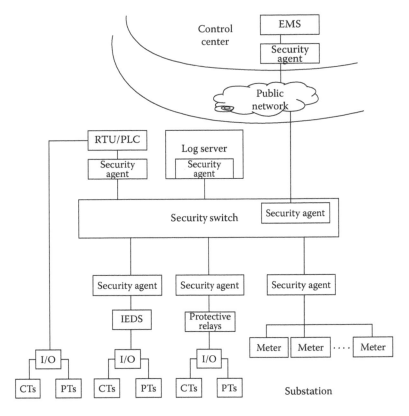

FIGURE 6.4 A security agent based framework for smart grid protection. (From Wei, D. et al., *IEEE Transactions on Smart Grid*, 2, 782–795, 2011.)

AMI security, specification-based IDS shows its superiority over the signature-based and anomaly-based detection techniques due to the following [39]:

a. A greater accuracy of specification-based IDS in AMI applications.
b. The signature-based IDS makes use of a black list approach, which needs an attack data set. In terms of AMI, it is difficult to prepare an empirical attack data set.
c. The development of specification-based IDS for AMI is cost effective.

6.6.2 PROTECTION FROM PROTOCOL-WISE CYBER ATTACK

SCADA is widely used in critical power system infrastructure. In case of multiple stakeholders, sometimes authentication, encryption, and firewalls may not mitigate the security issues in a large SCADA network [40]. Moreover, focusing securing issues considering only the SCADA network as a single entity will not solve the problem, and therefore, it is important to ensure the cyber security of the individual devices in the network [40]. Different communication protocols are used among the SCADA devices for successful automation and operation of a smart grid. The evolution of the proprietary and industrial SCADA protocols started in the early 1980s when Modbus, Modbus Plus, and proprietary and vendor-specific protocols were first developed [41]. The distributed networking protocol (DNP) first appeared in 1990 by Westronic, Inc., as an open protocol. The DNP3 protocol is based on the IEC 60870-5 protocol. Although the DNP3 protocol is designed for reliable data communication, it is still vulnerable to cyber attack. Therefore, a rule-based data set security for DNP3 devices is proposed in [40] to protect the smart grid from cyber terrorists. For simulating

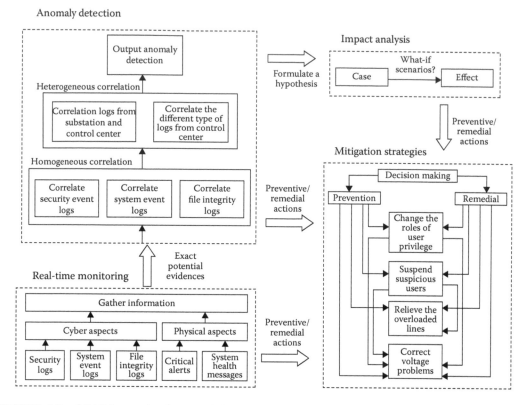

FIGURE 6.5 SCADA security framework based on real time monitoring and anomaly detection. (From Ten, C.-W. et al., *IEEE Transactions on Systems, Man and Cybernetics, Part A: Systems and Humans*, 40, 853–865, 2010.)

protocol attack, a SCADA simulation framework is developed in [42] in which attack on a Modbus protocol is illustrated. Guidelines and the best practices for the development of smart grid protocols considering design principles are discussed [43].

6.6.3 Protection from Topology-Wise Cyber Attacks

A smart grid is also vulnerable to topology-wise cyber attacks. For example, based on the knowledge of the power system topologies, an intruder may attack the bad data detection algorithms of the current state estimators [44]. Another topology-based cyber attack is proposed [45], in which an attack on the electric circuit breaker will cause the isolation of the generation units from the power grid. It has been shown [46] that a cyber attack on confidentiality with proper topological knowledge can lead to an integrity and availability attack. Therefore, an information flow security-based model is proposed for mitigating these security issues. An optimum interlink placement strategy [47] against random attacks in the cyber-physical network is proposed, which demonstrates that the strategy ensures better security compared with all other possible strategies, including strategies using random allocation and unidirectional interlinks and in the case when the topology of the cyber and physical networks are unknown to each other.

6.7 SECURITY ISSUES FOR FUTURE SMART GRID

To make the grid smarter, significant initiatives are taken throughout the world. These measures will not only modernize the grid but also improve the overall system efficiency, stability, and obviously reliability. But security issues must be maintained to ensure the uninterrupted power supply to the end users and to protect the national electricity grid from terrorist attacks. It is important to mention that a properly designed defense framework against cyber attack should address all aspects related to the cyber-crime in a complex cyber-physical electricity grid infrastructure. That means, not only should targeted cyber attack be considered, but also, unintentional ICT–related anomalies should be addressed, e.g., human operator errors, software errors, equipment failures, and obviously natural disaster–related problems.

In the process of making the power grid smarter, more automated control is being introduced in the grid. The risk of cyber attack will increase as the grid becomes more automated. Especially, control centers are the main target by the cyber terrorists. Energy utilities are applying advanced techniques and cyber security plans to avoid cyber attacks. Advanced intrusion detection and prevention techniques can be implemented in different entry points of the complex grid. Security management systems are being implemented in different utilities. Energy providers are also adopting different risk-management strategies and defense approaches against cyber attack.

It is obvious that the smart grid is providing lots of benefits, including energy-efficient smart homes, greener technology such as solar and wind, cost-effective demand-side management, smart charging stations for electric cars, and so on. In order to ensure these benefits, smart grid security measures must be maintained.

6.8   CONCLUSIONS

In recent years, the numbers of cyber attacks are increasing rapidly. The intelligent cyber terrorists with detailed and advanced power system knowledge may be able to create an integrity, availability, or confidentiality attack on the network. Protection of a smart grid from cyber attack is not only a concern of the engineers, researchers, and the utility operators; it is also the responsibility of the government to ensure the security of this national critical infrastructure.

This chapter is written for the general readers so that they could be able to easily grasp some of the concepts in the area of cyber security for a smart grid. At the beginning, a brief overview of smart grids and some recent cyber security incidents of this critical infrastructure are discussed. The key security requirements of a smart grid, which are availability, integrity, and confidentiality, are also discussed. Based on the existing research, an overview of smart grid anomalies is discussed thoroughly. The protection frameworks of a smart grid against component-wise, protocol-wise, and topology-wise cyber attacks are also reviewed in this chapter.

Cyber security is very crucial for the reliable and secured operation of a critical smart grid infrastructure. At present, only bad data detection (BDD) algorithms are used for data security in the state estimation. However, an adversary can attack the cyber-physical grid through any of the entry points of the cyber system and impact direly on the physical assets. For enhanced smart grid reliability and security, intrusion detection algorithms should be placed throughout the system.

AUTHORS' BIOGRAPHIES

Adnan Anwar received the BSc degree in electrical and electronic engineering from Islamic University of Technology (IUT), the organization of Islamic Conference. He has completed his masters degree from the University of New South Wales, Canberra, Australia. He joined the University of Asia Pacific (UAP) as a lecturer in 2009. Currently, he is working with National ICT, Australia (NICTA) at the "Future Energy System" project. His research interests include computational intelligence for the smart grid and its applications.

 **Abdun Naser Mahmood** received the BSc degree in applied physics and electronics and the MSc degree in computer science from the University of Dhaka, Bangladesh, in 1997 and 1999, respectively. He completed his PhD degree from the University of Melbourne in 2008. He joined the University of Dhaka as a lecturer in 2000, assistant professor in 2003, when he took a leave of absence for his PhD studies. Currently, he is working as a lecturer at the University of New South Wales with the School of Engineering and Information Technology. His research interests include data mining techniques for network monitoring and algorithm design for anomaly detection and intrusion detection.

REFERENCES

1. McMillan, R., Siemens: Stuxnet worm hit industrial systems, *COMPUTERWorld*, Sept. 14, 2010.
2. Cherry, S., with Langner, R., How Stuxnet is rewriting the cyberterrorism playbook, *IEEE Spectrum*, October 13, 2010.
3. U.S.-Canada Power System Outage Task Force, Final report on the August 14, 2003 blackout in the United States and Canada: Causes and recommendations, April 2004. Available at https://reports.energy.gov/BlackoutFinal-Web.pdf.
4. Repository for Industrial Security Incidents (RISI). Annual Report 2011, Available at http://www.securityincidents.net/index.php/products/indepth/risi_annual_report/.
5. 2011 Report on control system cyber security incidents. Available at http://community.controlglobal.com/content/risi-cyber-incident-report-2011-calendar-year-out-risi-cybersecurity-pauto-automation-mfg-ma.
6. Smart Grid Interoperability Panel — Cyber Security Working Group, *Guidelines for Smart Grid Cyber Security: Vol. 1, Smart Grid Cyber Security Strategy, Architecture, and High-Level Requirements*, August 2010.
7. NETL, The NETL modern grid initiative: Powering our 21st-century economy: Modern grid benefits. Department of Energy, 2007.
8. Liu, H., Chen, X., Yu, K., and Hou, Y., The control and analysis of self-healing urban power grid, *IEEE Transactions on Smart Grid*, vol. 3, pp. 1119–1129, Sept. 2012.
9. Mo, Y., Kim, T.H.-H., Brancik, K., Dickinson, D., Lee, H., Perrig, A., and Sinopoli, B., Cyber–physical security of a smart grid infrastructure, *Proceedings of the IEEE*, vol. 100, pp. 195–209, Jan. 2012.
10. Sridhar, S., Hahn, A., and Govindarasu, M., Cyber–physical system security for the electric power grid, *Proceedings of the IEEE*, vol. 100, pp. 210–224, Jan. 2012.
11. The Smart Grid Interoperability Panel Cyber Security Working Group, Introduction to NISTIR7628 Guidelines for Smart Grid Cyber Security, September 2010. Available at http://csrc.nist.gov/publications/nistir/ir7628/introduction-to-nistir-7628.pdf.
12. Naka, S., Genji, T., Yura, T., and Fukuyama, Y., A hybrid particle swarm optimization for distribution state estimation, *IEEE Transactions on Power Systems*, vol. 18, pp. 60–68, Feb. 2003.
13. Hug, G., and Giampapa, J. A., Vulnerability assessment of AC state estimation with respect to false data injection cyber-attacks, *IEEE Transactions on Smart Grid*, vol. 3, pp. 1362–1370, Sept. 2012.
14. Liu, Y., Ning, P., and Reiter, M. K., False data injection attacks against state estimation in electric power grids, *Proc. ACM Conf. Computer Communication Security*, pp. 21–32, 2009.
15. Kosut, O., Jia, L., Thomas, R. J., and Tong, L., Malicious data attacks on the smart grid, *IEEE Transactions on Smart Grid*, vol. 2, pp. 645–658, Dec. 2011.
16. Huang, Y., Esmalifalak, M., Nguyen, H., Zheng, R., Han, Z., Li, H., and Song, L., Bad data injection in Smart Grid: Attack and defense mechanisms, *Communications Magazine, IEEE*, vol. 51, pp. 27–33, January 2013.
17. Xie, L., Mo, Y., and Sinopoli, B., Integrity data attacks in power market operations, *IEEE Transactions on Smart Grid*, vol. 2, pp. 659–666, Dec. 2011.
18. Huang, Y., Esmalifalak, M., Nguyen, H., Zheng, R., Han, Z., Li, H., and Song, L., Bad data injection in Smart Grid: Attack and defense mechanisms, *Communications Magazine, IEEE*, vol. 51, pp. 27–33, January 2013.
19. Yuan, Y., Li, Z., and Ren, K., Quantitative analysis of load redistribution attacks in power systems, *IEEE Transactions on Parallel and Distributed Systems*, vol. 23, pp. 1731–1738, Sept. 2012.

20. Yuan, Y., Li, Z., and Ren, K., Modeling load redistribution attacks in power systems, *IEEE Transactions on Smart Grid*, vol. 2, pp. 382–390, June 2011.
21. Sridhar, S., Hahn, A., and Govindarasu, M., Cyber–physical system security for the electric power grid, *Proceedings of the IEEE*, vol. 100, pp. 210–224, Jan. 2012.
22. Huang, Y.-L., Cardenas, A. A., Amin, S., Lin, Z.-S., Tsai, H.-Y., and Sastry, S., Understanding the physical and economic consequences of attacks on control systems, *International Journal of Critical Infrastructure Protection*, 2009.
23. Miller, R. H., and Malinowski, J. H., *Power System Operation*, McGraw-Hill Professional, 1994.
24. Mohajerin Esfahani, P., Vrakopoulou, M., Margellos, K., Lygeros, J., and Andersson, G., Cyber attack in a two-area power system: Impact identification using reachability, in *Proc. Amer. Control Conf.*, pp. 962–967, Jul. 2010.
25. Huang, Y., Cardenas, A., Amin, S., Lin, S.-Z., Tsai, H.-Y., and Shankar Sastry, S., Understanding the physical and economic consequences of attacks against control systems, *International Journal of Critical Infrastructure Protection*, vol. 2, pp. 72–83, October 2009.
26. Sridhar, S., and Manimaran, G., Data integrity attacks and their impacts on SCADA control system, *Proc. Power Energy Soc. General Meeting*, Jul. 2010.
27. Saadat, H., *Power System Analysis*, McGraw-Hill Primis Custom Publishing, 2002.
28. ABB, Product guide, fiedlbus and network communications. Available at http://www.abb.com/product/us/9AAC115770.aspx.
29. Kothari, D. P., and Nagrath, I. J., *Modern Power System Analysis*, Tata McGraw-Hill Education, 2003.
30. Phillips, L. R., Baca, M., Hills, J., Margulies, J., Tejani, B., Richardson, B., and Weiland, L., Analysis of operations and cyber security policies for a system of cooperating flexible alternating current transmission system (FACTS) devices, Dec. 2005.
31. Valenzuela, J., Wang, J., and Bissinger, N., Real-time intrusion detection in power system operations, *IEEE Transactions on Power Systems*, vol. 28, pp. 1052–1062, 2013.
32. Dolezilek, D., and Hussey, L., Requirements or recommendations? Sorting out NERC CIP, NIST, and DOE cybersecurity, *Proc. 2011 64th Annu. Conf. Protective Relay Engineers*, 2011.
33. Wei, D., Lu, Y., Jafari, M., Skare, P. M., and Rohde, K., Protecting smart grid automation systems against cyberattacks, *IEEE Transactions on Smart Grid*, vol. 2, pp. 782–795, Dec. 2011.
34. Wei, D., Jafari, M., and Lu, Y., On protecting industrial automation and control systems against electronic attacks, *IEEE International Conference on Automation Science and Engineering*, pp. 176–181, Sept. 22–25, 2007.
35. Coutinho, M. P., Lambert-Torres, G., da Silva, L. E. B., Martins, H. G., Lazarek, H., and Neto, J. C., Anomaly detection in power system control center critical infrastructures using rough classification algorithm, *3rd IEEE International Conference on Digital Ecosystems and Technologies*, pp. 733–738, June 1–3, 2009.
36. Coutinho, M. P., Lambert-Torres, G., da Silva L. E. B., and Lazarek, H., Improving detection attacks in electric power system critical infrastructure using rough classification algorithm, *Proceedings of the Second International Conference on Forensic Computer Science*, Brazil, vol. 2, pp. 18–23, 2007.
37. Ten, C.-W., Manimaran, G., and Liu, C.-C., Cybersecurity for critical infrastructures: Attack and defense modeling, *IEEE Transactions on Systems, Man and Cybernetics, Part A: Systems and Humans*, vol. 40, pp. 853–865, July 2010.
38. Sheng, S., Chan, W. L., Li, K. K., Xianzhong, D., and Xiangjun, Z., Context information-based cyber security defense of protection system, *IEEE Transactions on Power Delivery*, vol. 22, pp. 1477–1481, July 2007.
39. Berthier, R., Sanders, W. H., and Khurana, H., Intrusion detection for advanced metering infrastructures: Requirements and architectural directions, *2010 First IEEE International Conference on Smart Grid Communications (SmartGridComm)*, pp. 350–355, Oct. 4–6, 2010.
40. Mander, T., Cheung, R., and Nabhani, F., Power system DNP3 data object security using data sets, *Computers & Security*, vol. 29, pp. 487–500, June.
41. Ten, C.-W., Manimaran, G., and Liu, C.-C., Cybersecurity for electric power control and automation systems, *Proc. eNetworks Cyberengineering Workshop, IEEE-SMC*, pp. 29–34, 2007.
42. Queiroz, C., Mahmood, A., and Tari, Z., SCADASim: A framework for building SCADA simulations, *IEEE Transactions on Smart Grid*, vol. 2, pp. 589–597, Dec. 2011.
43. Khurana, H., Bobba, R., Yardley, T., Agarwal, P., and Heine, E., Design principles for power grid cyber-infrastructure authentication protocols, *43rd Hawaii International Conference on System Sciences (HICSS)*, pp. 1–10, Jan. 5–8, 2010.
44. Xie, L., Mo, Y., and Sinopoli, B., Integrity data attacks in power market operations, *IEEE Transactions on Smart Grid*, vol. 2, pp. 659–666, Dec. 2011.

45. Srivastava, A., Morris, T., Ernster, T., Vellaithurai, C., Pan, S., and Adhikari, U., Modeling cyber-physical vulnerability of the smart grid with incomplete information, *IEEE Transactions on Smart Grid*, vol. 4, pp. 235–244, March 2013.
46. Gamage, T. T., Roth, T. P., McMillin, B. M., and Crow, M. L. Mitigating event confidentiality violations in smart grids: An information flow security-based approach, *IEEE Transactions on Smart Grid*, vol. 4, pp. 1227–1234, 2013.
47. Yagan, O., Qian, D., Zhang, J., and Cochran, D., Optimal allocation of interconnecting links in cyber-physical systems: Interdependence, cascading failures, and robustness, *IEEE Transactions on Parallel and Distributed Systems*, vol. 23, pp. 1708–1720, Sept. 2012.

7 Intrusion Detection and Prevention in Cyber Physical Systems

Mohamed Azab and Mohamed Eltoweissy

CONTENTS

7.1 INTRODUCTION

Cyber-physical systems (CPS) are increasingly becoming vital to modernizing the national critical infrastructure systems, ranging from health care, transportation, and energy to homeland security and national defense. Advances in cyber-controlled systems are needed to help improve their current capabilities as well as their adaptability, automaticity, efficiency, reliability, safety, and usability.

CPS come with large-scale heterogeneous compositions of interacting cyber and physical devices with differing capabilities and requirements.

Due to the proliferation of increasingly sophisticated cyber threats with exponentially destructive effects, intrusion and attack detection/resolution (IADR) systems must systematically evolve their detection, understanding, attribution, and mitigation capabilities. Unfortunately, most of the current IADR systems fall short of adequately providing defense services while maintaining operational continuity and stability of the target of defense (ToD) in the presence of advanced persistent attacks.

CPS attacks usually target valuable infrastructure assets, taking advantage of potential weaknesses in their defense systems. Such weaknesses might arise from the exponential increase in the volume of information flowing between cyber and physical processes that exceeds the analysis and investigation capabilities of the current IADR systems [1,2]. Further, most of these defense systems use uncoordinated combinations of disparate tools to provide detection and resolution services for the ToD components. Such isolation and lack of awareness of and cooperation between these tools may lead to massive resource waste due to unnecessary redundancy and potential conflicts that can be utilized by a resourceful attacker to penetrate the system. An adversary might induce such conflicts to facilitate system penetration. These ad hoc mixtures of security tools have negative impacts not only on security aspects, but also on related system qualities such as performance, management, and resilience.

Recent research argued against the suitability of the current IADR solutions to CPS environments [1,2]. We assert the need for new IADR platforms that efficiently coordinate defense missions and tools in real time with the following goals:

- Achieve asymmetric advantage to CPS defenders, prohibitively increasing the cost for attackers
- Ensure resilient operations in the presence of persistent and evolving attacks and failures
- Facilitate defense alliances, effectively and efficiently diffusing defense intelligence and operations transcending organizational boundaries

We surmise that CPS defense solutions should comprehensively address these goals in order to present a CPS-ready defense solution. These solutions should enable self and situation awareness, a resilient adaptive defense, and cooperative autonomous control and sharing among cooperating organizations without violating their individual privacy policy. Enabling such features makes it possible to successfully provide defense services to mission-critical heterogeneously composed systems such as CPS while maintaining the operation timeliness and stability in the presence of persistent attacks. In this chapter, we list the latest advances available to support the aforementioned aspects illustrating their capabilities and limitations. This chapter focuses on solutions supporting design time self-defense and intrinsic component resilience against attacks and failures and the available mechanisms to provide operation-time defense services. Additionally, the chapter presents a quick overview of the CARD (cooperative autonomous resilient defenses) realized as a CPS-ready defense cloud under the name CyPhyCARD [3]. CyPhyCARD is designed to comprehensively address the aforementioned limitations offering an evolutionary cyber and CPS IADR system. The presented defense platform, termed CyPhyCARD (cooperative autonomous resilient defenses for cyber-physical systems), is a biologically inspired, distributed, dynamically configurable, runtime programmable platform that manages a large number of cyber and physical resources and service upon which evolutionary defenses can be built to protect participant CPS applications. CyPhyCARD presents a unified defense platform to monitor, manage, and control the heterogeneous composition of ToD components. CyPhyCARD relies on three interrelated pillars to construct its defense platform. CyPhyCARD comprehensively unifies the efforts of the constructing pillars building a large scale, intrinsically resilient, self- and situation-aware, cooperative, and autonomous IADR cloud that provides adequate, prompt, and pervasive defense services for large-scale, heterogeneously composed platforms such as CPS.

CyPhyCARD pillars are the following:

- CyberX, an autonomous management platform for CyPhyCARD's cell oriented architecture– (COA) based foundation. CyberX enables application elasticity and autonomic adaptation to changes by runtime diversity employment, enhances the application resilience against attacks and failures by multimodal recovery mechanism, and enables unified application execution on heterogeneously composed platforms by a smart employment of a fine-grained environment-virtualization technology.
- ChameleonSoft encrypts software execution behavior by smart employment of multi-dimensional runtime diversity across time, space, and platform heterogeneity, inducing a trace-resistant, moving-target defense that works on securing the CyPhyCARD platform against software attacks.
- Evolutionary sensory system (EvoSense) realizing a pervasive, intrinsically resilient, situation-aware sense and response system to seamlessly effect a biological immune system such as defense. EvoSense acts as a middle layer between the defense service provider(s) and the target of defense (ToD) creating a uniform defense interface that hides the ToD's scale and heterogeneity concerns from defense-provisioning management.

CyPhyCARD was extensively evaluated both qualitatively and quantitatively [3]. The efficacy of the presented approach is assessed *qualitatively*, through a complex synthetic CPS attack scenario. In addition to the presented scenario, multiple prototype packages were devised for each pillar to assess their applicability in real execution environment and applications. The efficacy and the efficiency of the presented approach were comprehensively assessed *quantitatively* by a set of custom-made simulation packages simulating each CyPhyCARD pillar for performance and security evaluation. The evaluation illustrated the success of CyPhyCARD and its constructing pillars to efficiently and effectively achieve its design objective with reasonable overhead. In this chapter, we will only present a brief version of the qualitative evolution of CyPhyCARD, and more details can be found [3].

7.1.1 THE BLACKWIDOW ATTACK SCENARIO

To motivate our research, throughout the remainder of this chapter, we will be referring to the following working scenario depicting a hypothetical CPS attack named the BlackWidow attack. The name came from the similarity between the operational characteristics and the destructive effect of the attack and the deadly Black Widow spider.

Definition: The *BlackWidow* malware (BlackWidow for short) is our synthetic experimental attack that is designed to split into a set of code parts and spread in different directions and locations to decrease the probability of detection. The distribution of parts and the interconnection between the parts in different hosts weave a large web. This web is bidirectionally traversed to send any harvested data from the attacked target and to update the malware with new tools and missions. The BW is designed to be as generic as possible; it is not oriented to any specific application. BW exploits system weak points "Ex, zero day exploits" to penetrate the system to spread its initial web seeds that will help in constructing the whole web. By constructing the BW web, the attacker can start to direct the BW toward its designated mission based on the attacker target. These directions might be remotely assigned through the Internet or preprogrammed in Internet-inaccessible locations.

7.1.1.1 Attacker Possible Goals
- Espionage "stealing secrets as a first wave to be used to construct the second wave"
- Take control of organization's property for one's own gain
- Physical property manipulation

7.1.1.2 Attacker Tools and Capabilities

- Zero-day system exploits
- Social engineering methods to recruit insider agents via social networks
- Well trained and funded attackers
- Stolen certificates and digital keys
- Small lab to mimic the attacked system and its defense system

7.1.2 DESIGN ASPECTS

The attack is designed to be stealthy by hiding from the defense system sensors searching for attack signatures. The attack will target an intermediate host machine that will contain the worm and command and control channel communications.

In order to do so, the worm is designed to not harm the host or change any of its settings that might raise the anti-malware (AM) alerts. The malware will use minimal resources and will work in a very slow fashion not to alert the network defense systems by its existence.

The only way to detect this malware is through deep analysis of the logs of all the communicating nodes, which is computationally very costly to the current systems that share the same host machines. Further, in order to deeply analyze and correlate strange communications patterns spreading all over the network, a global view for all the communicating entities within the network will be needed.

The malware is equipped with a self-destruct timer that automatically resets upon successful communication with the attacker. The self-destructive code adds to the sophistication of the attack that removes any traces of the worm and attacker actions while inflicting damage to the target resources as a last resort.

The worm is later updated to use stolen digital certificates to authenticate its existence in the host machine in the form of drivers.

The malware is intended to be targeted, but due to the intentionally random deployment method, the code works in two modes as follows: (1) benign mode in which the malware infects other machines that do not belong to the target space. The machines might be used later in case of target change or as a base for future attacks. And (2) malicious mode, in which the worm works only on the target host systems. The attacker feedback can determine the mode. The default will be benign unless the attacker changes that or predetermined targets have been programmed.

7.1.3 COMMERCIAL SECURITY EXAMPLE

7.1.3.1 Attack-Specific Goals

- Operation disruption to cause losses
- Launch same (low-cost) attack on competitors to maximize gain

7.1.3.2 Attack Procedure (on Air-Gapped Target)

The attacker uses a phishing attack that targets users' emails and social network personal pages. The attacker uses social networks as a source of information to generate more convincing phishing emails. These emails will be directed from one of the closely related contacts to the victim (Figure 7.1).

The attacker selects a group of employees working in different branches of ABC. These branches are distributed in various geographical locations, and the victims that will be the malware couriers have no direct relationship with each other. This will increase the chance of the attack's success in the case that the same phishing technique is used with different targets. The BW is programmed to search the user network for connected computers; then it starts using one of the zero days exploits to clone itself into these computers.

The attack victims will receive parts of the malware. Each of these parts will contain a fraction of the designated mission and a simple communication module. The communications module will

FIGURE 7.1   Commercial security example.

be used to open a direct channel with the attacker and to search and establish communication with other parts. Directions to other parts' locations might be sent by the attacker to minimize the search time.

The attacker uses malware fractions to construct logical executable entities in the form of mobile software agents targeting different objectives. The first objective will be to search and infiltrate the network for data stores.

The malware will sniff network traffic searching for predetermined signatures for such locations. The second objective will be to attack such data stores using the zero day exploits and the stolen certificates to locate targeted industrial secrets and any available access keys to the protected area behind the air gap. The malware will frequently update the attacker on its findings based on a predetermined update methodology. After successful reception of this data, the attacker will use it to generate legitimate keys to access the air gap.

The attacker will use the malware to locate the workstations controlling the surveillance cameras. In locations with no surveillance cameras, the malware might use any available user-connected web cameras. The malware will record periodic video feeds to be sent to the attacker. These videos with the help of the attacker-generated access keys will guide a recruited insider into infecting the air gap with a copy of the BlackWidow.

The malware controlling the video cameras will make sure that this process will not be recorded on any of the cameras to protect the recruited insider.

The air gap malware is programmed to increase the operational hours of certain machines that use specific raw materials manufactured by XYZ to increase XYZ profits. The malware can easily identify such machines by searching a predetermined fixed identifier that must be added to all the programming files targeting such machines. Further, the attacker will use the stolen secrets and designs to equip the malware with the needed logic to randomly manipulate the operational motors frequency in the production machines to induce random defects in the output products to lower its quality. Doing so shall cause multiple financial problems to ABC. XYZ shall benefit from ABC's loss due to its low-quality products. Additionally XYZ will maliciously gain both financially and more control over ABC's production lines by, for example, carefully adjusting the amount of consumed and supplied raw materials.

We will revisit this scenario again to illustrate how CyPhyCARD invalidates the attack design invariants and attacker assumptions.

The remainder of the chapter is organized as follows: Section 7.2 illustrates the CPS defense provisioning landscape; Section 7.3 presents details about the CARD concept realized by the

CyPhyCARD defense cloud; Section 7.4 presents a brief qualitative evaluation of CyPhyCARD; and finally, Section 5 concludes the chapter.

7.2 CPS DEFENSE PROVISIONING LANDSCAPE

7.2.1 Overview

CPS IADR solutions' main objective is to enable efficient, resilient, pervasive, and prompt attack detection and resolution for heterogeneously composed targets. Doing so entails utilizing a hydride mixture of technologies that can work together to support one or more of these objectives. Figure 7.2 illustrates the landscape of CPS defense provisioning classified into two main classes, design time defense and operation time defense.

7.2.2 Design Time Defense

Design time defense class describes the contemporary approaches addressing the idea of building an intrinsically resilient product that insures safe execution in the presence of attacks. This class includes a design time defense mechanism to block certain attack categories and techniques built for fault tolerance, minimizing the cost of successful attacks.

In the following subsections, we list the variant efforts presented by the current literature focusing on techniques utilized toward building attack-resilient software products.

7.2.2.1 Attack/Failure Resilient Software

7.2.2.1.1 Elastic Software Design: Software Modularization

Design time security can be effectively realized through enabling elastic, dynamic, and adaptable software products with intrinsic support for situation- and context-aware fault tolerances. Currently, software products depend mostly on static or partially dynamic architectures in which data, logic, and/or physical resources are primarily tightly coupled. Multiple attempts have been presented in the literature to partially decouple these design concerns through what is termed as application modularization.

The CyberX managed cell oriented architecture (COA) [4] is the first architecture to separate the main design concerns through an intelligent modularization of the application into a set of cells. The entire application is presented as an organism modularized into a set of cells [3]. Later in this section, we will briefly describe the COA, and further details can be found [4]. There are other techniques in the literature that worked on application modularization for different objectives. We

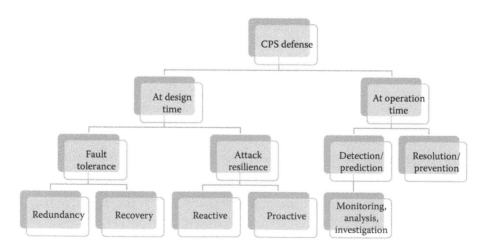

FIGURE 7.2 CPS defense provisioning landscape.

will illustrate the main approaches working toward modularizing applications into compostable components that can adapt to certain aspects.

COA modularizes the application in terms of cells, service-oriented architecture (SOA) modularizes the application in terms of services, object-oriented architecture (OOA) modularizes the application in terms of objects, and aspect-oriented architecture (AsOA) modularizes the application in terms of aspects "quality attributes." [7–10]. An application module is sometimes called components. OOA, AsOA, or SOA modularize software systems into a set of components [11].

Component-oriented design was introduced to create independent entities for different modules in a software application [11]. "Define a software component as unit of composition with contractually specified interfaces and explicit context dependencies only."

Generally speaking, a component can be represented as a closed composable box reflecting certain functionality and behavior at runtime and with interfacing capability through clearly defined inputs and outputs [10]. The component can communicate with other components and the surrounding environment through such interface. A clear characterization for the component was defined [11].

Several versions of the component modularization were presented industry-wise and as a research work, for example, the COM [12] from Microsoft, the EJB specification from SUN [13], CORBA [14] from the OMG, etc. Additionally the work presented such as Fractal [15], SOFA [16], etc. is a good research work related to software modularization. Fractal was one of the approaches that enabled the component to modify its internal structure during the execution. The program architecture can be modified at runtime enabling the application to dynamically change at runtime.

Unfortunately none of these solutions except for CyberX COA considered the real meaning of adaptation to changes at the application or the infrastructure level. More details about the conventional software modularization architectures and CyberX COA is presented in the next section. CyberX COA is described in further depth later in this section.

7.2.2.1.1.1 Modularized Software Architectures *Aspect-oriented software architecture (AsOA)* is one of the well-known software modularization architectures. AsOS refers to a set of emerging mechanisms that defines methods of modularizing software systems [10]. The concept of modularization started with Parnas in the 1970s [11]. Parnas defined modularization as the process of isolating and localization of quality attribute objectives. A quality attribute objective can represent any interest that the developers might care for about a system. Quality attribute objectives can include high-level objectives, such as security, robustness, or reliability. Low-level quality attribute objectives represent technical aspects such as caching and synchronization [15].

Separating such quality attribute objectives enabled programmers to focus on small modules, which improved the overall application quality and minimized the chance of failure due to attacks or design faults.

Separation of quality attribute objectives is an efficient way for software designers to effectively split the application objective or the problem that the application is designed to solve into multiple isolated modules that target specific quality attribute objectives.

Object-oriented programming (OOP), for example, is one of the techniques that works on the concept of quality attribute objective separation by fractionizing the entire application into a set of objects that targets specific functional quality attributes [16].

Aspect-oriented programming was defined in 1996 by Kickzales and his group at the Xerox PARC research center [15]. It was an enhanced version of the OOP to complement it in order to obtain applications that are clearer and better structured [17].

Service-oriented architecture (SOA) is a standard to design software applications based on services that interact with each other. Authors [18] define SOA as "a paradigm for dealing with business processes distributed over a large landscape of existing and new heterogeneous systems that are under the control of different owners." SOA aims at facing several challenges such as interoperability and heterogeneity. Heterogeneity refers to variation of resources and geographical location of the service provider, consumer, system developers, and owners.

SOA as a standard does not apply to a specific technology. The most mutual application example of SOA is Web services [10,19]. Web services are a way to establish a SOA solution by using a specific implementation strategy.

The service component architecture (SCA) was developed as a more established version of the SOA. SCA provides a platform to achieve delivery, support, and management of distributed applications compliant with the rules of SOA [20]. SCA utilizes software components to devise services.

SCA is a set of specifications defining a formal method for developing an application using SOA. It is endorsed by many well-known software manufacturers, including IBM, Oracle IONA, BEA, SAP, TIBCO, and Sun.

SCA highlights the decoupling of service employment and of service assembly from the details of infrastructure abilities and from the details of the access methods used to invoke services [10].

The SCA specification supports service implementations designed via many programming languages, including declarative languages, such as XQuery and SQL. SCA also supports many programming styles, including asynchronous and message-oriented styles, in addition to the synchronous call-and-return style [20]. Also it includes object-oriented and procedural languages, such as Java, PHP, C++, COBOL, and XML-centric languages, such as BPEL and XSLT.

Attempts were presented toward enabling software re-programmability and dynamic elasticity. Agent-oriented architecture (AOA) utilized autonomic building blocks, and SOA and OOA used nonautonomic components. Using autonomic building blocks facilitated supporting nondeterministic behavior change in AOA by explicit use of soft computing [21]. However, supporting online composability is not clear in AOA while in OAA and SOA it is enabled either by aggregation [22] or by service composition [23].

The cell-oriented architecture (COA), is a unique architecture, as it comprehensively supports intrinsic separation of design concerns needed for enabling runtime re-programmability, intrinsic autonomic online composability, and dynamic software adaptation and elasticity.

The cell is the basic building block in COA. The COA cell is inspired from the biological cell in its independent, generic, composable construction. A COA cell is an abstraction of a mission-oriented autonomous active resource. Generic cells, termed stem cells, are seamlessly created by the host-side middleware or the COA cell DNA (CCDNA). Further, they participate in emerging tasks through a process called specialization. The CCDNA is a middleware program that allows a physical workstation to host cells and facilitates cell physical resource allocation and management.

Applications built over COA can be envisioned as a group of cooperating roles representing mission objectives. The term "organism" is used to represent a role player that performs a dedicated mission. An organism might be composed of a single or multiple cells based on its objectives. Figure 7.3 illustrates the different components of the COA.

Conceptually, the cell is the smallest active resource in a distributed computing platform. Cells are intelligent and independent, autonomous, single-application capsules, a "sandbox" that acquires, on the fly, application-specific functionality in the form of an executable code variant, "The specialization process." Cells act as a simple virtualization environment isolating the executable logic from the underlying physical resources. The cell is dynamically composable into larger structure "organisms" representing complex multi-tasking applications.

The COA cell separates logic from physical resource management by constructing an intelligently managed, elastic, thin virtualization layer between the application and the underlying physical resources. Such construction facilitates unifying the execution platform for distributed applications regardless of the configuration of the host platform. Unifying the execution environment waives the load of the building platform/OS-specific application for each targeted platform. In addition, the maintainability issues are divided between the developer and the technology owner. Software developers are concerned with maintaining the application itself while the technology owner is responsible for maintaining the execution platform. Partially elastic virtualization approaches were presented for loosening the bond between physical and logical resources, in which applications are

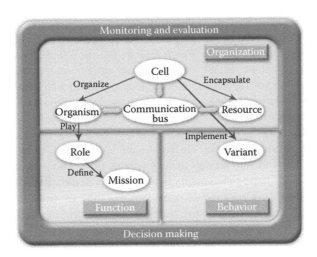

FIGURE 7.3 Components of our COA.

partially compiled at the production phase to be executed over a virtual machine host [7,11]. These techniques can be used to build a uniform execution environment for distributed applications. However, these approaches presented static elasticity and partial separation of design concerns. They did not separate data from logic and physical resources. Such separation is a key enabler for supporting intrinsic fault-tolerance, live-mobilization, and runtime adaptation to a frequently changing execution environment. These features are of extreme importance for diversity application as presented in the next subsections.

7.2.2.2 Diversity Employment toward Resilient and Efficient Execution

Software diversity has a long history of research work in the field of software security and fault tolerance dating back to the 1970s [7]. Component diversity was investigated in Genesis [16], in which the idea of providing both design diversity in the form of multiple variants representing different designs of the same specification as well as data diversity were proposed. A compiler-guided code variance approach [24] aimed to present automated massive-scale software diversity by the help of automated variant generation and utilizing multicore platforms. More advanced diversity employment approaches with the objective of anomaly detection through detecting flow deviation but with fewer constraints were presented [25,26]. A major drawback of such solutions is the need for virtualizing every input to the whole set of executing variants at the same logical point to be able to detect the abnormal deviation of the execution flow.

Utilizing runtime hot shuffling of software variants for quality attribute hot manipulation was first investigated by the ChameleonSoft software behavior encryption approach [5]. Diversity application entails a high chance of failure [27]. One of the unique features presented by this solution is the intrinsic support for failure recovery. ChameleonSoft is a comprehensive solution that provides an elastic, autonomous, resilient, situation-aware platform targeting different quality attributes while dynamically shuffling its software components to suit changes in the surroundings. The following subsections introduce more details about the variant techniques for diversity employment for different objectives.

7.2.2.2.1 Design Time Diversity

Basically, software diversity was presented as multiple independent solutions as a security measure and for fault tolerance. The realization software diversity was presented through the development of multiple independent versions of a program by different teams using different languages [7]. The main goal behind this approach was to increase the attacker's confusion by changing the behavior of the software, which will make system exploitation harder. They expected that at any given time the majority of these versions would be working correctly [7,8].

Some research work showed that there is a high probability that a multivariant software approach might face many coincidental failures [9,28]. On the contrary, other research work suggested that from the cost and the reliability point of view, the multivariant approach is much better than the one "good" version, especially in mission-critical applications in which the cost of failure could be very high [29].

Design time diversity aims to devise the same software in multiple designs to diversify the software product [32,33]; the objective was to defeat the mono culture of software development and to increase the attacker search space for vulnerabilities. Different techniques [30,31] were designed to automate inducing light changes in the software product at development time. The basic idea is that the diverse software replicas maintain the same functionality but differ only in their implementation details.

The main problem facing these approaches is the fact that they are static, and they can easily be predicted by runtime analyzers working on the attacker-targeted field of operations.

7.2.2.2.2   Load Time Diversity

System call randomization is a good mitigation mechanism against a wide set of code injection attacks; it aims to randomize the mapping of system calls [24]. The attacker mission to counterfeit such defense relies on guessing the system call numbers. The main issue is that the realization of this technique requires kernel recompilation with the new randomized system call mapping, and it necessitates that the binaries are rewritten to reflect the new system calls. These requirements invalidate such an approach in addition to the fact that static redesign of the kernel is a very complicated task [10]. Even with dynamic instrumentation [15], it is still considered impractical due to the excessive overhead. Additionally, it is a static solution that works only against one class of attacks and is not valid for other classes of attacks.

Pointer randomization: This approach works on randomizing the stored pointer representation values. The work presented [24] is a good example of such a mechanism. The authors perform an XOR operation on the pointer values with a random integer mask that gets generated at the bootstrap time. This mechanism works on mitigating attacks targeting corruption of pointer values. Attackers trying to mitigate such an attack have to guess the value of the random integer mask used at bootstrap time to devise the desired pointer value for corruption. The main disadvantage of such a solution is that it is static randomization. The values remain the same after bootstrapping and can be analyzed or guessed by the attacker with tools working on the same host especially for long-lived applications. Additionally, it works only with one class of attacks. Attacks such as buffer overflow, for example, cannot be mitigated with such a mechanism. Further, it is useless with languages that do not provide an accurate type of information or languages working with untyped buffers. With such languages, the corresponding pointer value(s) cannot be protected.

Address space layout randomization is one of the most successful and most commonly used mechanisms in many operating systems. Multiple implementations were presented to realize address space layout randomization [34–36]. These approaches focused on randomizing the base address of memory sections. It works fine with some attack classes such as buffer overflow attacks while it shares the same problem of static diversity approaches. These mechanisms provide static diversity that can be detected by a resourceful attacker with tools executing on the same machine running the targeted software.

7.2.2.2.3   Runtime Diversity

Diversity has been realized in various ways. Some work presented it in the form of a confusion induction paradigm [37,38] in which diversity is used to confuse the attack in order to complicate the attack process. An example for leveraging diversity for confusion induction is presented in the form of a load-time binary transformation as the one mentioned before and the one presented in [39]. Others presented a different solution for diversity realization based on virtual machines called "private machine architecture" [40]. They used randomization to promote heterogeneity at the machine level aiming to increase the cost of broad-based binary attacks. Moreover, some commercial operating systems realized the ideas of operating system randomization [41,42]. System call mappings, global library entry points, and stack placement randomization were used to induce diversity as a mitigation for buffer overflow attacks.

Component diversity was investigated in Genesis [31], in which the idea of providing both design diversity in the form of multiple variants representing different designs of the same specification as well as data diversity were proposed. Data diversity uses multiple copies of a single implementation operating on different data inputs but yielding the same desired results.

Massive-scale software diversity was presented with the help of automated variant generation and utilizing multicourse platforms. A compiler-guided code variance approach aims to present such automation [37]. A realization of this massive-scale software diversity approach for the purpose of detecting anomalies by replicated execution was first presented [24,43,44]; they mixed diversity with parallelism and check pointing. They execute different variants of a program in a muticore environment while monitoring any deviation in the program flow to issue an intrusion alert.

A major drawback of existing solutions is the need for virtualizing every input to the whole set of executing variants at the same logical point to be able to detect the abnormal deviation of the execution flow. More advanced approaches with the objective of anomaly detection through detecting flow deviation but with fewer constraints were presented [25,45–47].

These approaches generally apply different types of diversity mainly for reliability by replication or for intrusion detection by program flow deviation detection at runtime. Utilizing runtime hot shuffling of software variants for behavior encryption was first investigated by ChameleonSoft [5]. Furthermore, these solutions used diversity to target specific quality attributes. Failure recovery mechanisms were not investigated as most of these solutions presented static diversity with a low probability of failure. Another drawback of these solutions is the massive use of resources to realize diversity using heavy virtualization techniques and multicore or multiprocessor platforms. ChameleonSoft is one of those mechanisms that were designed to support legacy systems with limited resources. It can dynamically tailor its tasks to suit the dynamic change in resource availability.

ChameleonSoft is a diversity-based defense mechanism against software attacks. ChameleonSoft is founded over a cell-oriented architecture (COA)–based infrastructure managed by CyberX [4]. The elastic foundation of cells facilitating online programmability, hot code swapping, and automated recovery enabled what was termed as "ChameleonSoft Behavior Encryption (or CBE)" akin to message encryption.

CBE applies spatiotemporal diversity in a way that makes the attack target in continual random motion evading attackers. CBE leverages the COA intrinsic separation of concerns to realize temporal and spatial diversity. Temporal diversity is applied by shuffling multiple functionally equivalent, behaviorally different software variants at runtime. In addition, CBE realizes spatial diversity by enabling runtime seamless migration of cells from one physical host node to another. The goal behind that is to hide the potentially targeted software flaws that might be used to penetrate the system.

CyberX divides the missions of a huge software program into smaller tasks. Each of these tasks is assigned to one or more cells executing sets of similar function and different-behavior executable variants. These sets might have different objectives targeting different quality attributes. Reliability, performance, robustness, and mobility are examples of such attributes. ChameleonSoft shuffles variants and sets to induce diversity. The scope of diversity application extends beyond security goals to the other quality attributes. The system might shuffle to a variant that aims at high system performance in highly loaded but low security–risk situations. Alternatively, the system would resort to a higher security, perhaps lower performance, variant in higher risk situations.

Researchers [48] mentioned that multivariant systems without appropriate recovery mechanisms might face a larger amount of coincidental failures. ChameleonSoft relies on a CyberX autonomous recovery system to handle any coincidental failures that might occur due to diversity application. Such support increases the system resilience against international and unintentional failures.

ChameleonSoft autonomously and seamlessly changes the shuffling policy at runtime to suit the continual dynamic changes of the surroundings. Figure 7.4 illustrates ChameleonSoft's reliable

FIGURE 7.4 ChameleonSoft reliable behavior encryption.

behavior encryption realized through smart employment of online configurability, multidimensional diversity, and automated recovery managed by ChameleonSoft and CyberX.

Design time defense class represents a promising trend in complicating the attack process, especially those targeting running software-based products. Design time defense solutions are mostly proactive solutions working on minimizing the chance of successful attacks. The next subsections describe another defense class that includes solutions working on securing running applications at the time of operation. As presented later, in order to insure system resilience against sophisticated attacks and threats, modern defense solutions utilize hybrid mixtures of techniques from the two classes.

7.2.3 OPERATION TIME DEFENSE

Operation time defense class describes conventional defense services provisioned at time of operation. This class includes either detection/prediction or resolution/prevention techniques. Attack detection/prediction mechanisms are prerequisite for resolution or prevention. There is no resolution or prevention unless you are fully aware of the attack aspects, entry points, and pattern of dispersion. The monitoring and analysis mechanisms are major players in this game. The following subsections list the variant mechanisms available for attack detection/prediction focusing on the latest advances in the field of cyber and cyber physical systems monitoring and analysis techniques.

7.2.3.1 Cyber and CPS Monitoring and Evaluation Solutions

Defense services for CPS are highly dependent on the promptness and accuracy of the monitoring and analysis (M&A) mechanisms employed. Traditional M&A approaches do not treat sensing and effecting for cyber components and physical components seamlessly. The current M&A mechanisms were designed based on a set of assumptions that unintentionally neglect the real-time interaction and the tight coupling between these converging components. The *assumption* was *that physical components were protected by isolation and parameter defense* while *real-time response was not a primary factor for cyber components.* Further, they assumed *that there is no need to employ privacy preservation techniques* as the target of defense (ToD) privacy is implicitly protected by the cyber and physical parameter defense. Additionally, they assumed *that resource heterogeneity and scale could still be resolved by a distributed set of heterogeneous, pre-deployed, platform-dependent defense tools with fixed resource profiles.*

Research works [54,55] as well as our own [3] have disputed the validity and correctness of such assumptions as they lead to drastic *problems and limitations* negatively impacting the quality and promptness of the CPS defense service provisioning. Current CPS defense service providers (DSPs) fail to provide trustworthy robust and reliable *monitoring and evaluation* of the ToD components due to the use of scattered, uncoordinated, uncooperative, unaware, isolated, and heterogeneous monitoring tools and reporting mechanisms. Such limitations *increase the use of resources* due to redundancy, *increase the risk of conflicts and failures* due to limited awareness and coordination, *lower the defense quality* due to the poor and boundary limited feedback, and *increase the latency in defense provisioning and in detecting attacks giving the attacker the advantage* to spread the attacks through multiple networks. The tool heterogeneity and uncooperative nature massively *complicate automating its management*; the static nature of such tools *complicates attempts to autonomously adapt to changes in the surroundings.*

Research presented [56–59] attempted to resolve some of the problems resulting from such assumptions using more flexible sensing and control elements. They devised a mobile multi-agent–based attack detection system. The presented solutions were situation unaware and offered limited defense tools pervasiveness and coordination. Generally speaking, provisioning defense services while sharing the same host with the ToD exposes the ToD to DoS attacks and limits the system's scalability and interoperability.

Works [58,59] utilized a multidisciplinary approach to intelligently resolve some of the presented limitations. They combined multiple artificial intelligence techniques to build a complex smart attack detection system. Unfortunately, these techniques were bounded by the available technology constraints; they were designed to provision dedicated defense service while sharing the ToD host or host network. They were unable to overcome the curse of complex system dimensionality. With the increase of system complexity and the numerousness of input features, the processing time involved with clustering system events might badly affect the system and attack detection timeliness. Time constraints may sometimes force the system to prune less important features (dimensionality reduction) to maintain system timelines. However, the pruning approach is not always possible as it might compromise the detection accuracy.

All the above mentioned approaches were mainly concerned with defense service provisioning for cyber components. The work presented [60,61] is a hardware-based static detection system capable of supporting the requirements of both cyber and physical components. Using hardware-based detection and analysis techniques guarantees prompt and resource-efficient responses for quickly spreading attacks. A major disadvantage of technology is its limited flexibility, adaptability, interoperability, and maintainability. These systems are designed to work for specific targets and cannot seamlessly adapt to match different targets.

Multiple attack detection solutions were presented utilizing mixtures of the above mentioned methodologies employing different M&A techniques [62,63]. Unfortunately, *none of these systems were capable of presenting a comprehensive, autonomous, interoperable, globally situational aware, and scalable solution* that can guarantee adequate defense provisioning quality and promptness while maintaining the ToD survivability, operability, and privacy.

The next subsection closely gives a comprehensive study about the available mechanisms for detecting and mitigating one of the major attack classes that threaten both cyber and cyber-physical systems, malware-based attack class.

7.2.3.1.1 Malware Detection and Resolution Solutions

A malware is malicious software designed to infiltrate or damage a cyber system or cyber physical system (CPS) without the owner's informed consent [49]. There are many malware types with different shapes and entry points. Most of these software objects share similar purposes while they are expected to behave differently at time of infection. *Viruses*, worms, *botnets*, wabbits, Trojan horses, exploits "backdoors," spyware "scumware," stealware, parasiteware, "adware," *rootkits*, *blended threats*, *evolving threats*, keyloggers, and hoaxes are examples of the different malware types. Figure 7.5 lists the different types of attacks and the usability ration of each one of them [50].

Each malware group has its own way of being undetected. Modern malware detection tools utilize multiple detection mechanisms to be able to detect multiple malware categories as presented in Figure 7.5. Malware, especially viruses, are either memory resident or non-memory resident. Non-memory resident are simple attacks that can easily be detected at an entry point with a cleaver detection tool.

The memory resident attacks are more complex and efficient; they stay in memory and hide their presence from detection tools. These attacks are fast and infectious, aiming to infect as many

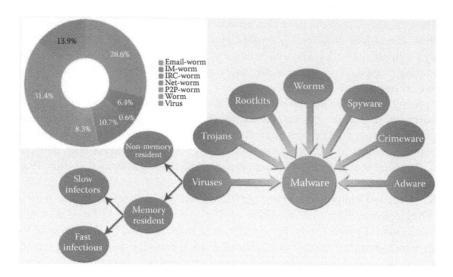

FIGURE 7.5 Classification of malware-related attacks.

files as possible locally within the infected host or remotely through the host network and network shares. The second category of memory resident attacks is the slow infectors. Slow infectors are the most dangerous type of malware as they use stealth and encryption techniques to stay undetected as long as they can. They are powerful attacks that can be a combination of multiple processes working together toward certain objectives.

Malware detectors use signature-based detection techniques to detect known attacks. Signature-based detection became a very efficient way of detecting known threats [51]. Finding a specific signature in one of the executable codes can accurately identify any enclosed threats within such code. Attack signatures are frequently updated and stored on the local anti-malware database. Unfortunately, this technique is inefficient if the attack has a malformed signature either by the programmer or by a mutation engine.

Heuristic techniques are one the most efficient ways to detect such mutated attacks. Heuristic and meta-heuristic techniques are used to spot unknown or known attacks with polymorphic behavior.

By definition, a heuristic technique is an informal technique to solve problems efficiently and in a way close to the optimal path [51]. Heuristic techniques are commonly used to rapidly reach a solution that is somehow close to the best possible solution. The meta-heuristic technique is a heuristic method for solving many of the computational problems by combining user-given black-box procedures in a hopefully efficient way [51].

Most of the modern malware detection techniques that use meta-heuristics to detect attacks utilize a set of isolated tools utilizing different techniques hoping to detect one of the attacks that there is no specific way to detect. Most of these tools utilize one of the following mechanisms: pattern matching, automatic learning, environment emulation, neural networks, data mining, Bayes networks, and hidden Markov models. There are other meta-heuristic techniques, but most of them are built based on one or more of the aforementioned mechanisms (Figure 7.6).

The main concept of heuristic-based detection techniques is to detect attacks without knowing too much about their internal structure. Heuristic techniques mainly focus on examining the behavior and the characteristics of the executing software to anticipate whether it is acting maliciously or not. The most successful heuristic-based detection technique is named as the heuristic scanning technique, which utilizes a mixture of multiple meta-heuristic techniques, such as pattern matching, automatic learning, and environment emulation.

Heuristic scanning in the common sense uses pattern matching to examine the assembly language instruction execution sequence and qualifies them by their potential dangerousness. Heuristic scanning

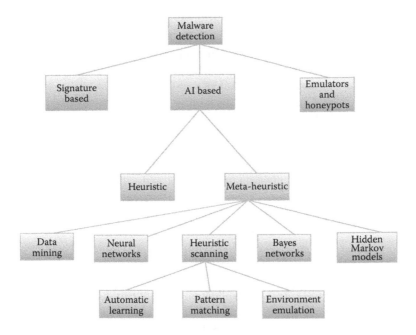

FIGURE 7.6   Classification of malware detection mechanisms.

usually follows a set of built-in rules with pre-assigned weight on each rule. In case of violation of any of the rules, the weight of the violated rule is added to the total violated rule by the same program or process. The program is flagged as malicious only if the total sum of added weights exceeds a certain threshold. Figure 7.7 illustrates the idea of a single layer classifier with predetermined threshold.

The feedback from the different scanners are fed into a global summarizing point that follows a certain meta-heuristic mechanism as illustrated in Figure 7.7. The overall result will decide whether to flag the scanned object or not.

As the detection techniques get more clever, the modern attacks or malware also emerge to more complicated attacks utilizing more sophisticated stealth techniques. Such techniques give them the advantage of being invisible to traditional scanners. Moreover the use of real-time encryption and anti-heuristic sequences make them look totally harmless to traditional malware scanners.

Heuristic scanners that use a single meta-heuristic mechanism that focuses only on monitoring the execution flow of the instructions of a certain program are deceivable by code obfuscation. Code obfuscation occurs by embedding some meaningless instructions within a malicious code. The same technique deceives detectors utilizing heuristic and signature scanning combined together.

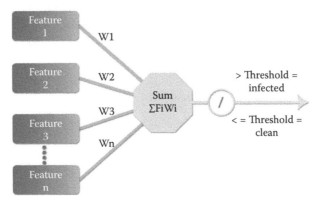

FIGURE 7.7   Single layer classifier.

One of the successful mechanisms to resolve the aforementioned problem is the use of artificial runtime environment emulation. However, it is not a lightweight detection mechanism, but it has high success rates in detecting unknown attacks. Environment emulation utilizes the idea of virtual machines; the malware detection tool provides a virtual machine with an independent and isolated operating system and allows malware to perform its routines freely within the virtual environment. The execution behavior of the suspicious application is being continuously examined while the malware is not aware. Most of the stealth and anti-heuristic techniques are irrelevant in this case as the detection tools scan the behavior from outside the box with a clear vision of what is really happening inside.

The main problem facing such a technique is the massive resource consumption and the expected delay needed to construct the virtualization environment and infiltrate the harmful instructions from being executed on the real machine.

Another problem that arises with using heuristic methods for detecting malware is the possibility of false positives. A false-positive event occurs when a benign program gets flagged as malicious by the heuristic scanner. The problem occurs frequently, especially with noncommercial programs having suspicious routines through their encryption functionalities.

The use of automatic learning is a good resolution of such a problem, in which the detector learns from its mistakes. The main issue with this technique is it requires an advanced user. In order to resolve such a problem autonomically, detection scanners have to increase their scanning depth and combine feedback from multiple heuristic mechanisms. Also, external consultation is one of the most efficient techniques, in which an external resourceful node gets consulted for guidance related to suspicious programs with weights that parley across the threshold line. The only issue with that solution is the possibility of a privacy violation due to sending specifics about the suspicious events.

Recently more complicated attacks were introduced that depend on infecting and controlling multiple hosts creating an automated taskforce targeting multiple objectives. Such attacks usually have dynamic objectives and construction components. Additionally, they frequently and autonomically get updated using a dynamic up/down link between the attacker and the malware itself. Detecting such attacks is a very complicated task given the uncooperative nature of the conventional modern detection tools and the fact that they share the same host or host network with their ToD.

Sharing the same network or host with the ToD makes them an easy target for attackers to deceive or destroy [52,53]. Additionally, the successfulness of the malware detector depends mostly on the fast real-time and deep analysis of the scanner feedback. Such a process, especially when it involves creating a runtime emulated execution environment is a computationally costly process for a tool sharing the ToD resources.

In this section, we overviewed the list of modern detection mechanisms available to identify cyber and cyber-physical systems attack indications. We also clarified a list of limitations facing these defenses and ways to resolve such limitations. The next subsection presents a brief overview of the contemporary CPS–targeted resolution mechanisms being used to mitigate such threats. In Section 7.3, we present a revolutionary defense approach that comprehensively addresses the presented monitoring, detection, and resolution limitations presenting a unique defense approach suitable for large-scale cyber and cyber-physical systems.

7.2.4   THREAT RESOLUTION IN CPS ENVIRONMENTS

In addition to the limitations presented in the previous two subsections, in regards to monitoring and evaluation and analysis of feedback, the control phase, *in which the defense system takes actions regarding detected threats*, faces a serious set of limitations [53]. The limitations are mainly due to the lack of cooperation and awareness that limit the defense tools' capability to resolve or even contain persistent fast-spreading attacks.

For example, it is too hard for such uncoordinated, scattered tools to marshal and coordinate task forces to hunt down the attacks spreading all over the network or a set of interconnected networks as it is hard to control the DSP and the ToD tools and equipment to block attack access to the shared network. Furthermore, without appropriate global control and situational awareness it is too hard to block the source of dynamic remote attacks. Such limitations can be utilized to cause DoS attack by keeping the DSP busy treating infected files and strike more and more files.

Research work has been focusing on presenting a resolution for some of the control problems in CPS environments. Researchers [64] presented what is called autonomous multi-agent cooperative problem solving (TEAM-CPS) and successfully applied it to one of the critical CPS, the public telephone networks. They used multiple intelligent agents that were designed to work together to provide distributed control for such a system. Unfortunately, the system was not scalable enough to suit large-scale systems. The limitations against this approach and other agent passed approaches [65,66] is the high resource consumption nature of the agents and the fact that they are designed to share the host resources. These limitations limit the approach capability to scale.

From another perspective, the use of intelligent agents lacks the support of the physical part of the network. The used agents are not aware of the interactions between the cyber and the physical parts of the system. Such unawareness increases the chance of conflicts, errors, and failures.

A more advanced version of this line of research was presented [53,66] as they used multiple AI techniques to control a pool of mobile agents performing control tasks. The use of AI guided the management platform toward smarter decisions. Unfortunately, they shared the same problem as their insisters: the lack of situational awareness and the inconsideration of isolating the control platform from the host under control. Such limitations limited the scalability of such systems and their ability to suit CPS applications.

An evolutionary monitoring analysis sharing and control (MASC) tool named EvoSense was presented [6], introducing a new paradigm for defense service provisioning that intrinsically and comprehensively address the aforementioned limitations facing existing systems. EvoSense is a biologically inspired, intrinsically resilient, intelligent, situation-aware, sense-and-effect system to realize a biological immune system–like defense provisioning. EvoSense acts as an intelligent elastic middle layer between the DSP and the ToD enabling remote defense provisioning and creating a uniform defense interface that hides ToD scale, resource heterogeneity, and complexity concerns from the control and management concerns. This uniform representation enables interoperable and cooperative defense services. Further, such isolation maintains defense provisioning survivability in case of ToD failure or DoS attacks.

EvoSense is founded over our biologically inspired, intrinsically resilient, adaptable cell oriented architecture (COA) [23,43]. The COA provides intrinsic, dynamic, distributed, resilient resource management and allocation needed to support pervasive MASC.

EvoSense manages a vast number of elastic and intelligent containers (cells) to host/abstract cyber/physical sensing and effecting tools. EvoSense mimics the human bloodstream circulation effect by utilizing its adaptable infrastructure to circulate these context-driven, functionally customizable sensor and effector cells into the ToD body to pervasively monitor, analyze, and control the ToD components. EvoSense sensors and effectors are used to execute defense missions provisioned by a DSP. A defense mission is a mixture of sensing and effecting tasks involving information gathering, partial analysis, control, and manipulation of the ToD elements. EvoSense utilizes such pervasive activities to build real-time global views of the entire ToD network, reflecting the quality of the defense service provision and the current state at each point. These views are intelligently analyzed to facilitate defense service evolution.

EvoSense alternates/mixes different defense/control missions from different DSPs to provision defense services to the same ToD host in a process called ToD vaccination. The ToD vaccination process involves sharing defense experience and tools between DSPs in terms of abstract missions and sensing and effecting packages. Using such a ToD vaccination mechanism enables the defense platform to continuously evolve its services and capabilities. Such evolution can lead to more accurate and prompt detection of known attacks and a better chance of detecting unknown attacks. Vaccines are autonomously checked for privacy violations and maliciousness before utilization or storage. This ToD vaccination is similar to biological systems in which antibodies can be extracted from one immune body to another to create a healthy up-to-date defense community [13]. EvoSense can be considered to be one of the first solutions capable of providing such features comprehensively and pervasively with low overhead.

7.3 THE CARD CONCEPT

In the previous section, we presented an overview of the latest efforts that were presented by the current literature that can be utilized toward the realization of resilient and efficient defense service provisioning for CPS. We illustrated the various techniques available to enable software elasticity needed to facilitate efficient and dynamic adaptation to changes within the CPS domain. Additionally, we presented the various techniques available to enable software diversity that can be utilized to realize a moving-target defense for platform security. Finally, we presented the different attack detection and resolution mechanisms being used within the cyber and CPS domains. We observed that despite the existence of a solid and concrete research base addressing these various design aspects, most of these solutions fall short of realizing the needed level of quality, efficiency, and effectiveness to support CPS defense. We assert the *need for new defense platforms that effectively and efficiently coordinate defense missions and tools in real-time to achieve the following goals:*

- Achieve asymmetric advantage to CPS defenders, prohibitively increasing the cost for attackers
- Ensure resilient operations in the presence of persistent and evolving attacks and failures
- Facilitate defense alliances, effectively and efficiently diffusing defense intelligence and operations transcending organizational boundaries

The proposed solution aims to comprehensively address these goals in order to present an evolutionary defense platform that would enable self and situation awareness, resilient adaptive defense, and cooperative autonomous control and sharing among cooperating organizations without violating their individual privacy policy. Enabling such features makes it possible to successfully provision defense services to mission-critical heterogeneously composed systems such as CPS while maintaining the operation timeliness and stability in the presence of persistent attacks.

For that, we present CyPhyCARD, a biologically inspired, distributed, dynamically configurable, runtime programmable platform that manages a large number of cyber and physical resources and services upon which evolutionary defenses can be built to protect participant organizations. Figure 7.8 presents an abstract view of CyPhyCARD.

CyPhyCARD features a set of platform-managed capabilities and services through a biologically inspired architecture and methodologies to effect trace-resistant, resilient, and allied defenses. CyPhyCARD provisions its services via an evolutionary sensory system, EvoSense, working through an intrinsically resilient and autonomously managed adaptable platform, CyberX, and protected by novel moving-target defense mechanism, ChameleonSoft. Figure 7.9 presents CyPhyCARD goals and features, which are described as follows:

Goals:
- Resilient operations by managing automatic failure recovery and containment and adapting structure, function, and performance to varying network scales and contexts
- Trace-resistant moving-target defense by multidimensional mobilization of the attack target evading attackers
- Allied defense by isolating the defense provisioning design concerns sensing, effecting, control, and physical resources; enabling trustworthy automated defense sharing and cooperation

FIGURE 7.8 Abstract view of CyPhyCARD.

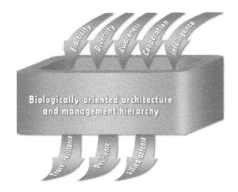

FIGURE 7.9 CyPhyCARD goals and features.

Features:

- Awareness by providing pervasive monitoring and analytics for self- and situation-awareness distributed throughout the targeted systems
- Elasticity right-sized resources and services by autonomically marshaling and adaptively provisioning resources (cyber and physical) and services (monitoring, detection, and response) to effect appropriate evolutionary immune responses
- Intelligence by using autonomic, independent, self- and situation-aware, smart building blocks to build the entire defense platform

- Diversity to induce software behavior encryption (i.e., inducing adequate confusion and diffusion similar to message encryption)
- Cooperative defense by enabling mixed initiative and fully autonomic cooperative tipping and cueing among participating organizations without violating their individual policies

To realize these capabilities, CyPhyCARD construction is based on three main contributions:

- Biologically Inspired Management Platform (*CyberX*)
  - Manages a distributed construction of composable basic building blocks termed "cells"
    - Enable cell dynamic runtime configuration
    - Support the cell self-monitoring
    - Enable the cells to dynamically adapt to changing internal and external conditions and acquire resources on demand based on the dynamics of the tasks on hand
  - A multimode, autonomous, situation-aware recovery system for enhanced system resilience
- Software Behavior Encryption System (*ChameleonSoft*)
  - Employs runtime multidimensional software diversity to induce confusion and diffusion to, in effect, induce spatiotemporal software behavior encryption
  - ChameleonSoft mobilize running cells among heterogeneously configured hosts in a way that makes the attack target in a continuous random motion inducing trace-resistant moving target defense
  - An elastic software platform that dynamically and autonomously changes diversity application and recovery policies to match the surrounding frequent changes
- Evolutionary Sensory System (*EvoSense*)
  - Defense service provisioning by autonomous abstraction and virtualization of heterogeneous compositions of physical resources, conventional defense services, and autonomously customized formations of sensing and effecting tools
  - Enable smart pervasive sensor circulation for enhanced detection efficiency and better resource utilization
  - Early enable trustworthy cooperative autonomous control and sharing of defense intelligence among interconnected CyPhyCARDs and/or target of defense (ToD) systems to enhance attack detection and deterrence

The next subsections give a brief overview of CyPhyCARD's constructing pillars participating in the realization of the CARD concept and CyPhyCARD defense cloud.

7.3.1 CyberX Managed CyPhyCARD Foundation

CyberX, a situation-aware trustworthy management platform that utilizes the COA features to realize the aforementioned pillars. COA is a biologically inspired architecture with active components termed cells that support development, deployment, execution, maintenance, and evolution of software. Cells separate logic, state, and physical resource management.

Conceptually, the cell is the smallest active resource in a distributed computing platform. Cells are intelligent, and independent, autonomous, single-application capsules "sandbox" that acquires, on the fly, application-specific functionality in the form of an executable code variant, "the specialization process." Cells act as a simple virtualization environment isolating the executable *logic* from the underlying *physical* resources. Figure 7.10 illustrates an abstract view of a COA cell at runtime. The cell is dynamically composable into larger structures, "organisms," representing complex multitasking applications.

A single workstation can host one or more cells, providing a flexible way to share the physical resources among multiple applications.

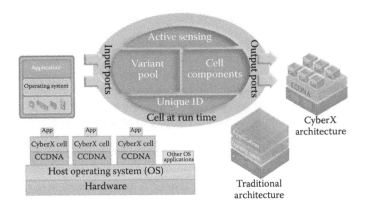

FIGURE 7.10 COA cell at runtime.

Cells are dynamically composable into organisms that are bound to functional roles at runtime. CyberX manages such construction to enable online re-programmability, hot code swapping, local/global situation awareness, and automated recovery.

CyberX enables applications to dynamically adapt to runtime changes in their execution environment via runtime diversification of multiple similar-function, quality objective–different code variants. Reliability, performance, robustness, survivability, compatibility, scalability, and mobility are examples of such attributes.

CyberX utilizes the COA feature of enabling the application to exchange real-time status and recommendation messages with the host cell for administrative purposes to enhance the cell local application awareness and to enable application-driven adaptation. CyberX uses these messages to guide the cell runtime quality-attribute manipulation toward accurate and prompt adaptation. Further, CyberX collects, analyzes, and trustworthy-shares these messages and status reports constructing a real-time sharable global view of the cell network.

CyberX enhances the system resilience by multiple recovery modes to cover different application requirements and host configurations. CyberX offers a prompt and accurate fine-grained recovery for resourceful hosts executing critical applications and a more resource efficient course-grained recovery for less critical applications. CyberX uses the COA's loosely coupled features to allow applications to seamlessly change their current active recovery modes based on context, environment, or application-objective change.

CyberX contributions are as follows:

- A biologically inspired architecture with the following capabilities
  - Intrinsic separation of design concerns (data, logic, and physical resources)
  - Employing a mission-oriented application design and inline code distribution to enable adaptability and online dynamic re-tasking
- Elastic system design and platform-managed control enabling the following:
  - Runtime diversity employment for hot manipulation of quality attributes to effect trace-resistance and moving target defense
  - Multimodal, autonomous, situation-aware recovery system for enhanced system resilience
  - Dynamic and autonomous change of shuffling and recovery policies according to runtime changes in the execution environment

The next subsections illustrates how CyberX-managed COA was utilized to enable software behavior encryption for moving-target defense.

7.3.2 CHAMELEONSOFT: SOFTWARE BEHAVIOR ENCRYPTION FOR MOVING-TARGET DEFENSE

Inspired by the resilience of diverse biological systems in the sea chameleons, we propose a diversity-based defense mechanism against software attacks, termed ChameleonSoft. Sea chameleons or cephalopods employ multi-layer diversity for different purposes. For example, they leverage their capability to change their body color, texture, and appearance to induce diversity. Diversity is used to camouflage for defense, disguise for hunting, and change color for communication [67]. Similarly, ChameleonSoft utilizes spatiotemporal software diversity to enhance software system security, survivability, and resilience.

ChameleonSoft is founded over cell-oriented architecture (COA)–based infrastructure managed by CyberX. Such construction supports online programmability, hot code swapping, and automated recovery. These features together enable what we term as "ChameleonSoft behavior encryption" (or CBE) akin to message encryption.

CBE applies spatiotemporal diversity in a way that makes the attack target in continual random motion evading attackers. CBE leverages the COA intrinsic separation of concerns to realize temporal and spatial diversity. Figure 7.11 illustrates the software Chameleonization process. CyberX divides the missions of a huge software program into smaller tasks. Each of these tasks is assigned to one or more cells executing sets of similar function and different-behavior executable variants. These sets might have different objectives targeting different quality attributes. Reliability, performance, robustness, and mobility are examples of such attributes. ChameleonSoft shuffles variants and sets to induce diversity. ChameleonSoft shuffles these variants locally for *temporal* diversity. ChameleonSoft migrates the live cells between heterogeneous and homogeneous platforms to realize the *spatial* diversity. The scope of diversity application extends beyond security goals to the other quality attributes. The system might shuffle to a variant that aims at high system performance in highly loaded but low security–risk situations. Alternatively, the system would resort to a higher security, perhaps lower performance variant in higher risk situations.

Researchers [68] mentioned that multivariant systems without an appropriate recovery mechanism might face a larger amount of coincidental failures. ChameleonSoft relies on CyberX's autonomous recovery system to handle any coincidental failures that might occur due to diversity application. Such support increases the system resilience against international and unintentional failures.

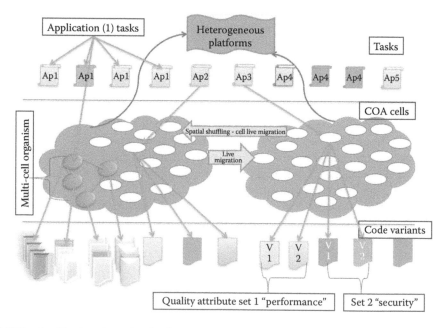

FIGURE 7.11   Application chameleonization.

Inspired by the sea chameleon dynamic, change occurs in response to frequent changes in the environment; ChameleonSoft autonomously and seamlessly changes the shuffling policy at runtime to suit the continual dynamic changes of the surroundings.

7.3.2.1 Software Behavior Encryption

Claude Shannon in 1949 introduced the confusion and diffusion properties of operation as a way to quantify the strength of a secure cipher. We present a key such as mapping between the key in message encryption and the CBE key to enable quantification. We built our mapping based on the fact that both keys have similar semantics, but they are not exactly equivalent. Message encryption depends on a key, and CBE depends on a set of parameters that may be constructed as a key or genetic material. We used measures of confusion and diffusion to evaluate the strength of our CBE. CBE is an encryption technique with added unique characteristics.

We consider CBE to be a multi-round encryption mechanism, in which the output of a single round is always valid for use directly without decryption within the lifetime of the round. Additionally, CBE has no limits for the number of rounds needed to produce the final output. CBE uses the output of each round as an input to the next round in order to increase the complexity of the cipher linearly over time.

CBE is an encryption scheme that does not need any key management or exchange mechanism. The reason behind that resides in the fact that CBE output is useable without decryption. Additionally, CBE is an event-driven encryption scheme in which the encryption key, the inputs, and the outputs have multiple elements representing different events affecting the encryption processes.

In our system, rounds are time slots. A single time slot might contain multiple temporal or spatial shuffles for confusion induction or random independent distributed variant changes for diffusion induction.

Figure 7.12 gives an abstract view of the behavior encryption process. The process involves multiple rounds of confusion and diffusion guided by dynamic parameters. These parameters represent the key to our encryption mechanism. The confusion process is responsible for temporal and spatial change in the current behavior by manipulating the cell location and/or the executing variants. The diffusion process is a random change in the execution behavior of multiple cells based on independent decisions guided by distributed recommendations to diffuse the changes all over the network in an intractable way. More details about ChameleonSoft software behavior encryption and the software Chameleonization process can be found in [5].

7.3.3 Bio-Inspired Evolutionary Sensory System for Cyber-Physical System Defense

Cyber-physical systems (CPS) promise advances toward smarter infrastructure systems and services, significantly enhancing their reliability, performance, and safety. Current CPS monitoring, analysis, sharing, and control (MASC) technologies offer disparate and largely inadequate services for the realization of effective and efficient CPS security. Most current technologies did not consider

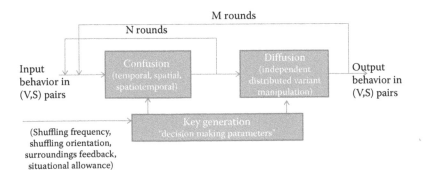

FIGURE 7.12 Behavior encryption process.

that cyber and physical convergence would need a new paradigm that treats cyber and physical components seamlessly and pervasively. Further, information sharing was severely curtailed by enforcing parameter defense to preserve the privacy of the system to be secured, the ToD these limitations negatively impact the quality, reliability, survivability, and promptness of security services.

EvoSense is an evolutionary system designed to enable real-time pervasive MASC toward autonomous context-aware security service provisioning. EvoSense uses COA cells to encapsulate attack investigation and resolution tools defined as binary code variants constructing a set of platform-independent sensing and effecting cells. EvoSense constructs a biological immune system–like security environment by circulating generic streams of such capsules into the ToD body to induce a bloodstream-like effect.

EvoSense's main contributions can be outlined as follows:

- Enable pervasive autonomously managed monitoring and analysis
- Uniform defense service provisioning for heterogeneously composed multi-enclave CPS systems
- Enable trustworthy, interoperable multi-organization cooperative, dynamic, autonomous defense
- Facilitate early failure/attack detection and resolution

7.3.3.1   Overview

EvoSense manages and controls sensing and affecting cells based on specific mission objectives provided by the DSP. EvoSense works as a middle layer between the DSP and the ToD as illustrated in Figure 7.13. EvoSense leverages the uniform abstract representation of sensing and affecting cells to circulate sensors and effectors intelligently throughout the ToDs. Additionally, EvoSense leverages such features to enable security service interoperability in which different DSPs can share in defense provisioning for the same ToD in a privacy-preserving manner.

EvoSense defense provisioning includes two main modes: (1) *DSP-guided mode* in which EvoSense blindly executes predetermined security missions provided by the DSP, and (2) *evolutionary mode*, which involves evolutionary sensing and affecting. Evolutionary sensing aims to detect malicious abnormal behaviors without prior knowledge of that behavior. The process involves analyzing and correlating different information feeds from multiple sources to zoom in on abnormal behavior deviation identifying possible attack indicators. On the other hand, evolutionary affecting involves utilizing the pervasive control feature of EvoSense to autonomously deploy safe-resolution tools (i.e., tools that don't conflict with the running applications) or to contain such attacks within certain perimeters while waiting for administrators to provide clear resolution procedures to execute. Figure 7.14 illustrates the EvoSense evolutionary security process.

FIGURE 7.13   EvoSense abstract view.

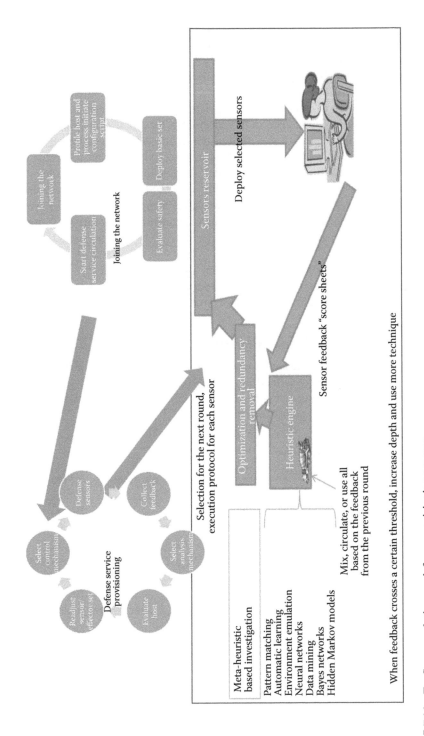

FIGURE 7.14 EvoSense evolutionary defense provisioning process.

Joining an EvoSense-equipped DSP network procedure starts by installing COA middleware on the host machines, registering the host's configuration and its security and privacy policies to the DSP host database. Then EvoSense starts to create a profile for this host. The host configuration profile presents all the details regarding the host platform, computational capabilities, the organization/enclave ID(s) for that host, if any, and any special consideration regarding the applications running on it. The security and privacy policy defines the needed security level, the scope of cooperation, and the type of allowable sharing materials.

Upon registration of a new cyber/physical host, EvoSense is notified to start the initial evaluation of the host to determine *the basic sensor deployment-package* composition. EvoSense interprets the host record in the DSP database to identify the appropriate types of sensors and effectors that match the host configuration profile to be included in the sensor/effector circulation stream.

The host is under full time evaluation and the sensor/effector deployment package evolves over time. The process is guided by the global sensing feedback not only at the host but also throughout the network. The feedback is analyzed on the DSP side to enable investing more resource searching for attack indications, without any effect on the ToD hosts. EvoSense circulates security missions (sensors, effectors, control and management logic) while favoring the activation of security tools targeting attacks that match the host profile. Using dynamic host profile–based circulation enhances the attack detection accuracy and promptness and helps optimize resource usage on the host and on the DSP.

The entire defense delivery process is managed by distributed intelligent management units working on the DSP side in a hierarchal fashion to support large-scale networks.

That was a brief overview of EvoSense, and more details can be found in [6].

7.4 CYPHYCARD QUALITATIVE EVALUATION

In this section, we intend to discuss the ability of CyPhyCARD to mitigate CPS attacks such as the BlackWidow (BW) attack that was described as a case study "attack scenario" in Section 7.1. We will list the attacker assumptions supporting the BW attack, followed by an illustration of how the CyPhyCARD defense cloud works against such assumptions.

7.4.1 THE BW ATTACKER ASSUMPTIONS

The following is the list of the BlackWidow attack designer assumptions that represents the pillars supporting his attack:

1. The defense system shares the same network or host with the target of attack/defense system. [Note the defense system might be exposed to attack by compromising the ToD.]
2. The attack target defense system, or major parts of it, uses COTS security products. [Note a majority of defense systems are signature based, so that it is probably easy to bypass with custom code.]
3. The system is not capable of being fully situation aware of all its components in a massive-scale network in real time.
   - Building a very slow-motion worm will increase the log file sample size needed to detect it.
   - The attack will spread in small parts in the target network hosted by geographically remote locations. This will make it more difficult to detect attacker activity unless a deep nearly network-scale analysis can be conducted to correlate all disparate logs.
4. The defense system management workstations (that the administrators use) share the same network with the target of defense. [Note stolen passwords can simply be used to modify rules of IDS, routers, switches, firewalls, proxies, etc.]

5. Attack hosts will not be manipulated in a detectable way so as not to alert the host AM. These hosts will be used only to launch the attack on the primary target. [Note this might be possible by using zero day exploits and malware code never seen before.]
6. Host-based defense systems usually use malware signatures as an indication for infection from various forms of malware.
7. It is not feasible to monitor all the host behavior patterns while sharing the same workstation that is performing user tasks.
8. Defense systems are not resilient against attacks and have weak recovery mechanisms. [Note most of them assume that they will not be the target of an attack as long as they were able to secure their ToD. Additionally, usually they have no intrinsic failure recovery.]
9. Cyber security is oblivious of and is not coordinated with physical security to protect the target cyber-physical system. Human intervention is needed to facilitate such coordination. [Note the attack can make them conflict with each other to bypass both of them.]

7.4.2 CyPhyCARD Invalidating the BW Attacker Assumptions

CyPhyCARD is designed to provide defense services in total isolation from the ToD, invalidating assumptions 1 and 4.

CyPhyCARD's EvoSense is a buffer between the DSP and ToD. Neither EvoSense nor the CyPhyCARD share the network or the hosts of the ToD. The defense services are delivered to the ToD in a separate network that connects the ToD to CyPhyCARD. The defense delivery vehicles are secured using our ChameleonSoft moving-target defense, which invalidates assumption 8.

CyPhyCARD is an active defense system founded over a CyberX–managed ChameleonSoft secured resilient foundation. One of the main tasks of ChameleonSoft is to monitor and secure the COA–based foundation against threats and attacks. Having dedicated and management-isolated systems such as ChameleonSoft and CyberX handling such details gives EvoSense more to focus on provisioning defense services to the ToD increasing the overall quality of provisioned service. Additionally, CyPhyCARD is designed to support large-scale systems and computationally expensive tasks. The CyPhyCARD design supports distributing the tasks over a hierarchy of independent management entities composed of fine-grained components managed by CyberX. The fine granularity of such components and the isolation between its logic, data, and physical resources enabled CyberX to fractionize large tasks over multiple hosts, constructing a cloud-like platform with virtually infinite resources. With that unique feature, CyPhyCARD invalidates assumption 7.

CyPhyCARD's EvoSense uses signature-based detection tools as a part of its arsenal while the major part of that arsenal relies on an evolutionary sensory system. The CyPhyCARD evolutionary sensory system utilizes multiple intelligent mechanisms to detect unknown attacks based on monitoring suspicious activities and up normal behavior, and that invalidates assumption 6.

CyPhyCARD is not a commercial product available for conventional users even though the foundation of CyPhyCARD is highly dynamic and autonomous, inducing a high level of dissimilarity between identical copies of the same system, and that invalidates assumption 2.

One of the main objectives of CyPhyCARD's EvoSense is to promote the defense system situational awareness of the different ToD components and to isolate the platform composition heterogeneity, enabling seamless defense provisioning. EvoSense pervasive monitoring and analysis and the intrinsic trustworthy sharing and cooperative defense enhance the situational awareness of all ToD components. EvoSense collects events from different entities of the ToD and correlates the collected information to generate a global image of the entire system to be analyzed by high management units. Doing so enables CyPhyCARD to detect slow-moving attacks and attacks using remote bots to launch attacks on remote hosts. The aforementioned aspects successfully invalidate assumptions 3, 5, and 9.

By invalidating all the attacker assumptions, it is hard for such an attack to succeed in attacking a CyPhyCARD protected system. More detailed qualitative and quantitative evaluation of CyPhyCARD effectiveness and efficiency in defense service provisioning for CPS applications can be found in [3].

7.5   CONCLUSION

In this chapter, we overviewed the domain of cyber and CPS IADR, illustrating the various techniques available to provision or to facilitate defense provisioning at design time and operation time. The study clarified the limitations of the current solutions and the need for a radical change not only on the defense provisioning technology, but also on the foundation utilized to provision defense services. The study illustrated the need for CPS–ready IARD solutions capable of efficiently coordinating defense missions and tools in real time to accomplish the following objectives:

- Achieve asymmetric advantage to CPS defenders, prohibitively increasing the cost for attackers
- Ensure resilient operations in the presence of persistent and evolving attacks and failures
- Facilitate defense alliances, effectively and efficiently diffusing defense intelligence and operations transcending organizational boundaries

For that, we presented the CARD concept as a solution to achieve these objectives and the CyPhyCARD platform as a realization of such a concept. CyPhyCARD provides the means to guarantee continuity of operations as well as to deter attacks and prohibitively increase the cost on potential attackers targeting CPS.

CyPhyCARD presents a unified resilient platform to monitor, manage, and control the heterogeneous composition of CPS components. Such unification of control with the help of CyPhyCARD autonomous management capability expands the applicability of such a system in multiple domains related to cyber and CPS.

CyPhyCARD uses its resilient cloud-like infrastructure to host defense services and to perform all the heavy tasks related to defense provisioning waiving a large computationally heavy load from the ToD. Waiving that load in addition to CyPhyCARD utilization of platform-independent sensing and effecting capsules for defense provisioning expands the system support to various host configuration and legacy systems.

CyPhyCARD provides the means to automate trustworthy multi-organization information sharing to enable early attack alarm and enhance the defense system global situation-awareness toward more accurate decision making. Enabling such features makes it possible to successfully provide defense services to mission-critical heterogeneously composed systems such as CPS while maintaining the operation timeliness and stability in presence of persistent attacks.

AUTHORS' BIOGRAPHIES

Mohamed Eltoweissy is chief scientist for cyber security research at Pacific Northwest National Laboratory. Before joining PNNL, Eltoweissy was an associate professor in the Bradley Department of Electrical and Computer Engineering at Virginia Tech.

Eltoweissy's current research interests crosscut the areas of trustworthy engineering, networking architecture and protocols, and distributed systems for large-scale, ubiquitous, cyber-physical systems. Eltoweissy's contributions include concern-oriented architecture and a cell-based network model for next-generation networks, dynamic key management for sensor and ad hoc networks, reputation management in ad hoc networks and service environments, and elastic sensor-actuator networks.

Eltoweissy received his PhD in computer science from Old Dominion University in 1993 and his MS and BS in computer science and automatic control from Alexandria University, Egypt, in 1989 and 1986, respectively. He has more than 135 publications in archival journals and respected books and conference proceedings. He also has an extensive funding record (more than $10M).

 **Mohamed Azab** is associate professor at the City of Scientific Research and Technological Applications, Alex, Egypt. Mohamed's current research interests crosscuts the areas of trustworthy engineering, networking architecture and protocols, and distributed systems for large-scale ubiquitous cyber-physical systems (CPS). Mohamed's contributions include cooperative autonomous resilient defense platforms for CPS, a software behavior encryption approach for moving-target defense, and an evolutionary sensory system for CPS monitoring, analysis, sharing, and control.

Mohamed received his PhD in computer engineering at Virginia Tech in 2013 and his MS and BS in computer engineering at AAST, Egypt, 2006 and 2002, respectively. He has two active U.S. Patents, and multiple publications in archival journals and respected conference proceedings. Mohamed's work was selected twice as one of the top 10 security projects in the domain of Homeland Security in 2012 and 2013 in a nationwide prestigious competition conducted and hosted by The Department of Homeland Defense Foundation, United States.

REFERENCES

1. A. Cardenas, S. Amin, B. Sinopoli, A. Giani, A. Perrig, and S. S. Sastry, Challenges for securing cyber physical systems, in *Workshop on Future Directions in Cyber-physical Systems Security*, 2009.
2. GAO, Critical infrastructure protection: Challenges and efforts to secure control systems. *United States General Accounting Office (GAO)*, pp. 4–354, 2004.
3. M. Azab, Cooperative autonomous resilient defense platform for cyber-physical systems, PhD dissertation, Virginia Tech, 2013.
4. M. Azab and M. Eltoweissy, CyberX: A biologically inspired platform for cyber trust management, 8th International Conference on Collaborative Computing, Oct. 2012.
5. M. Azab and M. Eltoweissy, ChameleonSoft: Software behavior encryption for moving target defense, *Mobile Networks and Applications (MONET)*, vol. 18, pp. 271–292, April 2013. doi: 10.1007/s11036-012-0392-0.
6. M. Azab and M. Eltoweissy, Bio-inspired evolutionary sensory system for cyber-physical system defense, *IEEE Technologies for Homeland Security*, Nov. 2012.
7. C. Grim, Application virtualization, 2012. Available at http://www.vmware.com/products/thinapp/overview.html.
8. G. Lawler, Distributed architecture for the object oriented methods for interoperability, Naval Postgraduate School, 2003.
9. C. Hahn, C. Madrigal-Mora, and K. Fischer, Interoperability through a platform-independent model for agents, in 3rd International Conference on Interoperability for Enterprise Software and Applications, 2007.
10. C. Szyperski, *Component Software beyond Object-Oriented Programming*, 2nd ed. Addison Wesley, Boston, 2002.
11. L. Parnas, On the criteria to be used in decomposing systems into modules, *Communications of the ACM*, vol. 15, pp. 1053–1058, 1972.
12. D. Box, *Essential COM*. Addison Wesley, Boston, 1998.
13. T. Jackson, B. Salamat, G. Wagner, C. Wimmer, and M. Franz, On the effectiveness of multi-variant program execution for vulnerability detection and prevention, in International Workshop on Security Measurements and Metrics (MetriSec 2010), 2010.
14. D. Schmidt, Tutorial on the lightweight CORBA component model (CCM), 2012. Available at http://www.slideshare.net/jwillemsen/omg-corba-component-model-tutorial.
15. E. Bruneton, T. Coupaye, M. Leclercq, V. Quéma, and J. Stefani, The FRACTAL component model and its support in Java: Experiences with auto-adaptive and reconfigurable systems, *Software Practice & Experience*, vol. 36, no. 11–12, pp. 1257–1284, 2006.
16. F. Plasil, D. Balek, and R. Janecek, Sofa/dcup: Architecture for component trading and dynamic updating, in International Conference on Configurable Distributed Systems, 1998.
17. R. Filman, T. Elrad, S. Clarke, and M. Aksit, *Aspect Oriented Software Development*. Addison Wesley, Boston, 2005.

18. G. Kiczales, J. Lamping, A. Mendhekar, C. Maeda, C. V. Lopes, J. Loingtier, and J. Irwin, Aspect-oriented programming, *ECOOP*, pp. 220–242, 1997.

19. C. Quintero et al., Architectural aspects of architectural aspects, Springer EWSA 2005. LNCS, vol. 3527, pp. 247–262, 2005.

20. N. Josuttis, SOA in practice: The art of distributed system design, 2007.

21. C. Carrascosa, A. Terrasa, A. García-Fornes, A. Espinosa, and V. Botti, Behaviour management in real-time agents, in *Fifth Iberoamerican Workshop on Multi-Agent Systems*, 2004, pp. 1–11.

22. A. Tolk, S. Diallo, C. Turnitsa, and L. Winters, Composable M&S web services for net-centric applications, *Journal of Defense Modeling and Simulation*, pp. 27–44, 2006.

23. P.-O. Östberg and E. Elmroth, GJMF—A composable service-oriented grid job management framework, 2010. Available at http://www.cs.umu.se/ds.

24. S. Forrest, A. Somayaji, and D. Ackley, Building diverse computer systems, in *6th Workshop on Hot Topics in Operating Systems (HotOS-VI)*, pp. 67–72, 1997.

25. T. Jackson, B. Salamat, G. Wagner, C. Wimmer, and M. Franz, On the effectiveness of multi-variant program execution for vulnerability detection and prevention, in International Workshop on Security Measurements and Metrics (MetriSec 2010), 2010.

26. M. Franz, E unibus pluram: Massive-scale software diversity as a defense mechanism, in New Security Paradigms Workshop 2010 (NSPW 2010), 2010.

27. A. Avizienis and L. Chen, On the implementation of n-version programming for software fault tolerance during execution, *IEEE COMPSAC 77*, pp. 149–155, 1977.

28. C. Zeigler and B. P. Seo, DEVS namespace for interoperable DEVS/SOA, in 2009 Winter Simulation Conference, 2009.

29. D. Gisolfi, Web services architect: Part 1, An introduction to dynamic e-business, 2012. Available at http://www.ibm.com/developerworks/webservices/library/ws-arc1/.

30. R. Ommering, Building product populations with software components, University of Groningen, 2004.

31. M. Chew and D. Song, Mitigating buffer overflows by operating system randomization. Carnegie Mellon University, pp. 2–197, 2002.

32. R. Feldt, Generating multiple diverse software versions with genetic programming, in 24th EUROMICRO Conference (EUROMICRO '98), 1998.

33. L. Hatton, N-version design versus one good version, *IEEE Software*, vol. 14, pp. 71–76, 1997.

34. R. Pucella and F. Schneider, Independence from obfuscation: A semantic framework for diversity, in IEEE Computer Security Foundations Workshop, 2006.

35. PaX, PaX, 2001. Available at http://pax.grsecurity.net.

36. C. Cowan, S. Beattie, J. Johansen, and P. Wagle, PointGuard: Protecting pointers from buffer overflow vulnerabilities, in USENIX Security Symposium, 2003.

37. J. Xu, Z. Kalbarczyk, and R. K. Iyer, Transparent runtime randomization for security, in Symposium on Reliable and Distributed Systems (SRDS), 2003.

38. R. P. Wilson and M. S. Lam, Efficient context-sensitive pointer analysis for C programs, in ACM SIGPLAN Conference on Programming Language Design and Implementation, 1995.

39. F. Cohen, Operating system protection through program evolution, *Computers and Security*, 1993.

40. C. Pu, A. Black, C. Cowan, and J. Walpole, A specialization toolkit to increase the diversity of operating systems, in ICMAS Workshop on Immunity-Based Systems, 1996.

41. J. E. Just and M. Cornwell, Review and analysis of synthetic diversity for breaking monocultures, in *ACM Workshop on Rapid Malcode (WORM '04)*, pp. 23–32, 2004.

42. D. A. Holland, A. T. Lim, and M. I. Seltzer, An architecture a day keeps the hacker away, *SIGARCH Computer Architecture News*, vol. 33, pp. 34–41, 2005.

43. J. C. L. Knight, J. W. Davidson, D. Evans, A. Nguyen-Tuong, and C. Wang, Genesis: A framework for achieving software component diversity, Technical Report AFRL-IF-RS-TR-2007-9, University of Virginia, January, 2007.

44. B. Salamat, T. Jackson, A. Gal, and M. Franz, Intrusion detection using parallel execution and monitoring of program variants in user-space, in *Eurosys 2009*, 2009.

45. B. Salamat, A. Gal, and M. Franz, Reverse stack execution in a multi-variant execution environment, in Workshop on Compiler and Architectural Techniques for Application Reliability and Security (CATARS '08), 2008.

46. B. Salamat, T. J. A. Gal, K. Manivannan, G. Wagner, and M. Franz, Multi-variant program execution: Using multi-core systems to defuse buffer-overflow vulnerabilities, in International Workshop on Multi-Core Computing Systems (MuCoCoS 2008), 2008.

47. M. Franz, E unibus pluram: Massive-scale software diversity as a defense mechanism, in New Security Paradigms Workshop 2010 (NSPW 2010), 2010.
48. A. Avizienis and L. Chen, On the implementation of n-version programming for software fault tolerance during execution, *IEEE COMPSAC 77*, pp. 149–155, 1977.
49. C. Zou, W. Gong, D. Towsley, and L. Gao, The monitoring and early detection of internet worms, *IEEE/ACM Transactions on Networking (TON)*, vol. 13, pp. 961–974, 2005.
50. Symantec, W32.bugbear@mm, 2002. Available at http://securityresponse.symantec.com/avcenter/venc/data/w32.bugbear@mm.%html.
51. X. Chen, J. Andersen, Z. M. Mao, M. Bailey, and J. Nazario, Towards an understanding of anti-virtualization and anti-debugging behavior in modern malware, in International Conference on Dependable Systems and Networks, 2008.
52. S. Sze and W. Tiong, A comparison between heuristic and metaheuristic methods for solving the multiple traveling salesman problem, World Academy of Science, Engineering and Technology, 2007.
53. W. Podgórski, Artificial intelligence methods in virus detection and recognition—Introduction to heuristic scanning, 2012. Available at http://podgorski.wordpress.com.
54. J. C. Knight and N. G. Leveson, An experimental evaluation of the assumption of independence in multiversion programming, *IEEE Transactions on Software Engineering*, vol. 12, pp. 96–109, 1986.
55. N. Jorstad and T. S. Landgrave, Cryptographic algorithm metrics, in 20th National Information Systems Security Conference, 1997.
56. J. Haack, G. Fink, E. Fulp, and W. Maiden, Cooperative infrastructure defense, in Workshop on Visualization for Computer Security (VizSec), 2008.
57. W. M. Maiden, DualTrust, a trust management model for swarm-based autonomic computing systems, Washington State University, 2010.
58. W. M. Maiden, I. Dionysiou, D. A. Frincke, G. A. Fink, and D. E. Bakken, DualTrust: A distributed trust model for swarm-based autonomic computing systems, *Data Privacy Management and Autonomous Spontaneous Security*, 2010.
59. Y. Lee, A pre-kernel agent platform for security assurance, in IEEE Symposium on Intelligent Agent (IA), 2011.
60. A. Abraham, R. Jain, J. Thomas, and S. Y. Han, D-SCIDS: Distributed soft computing intrusion detection system, *Journal of Network and Computer Applications*, vol. 30, pp. 81–98, 2007.
61. S. Wu and W. Banzhaf, The use of computational intelligence in intrusion detection systems: A review, *Applied Soft Computing*, vol. 10, pp. 1–35, 2010.
62. S. Mukherjee, FPGA based network security architecture for high speed networks, MTech, 2001.
63. M. Otey, A. Parthasarathy, A. Ghoting, S. Li, S. Narravula, and D. Panda, Towards NIC based intrusion detection, in the *9th ACM SIGKDD International Conference on Knowledge Discovery and Data Mining*, pp. 723–728, 2003.
64. I. Santos, Y. Penya, J. Devesa, and P. Bringas, N-Grams-based file signatures for malware detection, in 11th International Conference on Enterprise Information Systems (ICEIS), 2009.
65. S. Prayurachatuporn and L. Benedicenti, Increasing the reliability of control systems with agent technology, ACM SIGAPP Applied Computing, 2001.
66. R. Lemos, White House network attack highlights need for stronger defenses, 2012. Available at http://www.eweek.com/security/white-house-network-attack-highlights-need-for-stronger-defenses/.
67. E. H. Spafford, Computer viruses as artificial life, *Journal of Artificial Life*, vol. 1, pp. 249–265, 1994.
68. A. Avizienis and L. Chen, On the implementation of n-version programming for software fault tolerance during execution, *IEEE COMPSAC 77*, pp. 149–155, 1977.

Steven Zittrower and Cliff C. Zou

CONTENTS

8.1   INTRODUCTION

Encryption is a method that secures information by making it illegible or indistinguishable from random noise to anyone who does not have some privileged information, a key. The practice of using cryptography to encrypt sensitive information has been around for millennia. For thousands of years, a major tenet was that the encrypted information was unusable until decrypted. This served well until recently, when the vast number of documents needing to be encrypted has made decrypting individual documents to find query results infeasible in practice. Searchable encryption was invented to solve the problem of how to find keywords in documents that are encrypted without decrypting the entire corpus set.

Searchable encryption is not a new concept, but all current methods have failed in various aspects that keep them from becoming common or mainstream. Most proposed methods utilize advanced mathematical structures such as Bloom filters or trap doors, but they typically only allow for Boolean searches and do not support phrase searching [1–3]. Sub-word matching, exact matches, regular expressions, natural language searches, frequency ranking, and proximity-based queries are all forms of searching that modern search engines employ and users expect to have. For example, being able to search for "heart attack" and distinguish between results related to myocardial infarction (heart attack) as opposed to "an anxiety attack that caused heart palpitation" is important for the adoption of any searchable encryption scheme. Current methods are incapable of performing this kind of phrase searching. Even ranked word proximity searches, a search that ranks results based on how close the query keywords are together, has not been fully implemented by previous research. The closest previous methods stop at ranking documents only by the number of times a keyword appears in the documents and whether the keyword is within predefined locations [4].

Cloud computing, and specifically data as a service (DaaS), is one of the fastest growing technologies in computing today. A recent study by Market Research Media estimated that U.S. spending on cloud computing will experience a 40% compound annual growth over the next five years [5]. This is driven by a substantial cost savings for storing data on the cloud. Reports show that the cost of storing data on the cloud can be up to three times cheaper than onsite storage [6]. With the growing adoption of cloud computing, it is important to have encrypted searching methods that work between clients and cloud servers.

A recent string of widely publicized data breaches in the cloud, such as an attack on the Gmail accounts of U.S. government officials [7] and a massive attack on Sony in which thousands of credit card numbers and millions of customers' personal information were lost [8], have shown that third-party cloud providers cannot be fully trusted to safeguard data. These attacks have further illustrated the need for securely encrypting private information.

By making use of a trusted client-side server to encrypt and decrypt words and metadata, we can store our files and search index offsite on untrusted clouds while ensuring the integrity of the encrypted data and fulfilling potential government or industry regulations on sensitive data.

We consider the scenario in which an organization outsources its internal data to a public cloud, or generally speaking, we consider the case in which the data owner has the authority and ability to set up a trusted proxy for access to its encrypted data in the cloud. All of the organization's employees are considered to be "clients" for the encrypted data search. It would be easy and practical for the organization to set up a trusted proxy between the cloud and its employees. The trusted proxy does all the encryption and decryption of the encrypted data stored on the cloud; that is, clients have no knowledge of the security keys. Thus, if an employee's computer is compromised or the employee is an inside attacker, once permissions of this employee have been revoked, the encrypted data is still safe on the cloud. This chapter presents a novel approach to allow for phrase searching and query proximity ranking for search queries on encrypted data in the cloud. Neither the source documents nor the search index database needs to be hosted on local or trusted servers. Both of them will be encrypted and hosted in remote public cloud servers. Furthermore, we present a technique to incorporate headlining (i.e., returning words that appear near the found searched terms) in our method.

Contributions discussed in this chapter include the following:

- An encrypted searching method able to search for words and phrases composed of multiple keywords
- A corresponding ranking algorithm that ranks results based on query location and frequency
- A complete prototype of our proposed search methods using a realistic large-scale dataset of more than 500,000 documents that can complete encrypted searches within seconds
- A comprehensive experimental evaluation on the overhead, speed, bandwidth, and security of our method

The rest of the chapter is organized as follows. Section 8.2 discusses related work and previous research in encrypted searching. In Section 8.3 we present our method for encrypted phrase and proximity-ranked searching and discuss the implementation of these methods in Section 8.4. We analyze our results and evaluate our design in Section 8.5. Section 8.6 covers security attacks and improvements. Section 8.7 covers future research directions and impacts of other solutions. We conclude in Section 8.8.

8.2 RELATED WORK AND BACKGROUND

In the past, most keyword searching encryption schemes focused on a searchable index of words that remain hidden to the server until a one-way trapdoor function is given [9]. These indexes have more recently been stored as a Bloom filter to decrease the size of the index and increase the security by reducing the chance of active server attacks by allowing for false positives [2,3,10]. Bellovin and Cheswick [10] published a method for storing an index using Bloom filters and its corresponding cipher functions such that neither the querier nor the receiver knew of each other's search or collection. Bellovin went on to modify this paper [3] to support database searching functions. Most related works in this field focus on single-keyword searches or Boolean searches. However, recently, papers on multi-keyword ranked searches [11] and very limited proximity ranking [1] have been published.

Aviv et al. [2] developed a method to securely search files on a remote storage-based server. They encrypt and hash the words into a Bloom filter, thus keeping the index secure. However, their method provides no way of including phrases or proximity-ranked results as their index does not store any keyword location data.

This method was further improved [11,12] by creating a design that supports multi-keyword searches and ranked searching. Although this is a leap ahead of previous work, as it provides ranked results and multiple keyword searching, it still fails to include any ranking based on word location proximity or phrase searching capabilities.

Encrypted database research, especially that in the area of the publisher/subscriber model, has produced interesting results that corollary to our research. Raiciu et al. [13] and Srivatsa et al. [14] both developed methods of maintaining confidentially in a content-based publish/subscribe. While our model technically only has one subscriber (the trusted client-side server), further research in this area could potentially allow for direct cloud-to-client communication.

Another area of research that is similar to ours is public-key searchable encryption. Boneh et al. [15] published a method to allow a public-key encrypted document's owner to provide a gateway server a specialized trapdoor to test whether a word is contained in the owner's encrypted documents. Many extensions have been given to allow multiple keywords [16] and conjunctive searching with keyword subsets [17]. While these are similar to our end goal, they are very limited in scope as the documents must be encrypted with a single user's private key and keywords to search for must be known in advance. Also, while conjunctive and disjunctive searching is possible, proximity ranking is not.

Current research focuses on two fronts: adding features to previous designs (such as keyword ranking, proximity ranking, predicate and disjunctive searches, and Boolean operators) [11,18,19] and creating more computationally efficient encrypted searching designs [20].

Artzi et al. introduced the closest design that does support proximity ranking [1]. It divides each document into 64 separate sections and stores the hashes of this metadata along with each keyword separately in a Bloom filter. This allows the search engine to tell whether a word is within a generous range of another. While this does support limited proximity ranking, it still lacks support of phrase searching.

Our model is unique and novel as it implements phrase and proximity-based ranking of search results. It abandons using a Bloom filter to store document information in favor of a relational database. Our method trades the small storage size and the secure nature of Bloom filters for a more flexible, but larger, data structure. We then take extreme caution and diligence to prevent information leakage related to active and passive attacks on the database, search query, and search results.

Where previous models were limited in their search functionality and, therefore, unlikely to be used in commercial settings, our model allows for a full complement of modern search features, including but not limited to stemming (reducing words to their root), lexicographic parsing, Boolean searching, phrase searching, and frequency and proximity ranking of the results. Currently, no other research offers a full set of these features.

8.3   PROPOSED ENCRYPTED PHRASE SEARCHING

"Proximity-ranked searching" implicitly ranks documents by a function, f, that is directly proportional to the distance the multiple keywords in the search phrase appear from each other. In addition, our advanced search ranking algorithm (presented later in Section 8.3.6) also implements search querying techniques presented in previous research, such as Boolean searching [21] and multi-keyword ranking [11].

To allow for proximity ranking, the location information of keywords must be preserved in the encrypted index created from the data corpus. This is a challenge that previous research relying on Bloom filters cannot easily overcome. Instead of using a highly compressible index, such as a Bloom filter, we make use of a standard database to store the three valuable components to each document: document reference, keywords, and keyword locations.

8.3.1   OVERVIEW

In this section, we describe the basic architecture and system overview of the method we present to enable encrypted phrase and proximity-ranked searching. In Sections 8.3.3 and 8.3.5, we formally define the indexing and searching methods, respectively. Section 8.4 covers the implementation and architectural details of our phrase ranking methods and algorithms.

Our architecture makes use of an encrypted index that is generated prior to searching. A trusted client-side server generates the encrypted index and transfers this index to an untrusted cloud server. Further details on this index and how to create it are discussed in Section 8.3.3.

Figure 8.1 outlines the general process of our proposed encrypted phrase searching. First, the client sends a plain text search query to a trusted client-side server (step 1). The client-side server encrypts all keywords in the search query individually using symmetric-key encryption; it then truncates the encrypted keywords to a set number of bits to improve security by allowing for collisions and queries the untrusted cloud server for the documents containing the set of truncated encrypted keywords (the order of these encrypted keywords will be randomized) (step 2). The cloud server does a database query of its encrypted index and returns to the client-side server encrypted data that corresponds to document paths, a truncated encrypted keyword index offset, and encrypted keyword locations (step 3). The client-side server decrypts this data first. From the newly decrypted keyword index offset, it can then determine which returned results are actually for

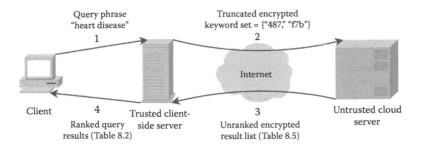

FIGURE 8.1 Flowchart of the proposed encrypted phrase searching procedure. For a company that outsources its dataset to an untrusted public cloud, a "trusted client-side server" is set up internally. The "client" represents any company employee or user.

the keywords searched and which are simply collisions. It discards those collisions and then runs a newly proposed ranking algorithm (presented in Section 8.3.6) that filters and/or sorts the pertinent returned documents based on relevant keyword locations and frequency. Finally, it sends this ranked listing to the original client (step 4). At this point, the client can peruse the results for the desired documents and, if desired, perform a request to the untrusted cloud server to retrieve the desired encrypted documents.

Some prior research on encrypted searching does not have a trusted client-side server in their architectures. We believe it is practical and reasonable to assume that the data owner can set up their own trusted server locally, which is not difficult for a data owner and does not introduce much overhead cost. In addition, the trusted local server can greatly simplify the networking architecture and protocol design in encrypted searching and improve data security against attacks.

Insider attacks, intrusion detection, and intrusion prevention are possible through the client-side server. Because all traffic is routed through a centralized server before queries are processed and before results are decrypted, the client-side server acts as a middleman who can inspect queries and results for authenticity, signs of tampering, or abuse. An easy-to-implement intrusion detection scheme for preventing unauthorized access that would be of use is a public-private key. The client digitally signs each search query with his or her private key before it is sent to the trusted client-side server. The client-side server verifies that the client did, in fact, generate the query by using the client's public-key. Furthermore, by reversing the process, results from the cloud can be digitally encrypted by the trusted-client server so that only the authorized recipient can decrypt the search results.

Intrusion prevention and detection measures from the cloud are based upon the hashes and encryption of all cloud index items and that the decrypted data follows a well-defined format (Table 8.1). If an attacker or malicious cloud provider without knowledge of the secret key (κ) were to modify the encrypted index, any changes would almost certainly not decrypt in the expected format. By checking the returned and decrypted result format for errors, it is possible to detect data corruption, intrusion, and tampering.

8.3.2 Notations

This section describes the notations and assumptions made for our model.

δ: The document containing keywords to be searched for
κ: The encryption key, known only to the client-side server
k_i and K: The individual keywords and list of keywords, respectively, that the user wishes to query for

k_i' and K': k_i and K after being encrypted, respectively. $E(k_i, \kappa) = k_i'$ where E is some symmetric-key cryptographic function

l_i: The encrypted locations of k_i' in δ

R: Proximity ranking function. Inputs documents, keywords, and locations and returns a ranking for each document

τ: Encrypted keyword truncation index used to map the encrypted truncated keyword with its full counterpart

β: Number of bits used to store each of the encrypted keywords

8.3.3 INDEXING

In our model, prior to searching for an individual document δ, the trusted client-side server must generate an encrypted index of the corpus. Then, the index is sent to the untrusted cloud server. Searching and returning of query results takes place by running SQL queries over the encrypted index.

For illustration purposes, Table 8.1 shows a subset of four documents from our example corpus that could be returned from the search query 'heart disease'. The weighted rankings of each of these documents is listed in Table 8.2. DocID 13 is not listed in the ranking table because it does not contain the word 'disease'. This example will be used in the following sections to illustrate our searching and ranking methods.

The unencrypted database index of the illustrated four documents (in Table 8.1) is shown in Table 8.3 and the corresponding partially encrypted version is shown in Table 8.4. Each row in the encrypted index table corresponds to one document δ in the corpus. Each row contains two columns: an arbitrarily assigned unique document ID (DocID) and a specialized data structure that contains truncated symmetric-key encrypted keywords associated with encrypted versions of the keyword's location in δ (Word Vectors). In addition, this data string contains an offset that is used to map the truncated encrypted keyword with its full version (stored on the trusted client-side server).

Table 8.2 depicts the offset and the keyword locations unencrypted to better show the structure of the string. In actuality, these characters are concatenated and encrypted together using a block cipher, thus making it unfeasible to determine the offset or keyword locations without the decryption key κ. Without loss of generality, we assume that the cryptographic keys used for both

TABLE 8.1

Four Example Documents Sorted by DocID

DocID	Content
3	… it was a *disease* of the *heart* that induced …
5	… *heart disease* is the leading cause of death in the …
10	… his *diseased* ideas led to his employees becoming *disheartened*…
13	… his small *heart* grew three sizes that day …

TABLE 8.2

Document Sorted in Order of Suggested Ranks for Search Query "Heart Disease"

Ranking	DocID
0.957	5
0.570	3
0.493	10

TABLE 8.3

Unencrypted Representation of the Database That the Cloud Server Stores

DocID	Word Vectors						
3	*diseas:3*	*heart:6*	induc:8				
5	*heart:1*	*diseas:2*	led:5	caus:6	death:8		
10	his:1,6	*diseas:2*	idea:3	led:4	employe:7	becom:8	*heart:9*
13	his:1	small:2	*heart:3*	grew:4	three:5	size:6	day:8

Note: Keywords are to the left of the colon and the location in the documents is in bold. Multiple locations are delimitated by commas.

encryptions are the same key κ and that κ can be used for decryption as well. Only the trusted client-side server has access to the value of κ.

Once the encrypted index is transferred to the untrusted cloud server, an inverted index, Table 8.3, based on the encrypted index, is generated by the cloud server to facilitate the searching speed of the index.

8.3.4 KEYWORD TRUNCATION

A main attack point on the proposed scheme thus far is that it is highly susceptible to statistical frequency analysis attacks. If each keyword were encrypted individually using a deterministic encryption method, a nosey cloud provider could compare the encrypted index with a language probability table to estimate which words map to which encrypted words. To combat this problem, we truncate the encrypted words to a predefined number of bits β. Therefore, numerous collisions are created because the entire encrypted keyword space size has been reduced to 2^β as seen in Figure 8.10.

This method can also thwart a separate analysis attack based on multiple keyword searches. Because keywords are likely to be related to each other, it would be possible for a malicious cloud provider or user to create associations between multiple encrypted keywords. If even one encrypted keyword is decrypted, such a table could reveal a large amount of information about the data. To illustrate this point, take the following example, in which, for simplicity, encrypted words are only five alphanumeric characters long. Without this feature, if the search terms "United Nations," "United States," "United Airlines," and "United Healthcare" with unique encrypted keywords returned of "ABCEF 1A3B5," "ABCEF 6C8D0," "ABCEF 2E4F6," and "ABCEF 5A7B9," respectively, had previously been searched for, an attack could map store this information. It could now be inferred that the encrypted value "ABCEF" is likely a common preceding word or adjective; thus, an attacker has gained information about a distinct encrypted keyword. In addition, with enough analysis of this type, if it is ever guessed that "ABCEF" corresponds to "united," each other encrypted word in the searches are now known to likely be a term related to "united." Having a random, many-to-one, mapping of keywords to encrypted keywords prevents attacks of this nature from reducing the security of the index.

The trusted client-side server creates a unique keyword truncation index number for each encrypted keyword. A table that is stored on the client-side server maps the truncated bits and index number with the fully encrypted keyword. Each index number is stored along with the keyword locations in the encrypted index. This string is encrypted using AES and a randomized salt. As many multiple keywords now map to the same bits, it makes any statistical frequency analysis attack far less useful.

The security gained from the truncated encrypted keyword collisions does come at a cost though. Because it is impossible, prior to decryption, to determine which keywords in the collision set were actually being searched for, they must all be returned, decrypted, and then filtered. Therefore, as shown in Figures 8.6 and 8.10, the more collisions there are, the more bandwidth and computation power that is required per search.

8.3.5 Searching

In this section, we outline functions and methods that can be called to search documents from a client to an untrusted cloud server without transmitting or leaking nontrivial data to the cloud server.

When the search begins, the client sends the query phrase with multiple keywords, $k_1, ..., k_n$, to a client-side server, which concatenates the keywords to a list, K (step 1 in Figure 8.1). The client-side server then encrypts each $k \in K$ using κ in which the order of keywords is randomized. Each keyword in this list is then truncated to β bits to create the encrypted keyword list, K'. In our reference example shown in Figure 8.1, the client searches for "heart disease." Therefore, with $\beta = 12$ bits, this phrase is transformed into "487 f7b." The client-side server then transfers this encrypted query, K', to the untrusted cloud server (step 2). In Section 8.4.5.2 we discuss other improvements and performance enhancements that can be implemented during this phase, such as stemming (reducing words to their root form) and the removal of commonly found words.

The untrusted cloud server parses K' into individual encrypted keywords k' and, using the inverted index (Table 8.3), efficiently determines the documents, δ, that contain a k'. It then references Table 8.2 to find the encrypted location(s), l_i', for each k_i' in δ. In our example, only documents 3, 5, and 10 contain both encrypted keywords 487 and f7b, so these DocIDs, the keyword locations, and the truncated keyword index as shown in Table 8.4 are sent back to the trusted client-side server (step 3).

The client-side server parses the results that the cloud server returns, which include the document's IDs, paths, and associated encrypted keywords, index, and encrypted locations l'. Each l_i' is decrypted to the truncation index τ and l_i. A proximity ranking function R, hosted by the client-side server, is utilized to meaningfully rank the results as shown in Table 8.5. This proposed ranking algorithm is presented next.

8.3.6 Ranking and Phrase Searching

An efficient method of document ranking is critical to the success of our method. To significantly outperform previous Boolean-based encrypted searching methods, we need to develop a strong correlative metric of relevance between keyword queries and documents. Furthermore, to enable both phrase searching and proximity-based ranking, the ranking algorithm must, at a minimum, use the distance between keywords in its formula.

In this chapter, we develop a new ranking algorithm that is based on a relevance-ranking algorithm presented in [22]. To facilitate the ranking, the authors [22] define two terms: extents and covers. An extent is defined as an ordered pair of location indexes, (p, q), in which, within the range of

---

TABLE 8.4

Partially Encrypted Version of Table 8.1 That Is Stored on the Cloud Server

DocID	Word Vectors						
3	*f7b:0-3*	*487:0-6*	477:0-8				
5	*487:0-1*	*f7b:0-2*	55d:0-5	d37:0-6	ff3:0-8		
10	110:0-1,6	*f7b:0-2*	aef:0-3	55d:0-4	7e9:0-7	498:0-8	*487:0-9*
13	110:0-1	99f:0-2	*487:0-3*	2f3:0-4	498:1-5	667:0-6	eef:0-8

Note: Both the keywords and the locations have been encrypted with a symmetric-key cipher. The encrypted keywords have been truncated to 12-bits. To improve readability for the reader, the index of the keyword in the keyword collision table (the number succeeding the colon), and the location data are shown unencrypted here; they are, in fact, encrypted in the actual implementation.

TABLE 8.5

Inverted Index Generated from Table 8.2 That Shows Which Document Contains Each Keyword

Word	DocID	Word	DocID
110	10,13	his	10,13
477	3	induce	3
487	3,5,10,13	heart	3,5,10,13
498	10,13	become/three	10,13
...	...	...	...
f7b	3,5,10	disease	3,5,10
ff3	5	death	5
(a) Encrypted		(b) Unencrypted	

Note: (a) is the version the cloud server stores and (b) is an unencrypted version, not stored by the cloud, for reference only. Note that "become" and "three" map to the same location when truncated.

these indexes, every keyword is contained, inclusively. Any extent that does not contain an extent of smaller size within it is called a *cover*, *c*. The ranking score, *R*, thus increases if documents contain more covers and the cover distance $(q - p)$ is small.

$$(1)R = \sum_{c\in C} r_c \tag{8.1}$$

$$r = \begin{cases} 1.0, & p-q+1 \le H \\ \dfrac{H}{p-q+1}, & \text{otherwise} \end{cases} \tag{8.2}$$

$$r = \begin{cases} 1.0, & p-q+1 = |K| \\ 0, & \text{otherwise} \end{cases} \tag{8.3}$$

$$r = \begin{cases} 1.0, & p-q+1 = |K| \text{ and } l_1 < l_2 < \ldots < l_{|K|} \\ \dfrac{H}{p-q+1}, & \text{otherwise} \end{cases} \tag{8.4}$$

R is calculated by summing the partial ranking score of each cover in the complete cover set, *C*, as show in Equation 8.1. Three additional equations are used for three different search types.

Non-phrase proximity–ranked search (Equation 8.2): The default non-phrase search scores the documents based on the keyword query location. Each cover is given a ranking between 0 and 1. A score of 1 is given if all the words in the cover, $p - q + 1$, are no more than *H* words apart. Otherwise, it is given a score inversely proportional to the distance of the cover. Previous research has shown that $H = 16$ produces good results [22].

Unordered-phrase searching (Equation 8.3): Unordered-phrase searching is defined as a search for a list of words that appear together with no other words in between, but the order of the words is not considered. This is useful over traditional phrase searching if the order of the words is commonly transposed. This is oftentimes the case in some search phrases, such as dates (i.e., "January 1, 2011" vs. "1 January 2011"). A score of 1 is given to each cover that contains all keywords successively, that is, $(p - q + 1) = |K|$ where $|K|$ is the magnitude of the keyword set. All other covers receive a score of 0. Intuitively, this counts the number of times each phrase is contained in a document and gives it a rank equal to that count.

Phrase searching (Equation 8.4): Phrase searching is very similar to semi-phrase searching except the ordering of the words matters. A search for "January 1, 2011" would not find a document that only contained "1 January 2011." Therefore, a score of 1 is only given to a cover if its cover distance is $|K|$ and the locations of each keyword, l_i, in that cover are in ascending order relative to their original search query index location.

After ranking, the results are returned to the client (step 4 in Figure 8.1). The client selects the document(s) that he or she wants to read and, via the client-side server, makes a second communication requesting the fully encrypted versions from the cloud. These documents are decrypted by the client-side server and returned to the client in plain text.

8.3.7 HEADLINING

"Headlining," often called "output contexting" or, informally, "snippets," is when the search engine returns to the querier a set number of words or lines that appear before or after the matched search term(s). Headlining is present in many commercially available unencrypted search engines and text search utilities [23]. The content column in Table 8.6 shows an example of headlining for the search query "heart disease." This is an important and key feature as it gives the client a context of how the search term(s) was used in the document, allowing them better insight as to whether to read the full document or not.

8.3.7.1 Naïve Solution

In unencrypted search engines, headlining is possible by returning the indexed words that appear next to the search keywords. Most search engines store word locations in their database. Depending on what indexes are present, headlining can take advantage of spatial locality and simply return the previous and subsequent row. If the document is not indexed by word location, a separate query may have to be processed, but in either case, the overhead is minimal.

Headlining in encrypted search engines is much more difficult as word locations are encrypted and the cloud server has no knowledge of their true values. There is a naïve solution to the problem, however. Because the cloud server does return the encrypted document identifiers, the client-side server can decrypt these values and then create a second request for the full documents. The

---

TABLE 8.6

Encrypted Unranked Results Generated by the Cloud Server and Returned to the Trusted Client-Side Server from the Search Phrase "Heart Disease"

DocID	Encrypted Results	
3	f7b:488Burh1fH	487:F1vFFNWp =
5	487:AjDL7i1Bo = =	f7b:1tsaFlvlBhY
10	F7b:XnSh0NB+u	487:JnhVD5N7a

Note: The keyword truncation index and the location data are shown in their true encrypted form (in Base 64). DocID 13 is not returned because it does not contain both of the search terms.

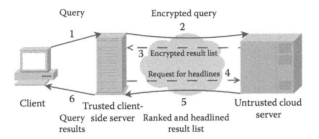

FIGURE 8.2 Headlining is made possible by adding a second handshake between steps 4 and 5. Steps 1, 2, and 3 are the same as the corresponding steps in Figure 8.1.

client-side server could then search the full documents for the corresponding keywords and create headlines in this manner.

This solution is poor. The bandwidth required to send a potentially large number of fully encrypted documents would create a bottleneck for even the fastest Internet connections. This could be substantially alleviated by only requesting the documents ranked highest from the ranking function. However, by reducing the bandwidth overhead, we increase the potential information leakage. By immediately requesting the full documents of the top results, we give the untrusted cloud server insight into what is contained in the encrypted documents. To efficiently implement headlining, we need an elegant, lighter weight, and more secure solution.

8.3.7.2 Proposed Solution

To implement headlining without the downfalls of the naïve solution in our proposed encryption search engine, we can first divide full documents into fixed-sized parts and then conduct document encryption on each part (see Figure 8.11). Each part would be stored with an encrypted unique identifier that includes both the full document's ID and the part's section number. The details of document splitting and its security repercussions are discussed in Section 8.6.3.

A second handshake is then added between the trusted client-side server and the untrusted cloud server. As shown in Figure 8.2, after receiving the unranked encrypted result list (step 3), the client-side server proceeds as normal, decrypts the results, and ranks them. From the top results, the client-side server then determines the subsection names and queries the cloud for these encrypted subsections of the documents (step 4). After the cloud returns these subsections of documents (step 5), the client-side server decrypts them, formats the output, and returns the headlining to the client (step 6).

While our method does allow for such advanced search techniques as headlining, extreme care must be taken to ensure additional information is not transmitted to the untrusted cloud. As discussed in Section 8.6.3, the naïve approach described above leaks information regarding query ranks and individual word locations. Given a large set of search histories, it is conceivable that a malicious cloud could attack the encrypted documents via frequency-based analysis attacks.

For example, to ensure not exposing additional information to the untrusted cloud, all documents' fragmented parts and their document IDs and section IDs are encrypted. The cloud cannot tell whether any two encrypted document parts belong to the same document or not. In this way, the cloud cannot infer the query ranks of documents based on the headlining query in step 4.

8.4 IMPLEMENTATION

The following sections of the chapter are divided into three parts in which we detail a phrase ranking encrypted search application we developed to test our design model and obtain experiment results in speed, bandwidth, size, and security. In Section 8.5, we show our experimental results and evaluate our design compared to similar other encrypted and non-encrypted searching designs. Section 8.6 covers security. Future work and further research paths are covered in Section 8.7.

8.4.1 Design Goals

To create usable searching for documents, we must ensure that the following goals and requirements are obtained concurrently.

Intelligent results ranking: Instead of designing a system that return results arbitrarily, by Boolean operators, or word counts as previous research has done, our design must rank the results by an efficient algorithm that ranks documents with keywords that appear closer together higher.

Minimal bandwidth overhead (efficient): The system must be able to return real-time results at high-speeds and utilize only a modest amount of bandwidth.

Minimal information leakage: Ideally, no information other than the outcome of a search would be leaked to the server. In practice, this strict definition is rarely held with perhaps [24] being the only notable exception. We relax this restriction and leak some information that cannot be used to reconstruct data or searches, such as user's search patterns and frequency data associated with encrypted keywords. In Section 8.6, we outline potential attacks that target these leaks and discuss techniques to avoid these.

8.4.2 OpenFTS

To build a working implementation of our encrypted phrase-ranking search, we modified and rewrote the free and open source application OpenFTS written and designed by Bartunov, Sigaev, and Wickstrom [25]. Specifically, OpenFTS is a search engine written in Perl for PostgreSQL. Because PostgreSQL's TextSearch (tsearch2) functionality is inherently made for natural languages and not for encrypted data and custom data structures, it has strict limits on the size of the database rows and type of data allowed in it. MySQL has looser limits on these, and therefore, when rewriting OpenFTS, we modified it such that it would be compatible with MySQL.

OpenFTS's Perl front end allows custom configuration of an indexer, parser, stemmer, dictionaries, search functions, and other cosmetic methods that are not of integral importance to the novelty or functionality of our search method but instead show that our method can be extended to include all of these modern searching devices.

The indexer was completely rewritten to encrypt the corpus of documents prior to sending them to the cloud server. The search function wrapper was modified to encrypt the query and decrypt the results to be further ranked and displayed to the end user.

8.4.3 MySQL Full-Text Search

Full-Text Search is a natural language text search engine that has been integrated into MySQL natively since version 3.23 [26]. It provides the functions and storage of the encrypted documents, location values, and document names.

We chose to use this implementation for its lack of restrictions on the full-text data type field and its support of inverted indexes. Whereas a traditional index maps keys to values (or documents to words in our case), an inverted index reverses this and maps words to the documents that contain them (see Table 8.3). Native support of inverted indexes is a necessity for our search engine to be scalable and efficient when indexing a large repository of documents. While it does support this natively, the indexing built into MySQL would have attempted to index the encrypted location data just as if it were a keyword. This would have created giant index tables and have rendered any index useless. However, through custom modifications to the MySQL source code, we were able to restrict the indexing to only the pertinent data, that is, the truncated encrypted keywords.

8.4.4 Cloud Database Representations

While we built our preliminary implementation using a relational database and Perl, preliminary results (Figure 8.4) indicated that very large datasets might not scale as efficiently as we had hoped. Using a database designed from the ground up for clusters and large cloud computing is one solution to improve performance and help achieve part of our second design goal (efficiency and speed). To this end, we rebuilt, from the ground up, a new version of our system that was based on a cloud, nonrelational, document-oriented database.

While the features of most NoSQL and cloud databases are quite limited to that of the mature and rich feature-set of MySQL, they typically do offer benefits that MySQL does not. Specifically, they offer easy-to-implement horizontal scalability (sharding) to distribute a database over a cluster of computers as well as replica sets and database mirroring. Map/reduce functions replace complex SQL queries to aggregate our encrypted data. However, perhaps the biggest advantage of a NoSQL database is the document-oriented storage. While this does add significant space overhead and increases the total size of the database on the disk, this greatly reduces the complexity, increases the verbosity, and allows for much more efficient sharding because each document is self-contained and can be moved individually.

The overall design of our system transcends any specific database requirements. However, for our experiments we used MongoDB. The same index architecture described in Section 8.3.3 is used with the modification that, instead of each row in the index corresponding to a specific encrypted document, each encrypted document and a set of the truncated and hashed words in that document are stored in their own JSON-like document as shown in Figure 8.3. To allow for quick accessing and querying, the MongoDB database is then indexed on the encrypted document's *docId* and the encrypted word's *truncHash*.

8.4.5 Implementation Outline

To implement a secure searching scheme, we took dedicated care to ensure that our design goals were never broken. Therefore, the trusted client-side server must accomplish all of the indexing, encryption, and decryption.

8.4.5.1 Indexing

Indexing of the corpus takes place prior to keyword searches and is completed by the client-side server. Future and continuous indexing is possible as each document is self-contained in its own encrypted form as shown in Table 8.1 and Figure 8.6. However, recreating the inverted index is a time-consuming task. It is assumed that the encrypted index is updated at an order of magnitude less frequent than keyword searching takes place.

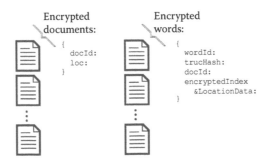

FIGURE 8.3 Every document and a set of its words are stored in JSON-like documents in our cloud database. Each encrypted word is linked to its containing document via the *docId* key. The locations for the word and its hash-collision value are stored in the *encryptedIndex&LocationData* field.

Scripts parse each unencrypted plain text document into its root stems. For example, *diseases* and *diseased* would both become the keyword *disease*. At this point, very common words, such as the conjunctions *and* and *or* as well as other words that appear in most documents but provide little insight or distinguishing value are removed (these common words are called *stop-words*). We encrypt each keyword using a symmetric-key cipher. The location of each keyword in the document is also encrypted. In our implementation, we used AES for its security (any kind of symmetric encryption algorithm can be used in practice). The encrypted keyword is then truncated to a specified number of bits, β. The client then searches the truncated index array for the index number corresponding to this encrypted keyword. If the full encrypted keyword is not already contained in the index array, it is appended to the end, and the truncated index becomes one greater than the previous maximum truncated index for the corresponding bits. The index and location data are salted and encrypted via AES. For the MySQL representation, this is then appended to the encrypted truncated keyword and transferred to the cloud to be stored in a custom-made MySQL structure. Because the NoSQL cloud database is schema-free, we can avoid this complexity and transfer the encrypted truncated keyword and location data separately.

Finally, once the encrypted index is transferred to the untrusted cloud server, an inverted index of the table is created to allow queries to be a function of the number of unique encrypted keywords.

8.4.5.2 Searching

Our implementation of searching closely follows that described in Section 8.3.5. Just as in indexing we modified the OpenFTS code to parse the keyword string for stop-words and stem each keyword to its root, we then encrypt and truncate each keyword using the same AES algorithm, salt, and β value that were used in indexing. A SQL or MongoDB query is formed and transferred to the cloud to run against its database.

In the MySQL implementation, the query is first compared against the inverted index to find which documents (and their corresponding rows in the index) contain the keyword set. Then these rows are analyzed, and the encrypted truncated keyword index and keyword locations are returned to the client-side server.

In the MongoDB implementation, a query will first collect all matching encrypted word's *truncHashes* and return the *docIds* and *encryptedIndex&LocationData*. On conjunctive searches, documents without a full set of matched *truncHashes* will be filtered. The location data is then aggregated by *docId* and returned to the client-side server for decryption.

Our modified OpenFTS code then decrypts the keyword index and locations using the same symmetric key that they were encrypted with. It discards any results with truncated keyword indexes that do not correspond to the keyword being searched and then calls the ranking function described in Section 8.3.6. All document ranks are then normalized, sorted, and thresholded to the maximum number of results requested. This sorted list is finally returned to the client.

8.5 EVALUATION

To evaluate our proposed encrypted phrase searching and ranking search engine, we indexed our encrypted modified search engines and an unencrypted standard OpenFTS/MySQL full-text search database as our control with more than 500,000 emails. Numerous queries were run to compare the two search engines for speed, bandwidth, size, and security. It is expected that our methods would add certain overhead to all of the benchmarks.

8.5.1 DATA SET AND EXPERIMENT SETUP

For our sample data set, we used a collection of more than 500,000 emails from the former Enron Corporation that were made public by the Federal Energy Regulatory Commission during their investigation of Enron in 2003. This plain text email archive, with attachments removed, contains more than 1.8 GB's worth of data. We formatted the data to be compatible with our indexer and removed attachments and nontext words, such as XML tags and binary data. The email archive we used, along with a comprehensive description of the data set, can be found at http://www.cs.cmu. edu/~enron/.

So far, we have found little previous research on encrypted search engines that have ever tested their system on a similarly sized corpus. Many used corpuses of size less than 1% of ours [2,11] while others [1] stopped their results at 100,000 documents.

We used four commodity computers to conduct the experiments. For the MySQL experiments, one computer behaves as the client-side server and another computer behaves as the cloud server. For the MongoDB experiments the data was sharded across three computers with one of the three computers also acting as the shard server; the last computer takes the role of the client-side server. Each computer was installed with Ubuntu 11.10, MySQL 5.1.58, MongoDB 2.4, Perl 5.12.4, and OpenFTS 0.40 as well as the custom-built software described in Sections 8.3 and 8.4. These computers were connected through Ethernet LAN. We used a Linux IP network monitor, IPTraf, to capture the network traffic between the client-side server and the cloud server [27].

8.5.2 Speed

For our search speed experiments, we eliminated the network overhead, lag, and transfer times associated with communicating across a WAN and analyzed these aspects in Section 8.5.3. Instead, we only calculate the time it takes for the cloud server to run its queries and return with the results. Furthermore, to eliminate external factors, such as initial index caching and set-up times, all searches are run on a hot database.

The speed of individual search queries varies proportionally to the number of documents containing the set of keywords in the query and the number of keywords in the query. The latter is due to the overhead of filtering keyword results in conjunctive searches that are not contained in all documents. Figure 8.4 shows this relationship for queries contained in 100 documents to 22,000 documents. Most reasonably, descriptive queries are returned in well under 10 seconds. It should be noted that many extremely common words, such as conjunctions and pronouns, are included in our stop-word set and thus not included in the index. The difference between MongoDB and MySQL in

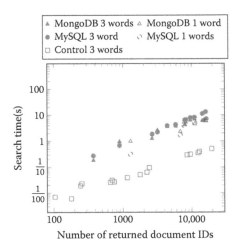

FIGURE 8.4 The average search time in relation to the number of documents returned with a total corpus size of 517,214 documents and $\beta = 12$ bits. Search time is proportional to the number of documents returned and the number of keywords searched for. For comparison, the times for an unencrypted search are provided as well.

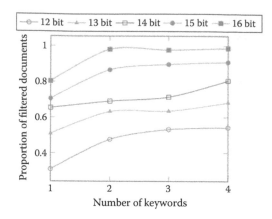

FIGURE 8.5   The proportion of documents for each keyword bit-size that make it past the truncated keyword index filter, that is, the proportion of documents that contain the word(s) that we searched for.

this regard is not significant. However, MongoDB tends to perform slightly worse when the number of returned results is small but better on larger return sets.

While the more keywords used increases the search time for encrypted searches, it is mitigated by the fact that it also considerably decreases the number of documents returned. It is worth noting that for unencrypted searches adding additional keywords adds relatively no overtime time (Figure 8.5).

A prohibitive part of extremely large search returns is the bandwidth considerations of transferring the results to the client-side server to be ranked. Because documents cannot be excluded prior to being decrypted, the server must either arbitrarily trim its result set (thus risking filtering a document the user was actually searching for) or return megabytes' worth of data to be filtered by the client-side server. Server trimming and suggesting the user create more descriptive search queries are compromises that we could implement to handle the problem gracefully.

8.5.3   BANDWIDTH USAGE

In the encrypted method, bandwidth is dependent on the number of documents returned, the number of query keywords, and the number of instances the query words appear in those documents. However, the unencrypted comparison engine is only dependent on the number of documents returned. For example, "stock" appears often in the documents in our testing data set.* It is located in 14,828 emails out of the 517,214 emails in the data set with a total of 63,316 appearance times overall for an average of 4.27 times per email. However, another 1412 documents contain words that encrypt to the same bits as "stock" (when truncated). These additional documents are returned as well. The bandwidth required to search for "stock" in our encrypted MySQL database is roughly 1214 KB and even larger in MongoDB. "Dear," on the other hand, is a word that typically begins letters in the English language but rarely appears otherwise. It is contained in 20,093 emails but only 1.12 times per email. In addition, 1076 other documents have keywords that collide with "dear." Therefore, the bandwidth needed to search for "dear," 1094 KB (MySQL), is less than that of "stock" even though there are almost 5000 more emails with "dear" in them. In contrast to the encrypted searches, both of these search terms lie almost directly on the line of best fit for the comparable unencrypted searches and require 1.6 to 3.8 times less bandwidth than their encrypted MySQL counterparts.

---

* "Stock" and "stock price" were routinely used multiple times per email in the Enron company-wide emails.

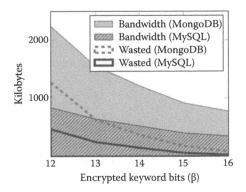

FIGURE 8.6 The average bandwidth used for a three-word search phrase. The fewer bits per index word used results in roughly 21% more bandwidth needed to transfer the database result set and the more filtered results (wasted bandwidth, that is, bandwidth associated with documents that were returned only because of keyword collisions).

Figure 8.6 compares the overall bandwidth usage for an average three-word search with different β values for both the MySQL and MongoDB implementations. The size of the data that is eventually filtered out due to hash collisions is shown with dashed lines. As stated previously, MongoDB adds considerable overhead due to each truncated hashed keyword being contained in its own JSON-like document in the database. This is an unavoidable artifact of NoSQL databases and the design choice to index each truncated keyword separately. The size was slightly reduced by reducing the length of the key names (contained in each and every document) to only 8 bits.

A considerable amount of bandwidth transferred is due to the salting of the AES encrypted blocks. In fact, because each keyword's location and truncated keyword index is salted individually and each salt is 8 bytes plus an attached header, between 25% and 50% of the bandwidth is due to the salt. By reducing the size of the salt or removing the header altogether, this overhead can be greatly reduced while the former sacrifices security; the latter's only consequence is slightly more complexity on the client-side server for decryption.

The bandwidth needed to perform a search varies by the number of keywords specified. Figure 8.7 compares bandwidth usage for searches between one and three keywords. While the increase in the number of keywords used does increase the bandwidth by roughly 90% per keyword, this effect is countered by the fact that adding keywords substantially decreases the

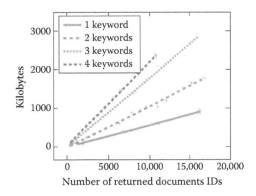

FIGURE 8.7 Bandwidth needed for 12-bit truncated keywords with variable number of keywords in the search query with the MySQL implementation. The trend line for each group is shown in the graph.

number of documents returned. For example, to return 10,048 documents with one keyword, a relatively uncommon word, "green," was chosen. However, to return roughly the same number of documents with four keywords, four of the most common words in the English language had to be used ("make," "time," "first," "like"). Each of these words is between 10 to 50 times more common than "green" [28].

8.5.4 DATABASE SIZE

The database size is the last portion of our model that we analyze. It is expected that the encrypted index adds overhead compared to a non-encrypted index, which has a high rate of compression. These compression techniques are rendered useless due to the randomized nature of the encryption algorithms in our encrypted search. In addition, our index size is expected to be much larger than previous work that used Bloom filters and database indexes without storing location information. Bloom filter sizes are typically a function of the number of unique words in a document. Our inverted index is also a function of the unique words; however, the size of our non-inverted index is proportional to the number of total words.

Figure 8.8 compares the overall storage size for our encrypted databases and a standard MySQL Full-Text search database indexed with the same documents but unencrypted. The MySQL encrypted database is larger but by a relatively small amount. For a database size of 2.6 GB, our encrypted solution is only 1.15 GB larger than its unencrypted counterpart. The MongoDB encrypted database is significantly larger than both by roughly a factor of four. This is due to the extensive overhead and repeated metadata encountered by storing each document and individual truncated hashed keyword as a MongoDB document.

Direct comparison with other encrypted searching schemes is difficult as much of the previous work either did not publish results of the size of their system or focused on much smaller sample corpus sizes than ours, often with less than 5000 documents [11]. However, to further show the claim that our approach is efficient, Figure 8.8 does show that the size needed to store both of the encrypted databases tested and original documents scale linearly with the corpus size.

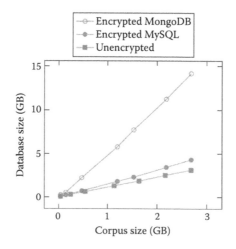

FIGURE 8.8   Relationship between the size of an unencrypted corpus of data plus an index and the encrypted corpus and encrypted index for both MySQL and MongoDB.

8.6 SECURITY ANALYSIS

In Sections 8.6.1 and 8.6.2, we analyze an attack on the encrypted index as well as the tradeoff between the number of bits used in the encrypted keywords and the bandwidth usage. Finally, in Section 8.6.3, we propose a solution for encrypting documents in parts (introduced in Section 8.3.7.2), which improves the overall security of the system.

8.6.1 FREQUENCY ANALYSIS OF ENCRYPTED KEYWORDS

Our proposed method still has areas that could be attacked. Even though there is a many-to-one relationship between keywords and their encrypted counterparts, not all encrypted values are equally distributed. For example, in a 13-bit keyword truncated index, the encrypted keyword "0E18" is contained in 262,941 documents (roughly half of the corpus) while "1C91" is in only 1005 documents. This is not all that surprising as the extremely common word, "Enron," encrypts to "0E18" while a much more rare word (such as jackal, among others) encrypts to "1C91." Nevertheless, despite the fact that multiple keywords encrypt to the same values of "0E18" and "1C91," a very large index value suggests that a common word may map to this (see Figure 8.9). For larger truncated bit values this disparity typically only increases.

To prevent information leakage, in a perfect model, all encrypted keyword strings would be uniformly distributed across documents instead of arbitrarily assigned by truncating encrypted values. Because the unencrypted to encrypted keyword map is completely contained on the client-side server, an algorithm to create a model to perform this could be implemented. A random sampling of documents could be taken. At this point, keywords contained in all or almost all documents (such as email headers and company names) could be added to the stop-word list and removed from the index. Finally, instead of the encrypted keywords being sorted into bins by a truncated value, they could be arranged such that it approximates a uniform distribution. Thus, the spikes in Figure 8.9 would be reduced, and the mean and median value's difference would decrease.

8.6.2 ANALYSIS OF KEYWORD COLLISIONS

In the previous section, it was explained that using more bits used for the truncated encrypted keyword leads to reduced security from an attack on the index. In addition, the more bits used for

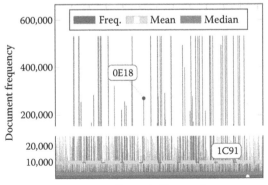

FIGURE 8.9   The number of documents that contain the truncated encrypted keyword ($\beta = 13$). Each line corresponds to a single encrypted keyword. Note that a few major outliers dominate the set. An analysis attack can conclude that these encrypted keyword values likely correspond to common words.

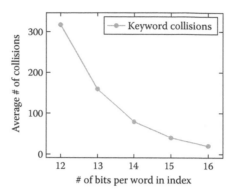

FIGURE 8.10 Relationship between the number of bits used to encrypt words and the average number of collisions between encrypted keywords.

truncated encrypted keywords also reduces the number of collisions (Figure 8.10). However, using more bits for encryption greatly decreases the bandwidth and thus the speed of searches (Figure 8.6). Therefore, there is an inverse relationship between the security of the database and bandwidth and the speed of the searches. It is important to understand the data set being used and to choose a sufficient β such that the collisions sufficiently interrupt any brute force or analysis attacks but also manages bandwidth considerations.

8.6.3 HEADLINING DOCUMENT RETRIEVAL

In Section 8.3.7, we suggested a method to implement headlining in our search engine. The headlining implementation may be vulnerable to an additional security attack. For headlining, the trusted client-side server would request the documents with the highest ranked scores, decrypt them, and then show textual context around the search terms found. Because each search results in an immediate request for the highest ranked documents, a malicious cloud server could associate the encrypted search keys with the headlining documents requested. Because it is known that a higher ranked document likely has the search keywords in closer proximity than a lower ranked document, with enough searches that return a single document, a malicious cloud server can begin to map encrypted keywords together. To alleviate the large amount of bandwidth needed to send multiple files that are potentially very large across the network, we suggested in Section 8.3.7.2 encrypting each document into fixed-sized parts. Incidentally, this method, as explained below, can also be used to diminish the security attack presented above.

Figure 8.11 shows a standard method of associating each document with exactly one fully encrypted version. Document 5 is always associated with encrypted document α. If document 5 contained its corresponding contents from Table 8.6, a search for "heart disease" would likely request

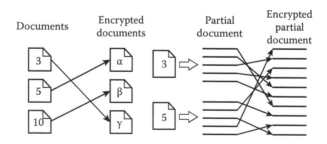

FIGURE 8.11 Separating documents into parts and encrypting them creates a many-to-many relationship. The cloud does not know which set of partial documents constitutes a full document.

this document for headlining. A malicious attacker with access to the cloud's database could know that α contains the encrypted keywords and likely contains them in close proximity. This information can be used by itself or be used in conjunction with other leaked data (such as a specific keyword's encrypted values) to further reduce the security of our system. While papers [19,29,30] have proposed workarounds, leaking a user's results and search patterns is a problem with almost every encrypted search method [20,21]; we can reduce the severity of it in ours by implementing headlining and encrypting in parts.

Encrypting in parts works as follows. Each document is split into a variable number of parts, depending on the length of the document. These partial documents have a metadata field that stores what original documents they belong to and where they are located in each original document. For example, document 5 is split into N partial documents, 5.1, 5.2, ..., 5.N. Each of these partial documents is encrypted separately and ordered arbitrarily on the cloud server. If a search for "heart disease" returns with the information that document 5 contains the phrase starting at location index 12, the trusted client server will determine this corresponds to the third partial document of 5 and request only 5.3 be returned. Using this method, the cloud server cannot exploit the headlining request to piece together encrypted partial documents to make an encrypted full document. Figure 8.11 shows the one-way, many-to-many mapping between partial documents and encrypted partial documents.

In this way, the client-side server requests an encrypted partial document instead of a full document while headlining. A malicious cloud server would only know that there is a partial document in which one or more of these encrypted keywords are present, in other words, that the search returned a non-empty result set. Because headlining requests many encrypted partial documents at once, the cloud server would not even be able to tell which full documents contain the partial documents that were requested. Finally, encrypting in parts actually offers the potential of reducing space by associating redundant data via links similar to data duplication in hard disks.

8.7 FUTURE WORK

The field of encrypted searching is wide and only truly in its infant stages. While our method does allow for proximity ranking and phrase searching, two important missing links, it still falls short on many others. The Holy Grail of encrypted searching is the ability for data owners to separate themselves from the management of the data users while having untrusted cloud providers continue to filter ranked results. We strategically avoid this by having a trusted client server that acts as a middleman and routes traffic and decrypts partial results. The research is moving in a direction in which this may be possible.

Current research by W. Lou and Y. T. Hou is taking the approach of encrypted trap door functions to new levels. Recent publications [4,31] have allowed for ranking of the returned documents based on relevancy scores, bringing the feature set of this technique close to the previously described Holy Grail.

Our continuing research is aimed at managing users efficiently and removing the need for a centralized client-side server. User provisioning is key to our collaborative searching model. While revocation and creation of new user accounts is trivial with our client-side server model, the ability to have user classes is not. Allowing a subset of the users to search through only a subset of documents can be managed by filtering the results at the client-side server; however, this method is, at its core, document filtering based on criteria and offers little value to the encrypted searching community.

Two better methods are in the works: a method that transfers the user privilege level to the cloud and only returns the results that are equal to or below the user's level and a method that will transfer a key to the client-side server and return all results, but using the transferred key, only those that are equal to or below the user's level are able to be decrypted.

In the near future, with the increased feature sets and performance of encrypted searching, we predict that it will enter the mainstream computing environment. Once this occurs, user privacy as well as a cloud server's legal protection will drive the expectation that all data on cloud servers be encrypted [32].

8.8 CONCLUSION

We propose a unique and novel encrypted keyword searching design with proximity ranking and phrase searches within the cloud. We design a four-step solution that safeguards the document's contents while still allowing for efficient searching and ranking of results that is a function of the number of unique keywords. We have developed two fully functional prototypes that can work within the confines of real-world response times on a large-scale data set. In practice, we show that the size of overhead of the encrypted indexed database is a linear function of a non-encrypted index. Finally, whereas non-encrypted proximity ranking models have a roughly static bandwidth usage per search, our model is dependent on the number of documents with the query keyword set.

AUTHORS' BIOGRAPHIES

Steven Zittrower is a PhD student at the University of Central Florida under the direction of Dr. Cliff Zou. Previously, he received his master's degree in computer science at Central Florida and his bachelor's degree in computer engineering and mathematics at Vanderbilt University in Nashville, TN. His interests include network security, cryptography, searching, and algorithmic studies. In his spare time, he enjoys programming, running, biking, and travel. He currently resides in Orlando, FL, USA.

Cliff C. Zou received the PhD degree in the Department of Electrical and Computer Engineering from the University of Massachusetts, Amherst, MA, in 2005.

He is an associate professor in the Department of Electrical Engineering and Computer Science, University of Central Florida. His research interests include computer and network security, computer networking, and performance evaluation. Dr. Zou is a member of ACM and senior member of IEEE.

REFERENCES

1. S. Artzi, A. Kieżum, C. Newport, and D. Schultz, Encrypted keyword search in a distributed storage system, Massachusetts Institute of Technology, Tech. Rep. 1738, Feb. 2006.
2. A. Aviv, M. Locasto, S. Potter, and A. Keromytis, SSARES: Secure searchable Automated remote email storage, in *Computer Security Applications Conference, 2007. ACSAC 2007. Twenty-Third Annual*, Dec. 2007, pp. 129–139.
3. M. Raykova, B. Vo, S. M. Bellovin, and T. Malkin, Secure anonymous database search, in *Proceedings of the 2009 ACM Workshop on Cloud Computing Security*, ser. CCSW '09. New York: ACM, 2009, pp. 115–126.
4. C. Wang, N. Cao, K. Ren, and W. Lou, Enabling secure and efficient ranked keyword search over out-sourced cloud data, *IEEE Transactions on Parallel and Distributed Systems (TPDS)*, 2012.
5. US federal cloud computing market forecast 2010–2015, tabular analysis, Market Research Media.
6. T. Schadler, Should your email live in the cloud? A comparative cost analysis, Forrester Research, Tech. Rep., 2009.
7. E. Grosse, Ensuring your information is safe online, http://googleblog.blogspot.com/2011/06/ensuring-your-information-is-safe.html, June 2011.
8. Sony Online Entertainment, Sony Online Entertainment announces theft of data from its systems, [Press Release] http://www.soe.com/securityupdate/pressrelease.vm, May 2011.
9. D. X. Song, D. Wagner, and A. Perrig, Practical techniques for searches on encrypted data, in *IEEE Symposium on Security and Privacy*, vol. 3, Berkeley, CA, May 2000, pp. 44–55.

10. S. M. Bellovin and W. R. Cheswick, Privacy-enhanced searches using encrypted Bloom filters, Department of Computer Science, Columbia University, Tech. Rep., Sept. 2004.

11. C. Wang, N. Cao, J. Li, K. Ren, and W. Lou, Privacy-preserving multi-keyword ranked search over encrypted cloud data, in *The 30th IEEE International Conference on Computer Communications (IEEE INFOCOM)*, Apr. 2011.

12. C. Wang, N. Cao, J. Li, K. Ren, and W. Lou, Secure ranked keyword search over encrypted cloud data, in *The 30th IEEE International Conference on Distributed Computing Systems (ICDCS)*, Jun. 2010, pp. 253–262.

13. C. Raiciu, D. Rosenblum et al., Enabling confidentiality in content-based publish/subscribe infrastructures, in *Proc. of the 2nd Int. Conf. on Security and Privacy in Communication Networks*, Aug. 2006.

14. M. Srivatsa and L. Liu, Securing publish-subscribe overlay services with eventguard, in *ACM Conference on Computer and Communications Security*, 2005, pp. 289–298.

15. D. Boneh, G. D. Crescenzo et al., Public key encryption with keyword search, in *EUROCRYPT*, 2004, pp. 506–522.

16. J. Baek, R. Safavi-Naini et al., Public key encryption with keyword search revisited, in *Computational Science and Its Applications*, 2008, pp. 1249–1259.

17. B. Zhang and F. Zhang, An efficient public key encryption with conjunctive-subset keywords search, *Journal of Network Computer Applications*, 2011, pp. 262–267.

18. J. Katz, A. Sahai, and B. Waters, Predicate encryption supporting disjunctions, polynomial equations, and inner products, in *EUROCRYPT*, 2008, pp. 146–162.

19. E. Shen, E. Shi, and B. Waters, Predicate privacy in encryption systems, in *Proceedings of the 6th Theory of Cryptography Conference on Theory of Cryptography*, ser. TCC '09. Berlin: Springer-Verlag, 2009, pp. 457–473.

20. P. van Liesdonk, S. Sedghi, J. Doumen, P. Hartel, and W. Jonker, Computationally efficient searchable symmetric encryption, in *Secure Data Management*, ser. Lecture Notes in Computer Science, vol. 6358, W. Jonker and M. Petkovic, Eds. Berlin: Springer, 2010, pp. 87–100.

21. P. Golle, J. Staddon, and B. Waters, Secure conjunctive keyword search over encrypted data, in *ACNS 04: 2nd International Conference on Applied Cryptography and Network Security*. Berlin: Springer-Verlag, 2004, pp. 31–45.

22. C. L. A. Clarke, G. V. Cormack, and E. A. Tudhope, Relevance ranking for one to three term queries, *Inf. Process. Manage.*, vol. 36, pp. 291–311, January 2000.

23. H. Joho and J. Jose, A comparative study of the effectiveness of search result presentation on the Web, in *Advances in Information Retrieval*, ser. Lecture Notes in Computer Science. vol. 3936, Berlin: Springer, 2006, pp. 302–313.

24. O. Goldreich, S. Goldwasser, and S. Halevi, Public-key cryptosystems from lattice reduction problems. Berlin: Springer-Verlag, 1996, pp. 112–131.

25. OpenFTS, http://openfts.sourceforge.net.

26. MySQL, http://www.mysql.com.

27. IPTraf, http://iptraf.seul.org.

28. J. B. Michel, S. Pinker, Y. K. Shen, A. P. Aiden, A. Veres, M. K. Gray, T. G. B. Team, J. P. Pickett, D. Hoiberg, D. Clancy, P. Norvig, J. Orwant, M. A. Nowak, and E. Lieberman-Aiden, Quantitative analysis of culture using millions of digitized books, *Science*, vol. 331, pp. 176–182, 2011.

29. M. Abdalla, M. Bellare, D. Catalano, E. Kiltz, T. Kohno, T. Lange, J. Malone-lee, G. Neven, P. Paillier, and H. Shi, Searchable encryption revisited: Consistency properties, relation to anonymous IBE, and extensions, in *CRYPTO 2005*. Springer-Verlag, 2005, pp. 205–222.

30. J. Bethencourt, D. Song, and B. Waters, New techniques for private stream searching, *ACM Trans. Inf. Syst. Secur.*, vol. 12, pp. 16:1–16:32, January 2009.

31. M. Li, S. Yu, W. Lou, and Y. T. Hou, Toward privacy-assured cloud data services with flexible search functionalities, in *Third International Workshop on Security and Privacy in Cloud Computing (ICDCS-SPCC 2012)*, Macau, China, 2012.

32. E. Limer, How Megas clever encryption will protect you, but mostly Kim Dotcom, http://gizmodo.com/5977265/how-megas-encryption-will-protect-you-but-mostly-kim-dotcom, January 2013.

9 Intrusion Detection for SCADA Systems

Alaa Atassi, Imad H. Elhajj, Ali Chehab, and Ayman Kayssi

CONTENTS

9.1 INTRODUCTION

Supervisory control and data acquisition (SCADA) systems are used in industrial systems that run automated processes to perform various industrial tasks. SCADA manages and controls a variety of systems, including cooling, ventilation, and power distribution and generation in addition to sensitive processes such as nuclear fusion. Statistics show that roughly 80% of the power facilities in the United States are controlled by SCADA systems [1]. A SCADA system allows for convergence and interconnectivity among many networks and nodes through many types of protocols, including the Internet protocol (IP) [2]. This wide scope makes the system vulnerable to widely known attacks in addition to the vulnerabilities in SCADA systems themselves.

However, traditionally, when designing SCADA systems, the main concern was performance. The security of SCADA systems had not been the main focus until relatively recently after several security incidents had been reported. In March 2000, the communication among pumping stations in Maroochy water services in Australia were lost, and the pumping stations did not operate properly. It was thought that alarms were raised due to a technical problem, but the staff discovered that someone had hacked the system and caused this cyber incident [3]. In August 2003, a computer worm bypassed the control room firewall and affected the SCADA control systems at the Davis-Besse nuclear power plant network in Ohio [4]. This trend culminated with Stuxnet [5], a SCADA-specific malware discovered in July 2010. Stuxnet is a sophisticated malware that attacks specific types of PLCs and modifies their control to behave erratically.

These attacks led researchers to analyze SCADA systems vulnerabilities. Vinay and Ronald assessed the security of several protocols and concluded that the hardware and software of the commercial off-the-shelf protocols concentrate on the performance of SCADA systems and mostly fail to increase their security, leading to several vulnerabilities at different OSI layers [2]. Others addressed common protocols used in SCADA systems and provided recommendations emphasizing access control, including firewalls and intrusion detection systems, running vulnerability assessment, introducing cryptography, paying more attention to each device and OS security as well as providing a proper management to organize the security of SCADA systems [6].

Thomas Kropp [7] gives an example of one SCADA system that employs TCP/IP protocol and common operating systems for monitoring purposes. Such a system is vulnerable to both OS and TCP vulnerabilities. Applying patches for the OS in such systems is not an option because the system is not to be interrupted. Moreover, the same problems and attacks that apply to TCP can be executed against SCADA systems. Turk [8] introduces previous work on cyber attacks over control systems and discusses their serious consequences on the production processes. According to Turk, the main obstacles that face SCADA and its reduced security are the lack of awareness, the lack of efficient analysis, and the excess attention on financial repercussions. Luders has applied DoS and scanning attacks on PLCs from several vendors using the Ethernet protocol. Results show that 32% of the devices were vulnerable to DoS attacks in addition to 21% of them crashing during the scanning process, and 61% were scanned successfully [9]. More general attacks against PLCs are proposed by Kabay such as PLC password cracking and turning the device on and off remotely in addition to DoS attacks [10].

9.2 PREVIOUS WORK

In this section, we discuss the work done in the field of intrusion detection systems, particularly SCADA-specific intrusion detection systems. In addition, we compare our proposed method with previous work. Articles [11–21] discuss the work done on intrusion detection using the misuse detection techniques. Misuse intrusion detection is an approach based on using prior knowledge about an attack. On the other hand, in anomaly-based approaches [22–26], all the anomalies are considered as malicious activities. Unlike misuse-based approaches, in anomaly-based approaches the model is built depending on the normal behavior and activities of the system. Hybrid intrusion detection systems were designed to combine the properties of both the misuse-based and the anomaly-based detection [27–31]. Hybrid detectors offer the ability to inspect unknown attacks that deviate from the normal behavior of the network as well as previously known attacks. However, the work done lacks the detection of control-specific attacks that target SCADA systems [11–31].

Model-based intrusion detection for SCADA systems is designed [32]. It basically works on detecting the malicious code by checking the requests and the responses in a Modbus TCP/IP SCADA network. The model is designed by calculating a variable for a request and determining whether it suits a certain device or not; then the response is also monitored to check its conformity with the sent request. The limitation of this system is that it only detects the wrong command or response validity; attacks with valid command codes will pass undetected. An environment is provided that is distributed over the whole SCADA network to allow monitoring for network activities and hence the detection of attacks. The exact attack scenario has been defined [33]. The main drawbacks of this system are the complex design, the need for further offline analysis by an expert and attacks are not detected in real time. A forensic system with a snort IDS has been designed [34]. The procedure starts by scanning the environment and recording the malicious activities; next, the activities are replayed and vulnerabilities are analyzed. When a malicious activity matches a vulnerability, we consider it as an intrusion, and a snort rule is created and tested. This system needs a high knowledge of building snort rules in addition to the complexity of network traffic analysis. An automatic software protection system has been proposed [35]. It monitors SCADA Modbus TCP/IP protocol and detects the attacks against it. The HMI attack is being detected through an anomaly-based detector that detects any deviation from the normal behavior of SCADA requests and responses by observing the Modbus header. Only Modbus TCP/IP protocol attacks are being detected, but Ethernet attacks will pass undetected.

An intrusion detection system based on neural networks for critical infrastructures was proposed [36]. The main contribution is adding a new window size feature to the set of features that are used in the neural networks training phase. Determining the proper window size for each type of attack is accomplished by an attribute extraction approach during the training phase. The neural network algorithm determines the boundaries of the normal and intrusive behaviors from the structured data set. This system only detects DoS and scanning attacks; a command-response injection will pass undetected. Researchers [37] implemented a detection technique that detects DoS attacks in addition to SCADA command and response attacks using a neural network algorithm. The training data set includes samples from normal behavior as well as some examples of false responses from MSU SCADA laboratory. The chosen input features are the water level, the command response frequency, RTU operating mode, and the state of the water tank pump. The detection rate of this system is high for the man-in-the-middle and DoS–based response injection but only 12% for the replay-based response injection. Moreover, the selected features and the built data set are only valid for the system used in the testing experiment; new feature selection is needed for each SCADA system.

An anomaly-based approach is proposed [38] based on pattern matching. The detection engine is trained for the normal behavior to build the normal profile of system indicators. These indicators are parameters such as CPU, link, and login information of the SCADA traffic. When the detection engine detects a non-predetermined behavior, an alarm is triggered. SCADA attacks that are based on normal behavior will pass undetected. A hybrid (anomaly and misuse) based detection system was proposed [39]. The system works as an application layer detector. The hardware of the intrusion detection system consists of three types of parallel detection. The interval-based sensors detect the variations in the normal frequencies of intervals between events. The procedure-based sensors observe the data of the execution patterns of different procedures. The misuse detectors observe the application-based codes looking for attacks based on known vulnerabilities. The limitation of this system is the complicated design, which requires placing sensors in each SCADA application.

A misuse detection system based on data mining algorithms was proposed [40]. The distributed architecture of this system sniffs the network data to extract the detection features and builds a profile of the current network status depending on the data mining algorithms. A set of rules extracted from the network status will be used in another classification process to detect attacks. Researchers [41] designed a Modbus/DNP3–based intrusion detection for critical infrastructure. Their method depends on the state of the system components and the correlations between these states. Each state is described by the registers and coils status for each particular component. The attack is detected when a variation from the built knowledge takes place. The main drawback of this system is its dependency on the Modbus/DNP3 communications protocol. Researchers [42] introduced a survey on intrusion detection for critical infrastructures. They stated that the IDS based on writing the normal and abnormal rules for a system will not give high detection efficiency, and at the same time, it gives a high false positive rate. They also stated that the normal anomaly-based and classification techniques still face the same issues of the regular intrusion detection systems. Moreover, they suggested using multi-agents, such as the mobile agents, to avoid the central point of failure in detection. Then they suggested a multi-layer framework that analyzes SCADA systems using multiple sensors.

The previously discussed works [32–42] either have some detection limitations against certain attacks or are specific to a certain protocol of SCADA systems and cannot be generalized. SCADA intrusion detection articles introduce stateless detection systems and take their detection decisions based on single packet validity regardless of the sequence of packets. The system presented by Fovino et al. [41] is stateful, but it is based on the memory status in devices and not packets exchanged, which requires the detection engine to send queries to the system devices to read their memory status. This option is not preferred in most environments as it generates additional traffic and needs synchronization between devices. Based on the previously discussed work on SCADA intrusion detection systems, no detection technique detects all types of SCADA intrusions. Most of them either do not detect replay attacks or cannot detect attacks in real time. Our proposed solution

	Real time detection	Detecting SCADA specific attacks	Scalable for all applications	Detects denial of service	Detects scanning attacks	Detects command response injection	Detects replay attacks	Detects man-in-the-middle based attacks
Our system	✓	✓	✓	✓	✓	✓	✓	✓
Misuse detection techniques [11–21]	✓	✗	✗	✓	✓	✗	✗	✗
Anomaly detection techniques [22–26]	✓	◐	✗	✓	✓	✗	✗	✗
Hybrid detection techniques [27–31]	✓	◐	✗	✓	✓	✗	✗	✗
Using model-based intrusion detection for SCADA networks [32]	✓	✓	✗	✗	✗	✓	✗	◐
A simulation environment for SCADA security analysis and assessment [33]	✗	✓	✗	✓	✓	✓	✓	✓
SCADA forensics with snort IDS [34]	✓	✓	✗	✓	✓	✗	✗	✗
A testbed for analyzing security of SCADA control systems (TASSCS) [35]	✓	✓	✗	✓	✓	✓	✗	✗
Neural network based intrusion detection system for critical infrastructures [36]	✓	✗	✗	✓	✓	✗	✗	✗
On SCADA control system command and response injection and intrusion detection [37]	✓	✓	✗	✓	✓	✓	✗	✗
Anomaly-based intrusion detection for SCADA systems [38]	✓	✓	✓	✓	✓	✗	✗	✗
Intrusion detection for embedded systems [39]	✓	✓	✗	✓	✓	◐	◐	◐
High-speed IDS in support of critical infrastructure protection [40]	✗	✓	✓	✓	✓	◐	◐	◐
Modbus/DNP3 state-based IDS [41]	✓	✓	✗	✓	✓	✓	◐	◐

FIGURE 9.1   Intrusion detection systems comparison.

is to design an anomaly intrusion detection system based on understanding the normal sequences of SCADA control systems and to detect all illegitimate system events or sequence transitions.

Figure 9.1 summarizes the capability of each detection system. Most of the misuse-, anomaly-, and hybrid-based approaches detect DoS attacks and scanning attacks in real-time but fail to detect other types of intrusions on SCADA. Other SCADA–specific detection techniques, discussed earlier, detect more SCADA attacks but fail to detect them all, and some are not real-time detectors. Our approach detects most SCADA attacks in real time, such as command injection, replay, and man-in-the-middle attacks with high detection accuracy.

9.3   SYSTEM DESIGN

The design of SCADA networks is clearly different from regular Ethernet networks. The protocols used over the Ethernet operate differently than the ones in SCADA systems. Hence, the widely known intrusion detection systems will not give high detection accuracy if used to detect SCADA intrusions. New detection features and packet fields have to be specified in order to improve performance. Generally, we can differentiate the properties of SCADA communications from regular Ethernet communications as follows:

- SCADA communications can be represented with sequential patterns or a limited number of event sequences.
- A limited number of packet types is exchanged to achieve a certain industrial control process.
- Industrial control–specific protocols are used in SCADA systems, such as BACnet, Omron, Modbus, ISO-TSAP, etc.
- The effect of some widely known attacks might have devastating consequences on SCADA systems, for example, a replay attack with a legitimate packet that opens a water pump while the water level is still high.

Our approach is based on learning the legitimate sequences and defining Markov chains to model them. Then this model is used to detect any deviation from normal behavior.

9.3.1   MARKOV CHAINS

A Markov process is a type of stochastic process with added dependency. Each of the random variables depends only on the variable preceding it and is conditionally independent of all other variables. We call a discrete stochastic process $X_1, X_2, ... X_n$ a Markov chain or process if the following statement is true for $n = 1, 2, ...,$ and so on.

$$Pr(X_{n+1} = x_{n+1} | X_n = x_n, X_{n-1} = x_{n-1}, ..., X_1 = x_1) = Pr(X_{n+1} = x_{n+1} | X_n = x_n) \tag{9.1}$$

$$\forall \, x_1, x_2, ..., x_n, x_{n+1} \in X.$$

The probability mass function of these random variables can be written as follows:

$$p(x_1, x_2, ..., x_n) = p(x_1)p(x_2|x_1)p(x_3|x_2)...p(x_n|x_{n-1}) \tag{9.2}$$

Another type of this process is the time-invariant Markov chain. We call a Markov chain or process time invariant if the conditional probability $p(x_{n+1}|x_n)$ does not depend on n, that is, for $n = 1, 2, ...,$ etc.

$$Pr\{X_{n+1} = b | X_n = a\} = Pr\{X_2 = b | X_1 = a\} \text{ for all } a, b \in X \tag{9.3}$$

In our system design, we assume that a Markov chain is time invariant unless otherwise stated. Moreover, we consider a one-step transition probability for the Markov model between each system state and the other. Generally, the transition probability, $P_{i,j}$, is described as the probability the system is in a state (j) at time ($t + 1$) if the system is in state (i) at time t. When the system has a finite number of states (1, 2, ..., s), the Markov model can be described by a matrix of transition probability:

$$P_{i,j} = \begin{bmatrix} p_{1,1} & p_{1,2} & \cdots & p_{1,s} \\ p_{2,1} & p_{2,2} & \cdots & p_{2,s} \\ \vdots & \vdots & \ddots & \vdots \\ p_{s,1} & p_{s,2} & \cdots & p_{s,s} \end{bmatrix}$$

where

$$\sum_{j=1}^{s} p_{i,j} = 1.$$

Another term to define is the initial probability of a certain state. The distribution of such probabilities is represented by

$$Q = [q_1, q_2,....., q_s]$$

The initial probability defines the probability that the system is in state (i) at time $t = 0$. To compute the probability of a certain sequence of states, $X_1, X_2, ..., X_S$, occurring in the context of the Markov chain model, we use

$$Pr\{X_1, X_2,..., X_S\} = q_{x_1} \prod_{t=2}^{S} p_{x_{t-1},x_t} \tag{9.4}$$

Assume that we have N system states and each state is represented by X_i as follows:

$$X_0, X_1, X_2, ..., X_{N-1}$$

To estimate the initial probability for each system state, we use the formula

$$q_i = \frac{N_i}{N} \tag{9.5}$$

where N_i is the number of the system states X_t in the state (i), and N is the total number of system states (system observations). To estimate the transition probabilities among the system states, the following formula is used:

$$P_{i,j} = \frac{N_{i,j}}{N_i} \tag{9.6}$$

where $N_{i,j}$ is the number of the system states pairs or observation pairs X_t and X_{t+1} with X_t in the state (i) and X_{t+1} in the state (j), and N_i is the number of the system state pairs or observation pairs X_t and X_{t+1} with X_t in the state (i) and X_{t+1} in any one of the system states 1, 2, ..., $N-1$.

9.3.2 Design Modules

The proposed SCADA intrusion detection is an anomaly-based detector based on the Markov chain model. It has three basic modules: (1) feature extracting and parsing module, (2) learning module, and (3) detection module.

9.3.2.1 Feature Extracting and Parsing Module

This module is used in two phases, the learning and the detection phases. It monitors the control traffic packet by packet to prepare it either for the training or detection phase. This module works as follows:

1. The module examines the packets included in the control process.
2. For each packet, IPs, MAC addresses, ports, and control fields are chosen as protocol features. These fields are chosen differently for each protocol to represent the current state.
3. The chosen fields are parsed from the original packets and forwarded to the hashing module.
4. The hashing module hashes these fields to create a packet digest.
5. Each message digest is forwarded either to the learning or to the detection module depending on the system state.

9.3.2.2 Learning Module

Because our detection model is anomaly based, the learning phase is very important to identify the normal sequences of packets. The normal behavior of the system is the basic key feature of the anomaly-based detection. First, the learning module receives the packet digests from the parsing module as a sequence of packets. The role of the learning module is to learn the sequences of packets depending on the Markov chain formulas and to calculate the initial probabilities of the system states in addition to the transition probabilities between each two system states.

The learning module recognizes each packet digest as a new system event from the sequence of events. Because each digest represents a fingerprint of a certain parsed packet, the similar digests represent the same packet and hence a similar system event. For each system event X_i, the initial probability q_i is calculated using Equation 9.5. Moreover, for each two consecutive system events, X_i and X_j, the transition probability is calculated using Equation 9.6. The initial and transition probabilities calculations are done for all packet sequences captured during the learning process. If we have a total of S system events during the learning process, then Q_s initial matrix with S number of elements and P_{sxs} are saved as a normal profile for the sequence probabilities to be used later in the detection phase by the malicious sequence detection module. The learning module saves the S states in a database in order to use them in the detection module.

If the sequence has the events X_k and X_l separately but not consecutively, the transition probability of this sequence P_{kl}, is assigned a very low probability, P_σ, by the learning module to avoid zero transition probabilities. Figure 9.2 illustrates the learning module algorithm.

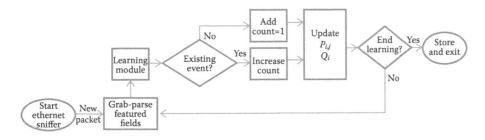

FIGURE 9.2 The learning module algorithm.

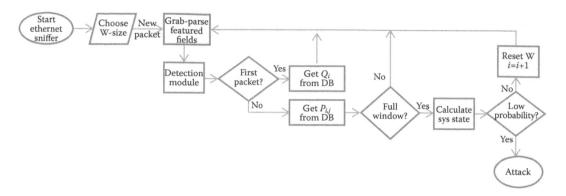

FIGURE 9.3   Detection module algorithm.

9.3.2.3   Detection Module

The detection module examines the current system states from the system events sniffed from the embedded parsing and hashing module similar to the learning module. The detection decision is based on the value of the system state probability. If the probability is high, it is more likely that it represents a sequence of normal system events. On the contrary, when the system state probability is low, it means one or more new system events have been injected into the normal sequence or a known system event has occurred in an unusual order.

Upon receiving new packets, the detection module calculates the system state probability for a window (W) of system events that contains n packets or system events. The purpose of the window-based calculation is to correlate multiple system events to each other. Because in a Markov chain each system event depends only on the previous state, taking a window of m events correlates more system events in one system state probability value. For example, choosing a window size of $W = 3$, the detection module calculates the state of three system events, one event for the initial probability and two events with transition probabilities system states. The values of the initial and transition probabilities used by this module to calculate the system state are examined from the initial and transition matrices calculated in the learning process. The system state probability is calculated according to Equation 9.4. The value of this probability is the key feature of making the detection decision as mentioned earlier. When a new system event is received, the window is shifted by one system event to the right, and the new probability is calculated for the new window that includes the new system event. Figure 9.3 illustrates the algorithm of the detection module.

9.4   EXPERIMENTAL SETUP AND RESULTS

In this section, we describe the experimental setup whereby we assess the detection accuracy of our SCADA intrusion detection system.

9.4.1   THE DETECTION ENGINE

The detection engine is implemented on Linux Ubuntu 11.04. The parsing, learning, and detection module codes are written in C language. The Pcap library is used because the code contains a live sniffer to capture network traffic. The learning phase, as explained in the system design, takes place before setting up the detection engine to start the detection process. The learning module extracts the learning data from the data set captured from the American University of Beirut (AUB) control infrastructure described in the next section. After the learning module extracts the normal sequence of system events and calculates the initial and transition probabilities, the detection module is ready to detect any abnormal sequence. We conduct our tests on the captured data set by applying different types of attacks.

9.4.2 Data Set Description

The data used for training and testing is captured from the American University of Beirut (AUB) Building Management System (BMS) control infrastructure. The data is captured using the Wireshark network sniffer [43] and saved to files because the BMS system is running on a 24/7 basis, serving different control procedures in many buildings. The BMS network of AUB has three sub–BMS systems:

- BMS of the power plant has seven direct digital controllers (DDCs), which include the load shedding of the chillers of six buildings.
- BMS of the cooling tower has one DDC.
- BMS of the pump room has two DDCs and includes the pump room station and one additional building.

In this experiment, we sniff the data of the pump room BMS system. There will be an exchange of information with other BMS systems, but mainly, we will describe the system that controls the water pumps. The water pumps are controlled by the Siemens BMS system via Variable Frequency Drives (VFD). The ventilation of pump room exhaust and fresh air fans, the fuel level, and the system fire pressure are also connected to the BMS. There are two main tanks and an elevated tank. The cold water is stored in the main tanks. Each tank is equipped with a pressure sensor (to check the water level) and a float switch. The cold water is lifted from the main tanks to the elevated tank by three identical water pumps, one duty and two standby, controlled by three Variable-Frequency Drives. The elevated water tank is the source of water distribution to different users.

This BMS also controls a fire alarm system with a set of two identical diesel fire pumps and one jockey pump in addition to a pressure sensor and main fuel tank with a solenoid valve and fuel meter model. Moreover, the BMS controls two fresh air and exhaust fans that form the room's ventilation system. The ventilation system is also equipped with a room temperature sensor in addition to a VFD for each fan.

The sequential operation of the water pumps can be summarized as follows: cold water will be lifted by the duty pump from the main tank to the elevated tank when the water level in the main tank is above the low level 3 and the water level in the elevated tank is below level 1. The duty water pump will stop either when the elevated tank is at high level or when the water level in the connected main tank is below low level. In the fire system, the level is sensed by the respective pressure sensor, and the diesel fire pumps are supplied by the fuel accordingly. DDS controls the solenoid valve according to the level in the main fuel tank. When the fuel level reaches the overview level, the solenoid valve will be closed after a minute. An audible alarm will be generated at the filling station if the fuel level reaches the high level during the filling process.

In the ventilation system controls, fans will start up automatically from the DDC depending on a predefined time schedule. The DDC will generate a fault schedule if one of the fans failed to start or stop during the operation.

The data is collected for the SCADA and BMS system, which includes monitoring and control devices. The control data was mirrored to a switch port in order to collect the control packets of all systems that should be monitored. The control protocol used to exchange the control data in this setup is BACnet/IP. We captured BACnet control data for two working days separately, a weekend, and two consecutive weeks.

9.4.3 BACnet Protocol Features

As we mentioned previously in the system design, each system event is characterized by specific protocol features extracted from the packet fields. In our testing environment, the BACnet protocol is used and the headers in BACnet have been chosen to represent each packet in the learning and detection phase. The BACnet features, illustrated in Table 9.1, are specific to the BACnet protocol

TABLE 9.1

BACnet/IP Detection Features

Feature	OSI Layer
Source/destination MAC addresses	Data link layer
Source/destination IP addresses	Network layer
Time to live	Network layer
Layer 4 protocol type	Network layer
Source/destination port addresses	Transport layer
BACnet type	Application layer
BACnet function	Application layer
BACnet BVLCI length	Application layer
BACnet control byte	Application layer
Other BACnet data	Application layer

regardless of the vendor. The features were chosen to generalize the detection algorithm and, hence, to make it application independent. To apply this method of detection to other protocols, only a few fields need to be replaced. For example, when detecting the control attacks on OMRON devices, which work over UDP protocol, we only change the application layer features. Instead of BACnet features, we take only the first two bytes of the payload that represent the command and response codes of the control instructions in the OMRON protocol. It is worth noting that most of the vendors with protocols over UDP choose the first two payload packets for the command and response codes.

Table 9.1 lists all BACnet features used. These bytes are chosen and parsed from the packet depending on the value of the control byte. Figure 9.4 illustrates the types of bytes taken as features depending on the control byte value {0, 8, 20, 28, 80}. The parsing code reads the control bytes value and parses the packet accordingly.

APDU stands for the application layer protocol data unit, which is part of the BACnet protocol [44]. This part of the code describes the services and function of BACnet in addition to the control data values. BVLC field is the BACnet Virtual Link Control Field. The network protocol data unit (NPDU) is another part of BACnet protocol and has the Control Byte field. The NPDU describes the network addresses of the source and destination devices as specified in the BACnet setup in addition

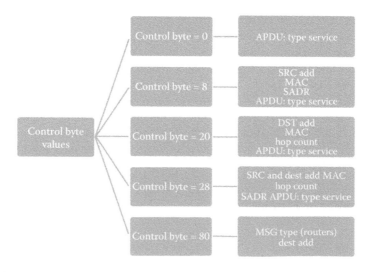

FIGURE 9.4 The APDU features parsed according to the control bytes value.

to the hop count between these sources and destinations. The NPDU describes the BMS system, and it is very dependent on the network topology. Hence, the values of the NPDU field reflect the type of the network topology. The APDU defines the type of the request or reply and whether they are confirmed or unconfirmed in addition to the service attached with this request/reply and the control values, such as pressure and temperature.

9.4.4 DETECTION SYSTEM ANALYSIS FOR NO ATTACK CASE

In this section, we study the behavior of our detection system without applying any type of attack in order to examine false positive (FP) and true negative (TN) rates. To study the false positive rate of our systems, we take into account the effect of the training phase on the detection accuracy of the intrusion detection system. Data sets are divided into multiple groups to study the impact of training on the testing results. The false positive rate is the number of detection windows mistakenly flagged as attacks over the total number of windows in the testing data sets. In this section, we study the FP and TN rates for different detection window sizes of $W = 2$ and $W = 3$.

Trial 1: The two weeks of data set was divided into two sets. The data set has 1,919,318 system events. We use the first week for training with 956,088 system events, and the second week is used for testing with 963,230 system events. In this case, without performing any attacks on the data set, the detection code detected 1312 events as intrusions. Hence, the false positive rate is 0.136%, and the true negative rate is 99.864%.

Trial 2: The data set was divided into quarters, half a week each. We took the first set for learning with 479,830 system events, and the rest of the system events are used for testing. Similarly, without performing any attack, the detection code detected more intrusions than in the previous case and mistakenly considered 2577 system events as attacks. This gives a 0.179% false positive rate and a true negative rate of 99.821%.

Trial 3: The data set was divided into seven groups of two days each. The first group with 274,188 system events is used for learning, and the six remaining groups are used for testing with 1,645,130 system events. The result of this trial is 10,790 system events detected mistakenly as intrusions. Hence the false positive rate of this trial is 0.655%, and the true negative rate is 99.345%.

Trial 4: The data set is divided into 14 groups; each has one day of system events. A single day is used for training, and the remaining 13 days are used for testing. This means 137,094 for learning and 1,782,224 for testing system events. The detection engine detected 16,913 false positives, which means a false positive rate of 0.949% and a true negative rate of 99.051%. Table 9.2 summarizes the results for the four trials.

Then a cross validation was done in which all the combinations in each trial are considered by alternating the learning group among all sets. For example in trial 4, we learn on group 2 and test on the rest of the group; then we learn on group 3 and test on the rest until we take all the combinations. Table 9.3 provides the FP rates for all trials.

TABLE 9.2
Results of False Positive Test Rates

	Trial 1	Trial 2	Trial 3	Trial 4
Dataset size	1,919,318	1,919,318	1,919,318	1,919,318
Number of training days	7	3.5	2	1
Number of testing days	7	10.5	12	13
Number of training events	956,088	479,830	274,188	137,094
Number of testing events	963,230	1,439,488	1,645,130	1,782,224
Number of detected attacks	1312	2577	10,790	16,913
False positive rate	0.136%	0.179%	0.655%	0.949%

TABLE 9.3

False Positive Rates of the Extended Experimental Trials ($W = 3$)

Number of Groups/ Learning Group	Two Groups	Four Groups	Seven Groups	14 Groups
Learn on 1st group	0.136%	0.18%	0.655%	0.95%
Learn on 2nd group	0.64%	0.303%	0.354%	0.83%
Learn on 3rd group		0.625%	0.731%	0.46%
Learn on 4th group		7.55%	0.38%	0.92%
Learn on 5th group			0.68%	0.83%
Learn on 6th group			0.75%	0.99%
Learn on 7th group			6.54%	0.49%
Learn on 8th group				0.89%
Learn on 9th group				1.01%
Learn on 10th group				0.85%
Learn on 11th group				0.82%
Learn on 12th group				6.44%
Learn on 13th group				6.36%
Learn on 14th group				6.14%
Average	0.39%	2.16%	1.44%	2.00%
Standard deviation	0.36%	3.60%	2.25%	2.34%

All the previous results were calculated for window size $W = 3$. To study the effect of the window size on the detection accuracy, we consider $W = 2$ and apply cross validation again for the no attack case. Table 9.4 shows the results for the $W = 2$ detection window, which gives lower FP rates as a low transition affects fewer windows because the windows are smaller.

TABLE 9.4

False Positive Rates of the Extended Experimental Trials ($W = 2$)

Number of Groups/ Learning Group	Two Groups	Four Groups	Seven Groups	14 Groups
Learn on 1st group	0.07%	0.08%	0.34%	0.489%
Learn on 2nd group	0.329%	0.15%	0.191%	0.443%
Learn on 3rd group		0.32%	0.38%	0.266%
Learn on 4th group		5.22%	0.196%	0.478%
Learn on 5th group			0.47%	0.48%
Learn on 6th group			0.391%	0.519%
Learn on 7th group			4.539%	0.257%
Learn on 8th group				0.466%
Learn on 9th group				0.529%
Learn on 10th group				0.447%
Learn on 11th group				0.43%
Learn on 12th group				4.119%
Learn on 13th group				4.65%
Learn on 14th group				4.34%
Average	0.2%	1.44%	0.93%	1.28%
Standard deviation	0.18%	2.52%	1.59%	1.68%

9.4.5 Attacker Model

In this section, the attacker model describing the different attacks simulated is introduced with the results for each case. For each attack scenario, false positives (FPs), true negatives (TNs), true positives (TPs), and false negatives (FNs) are calculated to evaluate the detection accuracy. TP and FN values are attack-dependent values, where TP rate is the number of detected attacks over the total number of attacks attempted and FN rate is the number of non-detected attacks over the total number of attacks attempted. In calculating TP and FN, all windows with low probability that are a result of one attack are counted as one attack only. On the contrary, the FP and TN rates are independent of attacks. We count the number of low probability windows to calculate these rates. For example, if the learning module is trained with the following sequence: {A, B, C, D, E, F, G}, and in the detection phase, we get the following sequence: {A, B, **A**, C, D, E, **T**, F, G}, in which **A** is a legitimate system event and **T** is an injected malicious event, then the BA and AC transitions are legitimate, but the engine is not trained for these legitimate transitions. If we choose a window size $W = 2$ for detection, two windows, BA and AC, would have low probability and will be considered as false positives. However, the injected system event **T** gives two windows of low probability, but we count them as one attack. TP is set to 100% because detecting one low transition is sufficient to detect the injected packet, and the FN is 0%.

9.4.5.1 Replay Attack Analysis

The purpose of the replay attack is to execute a legitimate function but in abnormal conditions or at a different time. This might lead to bad consequences in SCADA systems. For example, in our experiment, we have the following transitions:

(1) Learned Legitimate Transition:
Packet from SRC Network address: 0×01, type: Request, Service: Notification
Followed by
Packet from SRC Network address: 0×03, type: Request, Service: Notification
     Instead, the attacker takes the first request sent by the network address 0×01 and replays it after the packet is being forwarded by network address 0×03.
(2) Attack Malicious Transition:
Packet from SRC Network address: 0×03, type: Request, Service: Notification
Followed by
Packet from SRC Network address: 0×01, type: Request, Service: Notification

As a result, the detection system detects this transition as an intrusion as illustrated in Figure 9.5, which shows the log of the state probability. Clearly, this probability drops significantly when the relay attack is conducted.

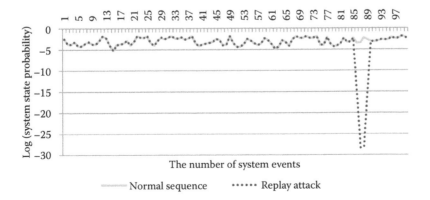

FIGURE 9.5   The system state analysis of replay attacks.

9.4.5.1.1   Replay Attack Results

To analyze the false negatives, the data set was divided into two sets. The data for the first week was used for training and the data for the second week for detection. In this scenario, the attacker has knowledge of the system sequence, and hence, the attacker will replay a captured packet but will not drop any packet. Three devices (1, 3, and 2098180) with a total of seven types of system events cause device number 2 to forward a request to device number 6. Here, we replayed the legitimate request packets sent by device 1 or 3. The total number of replayed packets in the test was 2451, which is the total number of system events in which devices 1 or 3 cause device number 2 to forward a request to device 6. The system was able to detect 2435 attacks correctly and 16 replayed events passed undetected. As a result of a window size $W = 3$, the false negative (FN) rate of this trial is 0.652%, and the detection accuracy (TP) is 99.348%. The false positive rate (FP) for this trial is 0.136%, and the true negative (TN) rate is 99.864%.

Next, we flipped the two weeks of learning and testing, making the second week for learning and the first week for testing. We replayed the same packets from devices 1 and 3 for 4340 times, in which 4340 is the number of system events that cause device 2 to forward a request to device 6 in the whole testing data set. The system was able to detect 4303 attacks correctly and missed 37 replayed events. As a result, the false negative (FN) rate of this trial is 0.85%, and the detection accuracy (TP) is 99.15%. The false positive rate (FP) for this trial is 0.64%, and the true negative (TN) rate is 99.36%.

In the following scenario, we repeat the same attacks but using a detection window size of $W = 2$. We use the data of the first week for learning and the second week for testing, and we get the following results: FN 0.652%, TP 99.348%, FP 0.07%, and TN 99.93%. Then, we learn from the data of the second week and test using the data of the first week. We get the following results: FN 0.85%, TP 99.15%, FP 0.33%, and TN 99.67%. Results are comparable to the ones with $W = 3$.

9.4.5.2   Man-in-the-Middle Attack (MIM) Analysis

MIM is a type of active eavesdropping in which the attacker relays connections between two victims after making independent connections between them. By this, the attacker makes each of the victims believe that they are talking to the other victim, and the attacker can fully control the communication stream. The attacker can modify the messages between the two parties and impersonate their identities.

The following is an example of legitimate transitions between three system events, one as a main request and two as a forwarded request and a reply:

Sequence of Legitimate Transitions
   Packet from Device A, type: Request, Service: Who is
   Followed by
   Packet from Device B, type: Request, Service: I am
   OR
   Packet from Device A, type: Request, Service: Who is
   Followed by
   Packet from Device C, type: Request, Service: Who is, Dest address.

Hence, from our data set, the learning module is trained to accept a reply from device B and a forwarded request to another destination address by device C only if device A sends a request with a "who is" service.

Sequence of Attack Malicious Transition
   Packet from Device A, type: Request, Service: Who is (Deleted Request)
   Followed by
   Packet from Device B, type: Request, Service: I am (Injected without Request)
   OR
   Packet from Device A, type: Request, Service: Who is (Deleted Request)
   Followed by
   Packet from Device C, type: Request, Service: Who is, Dest address. (Injected)

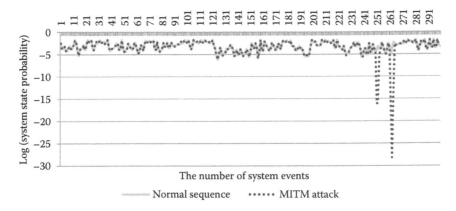

FIGURE 9.6 The system state analysis of the man-in-the-middle attacks.

As shown previously in the transitions, the attacker deletes the requests sent by device A and injects a response of device B and a forwarded request of device C. The detection engine detects these malicious injections of replayed packets, and the system state probability decreases significantly as illustrated in Figure 9.6.

In this scenario, the data was also divided into two sets, one for learning and one for testing. The attacker is assumed to be capable of analyzing the network for a long time in order to attempt to perform undetectable attacks and strategic injections. To calculate the false negative rate, the attacker tries to trick the detection engine by injecting packets knowing what the normal sequences are. Hence, we performed a large number of attacks in the testing data set in week two with 963,230 system events.

9.4.5.2.1 Man-in-the-Middle Attack Results

Three devices (1, 3, and 2098180) with a total of seven types of system events cause device number 2 to forward a request to device number 6. We analyzed the system events sent by these three devices to perform the attacks. Attacker model in this case allows the attacker to drop each packet sent by device number 2098180 and inject a legitimate request packet from device 1 or 3. The total number of man-in-the-middle injection packets was 2392, which is the total number of system events in which device 2098180 caused device number 2 to forward a request to device number 6. The system was able to detect 2307 attacks correctly and 85 system events considered mistakenly as normal transitions. As a result, FN = 3.55%, TP = 96.45%, FP = 0.136%, and TN = 99.864%.

Next, we flipped the two weeks of learning and testing, and we replayed the packets from devices 1 and 3 for 4340 times as man-in-the-middle attacks after deleting the requests, in which 4340 is the number of system events in the whole testing data set that caused device 2 to forward a request to device 6. The system was able to detect 4189 attacks correctly, and 151 replayed events passed undetected. As a result, FN = 3.47%, TP = 96.53%, FP = 0.64%, and TN = 99.36%. We repeated the same attacks but using a detection window size of 2. When we learn the first week and test the second week, we get the following: FN = 3.55%, TP = 96.45%, FP = 0.07%, and TN = 99.93%. Similarly, when learning the second week and testing the first week, we get FN = 3.47%, TP = 96.53%, FP = 0.33%, and TN = 99.67%. The results for the two window sizes are comparable.

9.4.5.3 Malicious Command/Response Injection

The attacker in this case injects legitimate BACnet request and response event packets but not similar to those in the learning phase. The total injected packets were 600 (we chose this number of injections randomly to test the accuracy) system events, and all of them were detected with a window size of $W = 3$. Hence, the detection accuracy of command-response injection is 100%. Figure 9.7 shows how the probability drops significantly for one of the detected injection commands. The false positive rate (FP) for this trial is 0.136% and the true negative (TN) rate is 99.864%.

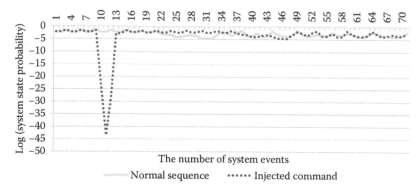

FIGURE 9.7   Command injection attack.

Similar to the previous trial, we flipped the learning and testing weeks. We made 900 new attack attempts, and all of these attacks were detected with 100% detection accuracy. Then, we changed the window size to $W = 2$ and repeated the same attacks, and we got a detection accuracy of 100%. Table 9.5 shows a summary of the false negative rates and detection accuracies of the three previous attacks.

TABLE 9.5

Detection Accuracy and False Negative Rates

Window Size = 3	Number of Attacks	Detected Attacks	Undetected Attacks	Detection Accuracy (TP)	False Negative Rate (FN)	True Negative Rate (TN)	False Positive Rate (FP)
MITM Attack Trial 1	2392	2307	85	96.45%	3.55%	99.864%	0.136%
MITM Attack Trial 2	4340	4189	151	96.53%	3.47%	99.36%	0.64%
Replay Attack Trial 1	2451	2435	16	99.348%	0.652%	99.864%	0.136%
Replay Attack Trial 2	4340	4303	37	99.15%	0.85%	99.36%	0.64%
Injection Attack Trial 1	600	600	0	100%	0%	99.864%	0.136%
Injection Attack Trial 2	900	900	0	100%	0%	99.36%	0.64%

Window Size = 2	Number of Attacks	Detected Attacks	Undetected Attacks	Detection Accuracy (TP)	False Negative Rate (FN)	True Negative Rate (TN)	False Positive Rate (FP)
MITM Attack Trial 1	2392	2307	85	96.45%	3.55%	99.93%	0.07%
MITM Attack Trial 2	4340	4189	151	96.53%	3.47%	99.671%	0.329%
Replay Attack Trial 1	2451	2435	16	99.348%	0.652%	99.93%	0.07%
Replay Attack Trial 2	4340	4303	37	99.15%	0.85%	99.671%	0.329%
Injection Attack Trial 1	600	600	0	100%	0%	99.93%	0.07%
Injection Attack Trial 2	900	900	0	100%	0%	99.671%	0.329%

The results show the high TP and TN rates for all attacks and the two window sizes used. This shows that the method is not sensitive to the window size nor the training set used.

9.4.5.4 Denial-of-Service Attack Analysis

The denial of service (DoS) attack is an attempt by an attacker or multiple attackers (distributed DoS) to make a resource unavailable for network users. There are many types of such attacks, including SYN flood, ICMP flood, teardrop attacks, and many others. In SCADA systems, the experiments showed that DoS attacks are easy to conduct on control devices due to their limitation of processing and memory capabilities. By sending service requests at a high frequency, we were able to stop the functionality of a PLC and make it not respond to other requests.

In Figure 9.8, we show the response of our detection system when performing DoS attacks. The first pulse represents a DoS attack using a legitimate request by sending it at a very high frequency. The second pulse illustrates the decrease of the system state probability as a result of the SYN flood attack. Note the logarithmic scale used for the y-axis, which represents the system state probability. Because the packet digest of such attack is not included in the table of learned digests, the detection accuracy TP is 100% and FN = 0%.

9.4.5.5 Scanning Attacks Analysis

The purpose of the scanning attacks is to find the vulnerability of a certain system. By performing port scanning, the attacker can get information about the operating system, open ports, and services running. There are several types of scanning attacks, including port scanning and systems

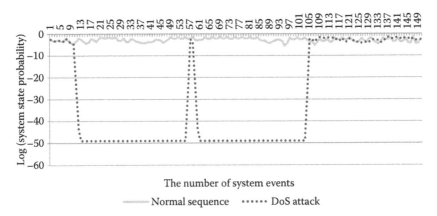

FIGURE 9.8 The system state analysis of DoS attacks.

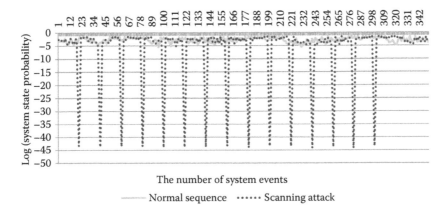

FIGURE 9.9 The system state analysis of scanning attacks.

fingerprinting. Using such attacks, an attacker can exploit the known vendor vulnerabilities of the control devices. Figure 9.9 illustrates the large decrease in system state probability when we injected probe packets among the normal system consecutive events. As we see, the probe packets come in fixed intervals to scan for open ports. It is worth noting that in this experiment we used a fixed interval for scanning; however, the detection would work as well for random interval scanners. Because the packet digest of such attack is not included in the table of learned digests, the detection accuracy TP is 100% and FN = 0%.

9.4.6 EXPERIMENTAL RESULTS ANALYSIS

The experimental results showed high detection accuracy for SCADA– and BMS–specific attacks. The lowest detection rate was above 96.45% for man-in-the-middle attacks, which is higher than any other detection algorithm in the field of SCADA and BMS detection systems. Moreover, we obtained high accuracies for replay, request/response injection, DoS, and scanning attacks. Although the detection accuracy is high, the number of false positive values is also high and sometimes reaches thousands because we are considering a very large number of system events. Such a problem will be solved in our future plan by designing an adaptive learning algorithm.

In addition, a limitation of our detection system is not considering the effect of time as a detection feature. The attacker can send a legitimate packet within a correct sequence but at a different time. Pushing a system event before or after its appropriate time might affect the whole SCADA and BMS systems because they sometimes have time-dependent processes.

9.5 CONCLUSION

In this chapter, we proposed an intrusion detection system based on Markov chains as an anomaly-based detection technique for SCADA systems. The results showed that the system was capable of detecting, with high accuracy, all SCADA intrusions, including injections, replays, and man-in-the-middle attacks. Moreover, the results showed that the period of the learning phase plays an important role in improving the detection accuracy of the detection system. However, the detection accuracy of the system is still high even for a one-day learning period because it is basically designed to scale for SCADA systems applications. We can summarize the advantages of our method as follows: (1) detects SCADA–specific attacks; (2) performs real-time detection; (3) shows high detection accuracy even with short learning periods; (4) high detection accuracy against replay and MITM attacks that are based on legitimate systems events injection; (5) low false positive (FP) rates.

However, our system has the following limitations, which will be addressed in future work: (1) time is not considered as a detection feature and hence might give low detection accuracy for time-dependent attacks; (2) legitimate system events could be mistakenly considered as intrusions; (3) learning module is not adaptive.

9.6 POTENTIAL AREAS FOR FUTURE WORK

We believe this is a rich area for research with several existing challenges that need to be addressed. We recommend potential areas for future research as follows:

1. Adaptive IDS, in which learning continues for a long time, hence improving the detection accuracy and reducing false alarms. However, the challenge with applying adaptive schemes is the risk of slow attacks being used to "teach" the IDS that the attack is actually legitimate traffic.
2. Internet of things (IoT) IDS: With the advent of IoT there is a need to address intrusions in this domain early on in the technology before the products are deployed. Therefore, we anticipate a need for intrusion detection research targeted at IoT type of devices and networks.

3. Identifying vulnerabilities in SCADA systems remains to be desirable, particularly that the security work in this area is relatively recent, and we suspect numerous vulnerabilities are waiting to be uncovered.

ACKNOWLEDGMENTS

Research funded by the Lebanese National Council for Scientific Research and the American University of Beirut University Research Board.

AUTHORS' BIOGRAPHIES

Alaa Atassi was born in Syria. He received his bachelor's degree, with distinction, in electronics and telecommunications engineering from Al-Baath University, Homs, Syria, in 2009. In 2012, he received his master's degree in electrical and computer engineering from the American University of Beirut (AUB). At AUB, he worked as a research assistant in the field of communications, wireless, and data networking with an emphasis on network security and industrial cyber security. He has published papers in low overhead anonymous routing and malicious node detection in wireless sensor networks. He is a member of the Syrian Engineers Association and a member of IEEE. In August 2012, he joined Innovative Contractors for Advanced Dimensions as information and communications technology engineer for special airport systems.

Imad H. Elhajj received his bachelor's of engineering in computer and communications engineering, with distinction, from the American University of Beirut in 1997 and the MS and PhD degrees in electrical engineering from Michigan State University in 1999 and 2002, respectively. He is currently an associate professor with the department of electrical and computer engineering. Dr. Elhajj is the vice-chair of the IEEE Lebanon Section, a senior member of IEEE, and a senior member of ACM. He is a member of the World Economic Forum Global Agenda Council on Robotics and Smart Devices. His research interests include cyber security, sensor and computer networks, multimedia networking, instrumentation, and robotics. Imad received the Most Outstanding Graduate Student Award from the Department of Electrical and Computer Engineering at Michigan State University in April 2001. Dr. Elhajj is recipient of the Teaching Excellence Award at the American University of Beirut, June 2011.

Ali Chehab received his bachelor's degree in EE from AUB in 1987, a master's degree in EE from Syracuse University in 1989, and a PhD degree in ECE from the University of North Carolina at Charlotte in 2002. From 1989 to 1998, he was a lecturer in the ECE department at the American University of Beirut (AUB). He rejoined the ECE department at AUB as an assistant professor in 2002 and became an associate professor in 2008. He received the AUB Teaching Excellence Award in 2007. His research interests include wireless communications security, cloud computing security, multimedia security, industrial security, trust in distributed computing, low energy VLSI design, and VLSI testing. He has about 130 publications. He is a senior member of IEEE and a member of ACM.

Ayman Kayssi was born in Lebanon. He studied electrical engineering and received the BE degree, with distinction, in 1987 from the American University of Beirut (AUB) and the MSE and PhD degrees from the University of Michigan, Ann Arbor, in 1989 and 1993, respectively. He received the Academic Excellence Award of the AUB Alumni Association in 1987. In 1993, he joined the Department of Electrical and Computer Engineering (ECE) at AUB, where he is currently a full professor. In 1999–2000, he took a leave of absence and joined Transmog, Inc., as chief technology officer. From 2004 to 2007, he served as chairman of the ECE Department at AUB. He teaches courses in electronics and in networking and has received AUB's Teaching Excellence Award in 2003. His research interests are in information security and networks and in integrated circuit design and testing.

He has published more than 160 articles in the areas of VLSI, networking, security, and engineering education. He is a senior member of IEEE and a member of ACM, ISOC, and the Beirut OEA.

REFERENCES

1. A. Daneels and W. Salter, What is SCADA? in *Proceeding of International Conference on Accelerator and Large Experimental Physics Control Systems*, pp. 39–343, 1999.
2. V. M. Igure and R. D. Williams, Security and SCADA protocols, *5th International Topical Meeting on Nuclear Plant Instrumentation Controls, and Human Machine Interface Technology (NPIC and HMIT)*, pp. 560–567, USA, 2006.
3. J. Slay and M. Miller, 2008, Lessons learned from the Maroochy water breach, *Critical Infrastructure Protection*, vol. 253, pp. 73–82, 2008.
4. D. Ryu, H. Kim and K. Um, Reducing security vulnerabilities for critical infrastructure, *Journal of Loss Prevention in the Process Industries*, vol. 22, pp. 1020–1024, 2009.
5. N. Falliere, L. O. Murchu and E. Chien, W32.Stuxnet dossier, Symantec Report version 1.3, Nov 2010.
6. V. M. Igure, S. A. Laughter and R. D. Williams, Security issues in SCADA networks, *Elsevier Computer and Security Journal*, vol. 25, pp. 498–506, 2006.
7. T. Kropp, System threats and vulnerabilities [power system protection], *Power and Energy Magazine*, IEEE, vol. 4, pp. 46–50, 2006.
8. R. Turk, Cyber incidents involving control systems, U.S. Department of Homeland Security, Oct 2005.
9. S. Luders, Control systems under attack? in CERN OPEN 2005 Conference, Cern, Geneva, Switzerland, 2005.
10. M. Kabay, Attacks on power systems: Hackers, Malware, Norwich University, 2010.
11. Z. Zhou, C. Zhongwen, Z. Tiecheng and G. Xiaohui, The study on network intrusion detection system of Snort, Networking and Digital Society (ICNDS), 2nd International Conference, pp. 194–196, China, 2010.
12. M. Attig and J. Lockwood, SIFT: Snort intrusion filter for TCP, *High Performance Interconnects, Proceedings 13th Symposium*, pp. 121–127, USA, 2005.
13. G. Yang, D. Chen, J. Xu and Z. Zhu, Research of intrusion detection system based on vulnerability scanner, *Advanced Computer Control (ICACC), 2nd International Conference*, pp. 173–176, China, 2010.
14. T. D. Tarman, E. L. Witzke, K. C. Bauer, B. R. Kellogg and W. F. Young, Asynchronous transfer mode (ATM) intrusion detection, *Military Communications Conference, MILCOM, Communications for Network-Centric Operations: Creating the Information Force*, pp. 87–91, vol. 1, USA, 2001.
15. B. H. Chung, S. H. Ryu, J. N. Kim and J. S. Jang, Kernel-level intrusion detection method using simplification and grouping, *Advanced Communication Technology, ICACT, the 7th International Conference*, pp. 251–254, Korea, 2005.
16. L. Lei-jun and P. Hong, A defense model study based on IDS and firewall linkage, *Information Science and Management Engineering (ISME)*, International Conference, pp. 91–94, China, 2010.
17. H. Salehi, H. Shirazi and R. A. Moghadam, Increasing overall network security by integrating signature-based NIDS with packet filtering firewall, *International Joint Conference on Artificial Intelligence*, pp. 357–362, USA, 2009.
18. H. Li and D. Liu, Research on intelligent intrusion prevention system based on Snort, *Computer, Mechatronics, Control and Electronic Engineering (CMCE)*, International Conference, pp. 251–253, China, 2010.
19. M. A. Qadeer, A. Iqbal, M. Zahid and M. R. Siddiqui, Network traffic analysis and intrusion detection using packet sniffer, *Second International Conference on Communication Software and Networks*, pp. 313–317, USA, 2010.
20. S. Roschke, F. Cheng and C. Meinel, An extensible and virtualization-compatible IDS management architecture, *Information Assurance and Security, IAS '09, Fifth International Conference*, pp. 130–134, China, 2009.
21. A. Farroukh, N. Mukadam, E. Bassil and I. H. Elhajj, Distributed and collaborative intrusion detection systems, *Communications Workshop, LCW, IEEE*, pp. 41–45, Lebanon, 2008.
22. P. M. Mafra, V. Moll, J. da Silva Fraga and A. O. Santin, Octopus-IIDS: An anomaly based intelligent intrusion detection system, *IEEE Symposium on Computers and Communications*, pp. 405–410, Italy, 2010.

23. U. Ahmed and A. Masood, Host based intrusion detection using RBF neural networks, *Emerging Technologies, ICET International Conference*, pp. 48–51, Pakistan, 2009.

24. S. Zaman and F. Karray, Lightweight IDS based on features selection and IDS classification scheme, *International Conference on Computational Science and Engineering*, pp. 365–370, Canada, 2009.

25. M. Deraman, J. M. Desa and Z. Othman, Multilayer packet tagging for network behaviour analysis, *Information Technology (ITSim), International Symposium*, pp. 909–913, Malaysia, 2010.

26. K. Lu, Z. Chen, Z. Jin and J. Guo, An adaptive real-time intrusion detection system using sequences of system call, *Electrical and Computer Engineering, IEEE CCECE, Canadian Conference*, pp. 789–792, vol. 2, Canada, 2003.

27. M. Jun and F. Shuqian, Research of intrusion detection system based on machine learning, *Computer Engineering and Technology (ICCET), 2nd International Conference*, pp. V7-713–V7-715, China, 2010.

28. Z. Quangang, A new model of intelligent hybrid detection system, *Networking and Digital Society (ICNDS), 2nd International Conference*, pp. 381–384, China, 2010.

29. Z. Xiao-hui, L. Wen-lang, Z. Jin-tao, C. Yan-ping and J. Shi-yao, Research on a high efficient intrusion prevention model, *Intelligent Information Technology and Security Informatics (IITSI), Third International Symposium*, pp. 720–723, China, 2010.

30. P. Jain and S. Goyal, An adaptive intrusion prevention system based on immunity, *International Conference on Advances in Computing, Control, and Telecommunication Technologies*, pp. 759–763, India, 2009.

31. R. C. Chen, K. F. Cheng and C. F. Hsieh, Using rough set and support vector machine for network intrusion detection, *International Journal of Network Security and Its Applications* 1.1, pp. 1–13, 2010.

32. S. Cheung, B. Dutertre, M. Fong, U. Lindqvist, K. Skinner and A. Valdes, Using model-based intrusion detection for SCADA networks, *Proceedings of the SCADA Security Scientific Symposium*, pp. 127–134, 2007.

33. C. Wang, L. Fang and Y. Dai, A simulation environment for SCADA security analysis and assessment, *ICMTMA Proceedings of the International Conference on Measuring Technology and Mechatronics Automation*, vol. 01, pp. 342–347, USA, 2010.

34. C. Valli, SCADA Forensics with Snort IDS, *Proceedings of WORLDCOMP2009, Security and Management*, pp. 618–621, USA, 2009.

35. M. Mallouhi, Y. Al-Nashif, D. Cox, T. Chadaga and S. Hariri, A testbed for analyzing security of SCADA control systems (TASSCS), *Innovative Smart Grid Technologies (ISGT), IEEE PES*, pp. 1–7, India, 2011.

36. T. Vollmer, O. Linda and M. Manic, Neural network based intrusion detection system for critical infrastructures, *Neural Networks, IJCNN, International Joint Conference*, pp. 1827–1834, USA, 2009.

37. W. Gao, T. Morris, B. Reaves and D. Richey, On SCADA control system command and response injection and intrusion detection, *ECrime Researchers Summit (eCrime)*, pp. 1–9, USA, 2010.

38. D. Yang, A. Usynin and J. W. Hines, Anomaly-based intrusion detection for SCADA systems, *5th Int. Topical Meeting on Nuclear Plant Instrumentation, Control and Human Machine Interface Technologies (NPIC&HMIT 05)*, Albuquerque, NM, Nov 12–16, 2006.

39. E. Naess, D. Frincke, A. McKinnon and D. Bakken, Configurable middleware-level intrusion detection for embedded systems, *25th IEEE International Conference on Distributed Computing Systems Workshops*, pp. 144–151, 2005.

40. S. D'Antonio, F. Oliviero, and R. Setola, High-speed intrusion detection in support of critical infrastructure protection, *Proc. of 1st International Workshop on Critical Information Infrastructures Security*, 2006.

41. I. Nai Fovino, A. Carcano, M. Masera, A. Trombetta and T. Delacheze-Murel, Modbus/DNP3 state-based intrusion detection system, *Proc. 24th Int. Conf. Advanced Information Networking and Applications*, pp. 729–736, 2010.

42. Á. MacDermott, Q. Shi, M. Merabti, and K. Kifayat, Intrusion Detection for Critical Infrastructure Protection, *The 13th Annual PostGraduate Symposium on the Coverage of Telecommunications, Networking and Broadcasting*, UK, June 2012.

43. Wireshark Sniffer, https://www.wireshark.org.

44. BACnet Tutorial, http://www.bacnet.org/Tutorial/BACnetIP/default.html.

10 Hardware Techniques for High-Performance Network Intrusion Detection

Weirong Jiang and Viktor K. Prasanna

CONTENTS

FIGURE 10.1   A sample Snort rule.

10.1   INTRODUCTION

The scale of the Internet has grown explosively to a giant open network. Unfortunately, network attacks require little effort and monetary investment to create, are difficult to trace, and can be launched from virtually anywhere in the globe [1]. A network intrusion detection system (NIDS) [2,3] is a critical network security facility that helps protect high-speed computer networks from malicious users. A NIDS examines network communications, identifies patterns of attacks, and then takes action either to terminate the connections or alert system administrators. While various techniques have been proposed for advanced NIDS, the most widely deployed is the signature-based NIDS. A signature-based NIDS, such as Snort [3], employs thousands of rules that contain intrusion patterns. Each Snort rule is divided into two logical sections: the rule header and the rule options. The rule header contains the rule's action and a classification filter that consists of five fixed fields: protocol, source IP address, source port, destination IP address, and destination port. The rule option contains alert messages and pattern information on how a packet payload should be inspected.

Figure 10.1 shows a sample Snort rule in which the section enclosed in parentheses is the rule option and the remaining part is the rule header. The results of the header classification identify the related rule options that will be checked in the follow-up deep packet inspection (DPI). Deep packet inspection is based on pattern matching, in which Snort employs two types of patterns: strings and regular expressions. Both header classification and deep packet inspection as the core functions of NIDS are computation-intensive, which has challenged the conventional computing architectures with demanding CPU, memory, and I/O requirements. For example, the current Ethernet link rate has been pushed beyond 100 Gbps [4], which requires processing a packet every 5 ns in the worst case (in which the Ethernet packets are of minimum size, i.e., 64 bytes). Given the explosive growth of network traffic, hardware techniques are required to accelerate these functions to prevent the NIDS from becoming the performance bottleneck of the network systems.

When examining today's hardware techniques, we have general-purpose processors, such as CPUs (central processing units) and GPUs (graphics processing units), on one end of the spectrum and application-specific integrated circuits (ASICs) on the other. Processors are highly programmable but usually deliver inferior performance for network processing due to the Von Neumann paradigm in which the bandwidth between the processor and the external memory is the limit (a.k.a., "memory wall" [5]). ASICs provide the best performance but require a complete and extremely expensive re-fabrication of the circuits. Fortunately, there exists some architecture between these two extremes. Reconfigurable hardware, such as a field-programmable gate array (FPGA), offers the best of both worlds. Modern FPGAs provide superior performance, and they can be reprogrammed on the fly [6]. This opens the door to the advanced hardware accelerators for NIDS as illustrated in the rest of this chapter.

10.2   HARDWARE TECHNIQUES FOR PACKET HEADER CLASSIFICATION

In NIDS, a packet may match multiple rule headers. Traditional network applications, such as firewall processing, require reporting only the highest priority matching rule, which we call the best-match packet classification [7,8]. In contrast, NIDS needs multi-match packet classification to find all rule headers that match a given packet [9–11].

10.2.1 BACKGROUND AND ANALYSIS

In multi-match packet classification, the 32-bit source and destination IP addresses (denoted SA/DA), the 16-bit source and destination port numbers (denoted SP/DP), and the 8-bit protocol (denoted Prtcl) fields from the rule header of a Snort rule are matched by the input packet header. We define SA, DA, SP, DP, and Prtcl as the five fields of a packet header rule. The IP addresses in SA/DA fields are specified as prefixes, which can represent either a network or a single host. The port numbers in SP/DP fields can be specified as any, a single number, or a range. The protocol field in the current version of Snort has only four values: tcp, udp, icmp, and ip. For the SA/DA and SP/DP fields, Snort supports specifying a list of values enclosed within square brackets. Snort also provides the negation operator "!". For example, ![50,90] indicates any port number except 50 and 90. In addition, Snort uses "EXTERNALNET" as an implicit negation of "HOMENET" in SA/DA fields.

Table 10.1 shows the statistics of 10 rule sets collected spanning five years from the Snort website [3]. Each column counts the number of unique values for each item. We have the following observations:

- The number of Snort rules is much larger than the number of unique rule headers. In other words, a rule header is shared by many rules in Snort.
- The number of rule headers remains quite small although it has increased gradually. The number of unique rule headers has almost doubled since 2005.
- Although the number of rule headers has been increasing gradually, the number of unique values for SA/DA fields tends to be small, less than 15.
- Unlike SA/DA fields, the number of values for SP/DP fields is increasing at a similar rate as that of rule headers. The number of unique SP/DP values is also on the same order of that of rule headers.
- The value of the protocol field is restricted to be tcp, udp, icmp, and ip. Thus the number of unique values of this field remains at four.

TABLE 10.1
Statistics of Snort Rule Headers

Rule Set ID	Snort Version	# Rules	# Rule Headers	# SA	# DA	# SP	# DP	# Prtl
0	2.3.0	3182	323	11	13	87	173	4
1	2.4.0	3462	340	11	13	91	183	4
2	2.3.0	8171	589	10	14	198	316	4
3	2.4.0	8346	594	10	14	198	320	4
4	2.6.0	9290	613	10	13	203	330	4
5	2.7.0	9244	594	10	13	190	327	4
6	2.8.0	9040	600	10	14	202	321	4
7	2.8.0	9277	620	10	13	204	336	4
8	2.8.0	9257	597	10	13	187	332	4
9	2.8.4	5662	609	10	13	184	344	4

Moreover, we examine the usage of those unique features provided by Snort rules, including the value list, the negation operator, and the range operator for port fields.

- Most of the port fields are specified as a single value. More than 85% of the unique values for SP/DP fields are specified as a single value, and only around 10% of port field values are specified as ranges.
- Negation operator is seldom used. Apart from the implicit negation by using "EXTERNALNET" in SA/DA fields, only the SP field has a couple of negation values.
- Each field uses few value lists. The number of value lists in SA/DA/SP/DP fields is 0/3/1/10, respectively. The value lists in SP/DP fields have no more than four values, and the value list in DA field contains up to 18 IP addresses.

10.2.2 TCAM–BASED APPROACHES

Ternary content addressable memory (TCAM) is a specialized ASIC widely used in network search engines. Most of the existing multi-match packet classification engines are based on TCAMs in which each input performs a parallel search over all entries in one clock cycle, and only the first matching index is output [10,12]. Figure 10.2 shows a TCAM storing three 4-bit ternary words: 1001, 1*1*, and *00*. The priority encoder is needed to obtain the highest matching entry out of the final match vector. Normally the top matching entry has the highest priority. In Figure 10.2, the input key 1001 matches both 1001 and *00*. But the entry 1001 has a higher priority than *00*. Hence, the output matching entry index is 00.

Some early work by Lakshminarayanan et al. [13] exploits the extra bits in each TCAM entry and finds all matching rules for a packet in multiple clock cycles. The number of clock cycles needed to classify a packet is linear to the number of matching rules. This results in low speed and high power consumption in the worst case.

One of the state-of-the-art TCAM-based multi-match packet classification solutions are proposed by Yu et al. [10], which are based on geometric intersection of rules. If two rules match a same packet header, several intersection rules that cover the overlap between the two rules are created and inserted into the TCAM. Only one TCAM lookup is needed to obtain all matching results. However, the number of intersection rules can be $O(N^D)$, in which N is the total number of rules and D is the number of fields. Although the authors later propose the set splitting

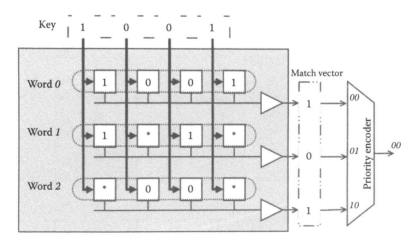

FIGURE 10.2 A 3 × 4 bits TCAM.

algorithm (SSA) [11] to split the rule set into two groups to remove at least half of the intersections among the rules, the worst-case memory requirement is still $O(N^D)$. Thus, this approach is expensive with respect to both memory and power consumption when the rule set has many intersections.

Faezipour et al. [12] propose the maximum–minimum intersection partitioning (MX-MN-IP) approach for TCAM-based multi-match packet classification. The power consumption is reduced by partitioning the entire rule set into several disjoint partitions so that only one partition is active in classifying a packet. Each partition is further partitioned so that each sub-partition needs only one clock cycle to output no more than one matching result. However, the MX-MN-IP scheme may need a large number of small TCAMs, which is not practical for real implementation. Because the number of partitions depends on the characteristic of the rule set, the power reduction ratio can vary a lot. As shown in [12], some rule sets can achieve only 5% power savings compared to conventional (non-partitioning) TCAM-based approaches.

10.2.3 ALGORITHMIC APPROACHES ON FPGA

TCAMs are expensive and not scalable with respect to clock rate, power consumption, or circuit area, compared to static random access memories (SRAMs) [8,14]. As the rule set size increases rapidly, alternate hardware platforms are needed for multi-match packet classification engines. State-of-the-art SRAM-based field programmable gate array (FPGA) devices, such as Xilinx Virtex-7 [15], provide a high clock rate and a large amount of on-chip dual-port memory with configurable word width. It takes a few milliseconds to reconfigure an entire FPGA, and the update frequency of NIDS rules is on the order of days. Thus, FPGA has become an attractive platform for realizing real-time network processing engines [9,14].

The bit vector (BV) algorithm [16] and its variants [17] are among the few existing packet classification algorithms that support returning all matching rules for a packet at the same time. The BV algorithm performs the parallel lookups on each individual field of a packet header at first. The lookup on each field returns a bit vector with each bit representing a rule. A bit is set to "1" if the corresponding rule matches in this field; otherwise the bit is set to "0". The result of the bitwise AND operation on these bit vectors gives the set of rules that matches a given packet. The BV algorithm can provide high throughput at the cost of low memory efficiency. Given N rules with D fields, because the projection of the N rules on each field may have $U = O(N)$ unique values and each value corresponds to one N-bit vector, the total memory requirement of BV algorithms is at least $U * N * D = O(N^2)$, which is undesirable [7,8].

By combining TCAMs and the original BV algorithm, Song et al. [9] present an architecture called BV-TCAM for multi-match packet classification on FPGAs. A TCAM performs prefix or exact match, and a multi-bit trie implemented in tree bitmap [18] is used for source or destination port lookup. It prevents range-to-prefix expansion for port fields. However, BV-TCAM still suffers from the $O(N^2)$ memory requirement inherited from the original BV algorithm.

Jiang et al. [14] make a key observation: If splitting a W-bit field into W subfields in which each subfield takes only 1 bit, the number of unique values in each subfield will be no more than two, i.e., the subfield value $\in[0,1]$. Then each subfield corresponds to $2N$-bit vectors, and the overall memory requirement for this W-bit field is $2W * N = O(WN)$ instead of $U * N = O(N^2)$ in the original BV algorithm. Such an algorithm is called the field-split bit vector (FSBV). It reduces the memory requirement when $2W < U$. Because W is a fixed number, FSBV achieves a linear memory increase with the number of rules. Figure 10.3 shows an example of applying the FSBV algorithm for matching the DP field (assuming 4 bits) of a packet against three rules. Splitting a field may result in many subfields, which leads to a lot of bit vectors to be merged via bitwise AND operations. Thanks to the rich resources and massive parallelism offered by FPGA, the FSBV architecture can be efficiently implemented in reconfigurable hardware.

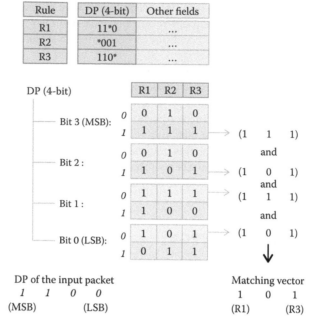

FIGURE 10.3   FSBV example: The packet matches both R1 and R3 on the DP field.

10.2.4 SUPPORTING SNORT FEATURES

Snort rule headers provide several unique features, including range, negation operators, and value list. Most of today's hardware accelerators do not support these features. This section showcases how to support these Snort features in the FSBV architecture.

10.2.4.1 Range

Both the TCAM and the FSBV solutions assume each rule is represented as a ternary string. To satisfy an assumption, a range needs to be converted into ternary strings. Most of the previous TCAM-based solutions convert a W-bit range into up to $2(W-1)$ prefixes [13]. Sasao [19] proposes an algorithm to convert a W-bit range into no more than $2(W-2)$ ternary strings. Rottenstreich et al. [20] have proven that a W-bit range can be encoded in W TCAM entries by optimal encoding.

After ranges are represented as ternary strings, we use the *expansion-aggregation* method (introduced later for the value list) to implement each range. The range-to-ternary-string conversion may increase the memory requirement. Each rule contains two port fields, which are specified in ranges. In the worst case in which all port fields of the N rules are specified as W-bit ranges, the total memory requirement will be $O(W^2N)$ rather than $O(WN)$.

10.2.4.2 Negation

A negated value may be converted into multiple ternary strings. This can affect the memory efficiency significantly [10]. Some TCAM-based work [10] reorganizes the rule set and inserts extra rules to remove negation. For BV-based algorithmic solutions, we consider a simple method that does not add any new rule. Given N rules with D fields, we assign an N-bit mask vector for each field. Initially all bits of a mask vector are reset to 0. If the ith rule ($i = 0, 1, ..., N-1$) has negated value in its jth field ($j = 0, 1, ..., D-1$), the ith bit of the mask vector for the jth field is set to 1.

For a field with negation, we use its unnegated value to build bit vectors. When performing packet classification, we merge the bit vectors of each field independently and obtain D partial matching vectors. The partial matching vector from the jth field ($j = 0, 1, ..., D-1$) is bitwise XORed with the mask vector of the jth field. If the ith bit of the mask vector is set, the matching result for the ith rule on this field will be negated. Such a method can be easily integrated into BV-based architectures, such as FSBV [14].

10.2.4.3 Value List

Snort allows SA/DA/SP/DP fields to be specified using a list of values. As shown in the earlier analysis, the current Snort rule set uses few value lists. A value list can be expanded to multiple values. Meanwhile, the range-to-string conversion also results in a list of values for a single field. If one rule has multiple fields in which each field is specified as a value list, this rule may be expanded to $\prod_{j=1}^{D} M_j$ rules, where D is the number of fields and M_j is the number of values in the list of the jth field.

To solve the above problem, we introduce a simple method called *expansion-aggregation*. For example, if a field of the ith rule is specified as a list of M values, the ith bit of all bit vectors for this field is expanded to M bits. When building the bit vectors for this field, each single value out of the M values is treated as a rule. To perform packet header classification, after all bit vectors of this field are bitwise ANDed to a single $(N + M - 1)$-bit vector, the M bits corresponding to the M values are ORed to result in one bit. Thus, the output partial matching vector of this field is still an N-bit vector.

10.2.5 Comparison

Table 10.2 compares the performance of the state-of-the-art hardware solutions for multi-match packet classification in NIDS.

We can see that the FSBV architecture achieves low memory requirement, which is comparable to TCAMs and is much less than BV-TCAM. Note that only FSBV can handle the negation and value list problems. Much higher memory consumption can be expected in other solutions to support Snort rule features. For both TCAM-SSA and MX-MN-IP in which the performance depends highly on the rule set, the performance comparison here considers the best case and assumes that each rule can be stored as one entry in TCAM without any expansion.

The throughput results of the FSBV and the BV-TCAM architectures are based on FPGA implementations, and those of the TCAM-SSA and the MX-MN-IP are based on TCAMs implemented as ASIC, which usually has a much higher clock rate than FPGA. We consider the clock frequency of TCAMs to be 250 MHz [11,12]. The original BV-TCAM paper [9] does not present the actual throughput results of the implementation. Instead it provides the predicted value. According to Table 10.2, the FSBV architecture achieves the highest throughput among the state-of-the-art solutions.

We also estimate the power consumption of SRAM and TCAM based on the data from [8]. The power consumption per bit of TCAMs is on the order of 3 μW, and that for SRAMs is less than 30 nW. Considering the 5% power savings, the power consumption of MX-MN-IP is calculated as 95% of the result of the TCAM-SSA. As two SRAM-based architectures, the FSBV and the

TABLE 10.2

Comparison of Hardware-Based Multi-Match Packet Classification Solutions

Approach	Platform	Throughput (Gbps)	Storage (bytes/rule)	Power (μW/rule)	Support for Snort Features
BV-TCAM [9]	FPGA	10	73.8	17.7	No
TCAM-SSA [11]	TCAM	20	13	312	No
MX-MN-IP [12]	TCAM	80	13	296	No
FSBV [14]	FPGA	100	17.4	4.2	Yes

BV-TCAM solutions are much more power-efficient than the TCAM-based approaches (TCAM-SSA and MX-MN-IP). Due to the lower memory requirement, the FSBV architecture achieves a fourfold reduction in power consumption compared with BV-TCAM.

10.3 HARDWARE TECHNIQUES FOR STRING MATCHING

The functions of NIDS rely on multi-pattern string matching, which scans the input stream to find all occurrences of a predefined set of string-based patterns rather than a single pattern [21,22]. Due to the explosive growth of network traffic, multi-pattern string matching has been a major perfor-mance bottleneck in NIDS, which has to scan the incoming traffic in real time on fast links (e.g., 100 Gbps Ethernet and beyond) [23,24]. For example, it has been reported that the string matching time accounts for 40% to 70% of the Snort running time [25]. Simple and efficient hardware-based multi-pattern string matching engines have become a necessity for high-speed NIDS [21].

10.3.1 Overview

Although string matching has been a classic problem for decades, multi-pattern string matching has sparked renewed research interest due to its application in NIDS [21]. Some comprehensive sur-veys can be found [21,26]. According to the implementation platform, the state-of-the-art solutions can be generally divided into three categories: multi-core processor–based [24,27,28], application-specific integrated circuit (ASIC)–based [23,29–31], and field programmable gate array (FPGA)–based [32–35] solutions. Each of the three hardware solutions has its own pros and cons. Advanced multi-core processor–based solutions can improve the aggregate throughput dramatically by using a large number of threads to process multiple input streams in parallel. On the other hand, it has been observed that the memory access pattern in string matching is irregular [24,27]. This results in relatively low per-stream throughput, which is critical for real-time network traffic processing. Although it is possible to split an input stream into several sub-streams with partial overlap among the sub-streams, additional complexity is introduced in scheduling, buffering, and ordering [30]. ASIC–based solutions provide impressively high per-stream throughput while their applicability is limited by the high implementation cost and low reprogrammability. Combining the flexibility of software and the near-ASIC performance, FPGA technology has become an attractive option for implementing high-performance string matching engines.

The majority of existing FPGA–based string matching solutions is based on pure logic [32,34]. Although they provide desirable high performance, it takes considerable time to resynthesize the design and reprogram the FPGA device. In case of pattern updates, the hardware-wired string matching engine has to be offline; thus, it is unable to detect network intrusion or viruses during that period. Hence, we resort to memory-based architectures, which support dynamic updates at run time. Most of the existing memory-based architectures [23,30,35] are based on the Aho–Corasick (AC) algorithm [36] for its ability to provide deterministic throughput. We revisit the AC algorithm in the next section to unveil the source of its memory inefficiency, which is the key limitation in hardware accelerators for large-scale string matching.

10.3.2 Understanding the Aho–Corasick Algorithm

The Aho–Corasick (AC) algorithm [36] is one of the earliest algorithms in multi-pattern string matching. Among all variants of AC algorithms, AC-DFA is widely adopted for its deterministic throughput. AC-DFA converts a pattern set, which contains N characters into a deterministic finite automaton (DFA) with $O(N)$ states. Once the DFA, which can be stored as a state transition table, is built, it reads in the input stream one character per clock cycle. Each input character is processed only once and results in exactly one state transition. Thus, it takes $O(M)$ time to process an input stream consisting of M characters. Figure 10.4 shows an example of the AC-DFA construction for

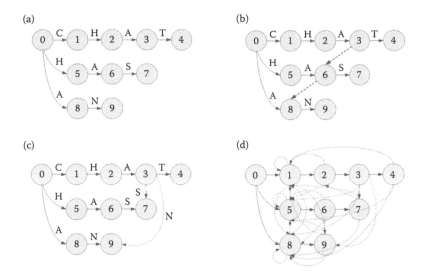

FIGURE 10.4 Constructing the AC-DFA for the strings {CHAT, HAS, AN}. (a) AC-Trie, (b) adding failure transitions, (c) changing to a DFA, and (d) final DFA.

the three string patterns: "CHAT," "HAS," and "AN." AC-DFA starts with constructing a trie (we call it AC-trie) in which the root is the default non-matching state. Each pattern to be matched adds states to the trie, one state per character, starting at the root and going to the end of the pattern. The transition edge between two states is stored as a *goto* function: $g(s_1,c) = s_2$, which means state s_1 receiving the character c will switch to state s_2. In the example shown in Figure 10.4a, $g(3,T) = 4$.

The AC-trie is then traversed, and failure transitions are added for each state. The failure transition of a state is used in case the *goto* function reports failure, i.e., the string matching on the current traversed path is not found. Initially, all nodes have the default failure transitions to the root. But it is possible that the suffix of the previously matched string is the prefix of another string in the trie. Hence, the failure transitions are updated to reuse the information associated with the last input characters (suffix) to recognize patterns that begin with that suffix without restarting from the root. To reuse as much history information as possible, the failure transition of a node (denoted N_1) is from it to such a node (denoted N_2) that the path from the root to N_2 is the longest prefix equal to the suffix ending at N_1. The failure transitions are represented as failure functions: $f(s_1) = s_2$, indicating there is a failure transition from state s_1 to state s_2, and we define s_2 as the failure state of s_1. Taking Figure 10.4b as an example, two prefixes "HA" and "A" are both the suffixes of "CHA," i.e., both states 6 and 8 are the candidates for the failure state of state 3. But because "HA" is longer, the failure transition of state 3 is to state 6, i.e., $f(3) = 6$.

The AC-trie with failure transitions (we call it AC-fail) is not a DFA yet because an input character may invoke multiple failure transitions. For example in Figure 10.4b, when state 3 receives the character "N," its own *goto* function will report failure. Then, via its failure transition, state 3 transits to state 6, which will check its *goto* function to see if the character "N" can be accepted. Because state 6's *goto* function still reports failure, state 6 has to consult its failure function, which directs it to state 8. Finally state 8 accepts "N" and transits to state 9. In other words, it takes two failure transitions and one *goto* transition for the input character "N" to be accepted. To convert the AC-fail into a DFA, Aho and Corasick [36] propose to combine the failure function with the *goto* function to obtain *next-move* functions: $\delta(s_1,c) = s_2$, which means state s_1 receiving the character c will switch to state s_2. In the above example, $\delta(3,N) = \delta(f(3) = 6,N) = \delta(f(6) = 8,N) = 9$ as shown in Figure 10.4c.

Figure 10.4d shows the complete DFA after adding all transitions. For the sake of readability, we do not show the default transitions to the root and remove all the labels on the transitions.

Unlike in an AC-fail, one character from the input stream results in exactly one transition in a AC-DFA. But the cost is that the memory requirement becomes higher due to the increasing number of transitions. For example, state 3 in Figure 10.4d will have six transitions, and it has only two transitions in Figure 10.4b. Such an increase in the number of transitions is caused by transition duplication due to the combination of the failure transitions with the *goto* transitions. For example, because $f(3) = 6$, $f(f(3)) = 8$, $f(f(f(3))) = 0$, the *goto* transitions of states 6, 8, and 0 may be all copied to state 3.

10.3.3 DEFLATING AC-DFA

Currently, there are two general approaches to reduce the memory requirement of AC-DFA. One is to minimize the number of states, and the other is to minimize the number of transitions. In most cases, these two approaches are orthogonal to each other and can be employed together to achieve higher memory efficiency.

10.3.3.1 Reducing the Number of States

Lin et al. [37] exploit the similarity between different states in an AC-DFA. The number of states is reduced by merging pseudo-equivalent states while maintaining the correctness of string matching. But the memory reduction achieved depends on the characteristics of the pattern set and is quite limited (e.g., 29% memory reduction is achieved for 1595 Snort string patterns [37]).

Alicherry et al. [29] divide each pattern into W-byte blocks, which are then used to construct a AC-DFA. This results in a "compressed" AC-DFA with fewer states and transitions. Meanwhile, the throughput can be improved by W times by running W instances of the AC-DFA in parallel, each of which accepts the same input data stream with a one-character offset (to ensure that no pattern is missed). However, because their architecture is based on TCAM, the improvements in memory requirement and throughput will be partially offset by the high cost of TCAM [38].

10.3.3.2 Reducing the Number of Transitions

As pointed out [30], there is very little space to reduce the number of states. Hence, a large body of work on memory-efficient string matching is to reduce the number of transitions. Tan et al. [31] propose the bit-split architecture to split a full AC-DFA into several partial state machines (PSM), each accepting a small portion (1 or 2 bits) of the input as transition labels. A partial match vector (PMV), one bit per pattern, is maintained at every state in the PSM to map the state to a set of possible matches. At every clock cycle, the PMVs from all PSMs are bitwise ANDed to generate a full match vector (FMV) to find the actual matches. However, there are substantial overheads in implementing a large number of PSMs in real hardware [39].

Lunteren [40] observes that a large fraction of state transitions are to the root or to the states in level 1. These transitions can be removed from the original AC-DFA by using a separate 256-entry on-chip table to keep track of them. The number of transitions can be further reduced by partitioning the pattern set into multiple subsets. But the performance of the partitioning scheme depends on the characteristics of the pattern set. In addition to [40], Song et al. [23] reduce more transitions by adding one buffer to "cache" the previous state. But it requires a dual-port memory to be accessed by both the cached state and the current state in parallel. The effective throughput is one character per clock cycle, which halves the potential throughput of using dual-port memory.

Note that the number of forward transitions in an AC-DFA with N states is always $N + 1$. Hence, there is little room to reduce the number of forward transitions. Yang et al. [35] and Pao et al. [38] propose to incorporate the pipeline architecture to remove all cross transition edges of an AC-DFA. Instead of being converted into a DFA, the AC-trie is mapped onto a linear pipeline. Each trie level is mapped to a stage containing a separate memory block. At each clock cycle, the input character is carried to all stages to invoke the state transition in each stage. Meanwhile, each stage forwards the output state to its next stage. Such pipelined solutions require an L-stage pipeline for mapping an L-level AC-trie. But the number of levels in an AC-trie corresponds to the length of the longest pattern. As we can see later, the length of the patterns in modern NIDS can be very large, making those pipelined solutions impractical to handle long patterns. As a workaround, Yang et al. [35] limit the pattern length to be smaller than 64. Pao et al. [38] propose to partition the long patterns into segments. Each segment is matched in the pipeline, and the segment IDs are used to build a high-level DFA for matching the entire pattern. Several small tables are needed to take care of the fragmentation when the string is matched in the middle of a segment. Such a solution complicates the overall architecture and is hard to extend for supporting multi-character input per clock cycle to achieve high throughput. Furthermore, [38] considers only the ASCII characters, which makes it less interesting for NIDS.

10.3.3.3 Depth-Bounded Pipeline

Existing pipelined string matching solutions aim to eliminate all cross transitions in a AC-DFA. But this results in a pipeline with unbounded depth. We generalize the problem and show that a linear pipeline with H stages can remove all cross transitions to the top H levels of an AC-DFA.

First we have the following definitions:

- The depth of a state in an AC-DFA is the directed distance from the root to that state.
- The ith level of an AC-DFA includes all the states whose depth is i, $i = 0, 1, \ldots$
- The depth of an AC-DFA, denoted L, is defined as the number of distinct levels (excluding level 0) in the AC-DFA. According to the AC-DFA construction procedure, the depth of a AC-DFA is equal to the length of the longest string pattern.
- The depth of a pipeline, denoted H, is the number of stages in the pipeline.

Figure 10.5 shows the system model of the depth-bounded pipelined AC-DFA. Given an AC-DFA with L levels, we map the states in level i of the AC-DFA to the ith stage of a linear pipeline, $i = 0$, 1, ..., $H - 1$ in which H is the pipeline depth and $H \leq L$. The remaining levels of the AC-DFA are placed in another (single) memory (denoted **AC-remain**). When $H = L$, AC-remain contains no state; we call such a model the fully pipelined AC-DFA. When L is large, we have to bound the pipeline depth so that the AC-DFA is partially pipelined where $H < L$. Because each memory block can have one active state, H stages along with AC-remain can maintain up to $H + 1$ active states simultaneously. At each clock cycle, the input character is delivered to AC-remain, and all the stages to invoke possible multiple state transitions in parallel.

In a H-stage pipeline, a state in stage i ($i = 0, 1, \ldots, H - 1$) will be active if and only if the last i characters match the prefix represented by the current state. As a result, there is no need for a failed matching in AC-remain to reuse the last i input characters, which have been matched by the first i stages. Thus all failure transitions in AC-remain to states in levels 0, 1, ..., $H - 1$ can be removed. Because cross transitions are generated based on the failure transitions, such a pipeline with H stages can remove all cross transitions to states in levels 0, 1, ..., H.

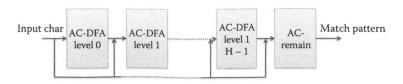

FIGURE 10.5   System model for the depth-bounded pipelined AC-DFA.

10.3.3.4 Analysis and Evaluation

We are interested in the following two questions:

- How many of the transitions in a AC-DFA are cross transitions?
- How many stages are needed for eliminating most of the cross transitions?

We use the string pattern sets from two widely used open source deep packet inspection (DPI) systems: Snort [3] and ClamAV [41]. We observe that

- As a whole, the cross transitions constitute the majority of the overall transitions. 99.52% and 99.61% of the transitions are cross transitions for Snort and ClamAV pattern sets, respectively.
- For both Snort and ClamAV pattern sets, the cross transitions dominate the transitions on almost every level until level 10. More than 99.9% of the cross transitions are on the top 10 levels of the AC-DFA. After level 10, the number of cross transitions decreases dramatically and becomes much smaller than the number of forward transitions.
- For the Snort pattern set, there is no cross transition beyond level 40. For the ClamAV pattern set, the last level containing cross transitions is level 145. On the other hand, the maximum pattern length for Snort and ClamAV pattern sets is 232 and 382, respectively. This indicates that, even if we want to eliminate all cross transitions, it is unnecessary to map an L-level AC-trie onto an L-stage pipeline. The actual pipeline depth needed can be much smaller.

A deeper pipeline results in further reduction in the number of cross transitions. The majority of transitions become the forward transitions when using more than eight and four stages, for Snort and ClamAV pattern sets, respectively. When using an eight-stage pipeline for Snort pattern set, 99.03% of the overall transitions are removed. For the ClamAV pattern set, a four-stage pipeline results in a 99.58% reduction in the number of the overall transitions.

10.3.4 THROUGHPUT MULTIPLICATION

The original AC-DFA can process only one character per clock cycle. To multiply the throughput, Alicherry et al. [29] propose the compressed AC-DFA, which can process $W(W \geq 1)$ characters per clock cycle. We define W as the input width. The compressed AC-DFA divides each pattern into W-byte blocks, which are used to build the AC-DFA. We apply the same idea to an AC-trie before converting it to a DFA. Figure 10.6 shows the compressed AC-trie with $W = 2$ for the example shown in Figure 10.4.

To avoid missing matching some patterns, W instances of the compressed AC-DFA should run in parallel. Each of them accepts the same input data stream with a one-character offset. For example, suppose there is an input stream "HANG." The first instance of the compressed AC-DFA reads the input stream as "HA" and "NG" while the second instance reads the input stream as "AN" and

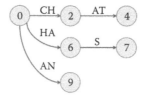

FIGURE 10.6 Compressed AC-trie ($W = 2$) for the strings {CHAT, HAS, AN}.

Input packet payload

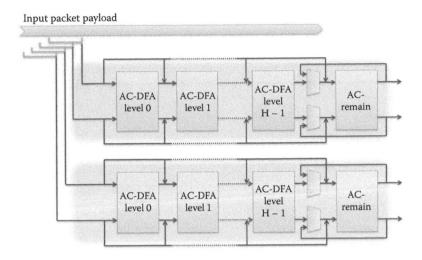

FIGURE 10.7   Multiple depth-bounded pipelined AC-DFAs for multi-character input ($W = 4$).

"G." Although the first instance fails to detect the matching pattern "AN," the second instance will eventually catch the matching pattern.

The depth-bounded pipeline architecture is simple and can be used for any AC-DFA. Combining the compressed AC-DFA with the pipelined scheme can make the architecture even more scalable. When W is larger, the depth of the resulting compressed AC-DFA becomes smaller, and fewer stages are needed to eliminate most of the cross transitions. The experimental results show that when $W = 8$ a six-stage pipeline can remove all of the cross transitions for the Snort string pattern set.

Figure 10.7 shows the depth-bounded pipeline architecture that supports a four-character input per clock cycle. Because dual-port memory is used in every stage, two different flows can access the same hardware pipeline in parallel. Hence, the number of hardware pipelines is half the number of the pipelined AC-DFA instances. During each clock cycle, each pipelined AC-DFA receives a W-character block from the input stream. Each W-character block is sent to all the stages, including the last stage that stores AC-remain. Each stage receives the W-character block, invokes the state transition by looking up its local state transition table, and forwards the output state to the next neighboring stage. The last stage storing AC-remain will ignore the state output from its previous stage unless its own state becomes fail. As discussed earlier, the main function of the previous H stages is to help reuse the last $H - 1$ input characters. As long as the last stage keeps matching the patterns, the information captured in the previous H stages is redundant.

10.3.5 COMPARISON

Table 10.3 compares the state-of-the-art solutions for high-performance multi-pattern string matching in NIDS. To support dynamic updates, only memory-based architectures are considered for ASIC– and FPGA–based solutions. For a fair comparison, the clock rates of the compared FPGA implementations are scaled to Xilinx Virtex-5 devices according to the maximum clock frequency. The values in parentheses are the original clock rates reported in the original papers. The results of the depth-bounded pipelined string matching architecture is based on the design with $W = 8$. Note that while most of the results are based on Snort pattern sets, the results of [24] and [28] are based on randomly generated binary patterns. This makes the results of [24] and [28] less comparable and also less interesting for NIDS.

TABLE 10.3
Performance Comparison of String Matching Solutions

Approaches	Platforms	# of Patterns	Pattern Length	# of Slices	Bytes/ Char	Clock Freq. (MHz)	Through- put (Gbps)	EffA	EffB
AC-DFA [24]	Cell/B.E.	8400	≤10	N/A	N/A	3200	2.5	N/A	N/A
AC-DFA [28]	GeForce 8600GT	4000	≤25	N/A	N/A	1200	2.3	N/A	N/A
CDFA [23]	0.18μmASIC	1785	No limit	N/A	3.3	763	6.1	1848	N/A
Bit-Split [39]	FPGA	1316	No limit	21,112	23	220 (200)	1.76	77	3.63
B-FSM [40]	FPGA	~8000	No limit	N/A	4.05	138 (125)	2.2	543	N/A
Field-Merge [35]	FPGA	6944	<64	12,027	6.33	285	4.56	720	60
Depth-Bounded Pipeline [42]	FPGA	9033	No limit	3168	6.12	178	11.4	1862	588

Considering the time-memory and the time-memory are a trade-off in hardware implementation, we define two new metrics:

$$EffA = \frac{Throughput}{Memory\ per\ char}\ (Mbps/Bytes)$$

and

$$EffB = \frac{Throughput}{Memory\ per\ char*\ \#Slices}\ (Kbps/Bytes)$$

According to Table 10.3, the FPGA implementations of the pipelined string matching architectures [35,42] outperform the multi-core processor–based solutions and achieve comparable performance to the ASIC–based solution with respect to the worst-case throughput. Even higher clock rates can be expected when the pipelined architecture is implemented in ASIC. The depth-bounded pipelined string matching solution is the only implementation of memory-based architectures that sustains more than 10 Gbps throughput while supporting more than 9 K string patterns from Snort. Its FPGA implementation achieves more than 2.5 × and 9 × improvements over the compared FPGA–based string matching engines with respect to EffA and EffB, respectively.

10.4 HARDWARE TECHNIQUES FOR REGULAR EXPRESSION MATCHING

Regular expression (regex) matching is an important mechanism used by modern NIDS, such as Bro [2] and Snort [3] to perform deep packet inspection against potential threats. Due to the large number of patterns to scan for and the increasing bandwidth of network traffic, regular expression matching is becoming not just a bottleneck, but itself a vulnerability of the NIDS [43].

10.4.1 BACKGROUND AND ANALYSIS

Basic regular expressions are regular languages constructed with character classes over a fixed alphabet. Table 10.4 lists the operators commonly used in a regular expression.

Because regular languages are exactly the class of languages that can be accepted by finite state automata, a basic regular expression matching engine can always be implemented as a finite

TABLE 10.4
Regular Expression Operators

Operator	Name	Example	Description
.	Concatenation	a_1a_2	a_2 right after a_1
|	Union	$a_1\|a_2$	Either a_1 or a_2
*	Kleene closure	$a*$	a zero or more times
+	Repetition	$a+$	a one or more times
?	Optionality	$a?$	a zero or one times
{m,n}	Constrained repetition	$a\{m,n\}$	a in m to n times
^	Start of string	$^\wedge a$	a at start of input
$	End of string	a$	a at end of input
[...]	Character class	$[a-c]$	Either a, b, or c
[^...]	Inverted character class	$[^\wedge abc]$	Neither a, b, nor c

state machine, either a non-deterministic finite automaton (NFA) or a deterministic finite automaton (DFA). In the NFA approach [44,45], individual regular expressions are processed in parallel independently. Each input character is sent to every state in every regular expression, and matching outputs are collected from all regular expressions running in parallel. More than one state in a NFA can be active at any time. A NFA can be converted to a DFA, in which the transitions between all valid combinations of the NFA states are compiled into a deterministic state transition table. A DFA maintains only one active state and performs a single state transition table lookup for each input character to determine the next active state. A DFA can be easily implemented in software on processor-based architectures. However, to represent all possible state combinations in the original NFA, the number of states in the minimal equivalent DFA can be $O(2^n)$ in the worst case, a phenomenon known as the state explosion [43,45]. In these cases, DFA–based approaches become infeasible to construct and accelerate. On the other hand, the parallel processing nature of the NFA makes it particularly suitable to accelerate in reconfigurable hardware, such as FPGA, which offers abundant parallelism and rich on-chip resources.

Note that all regular expressions are not created equally when implemented on hardware. Thus, when measuring the efficiency of a hardware solution, it is very important to take into account the complexity of the regular expressions being implemented. We define the following metrics to quantify the complexity of regular expressions when implemented in hardware matching engines:

- *State count:* Total number of states needed by the regular expression matching engine
- *State fan-in:* Maximum number of states that can immediately transition to any state
- *State fan-out:* Maximum number of states to which any state can immediately transition
- *Loop size:* Total number of transitions within a loop of state transitions
- *Branch-size delta:* Difference in number of transitions between two state transition paths with the same first and final states

The *state count* is originally used in [44] to describe the area requirement of a NFA–based regular expression matching engine. *State fan-in* and *state fan-out*, created by the use of union and Kleene closure operators, also affect logic complexity. We define *state fan-in* and *state fan-out* as the maximum number of signals entering and exiting any state, respectively, because the state machine runs at the speed of its slowest state transition. Note that, in general, *state fan-in* and *state fan-out* can be unequal to each other. The last two metrics, *loop size* and *branch-size delta*, would affect routing complexity when long and complicated regular expressions are implemented.

10.4.2   From Regular Expression to NFA

10.4.2.1   Parsing PCRE

Conventionally, the compilation of a regular expression (regex) starts from parsing the regex into a right-leaned (or left-leaned) parse tree representing the right-linear (or left-linear) production for the regular language [44]. When used for NIDS regular expressions in the Perl-compatible regular expression (PCRE) format, however, this approach is not concise for constrained repetitions. A repetition of {n} will be parsed as n identical concatenation nodes. A repetition of {m, n} will be converted to an (n − m)–level nested union node in the parse tree. It creates an unnecessarily deep tree, which, in turn, results in deep levels of recursion during the follow-up NFA construction.

To overcome the above limitation, Yang et al. [46] designed an efficient, simple, and modular parsing approach to capture the full semantics of PCRE. The approach transforms each regex into a token list data structure. Each token contains four fields: *val*, *rep*, *next*, and *child*. A token list is a multi-level linked list of tokens chained by the *next* and *child* fields. A concatenate operation is implied between a token and its next token except when the token's *val* field is the "union" (|); then a union operation is used instead. Depending on its *val* field, a token can be one of four types: (1) single character class, (2) union-op to a sub-regex, (3) parenthesis of a sub-regex, and (4) various PCRE–extended features. A type-1 or type-3 token may have a *rep* field representing the constrained ({m, n}) or closured (+ or *) repetition; a type-2 or type-3 token always points to a nested token list via the *child* field. The *val* field of a type-4 token stores a PCRE–extended feature, in which case the *child* field points to the corresponding raw sub-regex. Some of the features (e.g., ^ and $ in Table 10.4) can be implemented by tweaking the follow-up NFA construction; others cannot be handled by finite automata and will be either partially ignored (e.g., conditional) or used to cut short the regex (e.g., back reference). Conceptually, the token list data structure is a combination of the parse tree [44,45] and the opcodes [47,48]. Each token is powerful enough to efficiently represent a wide range of PCRE extensions. Although some of these extensions cannot be supported by finite automata, the token list data structure can still be useful for future regular expression matching solutions based on a more powerful automaton.

10.4.2.2   NFA Construction

The first algorithm used in NFA construction [44] is the McNaughton–Yamada algorithm [49]. The original McNaughton–Yamada algorithm generates a NFA with many intermediate nodes and redundant ε-transitions. A modified version is used [46,50] with the following distinct properties:

- Input ε-transitions to the union operator are sent to each operand individually, and output ε-transitions from all operands are collected and sent to the subsequent token(s).
- For the "*" and "+" operators, a pseudo state is created temporarily during token conversion to find all the feedback targets. The actual backward ε-transitions are made after the closured token has been converted.
- For the "*" operator, the input transitions into the token are sent directly to the subsequent token(s) without being aggregated by an extra state.
- Constrained repetitions are converted directly into proper NFA states without first being converted into multiple unions.

As a result, none of the regex operators produces extra states to propagate ε-transitions. Also note that recursion only occurs when there is a nesting of sub-regexes (due to unions or parentheses). In practice, the level recursion rarely exceeds 5. Figure 10.8 shows the NFA constructed for the example regex /b+c{5}(ab|a[ac])+d/ where the dashed lines represent the ε-transitions.

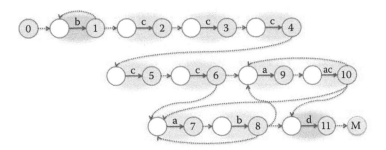

FIGURE 10.8   Example NFA for the regex /b+c{5}(ab|a[ac])+d/.

10.4.3   FROM NFA TO CIRCUIT

10.4.3.1   State Update Block

As shown in Figure 10.8, all pairs of nodes inside the shaded ovals have an identical structure. When constructing the NFA circuit, each of these pairs constitutes a state update block matching a single character class. All we need to do is to connect the inputs and outputs between various state update blocks as specified by the ε-transitions. Within each node pair, the right node corresponds to a 1-bit state register whereas the left node corresponds to an input ε-transition aggregator (implemented as an OR gate). The matching of the character class associated with the state is received as a 1-bit true or false signal to the AND gate. The state update block does not care about what the character class is. As a result, state update and transition are decoupled from character matching and classification.

There are two types of state update blocks: one accepting normal character matching and the other accepting negated character matching. This allows us to instantiate only one character matching circuit for both a character class and its negation, which potentially reduces the resource used for character matching by half. In addition, each state update block is also configured with one parameter: the number of input ports, determined by the number of "previous states" that immediately ε-transition to the current state. Figure 10.9 shows the NFA circuit matching the regex example of Figure 10.8.

10.4.3.2   Character Classification

A complex but important feature of PCRE is the use of character classes. A character class is effectively a union of one or more character symbols from the alphabet. Efficient implementation of character class matching can significantly reduce the circuit complexity.

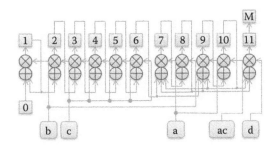

FIGURE 10.9   NFA circuit for matching the regex /b+c{5}(ab|a[ac])+d/.

Character classification takes one character as an input and generates one bit of matching result. For 8-bit characters, any character classification can be fully specified by 256 bits, one for the inclusion of each 8-bit value. Thus character classification of an n-state NFA can be implemented in memory of no more than $256 \times n$ bits. Furthermore, if two states use the same character class for matching inputs, they can share the same character classification output.

When implementing character classification on FPGA devices, the amount of on-chip memory can be a limiting factor on the number of regex engines that can be implemented. While there are many techniques to compress memory, simply aggregating the character classifications from several regex engines into one place could effectively alleviate the problem. When constructing the centralized character classification, we examine and compare each state's character class to the character class entries collected so far. If the character class of the current state is new, then a new entry is added to the character classification BRAM; if it is old, then a proper connection is made from the BRAM output of the previous character class entry to the input of the current state.

10.4.3.3 Multi-Character Input

Like the compressed AC-DFA discussed earlier for string matching, multi-character input can multiply the throughput. Some regular expression matching designs [51,52] adopt temporal transformations at the NFA-level, at which state transitions are extended forward in time (in terms of the number of clock cycles) to construct a new NFA with multi-character state transitions. An alternative is to adopt a circuit-level spatial approach to construct multi-character input regular expression matching engines. An example two-character input circuit for the regular expression /b+c{5} (ab|a[ac])+d/ is shown in Figure 10.10.

Compared to the temporal approaches [51] [52], the multi-character input construction with spatial stacking is simpler, faster, and more flexible. The resulting circuit can be optimized automatically and effectively by the FPGA synthesis and implementation tools at the circuit level.

10.4.3.4 Staging and Pipelining

A common issue of most NFA–based regular expression implementations on FPGA is the decline in achievable clock frequency with large numbers of regular expressions, supposedly due to the more complicated routing of signals. This is especially true with techniques such as centralized character classification in which a single character matching output can be used in many disparate states.

We use an aggressive staging and pipelining structure to improve the clock rate. The set of regular expression matching engines are first divided into multiple pipelines; each pipeline is further divided into multiple stages. Every input character goes into a pipeline in the first clock cycle; then it is forwarded to the next pipeline in the next clock cycle. Within a pipeline, all the regular expression

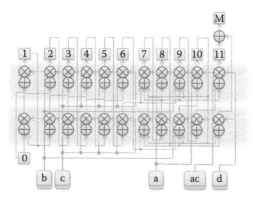

FIGURE 10.10   A two-character matching circuit for regex /b+c{5}(ab|a[ac])+d/.

TABLE 10.5
Comparison of FPGA-Based Regular Expression Matching Engines

	# Non-Meta Chars	Multi-Char Per Cycle	Throughput (Gbps)	# LUT Per State	Throughput Efficiency
Bispo et al. [53]	19,580	1	2.9	1.28	2.3
Clark et al. [51]	17,537	4	7.0	3.1	2.3
Mitra et al. [47]	N/A	1	0.8	~ 2.3	~ 0.35
Sourdis et al. [54]	69,127	1	2.42	0.66	3.67
Yamagaki et al. [52]	40,896	4	3.63	0.94	3.86
Yang et al. [50]	~ 15k	2	4.88	1.24	3.9
	~ 15k	4	7.46	2.2	3.4

engines share the same centralized character classification, whose output is buffered at every stage in the pipeline.

Matching outputs of all regular expression matching engines are prioritized with lower-indexed pipelines and lower-indexed stages having higher priority. Within a stage, matching outputs from different regular expression matching engines are priority-encoded. The encoded matching output is buffered to the next stages and pipelines in the same way as the input character classifications. This allows for a single matching output from all regular expression matching engines at any clock cycle.

10.4.4 COMPARISON

Table 10.5 shows the comparison of state-of-the-art NFA–based regular expression matching solutions implemented in FPGA. We define the *throughput efficiency*, in units of Gbps * state/LUT, as the concurrent throughput of the circuit divided by the number of LUTs the circuit used per state.

The FPGA implementation of [50] achieves higher throughput and throughput efficiency than others. The regular expression matching circuits of [52] can match eight characters per cycle but only at a much smaller scale (512 regexes), probably due to the complex multi-character circuit construction based on temporal extension. In [54], an aggressive shift-register lookup table (SRL) is used for constrained repetition, and common-prefix sharing is used to achieve very low resource usage per state. But the resource saving relies on the pattern properties of the regexes. Counters are used in [53] for matching repetition, which helps reducing the total LUT usage. Although [47] achieves lower performance than other solutions, it is worth mentioning that it utilizes a generic software-to-FPGA compilation and has performance numbers experimentally measured (rather than reported by the synthesis and place-and-route tools). [47] is also the only FPGA–based regular expression matching design able to handle true back references.

10.5 SUMMARY

Network intrusion detection systems (NIDS) have been widely used to secure the networks. However, the performance of NIDS must be capable of catching up with the explosive growth of network traffic to prevent the NIDS itself becoming the target of attacks. The core functions of modern NIDS include multi-match packet classification and deep packet inspection, which is based on multi-pattern string matching and regular expression matching. These functions are computation-intensive, especially when the size of the NIDS rule set is large. This has challenged conventional computing architectures with demanding CPU, memory, and I/O requirements. Dedicated hardware accelerators become a necessity to address these challenges.

This chapter gives a detailed introduction to each of the core functions of NIDS and the state-of-the-art hardware accelerators for each function. It reveals that the field programmable gate array (FPGA) technology has been an attractive platform for implementing these accelerators.

First, we discuss the hardware technology for accelerating multi-match packet classification in NIDS. We review both TCAM–based and FPGA–based solutions. We highlight the novel field-split parallel bit vector (FSBV) architecture, which requires a linear memory increase with the number of rules. Its FPGA implementation could store the full set of the current Snort rule headers using a small amount of on-chip resources and sustains 100 Gbps throughput for minimum size (40 bytes) packets. We also discuss the methods to support the unique Snort features in the BV–based architecture.

Second, we examine the hardware technology for high-performance string matching in NIDS. We give a detailed discussion on employing pipeline architectures for AC-DFA–based multi-pattern string matching. We revisit the classical AC algorithm and show that a H-stage linear pipeline can eliminate all the cross transitions to the top H levels of an AC-DFA. Analysis using real-life string pattern sets shows that a pipeline with no more than eight stages could remove more than 99% of the overall transitions in an AC-DFA. Also we present the scheme to support multi-character input per clock cycle to achieve multiplicative throughput improvement. The implementation of the depth-bounded pipelined string matching architecture on a state-of-the-art FPGA sustains more than 10 Gbps throughput while supporting the full set of string patterns from the latest Snort rule set.

Third, we investigate the hardware technology for accelerating regular expression matching used by NIDS. We review the existing approaches and focus on hardware accelerators for NFA–based regular expression matching. We describe the details of converting regular expressions into NFA and then mapping it to circuit. Various optimizations, such as multi-character matching, shared character classifier, and fine-grained pipelining, are discussed. The FPGA implementation of NFA–based regular expression matching engines can achieve high throughput up to 7 Gbps.

So far, the above three core functions of NIDS, i.e., multi-match packet classification, string matching, and regular expression matching, are studied in an isolated context. While there remain a lot of challenges for each of these three problems, an interesting effort would be the efficient integration of the hardware accelerators for them together. For example, as the packet header classification is usually the fastest while the string matching is slower and the regular expression matching is the slowest, we can filter the string patterns based on the header classification results and then filter the regular expression patterns based on the string matching results. By this means, we may reduce the size of the pattern set, which can lead to improved performance and power efficiency.

AUTHORS' BIOGRAPHIES

Weirong Jiang is currently a staff research engineer at Xilinx Research Labs, San Jose, CA, USA. He received his PhD degree in computer engineering in 2010 from the University of Southern California, Los Angeles. He received his MS degree in control science and engineering in 2006 and his BS degree in automation in 2004, both from Tsinghua University, Beijing. His primary research is on parallel algorithm and architecture design for high-performance low-power packet processing. His research interests also include network security, reconfigurable computing, software-defined networking, virtualization, data mining, and wireless networking. He has published two book chapters and more than 40 papers for top conferences and journals and received five best paper awards. He is a member of the IEEE and the ACM.

Viktor K. Prasanna is Charles Lee Powell Chair in engineering in the Ming Hsieh Department of Electrical Engineering and professor of computer science at the University of Southern California, Los Angeles. He serves as the director of the Center for Energy Informatics at USC. His research interests include high performance computing, parallel and distributed systems, reconfigurable computing, and embedded systems. He received his BS in electronics engineering from

Bangalore University; MS from the School of Automation, Indian Institute of Science; and PhD in computer science from Pennsylvania State University. He served as the editor-in-chief of the *IEEE Transactions on Computers* during 2003–2006. Currently, he is the editor-in-chief of the *Journal of Parallel and Distributed Computing.* He was the founding chair of the IEEE Computer Society Technical Committee on Parallel Processing. He is a fellow of the IEEE, the ACM, and the American Association for Advancement of Science (AAAS).

REFERENCES

1. R. Bajcsy, T. Benzel, M. Bishop, B. Braden, C. Brodley, S. Fahmy, S. Floyd, W. Hardaker, A. Joseph, G. Kesidis, K. Levitt, B. Lindell, P. Liu, D. Miller, R. Mundy, C. Neuman, R. Ostrenga, V. Paxson, P. Porras, C. Rosenberg, J. D. Tygar, S. Sastry, D. Sterne and S. F. Wu, Cyber defense technology networking and evaluation, *Commun. CAM,* vol. 47, pp. 58–61, 2004.
2. The Bro Project, The Bro network security monitor, Available: http://www.bro.org/.
3. Snort: The de facto standard for intrusion, Available: http://www.snort.org.
4. Efforts toward 400 gigabit Ethernet begin, March 25, 2013. Available: http://www.lightwave online.com/articles/2013/03/efforts-toward-400-gigabit-ethernet-begin.html.
5. W. A. Wulf and S. A. McKee, Hitting the memory wall: Implications of the obvious, *SIGARCH Comput. Archit. News,* vol. 23, no. 1, pp. 20–24, 1995.
6. D. Bacon, R. Rabbah and S. Shukla, FPGA programming for the masses, *Commun. ACM,* vol. 56, pp. 56–63, 2013.
7. P. Gupta and N. McKeown, Algorithms for packet classification, *IEEE Network,* vol. 15, pp. 24–32, 2001.
8. D. E. Taylor, Survey and taxonomy of packet classification techniques, *ACM Comput. Surv.,* vol. 37, pp. 238–275, 2005.
9. H. Song and J. W. Lockwood, Efficient packet classification for network intrusion detection using FPGA, in *FPGA '05: Proceeding of the AC/SIGDA International Symposium on Field Programmable Gate Arrays,* 2005.
10. F. Yu, R. H. Katz and T. V. Lakshman, Efficient multimatch packet classification and lookup with TCAM, *IEEE Micro,* vol. 25, pp. 50–59, 2005.
11. F. Yu, T. V. Lakshman, M. Motoyama and R. H. Katz, Efficient multimatch packet classification for network security applications, *IEEE Journal on Selected Areas in Communications,* vol. 24, pp. 1805–1816, 2006.
12. M. Faezipour and M. Nourani, Wire-speed TCAM-based architectures for multimatch packet classification, *IEEE Trans. Comput.,* vol. 58, pp. 5–17, 2009.
13. K. Lakshminarayanan, A. Rangarajan and S. Venkatachary, Algorithms for advanced packet classification with ternary CAMs, in *SIGCOMM '05: Proceedings of the Conference on Applications, Technologies, Architectures, and Protocols for Computer Communications,* 2005.
14. W. Jiang and V. K. Prasanna, Field-split parallel architecture for high performance multi-match packet classification using FPGAs, in *SPAA '09: Proceedings of the Twenty-First Annual Symposium on Parallelism in Algorithms and Architectures,* 2009.
15. Virtex-7 FPGA family, Xilinx, Available: http://www.xilinx.com/products/silicon-devices/fpga/virtex-7/index.htm.
16. T. V. Lakshman and D. Stiliadis, High-speed policy-based packet forwarding using efficient multi-dimensional range matching, *SIGCOMM Comput. Commun. Rev.,* vol. 28, pp. 203–214, 1998.
17. F. Baboescu and G. Varghese, Scalable packet classification, *IEEE/ACM Trans. Netw.,* vol. 13, pp. 2–14, 2005.
18. W. Eatherton, G. Varghese and Z. Dittia, Tree bitmap: Hardware/software IP lookups with incremental updates, *SIGCOMM Comput. Commun. Rev.,* vol. 34, pp. 97–122, 2004.
19. T. Sasao, On the complexity of classification functions, in *ISMVL '08: Proceedings of the 38th International Symposium on Multiple Valued Logic,* 2008.
20. O. Rottenstreich, R. Cohen, D. Raz and I. Keslassy, Exact worst-case TCAM rule expansion, *IEEE Transactions on Computers,* vol. 62, pp. 1127–1140, 2013.
21. P.-C. Lin, Y.-D. Lin, T.-H. Lee and Y.-C. Lai, Using string matching for deep packet inspection, *Computer,* vol. 41, pp. 23–28, 2008.
22. M. Crochemore and T. Lecroq, Sequential multiple string matching, in *Encyclopedia of Algorithms,* 2008, pp. 826–829.
23. T. Song, W. Zhang, D. Wang and Y. Xue, A memory efficient multiple pattern matching architecture for network security, in *INFOCOM '08: The 27th Conference on Computer Communications,* 2008.

24. D. P. Scarpazza, O. Villa and F. Petrini, High-speed string searching against large dictionaries on the Cell/ B.E. processor, in *IPDPS '08: IEEE International Symposium on Parallel and Distributed Processing*, 2008.

25. S. Antonatos, K. G. Anagnostakis and E. P. Markatos, Generating realistic workloads for network intrusion detection systems, *SIGSOFT Softw. Eng. Notes*, vol. 29, pp. 207–215, 2004.

26. T. AbuHmed, A. Mohaisen and D. Nyang, A survey on deep packet inspection for intrusion detection systems, *Magazine of Korea Telecommunication Society*, vol. 24, pp. 25–36, 2007.

27. O. Villa, D. Chavarria and K. Maschhoff, Input-independent, scalable and fast string matching on the Cray XMT, in *IPDPS '09: IEEE International Symposium on Parallel and Distributed Processing*, 2009.

28. G. Vasiliadis, S. Antonatos, M. Polychronakis, E. P. Markatos and S. Ioannidis, Gnort: High performance network intrusion detection using graphics processors, in *RAID '08: Proceedings of the 11th International Symposium on Recent Advances in Intrusion Detection*, 2008.

29. M. Alicherry, M. Muthuprasanna and V. Kumar, High speed pattern matching for network IDS/IPS, in *ICNP '06: Proceedings of the 2006 IEEE International Conference on Network Protocols*, 2006.

30. N. Hua, H. Song and T. V. Lakshman, Variable-stride multi-pattern matching for scalable deep packet inspection, in *INFOCOM '09: The 28th Conference on Computer Communications*, 2009.

31. L. Tan and T. Sherwood, A high throughput string matching architecture for intrusion detection and prevention, in *ISCA '05: Proceedings of the 32nd Annual International Symposium on Computer Architecture*, 2005.

32. I. Sourdis, D. N. Pnevmatikatos and S. Vassiliadis, Scalable multigigabit pattern matching for packet inspection, *IEEE Trans. VLSI Syst.*, vol. 16, pp. 156–166, 2008.

33. Z. Baker and V. K. Prasanna, A computationally efficient engine for flexible intrusion detection, *IEEE Transactions on Very Large Scale Integration (VLSI) Systems*, vol. 13, pp. 1179–1189, 2005.

34. Y. H. Cho and W. H. Mangione-Smith, Deep network packet filter design for reconfigurable devices, *ACM Trans. Embed. Comput. Syst.*, vol. 7, pp. 1–26, 2008.

35. Y.-H. E. Yang and V. K. Prasanna, Memory-efficient pipelined architecture for large-scale string matching, in *FCCM '09: 17th Annual IEEE Symposium on Field-Programmable Custom Computing Machines*, 2009.

36. A. V. Aho and M. J. Corasick, Efficient string matching: An aid to bibliographic search, *Commun. ACM*, vol. 18, pp. 333–340, 1975.

37. C.-H. Lin, Y.-T. Tai and S.-C. Chang, Optimization of pattern matching algorithm for memory based architecture, in *ANCS '07: Proceedings of the 3rd ACM/IEEE Symposium on Architecture for Networking and Communications Systems*, 2007.

38. D. Pao, W. Lin and B. Liu, Pipelined architecture for multi-string matching, *Computer Architecture Letters*, vol. 7, pp. 33–36, 2008.

39. H.-J. Jung, Z. Baker and V. K. Prasanna, Performance of FPGA implementation of bit-split architecture for intrusion detection systems, in *IPDPS '06: The 20th International Parallel and Distributed Processing Symposium*, 2006.

40. J. van Lunteren, High-performance pattern-matching for intrusion detection, in *INFOCOM '06: The 5th IEEE International Conference on Computer Communications*, 2006.

41. Clam AntiVirus, Available: http://www.clamav.net.

42. W. Jiang, Y.-H. E. Yang and V. K. Prasanna, Scalable multi-pipeline architecture for high performance multi-pattern string matching, in *IPDPS '10: IEEE International Symposium on Parallel & Distributed Processing*, 2010.

43. R. Smith, C. Estan and S. Jha, Backtracking algorithmic complexity attacks against a NIDS, in *ACSAC '06: Proceedings of the 22nd Annual Computer Security Applications Conference*, 2006.

44. R. W. Floyd and J. D. Ullman, The compilation of regular expressions into integrated circuits, *J. ACM*, vol. 29, pp. 603–622, 1982.

45. R. Sidhu and V. K. Prasanna, Fast regular expression matching using FPGAs, in *FCCM '01: Proceedings of the 9th Annual IEEE Symposium on Field-Programmable Custom Computing Machines*, 2001.

46. Y.-H. E. Yang and V. K. Prasanna, High-performance and compact architecture for regular expression matching on FPGA, *IEEE Transactions on Computers*, vol. 61, pp. 1013–1025, 2012.

47. A. Mitra, W. Najjar and L. Bhuyan, Compiling PCRE to FPGA for accelerating Snort IDS, in *ANCS '07: ACM/IEEE Sym. on Architecture for Networking and Communications Systems*, 2007.

48. PCRE: Perl compatible regular expression, Available: http://www.pcre.org.

49. R. McNaughton and H. Yamada, Regular expressions and state graphs for automata, *IEEE Trans. on Comput.*, vol. 9, pp. 39–47, 1960.

50. Y.-H. E. Yang, W. Jiang and V. K. Prasanna, Compact architecture for high-throughput regular expression matching on FPGA, in *ANCS '08: Proceedings of the 4th ACM/IEEE Symposium on Architectures for Networking and Communications Systems*, 2008.
51. C. R. Clark and D. E. Schimmel, Scalable pattern matching for high speed networks, in *FCCM '04: Proceedings of the 12th Annual IEEE Symposium on Field-Programmable Custom Computing Machines*, 2004.
52. N. Yamagaki, R. Sidhu and S. Kamiya, High-speed regular expression matching engine using multi-character NFA, in *FPL '08: Proceedings of the International Conference on Field Programmable Logic and Applications*, 2008.
53. J. Bispo, I. Sourdis, J. M. Cardoso and S. Vassiliadis, Regular expression matching for reconfigurable packet inspection, in *FPT '06: Proceedings of the IEEE International Conference on Field Programmable Technology*, 2006.
54. I. Sourdis, S. Vassiliadis, J. Bispo and J. M. Cardoso, Regular expression matching in reconfigurable hardware, *Journal of Signal Processing Systems*, vol. 51, pp. 99–121, 2008.

Section III

Artificial Intelligence Techniques for IDS

11 New Unknown Attack Detection with the Neural Network–Based IDS

Przemysław Kukiełka and Zbigniew Kotulski

CONTENTS

11.1 INTRUSION DETECTION SYSTEM DEFINITION

An intrusion detection system (IDS) could be defined as one of the security mechanisms that rely on monitoring and detection of attacks against information systems. The typical task of an IDS system could be, for example, detection of attacks targeted to blocking computer or service (DoS, denial of service), attempt of access to non-authorized resources, and installation of software-like worms or trojans. To locate our experiments within a general pattern of intrusion detection, we start from a presentation of the fundamentals of IDS models and approaches. Thus, intrusion detection systems could be classified according to three main criteria:

11.1.1 SOURCE OF ANALYZED INFORMATION

- *Host based IDS*—that use information available on protected host-like audit files, service logs, etc.
- *Network based IDS*—that analyze information flows in the network between hosts (for instance, TCP/IP packet header, statistic of the packet traffic). Often such an IDS uses a set of sensors distributed in a different place on the network, which, besides the collection of data, could make basic analyses and send high-level information to a central system that is responsible for the final decision about attack detection.

11.1.2 WAY OF ANALYSIS

- *Anomaly IDS*—that are looking for abnormal behavior of a monitored user or system. It is more effective for detection of unknown, new types of attacks.
- *Misuse IDS*—targeted for detection of well-known attacks, thanks to comparison of analyzed data with the data that is specific to attack behaviors (so-called signatures).

11.1.3 REACTION TO ATTACK

- *Active*—that after finding the attack the IDS tries to block it (for instance, by modifying firewall rules in order to block traffic from suspicious IP addresses or disconnecting the network). Active IDS are often called intrusion prevention systems (IPSs).
- *Passive*—that transfer only information about the attack to a human administrator.

Research in the area of intrusion detection systems (IDSs) starts in 1980 from the publication of Anderson [1] who proposed a first IDS that analyzed data from an audit file, in order to look for suspicious activities. For analysis of data, he applied statistical methods that use probability distribution for each of the analyzed parameters from the audit data. A decision about an alarm was taken in the case when a defined level of mean value was overdrawn.

In the first years of usage, mainly IDS signature (expert systems), state analysis, and different models of normal behavior were used. This IDS solution has limitations, which are described below:

- For misuse IDS, it is not possible to detect a new attack or a modified version of a well-known attack.
- For anomaly IDS, very often a big number of false alarms is observed.
- Preparation of a signature for misuse detection or models of user's normal behavior for anomaly detection are complicated and time-consuming tasks because of the still growing number of different activities of users and systems.
- Prepared models or signatures should be modified in order to work for new host operating systems or environments (especially host-based IDS dedicated to a particular operating system).

Therefore, since the 1990s, 20th-century research started analyzing machine learning algorithm systems (artificial intelligence) that could solve most of the issues presented above. That solution does not need to prepare a signature of attacks or a model of the normal user's behavior because both are created automatically in the learning process. Machine learning techniques are dedicated for classification based on noncompleted information and are able to effectively analyze large amounts of information provided from different sources. Many different types of systems and algorithms, such as decision trees, neural networks, immune systems, and genetic algorithms, were tested. We decided to focus, in this chapter, on neural networks.

Because of their generalization feature, neural networks are able to work with imprecise and incomplete data. It means that they can recognize patterns not presented during a network learning phase. That's why the neural networks could be a good solution for detection of a well-known attack that has been modified by an aggressor in order to pass through a firewall system. In that case, a traditional intrusion detection system (IDS), based on signatures of attacks or expert-defined rules, may not be able to detect such a new version of this attack.

Unfortunately, as could be noticed [2–5] and in the results of our research (see Table 11.2), some representation of the new attack or new normal traffic not presented during the training process cannot be properly classified by a neural network. A simple remedy could be adding a vector representing the new traffic to the learning data set and retraining the neural network. However, the blocking problem for such an approach is to obtain data that represent new, previously undetected attacks. In this chapter, we present a proposal of a new algorithm and a new IDS architecture based on the neural network technology that allows the collection automatically of new attack-representing data and to use them for retraining and updating weights and the number of hidden neurons in distributed network detectors.

In our research, we focus on MLP and SVM neural network architectures. The result of the investigation is the information about the classification accuracy, represented as a number of false alarms and undetected attacks in comparison to the number of validation vectors. New attacks and new normal traffic representations are added to the training data set in order to observe their influence on improvement of the classification process for new vectors in a test data set.

The rest of this chapter is the following: In Section 11.2, we introduce the concept of neural networks and introduce the neural networks' architectures often applied in IDS applications. In the most detail, we describe the architectures used in our own investigations. Section 11.3, describes the data set used in our research. It is KDD 99 with our extensions representing new attacks and new normal traffic not included in the original set. In Section 11.4, we present related work on the application of artificial neural networks for constructing intrusion detection systems and their effectiveness in detecting new, previously unknown attacks. Section 11.5 is the outline of the new IDS architecture that has a higher ability of detecting new attacks, and Section 11.6 contains the results of tests and experiments validating our proposal. Section 11.7 concludes the chapter, presenting possible future investigations concerning application of neural network–based IDS for new attack detection.

11.2 NEURAL NETWORKS

11.2.1 Neural Networks: A Way of Work

An artificial neural network is a system simulating the work of neurons in a human brain. In Figure 11.1 is shown a diagram of a neuron's operation.

The neuron consists of a number of inputs emulating dendrites of the biological neuron, an adder module, an activation function, and one output emulating an axon of the biological neuron. The importance of a particular input is indicated by its weight, which emulates the biological neuron's

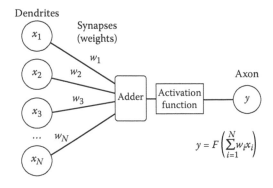

FIGURE 11.1 Artificial neuron's schema.

synapse. The input signals (assume we have n inputs) are multiplied by the values of weights w_i, $i = 1, 2,..., N$, and next the results are added in the adder block. The sum is sent to the activation block where it is processed by the activation function $F(.)$. In that way, we obtain the neuron's answer y for the input signals x_i, $i = 1, 2,..., N$. Thus, the way of work of a neuron in a neural network depends on values of w_i, $i = 0, 1, 2,..., N$ (calculated during the neuron's learning) and a shape of the function $F(.)$ (selected from a few usually used classes). This way, we obtain different classes of artificial neurons usually used in the neural network applications.

One of the most popular neuron models is a perceptron. The activation function $F(.)$ of the perceptron is a step function: bipolar or binary function. For $s = \sum_{i=1}^{N} w_i x_i$ it takes the value, respectively:

$$F(s) = \begin{cases} -1 & \text{for} & s \leq 0 \\ 1 & \text{for} & s > 0 \end{cases}$$

(11.1a)

or

$$F(s) = \begin{cases} 0 & \text{for} & s \leq 0 \\ 1 & \text{for} & s > 0 \end{cases}.$$

(11.1b)

The other possible activation functions are of sigmoidal shape (looking like a letter "S"), growing smoothly and monotonically from a minimal to a maximal value. Alike in the case of step functions, they can be bipolar or binary sigmoidal functions. Such functions can be written, for instance, as

$$F(s) = \frac{2}{1 + \exp\{-bs\}} - 1 = \frac{1 - \exp\{-bs\}}{1 + \exp\{-bs\}}$$

(11.2a)

or

$$F(s) = \frac{1}{1 + \exp\{-bs\}},$$

(11.2b)

respectively. The first one is a hyperbolic tangent-like function, and the second one is a logistic function. Usually in applications, we assume $0 < b \leq 1$; however, for $b \to \infty$, the first function (the bipolar sigmoidal function) tends to the bipolar step function, and the second one tends to the binary step function. The neurons using sigmoidal activation functions are called sigmoidal neurons.

A similar (but not smooth) activation function we can obtain using piece-wise linear maps. For example, for bipolar and binary effect we can use

$$F(s) = \begin{cases} -1 & \text{for} & s < -1 \\ s & \text{for} & -1 \leq s \leq 1 \\ 1 & \text{for} & 1 < s \end{cases}$$

(11.3a)

or

$$F(s) = \begin{cases} 0 & \text{for} & s < -0.5 \\ s & \text{for} & -0.5 \leq s \leq 0.5, \\ 1 & \text{for} & 0.5 < s \end{cases}$$

(11.3b)

respectively. The special kinds of activation functions, called radial basis functions, are used in neurons constituting so-called radial basis function (RBF) networks. Such real-valued functions have a property that their values depend only on the distance from the origin. Examples of the RBF used as activation functions could be the Gaussian function

$$F(s_1, s_2, ..., s_N) = \exp\left(\frac{-\sum_{i=1}^{N}(s_i - b_i)^2}{a^2}\right), \tag{11.4}$$

the multiquadratic function

$$F(s_1, s_2, ..., s_N) = \sqrt{\sum_{i=1}^{N}(s_i - b_i)^2 + a^2}, \tag{11.5}$$

and the inverse multiquadratic function

$$F(s_1, s_2, ..., s_N) = \frac{1}{\sqrt{\sum_{i=1}^{N}(s_i - b_i)^2 + a^2}}. \tag{11.6}$$

In the above RBF definitions, $s_1, s_2, ..., s_N$ are the activation function's input vector coordinates; the parameters b_i, $i = 1, 2, ..., N$ define the central point of the function (the origin's location in R^N) while a^2 affects the spread of the radius. More detailed information about a neural network can be found in [6].

The next important aspect of neuron and neural network applications is the learning procedure leading to fixing concrete values of the weights. Because one neuron cannot solve a complex problem, the neural networks composed of many neurons are used (the architectures of neural networks will be presented in another part in this section). The learning or, as we sometimes say, training procedure is also applied to the neural networks. The purpose of the learning of neurons (a neural network) is fixing values of weights (which are parameters of the estimated observation values) in such a way that the neuron (the neural network) for all values of observations (its inputs) gives the output, which is optimal or, in other words, which minimizes a cost function. The cost function $C(.)$, which is a real-valued convex function of observations, could be defined for each particular problem accordingly.

In neural network applications, three main learning approaches are used: supervised learning, unsupervised learning, and reinforcement learning. The choice of one of those approaches depends on what kind of information about a process we have, what is the purpose of learning, and what is the network's architecture. Let us start from a basic description of the three methods.

In supervised learning, we use a set of samples of pairs $(X^{(i)}, Y^{(i)})$, $i = 1, 2, ..., I$ where $X^{(i)}$ is an input value (the ith vector of observations), and $Y^{(i)}$ is a corresponding output value. In the learning procedure, we select such values of weights, which, for given values of actual observations, give the calculated neuron's outputs (or the network's outputs) nearest to the corresponding sample outputs. In other words, we wish to deduce the mapping implied by the sample data set tuning the weights' values. The quality of such an approximation is measured with a cost function, which expresses the mismatch between the exact sample data and results of the neural network–based approximation. In supervised learning, a commonly used cost function is the mean-squared distance. It is expressed by the averaged (over the set of observations) square of differences of actual values $\hat{y}_j(X, \mathbf{w})$, $j = 1$, 2,..., M of the outputs calculated for particular observations X with the weights $\mathbf{w}$ ($X = (x_1 x_2,..., x_N)$ being the vector of all inputs of the neuron/neural network while $\mathbf{w}$ is the vector of all weights, and their desired values y_j. Thus, the cost $C(.)$ for a single training sample (X, Y) can be expressed as

$$C(\mathbf{w}) = \sum_{j=1}^{M} (\hat{y}_j(X, \mathbf{w}) - y_j)^2 \tag{11.7}$$

and in a case of a larger training set $(X^{(i)}, Y^{(i)})$, $i = 1, 2,...,I$ it will be averaged over all samples:

$$C(\mathbf{w}) = \frac{1}{I} \sum_{i=1}^{I} \sum_{j=1}^{M} \left(\hat{y}_j(X^{(i)}, \mathbf{w}) - y_j^{(i)} \right)^2. \tag{11.8}$$

Another method of the weight selection is unsupervised learning. In the unsupervised learning, we use some sample observation data X and a cost function $C(.)$, which should be minimized. The cost function is defined on the observation data and the network's output. It depends on the task we want to describe and on some initial assumptions made on a basis of our knowledge: the properties of the model, its parameters, and the observed variables.

The third important approach to neural network training is reinforcement learning. In reinforcement learning, data X are usually not given, but they are generated by a network's interactions with the environment. At each instant of time t, the network performs an action $Y(t)$, and the environment generates an observation $X(t)$ according to its dynamics; the corresponding cost $C(t)$ should be calculated to valuate the network's action. The purpose of learning is estimation of such values of weights in the network that the expected cumulative cost is minimal. The reinforcement learning can be considered as a feedback system in which the output of a network has an effect on its input, helping to minimize the cost function. In probabilistic formalism, it can be considered as a Markov decision process in which a neural network describes transitions between states of a Markov chain, and the learning is identification of its transition probabilities. The trained Markov chain should minimize the cost.

Each of the above three approaches is, in fact, a class of algorithms in which a particular solution depends on the learning problem formulation. A learning algorithm is an essential element of a neural network's architecture.

As it is seen, a single neuron is very simple, and it can represent only simple functions. For higher generality, neurons are grouped in the networks called neural networks. As real neurons in a human's brain, they are located in parallel layers in which the neurons are interconnected according to some pattern in such a way that outputs of neurons in an earlier layer are inputs of neurons in a farther one. Such a pattern together with a definition of a learning algorithm and a specific activation function define the neural network's architecture. A detailed description of the learning methods can be found [7–9].

11.2.2 Multilayer Perceptron

One of the most frequently used neural network architectures is the multilayer perceptron (MLP) [10,11]. Such a network is built of several layers of neurons, and each neuron's output of the previous layer is connected with some neuron's input of the next layer, see Figure 11.2. The MLP architecture consists of input and an output layers and one or more hidden layers. The signal is transmitted through the network in one direction from the input to the output (this architecture is feedforward). The activation functions usually used in MLP networks are sigmoidal ones, both hyperbolic tangent (Equation 11.2a) and logistic (Equation 11.2b).

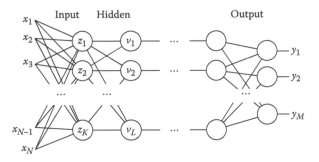

FIGURE 11.2 The MLP network.

Example architecture of the MLP network is presented in Figure 11.2. For such an architecture, we can express values of signals on the output layer versus signals on the input layer. The output signal of the ith neuron ($i = 1, 2,..., K$) after going through one layer is

$$z_i = F_i^1 \left(\sum_{j=0}^{N} w_{ij}^1 x_j \right). \tag{11.9}$$

Next, the output of the lth neuron ($l = 1, 2,..., L$) after going through two layers is

$$v_l = F_l^2 \left(\sum_{i=0}^{K} w_{li}^2 z_i \right) = F_l^2 \left(\sum_{i=0}^{K} w_{li}^2 F_i^1 \left(\sum_{j=0}^{N} w_{ij}^1 x_j \right) \right) \tag{11.10}$$

and so on. In Equation 11.9 and Equation 11.10, we assumed that superscripts are numbers of layers, w_{ij}^1 are weights of the ith neuron for the jth input in layer 1, (w_{li}^2 analogously in layer 2) and F_i^1, F_l^2 are corresponding activation functions. The MLP network formula (Equation 11.9) can represent the input layer activity and formula (Equation 11.10) for the first hidden layer. To model the next hidden layers and the output layers, one should iterate the formulae accordingly.

The MLP network undergoes a supervised learning. Adaptation of the weights w is a stepwise procedure running according to the formula:

$$\mathbf{w}(t + 1) = \mathbf{w}(t) + \Delta\mathbf{w} = \mathbf{w}(t) + \eta(t) \cdot \mathbf{p}(t) \tag{11.11}$$

where η is a learning coefficient, and $\mathbf{p}(t)$ is a direction vector in an n-dimensional space of all weights. Because the gradient of a function indicates the direction of its quickest growth (the quickest decrease when negated), it can be used for effective minimization of the cost function. In order to reach better efficiency and speed of the learning process, one can use the back propagation (BP) algorithm [12]. It runs in the following steps:

Step 1. Entering a vector of inputs x on the first layer and analysis of signals in the network propagating feed-forward. Using the formulas in Equations 11.9, 11.10, and so on, one obtains input signals for all layers and is able to calculate the derivatives of activation functions for all layers: $\dfrac{dF^1\left(u_1^1\right)}{du_i^1}, \dfrac{dF^2\left(u_1^2\right)}{du_i^2}, \ldots\ldots, \dfrac{dF^m\left(u_1^m\right)}{du_i^m}$, where m is the number of lay-

ers in the network, $u_i^k = \displaystyle\sum_{j=0}^{N} w_{ij}^k x_j^k$ and x_j^k is jth input of the kth layer of the network, $j = 1, 2,\ldots, N$, $k = 1, 2,\ldots, n$.

Step 2. Building a back propagation network by inverting the direction of the signal's flow, replacement of activation functions with their derivatives, and putting at the network's output a difference of the actual $\hat{y}_i$ and desired y_i output values, $i = 1, 2,\ldots, M$ (now playing a role of an input). For such a network, we calculate the backward differences. For the last (output) layer it will take the form:

$$\delta_i^2 = (\hat{y}_i - y_i)\frac{dF^2\left(u_i^2\right)}{du_i^2} \tag{11.12}$$

while for the hidden layer the difference is

$$\delta_i^1 = \sum_{k=1}^{M} (\hat{y}_k - y_k)\frac{dF^2\left(u_k^2\right)}{du_k^2} w_{ki}^2 \frac{dF^1\left(u_i^1\right)}{du_i^1}. \tag{11.13}$$

Step 3. Adaptation of the weights is according to formula (2.11) with application of results of steps 1 and 2 with

$$\Delta w_{ij}^2 = \eta \delta_i^2 v_j \tag{11.14}$$

for the output layer and

$$\Delta w_{ij}^1 = \eta \delta_i^1 x_j \tag{11.15}$$

for the hidden layer.

Step 4. The procedure defined by steps 1, 2, and 3 must be repeated for all vectors from the training set. The training goes until a stop condition (approaching either the expected cost value or the number of iterations and gradient limits).

Under the condition of continuity of the cost function $C(\mathbf{w})$, the algorithms based on gradient methods of optimization are the most effective ones. Assume that $\mathbf{w} = [w_1, w_2,\ldots, w_n]^T$ is the vector of all weights in a neural network. The cost function $C(\mathbf{w})$ can be expanded into a Taylor series at point $\mathbf{w}$ along some direction vector $\mathbf{p}$:

$$C(\mathbf{w}+\mathbf{p}) = C(\mathbf{w}) + [\mathbf{g}(\mathbf{w})]^T \cdot \mathbf{p} + \frac{1}{2}\mathbf{p}^T \cdot \mathbf{H}(\mathbf{w}) \cdot \mathbf{p} + \ldots \tag{11.16}$$

where

$$\mathbf{g}(\mathbf{w}) = \nabla C(\mathbf{w}) = \left[\frac{\partial C}{\partial w_1}, \frac{\partial C}{\partial w_2}, \ldots, \frac{\partial C}{\partial w_n}\right]^T \tag{11.17}$$

is a gradient vector of $C(\mathbf{w})$ and

$$\mathbf{H(w)} = \begin{bmatrix} \dfrac{\partial^2 C}{\partial w_1 \partial w_1} & \cdots & \dfrac{\partial^2 C}{\partial w_1 \partial w_n} \\ & \cdot & \\ & \cdot & \\ \dfrac{\partial^2 C}{\partial w_n \partial w_1} & \cdots & \dfrac{\partial^2 C}{\partial w_n \partial w_n} \end{bmatrix} \tag{11.18}$$

is the matrix of partial derivatives of the cost function $C(\mathbf{w})$ (its Hessian).

Now, we can say that the optimal weight in the kth iteration $\mathbf{w}_k$ minimizes $C(\mathbf{w})$ if $\mathbf{g(w}_k) = 0$, and the Hessian $\mathbf{H(w}_k)$ is positively definite. To minimize the cost function $C(\mathbf{w})$, one should select such a value of the learning coefficient η_k and the direction vector $\mathbf{p}_k$ that in the next iteration the cost is smaller, $C(\mathbf{w}_{k+1}) = C(\mathbf{w}_k + \eta_k \mathbf{p}_k) < C(\mathbf{w}_k)$. In practice, several particular methods of gradient optimization are used. Now, we will refer to some of them.

A simple version of the gradient method is the *method of steepest descent* [13]. It restricts the expansion (Equation 11.16) to the first two terms (it misses information given by Hessian). As the direction vector, it takes $\mathbf{p}_k = -\mathbf{g(w}_k)$, and the updates of weights are $\Delta \mathbf{w}_k = \eta_k \mathbf{p}_k + \alpha(\mathbf{w}_k - \mathbf{w}_{k-1})$ appropriate choice of constants η_k and α.

Some other method is the *variable metric method* [14], which uses the first three terms from the expansion (Equation 11.16). It uses the direction vector in the form $\mathbf{p}_k = -[\mathbf{H(w}_k)]^{-1}\mathbf{g(w}_k)$ or an analogous formula with approximate expressions for the Hessian. Two main algorithms of such a type are BFGS (Broyden–Fletcher–Goldfarb–Shanno) and DFP (Davidon–Fletcher–Powell). A computationally more effective variant of the method is the *one-step secant* algorithm.

Some methods resign with using Hessian in calculating the direction vector. For instance, the *conjugate gradient method* [15] estimates the actual value of the direction vector $\mathbf{p}_k$ using previous directions $\mathbf{p}_0, \mathbf{p}_1, \ldots, \mathbf{p}_{k-1}$. The expression for $\mathbf{p}_k$ is $\mathbf{p}_k = -\mathbf{g}_k + \beta_{k-1}\mathbf{p}_{k-1}$, where $\mathbf{g}_k$ is the value of the gradient at point $\mathbf{w}_k$, and β_{k-1} is the coefficient of conjugation. The versions of such an algorithm differ with methods of calculation of β_{k-1} (e.g., methods by Fletcher–Reeves, Polak–Ribiére, Powell–Beale). Quicker learning can be obtained using the scaled conjugate gradient algorithm proposed by Moller [15].

Another method that also avoids calculating Hessian is the *Levenberg–Marquardt algorithm* [16]. It requires calculating the Jacobi matrix $\mathbf{J(w)}$ containing first derivatives of the cost function $C(\mathbf{w})$. Now the gradient is calculated according to the formula

$$\mathbf{g(w)} = [\mathbf{J(w)}]^T \mathbf{e(w)} \tag{11.19}$$

and the approximate value of the Hessian in step k is

$$\mathbf{G(w}_k) = [\mathbf{J(w}_k)]^T \mathbf{J(w}_k) + \nu_k \mathbf{1} \tag{11.20}$$

where $\mathbf{e(w)}$ is a vector containing the values of the cost function for each output of the neural network, and ν_k is the Levenberg–Marquardt parameter. The algorithm works in such a way that at the beginning of the training when the actual value of $\mathbf{w}_k$ is far from the solution, then values of ν_k much greater than the eigenvalues of the matrix $[\mathbf{Jw}_k]^T \mathbf{J(w}_k)$ are applied, and optimization works with the method of steepest descent is applied with

$$\mathbf{p}_k \approx \frac{\mathbf{g(w}_k)}{\nu_k}. \tag{11.21}$$

Later, when the approximation error decreases, the parameter v_k decreases as well, and the matrix $[\mathbf{Jw}_k]^T \mathbf{J}(\mathbf{w}_k)$ is more significant in formula (Equation 11.20) and defining the direction vector.

The next effective method of learning is the *resilient backpropagation* [17] algorithm. In this method, the updates of weights are made on the basis of the sign of the gradient's coordinates without taking into account their absolute values:

$$(\Delta \mathbf{w}_k)_{ij} = -(\eta_k)_{ij} \, \mathrm{sgn}\left(\frac{\partial C(\mathbf{w}_k)}{\partial (\mathbf{w}_k)_{ij}} \right), \qquad (11.22)$$

where sgn is the sign function, and $\dfrac{\partial C(\mathbf{w}_k)}{\partial (\mathbf{w}_k)_{ij}}$ is the gradient of the cost function at step k. The training coefficient is adapted for each weight according to changes of the gradient values.

11.2.3 Other Networks' Architectures

The *support vector machine* (SVM) [10,18] is the feedforward neural network that consists of two layers (hidden and output) and that can use various types of the activation function. In the classification tasks, the first step of the SVM network work is to transform the nonlinearly separated input observations (with usage of a kernel function) to the space in which they can be lineally separated. The kernel functions are functions of observation data that are symmetric with two variables. They assign weights to points (say, $\mathbf{x}_i \in R^N$) around some other point (say, $\mathbf{x}_j \in R^N$). Examples of possible kernel functions are [19]

$$\text{Gaussian kernel} \quad K(\mathbf{x}_i, \mathbf{x}_j) = \exp\left\{ -\frac{\|\mathbf{x}_i - \mathbf{x}_j\|^2}{2a^2} \right\}$$

$$\text{polynomial kernel} \quad K(\mathbf{x}_i, \mathbf{x}_j) = (a\mathbf{x}_i \cdot \mathbf{x}_j + b)^p$$

$$\text{sigmoidal kernel} \quad K(\mathbf{x}_i, \mathbf{x}_j) = (a\mathbf{x}_i \cdot \mathbf{x}_j - b)$$

The transformation of variables should lead to the situation in which in the new space the kernel function (being a function of two variables) could be represented as a product of two functions of one variable. The second step of the learning phase is the maximization of the separation margin between two classes of the observations. The calculations are performed now in the new space of the transformed variables.

Recurrent neural networks (RNN) [20] are the networks in which connections between units can form cycles: They are networks of neurons with feedback connections. This introduces internal states allowing dynamic modeling of temporal behavior of the networks, see Figure 11.3. Unlike feedforward neural networks (e.g., MLP and SVM networks), the recurrent networks use their internal memory to process arbitrary sequences of inputs. They can be learned both with supervised and unsupervised procedures. In the literature, one can find many particular proposals of RNN. The *Elman neural network* [21] is a three-layer network, see Figure 11.3, in which cyclic connections are in the hidden layer. It introduces so-called context units, which allow remembering previous states of the hidden layer neurons and use them in the training procedure.

The *Jordan recurrent neural network* [22,23] is similar to the previous one with the difference that context units are connected with the output layer neurons. The context units play here a role of a state layer remembering the last state of the whole network.

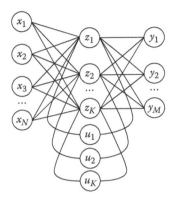

FIGURE 11.3   The Elman recurrent network scheme.

The *Hopfield neural network* [24] is a one-layer regular network in which every two neurons have a connection described by a connectivity weight. The weights have such a property that no neuron has a connection with itself, and connections of different neurons are symmetric. Their activation functions are the step functions (Equations 11.1a or 11.1b).

A *self-organizing map* (SOM) [25] is trained using unsupervised learning. It produces a low-dimensional discrete map of the input space of the training samples. The training of SOM is an unsupervised one and is based on a network's own criteria. Each node of SOM has its weight being a vector of dimension equal to the dimension of vectors of input data and has its position on a map space. Very often, SOM uses competitive learning in which the output neurons attempt to be activated. This activated neuron is a winning neuron (winner-takes-all neuron). The competition is forced by negative feedback paths in the network, so the neurons are organizing themselves, becoming active or not. Because the neurons have their positions at maps, the trained network represents a pattern drown by active neurons. Such a model was first described by Kohonen [25], so such a network is also known as the *Kohonen network*. In its original form, it is a feed-forward structure with an input layer and a computational layer constituting of an array of rows and columns in which each node of the computational layer is connected to all nodes of the input layer. The training involves four phases: *initialization* of weights with small random values; *competition* in which each neuron calculates its value of a discrimination function (DF, describing distance of its actual output from actual weights) and in which, finally, the neuron with the smallest value of DF is the winner; *cooperation* during which the winner determines location of the neighbors of excited neurons and makes them cooperate; and *adaptation* in which, through decreasing values of the discrimination function of the excited neurons and adequate adjustment of the connection weights, are obtained a similarity of the weight vector of the wining neuron and the network input vector.

Several extensions of SOM neural networks have been proposed. One of them is the *Pareto learning SOM* [4,26]. In this case, instead of completely determined, e.g., the Euclidean distance as a discrimination function (requiring a priori knowledge of the error surface defined by the problem), the Pareto optimality is applied.

Another possible extension is the application of *hierarchical self-organizing maps* (H-SOM) [27,28]. The key idea H-SOM is to use a hierarchical structure of multiple layers in which each layer consists of a number of independent self-organizing maps (SOM). One SOM is used at the first layer of the hierarchy. For every unit in this map, a SOM might be added to the next layer of the hierarchy. This principle can be repeated with the third and any further layers of the HSOM.

The precursor of a general SOM neural network was the *learning vector quantization* (LVQ) [29] artificial neural network. It uses a popular, in SOM, winner-takes-all learning approach. A goal of the algorithm is to approximate the distribution of a class using a reduced number of vectors from a codebook minimizing classification errors. It does not construct a map (as SOM does) and does not introduce the concept of a neighborhood.

As we already mentioned, some networks, e.g., SOM and LVQ networks, use the winner-takes-all learning approach. It is very useful in many applications. However, sometimes other training algorithms are better to be used. An example of a simple learning algorithm is *k-nearest neighbor* (K-NN) [30,31]. In this method, an object is classified by a majority of votes of his neighbors; it is assigned to the class most popular among its *k* neighbors. The best choice of *k* depends on data to classify. For $k = 1$, the method is called the nearest neighbor algorithm. To complete the definition, one should propose a metric to select neighbors. It can be Euclidean distance (for continuous variables) or Hamming distance (for discrete ones).

A *radial basis function network* (RBF) [32] is a network that uses radial basis functions as activation functions. The output *y* of the network is a linear combination of radial basis functions of the inputs and neuron parameters, see Figure 11.4.

It can be represented by the formula

$$y = \sum_{j=1}^{K} c_j z_j = \sum_{j=1}^{K} c_j F_j(w_1 x_1, w_2 x_2, ..., w_N x_N), \tag{11.23}$$

where *K* is the number of neurons in the second layer, c_j, $j = 1, 2,..., K$ are the weights of linear combination of the RBF network's output, $F_j(...)$, $j = 1, 2,..., K$ are the RBF of neurons in the second layer (the activation functions of one of the allowable forms, e.g., (2.4) – (2.6)), *n* is the number of inputs of the neural network, x_i, $i = 1, 2,..., N$ are the inputs of the network, and w_i, $i = 1, 2,..., N$ are their weights.

A *probabilistic neural network* (PNN) [33] is a multilayered feedforward neural network organized into four layers called the input layer, hidden layer, summation layer, and output layer. Each neuron in the input layer provides the same input values to the pattern layer neurons. In classification problems, $N - 1$ neurons are used for *N* categories. The pattern layer contains one neuron for each case in the training data set. It uses an exponential activation function (e.g., $\exp\{(w_i x_i - 1)/\sigma^2\}$) as a nonlinear operation of the network. It stores the values of the predictor variables for the case along with the target value. The input and pattern layers form a connected structure. The summation layer contains one neuron for each category of the target variable. The actual target category of each training case is stored with each neuron; the weights of signals coming out of a hidden neuron grow only for the neuron of the pattern layer, which corresponds to its category. The neurons of the summation layer add the outputs of the pattern layer for the class they represent. The output layer takes a final decision on classifying the sample as belonging to the specific category. It compares the outputs of neurons of the summation layer and chooses the most significant as the class indicator.

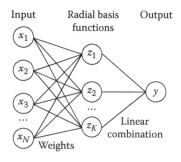

FIGURE 11.4   The radial basis function network.

The PNN can be also used for identification of unknown categories from the observed data [34]. This gives some alternatives to the approach presented in further sections of this chapter.

By *hybrid networks* [35], one understands the neural networks that unify several methodologies and cannot be included in a specific class. An approach incorporating elements of symbolic computations and artificial neural networks into one model is one possibility. Symbolic representations have advantages with respect to explicit, direct control, fast initial coding, dynamic variable binding, and abstract modeling. Including neural networks adds the possibility of learning, robustness, and generalization to similar input.

Another understanding of *hybrid networks* [36,37] is a combination of the network's layers of a different nature into one network, e.g., combining self-organizing and feedforward layers into one neural network model. Such a combination is closer to the biological paradigm than pure feedforward networks or classical associative memories and gives more flexibility in the network's training.

11.2.4 Neural Networks Used in Our Research

In our analysis, we made a number of experiments using different neural network architectures for new attack detection [38]. The most effective ones proved to be the MLP and the SVM neural networks.

The first series of tests has been performed with the MLP neural network (see Section 11.2.1). We used the network with three layers: the usual input and output layers and one hidden layer, and we trained it with the back propagation algorithm. In our research, we used the two following variants of the BP algorithm:

- Levenberg–Marquardt (*trainln*)
- Resilient back propagation (*trainrp*)

For the simulation process, the MATLAB® toolbox was used. The variants of the BP algorithm that were applied are followed by names of the learning MATLAB's functions given in parentheses.

The second neural network architecture that was applied for our experiment is the support vector machine (SVM). It was the feedforward neural network that consisted of two layers (hidden and output) and with the Gaussian kernel function. Parameters of the kernel function have been selected with a *n*-fold cross-validation method practically described [39]. In the simulation, *LibSVM* implementation of the SVM network was used.

11.3 INPUT DATA FOR THE DETECTION OF ATTACKS

In the first phase of our investigation, we used the KDD 99 data set as the input vectors for training and validation of the neural networks. This data set was prepared based on the data collected in the DARPA (Defense Advanced Research Project Agency) intrusion detection evaluation program. The MIT Lincoln Lab that participated in this program had set up simulation of a typical LAN network in order to acquire raw TCP dump data [40]. They simulated LAN network operating as a normal environment, which was infected with different types of attacks. The raw data was processed into connection records [2,41,65]. For each connection, 41 different features were extracted. Each connection was labeled as the normal one or as being under a specific type of attack. Four main categories of the attacks were simulated:

- *DoS* (denial of service)—An attacker tries to prevent legitimate users from using a service, e.g., TCP SYN Flood, Smurf, etc.
- *Probe*—An attacker tries to collect information about the target host, for example, scanning victims in order to get knowledge of available services, operating system version, etc.

TABLE 11.1
KDD 99 Data Subsets

Data Set	DoS	Probe	U2R	U2L	Normal
10% KDD	391,458	4107	52	1126	97,277
Corrected KDD	229,853	4166	70	16,347	60,593
Whole KDD	3,883,370	41,102	52	1126	972,780

- *U2R* (user to root)—An attacker has a local account on the victim host and tries to gain root privileges.
- *R2L* (remote to local)—An attacker does not have local account on a victim host and tries to obtain it.

The KDD 99 data set is divided in to three subsets: 10% KDD, corrected KDD, and whole KDD. Basic characteristics of the KDD 99 data sets are shown in Table 11.1. Table 11.1 includes the number of connections assigned to the particular class of an attack (DoS, Probe, etc.).

The 10% KDD data set is used for the training process of the IDS. It includes connections simulating 22 types of attacks and the normal traffic. The corrected KDD data set is used for the testing process of the IDS. It includes an additional 14 types of new attacks not presented in 10% KDD and in whole KDD. Thanks to them, it is possible to check if the IDS is able to detect a new attack not presented in the training phase.

In the second phase of investigation, we added to the KDD 99 data set the simulation results of 14 new attacks (generated with usage of *Metasploit Framework*) and a new normal traffic containing instant messaging, VoIP, audio streaming, and network games. These types of the network traffic were not presented before in the KDD 99 data set and could show how our proposal works for the real data.

11.4 LITERATURE REVIEW

Usage of neural networks for intrusion detection was presented in many publications. There are visible three main research streams that will be described in the next subsections:

11.4.1 PREPROCESSING OF INPUT DATA

An input data from an IP network or an audit log must be transferred to the numeric representation in order to be analyzed by the neural network. Because the number of features and vectors is very large and could negatively impact on the performance of the IDS, most welcome are solutions that allow reducing it. Two main ways of reduction are described in the literature:

11.4.1.1 Input Data Clustering

This solution assumes that data are clustered before going into the input of a neural network. It allows a decreasing amount of analyzed data because of the use of a group of data with similar features instead of individual vectors. In the paper [42], usage of a SOM neural network allows the creation of an input vector that includes a series of events related to a particular attack. In [43] was described usage of a neural network (also SOM) to preprocess input data in order to obtain a constant number of groups in which each of them consisted of a similar intensity of IP network flow.

11.4.1.2 Reduction of Input Vector Size

The second way of improving the performance of an IDS is decreasing the number of analyzing vector features. In order to achieve this goal in the papers [44] and [45] was proposed the choosing of the most important features related to each of the analyzed group of attacks. Usage of a FNT (flexible neural tree) algorithm allowed the reduction in number of analyzed features of a KDD vector from 41 to 4 (normal), 12 (probe), 12 (DoS), 8 (U2R), and 10 (R2L). Presented results of a simulation for a reduced to 12 features vector with a neural network show the accuracy of the attack detection from 95.08% to 100% and a false alarm rate from 0.1% to 0.8%. Compared to a simulation without features reduction proposed solution increased detection accuracy for the R2L and DoS attacks group.

In paper [2], the most important features related to a TCP/IP packet header from the DARPA data set was found with usage of a genetic algorithm.

Reduction of input data is accomplished with two methods: PBRM (the performance-based ranking method) and support vector decision function ranking were described in [46]. For each of five classes from the KDD data set was found the most relevant features. The PRBM method relies on the following algorithm: from the input data was deleted one feature; next, the process of learning and testing is conducted; and in the last step, results such as accuracy and duration of learning and testing phases was compared to obtain for classification learning with a complete 41-feature vector. SVDFR methods rely on the counting of weight with the usage of a decision function of support vectors. Relevance of each feature is indicated based on weight values. Results obtained for the two methods were similar for DoS, Probe, and R2L classes. Simulation with usage of a SVM classifier was shown similar results concerning classification accuracy and a shorter duration time of learning and testing phases for a reduced data set.

11.4.2 ARCHITECTURE OF IDS BASED ON NEURAL NETWORK

In the literature, there are presented two approaches of usage of neural networks in IDS:

- Combination of neural network and expert system—the neural network identifies suspicious events and transfers them to an expert system for more detailed analysis.
- Usage of the neural network as an autonomous system that is learning signatures of attacks or normal behaviors of the end user and, in the next step, based on its own analysis decides to treat monitoring traffic as an attack or normal.

An example of the first approach was described by Debar [47]. In this solution, the role of the expert system is to make a final decision about the generation of alarm. The decision is made based on information from the output of the neural network and analysis of audit data that rely on comparing it with well known signatures of attacks collected in the knowledge data base. The block schema of this system is presented in Figure 11.5.

The system consists of the following blocks:

- *Data acquisitions*—responsible for collecting the audit data.
- *Data formatting*—that preprocesses analyzed data to a representation accepted by the neural network and expert system.
- *Neural network*—responsible for analysis of audit data. Also in this block coding and decoding of audit data to numeric representation is conducted.
- *Expert system analysis and control of neural network*—block analysis output of neural network and translation of information to a form proper for intrusion detection. It is also responsible for system controlling of the neural network learning process.
- *Expert system analysis and decision*—module generates an alarm based on information from the neural network or comparison of analyzed data with the knowledge base that includes scenarios of known attacks.

This solution provides the following advantages: a decrease in the number of false alarms thanks to adaptation of thresholds based on information from the neural network; moreover, there is an

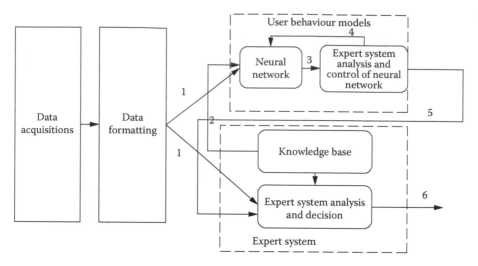

FIGURE 11.5   The block schema of an IDS system (based on Debar, H., Becke, M., and Siboni, D., *Proc. of the IEEE Computer Society Symposium on Research in Security and Privacy*, 240–250, 1992). (1) Retrieval and formatting of the audit records from the target system; (2) computation of complementary context-dependent inputs; (3) raw output of the artificial neural network; (4) supervised learning and output interpretation; (5) input from the model of the behavior of the user; (6) final decision and alarm generation.

increase in performance and accuracy because only suspicious events are transferred to the expert system. The main disadvantage is the necessity of updating the expert system when the neural network detects a new attack whose scenarios are not included in the knowledge base.

Consider the second approach (the neural network as an autonomous system); most of the known architecture of the neural network was analyses. Below is described some of the research examples.

A recurrent neural network was used in the case when the input data depended on an answer of the system in previous steps. For example, an analysis of usage of the Elman neural network for looking for intrusions in the UNIX command sequence was presented [21]. Research on the IDS based on Jordan and Elman recurrent neural networks that analyze SQL requests in order to find SQL injection attacks was considered [23].

A description of self-organizing map (SOM) usage for IDS was the subject of paper [48]. The neural network analyzed a distance between vectors representing an attack and normal traffic. In the case, when this distance was longer than a threshold, an alarm was generated. Usage of an improved SOM network (full Pareto learning SOM) that uses a new learning rate function was described [4]. The presented research results show that in comparison to SOM, there were obtained better classification results and a shorter time of learning.

The described above examples of usage of the SOM network was validated in offline analysis by usage of before collected data. Such an approach does not allow reacting to the attack in time when it occurs. An IDS (RT-UNNID, *real-time unsupervised neural-net-based intrusion detector*) based on a SOM network that, working in real time, was presented [49]. The schema of work of this solution is shown in Figure 11.6.

In the first step, *Sniffer* collects the packet data from an IP network. Next, this data are preprocessed to numeric representation that could be recognized by the neural network (module *UNN Engine*). Information about classification of an input vector as an attack or as normal traffic is transferred to the *Responder* module, which writes it in logs and generates an alarm for the suspicious traffic. The SOM network is learned as follows: In the first step, the network assigns vector to groups based on their similarity. After finishing of the clustering process, it was chosen a neuron's output responsible for representation of each group. For instance, if 50% vectors belong to the normal category, the whole group is labeled as normal. When the neuron's output does not indicate

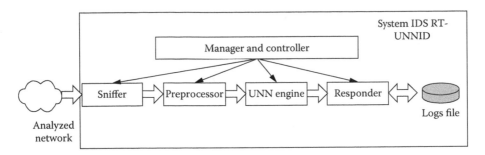

FIGURE 11.6 Schema of working RT-UNNID system (according to Amini, M., Jalili, R., and Shahriari, H. R., *Computers & Security*, 25, 459–468, 2006).

any group, it should be removed. In this work was also presented a comparison of results for usage as UNN Engine module SOM and ART neural network. Better results were obtained for ART architecture that was allowed to detect 97% of the presented attacks with a 2% false alarm rate. In comparison, the SOM neural network was obtaining a 95% accuracy detection rate of attacks with a 3.5% false alarm rate. The ART network also allows learning new patterns on each level of the learning process. Additionally, performance of tested neural networks was compared, and results shown that, for ART, time of learning is shortened and this architecture is able to more quickly classify input vectors.

The main advantage for the usage of SOM is the possibility of learning the system basing on unlabeled data. One of the disadvantages of SOM is the dependence of network performance on the neuron's number. The more features in the vector, the more inputs that are needed, and because of this SOM network's behavior, time of analysis is longer. In [50] was presented a solution that solves this drawback and, for the same detection accuracy, offers a shorter duration time for the analysis and learning processes. A proposed ICLN (*improved competitive learning network*) algorithm changes the way of neurons update by usage of an additional kernel function (with arguments depending on distance between the neurons) on which depend values of weights' updates. For a reduced to seven attacks and normal traffic KDD data set, there was obtained a 98% accuracy of classification.

Many publications described usage of the MLP network. Cannady [51] presented the neural network with four layers and nine input and two output neurons that represent the attack as "1" "0" or the normal traffic as "0" "1." It successfully detected three presented types of attack. Other examples of usage of the MLP are described [42,52].

Very high classification accuracy was achieved thanks to the SVM network. One of the first usages of this type of neural network for intrusion detection was presented by Mukkamala [53]. The described experiment used the KDD 99 data set; the tests showed that for the same detection accuracy (about 99%) the SVM learned and worked more quickly than the MLP network. One of the small disadvantages of the SVM network was the possibility of classification of only binary problems. In the case when it is important to recognize also a type of attack, a separated network for each class of the attack should be used [53].

Also usage of hybrid neural network architecture could improve detection accuracy. In [54] was presented an example of such a system consisting of RBF (radial basis function) and Elman neural networks. The proposed hybrid IDS was validated with DARPA input data; the results obtained showed good accuracy in detection of DoS and probing attacks. A mixture of MLP and SVM networks was used for classification of the SQL injection attack in paper [55]. Also, usage of clustering methods as a first module that preprocessed input data before neural network analysis could improve performance of the IDS. A hybrid IDS system consisting of SVM and the hierarchical clustering algorithm was described [56]. The IDS based on fuzzy clustering and the MLP network was presented [57,58]. Presented [57] test results showed a better classification accuracy of such an approach in comparison to SVM, K-NN (k-nearest neighbor), or H-SOM (hierarchical self-organizing map) architectures. Composition of LVQ (learning vector quantization) and k-nearest neighbor was described [59]. The proposed system was validated on a small part of the KDD data (3937 vectors) with an 89% classification success rate for all five classes.

Better classification results could be also obtained by using features and a training instance weighting algorithm [60].

11.4.3 New Attack Detection

In the literature, there are many papers concerning tests of usage of various neural network architectures for attack detection but only a few that focus on a new attack recognition issue. Bouzida and Cuppens [61] proposed to use a threshold from the above that should be their reaction of output neurons. In the case when this reaction is below the threshold, it might be a new attack, and this vector should be more deeply analyzed. Unfortunately, even if this solution is successful for some new types of attack, it cannot help in increasing the detection accuracy of new attacks from the U2R class.

In paper [2] was presented the usage of an expert system and the hybrid neural network RBF-SOM in order to adapt the system to identification of new classes of attacks.

A hybrid system consisting of the MLP neural network and a fuzzy inference module was proposed by Tai [62]. The results of their work showed the possibility of detecting one new attack (synk4- TCP SYN flood). Unfortunately, the tests have not been performed on a wider data set such as the KDD 99, so it is not possible to compare the approach [62] with that presented in this chapter, the new IDS architecture proposal. Recognition of previously unknown attacks with application of neural networks was also considered in [66,67].

11.5   THE PROPOSAL OF THE NEW IDS ARCHITECTURE

The main goal of the IDS architecture proposed in this section is to allow adapting the IDS system to the correct classification of new network traffic related to both normal behavior of an end-user and to new attacks. The block diagram of the architecture is presented in Figure 11.7.

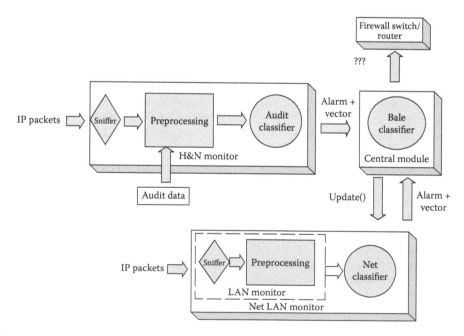

FIGURE 11.7   Block diagram architecture of the IDS proposal.

The IDS system proposed in Figure 11.7 is composed of three main modules: *H&N monitor*, *Net-LAN monitor*, and *central module*. The role of each module is the following:

11.5.1 H&N Monitor

The main task of this module is analyzing logs and a host's audit data in order to find an anomalous event that can be an aggressor's activity. When an attack is detected by *the audit detector*, a network packet associated with it should be identified. Based on that network data, the KDD 99 vector of the attack detected is created and is delivered with the alarm flag to the *central module* where it could be used to retrain *the base classifier*.

11.5.2 Net-LAN Monitor

This module analyzes network data provided by a sniffer and transforms it to the KDD 99 vector form. The neural network is used for the classification process. It takes a decision about whether a current vector is related to an attack or to normal traffic. In the case of the attack detection, the alarm flag accompanied by the KDD 99 vector is sent to *the central module*. Based on this KDD 99 vector, it is possible to perform additional analysis, and, finally, an eventual decision about classification of this alarm to the attack group or to the false alarm group is taken. For the additional analysis purpose, *the central module* can use various methods (in the simplest way, by analysis of a security officer). In a case of the false alarm, the provided KDD 99 vector can be used to retrain *the base classifier* and to update all classifiers in all *Net-LAN monitor* modules.

11.5.3 Central Module

This module obtains all alarms from distributed *Net-LAN* and *H&N monitor* modules and presents them to the end user of the IDS system. The second task of this module is retraining *the base classifier* with using the new learning data provided by *H&N* and *Net-LAN monitors*. *The base classifier* is the neural network that has the same architecture and weight values as *Net-classifier* in each *Net-Lan monitor* module. After the retraining process, information about the updated weights and the new number of hidden neurons is sent to all *Net-LAN monitor* modules.

An example of the network architecture that can use our solution is shown in Figure 11.8.

In our work, we decided that the *H&N monitor* module is located on a honeypot system. This localization has the following advantages:

- The honeypot system can be created with specific security rules that are less restrictive than the rules for other hosts in the protected network. In that case, the host with the installed honeypot system can be visible for an aggressor as an easier target to attack than other hosts. Thanks to this feature, it is more probable than for a real production server or for an end user host that the aggressor performs a new attack against it. As a result, we can collect the data that represent this new attack. Moreover, focusing an aggressor's attention on the honeypot could distract him from production servers and could increase other hosts' safety.
- The honeypot system only simulates some network services, and the size of the normal traffic destined for it is very limited. That's why it is easier to identify the data related to the new attacks.

The honeypot system in our proposal is located in the DMZ (*demilitarized zone*). Thanks to this localization, in a case of taking over the honeypot control by an aggressor, the risk of a successful attack against another host located in this internal network is lower because they are protected by the specific rules of a firewall. Moreover, the DMZ is less secure, so it could attract aggressors and make it easier to collect the data related to the new attacks.

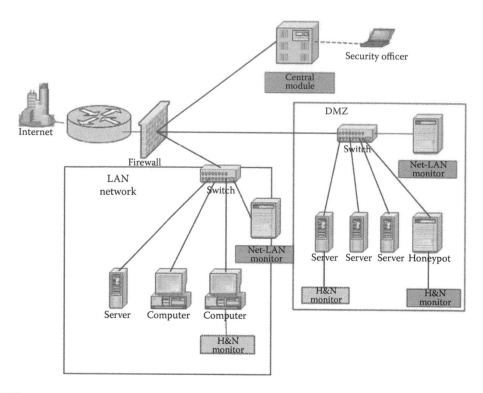

FIGURE 11.8   The network architecture with the IDS proposal.

In order to analyze all network traffic data, a *Net-LAN monitor* should be located in each real or virtual subnetwork.

11.6 RESULTS OF TESTS

Our investigation was divided into two phases. In the first phase, the accuracy of classification of a new pattern by the neural network was analyzed. The goal of the second phase was to build the prototype of the IDS in the proposed architecture and to check its effectiveness concerning detection of the new attacks and the normal traffic classification. The data sets used for each phase of investigation have been described in Section 11.3.

11.6.1 PHASE 1

For the simulation, we used two architectures of the neural network: MLP and SVM. For the training and validation, the KDD 99 data sets were used. More information about creation and training the neural network can be found [63].

During analysis of the test results, we noticed that both neural network architectures have a problem with classification of a new attack not presented in the learning phase.

- For the MLP network, the detection rate of a new attack was only 4.26% while, for the other attacks presented during the learning phase, it was 98%. The false alarm rate was 2.5%.
- For the SVM network, the detection rate of a new attack was only 18.7% while, for the other attacks presented during the learning phase, it was 97%. The false alarm rate was 2%.

TABLE 11.2

Accuracy of New Attack Detection from Corrected KDD Testing Data Set

Name of Attack	Number of Vectors in Test Data Set	Attack Detection Rate [%] (SVM)	False Alarm Rate [%] (MLP)
Snmpgetattack	7741	0.25	0.02
Named	17	29.4	52.94
Xlock	9	0	55.55
Xsnoop	4	50	50
Sendmail	17	47.06	52.95
Saint	736	96.06	82.2
Xterm	13	84.61	61.54
Mscan	1053	94.59	7.50
Proces stable	759	77. 08	1.45
Ps	16	37.5	81.25
Apache2	794	99.75	4.16
Udpstorm	2	50	100
Httptunnel	158	16.45	0.63
Worm	2	0	0
Mailbomb	5000	6.78	0.32
Sqlattack	2	100	100
Snmpguess	2406	0.17	0.04
Sum of new attacks	18,729	18.7	4.26

In Table 11.2, the accuracy of detection for each type of the new attacks from the test data set was presented. It could be noticed that for 17 new attacks only two were classified with a detection rate that equals 100%.

11.6.2 Phase 2

As we noticed in the first phase, the SVM network better classified a new pattern. That's why, for the second phase of the investigation, we decided to use only this neural network's architecture. The results of the tests are presented in Table 11.3 (new normal traffic) and Table 11.4 (new attacks).

The first row of each table corresponds to the situation in which the new normal traffic and the new attacks were not presented in the learning phase. In that situation for Table 11.3, false alarms were observed for four from 10 new normal vectors analyzed by a *Net-LAN monitor* module. For Table 11.4, it could be noticed that four new attacks were not detected. The new attacks not detected by the *Net-LAN monitor* were later detected by the *H&N monitor* located on the honeypot hosts. Thanks to it, we obtain the vectors for retraining the neural networks in the *central module* and for

TABLE 11.3

Results of Net-LAN Monitor Classification of the New Normal Traffic

Learning Data Set (Network Architecture)	Test Data Set	Number of False Alarms	Number of Not Detected Attacks	Remarks
"NaukaIbiza 2009 sm (SVM)"	*"Testowe_gadu3D"*	1347	21,380	False alarm concerns: *"sip-audio," "rtp-audio," "gadu-k,"* and *"radio"*
"NaukaDay55"	*"Testowe_gadu3D"*	1328	21,432	All the new normal vectors were properly classified

TABLE 11.4
Results of Detection of the New Attacks by Net-LAN Monitor

Learning Data Set (Network Architecture)	Test Data Set	Number of False Alarms	Number of Not Detected Attacks	Remarks
"NaukaIbiza2009sm" (SVM)	"Testowe+new31"	1343	21,384	Not detected: *cesarftp_mkd, slimp_ftp_list., mailcarrier_ smtp, goodtech_telnet*
net-klasyfikator after update (SVM)	"Testowe+new31"	1376	21,292	All new attacks were properly detected

updating *Net-LAN monitor* classifiers. The second row of each table represents the situation after this update. In both tables, we observe that all the new vectors were properly classified.

11.7   VISION OF FUTURE DEVELOPMENT OF IDS

Intrusion detection and prevention systems are the subject of extensive research both of individual investigators and state-owned organizations. The American agency NIST gave its own recommendations for constructing IDS [64]. This document presents different architectures of the networks to protect different technologies of network protection. However, in spite of the recommendations, considering anomaly-based systems a tool of network attack detection, they do not consider the neural network–based IDS explicitly.

From our investigation, we noticed that the neural networks properly classified the network traffic similar to the one presented during the learning phase. Therefore, they could be a good solution for detection of the attacks that were modified by an aggressor in order to cheat intrusion detection systems. Unfortunately, the new attacks and the new normal traffic that is significantly different from the one presented in the training phase cannot be classified with sufficiently good accuracy. The IDS architecture that we proposed could improve classification of the new network patterns. Our solution has the following advantages:

- It fixes problems with obtaining training data representing a new attack or new normal traffic.
- It adapts itself to new attack detection.
- Thanks to using the Net-LAN classifier, it is possible to react to an attack in real time and block it before it reaches a host under protection.
- It adapts the system to correct classification of the normal network traffic related to a new service not presented before in the training data (still, it should work out a method of making automatically a final decision about classification of alarms in *the central module*).

It is important to check if adding a new vector influences negatively the classification accuracy. For example, in a situation when we add new normal traffic to the learning data set and the number of not detected attacks increased significantly, the reason may be that the new vectors can be too much similar to an attack representation. In that case, a new feature should be added to KDD 99 vectors in order to classify reliably both traffic types. This is the main limitation of a presented solution. That's why, in the future, it should find a solution that allows not only relearning a neural network for a new attack but also automatically changing its architecture when it is needed. For instance, add additional inputs when new features need to be created. This system should adapt not only to the classification of attacks but also to recognition of new traffic generated by the new normal activity of the user.

Presented in this chapter is a solution that allows the collection of data that represents attacks from a honeypot system. In commercial solutions, such a honeypot could be represented by a network of honeypots with different operating systems and a large number of services that collect suspicious traffic and prepare new vectors for the relearning of neural networks or other machine learning IDS. Still, we should also find a solution for the collection of data that represent new normal behavior of a monitored user or system.

The future analysis of the usage of a neural network or other solution for intrusion detection needs a new data set for evaluation of IDS with new attacks and compares obtained results with other researchers. Moreover, based on this new data set, there also should be created a new updated set of features that allow the proper recognition of most new attacks and normal traffic. Currently, most of the publications still used for evaluation data are provided by the DARPA project in the years 1998 and 1999. Unfortunately, such a data set cannot prove the effectiveness of using neural network–based IDS to detect today's attacks.

It should be also mentioned that usage of a neural network is reasonable for a known attack only when the creation of a proper signature is complicated. For instance, attacks based on incorrect fragmentation of IP packets could be easily detected by checking two fields of the IP packet header: offset and length. A similar way of attack detection could be used for all other attacks that are based on sending modified, incompliant with specification packets. It seems that efficient IDS could be the combination of two modules: IDS based on signatures and responsible for detection of well-known attacks and, second, based on a neural network or other machine learning technology that could recognize modified versions of known attacks and even some new attacks as were proposed above.

AUTHORS' BIOGRAPHIES

Przemysław Kukiełka graduated from the University of Technology Wroclaw in 2002 with a MSc in electronic and telecommunication. He received his PhD in telecommunication from Warsaw University of Technology. Kukiełka is working now as a laboratory manager in the research and development department of Orange Poland. His current research project concerns intrusion detection with usage data mining technology and security aspects of video services. He has published 15 articles related to security and multimedia services.

Zbigniew Kotulski received his MSc in applied mathematics from Warsaw University of Technology and his PhD and DSc degrees from the Institute of Fundamental Technological Research of the Polish Academy of Sciences. He is currently professor and head of the Security Research Group, Department of Electronics and Information Technology at Warsaw University of Technology, Poland. Prof. Kotulski is the author or co-author of five books and more than 150 research papers on applied probability, cryptographic protocols, and network security.

REFERENCES

1. Anderson, J. P., Computer security threat monitoring and surveillance, Fort Washington, PA, 1980.
2. Horeis, T., Intrusion detection with neural networks-combination of SOM and RBF networks for human expert integration, http://ieeecis.org/_files/EAC_Research_2003_Report_Horeis.pdf, 2003.
3. Hwang, S., Lee, T.-J., Lee, Y.-J., A three-tier IDS via data mining approach, *Proc. of the 3rd Annual ACM Workshop on Mining Network Data (MineNet)*, pp. 1–6, San Diego, CA, USA, June 12, 2007.
4. Jiang, X., Liu, K., Yan, J., Chen, W., Application of improved SOM neural network in anomaly detection, *Proc. International Conference on Medical Physics and Biomedical Engineering, Physics Procedia*, vol. 33, pp. 1093–1099, 2012.
5. Pradhan, M., Pradhan, S. K., Sahu, S. K., Anomaly detection using artificial neural network, *International Journal of Engineering Sciences & Emerging Technologies*, vol. 2, pp. 29–36, 2012.
6. Haykin, S., *Neural networks: A Comprehensive Foundation* (2nd ed.). Prentice Hall, 1998.
7. Anthony, M., Bartlett, P. L., *Neural Network Learning: Theoretical Foundations*, Cambridge University Press, 2009.

8. Hinton, G., Sejnowski, T. J. [Eds.], *Unsupervised Learning: Foundations of Neural Computation*, MIT Press, 1999.

9. Mohri, M., Rostamizadeh, A., Talwalkar, A., *Foundations of Machine Learning*, MIT Press, Cambridge, MA, 2012.

10. Collobert, R., Bengio, S., Links between perceptrons, MLPs and SVMs. In Carla E. Brodley (Ed.), *Proc. of the Twenty-first International Conference on Machine Learning (ICML 2004)*, Banff, Alberta, Canada, July 4–8, 2004, ACM International Conference Proceeding Series, vol. 69. doi: 10.1145/1015330.1015415.

11. Rosenblatt, F., *Principles of Neurodynamics: Perceptrons and the Theory of Brain Mechanisms*, Spartan Books, Washington, DC, 1961.

12. Rumelhart, D. E., Hinton, G. E., Williams, R. J., Learning representations by back-propagating errors, *Nature*, vol. 323, pp. 533–536, 1986.

13. Snyman, J. A., *Practical Mathematical Optimization: An Introduction to Basic Optimization Theory and Classical and New Gradient-Based Algorithms*, Springer, 2005.

14. Battiti, R., First and second order methods for learning: Between steepest descent and Newton's method, *Neural Computation*, vol. 4, pp. 141–166, 1992.

15. Moller, M. F., A scaled conjugate gradient algorithm for fast supervised learning, *Neural Networks*, vol. 6, pp. 525–533, 1993.

16. Hagan, M., Menhaj, M. B., Training feed forward networks with the Marquardt algorithm, *IEEE Trans. on Neural Networks*, vol. 5, pp. 989–993, 1994.

17. Riedmiller, M., Braun, H., A direct adaptive method for faster backpropagation learning: The RPROP algorithm, *Proc. of the IEEE International Conference on Neural Networks*, pp. 586–591, 1993.

18. Cortes, C., Vapnik, V., Support-vector networks, *Machine Learning*, vol. 20, pp. 273–297, 1995.

19. Hastie, T., Tibishirani, R., Friedman, J., *The Elements of Statistical Learning*, Springer Series in Statistics, Springer 2008.

20. Elman, J. L., Finding structure in time, *Cognitive Science*, vol. 14, pp. 179–211, 1990.

21. Debar, H., Dorizzi, B., An application of a recurrent network to an intrusion detection system, *Proc. of the International Joint Conference on Neural Network*, pp. 478–483, 1992.

22. Jordan, M. L., Attractor dynamics and parallelism in a connectionist sequential machine, *Proc. of the Eighth Annual Conference of the Cognitive Science Society*. (Amherst, 1986), Hillsdale, Erlbaum, pp. 531–546, 1986.

23. Skaruz, J., Seredyński, F., Recurrent neural networks towards detection of SQL attacks, *Parallel and Distributed Processing Symposium IPDPS*, 2007, pp. 1–8, 2007.

24. Hopfield, J. J., Neural networks and physical systems with emergent collective computational abilities, *Proc. of the National Academy of Sciences of the USA*, vol. 79, pp. 2554–2558, 1982.

25. Kohonen, T., Self-organized formation of topologically correct feature maps, *Biological Cybernetics*, vol. 43, pp. 59–69, 1982.

26. Fieldsend, J. E., Singh, S., Pareto evolutionary neural networks, *IEEE Transactions on Neural Networks*, vol. 16, pp. 338–354, 2005.

27. Dittenbach, M., Merkl, D., Rauber, A., The growing hierarchical self-organizing map, *Proc. of the Int. Joint Conference on Neural Networks (IJCNN '2000)*, vol. 6, pp. 15–19, 2000.

28. Luttrell, S. P., Hierarchical self-organising networks, *Proc. of the 1st IEEE International Conference on Artificial Neural Networks*, London, pp. 2–6, 1989.

29. Kohonen, T., Learning vector quantization, In M. A. Arbib (Ed.), *The Handbook of Brain Theory and Neural Networks*, pp. 537–540. MIT Press, Cambridge, MA, 1995.

30. Bremner, D., Demaine, E., Erickson, J., Iacono, J., Langerman, S., Morin, P., Toussain, G., Output-sensitive algorithms for computing nearest-neighbor decision boundaries, *Discrete and Computational Geometry*, vol. 33, pp. 593–604, 2005.

31. Furaoa, S., Hasegawa, O., A fast nearest neighbor classifier based on self-organizing incremental neural network, *Neural Networks*, vol. 21, pp. 1537–1547, 2008.

32. Broomhead, D. S., Lowe, D., Multivariable functional interpolation and adaptive networks, *Complex Systems*, vol. 2, pp. 321–355, 1988.

33. Specht, D. F., Probabilistic neural networks for classification, mapping, or associative memory, *Proc. of the IEEE Conference on Neural Networks*, vol. 1, pp. 528, 1988.

34. Washburne, T. P., Specht, D. F., Drake, R. M., Identification of unknown categories with probabilistic neural networks, *Proc. IEEE International Conference on Neural Networks*, 1993. doi: 10.1109/ICNN.1993.298596.

35. Psichogios, D. C., Ungar, L. H., A hybrid neural network-first principles approach to process modeling, *AIChE Journal*, vol. 38, pp. 1499–1511, 1992.

36. Grossberg, S., Adaptive pattern classification: Parallel deployment and coding of neural feature detectors, *Biological Cybernetics*, vol. 23, pp. 121–134, 1976.
37. Rojas, R., *Neural Networks: A Systematic Introduction*, Springer, Berlin, 1996.
38. Kukiełka, P., Detection of attacks against information systems using adaptive methods, PhD thesis, Warsaw University of Technology, Warsaw, 2011.
39. Hsu, C. W., Chang, C.-C., Lin, C.-J., A practical guide to support vector classification, Department of Computer Science National Taiwan University, Taipei, Tajwan, available online at http://www.csie.ntu.edu.tw/~cjlin, 2009.
40. Lippmann, R., Haines, J. W., Fried, D. J., Korba, J., Das, K., The 1999 DARPA off-line intrusion detection evaluation, *Computer Networks*, vol. 34, pp. 579–595, 2000.
41. Lee, W., Stolfo, S. J., A data mining approaches for intrusion detection, *Proc. Seventh USENIX Security Symposium (SECURITY '98)*, vol. 7, p. 6, San Antonio, TX, 1998.
42. Cannady, J., Maheffey, J., The application of artificial neural networks to misuse detection. Initial results, *Proc. of the 1st International Workshop on Recent Advances in Intrusion Detection (RAID)*, Louvain-la-Neuve, Belgium, 1998.
43. Bivens, A., Palagiri, C., Smith, R., Szymanski, B., Embrechts, M., Network-based intrusion detection using neural networks, *Proc. ANNIE 2002 Conference*, pp. 10–13, ASME Press 2002.
44. Chen, Y., Abraham, A., Feature selection and intrusion detection using hybrid flexible neural tree, *Proc. of Second International Symposium on Neural Networks (ISNN-05)*, LNCS 3498, pp. 439–444, 2005.
45. Chen, Y., Abraham, A., Yang, B., Hybrid flexible neural-tree based IDS, *International Journal of Intelligent Systems*, vol. 22, pp. 337–352, 2007.
46. Mukkamala, S., Sung, A. H., Feature selection for intrusion detection using neural networks and support vector machines, *Journal of the Transportation Research Board of the National Academies*, vol. 1822, pp. 33–39, 2003.
47. Debar, H., Becke, M., Siboni, D., A neural network component for an intrusion detection system, *Proc. of the IEEE Computer Society Symposium on Research in Security and Privacy*, pp. 240–250, 1992.
48. Rhodes, B. C., Mahaffey, J. A., Cannady, J. D., Multiple self-organizing maps for intrusion detection, *Proc. of the 23rd National Information Systems Security Conference*, pp. 16–19, 2000.
49. Amini, M., Jalili, R., Shahriari, H. R., RT-UNNID: A practical solution to real-time network-based intrusion detection using unsupervised neural networks, *Computers & Security*, vol. 25, pp. 459–468, 2006.
50. Zhong, J., Ghorbani, A., Network intrusion detection using an improved competitive learning neural network, *Proc. of the Second Annual Conference on Communication Networks and Services Research*, pp. 190–197, 2004.
51. Cannady, J., Artificial neural networks for misuse detection, *National Information Systems Security Conference*, pp. 443–456, 1998.
52. Ryan, J., Lin, M. J., Miikkulain, R., Intrusion detection with neural networks, *Advances in Neural Information Processing Systems*, vol. 10, pp. 943–949, MIT Press, Cambridge, MA, 1998.
53. Mukkamala, S., Janoski, G., Sung, A. H., Intrusion detection using neural networks and support vector machines, *Proc. of the IEEE International Joint Conference on Neural Networks*, vol. 2, pp. 1702–1707, IEEE Computer Society Press, 2002.
54. Tong, X., Wang, Z., Yu, H., A research using hybrid RBF/Elman neural networks for intrusion detection system secure model, *Computer Physics Communications*, vol. 180, pp. 1795–1801, 2009.
55. Pinzon, C., Herrero, A., AIIDA-SQL: An adaptive intelligent intrusion detector agent for detecting SQL injection attacks, *Proc. of 10th International Conference on Hybrid Intelligent Systems*, pp. 73–78, 2010.
56. Horng, S.-J., Su, M.-Y., Chen, Y.-H., Kao, T.-W., Chen, R.-J., Lai, J.-L., Perkata, C. D., A novel intrusion detection system based on hierarchical clustering and support vector machines, *Expert Systems with Applications,* vol. 38, pp. 306–313, 2011.
57. Ghadiri, A., Ghadiri, N., An adaptive hybrid architecture for intrusion detection based on fuzzy clustering and RBF neural networks, *Communication Networks and Services Research Conference*, pp. 123–129, 2011.
58. Wang, G., Hao, J., Mab, J., Huang, L., A new approach to intrusion detection using artificial neural networks and fuzzy clustering, *Expert Systems with Applications,* vol. 37, pp. 6225–6232, 2010.
59. Naoum, R. S., Al-Sultani, Z. N., Learning vector quantization (LVQ) and k-nearest neighbor for intrusion classification, *World of Computer Science and Information Technology Journal (WCSIT)*, vol. 2, pp. 105–109, 2012.
60. Ghodratnama, S., Moosavi, M. R., Taheri, M., Jahromi, M. Z., A cost sensitive learning algorithm for intrusion detection, *Iranian Conference on Electrical Engineering (ICCE)*, pp. 1–7, May 2010.

61. Bouzida, W. Y., Cuppens, F., Neural networks vs. decision tress for intrusion detection, *IEEE/IST Workshop on Monitoring, Attack Detection and Mitigation (MonAM)*, pp. 81–88, 2006.
62. Tai, D.-R., Tai, W.-P., Chang, C.-F., A hybrid intelligent intrusion detection system to recognize novel attacks, In *Proc. IEEE 37th Annual 2003 International Carnahan Conference on Security Technology*, 2003.
63. Kukiełka, P., Kotulski, Z., Analysis of the different architectures of neural networks usage for intrusion detection systems, *Proc. of the International Multiconference on Computer Science and Information Technology, IMCSIT 2008*, pp. 807–811, IEEEXplore, 2008.
64. Scarfone, K., Mell, P., Guide to intrusion detection and prevention systems (IDPS), Recommendations of the National Institute of Standards and Technology, Sp 800–94, Revision 1 (Draft), NIST, July, 2012.
65. Lee, W., Stolfo, S. J., A framework for constructing features and models for intrusion detection systems, *ACM Transactions on Information and System Security (TISSEC)*, vol. 3, pp. 227–261, 2000.
66. Novikov, D., Yampolskiy, D. V., Reznik, L., Traffic analysis based identification of attacks, *International Journal of Computer Science and Applications*, vol. 5, pp. 69–88, 2008.
67. Muthukkumarasamy, V., Birkely, R., An intelligent intrusion detection system based on neural network, *IADIS International Conference Applied Computing*, pp. I-221–I-228, 2004.

12 Artificial Intelligence– Based Intrusion Detection Techniques

Zahra Jadidi, Vallipuram Muthukkumarasamy, and Elankayer Sithirasenan

CONTENTS

12.1 INTRODUCTION

Ever-growing high-speed networks should be able to provide quality Internet services. Improving the security of the Internet is a crucial challenge for researchers. An intrusion detection system (IDS) is an important mechanism to protect these widespread networks from malicious activities. Nowadays, the network is constantly growing and becoming heterogeneous. Thus, IDSs should be able to handle a high volume of data traffic and be capable of operating with different types of networks. The research community is trying to address these through different ways, for example, hardware-based IDS [1], flow-based intrusion detection [2], and distributed intrusion detection [3]. An intelligent system can be trained to adapt to environmental changes. Different methods of artificial intelligence (AI) have been deployed in intrusion detection, for example, artificial neural networks (ANNs), fuzzy logic, and genetic algorithms (GA). In addition, hybrid intelligent IDSs, such as evolutionary fuzzy neural networks (EFuNN) and evolutionary neural network (ENN)–based IDSs, are also used [4–6].

Most of these proposed methods cannot easily be performed in high-speed networks. An intelligent IDS should be able to operate in Gigabit per second (Gbps) traffic. Different researchers have considered the application of intelligent methods in high-speed networks. A flow-based intelligent IDS [7], a hardware-based intelligent IDS [8], a multi-agent–based intelligent IDS [9], and a distributed intelligent IDS [10] are some of the scalable methods and need to be evaluated with benchmark data sets. The majority of data sets, which are used for such evaluation of IDSs, are based on IP version 4 (IPv4). Limited address space and security concerns are two main challenges for IPv4. The IP version 6 (IPv6) protocol addresses these problems. However, there are still a number of security challenges in IPv6 and in the transition process from IPv4 to IPv6 [11,12]. Some of these vulnerabilities are common both in IPv4 and IPv6. Although a migration from IPv4 to IPv6 is inevitable, this process is gradual and takes time. Before the complete replacement, both protocols need to work together during the transition period, which brings additional security issues. In addition, there are specific attacks targeting IPv6. However, research on IPv6 intrusion detection is still in its infancy.

Most of the mentioned problems are related to wired networks. There are other types of environments, all of which suffer from a number of security threats, for example, grid computing, cloud computing, and wireless networks. Grid computing shares tasks over different machines without any knowledge about their locations [13]. Cloud computing provides a pool of resources as services on the Internet [14]. Wireless local area networks [15], mobile ad hoc networks [16], and wireless sensor networks are different types of wireless networks [17]. Several methods have been proposed to detect intrusions in wireless networks. The remainder of this chapter is organized as follows. Section 12.2 discusses different intrusion detection methods deployed in or proposed for wired networks. Section 12.3 investigates the application of artificial intelligence for intrusion detection. Section 12.4 explains the security challenges in IPv6. To provide comprehensive examination, Section 12.5 describes the application of artificial intelligence in other environments. Finally, Section 12.6 concludes this chapter.

12.2 INTRUSION DETECTION IN WIRED NETWORKS

Over the years, the number of attacks has grown extensively in wired networks. One way of dealing with these suspicious activities is the use of IDS. The spread of Gbps speed in wired networks has encouraged researchers to work on intrusion detection in high-speed networks.

12.2.1 INTRUSION DETECTION TECHNIQUES

An IDS should monitor traffic and detect malicious activities. IDSs can be categorized based on different modules. Figure 12.1 shows IDS classes upon three modules [18]: data source, data analysis,

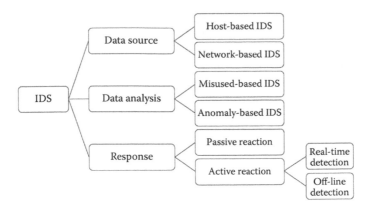

FIGURE 12.1   IDS classes.

and response. A data source can be gathered from either an individual computer (host-based IDS, HIDS) or network traffic (network-based IDS, NIDS).

There are two methods for analyzing the collected data: anomaly-based detection and misuse-based detection, which will be explained in the following sections. Anomaly- and misuse-based detection have general meaning for all environments. The third module specifies a suitable response for the suspicious data. This response can be passive or active in terms of behavior. As opposed to passive methods, active IDSs detect and respond to attacks [4,5].

12.2.1.1   Anomaly-Based Detection

The pattern of normal behavior is used in anomaly-based detection, which can be either self-learned or programmed [19]. In the self-learned anomaly detection, the normal behavior of a system is built automatically. On the other hand, in the programmed detection, a system developer provides the model of normal behavior. Although an anomaly-based IDS is able to detect unknown attacks, it has a high false alarm rate and cannot distinguish between different types of attacks. A number of anomaly detection methods are listed below [19–21], some of which are machine learning methods, such as neural networks:

- *Statistical techniques:* This technique uses a statistical model for defining normal behavior of the components of the system. All traffic out of this normal behavior will be known as anomalies. This technique assumes that the probability of normal data instances is higher in a stochastic model in comparison with the probability of an anomaly occurrence [20].
- *Clustering-based methods:* In this method, normal data belong to a cluster, and data not included in any cluster is detected as anomalies [20].
- *Information theoretic:* This method assumes that anomalies cause irregularities in information content of the data set. Different information theoretic measures are used to analyze the information content, for example, entropy and Kolmogorov Complexity [20].
- *Bayesian networks:* The probabilistic relationships among variables are encoded in the Bayesian method. The combination of this method with a statistical scheme offers better detection capability [22].
- *Data mining methods:* Data mining is the application of machine learning in large databases to provide simple models [23].
- *Neural networks:* This method is inspired by the human brain. Neural networks are flexible and adaptable to environmental changes. They can be deployed to create a user profile, to detect intrusion, and to predict the future behavior of the traffic [22].

- *Support vector machines (SVMs):* The SVM is based on statistical learning theory. One-class SVMs and multi-class SVM are well-known methods in classification and regression [24].
- *Nearest neighbor-based techniques:* In this method, the distance or similarity between two data instances is measured. Although normal data instances occur in dense neighborhoods, anomalies occur far from their closest neighbors [20].
- *Pattern matching:* Online learning is used in the pattern matching method to generate a traffic profile for each network. The profiles are used for anomaly detection. However, pattern matching may need to build traffic profiles for new networks, which results in a time-consuming process [21].
- *Group outlier:* The detection of rare events and malicious behavior is very important for network intrusion detection. There are different approaches to find such outliers in large data sets. A group outlier score (GOS) can differentiate between legitimate and illegitimate events in a network using outlier-based data association techniques [25].

12.2.1.2 Misuse-Based Detection

A misuse-based IDS, which is a programmed method, compares the user's activities with predefined signatures to find malicious traffic. Although this method is very accurate in detecting known attacks, it is not able to detect unknown attacks. Based on our knowledge, different misuse detection methods are shown in Figure 12.2 with a number of examples [26].

- *State modeling:* Intrusions are defined as states in this method. State-transition [27] and Petri-net [28] are two important methods of state modeling. These methods are different in the type of states that make up the intrusions. The state transition analysis technique (STAT) is an example of the state-transition method and is able to detect new attacks [29]. In this technique, the sequences of actions performed by attackers are specified to describe computer penetrations. There are different types of STAT techniques: host based (USTAT) [27], network based (NETSTAT) [30], and distributed multi-host (NSTAT). Analysis tools use a system's audit trail or network traffic to obtain required information. Then, they make a comparison between state changes and the state transition diagrams of known attacks. The STAT family was used [31] to propose STATL, a language for specifying attack actions. A state- or transition-based language is used in STATL to describe both network- and host-based attacks. Because having the whole state of a system is not possible, this language specifies and records only the part of a system that is necessary to define an attack signature. There are several attack languages. For example, P-Best [32], STATL, LogWeaver [33], CISL [34], BRO [35], Snort Rules [36], IDMEF [37], LAMBDA [38], and JIGSAW [39] are attack languages [40,41].
- *Expert system:* There are a set of rules in an expert system in which rules describe attack behavior. The expert system can be used to consider the security state of the system. Next-generation intrusion detection expert systems (NIDES) [42], EMERALD [43], and MIDAS [44] are expert system-based IDS techniques.

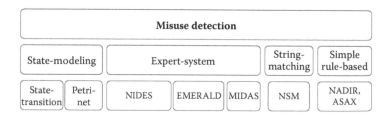

FIGURE 12.2 Misuse detection methods.

- *String matching:* Numbers of misuse- or signature-based IDSs use this technique, which is a substring matching of characters in texts. If there is a change in an attack signature, this method is unable to detect the attack. NSM is a model that is proposed [45].
- *Simple rule-based:* Expert knowledge about attacks can be modeled by the rule-based method. NADIR [46,47] and ASAX [48] are two methods that use a rule-based method.

12.2.2 INTRUSION DETECTION IN HIGH-SPEED NETWORKS

The state-of-the-art NIDSs should be applicable at the speed of Gbps. Various techniques have been used to improve the scalability of NIDSs. The techniques are shown in Figure 12.3 to the best of our knowledge.

12.2.2.1 Using Specialized Hardware

Hardware-based intrusion detection is a scalable method as it is able to inspect packets in high-speed networks. Most of the hardware-based NIDSs have been proposed to improve deep packet inspection (DPI), using some specialized hardware, such as a field-programming gate array (FPGA), an application-specific integrated circuit (ASIC), and ternary content addressable memories (TCAM) [49–55]. For example, a regular expression method is proposed using TCAM [51]. It is shown that this method is useful for throughput up to 18.6 Gbps. Another study reduces the input traffic of a software NIDS/network intrusion prevention system (NIPS) using a proposed pre-filtering mechanism based on FPGA [1,56].

12.2.2.2 Using Flow-Based Traffic for Intrusion Detection

A flow record is defined as a group of packets with a number of common properties, which pass a monitoring point in a certain time interval. Flow-based traffic contains only packet headers, and hence it reduces data. Flow-based IDS (FIDS) cannot detect attacks related to packet payload. Therefore, it is not a replacement for packet-based IDS. The FIDS can detect attacks such as denial of service (DoS), scans, worms, and botnets. DoS attacks caused by payload contents cannot be detected by FIDS [19]. For example, FIDS is not beneficial for a ping of death attack because this attack does not make a change in flow frequency and traffic volume. Several studies consider flow-based intrusion detection [57,58]. HiFIND is an online DoS–resilient flow-level intrusion detection system for a high-speed network [2]. Sketches are used in this technique to detect anomalies. A sketch is a one-dimensional hash table used for storing information. It records traffic for specific

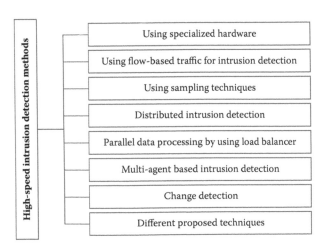

FIGURE 12.3 Intrusion detection methods in high-speed networks.

keys. HiFIND uses 2-D sketches, which hashes a set of flow-derived fields for each dimension. This method is employed to detect SYN flooding and port scans.

12.2.2.3   Using Sampling Techniques

Sampling data is a method used for anomaly detection [59–61] and change detection, for example, DoS attack detection. Cisco NetFlow [62] is a sampling technique to decrease the heavy load on router CPU in high-speed networks. However, sampling has negative impacts on the statistical characteristics of traffic and hence on the performance of intrusion detection. There are different types of sampling [19,63,64]:

- *Packet sampling:* There are two types of packet sampling methods: systematic and random. In systematic packet sampling, a time interval, or a sequence of packet arrival, is chosen to select a packet. In random packet sampling, the probability distribution function is used as a basis of sampling.
- *Flow sampling:* This method is more accurate than packet sampling. Random probability is used in random flow sampling to select flows.
- *Smart sampling:* This method is proposed to control the size of sampling data. Both the smart and the sample-and-hold sampling are flow-sampling methods proposed to reduce required memory.
- *Sample-and-hold:* The smart and sample-and-hold sampling methods try to provide precise traffic estimation for larger flows.
- *Adaptive packet sampling:* In order to have an accurate traffic statistic, this method identifies the current traffic load to adjust the sampling rate.
- *Selective flow sampling:* Although sampling techniques address the scalability problems, they affect anomaly detection efficiency. Selective flow sampling provides an appropriate balance between the performance and the amount of sampled information. Using small flows in selective flow sampling helps this method to improve the performance with less selected flow [65,66].

12.2.2.4   Distributed Intrusion Detection

Distributed intrusion detection systems (DIDS) are groups of IDSs or sensors that cooperate and work together. DIDS can be homogeneous or heterogeneous. In the homogeneous model, the DIDS contains sensors with the same type, and the heterogeneous model has a mixture of types. In addition, there are different types of management in DIDS, such as central management and hierarchical central management [67]. Two distributed intrusion detection methods are described as follows:

1. *Parallel data processing using load balancer:* A load balancer divides huge amounts of network traffic among multiple IDSs. Jiang et al. [68] introduces a high-performance NIDS called the HPMonitor. A high-efficiency detection engine and a flow-based dynamic load-balancing algorithm are used in the HPMonitor. The study also proposes an efficient load-balancing algorithm called the dynamic least load first (DLLF) algorithm. The DLLF divides the traffic based on the current value of the traffic function in each analyzer. A shift max algorithm (SMA) is the multi-pattern string matching algorithm proposed in this study. Another example is a stateful intrusion detection proposed [69]. The method divides the traffic and sends it to numbers of intrusion detection sensors. In this method, the portion of traffic required to detect an attack is sent to the sensor specified for the detection of that attack. In this proposed stateful intrusion detection method, there is no interconnection among sensors. However, this static technique is not very powerful in partitioning, especially in complex stateful signatures, in which there are more problems.

Foschini [70] extends the work [69] and proposes a similar parallel intrusion detection method. It also uses partitioning to divide traffic into reasonable and affordable sizes among intrusion detection sensors. The difference is that the sensors can communicate with others. This makes IDSs able to synchronize their scanning process. This method boosts the performance of high-speed intrusion detection as well, and no predefined relationships between packets and sensors are needed, and each packet can be sent to any sensors. In this case, we do not need any prior knowledge about packets. The SPANIDS load balancer is another method that utilizes a hash-based packet distribution mechanism [71]. In this method, network packets related to the same connection are forwarded to the same sensor node. Also, dynamic feedback from sensors helps SPANIDS to avoid overloading of sensor nodes. It is claimed [71] that this proposed technique can handle 1 Gbps and above.

2. *Multi-agent based intrusion detection:* Traditional IDSs are generally used to monitor a local area, and there is no interoperation between IDSs. An agent-based computing method is proposed to address this problem. In this method, intrusion detection is divided between a number of processors. As an agent-based IDS can obtain an overall view of the network, it will give a better detection rate. There are two types of agent-based methods: autonomous distributed agents and mobile agents. In the distributed agent–based IDS, agents can monitor traffic and share data with other agents [9]. Mobile agents are similar to distributed agents, but they also can move throughout the network to detect attacks [72]. A mobile agent distributed IDS (MADIDS) is an example proposed in [73]. A MADIDS provides a good performance for high-speed networks. If the observing IDS moves throughout the network, it will have a better detection performance. In a multi-agent method, IDS can move and share data about occurring attacks. Moving in the network lets agents find the better vantage point to detect attacks. A multi-agent–based IDS has the advantages of both network-based and anomaly-based IDS [3].

12.2.2.5 Change Detection

DoS attacks cause volume anomalies, and hence, there will be a change in traffic behavior. In this regard, change detection can be useful in detecting DoS attacks. For change detection, it should be determined whether the observed time series are statistically homogeneous or not. If they are not homogeneous, we should find the time of the change. There are different change detection methods [74]. For example, a wavelet-based, spectrum-based technique; sketch-based, signal processing approaches; an auto-regressive (AR) process; and change-point monitoring (CPM) [74,75] are some. Gao et al. [76] uses flow-based data to detect DoS attacks in high-speed networks. They use 2-D sketches. CPM is also a mechanism proposed to detect DoS attacks. This method is an instance of the sequential change point detection [74] in which a non-parametric cumulative sum (CUSUM) method is used to improve the detection mechanism. The CPM introduces a few variables to record the protocol behaviors. This strengthens CPM against flooding attacks.

12.2.2.6 Different Proposed Techniques

An IDS called the rule-based high performance network intrusion detection system (RHP-NIDS) is proposed for high speed networks [77]. RHP-NIDS divides the detection method into four steps: data capture, packet filter, application-protocol analysis, and a rule-based detection engine. Different optimization methods are employed in this IDS. For instance, use of zero-copy in the packet capture and a multi-rule packet filter mechanism improve performance. RHP-NIDS improves data collection and data analysis. Using the zero-copy technique improves the number of captured packets.

In the second step, RHP-NIDS uses a multi-rule packet filter at the user layer to reduce the input data. Uninteresting network packets are removed in this step to reduce data and to protect IDS from attacks. The third step is an application-protocol analysis. The proposed NIDS takes the application layer into consideration, while the traditional NIDS only performs analysis up to the transport layer.

Applying the application protocol analysis has the following advantages: 1) improving the detection rate; 2) detecting evasion attacks, which are used by attackers to avoid detection; and 3) boosting the security of the proposed NIDS. Finally, this study uses a rule-based detection engine, which is based on rule-based pattern recognition. This phase looks for interesting packets through complete matching. A rule-based detection can be applied in protocol analysis–based signature detection, in protocol-based anomaly detection, and in statistical-based anomaly detection.

Xinidis [78] provides an active splitter architecture, which utilizes early filtering to reduce the load on sensors. To improve scalability, several methods have been proposed, such as EMERALD [43], GriDS [79], and AAFID [80]. These methods have a hierarchical structure in which low-level IDSs send information to higher level IDSs. The common intrusion detection framework (CIDF) is proposed in [81] to enable the interoperation between intrusion detection components in a distributed environment. Mining audit data for automated models (MADAM) [82] reduces the gap between the discovery and the detection of new attacks by using a CIDF. It uses audit data to build signatures for new attacks. To provide real-time intrusion detection, many papers have improved detection mechanisms to be able to handle a high volume of traffic. For example, string matching and regular expression matching are used to provide an IDS with fast analysis [83,84].

12.3 APPLICATIONS OF ARTIFICIAL INTELLIGENCE IN INTRUSION DETECTION

Artificial intelligence is a well-studied approach for intrusion detection. Flexibility, learning ability, and adaptability are characteristics of AI–based IDS. ANNs, fuzzy systems, artificial immune systems, GA, and swarm intelligence have been widely applied to intrusion detection [4,5]. A brief overview of the applications of AI methods to intrusion detection is discussed in the following sections. AI–based, high-speed intrusion detection will also be considered.

12.3.1 INTELLIGENT IDS

AI methods are flexible methods and are adaptable to changes in the environment. For example, ANNs are capable of learning and generalizing noisy and incomplete data. In ANN, the weight coefficients are initialized in the first step. A training process is responsible for minimizing error by adjusting weight coefficients. Figure 12.4 shows different learning methods [4,23,85–87]. The ANNs can be combined with other algorithms in intrusion detection. In these hybrid models, one can optimize the network structure of the second one, for example, EFuNN and ENN [4,6]. ENN can detect the call sequences of an anomaly system. An adaptive neuro-fuzzy IDS is also a proposed method to detect intrusions [88].

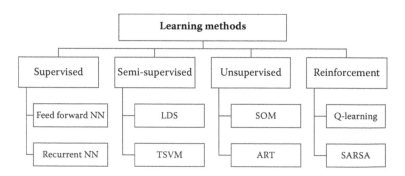

FIGURE 12.4   Learning methods.

12.3.1.1 Supervised Learning

The supervised method learns to map inputs to outputs using the correct values defined by the supervisor. A feedforward neural network (FFNN) and recurrent neural network (RNN) are two important methods that use supervised learning. A multi-layered feed-forward (MLFF) NN and radial basis function (RBF) are two examples of FFNNs. The calculation of the distance between inputs and the centers of hidden neurons is the basis of RBF classification. In comparison with the MLFF back-propagation (BP), the RBF is better for large data because it is faster [4]. A hierarchical RBF is proposed in [89] that combines anomaly and misuse detection. This proposed method enables IDS to detect known and unknown attacks. A comparison between the RBF and MLFF-BP shows that in misuse detection, the MLFF-BP has a better detection rate and lower false positives than the RBF although it takes more training time. The RBF has better performance in anomaly detection compared to misuse detection and has a shorter training time [4,89]. An Elman recurrent neural network and cerebellar model articulation controller (CMAC) neural network are two examples of RNNs, which are used for anomaly detection. A labeled data set is needed to train and evaluate a supervised IDS. A three-layer RNN is proposed in [90], which compares the performance of the Elman and RNN in misuse detection in computer networks. The results show that the RNN has better performance.

12.3.1.2 Unsupervised Learning

There is no supervisor in unsupervised learning, and it is trained using unlabeled data only. Unsupervised learning is similar to a statistical clustering, in which they identify various groups of inputs using their similarity [23]. The self-organizing maps (SOM) and the adaptive resonance theory (ART) are two examples of unsupervised learning. The SOM is an important neural network method used for the anomaly and misuse detection [4]. However, the performance of ART and SOM–based intrusion detection are compared in [91], which shows the higher detection performance of ART on both offline and online data.

12.3.1.3 Semi-Supervised Learning

The semi-supervised learning method combines the supervised and the unsupervised learning capabilities. In this method, often some unlabeled data is provided in a data set beside labeled data. When labeling is expensive, this method can be useful even with less labeled data [85]. The semi-supervised method can act as a supervised or an unsupervised learning according to the availability of labeled data. This method is employed for intrusion detection in several studies [86,87,92]. A semi-supervised learning-based method can be trained by both labeled and unlabeled data and has more accurate prediction. Low density separation (LDS) [93] and transductive SVM (TSVM) [94] are examples.

12.3.1.4 Reinforcement Learning

Reinforcement learning (RL) is a combination of the supervised and unsupervised learning. In reinforcement learning, there is an agent acting upon the environment. The state of the environment changes with the agent's actions, and the environment, in return, gives feedback for those actions. The feedback is either a reward or a punishment; therefore, RL is trained by rewards and punishments. For instance, when the system acts well, the teacher gives a reward. On the other hand, while getting a punishment, the system should improve itself. Thus, due to the existence of the feedback from the environment, RL is a form of supervised learning, but it is known as weak supervised learning because RL never presents the correct input/output pairs. The feedback information is evaluative and is not instructive, so this information can be right or wrong. The RL also has some further concepts. For example, a policy is the map between the states and the actions. A reward function gives a mapping between each state-action pair to a reward. The reward is a single number showing the desirability of that state. Moreover, there is a value function. The long-term desirability of a state is defined by the value function [95].

The hidden Markov models (HMM) and RL are deployed in [96]. They learn the state-transition probabilities to detect host-based intrusions. The reinforcement learning is used in [97] to train an agent-based IDS. The proposed DIDS has heterogeneous agents in which each agent has three layers: 1) signature-based intrusion detection, 2) an array of a SOM to detect anomalies, and 3) more analysis by collecting information. RL is also deployed in [98] in which a HMM, RL, and the behavioral analysis of IP addresses are used to detect a DoS/distributed denial-of-service (DDoS) attacks by DIDS. Q-learning [99] and SARSA [100] are two methods used in RL [101].

12.3.2 High-Speed Networks

In the increasing network throughput, an intelligent IDS should be able to handle a high volume of traffic. Based on our knowledge, this section lists AI–based intrusion detection techniques for high-speed networks.

12.3.2.1 Intelligent Flow-Based IDS

Different AI methods have been used in flow-based intrusion detection, such as HMM [102] and data-mining and visualization [103]. HMM-based IDS provides a low false-positive rate and a high detection rate. However, it takes a long time to model normal behavior. The privileged transition flows are used to propose an improved HMM-based IDS in [102]. This method reduces computational cost and improves performance. In the second example, data mining and an optimized visualization technique are combined to provide a high botnet detection rate in flow-based traffic [103]. This method visualizes processed and selected data as visualizing a large volume of raw data and is very time-consuming. Next, the study considers the application of three supervised machine learning algorithms, Bayesian networks, decision trees, and a multi-layer perceptron (MLP), in the classification of flow-based traffic [104]. Alshammari and Zincir Heywood [105] also provide a flow-based IDS. They use five learning algorithms, SVM, C4.5, AdaBoost, Naïve Bayesian, and RIPPER, to classify encrypted traffic. The results show that the C4.5 has the best performance in the classification of traffic. However, the traffic is limited to SSH and Skype protocols.

The first public labeled data set is provided in [106] for the evaluation of flow-based NIDSs. This data set includes network flows. Winter [107] modifies this data set and used it to train a one-class SVM (OC-SVM) to detect malicious activities. This modified data set is also employed to evaluate the GSA-based flow anomaly detection system (GFADS) proposed in [7]. The gravitational search algorithm (GSA) is a heuristic algorithm, which addresses the problem of local minima in backpropagation. GSA is employed in GFADS to train a MLP neural network, which is a feedforward neural network. This study compares the performance of the GSA with another heuristic algorithm, particle swarm optimization (PSO), and three gradient descent algorithms. The results show that the GSA is a beneficial algorithm for the flow-based IDS. Table 12.1 shows the results.

The gradient descent adaptive learning rate with momentum (GDX), gradient descent with adaptive rate (GDA), and gradient descent with momentum (GDM) are compared in this table with two heuristic algorithms. Four metrics are used to evaluate the algorithms. True positive is the correct detection of malicious traffic. True negative is the correct detection of benign traffic. A false positive is the wrong detection of benign traffic, and a false negative means fault in detecting malicious activities. The number of benign and malicious flows in the table offers better understanding of the algorithm efficiency.

Another study proposes flow-based anomaly detection based on an optimized MLP to detect attacks in high-speed networks [108]. This anomaly detector employs a modified GSA (MGSA) to optimize interconnection weights of a MLP.

12.3.2.2 Hardware-Based Intelligent IDS

Software-based IDSs can adapt to new attacks quickly, but they have limited detection speed. On the other hand, hardware-based IDSs have higher detection speed while they are ineffective against

TABLE 12.1

Performance Metrics of GSA-Based Anomaly Detector Compared to Other Algorithms

	Algorithms	GSA	PSO	GDX	GDA	GDM
Performance metrics	True Positive	7645	7642	7640	7560	7666
	False Positive	6	7	9	9	513
	True Negative	936	935	933	933	429
	False Negative	43	46	48	128	22
Data set information	Benign flows			942		
	Malicious flows			7688		
	Total traffic			8630		

Source: Jadidi, Z. et al., Flow-based anomaly detection using neural network optimized with GSA algorithm, in *Proc. IEEE ICDCS Workshops on the 2nd International Workshop on Network Forensics, Security and Privacy (NFSP)*, 2013, pp. 76–81.

unknown attacks. A block based neural network (BBNN) is an intelligent learning algorithm. An improved BBNN integrated with a high-frequency FPGA is proposed in [8]. The combination of a hardware-cored IDS and a BBNN provides flexibility to learn and detect unknown attacks with a high detection rate and low rate of false alarms. Flow records are extracted from a DARPA packet-based data set in this study. The proposed hardware-based IDS is evaluated using this generated flow-based data set. The results show that it has real-time intrusion detection.

12.3.2.3 Multi-Agent Intrusion Detection System

MFIRE is a multi-agent flow-based intrusion detection system [9] in which agents learn to detect attacks and share the data with other agents. MFIRE agents detect attacks using the SVM method. In the network, agents can move to find a good vantage point [9]. A distributed soft computing-based IDS (DSCIDS) is another agent-based method proposed in [109]. The DSCIDS consists of several distributed intelligent agents. These agents can communicate with each other. Three fuzzy rule-based classifiers were deployed in this paper to detect attacks. A multi-agent rein-forcement learning (MARL) is the next method proposed for intrusion detection [110]. MARL is used to detect a flooding-base DoS (FBDoS) and flooding-base DDoS (FBDDoS) attacks. It has a hierarchical architecture in which there are sensor agents (SA) and decision agents (DA). A SA is responsible for collecting and analyzing state information about the environment, and its information about the global state of the environment is limited. A DA receives the informa-tion of SAs. MARL uses a hierarchical architecture of DAs, which are based on reinforcement learning.

12.3.2.4 Distributed Intelligent IDS

DIDS is a solution to handle a high volume of network traffic. It includes several IDSs that can com-municate with each other. A distributed neural network learning algorithm (DNNL) is proposed in [10]. A DNNL is used in a distributed anomaly detection system. This distributed learning algo-rithm uses independent neural networks, which process subsets of training data in parallel. The par-allel neural networks help to overcome the problems of concentrated training. Initially, in DNNL, a large data set is divided randomly into smaller subsets. Each subset is sent to an independent neural network. These neural networks are trained by these subsets in parallel. Afterward, using the training results of each neural network, a new training data is created. Finally, there is concentrated learning using the new training data [10].

12.3.2.5 AI–Based Ensemble IDSs

Traditional IDSs are based only on single-classification techniques. Ensemble IDSs employ multiple classifiers, which complement the weakness of each other. A combination of multiple classifiers leads to decreased false alarms and improves the performance. The false alarm rate is an important factor in IDSs. The state-of-the-art IDSs should reduce false alarms, be able to handle a high volume of network traffic, and be adaptable to environmental changes. The ensemble IDS is an example. Multiple base classifiers are deployed in an ensemble in which the individual predictions of classifiers are combined to provide an accurate prediction. An ensemble for intrusion detection may present information at multiple abstraction levels. It also collects information from multiple sources. This information is understandable for the human level [111].

AI methods are effective in developing ensembles for intrusion detection. In this regard, a number of studies are listed here: A heterogeneous ensemble of linear genetic programming (LGP), an adaptive neural fuzzy inference system (ANFIS), and a random forest (RF) is proposed in [112] for intrusion detection. This ensemble model uses a rough-discrete PSO to select features for a specific class of KDD cup 99 data set. In the study, the final ensemble prediction is used to assign weights to classifiers. This heterogeneous ensemble improves the detection performance of all classes in the data set. In the next study [113], base classifiers are C4.5 decision tree [114], naïve Bayes [115], k-NN clustering [116], VFI-voting feature intervals [117], and OneR [118] classifiers. The third study [119] uses ANN and fuzzy clustering to propose FCANN. Different homogeneous training subsets were generated in FCANN from the heterogeneous training set. In the final example, Muda et al. [120] use a combination of clustering and classification in their model. The K-means algorithm–based clustering groups similar data in an earlier stage. The output of clustering is classified in the next stage using a naïve Bayes classifier.

12.4 CHALLENGES IN IPV6 NETWORKS

IPv6 is the next generation of Internet protocol. It was developed to overcome the weakness of IPv4, the main problems of which were the limited number of IP addresses and security. However, IPv6 suffers from several security problems, which can be addressed using IDSs. The characteristics of IPv6 compared to IPv4 and its existing threats are described in this section.

12.4.1 IPv6 vs. IPv4

There are several changes in IPv6 packet format in comparison to IPv4. Figures 12.5 and 12.6 show IPv6 and IPv4 packet headers [121–123]. Table 12.2 represents the difference between packet header fields in these protocols.

IPv6 header fields are described below [124,125]:

- *Version:* (four bits) IPv6 version field is equal to six.
- *Traffic Class:* (eight bits) This identifies the priority of a packet; thus network congestion causes the lowest priority packets to get dropped.
- *Flow Label:* (20 bits) Identifies packets related to the same flow.

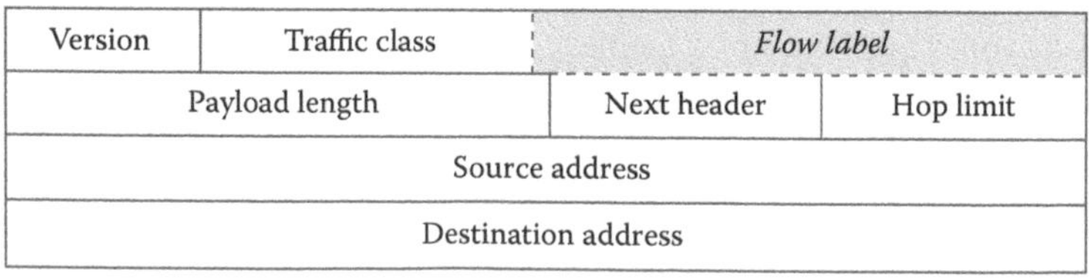

Version	Traffic class	*Flow label*	
Payload length		Next header	Hop limit
Source address			
Destination address			

FIGURE 12.5   IPv6 header.

Version	IHL	Type of service	Total length	
Identification			Flags	Fragment offset
Time to live		Protocol	Header checksum	
Source address				
Destination address				
Options				Padding

FIGURE 12.6 IPv4 header.

TABLE 12.2
Difference between IPv6 and IPv4 Packet Header Fields

	Name	IPv4	IPv6	
Common Fields	Version	Yes	Yes	
	Source address	Yes	Yes	
	Destination address	Yes	Yes	
Changed Names	Type of service	Yes	Traffic Class	
	Total length	Yes	Payload Length	
	Time to live	Yes	Hop Limit	
	Protocol	Yes	Next Header	
New Fields	Flow label	No	Yes	Shaded area in Figure 12.5
Removed Fields	IHL	Yes	No	Shaded area in Figure 12.6
	Identification	Yes	No	
	Flags	Yes	No	
	Fragment offset	Yes	No	
	Header checksum	Yes	No	
	Options	Yes	No	
	Padding	Yes	No	

- *Payload Length:* (16 bits) The size of payload in octets is identified by payload length. Payload is the length of the packet that follows the IPv6 header.
- *Next Header (NH):* (8 bits) Number of fields in IPv4 headers become optional extension headers in IPv6, which follow the header. NH specifies the extension header, which is similar to the protocol field in the IPv4 packet header. There can be zero, one, or more extension headers in the datagram. Figure 12.7 shows the format of the IPv6 packet.

The extension headers should be placed in a specific order, which is shown in Table 12.3 [122,124]. For example, the authentication header (AH) in this table verifies the authenticity and the integrity of the packets. In fact, AH ensure that the information has not been changed in the intermediate nodes. Also, the encapsulation security payload (ESP) header encrypts the packet to ensure the transmission of datagrams.

- *Hop Limit:* (8 bits) This is a counter for the remaining number of hops. The value decreases whenever the packet is handled by a router.
- *Source Address:* (16 bits) The IPv6 address of the source node.
- *Destination Address:* (16 bits) The IPv6 address of the destination node.

Base header	Extension header 1, ..., extension header N	Data

FIGURE 12.7 Format of IPv6 packet.

TABLE 12.3
Order of Extension Headers

Order	Extension Header
1	IPv6 header
2	Hop-by-hop options header
3	Destination options header
4	Routing header
5	Fragment header
6	Authentication header (AH)
7	Encapsulation security payload header (ESP)
8	Destination options header
9	Upper-layer header

IPv6 is a successor to IPv4. This protocol simplifies header format, and hence, it reduces the processing cost. Also, due to several modifications in the encoding method of the IPv6 header options, there is better forwarding, fewer restrictions on the length of options, and more flexibility in the introduction of new options. Moreover, Internet protocol security (IPsec) is mandatory in IPv6 [122]. Because IP datagrams are transmitted over unknown networks, their security is very important. In this regard, IPsec was developed to secure IPs. IPv6 also provides improvements in routing speed and quality of service (QoS). Differences between IPv4 and IPv6 are summarized in Table 12.4, which completes Table 12.2 [11,121].

Auto configuration is a feature of IPv6. Each device in a network needs an IP address. IPv4 used a stateful protocol, such as dynamic host configuration protocol (DHCP), to assign IP addresses. IPv6 also support DHCPv6. Moreover, IPv6 has a stateless auto-configuration procedure in which each node configures its IP address using local information. Another advantage of IPv6 is increasing support of mobility. In IPv6, mobile nodes can maintain their connections while they change their locations.

TABLE 12.4
IPv4 vs. IPv6

Services	IPv4	IPv6
Address	32 bits	128 bits
Checksum in header	Yes	No
Options in header	Yes	Moved to extension headers
Fragmentation permission	All routers and source nodes are permitted	Only the source node is permitted
IPsec support	Optional	It is mandated
Flow labeling	No	Yes
Address types	Unicast, multicast, and broadcast	Unicast, multicast, and anycast
IP configuration	DHCP	Auto configuration or DHCPv6
QoS	Differentiated services, integrated service	Differentiated services, integrated service, and flow labels
Address resolution protocol (ARP)	Used to find a physical address	Replaced by neighbor discovery
Internet group management Protocol (IGMP)	For management of local subnet group	Replaced by multicast listener Discovery (MLD) protocol
Domain name system (DNS)	Support for IPv4 using host address (A) resource records	Support for IPv6 using host address (AAAA) resource records
Mobility	Use mobile IPv4 (MIPv4)	MIPv6 with direct routing

12.4.2 SECURITY IN IPv6

The increasing use of the Internet results in difficulties for IPv4 networks. The limited number of IP addresses and the lack of security are two important problems of IPv4 networks. The Internet Engineering Task Force (IETF) proposes IPv6 to meet these requirements [11,121]. However, there are several types of attacks against IPv6. The migration from IPv4 to IPv6 will take time; therefore, they should work together in the transition period. There are different transition mechanisms. These mechanisms open up a number of new attacks. In the transition period, the security of both IPv4 and IPv6 should be considered [11,12]. Two IPv6 security headers, AH and ESP, provide IPsec security services.

Most security threats are at the application layer. In both IPv4 and IPv6, security services, which are provided by IPsec, are at the IP layer. Therefore, using IPsec does not prevent application layer attacks.

12.4.2.1 Security Threats

The attacking process of IPv6 is divided into three steps [126]: discovery, port scanning, and exploitation.

- *Discovery:* This is used to find active IPv6 addresses [126]. There are different discovery methods; for example, discovery through MAC addresses is used to enumerate active link-local addresses. In this method, ICMPv6 is used. The second technique is discovery through ICMPv6 requests to find global unicast addresses on an Internet host using PINGv6. The third method is discovery through the domain name system (DNS). As IPv6 address space is very large, DNS, which converts a domain to an IP address, is very important. This type of discovery may be used to enumerate the IPv6 address on the target domain. The final discovery method is using the combination of the three explained techniques.
- *Port Scanning:* After finding active IPv6 addresses, attackers use port scanning to find vulnerabilities on those machines.
- *Exploitation:* This is used to exploit the machine. Two common methods used to exploit a victim are stack-based buffer overflow and format string exploitation.

IPv6 security threats are grouped into three categories: i) IPv4 attacks, which can still be applied to IPv6; ii) IPv6 specific security threats; and iii) transition period threats.

12.4.2.1.1 Common Security Threats for IPv4 and IPv6

IPv6 was developed to improve security, but it still suffers from a number of security problems. Several attacks in IPv4 still exist in IPv6. For example, 1) the sniffing attack, which captures transmitted data in the network. Sniffing attacks can be avoided by IPsec. 2) The application layer attacks, which are very important and frequent. However, IPsec is not useful for application layer attacks. 3) Flooding attacks, such as DoS attacks. These attacks send a large volume of traffic to a system unable to process this traffic, and hence, the system becomes out of service. A Smurf attack is a DoS attack, which is common between IPv4 and IPv6 [126]. 4) Another group of attacks is called Rogue device. These devices are unauthorized devices introduced into a network, and this can be misused. If IPsec is used appropriately, this attack can be avoided. 5) Man-in-the-middle attacks also are not changed in IPv6. Man-in-the-middle allows the attacker to position between a source and destination and listen to data. The attacker can cause other attacks, such as stealing information and sniffing, etc. [11,12].

12.4.2.1.2 IPv6 Specific Threats

- *Attacks related to IPv6 routing header:* All nodes in IPv6 can process the routing header. On the other hand, access control based on a destination address can be avoided by using routing headers. This can cause some attacks, such as a DoS attack.

- *ICMPv6 and multicast security issues:* In IPv4, blocking ICMP messages is popular to improve the security of networks. However, In IPv6, ICMPv6 messages should be permitted because they are used by different important mechanisms, such as neighbor discovery. One of the disadvantages is that it is possible to send an error notification response to multicast addresses using ICMPv6. Then multiple responses are sent back to the victim system.
- *Attacks related to fragmentation:* In IPv6, fragmentation can be done only at the source node. DoS attacks can be performed by sending a large number of small fragments to a system. If the total number of fragments and their allowed arrival rate become limited, these problems can be avoided [11,12].

12.4.2.1.3   Threats in Transition Mechanisms

In the transition period, IPv4 and IPv6 should work simultaneously using different techniques, such as tunneling and dual-stack. Tunneling mechanisms allow IPv6 users to interconnect through the IPv4 environment using tunneling. The dual-stack technique uses two separated protocol stacks, IPv4 and IPv6. Datagrams, which come through the network interface of a dual-stack node, are analyzed. Then, datagrams are divided into IPv4 and IPv6 datagrams, which are sent to the IPv4 stack and the IPv6 stack, respectively. In the dual-stack configuration, the attacker can target both IPv4 and IPv6 applications.

In the aspect of security, the transition mechanisms result in a number of new vulnerabilities. As attackers may spoof network addresses in IPv6 and IPv4 packet headers, this mechanism can cause a DoS attack [11,12]. Consequently, IDS is an essential tool to protect IPv6 networks. IDS is effective in detecting discovery through an ICMPv6 request. Therefore, it can be used to detect an IPv6 ping sweep occurrence. In addition, IDS is very valuable in detecting port scanning risks, buffer overflow attacks, format string exploitation, and DoS attacks. IDS can monitor DNS logs to detect discovery through a DNS [126]. As explained earlier in this chapter, many attacks have similar behavior in both IP protocols. Therefore, many intrusion detection methods mentioned in Section 12.2 and Section 12.3 are also useful for IPv6.

12.5   APPLICATION OF ARTIFICIAL INTELLIGENCE IN OTHER ENVIRONMENTS

Nowadays, there are different types of environments, such as grid computing, cloud computing, and wireless networks. All of these environments suffer from several vulnerabilities, which can be misused by intruders. Thus, an IDS is a required tool in which the artificial intelligence can be applied to provide adaptable intrusion detection. This section describes the application of AI methods in different environments.

12.5.1   Grid Computing

To provide an analogy for grid computing, we can refer to power grids in which users have access to electricity with no care about where or how the electricity is generated. Similarly, grid computing enables sharing pools of resources across institutional boundaries. Therefore, in grid computing, individual users can have access to computing resources without any knowledge of the location of these resources or operating systems (OS) or hardware. Resources can be processors, storage space, data applications, and so on. In other words, grid computing is sharing tasks over multiple machines that can be spread over a large distance. In some cases, computers in a grid act as a part of that grid only when they are not busy. Otherwise, they perform their normal job. In other words, the machine that is normally used to run the application might be busy, so the job can then be run on another machine that is idle in the grid. The idea of grid computing was originated to create a toolkit able to handle computation management, storage management, etc. This toolkit should work with large grids, independent of their hardware or operating system, etc. It means computers in a grid do not need to have the same OS or hardware.

DoS and DDoS are important threats against grid environments. Hence, IDS is required in grid computing. In this regard, several methods have been proposed. For example, a high-level grid IDS (GIDS) uses functionality of both HIDS and NIDS and uses inter-IDS communication [13]. Artificial intelligence is also applicable to grid computing. For instance, a distributed soft computing IDS (DSCIDS) proposed for traditional networks is deployable in grid computing networks [127]. DSCIDS combines different classifiers to model precise and lightweight IDS. In this method, three fuzzy rule–based classifiers are used to detect intrusions [109]. This method can be used to detect different attacks in grid computing.

Another example is a model based on SVM proposed in [128] to detect DDoS attacks in grid computing. The SVM is used in this model to detect new DDoS attacks automatically. This model also uses a concentration tendency of network traffic (CTNT) for analysis of the characteristics of network traffic for DDoS attacks. The ratio between a specific type of packet and the total number of network packets is monitored by CTNT to compute the TCP flag rate and protocol rate. The results show that differences between normal and DDoS traffic are predictable. Traffic analysis results are used as input features of the SVM. This helped to automatically generate DDoS detection rules. The evaluation of this method shows its efficiency in detecting different DDoS attacks [128].

12.5.2 Cloud Computing

Cloud computing consists of hardware and software resources made available on the Internet. Existing email providers, such as Yahoo and Gmail, are examples of cloud computing. These providers house all of the required software and hardware to support email accounts. In this example, emails can be housed anywhere and can be accessed through the Internet. However, there is a difference between cloud computing and email. In cloud computing, users can choose the information intended to be accessed within the cloud. Therefore, information is available from anywhere by using any devices, such as laptops, tablets, or phones [14]. Cloud providers house the required software and hardware to run applications. Small businesses also can store their information in the cloud to avoid the cost of purchasing the hardware and storage space. To have access to the documents in the cloud, users need to have an Internet connection.

There are malicious activities in clouds because people store important information there. User activities and stored information cannot be controlled appropriately. In addition, data is accessible through an unsecured Internet connection. Therefore, the security aspect of cloud computing is very important [14]. Generally, the architecture of the cloud computing environment is divided into four layers: the hardware or datacenter layer, the infrastructure layer, the platform layer, and the application layer. The hardware layer is used to manage the physical resources in the cloud, such as servers, routers, etc. The infrastructure is also called the virtualization layer. It uses virtualization technologies to partition the physical resources and create a pool of computing resources and storage. The platform layer is on top of the infrastructure layer and contains operating system and application frameworks. The highest layer is the application layer that consists of the actual cloud application [129].

Cloud computing provides hardware and platform-level resources as services on an on-demand basis. This is a difference between cloud and grid computing. In cloud computing, applications have access to resources through services. Every aforementioned layer is as a service to the layer above while every layer is as a customer of the layer below. There are three types of services in clouds: software as a service (SaaS), platform as a service (PaaS), and infrastructure as a service (IaaS). SaaS provides on-demand applications through the Internet. Providing platform layer resources, such as OS support and a software development framework, are included in PaaS. IaaS is related to providing infrastructure resources, such as virtual machines (VMs) [129].

An IDS is an important tool to detect attacks in the cloud environment. In cloud computing, virtual machines allow us to run multiple operating systems. VMs are deployed in a cloud environment to make providers able to use resources efficiently. Virtualization techniques and integrated technologies are used in the cloud and run through the Internet. This causes a number of vulnerabilities. Several traditional attacks, such as DoS attack, DDoS, flooding, and IP spoofing, are also used by intruders against cloud computing. In addition, other existing attacks in cloud systems are as follows: i) insider attacks, ii) user to root attacks, iii) port scanning, iv) attacks on VM or hypervisor, and v) backdoor channel attacks [130]. The following description is about various defensive methods in cloud computing.

- *IDS and IPS:* IDS and intrusion prevention system (IPS) techniques can be used in the cloud environment. Signature-based, anomaly-based, and AI–based detection techniques are applicable in the cloud. A signature-based method is used to detect external intrusions when it is at the front end of the cloud. On the other hand, the IDS in the back end of cloud helps to detect external and internal attacks. Anomaly-based detection in the cloud is used to detect unknown attacks. The paper [130] described ANN–based anomaly detection as a beneficial method in unstructured network data that can classify data as normal and malicious. This paper introduces a fuzzy logic–based IDS. The fuzzy logic with ANN gives fast detection of unknown attacks in the cloud because it decreases the training time of ANN. Soft computing techniques of traditional IDSs are also helpful in cloud computing.

  Association rule, SVM, GA, and hybrid techniques are intelligent methods applicable to cloud computing IDS [130]. Soft computing techniques are used in [131] to propose a security model for the cloud computing environment. A reputation management system is used in this method to ensure the data security in the cloud computing. A reputation management system is a proficient reputation collection method from multiple nodes in the cloud. In the proposed method, the suitable nodes for transmission are identified using GA. A grid and cloud computing intrusion detection system (GCCIDS) is proposed in [132] in which misuse and anomaly detection methods are combined. The ANN is deployed to train the system. A prototype is developed in the paper using a middleware called Grid-M. However, GCCIDS can only detect specific attacks. Based on the monitoring location, there are different types of IDS for cloud computing [130]:
  i. HIDS
  ii. NIDS
  iii. Distributed IDS (DIDS): DIDS is used in a large network. It includes several IDSs, such as the HIDS, NIDS, etc., that can communicate with each other or with a central server to monitor network. A DIDS can consist of anomaly- and signature-based detection, so it is beneficial for detecting known and unknown attacks.
  iv. Hypervisor-based IDS: A hypervisor is a platform used for running VMs. A hypervisor-based IDS can be used to monitor and analyze packets exchanged between a hypervisor and VM, between VMs, and within the hypervisor-based virtual network. Hypervisor IDS is significant for intrusion detection in a virtual environment in the cloud computing.

  On the other hand, an IPS monitors network traffic to detect attacks; then it responds to the intrusions. There are two types of IPSs: HIPS and NIPS. A HIPS detects and prevents attacks on a VM, hypervisor, or host system.
- *IDPS:* The combination of IDS and IPS is used in an intrusion detection and prevention system (IDPS). An IDPS has four security functions: monitoring, detecting, analyzing, and responding to unauthorized activities [130,133]. Most of the existing cloud-based IDPS works in one layer separate from other layers. For instance, a cloud-based IDPS for the infrastructure layer is proposed in [134], which is based on a virtual machine monitor to protect it from attacks in this layer. This model provides a secure infrastructure layer that improves reliability and availability of the system. However, it has a limitation. When an attack causes the infrastructure to collapse, this model cannot stop the system and does not have any solution.

12.5.3 Wireless Networks

Wireless networks are very important because they offer mobility and independence from fixed installation. These networks are difficult to secure. Hence, several models have been proposed to increase the reliability of wireless networks. The AI–based intrusion detection in wireless sensor networks, mobile ad hoc networks, and wireless local area networks are three examples, which are considered in this section.

1. *Wireless local area networks:* Wireless local area networks (WLANs) are used in many different areas, such as conference rooms, industrial warehouses, etc. WLANs have several new vulnerabilities compared to fixed wired networks. Therefore, some traditional security mechanisms are ineffective in this area. AI–based anomaly detection in these networks has been considered in different studies. For example, two methods are proposed in [15] to detect anomalies in WLANs. HMM is used in the first method to check reflector DoS attacks. In addition, an ART is used in the second method. The ART is an unsupervised method, which can learn normal behavior. The methods provide real-time anomaly detection. A dynamic growing neural network (DGNN) is another example proposed in [135] for intrusion detection in wireless networks. The Hebbian learning rule is used in DGNN in which new neurons are added under certain conditions. This rule uses the combination of the winner-take-all (WTA) learning rule and ART/ARTMAP neural network. The results show that this method can detect new intrusions and also has a low false alarm rate.

2. *Mobile ad hoc network:* Wireless ad hoc networks are important in the wireless research community. An ad hoc network contains a set of autonomous nodes in which nodes move in and out of the network. Thus, wireless networks do not have a fixed infrastructure, and their topologies are constantly changing. Wireless ad hoc networks have different applications, such as virtual classrooms, conferences, and rescue missions in which moving persons can communicate. There are different attacks against wireless ad hoc networks, including DoS attacks [16]. Artificial intelligence is applicable in this area. An immune-based system is proposed in [136,137] to detect misbehaving nodes in mobile ad-hoc networks (MANET). An anomaly detection method for ad hoc networks is proposed in [138]. This method is based on a one-class SVM. In fact, information sharing between nodes is used to detect attacks. The SVM is used in this paper to classify normal and abnormal traffic.

3. *Wireless Sensor Networks:* These networks have been deployed in different areas, such as agriculture, industrial, and civil domains; machine health monitoring; health care applications; and traffic control [17]. A characteristic of a wireless sensor network (WSN) is its constrained resources. For example, it has limitations in computational capability, energy, memory, etc. A WSN is made of a large number of distributed autonomous sensors. These sensors monitor environmental conditions, such as pressure, temperature, and pollution. There are various network services, such as localization, data compression, and security, in each sensor. The physical, the data link, the network, the transport, and the application layers are five-layer communication protocol stacks and are used for the interconnection of sensor nodes. WSN suffers from several security vulnerabilities [17]. Therefore, intrusion detection in WSNs is an important research area. Energy consumption is critical in intrusion detection of WSNs. There are three types of intrusion detection for WSN: stateful protocol analysis, signature detection, and anomaly detection. The stateful protocol has predetermined profiles of benign protocol activities for each protocol state and compares these profiles with observed events to detect outliers. Stateful protocol analysis and misuse detection are not suitable for WSN because they need a large memory and cannot detect unknown threats. Anomaly detection is the

dominant technique to improve the security of WSNs. Several anomaly detection methods in WSNs are listed below [17]:

- Statistical techniques
- Computational intelligence
- Rule-based techniques
- Hybrid techniques
- Game theory techniques
- Graph-based techniques

SVM, ANN, SOM, GA, and association rule learning are examples of computational intelligence methods applicable to anomaly detection [17]. An anomaly detection method is proposed in [139] in which only important features of a data signal are used to detect anomalies. This proposed method is the combination of a discrete wavelet transform (DWT) and SOM, which is a competitive learning neural network. The results show that this hybrid method outperforms the SOM and DWT algorithms. This paper detects anomalies of WSN by training the SOM using the wavelet coefficients. The method provides efficient anomaly detection and reduces wasted energy by applying the DWT algorithm to sensors to reduce the size of transmitted data.

12.6 CONCLUSION

Our dependence on the Internet is increasing day by day. Attacks and malicious activities are very common in this cyber world. An intrusion detection system is an essential mechanism to protect computers and networks from attacks. While the Internet service providers can offer high bandwidth, detecting intrusions in the high-speed networks is a challenge for researchers. High-speed IDSs are required to handle this huge amount of traffic. Different high-speed intrusion detection techniques were described in this chapter. Use of artificial intelligence techniques has numbers of advantages due to their learning ability and adaptability. An artificial intelligence–based IDS is adaptable to environmental changes and is trained to detect even unknown attacks. The intelligent IDS may also be able to work in high-speed networks. This chapter described common artificial intelligence–based IDSs as well as a number of high-speed intelligent IDSs. Traditional IDSs were evaluated using IPv4 traffic. Migration to IPv6 provides new security challenges. Although, IPv6 is, in general, more secure than IPv4 due to the mandated IPsec, the transition process introduces a number of security problems. These security threats were considered in this chapter. Intrusion detection in other networks is as important as in wired networks. Artificial intelligence–based IDSs are applicable to many other environments as well. In this chapter, the application of artificial intelligence in grid computing, cloud computing, and wireless networks was also considered.

AUTHORS' BIOGRAPHIES

Zahra Jadidi is a PhD student in information and communication technology at Griffith University in Australia. She received her MSc in electronics engineering at Islamic Azad University (South Tehran Branch) in Iran, where she could publish several papers about artificial neural networks–based intrusion detection systems. She has more than 10 years work experience as a computer network support specialist. Her work experience helped her to become familiar with different networks, such as wired and wireless networks, routers, switches, and routing protocols. Her research interest is artificial intelligence and its application is in computer networks. The topic of her PhD research is artificial intelligence–based anomaly detection in high-speed computer networks.

    Dr. Muthukkumarasamy obtained a BScEng with first class honors from the University of Peradeniya, Sri Lanka, and obtained a PhD from Cambridge University, England. He is currently attached to the School of Information and Communications Technology, Griffith University, Australia, as a senior lecturer. His current research areas include investigation of security issues in wireless networks, sensor networks, trust management in MANETs, key establishment protocols, and medical sensor networks. He is currently leading the Network Security Research Group at the Institute for Integrated and Intelligent Systems at Griffith University. He has also received a number of best teacher awards.

Elankayer Sithirasenan received his PhD and master of software engineering degrees from Griffith University, Australia, in 2009 and 2004 respectively and his BSc degree in electrical and electronic engineering from University of Peradeniya, Sri Lanka, in 1991. He is currently a lecturer in information and communication technology at Griffith University, Gold Coast, Australia. His current research interests include wireless/wired network security, authentication and access control, disaster recovery, intrusion detection and prevention, outlier detection on multilevel, multivariate data sets, and software requirements analysis. He was a lecturer at the University of Peradeniya, Sri Lanka, from 2001 to 2003 and the director of Integrated Digital Systems, Sri Lanka, from 1998 to 2008.

REFERENCES

1. J. M. Gonzalez, V. Paxson, and N. Weaver, Shunting: A hardware/software architecture for flexible, high-performance network intrusion prevention, in *Proceedings of the 14th ACM Conference on Computer and Communications Security*, pp. 139–149, ACM, 2007.
2. Z. Li, Y. Gao, and Y. Chen, HiFIND: A high-speed flow-level intrusion detection approach with DoS resiliency, *Computer Networks*, 54, 1282–1299, 2010.
3. R. Zhang, D. Qian, C. Ba, W. Wu, and X. Guo, Multi-agent based intrusion detection architecture, in *Proceedings of 2001 IEEE International Conference on Computer Networks and Mobile Computing*, pp. 494–501, Oct. 2001.
4. S. X. Wu, and W. Banzhaf, The use of computational intelligence in intrusion detection systems: A review, *Applied Soft Computing*, 10, 1–35, 2010.
5. V. Engen, Machine learning for network based intrusion detection: An investigation into discrepancies in findings with the KDD cup '99 data set and multi-objective evolution of neural network classifier ensembles from imbalanced data. PhD diss., Bournemouth University, 2010.
6. S.-J. Han, and S.-B. Cho, Evolutionary neural networks for anomaly detection based on the behavior of a program, *Systems, Man, and Cybernetics, Part B: Cybernetics, IEEE Transactions on*, 36, 559–570, 2005.
7. Z. Jadidi, V. Muthukkumarasamy, E. Sithirasenan, and M. Sheikhan, Flow-based anomaly detection using neural network optimized with GSA algorithm, in *Proc. IEEE ICDCS Workshops on the 2nd International Workshop on Network Forensics, Security and Privacy (NFSP)*, pp. 76–81, 2013.
8. Q. A. Tran, F. Jiang, and J. Hu, A real-time netflow-based intrusion detection system with improved BBNN and high-frequency field programmable gate arrays, in *Trust, Security and Privacy in Computing and Communications (TrustCom), 2012 IEEE 11th International Conference on*, pp. 201–208, IEEE, 2012.
9. T. J. Wilson, MFIRE-2: A multi agent system for flow-based intrusion detection using stochastic search, No. AFIT/GCO/ENG/12-12. Air Force Inst of Tech, Wright-Patterson AFB OH Graduate School of Engineering and Management, 2012.
10. D. Tian, Y. Liu, and Y. Xiang, Large-scale network intrusion detection based on distributed learning algorithm, *International Journal of Information Security*, 8, 25–35, 2009.
11. E. Durdağı, and A. Buldu, IPV4/IPV6 security and threat comparisons, *Procedia-Social and Behavioral Sciences*, 2, 5285–5291, 2010.
12. D. Zagar, K. Grgic, and S. Rimac-Drlje, Security aspects in IPv6 networks implementation and testing, *Computers & Electrical Engineering*, 33, 425–437, 2007.
13. S. Kar, An anomaly detection scheme for DDoS attack in grid computing, PhD diss., 2009.
14. A. Huth, and J. Cebula, *The Basics of Cloud Computing*, 2011.
15. D. Tian, Q. Li, and S. Chen, Anomaly intrusion detection methods for wireless LAN, in *Natural Computation, 2008, ICNC '08. Fourth International Conference on*, vol. 5, pp. 179–182. IEEE, 2008.
16. A. Mishra, K. Nadkarni, and A. Patcha, Intrusion detection in wireless ad hoc networks, *Wireless Communications, IEEE*, 11, 48–60, 2004.
17. M. Xie, S. Han, B. Tian, and S. Parvin, Anomaly detection in wireless sensor networks: A survey, *Journal of Network and Computer Applications*, 34, 1302–1325, 2011.

18. H.-J. Liao, K.-Y. Tung, C.-H. R. Lin, and Y.-C. Lin, Intrusion detection system: A comprehensive review, *Journal of Network and Computer Applications* 2012.

19. A. Sperotto, G. Schaffrath, R. Sadre, C. Morariu, A. Pras, and B. Stiller, An overview of IP flow-based intrusion detection, *Communications Surveys & Tutorials, IEEE*, 12, 343–356, 2010.

20. V. Chandola, A. Banerjee, and V. Kumar, Anomaly detection: A survey, *ACM Computing Surveys (CSUR)*, 41, 15, 2009.

21. M. Thottan, and C. Ji, Anomaly detection in IP networks, *IEEE Transactions on Signal Processing*, 51, 2191–2204, 2003.

22. P. Garcia-Teodoro, J. Diaz-Verdejo, G. Maciá-Fernández, and E. Vázquez, Anomaly-based network intrusion detection: Techniques, systems and challenges, *Computers & Security*, 28, 18–28, 2009.

23. E. Alpaydin, *Introduction to Machine Learning*, MIT Press, 2004.

24. P. Winter, E. Hermann, and M. Zeilinger, Inductive intrusion detection in flow-based network data using one-class support vector machines, in *New Technologies, Mobility and Security (NTMS), 2011 4th IFIP International Conference on*, pp. 1–5. IEEE, 2011.

25. E. Sithirasenan, and V. Muthukkumarasamy, Substantiating anomalies in wireless networks using group outlier scores, *Journal of Software*, 6, 678–689, 2011.

26. S. Axelsson, Intrusion detection systems: A survey and taxonomy, vol. 99, Technical report, 2000.

27. K. Ilgun, USTAT: A real-time intrusion detection system for UNIX, Master's thesis, Computer Science Department, University of California, Santa Barbara, July 1992.

28. S. Kumar, and E. H. Spafford, A pattern matching model for misuse intrusion detection, in *Proceedings of the 17th National Computer Security Conference*, pp. 11–21, Baltimore, MD, USA, 1994. National Institute of Standards and Technology/National Computer Security Center.

29. G. Vigna, S. T. Eckmann, and R. A. Kemmerer, The STAT tool suite, in *DARPA Information Survivability Conference and Exposition, 2000, DISCEX '00, Proceedings*, vol. 2, pp. 46–55. IEEE, 2000.

30. G. Vigna, and R. A. Kemmerer, NetSTAT: A network-based intrusion detection system, *Journal of Computer Security*, 7, 37–71, 1999.

31. S. T. Eckmann, G. Vigna, and R. A. Kemmerer, STATL: An attack language for state-based intrusion detection, *Journal of Computer Security*, 10, 71–103, 2002.

32. U. Lindqvist and P. A. Porras, Detecting computer and network misuse through the production based system toolset (p-best), in *Proceedings of the 1999 IEEE Symposium on Security and Privacy*, pp. 146–161. IEEE, May 1999.

33. J. Goubault-Larrecq. An introduction to LogWeaver (v2.8). http://www.lsv.ens-cachan.fr/goubault/DICO/tutorial.pdf, September 2001.

34. R. Feiertag, C. Kahn, P. Porras, D. Schackenberg, S. Staniford-Chen, and B. Tung. A common intrusion specification language, http://www.isi.edu/brian/cidf/drafts/language.txt, June 1999.

35. V. Paxson, Bro: A system for detecting network intruders in real-time, *Computer Networks*, 31, 2435–2463, 1999.

36. M. Roesch. Snort, version 1.8.3. Available via www.snort.org, August 2001.

37. D. Curry, H. Debar, and B. Feinstein, Intrusion detection message exchange format data model and extensible markup language (XML) document type definition, IDWG, February (2002).

38. F. Cuppens, and R. Ortalo. LAMBDA: A language to model a database for detection of attacks, in *Proc. of Recent Advances in Intrusion Detection (RAID 2000)*, pp. 197–216, September 2000.

39. S. Templeton, and K. Levitt, A requires/provides model for computer attacks, in *Proceedings of New Security Paradigms Workshop*, pp. 31–38, ACM Press, September 2000.

40. J. Undercoffer, A. Joshi, and J. Pinkston, Modelling computer attacks: An ontology for intrusion detection, in *Proceedings of the 6th International Symposium on Recent Advances in Intrusion Detection (RAID 2003)*, pp. 113–135, Pittsburgh, PA. Lecture Notes in Computer Science, vol. 2820, September 2003.

41. P. Ning, and D. Xu, Learning attack strategies from intrusion alerts, in *Proceedings of the 10th ACM Conference on Computer and Communications Security*, pp. 200–209, ACM, 2003.

42. D. Anderson, T. Frivold, and A. Valdes, Next-generation intrusion-detection expert system (NIDES), Technical Report SRI-CSL-95-07, Computer Science Laboratory, SRI International, Menlo Park, CA, 94025-3493, USA, May 1995.

43. P. A. Porras, and P. G. Neumann, EMERALD: Event monitoring enabling response to anomalous live disturbances, in *Proceedings of the 20th National Information Systems Security Conference*, pp. 353–365, 1997.

44. M. M. Sebring, E. Shellhouse, M. E. Hanna, and R. A. Whitehurst, Expert systems in intrusion detection: A case study, in *Proceedings of the 11th National Computer Security Conference*, pp. 74–81, Baltimore, Maryland, October 17–20, 1988, NIST.

45. T. Heberlein, G. Dias, K. Levitt, B. Mukherjee, J. Wood, and D. Wolber, A network security monitor, in *Proceedings of the 1990 IEEE Symposium on Research in Security and Privacy*, pp. 296–304. IEEE, IEEE Comput. Soc. Press, Los Alamitos, CA, USA, 1990.

46. K. A. Jackson, D. H. DuBois, and C. A. Stallings, An expert system application for network intrusion detection, No. LA-UR-91-558; CONF-911059, Los Alamos National Lab, NM (United States), 1991.

47. J. Hochberg, K. Jackson, C. Stallings, J. F. McClary, D. DuBois, and J. Ford, NADIR: An automated system for detecting network intrusion and misuse, *Computers & Security*, 12, 235–248, 1993.

48. J. Habra, B. Le Charlier, A. Mounji, and I. Mathieu, ASAX: Software architecture and rule-based language for universal audit trail analysis, in Yves Deswarte et al., editors, *Computer Security—Proceedings of ESORICS 92*, vol. 648 of LNCS, pp. 435–450, Toulouse, France, November 23–25, 1992. Springer-Verlag.

49. C. R. Clark, W. Lee, D. E. Schimmel, D. Contis, M. Koné, and A. Thomas, A hardware platform for network intrusion detection and prevention, *Network Processor Design: Issues and Practices*, 3, 99–118, 2005.

50. S. Dharmapurikar, P. Krishnamurthy, T. S. Sproull, and J. W. Lockwood, Deep packet inspection using parallel bloom filters, *Micro, IEEE*, 24, 52–61, 2004.

51. C. R. Meiners, J. Patel, E. Norige, E. Torng, and A. X. Liu, Fast regular expression matching using small TCAMs for network intrusion detection and prevention systems, in *Proceedings of the 19th USENIX Conference on Security*, p. 8, USENIX Association, 2010.

52. F. Yu, R. H. Katz, and T. V. Lakshman, Gigabit rate packet pattern-matching using TCAM, in *Network Protocols, 2004, ICNP 2004. Proceedings of the 12th IEEE International Conference on*, pp. 174–183. IEEE, 2004.

53. J. Moscola, J. Lockwood, R. P. Loui, and M. Pachos, Implementation of a content-scanning module for an Internet firewall, in, pp. 31–38, IEEE, 2003.

54. I. Sourdis, and D. Pnevmatikatos, Pre-decoded CAMs for efficient and high-speed NIDS pattern matching, in *Field-Programmable Custom Computing Machines, 2004, FCCM 2004, 12th Annual IEEE Symposium on*, pp. 258–267, IEEE, 2004.

55. G. Vasiliadis, M. Polychronakis, and S. Ioannidis, MIDeA: A multi-parallel intrusion detection architecture, in *Proceedings of the 18th ACM Conference on Computer and Communications Security*, pp. 297–308, ACM, 2011.

56. H. Song, T. Sproull, M. Attig, and J. Lockwood, Snort offloader: A reconfigurable hardware NIDS filter, in *Field Programmable Logic and Applications, 2005. International Conference on*, pp. 493–498. IEEE, 2005.

57. N. Muraleedharan, A. Parmar, and M. Kumar, A flow based anomaly detection system using chi-square technique, in *Advance Computing Conference (IACC), 2010 IEEE 2nd International*, pp. 285–289. IEEE, 2010.

58. M. J. Chapple, T. E. Wright, and R. M. Winding, Flow anomaly detection in firewalled networks, in *Securecomm and Workshops, 2006*, pp. 1–6. IEEE, 2006.

59. P. Barford, J. Kline, D. Plonka, and A. Ron, A signal analysis of network traffic anomalies, in *Proc. ACM Sigcomm IMW02*, pp. 71–82, Marseille, France, Nov. 2002.

60. A. Lakhina, M. Crovella, and C. Diot, Mining anomalies using traffic feature distributions, in *ACM Sigcomm Computer Communication Review*, vol. 35, pp. 217–228, ACM, 2005.

61. M.-S. Kim, H.-J. Kong, S.-C. Hong, S.-H. Chung, and J. W. Hong, A flow-based method for abnormal network traffic detection, in *Network Operations and Management Symposium, 2004, NOMS 2004. IEEE/IFIP*, vol. 1, pp. 599–612, IEEE, 2004.

62. Cisco IOS Software NetFlow, http://www.cisco.com/warp/public/732/Tech/nmp/netow/.

63. J. Mai, C.-N. Chuah, A. Sridharan, T. Ye, and H. Zang, Is sampled data sufficient for anomaly detection? in *Proceedings of the 6th ACM Sigcomm Conference on Internet Measurement*, pp. 165–176, ACM, 2006.

64. K. Bartos, and M. Rehak, Towards efficient flow sampling technique for anomaly detection, in *Traffic Monitoring and Analysis*, pp. 93–106. Springer Berlin Heidelberg, 2012.

65. G. Androulidakis, and S. Papavassiliou, Improving network anomaly detection via selective flow-based sampling, *Communications, IET*, 2, 399–409, 2008.

66. M. Thottan, G. Liu, and C. Ji, Anomaly detection approaches for communication networks, in *Algorithms for Next Generation Networks*, pp. 239–261, Springer, London, 2010.

67. A. Servin, and D. Kudenko, Multi-agent reinforcement learning for intrusion detection: A case study and evaluation, in *Multiagent System Technologies*, pp. 159–170, Springer, Berlin, 2008.

68. W. Jiang, H. Song, and Y. Dai, Real-time intrusion detection for high-speed networks, *Computers & Security*, 24, 287–294, 2005.

69. C. Kruegel, F. Valeur, G. Vigna, and R. Kemmerer, Stateful intrusion detection for high-speed networks, in *Security and Privacy, 2002, Proceedings 2002 IEEE Symposium on*, pp. 285–293, IEEE, 2002.

70. L. Foschini, A. V. Thapliyal, L. Cavallaro, C. Kruegel, and G. Vigna, A parallel architecture for stateful, high-speed intrusion detection, in *Information Systems Security*, pp. 203–220, Springer, Berlin, 2008.

71. L. Schaelicke, K. Wheeler, and C. Freeland, SPANIDS: A scalable network intrusion detection load balancer, in *CF 05: Proceedings of the 2nd Conference on Computing Frontiers*, pp. 315–322, New York, USA, 2005, ACM.

72. P. Kabiri, and A. A. Ghorbani, Research on intrusion detection and response: A survey, *International Journal of Network Security*, 1, 84–102, 2005.

73. G. Luo, X. L. Lu, J. Li, and J. Zhang, MADIDS: A novel distributed IDS based on mobile agent, *ACM SIGOPS Operating Systems Review*, vol. 37, pp. 46–53, January 2003.

74. H. Wang, D. Zhang, and K. G. Shin, Change-point monitoring for the detection of DoS attacks, *Dependable and Secure Computing, IEEE Transactions on*, 1, 193–208, 2004.

75. M. Thottan, and C. Ji, Anomaly detection in IP networks, *Signal Processing, IEEE Transactions on*, 51, 2191–2204, 2003.

76. Y. Gao, Z. Li, and Y. Chen, A DoS resilient flow-level intrusion detection approach for high-speed networks, in *Distributed Computing Systems, 2006, ICDCS 2006. 26th IEEE International Conference on*, p. 39. IEEE, 2006.

77. W. Yang, B.-X. Fang, B. Liu, and H.-L. Zhang, Intrusion detection system for high-speed network, *Computer Communications*, 27, 1288–1294, 2004.

78. K. Xinidis, I. Charitakis, S. Antonatos, K. G. Anagnostakis, and E. P. Markatos, An active splitter architecture for intrusion detection and prevention, *Dependable and Secure Computing, IEEE Transactions on*, 3, 31–44, 2006.

79. S. Staniford-Chen, S. Cheung, R. Crawford, M. Dilger, J. Frank, J. Hoagland, K. Levitt, C. Wee, R. Yipi, and D. Z. Erkle, GriDS: A large scale intrusion detection system for large networks, *Proceedings of the 19th National Information Security Conference*, vol. 1, 361–370, 1996.

80. E. H. Spafford, and D. Zamboni, Intrusion detection using autonomous agents, *Comput Networks*, vol. 34, 547–570, 2000.

81. S. Staniford-Chen, S. B. Tung, and D. Schnackenberg, The common intrusion detection framework (CIDF), *Proceedings of the Information Survivability Workshop*, Orlando, FL, October 1998.

82. W. Lee, R. A. Nimbalkar, K. K. Yee, S. B. Patil, P. H. Desai, T. T. Tran, and S. J. Stolfo, A data mining and CIDF based approach for detecting novel and distributed intrusions, in *Recent Advances in Intrusion Detection*, pp. 49–65, Springer, Berlin, 2000.

83. S. Kumar, S. Dharmapurikar, F. Yu, P. Crowley, and J. Turner, Algorithms to accelerate multiple regular expressions matching for deep packet inspection, in *ACM Sigcomm Computer Communication Review*, vol. 36, pp. 339–350, ACM, 2006.

84. N. Tuck, T. Sherwood, B. Calder, and G. Varghese, Deterministic memory-efficient string matching algorithms for intrusion detection, in *INFOCOM 2004, Twenty-third Annual Joint Conference of the IEEE Computer and Communications Societies*, vol. 4, pp. 2628–2639, IEEE, 2004.

85. O. Chapelle, B. Schlkopf, and A. Zien, *Semi-Supervised Learning*, vol. 2, MIT Press, Cambridge, MA, 2006.

86. Y. Meng, Intrusion detection using disagreement-based semi-supervised learning: Detection enhancement and false alarm reduction, in *Cyberspace Safety and Security*, pp. 483–497, Springer, Berlin, 2012.

87. C.-H. Mao, H.-M. Lee, D. Parikh, T. Chen, and S.-Y. Huang, Semi-supervised co-training and active learning based approach for multi-view intrusion detection, in *Proceedings of the 2009 ACM Symposium on Applied Computing*, pp. 2042–2048, ACM, 2009.

88. S. Chavan, K. Shah, N. Dave, S. Mukherjee, A. Abraham, and S. Sanyal, Adaptive neuro-fuzzy intrusion detection systems, in *Information Technology: Coding and Computing, 2004, Proceedings, ITCC 2004, International Conference on*, vol. 1, pp. 70–74, IEEE, 2004.

89. J. Jiang, C. Zhang, and M. Kamel, RBF-based real-time hierarchical intrusion detection systems, in *Neural Networks, 2003, Proceedings of the International Joint Conference on*, vol. 2, pp. 1512–1516, IEEE, 2003.

90. M. Sheikhan, Z. Jadidi, and A. Farrokhi, Intrusion detection using reduced-size RNN based on feature grouping, *Neural Computing and Applications*, 21, 1185–1190, 2012.

91. M. Amini, R. Jalili, and H. R. Shahriari, RT-UNNID: A practical solution to real-time network-based intrusion detection using unsupervised neural networks, *Computers & Security*, 25, 459–468, 2006.

92. C.-H. Mao, H.-M. Lee, D. Parikh, T. Chen, and S.-Y. Huang, Semi-supervised co-training and active learning based approach for multi-view intrusion detection, in *Proceedings of the 2009 ACM Symposium on Applied Computing*, pp. 2042–2048, ACM, 2009.

93. O. Chapelle, and A. Zien, Semi-supervised classification by low density separation, 2004.
94. V. N. Vapnik, *The Nature of Statistical Learning Theory*, 2nd ed., Springer-Verlag, Berlin, Germany, 1999.
95. I. Bar-Gad, G. Morris, and H. Bergman, Information processing, dimensionality reduction and reinforcement learning in the basal ganglia, *Progress in Neurobiology*, 71, 439–473, 2003.
96. X. Xu, and T. Xie, A reinforcement learning approach for host-based intrusion detection using sequences of system calls, in *Advances in Intelligent Computing*, pp. 995–1003, Springer, Berlin, 2005.
97. P. Miller and A. Inoue, Collaborative intrusion detection system, in *North American Fuzzy Information Processing Society, NAFIPS 2003, 22nd International Conference of the*, pp. 519–524, 2003.
98. X. Xu, Y. Sun, and Z. Huang. Defending DDoS attacks using hidden Markov models and cooperative reinforcement learning, *Lecture Notes in Computer Science*, 4430, 196, 2007.
99. C. J. C. H. Watkins, and P. Dayan, Q-learning, *Machine Learning*, 8, 279–292, 1992.
100. R. S. Sutton and A. G. Barto, *Reinforcement Learning: An Introduction*, MIT Press, Cambridge, MA, 1998.
101. P. Stone, R. S. Sutton, and G. Kuhlmann, Reinforcement learning for robocup soccer keepaway, *Adaptive Behavior*, 13, 165–188, 2005.
102. S.-B. Cho, and H.-J. Park, Efficient anomaly detection by modeling privilege flows using hidden Markov model, *Computers & Security*, 22, 45–55, 2003.
103. A. Shahrestani, M. Feily, R. Ahmad, and S. Ramadass, Architecture for applying data mining and visualization on network flow for botnet traffic detection, in *Proceedings of the International Conference on Computer Technology and Development*, pp. 33–37, 2009.
104. M. Soysal, and E. G. Schmidt, Machine learning algorithms for accurate flow-based network traffic classification: Evaluation and comparison, *Performance Evaluation*, 67, 451–467, 2010.
105. R. Alshammari, and A. Nur Zincir-Heywood, Machine learning based encrypted traffic classification: Identifying SSH and Skype, in *Computational Intelligence for Security and Defense Applications, 2009, CISDA 2009. IEEE Symposium on*, pp. 1–8, IEEE, 2009.
106. A. Sperotto, R. Sadre, F. van Vliet, and A. Pras, A labeled data set for flow-based intrusion detection, in *IP Operations and Management*, pp. 39–50. Springer, Berlin, 2009.
107. P. Winter, Inductive intrusion detection in flow-based network data using one-class support vector machines, MSc Thesis, 2010.
108. M. Sheikhan, and Z. Jadidi, Flow-based anomaly detection in high-speed links using modified GSA-optimized neural network, *Neural Computing and Applications*, 1–13, 2012.
109. A. Abraham, R. Jain, J. Thomas, and S. Y. Han, D-SCIDS: Distributed soft computing intrusion detection system, *Journal of Network and Computer Applications*, 30, 81–98, 2007.
110. A. Servin, and D. Kudenko, *Multi-agent Reinforcement Learning for Intrusion Detection*. Springer, Berlin, 2008.
111. G. Kumar, and K. Kumar, The use of artificial-intelligence-based ensembles for intrusion detection: A review, *Applied Computational Intelligence and Soft Computing*, 21, 2012.
112. A. Zainal, M. A. Maarof, and S. M. Shamsuddin, Ensemble classifiers for network intrusion detection system, *Journal of Information Assurance and Security*, 4, 217–225, 2009.
113. E. Menahem, L. Rokach, and Y. Elovici, Troika: An improved stacking schema for classification tasks, *Information Sciences*, 179, 4097–4122, 2009.
114. J. R. Quinlan, *C4.5 Programs for Machine Learning*, Morgan Kaufmann, San Mateo, CA, 1997.
115. G. H. John and P. Langley, Estimating continuous distributions in Bayesian classifiers, in *Proceedings of the Conference on Uncertainty in Artificial Intelligence*, pp. 338–345, 1995.
116. D. W. Aha, D. Kibler, and M. K. Albert, Instance-based learning algorithms, *Machine Learning*, 6, 37–66, 1991.
117. G. D. Guvenir, Classification by voting feature intervals, in *Proceedings of the European Conference on Machine Learning*, pp. 85–92, 1997.
118. R. C. Holte, Very simple classification rules perform well on most commonly used datasets, *Machine Learning*, 11, 63–90, 1993.
119. G. Wang, J. Hao, J. Ma, and L. Huang, A new approach to intrusion detection using artificial neural networks and fuzzy clustering, *Expert Systems with Applications*, 37, 6225–6232, 2010.
120. Z. Muda, W. Yassin, M. N. Sulaiman, and N. I. Udzir, A K-means and naive Bayes learning approach for better intrusion detection, *Information Technology Journal*, 10, 648–655, 2011.
121. IPv6 Tutorial, www.sanog.org/resources/sanog5-pfs-ipv6-tutorial.pdf.
122. S. E. Deering and R. M. Hinden, Internet Protocol, Version 6 (IPv6) Specification. RFC 2460, December 1998.

123. J. B. Postel, (Ed.), Internet Protocol. Internet Request For Comments RFC 791, September 1981.
124. K. A. Gehrke, The unexplored impact of IPv6 on intrusion detection systems, Naval Postgraduate School, Monterey, CA, Dept of Computer Science, 2012, http://www.dtic.mil/cgi-bin/GetTRDoc?AD = ADA561931.
125. *Internet Protocol Version 6 (IPv6)*, chapter 15, http://alliedtelesis.com/media/fount/softwarereference/271/ar400/ipv6.pdf.
126. A. Pilihanto, A complete guide on IPv6 attack and defence, GIAC(GSEC) Gold Certification, SANS Institute InfoSec Reading Room, http://www.sans.org/reading_room/whitepapers/detection/complete-guide-ipv6-attack-defense_33904.
127. S. R. Hassan, M. Syrame, and J. Bourgeois, Protecting grids from cross-domain attacks using security alert sharing mechanisms, Future Generation Computer Systems, 2012.
128. J. Seo, C. Lee, T. Shon, and J. Moon, SVM approach with CTNT to detect DDoS attacks in grid computing, in *Grid and Cooperative Computing-GCC, 2005*, pp. 59–70, Springer, Berlin, 2005.
129. Q. Zhang, L. Cheng, and R. Boutaba, Cloud computing: State-of-the-art and research challenges, *Journal of Internet Services and Applications*, 1, 7–18, 2010.
130. C. Modi, D. Patel, B. Borisaniya, H. Patel, A. Patel, and M. Rajarajan, A survey of intrusion detection techniques in cloud, *Journal of Network and Computer Applications*, 2012.
131. G. R. Vijay, R. Mohan, and A. Reddy, An efficient security model in cloud computing based on soft computing techniques, *International Journal of Computer Applications*, 60, December 18–23, 2012.
132. K. Vieira, A. Schulter, C. B. Westphall, and C. Merkle Westphall, Intrusion detection for grid and cloud computing, *IT Professional*, 12, 38–43, 2010.
133. A. Patel, M. Taghavi, K. Bakhtiyari, and J. Celestino Jr., An intrusion detection and prevention system in cloud computing: A systematic review, *Journal of Network and Computer Applications*, 2012.
134. U. Tupakula, V. Varadharajan, and N. Akku, Intrusion detection techniques for infrastructure as a service cloud, in *Dependable, Autonomic and Secure Computing (DASC), 2011 IEEE Ninth International Conference on*, pp. 744–751, IEEE, 2011.
135. Y. Liu, D. Tian, and B. Li, A wireless intrusion detection method based on dynamic growing neural network, in *Computer and Computational Sciences, 2006, IMSCCS '06, First International Multi-Symposiums on*, vol. 2, pp. 611–615, IEEE, 2006.
136. J. Boudec and S. Sarafijanovic, An artificial immune system approach to misbehavior detection in mobile ad-hoc networks, Technical Report IC/2003/59, Ecole Polytechnique Federale de Lausanne, 2003.
137. S. Sarafijanovic and J. Boudec, An artificial immune system approach with secondary response for misbehavior detection in mobile ad-hoc networks, Technical Report IC/2003/65, Ecole Polytechnique Federale de Lausanne, 2003.
138. H. Deng, Q.-A. Zeng, and D. P. Agrawal, SVM-based intrusion detection system for wireless ad hoc networks, in *Vehicular Technology Conference, 2003, VTC 2003*, Fall, 2003 IEEE 58th, vol. 3, pp. 2147–2151, IEEE, 2003.
139. S. Siripanadorn, W. Hattagam, and N. Teaumroong, Anomaly detection in wireless sensor networks using self-organizing map and wavelets, *International Journal of Communications*, 4, 74–83, 2010.

13 Applications of Machine Learning in Intrusion Detection

Yuxin Meng, Yang Xiang, and Lam-For Kwok

CONTENTS

13.1 INTRODUCTION

With the rapid development of network technology, the need for and the dependency on networks, such as online services, have been definitely increased, which has also given rise to new vulnerabilities and threats (e.g., worms, Trojans, viruses). For example, the Internet has already become an important component of business models [1]; thus, many business operations should use Internet applications, such as e-banking and online transfers. To protect business and personal networks, intrusion detection is one major challenge for both research and practice.

To defend against a variety of attacks (either host or network attacks), intrusion detection systems (IDSs) have been widely deployed in current network environments and have become an essential component for protecting network security. *Intrusion detection* is the process of monitoring the events occurring in a computer system or network and analyzing them for signs of possible incidents that violate computer security policies or standard security practices [2]. Therefore, an intrusion detection system is a kind of software to automate the process of intrusion detection. The major functions of an IDS can be summarized as below:

- Recording relevant information on events
- Notifying security officers of important events
- Generating alarms (or alerts) when detecting intrusions

Based on the deployment, an IDS can be generally classified into two types: host-based IDS (HIDS) and network-based IDS (NIDS). A host-based IDS monitors the characteristics of a single host and the events occurring within that host for suspicious activity. On the other hand, a network-based IDS monitors and analyzes network traffic for particular events and application protocols to identify suspicious activities.

Based on the detection approaches, an IDS can be categorized into three folders: signature-based detection, anomaly-based detection, and specification-based detection. These detection approaches can be characterized as below:

- Signature-based detection. A *signature* is a kind of description to illustrate a known attack or exploit. This approach detects an attack (or potential incident) by comparing its available signatures with incoming observed events.
- Anomaly-based detection. This approach identifies an anomaly by comparing its normal profile with observed events. A normal profile can represent the normal behavior of users, hosts, or network connections.
- Specification-based detection. This approach is also known as stateful protocol analysis. The *stateful* means that an IDS is capable of understanding and tracking the state of network, transport, and application protocols that have a notion of state [2].

Traditionally, the above detection approaches can be treated as two views: misuse detection and anomaly detection. A signature-based IDS [3] (or *misuse detection*) is good at detecting known attacks but largely ineffective at detecting unknown threats and many variants on known threats, and an anomaly-based IDS [4] (or *anomaly detection*) can be very effective at detecting previously unknown threats. Thus, these two detection approaches are complementary methods [5], for which hybrid detection systems have also been developed [6].

Motivation and Target. Machine learning is a powerful technique and tool for intrusion detection, especially for anomaly-based detection. In the literature, a number of anomaly detection systems are developed based on massive distinct machine learning algorithms. In addition, machine learning algorithms can be used to construct false alarm filters for both signature-based detection and anomaly-based detection. In this case, machine learning techniques have a wide use to improve the performance of intrusion detection systems. In this chapter, we therefore focus on the applications of machine learning techniques in the field of intrusion detection.

Lee and Stolfo [7] first proposed a framework of MADAM ID that applied data mining techniques to intrusion detection. In particular, their framework utilized data mining algorithms to compute activity patterns from system audit data and extracted predictive features from the patterns. It then applied machine learning algorithms to the audit records according to the feature definitions and generated intrusion detection rules. Following this framework, a lot of machine learning algorithms are applied to developing an intrusion detection system.

Contributions. In this chapter, we begin by conducting a survey of introducing the applications of machine learning in the aspects of anomaly detection and false alarm filter construction, and we then identify several challenges and limitations, and further propose several potential countermeasures accordingly. Our contributions can be summarized as below:

- We first conduct a survey about the applications of machine learning in intrusion detection regarding two specific aspects of anomaly-based intrusion detection and false alarm filter construction.
- After understanding the recent development of machine learning techniques in intrusion detection, we then identify several challenges and limitations regarding the applications of machine learning in intrusion detection, such as issues related to feature extraction, algorithm selection, false alarm generation, and training data.

- To mitigate the above challenges and limitations, we further propose several countermeasures and directions accordingly, such as constructing newly well-defined data sets, selecting machine learning algorithms in an adaptive way, constructing an active learning-based false alarm filter, and automatically labeling unlabeled data by using a semi-supervised learning–based approach.

The remaining parts of this chapter are organized as follows. In Section 13.2, we give a survey by introducing the recent development of using machine learning techniques in anomaly-based detection and false alarm reduction by constructing an alarm filter. In Section 13.3, we analyze the applications of machine learning in intrusion detection and identify several challenges and limitations in this area. Section 13.4 describes the potential countermeasures and directions to tackle the above issues. Finally, we conclude the chapter in Section 13.5.

13.2   MACHINE LEARNING IN INTRUSION DETECTION

In this section, we mainly introduce the applications of machine learning schemes in intrusion detection. In particular, we conduct a survey in two aspects: anomaly-based detection and false alarm filter construction.

The above aspects are two major applications of machine learning in the area of intrusion detection:

- *Anomaly-based detection.* Machine learning algorithms are widely used in developing an anomaly-based detection system in which an algorithm can be utilized to establish a normal profile. Due to the ability of efficiently handling a large number of flow samples and multidimensional feature spaces, machine learning–based classification has been widely adopted during a multitude of research findings [8].
- *False alarm filter.* False alarms are a big problem for an IDS. To mitigate this issue, the construction of a machine learning–based false alarm filter is a promising way for both signature-based IDSs and anomaly-based IDSs. In addition, a false alarm filter is easy for design and flexible for deployment.

13.2.1   MACHINE LEARNING FOR ANOMALY-BASED DETECTION

As described above, Lee and Stolfo [7] first proposed a framework of applying data mining and machine learning to intrusion detection. The architecture of the framework is described in Figure 13.1.

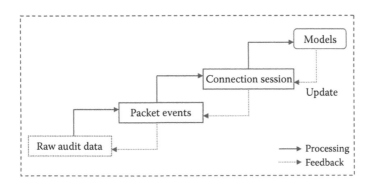

FIGURE 13.1   The framework of applying data mining to intrusion detection.

In Figure 13.1, raw (binary) audit data can be first processed into ASCII network packet information (or host event data), which is further summarized into connection records (or host session records), including many basic features, such as service, duration, etc. Data mining programs can then be applied to the connection records (in connection session) to compute the frequent patterns (i.e., association rules), construct additional features for the connection records, and establish models. This process of learning the detection models is iterative. Basically, poor performance of the classification models often indicates that more pattern mining and feature construction is needed.

Following this framework, a number of machine learning algorithms have been proposed and applied to intrusion detection, especially to anomaly-based detection.

13.2.1.1 Supervised Learning

Supervised learning is based on the use of training data to create a function, in which each of the training data contains a pair of the input vector and output (e.g., class labels). The learning (training) task is to compute the approximate distance between the input and output examples to create a classifier (model). When the model is created, it can be used to classify unknown examples (instance) into a learned class label [9].

13.2.1.1.1 K-Nearest Neighbor Classifier

K-nearest neighbor (KNN) is one of the most simple and traditional non-parametric techniques to classify objects based on the closest training examples in the feature space: An object is classified by a majority vote of its neighbors [10]. For example, if $k = 1$, then the object is simply assigned to the class of its nearest neighbor.

Liao and Vemuri [11] proposed an approach of using a k-nearest neighbor (KNN) classifier to classify program behavior as normal or intrusive. Specifically, the frequencies of system calls used by a program, instead of their local ordering, are used to characterize the program's behavior. Each system call can be treated as a "word," and each process (e.g., program execution) as a "document." Then, a KNN classifier can be used. Because there is no need to build a profile for each program and check every sequence during the new program execution, the calculation burden is greatly reduced. Their preliminary experiments with 1998 DARPA BSM audit data showed that the KNN classifier could effectively detect attacks and achieve a low false positive rate. For instance, the detection rate reaches 100% rapidly when the threshold is raised to 0.72, and the false positive rate remains as low as 0.44%.

Then, Pradeep Kumar et al. [12] focus on classification of sequential data and propose an approach of using a sliding window to extract sub-sequences of various lengths and giving classifications based on the KNN classifier. In the evaluation, they conducted experiments on the DARPA 1998 data set by varying the length of the sliding window from 1 to 5 and using different distance/similarity measures, such as Jaccard similarity, cosine similarity, Euclidian distance, and a binary weighted cosine (BWC) measure. The experimental results demonstrate that the sub-sequences can enhance the classification accuracy of KNN for sequential data, irrespective of the used distance/similarity metric. Later, Kuang and Zulkemine [13] proposed an anomaly intrusion detection method using the combined strangeness and isolation measure k-nearest neighbors (CSI-KNN) algorithm. This intrusion detection algorithm could analyze distinct characteristics of network data by using two measures: *strangeness* and *isolation*. Based on these two measures, a correlation unit raises intrusion alerts with associated confidence estimates. In addition, multiple CSI-KNN classifiers work in parallel and can deal with many types of network services so that the CSI KNN-based NIDS can work more efficiently than processing all network services together.

13.2.1.1.2 Support Vector Machine

In machine learning, support vector machines (SVMs) are supervised learning models with associated learning algorithms that analyze data and recognize patterns. SVM first maps the input vector into a higher dimensional feature space and then obtains the optimal separating hyper-plane in the higher dimensional feature space. Given a set of training examples, each of them can belong to one of two categories; an SVM training algorithm builds a model that assigns new examples into one category or the other. In addition, a decision boundary is determined by support vectors rather than the whole training samples and thus is extremely robust to outliers [9,14].

Fugate and Gattiker [15] described experiences and results of applying a support vector machine (SVM) to a computer intrusion detection (CID) data set. In the experiments, with comparison to an intuitively understandable method, such as Mahalanobis distance, SVM can be a valuable tool for gaining information regarding high-dimensional data as well as achieving good classification performance. Kim and Park [16] proposed a method of applying support vector machines to a network-based intrusion detection system, called SVM IDS. In the evaluation, they used the 1999 KDD data set on the SVM IDS with various kernel functions and regularization parameter C values. The results showed that SVM IDS is feasible in real implementation.

Later, Zhang and Shen [17] conducted a comparison between conventional SVM, Robust SVM, and one-class SVM and made a modification to them. Their preliminary experiments with the 1998 DARPA BSM data set indicate that their modified SVMs can be trained online, and the corresponding results outperform the original ones with fewer support vectors (SVs) and less training time without decreasing detection accuracy. Specifically, the running time of their modified algorithms can be reduced greatly due to the fewer support vectors, and the training time can be saved significantly by the effective decomposition of the original algorithms for faster convergence. Wang et al. [18] extended kernel methods to intrusion detection by introducing a new family of kernels suitable for intrusion detection. They particularly described two anomaly detectors that are based on kernel methods and a one-class SVM learning algorithm, respectively. The experimental results provide strong evidence that STIDE kernels and Markov chain kernels, in conjunction with one-class SVMs, could offer a more accurate and efficient alternative to a conventional anomaly detection algorithm (STIDE and Markov chain methods) for detecting anomalies in system call sequences.

Kim and Cha [20] performed an empirical study investigating the effectiveness of SVM (support vector machine) in detecting masquerade activities using two different UNIX command sets. The term of "common commands" was used as a feature aiming to more effectively reflect diverse command patterns conducted by various users. In the evaluation, the experimental results indicated that what they proposed could achieve an accuracy of 80.1% using the same data set containing only the command names. These combined experiments demonstrate that SVM is an effective approach to masquerade detection.

Joseph et al. [27] proposed CARRADS, a computationally efficient methodology for adapting the intrusion detection model in real time. Its initial detection engine is built based on the support vector machines (SVMs). Their experiments show that the CARRADS can provide high detection accuracy with low processing overhead. Several other related works about detecting anomalies and intrusions using SVM can be referred to [19,21–26,28,29].

13.2.1.1.3 Decision Tree

A decision tree classifies a sample through a sequence of decisions, in which the current decision helps to make the subsequent decision. Such a sequence of decisions is represented in a tree structure [9]. Decision trees present a system using a top-down strategy based on the divide and conquer approach in which the major aim is to partition the tree in many mutually exclusive subsets. Each subset partition corresponds to a classification sub-problem. A decision tree is composed of three basic elements: nodes, edges, and leaves.

Han and Cho [30] proposed an anomaly-based detection technique that combined multiple detectors to improve the performance of the conventional anomaly detection techniques. Specifically, they developed four detection methods that used system call events, resource usage of process, and file access events as the measure of normal behavior with appropriate modeling methods. In addition, they combined these multiple detectors using the decision tree. The proposed detection method had expected better performance because it could model normal behaviors from various perspectives. Experimental results with real data demonstrated the effectiveness of the proposed method, which could achieve a significantly low false positive rate against various types of intrusion (i.e., above 80%). Similarly, Amor et al. [31] also applied a decision tree to intrusion detection and proposed an extension of the inference method for classifying new instances containing uncertain attributes. The experimental results with the KDD 1999 data set showed that their approach was encouraging.

Later, Paek et al. [34] proposed an algorithm of sC4.5 for a small-size decision tree induction and for a specific data by complementing the split attribute selection criteria of C4.5 during the tree induction. Note that C4.5 is one of the most popular decision tree algorithms. The approach of sC4.5 is to select the next highest gain ratio attribute as the split attribute if the training data set is satisfied with the bias properties of C4.5. The experimental results indicate that sC4.5 can improve the performance of detection compared with the previous method C4.5 and reduce tree size. In addition, Ohta et al. [35] investigated an approach of decreasing false positives in network intrusion detection based on a decision tree classifier. To achieve a low false positive rate, they pointed out that the tree construction algorithm must select the attribute best suited to decrease the false positives. They then proposed a new function that evaluated the goodness of an attribute with respect to error type. The experiments showed that the proposed function could effectively build decision trees with fewer false positives. Several other related works about the use of decision trees in intrusion detection can be referred to [32,33,36].

13.2.1.1.4   Naïve Bayes Classifier

This classifier is a simple probabilistic classifier based on applying Bayes' theorem with strong (naïve) independence. A naïve Bayes classifier assumes that the presence or absence of a particular feature is unrelated to the presence or absence of any other feature, given the class variable.

Rezaul Karim et al. [37] proposed a collaborative IDS for MANET using the Bayesian method and used a set of features to guarantee the effectiveness of such an IDS, in which the Bayesian method could improve the efficiency in the detection procedure. Khor et al. [38] explored the possibility of employing a multiple classifier approach while only limited to several variations of Bayesian technique, namely naïve Bayes classifier, Bayesian networks, and expert-elicited Bayesian networks. The evaluation were conducted based on the DARPA data set, and the results showed that the multiple Bayesian classifier approach gave an insignificant increase of performance in detecting network intrusions as compared to a single Bayesian classifier. Later, Dash et al. [39] applied naïve Bayes in masquerade detection.

13.2.1.1.5   Neural Networks

The modern usage of this term often refers to artificial neural networks (ANNs), which are composed of artificial neurons or nodes. In most cases, an ANN is an adaptive system that changes its structure based on external or internal information that flows through the network. It can be utilized to model complex relationships between inputs and outputs or to find patterns in data.

Debar et al. [40] presented a possible application of using neural networks as a component of an intrusion detection system. Then, Doumas et al. [41] applied neural networks for recognition and classification of computer viruses.

Joo et al. [42] investigated the asymmetric costs of false positives and false negatives to enhance the IDS performance and proposed an approach of using a neural network model to consider the cost ratio of false negative errors to false positive errors. The results showed that the neural network model could provide high accuracy in intrusion detection. In addition, their simulation results showed that the effectiveness of intrusion detection could also be enhanced by considering the asymmetric costs of false negative and false positive errors. Then, Dass et al. [45] identified that ANN was not effective in a very dynamic environment and proposed a blackboard-based learning intrusion detection system, which was controlled by autonomous agents and has an online learning capability. They further showed that this feature could enable the system to adapt itself with the changing environment and to perform better than current detection systems. Gavrilis and Dermatas [50] presented a radial basis–function neural network detector for distributed denial of service (DDoS) attacks in public networks based on statistical features estimated in short time–window analysis of the incoming data packets. The proposed method was evaluated in a simulated public network and showed a detection rate better than 98% of DDoS attacks using only three statistical features estimated from one window of data packets of 6 seconds' length. Yang and Karahoca [54] presented an anomaly detection approach for network intrusion detection based on the cellular neural networks (CNN) model. The experiments with the KDD 1999 data set showed that the proposed CNN model was effective for intrusion detection: In comparison to a back propagation neural network, the CNN model exhibited an excellent performance with a higher attack detection rate and a lower false positive rate.

In addition, Stopel et al. [57] presented a new approach that used artificial neural networks (ANN) to detect the presence of computer worms based on measurements of computer behavior. As the measurement of a large number of system features may require significant computational resources, they evaluated the ANN's capability of detecting the presence of an unknown worm with three feature selection techniques. The results showed that, by using only five features, one could detect an unknown worm with an average accuracy of 90%. Fisch et al. [59] conducted a case study of radial basis function neural networks in intrusion detection. In the case study, they compared the classification abilities of radial basis function classifiers, multilayer perceptrons, the neuro-fuzzy system NEFCLASS, decision trees, classifying fuzzy-k-means, support vector machines, Bayesian networks, and nearest neighbor classifiers. Then, they explored the interpretability and understandability of the best paradigms and showed how structure optimization and feature selection for radial basis function classifiers can be done using evolutionary algorithms. Finally, they demonstrated that radial basis function classifiers are basically able to detect novel attack types. Several other related papers about utilizing neural networks in intrusion detection can be referred to [43,44,46,48,49,51–53,55,56,58,61].

13.2.1.1.6 Fuzzy Logic

Fuzzy logic is a form of many-valued logic or probabilistic logic, and it may have a truth value that ranges in degree between 0 and 1. That is, in fuzzy logic, the degree of truth of a statement can range between 0 and 1, and it is not constrained to the two truth values (i.e., true, false) [9].

Dickerson and Dickerson [62] proposed a fuzzy intrusion recognition engine (FIRE) for an anomaly-based intrusion detection system, which used fuzzy logic to assess whether malicious activity is taking place on a network. FIRE used a fuzzy analysis engine to evaluate the fuzzy inputs and trigger alert levels for the security administrator. Then, Dickerson et al. [63] further presented several intrusion scenarios with the fuzzy systems for detecting the intrusions. Their results showed that the fuzzy systems could easily identify port scanning and denial of service attacks, and it can be effective at detecting some types of backdoor and Trojan horse attacks.

Later, Liao et al. [70] proposed an approach based on fuzzy logic and an expert system for network forensics, which could analyze computer crimes in the network environment and make digital evidence automatically. Experimental results showed that their system could classify most kinds of attack types (i.e., a classification rate of 91.5% on average) and provided analyzable and comprehensible information for forensic experts. Li et al. [71] proposed a novel approach named *fuzzyVIDS*, which enabled dynamic resource provision for a NIDS virtual appliance. It used a fuzzy model to characterize the complex relationship between performance and resource demands and used an online fuzzy controller to adaptively control the resource allocation for NIDS under varying network traffic. Several related works about using fuzzy in intrusion detection can be referred to [64–69,72–75].

13.2.1.1.7 Genetic Algorithms

A genetic algorithm (GA) is a search heuristic that mimics the process of natural evolution. It usually starts by randomly generating a large population of candidate programs and is an iterative process. A typical genetic algorithm requires (1) a genetic representation of the solution domain and (2) a fitness function to evaluate the solution domain.

Helmer et al. [76] designed an essential component of a multi-agent distributed knowledge network system for intrusion detection. In the study, they explored the performance of the rule learning algorithm on this task with and without feature subset selection using a genetic algorithm. The selection of feature subset is shown to significantly reduce the number of features used while improving the accuracy of predictions. Song et al. [77] proposed a generic method but not specific to a particular GP structure. In the experiments, significant generalization was demonstrated, with attacks previously unseen detected and attack classes with representation rates in training data of less than 1% also being detected. Banković et al. [78] presented a serial combination of two genetic algorithm-based intrusion detection systems, and the designed system was simple, accurate, adaptive and fast without introducing significantly computational overhead. In real-world applications, a genetic algorithm is usually used to optimize other algorithms (i.e., constructing hybrid algorithms).

13.2.1.1.8   Hybrid Classifiers

For an IDS, the ultimate goal is to achieve the best possible accuracy of detecting attacks. This objective leads to the design of hybrid approaches to solve this problem. The idea behind a hybrid classifier is to combine several machine learning techniques (e.g., [85]) so that the performance can be significantly improved. For example, a hybrid approach typically consists of two functional components as below [9]:

- The first one takes raw data as input and generates intermediate results.
- The second one then takes the intermediate results as its input and generates the final results.

In intrusion detection, many hybrid classifiers are developed, and we list some genetic algorithm–based hybrid classifiers in Table 13.1.

13.2.1.2   Unsupervised Learning

From the view of machine learning, unsupervised learning refers to the problem of trying to identify hidden structure in unlabeled data. Because the examples for a learner are unlabeled, there is no error or reward signal to evaluate a potential solution, which distinguishes unsupervised learning from supervised learning.

For example, Yamanishi and Takeuchi [92] focused on the problem of detecting outliers from unlabeled data and developed *SmartSifter*, an online outlier detection algorithm based on unsupervised learning from data. Then, Luo et al. [93] proposed an intrusion detection algorithm based on unsupervised clustering (UC) and a support vector machine (SVM). The experiment with KDD 99 data sets showed that their approach could detect intrusions efficiently in the network connections.

Later, Zanero and Savaresi [94] identified that IDSs were increasingly limited by their need of an up to date and comprehensive knowledge base and introduced a two-tier architecture to overcome this problem: The first tier was an unsupervised clustering algorithm that reduced network packets' payload to a tractable size while the second tier is a traditional anomaly detection algorithm. Jalili et al. [95] presented a novel method for detecting DDoS attacks, which was based on a statistical pre-processor and an unsupervised artificial neural net. This unsupervised neural net was used to

TABLE 13.1

Hybrid Classifiers Based on Genetic Algorithms

	Neural Network	SVM	Fuzzy	KNN	Decision Tree
Genetic Algorithm	[82,90]	[79–81]	[83,84,87,89]	[86,88]	[91]

analyze and classify traffic as either a DDoS attack or normal. Experimental results showed that their approach could accurately and efficiently detect DDoS attacks.

Lu and Traore [99] proposed a new unsupervised anomaly detection framework for detecting network intrusions in real-time. The proposed framework consisted of new anomalousness metrics named *IP weight* and an outlier detection algorithm based on a Gaussian mixture model (GMM). IP weights could convert the features of IP packets into a four-dimensional numerical feature space. Then, Tsai and Yen [103] presented a new mixed clustering algorithm named HDG-clustering for unsupervised anomaly detection. Experimental results with the 1999 KDD cup data set indicated that the proposed approach could outperform several existing techniques, such as SVM and KNN. Later, Said et al. [105] investigated the problem of detecting intrusion using distance-based outlier detection that was an unsupervised and efficient approach to detect outliers.

Casas et al. [106] presented *UNIDS*, an unsupervised network intrusion detection system which was capable of detecting unknown network attacks without using any kind of signatures, labeled traffic, or training. It used a novel unsupervised outlier detection approach based on sub-space clustering and multiple evidence accumulation to pinpoint different kinds of network intrusions and attacks, such as DoS/DDoS. The experimental results showed that it could drastically reduce the overall analysis time of the system. Recently, Song et al. [107] indicated that it was still not easy to deploy unsupervised learning–based anomaly detection into a real network environment as it requires several parameters during their building process, and thus IDS operators and managers suffer from tuning and optimizing the required parameters based on changes of their network characteristics. They then proposed a new anomaly detection method that could automatically tune and optimize the values of parameters without predefining them. The experimental results showed that the performance of the proposed method was superior to that of the previous one. Several other works regarding unsupervised learning intrusion detection can be referred to [96–98,100–102,104].

13.2.2 Machine Learning for Constructing False Alarm Filters

False alarms (false positives) are a big problem for an IDS (either a signature-based IDS or anomaly-based IDS) and are especially a key limiting factor for the development of these detection systems [108]. Take an anomaly-based detection system as an example; there may be thousands of alarms produced a day, among which most are false alarms. The big number of false alarms is a heavy burden for a security officer to handle. To mitigate this issue, we advocate that constructing an alarm filter is a promising solution. Constructing a false alarm filter is another application of machine learning in intrusion detection. Although most machine learning algorithms can be directly applied to an anomaly detector, a false alarm filter is easier to design and more flexible to deploy (i.e., establishing another mechanism to reduce false alarms).

The high-level construction and deployment of the false alarm filter is presented in Figure 13.2. As shown in the figure, the false alarm filter consists of two major components: a *classifier* and

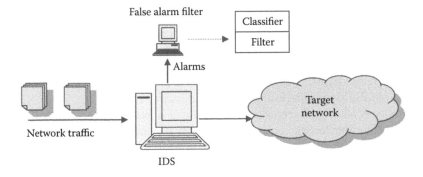

FIGURE 13.2 The construction and deployment of the false alarm filter.

a *filter*. The classifier can be either a single algorithm or an ensemble classifier while the filter is mainly used to reduce alarms based on the selected classifier.

For the deployment, such a false alarm filter is usually deployed close to an IDS. The IDS can examine incoming network traffic and forward its generated alarms to the false alarm filter. The false alarm filter can filter out false alarms based on its classifier. The output of the alarm filter can be treated as true alarms.

Spathoulas and Katsikas [117] developed a false alarm filter that consists of three components: NRA, HAF, and UFP. In particular, the NRA component is based on the assumption that a true positive alert must be part of a neighboring (in time) set of alerts with similarities in source or destination IPs. The HAF component is based on the observation that actual attacks tend to increase the signature-related frequency of alerts while the UFP component is the simplest of the three that aims to detect and discard usual false positives (FPs) in a network. The experimental results with the DARPA data set indicated that the proposed filter could reduce the number of alarms by 29% while reducing the number of FPs by 74%.

In addition, Pietraszek [109] indicated that IDSs had been observed to trigger thousands of alerts per day, and most of them are false positives. They then proposed a machine-learning based system, called ALAC (adaptive learner for alert classification) to reduce false positives by classifying alerts into true positives and false positives. The system could be configured to process autonomously alerts that were classified with high confidence. In particular, in the training phase, this system classifies alerts into true or false positives. Then, this system computes a parameter of classification confidence and presents this classification to a human analyst. The analyst's feedback could be used to generate training examples and build/update the classifiers. In the evaluation, they showed the effectiveness of this system. For instance, they showed that the system was useful in recommender mode, in which it could adaptively learn the classification from the analyst.

Then, Law and Kwok [110] proposed an approach of reducing the number of false alarms using a KNN (k-nearest-neighbor) classifier. Specifically, they model the patterns of normal alarms to describe the sequence of incoming alarms, and then identify the anomalies by identifying deviations from that model. The KNN classifier is used to classify new data points into normal or abnormal based on the Euclidean distances. Alharby and Imai [111] presented an approach to mine historical alarms to learn how future alarms could be handled more efficiently. In particular, they mainly designed an algorithm for detecting anomalies by using continuous and discontinuous sequential patterns and their experiments with real-world data showed that the presented model could handle IDSs alarms efficiently.

In addition, many supervised learning algorithms, such as support vector machine (SVM) [112], neural networks [113], and fuzzy set [114] have been applied to reducing false alarms for an IDS. Later, several semi-supervised learning and active learning have been studied in this field because traditional supervised learning algorithms usually demand a large number of labeled instances during the training process.

For example, Chiu et al. [115] developed a semi-supervised learning–based mechanism to establish an alert filter. This filter only needs a very small amount of label information and can make the alarm filter be more practical for the real deployment. In particular, they used a network connection feature instance (NCF instance) to represent the corresponding cluster of alerts. These instances could be used to train the machine learning–based analysis engine to classify incoming alerts into suspicious alerts or false alarms. In the evaluation, the results indicated that their approach could reduce up to 85% of false alarms and still keep a high detection rate.

In the community of machine learning, active learning is a form of supervised machine learning in which a learning algorithm has the capability of interactively querying a user for some useful information to obtain the desired outputs. It usually consists of two components: a classifier and a query function. For instance, Li and Guo [116] proposed a novel supervised network intrusion detection method based on both a TCM-KNN (transductive confidence machines for k-nearest neighbors) machine learning algorithm and a method of active learning–based training data selection. In the experiment, they compared the performance of SVM, neural network, KNN, and TCM-KNN. The experimental results indicated that the proposed method is more robust and effective than the state-of-the-art intrusion detection methods.

13.3 CHALLENGES AND LIMITATIONS

As described above, machine learning has been widely applied to intrusion detection, especially to anomaly-based detection. Although it has proven its value in improving the performance of intrusion detection, it still suffers from several issues:

- Feature extraction
- Algorithm selection
- False alarms
- Training data

13.3.1 FEATURE EXTRACTION

To apply any machine learning algorithms to intrusion detection, the first issue is how to appropriately extract features. Take the KDD Cup 1999 data set (KDD1999) as an example; it derives from the DARPA packet traces and includes a wide variety of intrusions simulated in a military network environment. The full KDD 1999 data set includes 4,898,431 records, and each record contains 41 features. The features of the KDD 1999 data set are described in Figure 13.3.

The figure shows that each item of the KDD 1999 data set has 41 features whereas there are many other approaches for feature selection. Therefore, the challenge is that it is not known which method can perform the best especially under what classification techniques for intrusion detection [9].

13.3.2 ALGORITHM SELECTION

Another challenge is how to select an appropriate machine learning algorithm in constructing an intrusion detector or a false alarm filter. In the literature, each machine learning–based approach claims that they can achieve a better result (e.g., classification accuracy) than other approaches, but there is no available metric to provide an overall evaluation. In addition, the filtration accuracy of an algorithm may be fluctuant (i.e., in some scenarios, the accuracy is not good but quite good in other scenarios) due to the inherent limitations of machine learning algorithms.

Category	Specific features
TCP connection basic characteristic	duration, protocol_type, service, flag, src_bytes, dst_bytes, land, wrong_fragment, urgent
TCP connection content characteristic	hot, num_failed_logins, logged_in, num_compromised, root_shell, su_attempted, num_root, num_file_creations, num_shells, num_access_files, num_outbound_cmds, is_hot_login, is_guest_login
Time-based network traffic	count, srv_count, serror_rate, srv_seror_rate, rerror_rate, srv_rerror_rate, same_srv_rate, diff_srv_rate, srv_diff_host_rate
Host-based network traffic	dst_host_count, dst_host_srv_count, dst_host_same_srv_rate, dst_host_diff_srv_rate, dst_host_same_src_port_rate, dst_host_srv_diff_host_rate, dst_host_serror_rate, dst_host_srv_serror_rate, dst_host_srv_serror_rate, dst_host_rerror_rate, dst_host_srv_rerror_rate

FIGURE 13.3 The features of KDD 1999 data set.

Moreover, to choose one single algorithm may be no longer a good candidate in the evaluation. To further improve the performance of detection, designing more efficient algorithms is required, such as hybrid classifiers and ensemble classifiers (i.e., combining multiple classifiers). Again, the challenge is how to appropriately select such a combination.

13.3.3 FALSE ALARMS

False alarms are a big challenge for an IDS. Axelsson [108] suggested that one false alarm in 100,000 events was the minimum requirement for an intrusion detection system to be effective. In this case, the primary and probably the most important challenge that needs to be met is the development of effective strategies to reduce the high rate of false alarms.

We identified that for an anomaly-based detection, the detection accuracy of these detection systems depends heavily on the pre-established normal profile. As described earlier, a normal profile is used to present a normal event. However, it is very hard to establish a good quality normal profile in most cases because network traffic is too dynamic and is very hard to predict [118]. Therefore, a lot of generated alarms are false alarms in a real network environment. For example, some traffic mutations can easily violate the normal profile and cause an anomaly-based NIDS to produce many false alarms.

For a signature-based IDS, the detection capability of these systems is mainly depending on the stored signatures. That is, the detection accuracy is limited to the number and content of their available signatures. But in real settings, the number of signatures is limited and these available signatures are difficult to cover all known attacks and exploits. In addition, such kind of IDSs is weak in detecting multi-step attacks. Therefore, a lot of false alarms may be produced during the detection.

13.3.4 TRAINING DATA

Traditional supervised machine learning approaches usually require a large number of labeled data in the phase of training whereas in real-world applications, the number of available labeled data is very small. Therefore, this is a big challenge for a machine learning–based IDS. Based on our work [119], we identify and summarize some common characteristics for intrusion detection as below:

- *Limited samples.* This characteristic is due to the fact that few security experts can provide a large number of attack examples or false alarm examples. In actuality, the number of attack examples, especially for some novel attacks, is very small in real scenarios. This situation is the same for the false alarm reduction: massive unlabeled alarms are available while only a few labeled alarms can be obtained. Therefore, with an extremely small number of training examples, it is a very difficult task for many supervised machine learning algorithms to achieve a high accuracy.
- *Asymmetrical training samples.* Typical machine learning algorithms usually assume that both positive and negative examples (instances) are distributed approximately equally. However, in the aspect of network intrusion detection, positive (or normal) examples are easily obtained and widely available. But the number of available negative (or malicious) examples is very small, and these examples can be further divided into many different sub-classes. This situation is also similar in false alarm reduction. With only a few negative examples, it is very hard for training an algorithm to achieve a high accuracy of detecting negative instances.

13.4 POTENTIAL COUNTERMEASURES

To mitigate the above issues, in this section, we identify several potential directions and countermeasures accordingly, such as constructing newly well-defined data sets, selecting a machine learning algorithm in an adaptive way, constructing an active learning–based false alarm filter and automatically labeling unlabeled data by using a semi-supervised learning–based approach.

13.4.1 DATA SET CONSTRUCTION

There are many approaches for extracting features, so the first challenge is how to appropriately extract features. To resolve this issue, we should work in collaboration and test some candidates. In addition, expert knowledge should be considered when deciding which approach of extracting features should be used. In this case, constructing some new, widely available and well-known data sets by recognized laboratories and universities is a promising way to mitigate this challenge.

For example, although the KDD 1999 data set is more than a decade old, it is the only well-known and widely available data set in the area of intrusion detection. This data set is still widely used in a baseline evaluation aiming to explore the performance of many newly proposed intrusion detection–related algorithms.

13.4.2 INTELLIGENT ALGORITHM SELECTION

To select an appropriate machine learning algorithm is a big challenge because the filtration accuracy of an algorithm may be fluctuant.

To resolve this issue, we proposed an approach of *intelligent algorithm selection* that selects a machine leaning algorithm in an adaptive way [120]. In particular, we constructed an adaptive false alarm filter that could select the best algorithm from a pool of algorithms. The high-level architecture of this intelligent false alarm filter is presented in Figure 13.4.

There are four major components: *alarm standardization, alarm processing, intelligent algorithm selection,* and *false alarm reduction.* The component of *alarm standardization* has two phases: feature extraction and format conversion. The feature extraction is depending heavily on an IDS; that is, for different IDSs, selected features may be a bit different. After extracting these predefined features, all the incoming alarms can be converted during the format conversion. The component of *alarm processing* is responsible for storing these alarms. In the component of *intelligent algorithm selection,* the false alarm filter can select the most appropriate machine learning algorithm in an adaptive way. Finally, the component of *false alarm reduction* can perform alarm reduction based on the selected algorithms.

In the evaluation, we showed that the intelligent false alarm filter could maintain the reduction accuracy at a high and stable level by selecting the algorithm in an adaptive way. Note that this *intelligent algorithm selection* can also be directly used in anomaly detection that selects an appropriate

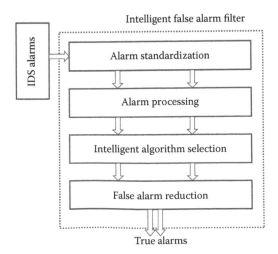

FIGURE 13.4 The architecture of the intelligent false alarm filter.

algorithm in detecting intrusions. By selecting the algorithm in an adaptive way, it is expected that the detection accuracy can be improved and maintained at a stable level.

13.4.3 ACTIVE LEARNING–BASED ALARM REDUCTION

False alarms are a big challenge for an IDS; to mitigate this issue, we advocate that considering expert knowledge during alarm reduction is a promising solution.

In [121], we proposed an approach of constructing a false alarm filter using active learning. Active learning is a form of supervised machine learning in which a learning algorithm has the capability of interactively querying a user/expert for some useful information and thus obtaining the desired outputs. It usually consists of two components: a classifier and a query function.

The classifier can be any type of schemes, such as Bayesian networks and support vector machines. For the query function, it mainly decides the next examples that should be labeled. The query function is the most significant part of active learning and is also the major difference from a traditional machine learning algorithm. By labeling the most relevant examples (or instances), an active learner can minimize the number of queries required. That is, active learning can achieve good performance by only using as few labeled examples as possible.

In Figure 13.5, we describe the pseudo code of our designed active learning algorithm. In the evaluation, the experimental results of the first experiment showed that the active learner could achieve a better classification accuracy and hit rate than several other traditional supervised classifiers and

---

Input: (1) Let U denotes the unlabeled dataset, L denotes the labeled dataset, pl denotes a pool, $|pl|$ denotes the size of the pool, $P_{Distance}$ denotes the Euclidean distance from the closest point in the positive cluster and $N_{Distance}$ denotes the Euclidean distance from the closest point in the negative cluster. (2) Let $A = \{A_1, A_2, ..., A_i, ...\}$ denotes an incoming alarm stream.

Phase1:
Query function: initiate the pool pl.

While ($U \neq \emptyset$).
 { **for** i=1 to $|U|$ **do**
 calculate $P^i_{Distance}$, $N^i_{Distance}$ and $E^i_{Distance} = |P^i_{Distance} - N^i_{Distance}|$
 end for }

 for i=1 to $|pl|$ **do**
 for j=1 to $|U|$ **do**
 {find the smallest $E^j_{Distance}$,
 query for labeling this instance j,
 add j to pl and remove j from U. }
 end for
 end for
Output: pool pl.

Phase2:
Classifier: classify incoming alarm stream.

 for all labeled instances x in L, from i=1 to $|L|$ **do**
 calculate $d(x_i, A)$ and order $d(x_i, A)$ from lowest to highest.
 select the K nearest instances to A.
 assign A the most frequent class in L.
 end for
Output: labeled alarm stream A.

FIGURE 13.5 Pseudo code: The designed active learning algorithm. (From Y. Meng, and L.-F. Kwok, Proceedings of the 9th Information Security Practice and Experience Conference (ISPEC), 1–16, 2013.)

that the active learner could approximately reduce the required number of labeled alarms by half. Moreover, the second experiment indicated that the designed false alarm filter was encouraging and could perform well in a network environment, achieving both a classification accuracy and a hit rate above 90%.

13.4.4 Semi-Supervised Learning

To mitigate the issue of labeled data, semi-supervised learning is a promising technique, which can automatically exploit unlabeled data in addition to labeled data without human intervention.

In [122], we conducted a study of applying disagreement-based semi-supervised learning to anomaly detection. Disagreement-based semi-supervised learning is a method in which multiple learners are trained for the task, and the disagreements among the learners are exploited during the semi-supervised learning process. This method has many advantages, such as avoiding the model assumption violation, the non-convexity of the loss function, and the poor scalability of the learning algorithms.

In the evaluation, we conducted two major experiments to respectively evaluate the performance of the disagreement-based algorithm and to evaluate its performance together with active learning. The experimental results indicate that the disagreement-based method can outperform traditional supervised machine leaning schemes by utilizing unlabeled data and that the performance can be further improved by co-working with active learning.

13.5 CONCLUSION

Machine learning is a useful technique to solve the problem of intrusion detection (i.e., classifying incoming events into normal or abnormal), and it has been widely applied to intrusion detection, especially to anomaly-based detection. In this chapter, we conduct a survey by reviewing the applications of machine learning in intrusion detection regarding two aspects: *anomaly-based detection* and *false alarm filter construction*. We then identify several challenges and limitations with respect to feature extraction, algorithm selection, false alarms, and training data. Finally, we accordingly propose several potential countermeasures and directions to tackle these issues, such as constructing newly well-defined data sets, selecting a machine learning algorithm in an adaptive way, constructing active learning–based false alarm filter, and automatically labeling unlabeled data by using a semi-supervised learning–based approach.

Overall, a machine learning technique and its rapid development can continue to improve the performance of intrusion detection systems while it has some inherent limitations, such as fluctuant performance. To enhance the applications of machine learning in intrusion detection, expert knowledge can be considered to improve the utilization by continuously tuning these machine learning classifiers.

AUTHORS' BIOGRAPHIES

Yuxin Meng received his bachelor's degree in computer science (information security) from Nanjing University of Posts and Telecommunications, China, in 2009 and obtained his PhD degree in Computer Science from the City University of Hong Kong in 2013. His research interests are information security, such as network security, intrusion detection, web security, vulnerability and malware detection, cloud technology in security, access control, and mobile authentication. He is also interested in cryptography, especially its use in network protocols. In addition, he is working on the application of intelligent technology in information security. He has actively served as a reviewer for many conferences and journals.

Yang Xiang received his PhD in computer science from Deakin University, Australia. He is currently a full professor at the School of Information Technology, Deakin University. He is the director of the Network Security and Computing Lab (NSCLab). His research interests include network and system security, distributed systems, and networking. In particular, he is currently leading his team developing active defense systems against large-scale distributed network attacks. He is the chief investigator of several projects in network and system security, funded by the Australian Research Council (ARC). He has published more than 130 research papers in many international journals and conferences, such as *IEEE Transactions on Computers,* *IEEE Transactions on Parallel and Distributed Systems, IEEE Transactions on Information Security and Forensics,* and *IEEE Journal on Selected Areas in Communications.* He is a senior member of the IEEE.

Lam-For Kwok received his PhD degree in information security from Queensland University of Technology, Australia. He is currently an associate professor of the Department of Computer Science at City University of Hong Kong. His research interests include information security and management, intrusion detection systems, and computers in education. He has extensive teaching and academic planning experience. He is the associate director of the AIMtech Centre (Centre for Innovative Applications of Internet and Multimedia Technologies) and the InPAC Centre (Internet Security and PKI Application Centre) at City University of Hong Kong. He actively serves the academic and professional communities and has been acting as program chairs and organizing chairs of international conferences, assessors, and panel judges of various awards. He is a fellow of the Hong Kong Institution of Engineers and British Computer Society.

REFERENCES

1. Shon, T., Moon, J.: A hybrid machine learning approach to network anomaly detection. *Information Sciences* 177, 3799–3821, 2007.
2. Scarfone, K., Mell, P.: *Guide to Intrusion Detection and Prevention Systems (IDPS).* NIST Special Publication 800-94, February 2007.
3. Roesch, M.: Snort: Lightweight intrusion detection for networks. In: *Proceedings of the 13th Large Installation System Administration Conference (LISA),* pp. 229–238, 1999.
4. Ghosh, A. K., Wanken, J., Charron, F.: Detecting anomalous and unknown intrusions against programs. In: *Proceedings of the 1998 Annual Computer Security Applications Conference (ACSAC),* pp. 259–267, 1998.
5. Liao, H.-J., Richard Lin, C.-H., Lin, Y.-C., Tung, K.-Y.: Intrusion detection system: A comprehensive review. *Journal of Network and Computer Applications* 36, 16–24, 2013.
6. Ali, A. M., Halim, Z. A., Gökhan, C. K.: A hybrid intrusion detection system design for computer network security. *Computers and Electrical Engineering* 35, 517–526, 2009.
7. Lee, W., Stolfo, S. J.: A framework for constructing features and models for intrusion detection systems. *ACM Transactions on Information and System Security* 3, 227–261, 2000.
8. Nguyen, T. T. T., Armitage, G.: A survey of techniques for Internet traffic classification using machine learning. *IEEE Communications Surveys & Tutorials* 10, 56–76, 2008.
9. Tsai, C.-F., Hsu, Y.-F., Lin, C.-Y., Lin, W.-Y.: Intrusion detection by machine learning: A review. *Expert Systems with Applications* 36, 11994–12000, 2009.
10. Manocha, S., Girolami, M. A.: An empirical analysis of the probabilistic K-nearest neighbor classifier. *Pattern Recognition Letters* 28, 1818–1824, 2007.
11. Liao, Y., Vemuri, V. R.: Use of k-nearest neighbor classifier for intrusion detection. *Computers and Security* 21, 439–448, 2002.
12. Pradeep Kumar, N., Venkateswara Rao, M., Radha Krishna, P., Bapi, R. S.: Using sub-sequence information with kNN for classification of sequential data. In: G. Chakraborty (ed.): *ICDCIT 2005,* LNCS 3816, pp. 536–546, 2005.

13. Kuang, L., Zulkemine, M.: An anomaly intrusion detection method using the CSI-KNN algorithm. In: *Proceedings of the 2008 ACM Symposium on Applied Computing (SAC)*, pp. 921–926, 2008.

14. Vapnik, V.: *Statistical Learning Theory*. New York: John Wiley, 1998.

15. Fugate, M., Gattiker, J. R.: Computer intrusion detection with classification and anomaly detection, using SVMs. *International Journal of Pattern Recognition and Artificial Intelligence* 17, 441–458, 2003.

16. Kim, D. S., Park, J. S.: Network-based intrusion detection with support vector machines. In: H.-K. Kahng (ed.): *ICOIN 2003*, LNCS 2662, pp. 747–756, 2003.

17. Zhang, Z., Shen, H.: Online training of SVMs for real-time intrusion detection. In: *Proceedings of the 18th International Conference on Advanced Information Networking and Applications (AINA)*, pp. 568–573, 2004.

18. Wang, Y., Wong, J., Miner, A.: Anomaly intrusion detection using one class SVM. In: *Proceedings of the 5th Annual IEEE SMC on Information Assurance Workshop*, pp. 358–364, 2004.

19. Zheng, Q., Li, H., Xiao, Y.: A classified method based on support vector machine for grid computing intrusion detection. In: H. Jin, Y. Pan, N. Xiao, and J. Sun (eds.): *GCC 2004*, LNCS 3251, pp. 875–878, 2004.

20. Kim, H.-S., Cha, S.-D.: Empirical evaluation of SVM-based masquerade detection using UNIX commands. *Computers and Security* 24, 160–168, 2005.

21. Zhang, Z., Shen, H.: Application of online-training SVMs for real-time intrusion detection with different considerations. *Computer Communications* 28, 1428–1442, 2005.

22. Gao, H.-H., Yang, H.-H., Wang, X.-Y.: Kernel PCA based network intrusion feature extraction and detection using SVM. In: L. Wang, K. Chen, and Y.S. Ong (eds.): *ICNC 2005*, LNCS 3611, pp. 89–94, 2005.

23. Lee, H., Song, J., Park, D.: Intrusion detection system based on multi-class SVM. In: D. Slezak et al. (eds.): *RSFDGrC 2005*, LNAI 3642, pp. 511–519, 2005.

24. Chen, R.-C., Chen, S.-P.: An intrusion detection based on support vector machines with a voting weight schema. In: H.G. Okuno and M. Ali (eds.): *IEA/AIE 2007*, LNAI 4570, pp. 1148–1157, 2007.

25. Seo, J.: An attack classification mechanism based on multiple support vector machines. In: O. Gervasi and M. Gavrilova (eds.): *ICCSA 2007*, LNCS 4706, Part II, pp. 94–103, 2007.

26. Yu, J., Lee, H., Kim, M.-S., Park, D.: Traffic flooding attack detection with SNMP MIB using SVM. *Computer Communications* 31, 4212–4219, 2008.

27. Joseph, J. F. C., Das, A., Lee, B.-S., Seet, B.-C.: CARRADS: Cross layer based adaptive real-time routing attack detection system for MANETS. *Computer Networks* 54, 1126–1141, 2010.

28. Yan, M., Liu, Z.: A new method of transductive SVM-based network intrusion detection. In: D. Li, Y. Liu, and Y. Chen (eds.): *CCTA 2010*, Part I, IFIP AICT 344, pp. 87–95, 2011.

29. Agrawal, P. K., Gupta, B. B., Jain, S.: SVM based scheme for predicting number of zombies in a DDoS attack. In: *Proceedings of the 2011 European Intelligence and Security Informatics Conference (EISIC)*, pp. 178–182, 2011.

30. Han, S.-J., Cho, S.-B.: Combining multiple host-based detectors using decision tree. In: T. D. Gedeon and L. C. C. Fung (eds.): *AI 2003*, LNAI 2903, pp. 208–220, 2003.

31. Amor, N. B., Benferhat, S., Elouedi, Z., Mellouli, K.: Decision trees and qualitative possibilistic inference: Application to the intrusion detection problem. In: T. D. Nielsen and N. L. Zhang (eds.): *ECSQARU 2003*, LNAI 2711, pp. 419–431, 2003.

32. Li, X.-B.: A scalable decision tree system and its application in pattern recognition and intrusion detection. *Decision Support Systems* 41, 112–130, 2005.

33. Baik, S., Bala, J.: A decision tree algorithm for distributed data mining: Towards network intrusion detection. In: A. Laganà et al. (eds.): *ICCSA 2004*, LNCS 3046, pp. 206–212, 2004.

34. Paek, S.-H., Oh, Y.-K., Lee, D.-H.: sIDMG: Small-size intrusion detection model generation of complimenting decision tree classification algorithm. In: J. K. Lee, O. Yi, and M. Yung (eds.): *WISA 2006*, LNCS 4298, pp. 83–99, 2007.

35. Ohta, S., Kurebayashi, R., Kobayashi, K.: Minimizing false positives of a decision tree classifier for intrusion detection on the internet. *Journal of Network and Systems Management* 16, 399–419, 2008.

36. Abbes, T., Bouhoula, A., Rusinowitch, M.: Efficient decision tree for protocol analysis in intrusion detection. *International Journal of Security and Networks* 5, 220–235, 2010.

37. Rezaul Karim, A. H. M., Rajatheva, R. M. A. P., Ahmed, K. M.: An efficient collaborative intrusion detection system for MANET using Bayesian approach. In: *Proceedings of the 9th ACM Symposium on Modeling, Analysis and Simulation of Wireless and Mobile Systems (MSWiM)*, pp. 187–190, 2006.

38. Khor, K.-C., Ting, C.-Y., Amnuaisuk, S.-P.: Comparing single and multiple Bayesian classifiers approaches for network intrusion detection. In: *Proceedings of the 2nd International Conference on Computer Engineering and Applications (ICCEA)*, pp. 325–329, 2010.

39. Dash, S. K., Reddy, K. S., Pujari, A. K.: Adaptive Naive Bayes method for masquerade detection. *Security and Communication Networks* 4, 410–417, 2011.

40. Debar, H., Becker, M., Siboni, D.: A neural network component for an intrusion detection system. In: *Proceedings of the 1992 IEEE Symposium on Security and Privacy*, 240–250, 1992.

41. Doumas, A., Mavroudakis, K., Gritzalis, D., Katsikas, S.: Design of a neural network for recognition and classification of computer viruses. *Computers and Security* 14, 435–448, 1995.

42. Joo, D., Hong, T., Han, I.: The neural network models for IDS based on the asymmetric costs of false negative errors and false positive errors. *Expert Systems with Applications* 25, 69–75, 2003.

43. Liu, Z., Bridges, S. M., Vaughn, R. B.: Classification of anomalous traces of privileged and parallel programs by neural networks. In: *Proceedings of the 12th IEEE International Conference on Fuzzy Systems (FUZZ)*, pp. 1225–1230, 2003.

44. Liu, Y.-H., Tian, D.-X., Wang, A.-M.: ANNIDS: Intrusion detection system based on artificial neural network. In: *Proceedings of the 2003 International Conference on Machine Learning and Cybernetics*, pp. 1337–1342, 2003.

45. Dass, M., Cannady, J., Potter, W. D.: A blackboard-based learning intrusion detection system: A new approach. In: P. W. H. Chung, C. J. Hinde, M. Ali (eds.): *IEA/AIE 2003*, LNAI 2718, pp. 385–390, 2003.

46. Ng, W. W. Y., Chang, R. K. C., Yeung, D. S.: Dimensionality reduction for denial of service detection problems using RBFNN output sensitivity. In: *Proceedings of the 2003 International Conference on Machine Learning and Cybernetics*, pp. 1293–1298, 2003.

47. Li, J., Zhang, G.-Y., Gu, G.-C.: The research and implementation of intelligent intrusion detection system based on artificial neural network. In: *Proceedings of the 2004 International Conference on Machine Learning and Cybernetics*, pp. 3178–3182, 2004.

48. Jing-Xin, W., Zhi-Ying, W., Kui, D.: A network intrusion detection system based on the artificial neural networks. In: *Proceedings of the 3rd International Conference on Information Security (InfoSecu)*, pp. 166–170, 2004.

49. Kim, W., Oh, S.-C., Yoon, K.: Intrusion detection based on feature transform using neural network. In: M. Bubak et al. (eds.): *ICCS 2004*, LNCS 3037, pp. 212–219, 2004.

50. Gavrilis, D., Dermatas, E.: Real-time detection of distributed denial-of-service attacks using RBF networks and statistical features. *Computer Networks* 48, 235–245, 2005.

51. Zhang, C., Jiang, J., Kamel, M.: Intrusion detection using hierarchical neural networks. *Pattern Recognition Letters* 26, 779–791, 2005.

52. Cha, B., Park, K., Seo, J.: Neural network techniques for host anomaly intrusion detection using fixed pattern transformation. In: O. Gervasi et al. (eds.): *ICCSA 2005*, LNCS 3481, pp. 254–263, 2005.

53. Wei, X., Huang, H., Tian, S.: A modified RBF neural network for network anomaly detection. In: J. Wang et al. (eds.): *ISNN 2006*, LNCS 3973, pp. 261–266, 2006.

54. Yang, Z., Karahoca, A.: An anomaly intrusion detection approach using cellular neural networks. In: A. Levi et al. (eds.): *ISCIS 2006*, LNCS 4263, pp. 908–917, 2006.

55. Tian, D., Liu, Y., Li, B.: A distributed hebb neural network for network anomaly detection. In: I. Stojmenovic et al. (eds.): *ISPA 2007*, LNCS 4742, pp. 314–325, 2007.

56. Horng, S.-J., Fan, P., Chou, Y.-P., Chang, Y.-C., Pan, Y.: A feasible intrusion detector for recognizing IIS attacks based on neural networks. *Computers and Security* 27, 84–100, 2008.

57. Stopel, D., Moskovitch, R., Boger, Z., Shahar, Y., Elovici, Y.: Using artificial neural networks to detect unknown computer worms. *Neural Computing and Applications* 18, 663–674, 2009.

58. Wu, H.-C., Huang, S.-H. S.: Neural networks-based detection of stepping-stone intrusion. *Expert Systems with Applications* 37, 1431–1437, 2010.

59. Fisch, D., Hofmann, A., Sick, B.: On the versatility of radial basis function neural networks: A case study in the field of intrusion detection. *Information Sciences* 180, 2421–2439, 2010.

60. Govindarajan, M., Chandrasekaran, R.: Intrusion detection using neural based hybrid classification methods. *Computer Networks* 55, 1662–1671, 2011.

61. Bukhtoyarov, V., Semenkin, E.: Neural networks ensemble approach for detecting attacks in computer networks. In: *Proceedings of the 2012 IEEE Congress on Evolutionary Computation (CEC)*, pp. 1–6, 2012.

62. Dickerson, J. E., Dickerson, J. A.: Fuzzy network profiling for intrusion detection. In: *Proceedings of the 19th International Conference of the North American Fuzzy Information Processing Society*, pp. 301–306, 2000.

63. Dickerson, J. E., Juslin, J., Koukousoula, O., Dickerson, J. A.: Fuzzy intrusion detection. In: *Proceedings of the 2001 Annual Conference of the North American Fuzzy Information Processing Society*, pp. 1506–1510, 2001.

64. Xin, J., Dickerson, J. E., Dickerson, J. A.: Fuzzy feature extraction and visualization for intrusion detection. In: *Proceedings of the 2003 IEEE International Conference on Fuzzy Systems*, pp. 1249–1254, 2003.

65. Orfila, A., Carbó, J., Ribagorda, A.: Fuzzy logic on decision model for IDS. In: *Proceedings of the 2003 IEEE International Conference on Fuzzy Systems*, pp. 1237–1242, 2003.

66. Petrovskiy, M.: A fuzzy kernel-based method for real-time network intrusion detection. In: T. Böhme, G. Heyer, H. Unger (eds.): *IICS 2003*, LNCS 2877, pp. 189–200, 2003.

67. Li, D., Wang, K., Deogun, J. S.: FADS: A fuzzy anomaly detection system. In: G. Wang et al. (eds.): *RSKT 2006*, LNAI 4062, pp. 792–798, 2006.

68. Su, M.-Y., Yeh, S.-C., Chang, K.-C., Wei, H.-F.: Using incremental mining to generate fuzzy rules for real-time network intrusion detection systems. In: *Proceedings of the 2008 International Conference on Advanced Information Networking and Applications (AINA)*, pp. 50–55, 2008.

69. Marín-Blázquez, J. G., Martínez Pérez, G.: Intrusion detection using a linguistic hedged fuzzy-XCS classifier system. *Soft Computing* 13, 273–290, 2009.

70. Liao, N., Tian, S., Wang, T.: Network forensics based on fuzzy logic and expert system. *Computer Communications* 32, 1881–1892, 2009.

71. Li, B., Li, J., Wo, T., Wu, X., Arshad, J., Liu, W.: A fuzzy-based dynamic provision approach for virtualized network intrusion detection systems. In: T. H. Kim and H. Adeli (eds.): *AST/UCMA/ISA/ACN 2010*, LNCS 6059, pp. 115–128, 2010.

72. Acampora, G.: Exploiting timed automata based fuzzy controllers for designing adaptive intrusion detection systems. *Soft Computing* 16, 1183–1196, 2012.

73. Alsubhi, K., Aib, I., Boutaba, R.: FuzMet: A fuzzy-logic based alert prioritization engine for intrusion detection systems. *International Journal of Network Management* 22 , 263–284, 2012.

74. Shiaeles, S. N., Katos, V., Karakos, A. S., Papadopoulos, B. K.: Real time DDoS detection using fuzzy estimators. *Computers and Security* 31, 782–790, 2012.

75. Geramiraz, F., Memaripour, A. S., Abbaspour, M.: Adaptive anomaly-based intrusion detection system using fuzzy controller. *International Journal of Network Security* 14, 352–361, 2012.

76. Helmer, G., Wong, J. S. K., Honavar, V., Miller, L.: Automated discovery of concise predictive rules for intrusion detection. *Journal of Systems and Software* 60, 165–175, 2002.

77. Song, D., Heywood, M. I., Zincir-Heywood, A. N.: Training genetic programming on half a million patterns: An example from anomaly detection. *IEEE Transactions on Evolutionary Computation* 9, 225–239, 2005.

78. Banković, Z., Bojanić, S., Nieto-Taladriz, O.: Evaluating sequential combination of two genetic algorithm-based solutions for intrusion detection. *Advances in Soft Computing* 53, 147–154, 2009.

79. Ohn, S.-Y., Nguyen, H.-N., Kim, D. S., Park, J. S.: Determining optimal decision model for support vector machine by genetic algorithm. In: J. Zhang, J.-H. He, and Y. Fu (eds.): *CIS 2004*, LNCS 3314, pp. 895–902, 2004.

80. Chen, R., Chen, J., Chen, T., Hsieh, C., Chen, T., Wu, K.: Building an intrusion detection system based on support vector machine and genetic algorithm. In: J. Wang, X. Liao, and Z. Yi (eds.): *ISNN 2005*, LNCS 3498, pp. 409–414, 2005.

81. Shon, T., Seo, J., Moon, J.: SVM approach with a genetic algorithm for network intrusion detection. In: P. Yolum et al. (eds.): *ISCIS 2005*, LNCS 3733, pp. 224–233, 2005.

82. Ramasubramanian, P., Kannan, A.: A genetic-algorithm based neural network short-term forecasting framework for database intrusion prediction system. *Soft Computing* 10, 699–714, 2006.

83. Abadeh, M. S., Habibi, J., Lucas, C.: Intrusion detection using a fuzzy genetics-based learning algorithm. *Journal of Network and Computer Applications* 30, 414–428, 2007.

84. Özyer, T., Alhajj, R., Barker, K.: Intrusion detection by integrating boosting genetic fuzzy classifier and data mining criteria for rule pre-screening. *Journal of Network and Computer Applications* 30, 99–113, 2007.

85. Shon, T., Moon, J.: A hybrid machine learning approach to network anomaly detection. *Information Sciences* 177, 3799–3821, 2007.

86. Su, M.-Y., Chang, K.-C., Wei, H.-F., Lin, C.-Y.: Feature weighting and selection for a real-time network intrusion detection system based on GA with KNN. In: C. C. Yang et al. (eds.): *ISI 2008 Workshops*, LNCS 5075, pp. 195–204, 2008.

87. Fries, T. P.: A fuzzy-genetic approach to network intrusion detection. In: *Proceedings of the 10th Annual Conference on Genetic and Evolutionary Computation*, pp. 2141–2146, 2008.

88. Su, M.-Y.: Real-time anomaly detection systems for denial-of-service attacks by weighted k-nearest-neighbor classifiers. *Expert Systems with Applications* 38, 3492–3498, 2011.

89. Abadeh, M. S., Mohamadi, H., Habibi, J.: Design and analysis of genetic fuzzy systems for intrusion detection in computer networks. *Expert Systems with Applications* 38, 7067–7075, 2011.

90. Zhou, L.-P., Li, B.-R.: The study on the intrusion detection algorithm analysis using the improved genetic optimized neural network. *Journal of Convergence Information Technology* 8, 571–577, 2013.

91. Stein, G., Chen, B., Wu, A. S., Hua. K. A.: Decision tree classifier for network intrusion detection with GA-based feature selection. In: *Proceedings of the 43rd Annual Southeast Regional Conference*, pp. 136–141, 2005.

92. Yamanishi, K., Takeuchi, J.-I.: Discovering outlier filtering rules from unlabeled data. In: *Proceedings of the 7th ACM SIGKDD International Conference on Knowledge Discovery and Data Mining*, pp. 389–394, 2001.

93. Luo, M., Wang, L., Zhang, H., Chen, J.: A research on intrusion detection based on unsupervised clustering and support vector machine. In: S. Qing, D. Gollmann, and J. Zhou (eds.): *ICICS 2003*, LNCS 2836, pp. 325–336, 2003.

94. Zanero, S., Savaresi, S. M.: Unsupervised learning techniques for an intrusion detection system. In: *Proceedings of the 2004 ACM Symposium on Applied Computing*, pp. 412–419, 2004.

95. Jalili, R., Imani-Mehr, F., Amini, M., Shahriari, H. R.: Detection of distributed denial of service attacks using statistical pre-processor and unsupervised neural networks. In: R. H. Deng et al. (eds.): *ISPEC 2005*, LNCS 3439, pp. 192–203, 2005.

96. Laskov, P., Düssel, P., Schäfer, C., Rieck, K.: Learning intrusion detection: Supervised or unsupervised? In: F. Roli and S. Vitulano (eds.): *ICIAP 2005*, LNCS 3617, pp. 50–57, 2005.

97. Xiang, G., Min, W., Rongchun, Z.: Applying fuzzy data mining to network unsupervised anomaly detection. In: *Proceedings of the 2005 International Symposium on Communications and Information Technologies*, pp.1249–1253, 2005.

98. Rouil, R., Chevrollier, N., Golmie, N.: Unsupervised anomaly detection system using next-generation router architecture. In: *Proceedings of the 2005 IEEE Military Communications Conference (MILCOM)*, pp. 1654–1659, 2005.

99. Lu, W., Traore, I.: A new unsupervised anomaly detection framework for detecting network attacks in real-time. In: Y. G. Desmedt et al. (eds.): *CANS 2005*, LNCS 3810, pp. 96–109, 2005.

100. Jiang, S., Song, X., Wang, H., Han, J.-J., Li, Q.-H.: A clustering-based method for unsupervised intrusion detections. *Pattern Recognition Letters* 27, 802–810, 2006.

101. Amini, M., Jalili, R., Shahriari, H. R.: RT-UNNID: A practical solution to real-time network-based intrusion detection using unsupervised neural networks. *Computers and Security* 25, 459–468, 2006.

102. Cermak, G., Keyzer, K.: Unsupervised intrusion detection using color images. In: G. Bebis et al. (eds.): *ISVC 2007*, Part II, LNCS 4842, pp. 770–780, 2007.

103. Tsai, C.-F., Yen, C.-C.: Unsupervised anomaly detection using HDG-clustering algorithm. In: M. Ishikawa et al. (eds.): *ICONIP 2007*, Part II, LNCS 4985, pp. 356–365, 2008.

104. Song, J., Takakura, H., Okabe, Y., Kwon, Y.: Unsupervised anomaly detection based on clustering and multiple one-class SVM. *IEICE Transactions on Communications* E92-B, 1981–1990, 2009.

105. Said, D., Stirling, L., Federolf, P., Barker, K.: Data preprocessing for distance-based unsupervised intrusion detection. In: *Proceedings of the 9th Annual International Conference on Privacy, Security and Trust (PST)*, pp. 181–188, 2011.

106. Casas, P., Mazel, J., Owezarski, P.: Unsupervised network intrusion detection systems: Detecting the unknown without knowledge. *Computer Communications* 35, 772–783, 2012.

107. Song, J., Takakura, H., Okabe, Y., Nakao, K.: Toward a more practical unsupervised anomaly detection system. *Information Sciences* 231, 4–14, 2013.

108. Axelsson, S.: The base-rate fallacy and the difficulty of intrusion detection. *ACM Transactions on Information and System Security* 3, 186–205, 2000.

109. Pietraszek, T.: Using adaptive alert classification to reduce false positives in intrusion detection. In: E. Jonsson et al. (eds.): *RAID 2004*, LNCS 3224, pp. 102–124, 2004.

110. Law, K.-H., Kwok, L.-F.: IDS false alarm filtering using KNN classifier. In: C. H. Lim and M. Yung (eds.): *WISA 2004*, LNCS 3325, pp. 114–121, 2004.

111. Alharby, A., Imai, H.: IDS false alarm reduction using continuous and discontinuous patterns. In: J. Ioannidis, A. Keromytis, and M. Yung (eds.): *ACNS 2005*, LNCS 3531, pp. 192–205, 2005.

112. Davenport, M. A., Baraniuk, R. G., Scott, C. D.: Controlling false alarms with support vector machines. In: *Proceedings of the 2006 International Conference on Acoustics, Speech and Signal*, pp. 589–592, 2006.

113. Wang, J., Wang, Z., Dai, K.: A network intrusion detection system based on the artificial neural networks. In: *Proceedings of the 3rd International Conference on Information Security*, pp. 166–170, 2004.

114. El-Semary, A., Edmonds, J., Gonzalez, J., Papa, M.: A framework for hybrid fuzzy logic intrusion detection systems. In: *Proceedings of the 2005 International Conference on Fuzzy Systems*, pp. 325–330, 2005.
115. Chiu, C.-Y., Lee, Y.-J., Chang, C.-C., Luo, W.-Y., Huang, H.-C.: Semi-supervised learning for false alarm reduction. In *Proc. of the 10th Industrial Conference on Advances in Data Mining: Applications and Theoretical Aspects*, pp. 595–605, 2010.
116. Li, Y., Guo, L.: An active learning based TCM-KNN algorithm for supervised network intrusion detection. *Computers and Security* 26, 459–467, 2007.
117. Spathoulas, G. P., Katsikas, S. K.: Reducing false positives in intrusion detection systems. *Computers and Security* 29, 35–44, 2010.
118. Sommer, R., Paxson, V.: Outside the closed world: On using machine learning for network intrusion detection. In: *Proceedings of the 2010 IEEE Symposium on Security and Privacy*, pp. 305–316, 2010.
119. Meng, Y., Kwok, L.-F.: Enhancing false alarm reduction using pool-based active learning in network intrusion detection. In: R. H. Deng and T. Feng (eds.): *ISPEC 2013*, LNCS 7863, pp. 1–15, 2013.
120. Meng, Y., Kwok, L.-F.: Adaptive false alarm filter using machine learning in intrusion detection. In: *Proceedings of the 6th International Conference on Intelligent Systems and Knowledge Engineering (ISKE)*, pp. 573–584, 2011.
121. Meng, Y., Kwok, L.-F.: Enhancing false alarm reduction using pool-based active learning in network intrusion detection. In: *Proceedings of the 9th Information Security Practice and Experience Conference (ISPEC)*, pp. 1–16, 2013.
122. Meng, Y., Kwok, L.-F.: Intrusion detection using disagreement-based semi-supervised learning: Detection enhancement and false alarm reduction. In: *Proceedings of the 4th International Symposium on Cyberspace Safety and Security (CSS)*, pp. 483–497, 2012.

Section IV

IDS for Wireless Systems

14 Introduction to Wireless Intrusion Detection Systems

Jonny Milliken

CONTENTS

14.1 WIRELESS INTRUSION DETECTION SYSTEMS

Security in IT systems is an increasingly important area of research as users have come to accept that every system connected to the Internet is vulnerable. These vulnerabilities can come from known threats, zero-day attacks, malware, or DoS (denial of service) attacks. Some systems that aim to protect against these attacks include firewalls and antivirus systems. Each of these defenses only covers a fraction of computer security however. Firewalls are barriers and do not inform about activity within the network while antivirus systems only protect against malicious software on hosts. There are many more protocol and network level threats, which these options do not protect against.

The primary means of defense against these kinds of attacks is with an IDS (intrusion detection system). An IDS monitors the network environment and alerts a human operator to the presence of an attack or abnormalities. An IDS is also useful for detecting attacks that are difficult and resource intensive to prevent (such as DoS) but can be mitigated once they have begun. WIDS (wireless intrusion detection systems) are designed to mitigate the risks of attacks in WiFi networks by monitoring traffic broadcast over the wireless medium of a network for suspicious activity.

14.1.1 THE BASIC STRUCTURE OF A WIRELESS INTRUSION DETECTION SYSTEM

The rudimentary functions of a WIDS encompass many areas, from data collection and attack detection through to attack reporting to a discerning human or automated response system. Most research work concentrates on one specific area of WIDS performance without consideration of the operation of the whole. This can make it difficult to identify how disparate research investigations and conclusions relate to or impact on each other. Hence, it is useful for researchers to have an appreciation of the whole of the system. This section will outline the operation of a typical WIDS, categorized into six sections:

- Threat identification
- Architecture considerations
- Data collection
- Detection strategy

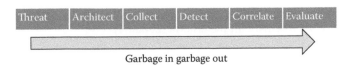

FIGURE 14.1 Structure of a WIDS.

- Correlation method
- Evaluation

The first step in the process is to identify which attacks are *threats* to the network. There are hundreds of attacks that can be lobbied against a system, and it is critically important to identify which of these are priorities because no IDS exists that can reliably detect all known and zero-day attacks.

Once the attacks are identified, the *architecture*, topography, and topology of the network must be investigated. This reveals the resources available and the potential placement locations for data monitors. Once these are known, the best way of detecting the attacks using the available resources is described using a series of metrics based on the *data collection* methods. The metrics in question can come from many sources and operate on many OSI (open systems interconnection) layers.

Once the information sources for attack discovery are known, a *detection* method must be selected. This is an area of mature research as this is the first stage of active intelligence and decision making in the system. It is possible to have a system based on anomaly, signature, specification, or hybrid detection, trained using any number of machine learning algorithms.

In order to reduce the volume of potential alerts, which can confound a human at the evaluation stage, *alert correlation* is used to refine the WIDS output. The outcome of the correlation process must then be displayed in a descriptive way to the human operator or automated response system for *evaluation*.

These six categories are applicable for any IDS although the focus in the descriptions will concentrate on Wireless IDSs. The most important categories in this system are the first and last as they encompass the critical link a WIDS is designed to provide: evaluation if a threat (or attack) has occurred. The four intervening stages should be focused toward ensuring that this link is as reliable as possible. Hence, one of the critical factors to appreciate from the classification outlined here is that all subsequent categories are reliant on the performance of previous sections; see Figure 14.1. Poor choices in the design or performance of lower layers can impact on the performance of the entire system further up the chain, leading to cascading suboptimal design.

14.2 THREAT IDENTIFICATION

Network attacks compromise the integrity, confidentiality, and availability of systems. Before a WIDS can begin protecting a system, it must know what it needs to protect the system against. The nature of the threat will govern the characteristics and success of the defense system. However, when the threat is not explicitly known, approximations must be made. Unfortunately, there is no common, standard way of classifying attacks. As a result, it can be very difficult to determine the critical attacks against networked systems. Many approaches for categorization and identification of attacks have been proposed, all of which try to balance completion with accuracy, in the form of taxonomies (Figure 14.2).

A taxonomy is the study of the means of classification, in this case, the way in which attacks are classified. Taxonomies play an important feedback role in a WIDS too because identification

FIGURE 14.2 Threat identification within WIDS categorization.

of attacks is necessary as a barometer for the success of the system. Many taxonomies have been proposed, but none have yet to satisfy all the criteria set out [1]:

• Accepted	• Deterministic	• Have established terminology
• Comprehensible	• Mutually exclusive	• Unambiguous
• Complete	• Repeatable	• Useful

The goal of many taxonomies is to comprehensively encompass *all relevant attacks*. This is academically desirable but does not necessarily address the most common practical limitation: clarity for those of limited technical backgrounds. As network attacks become increasingly common, it becomes more important for non-academics to be able to act securely and know the threats they are subject to. No key taxonomy has yet arisen that is both sufficiently comprehensive and easy to understand.

The complexity of a taxonomy is generally dictated by the volume of attacks it wishes to cover. Reducing this attack space to a manageable level would assist in presentation and interpretation. A subset of potential attacks is given [2] although it is incomplete:

• External misuse	• Bypassing controls	• Worms
• Hardware misuse	• Eavesdropping	• Viruses
• Masquerading	• Interference	• DoS
• Preparatory abuse	• Authorization attacks	• Spoofing
• Race condition	• MITM (man in the middle)	• Buffer overflow
• Privilege escalation	• Social engineering	• Password attacks
• Vulnerabilities	• Access rights	• Communication based
• Misconfiguration		

Some notable academic investigations into taxonomies include the following:

- *Purdue University* [3]—Taxonomy based on system logs states that a thesaurus of vulnerability terms is needed to remove confusion.
- *Straub and Widom* [4]—Describes a means of classifying attackers based on their motivation as opposed to the attacks themselves and links these to potential responses.
- *AVOIDIT* [5]—Categorizes attacks based on attack method, attack target, operational impact, information impact, and remediation options. Includes a comparison of [1] and [2].
- *Defense-Centric* [6]—Advocates that taxonomies are more useful if built from the defender's point of view rather than from the attacker's.
- *IDS Taxonomy* [7]—Develops a means of comparing the performance of IDSs against each other.
- *Communities* [8]—Investigates the impact on communities from cyber attacks with a separation between the intrusive event and the impact of the event.

In each of these cases, attacks have been defined and named differently based on the authors' experience. There is no formal method applied that would attempt to ensure that all attacks within a particular technology, protocol, or device have been identified. It is possible to list every possible threat that a device may be susceptible to, but this could create many false alarms at evaluation, which can mask the real dangers. No IDS protects against all existing attacks, so the most critical need to be identified instead [9].

14.3 ARCHITECTURE

Once the important threats that can be levied against a vulnerable system have been identified, the next decision concerns where to place the components of the WIDS (Figure 14.3). The architectural structure

Threat	Architect	Collect	Detect	Correlate	Evaluate

FIGURE 14.3 Architecture considerations within WIDS categorization.

can play a huge role in detection ability [10]. This choice is dependent upon the availability of resources, equipment, monitoring points, communication channels, etc. Choices may also be dictated by how distributed the network is. For example, if there are many network locations that need to be protected, then selecting data collection points closer to centralized network switching positions may be prudent.

If an inappropriate architecture is selected, then a WIDS can severely hamper network performance by consuming excessive resources or not having sufficient information available in order to make accurate detection decisions further on in the process. Despite this, very limited research has investigated how to optimally select detection locations.

14.3.1 Embedded vs. Overlay

Depending on the availability of computing resources, a WIDS can be more effectively installed as either an *embedded* or an *overlay* system. An overlay monitoring network is a system that is independent from the network that is to be monitored and is designed to collect the same data from the wireless medium but with minimal network disruption [11]. This is in contrast to an embedded system, which connects directly with the equipment that is to be monitored. This often includes routers or switches and WLAN access points. There are positive and negative aspects for each approach to WLAN monitoring, as summarized below.

14.3.1.1 Embedded

The traffic that the WIDS must analyze already passes through the network, requiring protection, so the optimal solution would seem to be an embedded system. This utilizes the spare capacity in bandwidth and processing power from the existing equipment to monitor, track, and communicate intrusion information. There are several benefits to this approach:

- Low detection latency
- Low response latency
- Low or potentially zero equipment cost
- Existing communication channels are used

Nonetheless, there are drawbacks to this implementation. The reason for this is resource, rather than technology, based:

- Infringes on existing network performance
- Crashing the network node crashes the defense
- No redundancy
- May require router upgrades or modification
- Self DoS conditions

Any additional load that is placed on the existing infrastructure is very likely to have a performance trade-off. One solution would be to replace the network components with upgraded systems, but then an embedded solution loses its main cost benefit over overlay solutions. There are security considerations too; if an adversary crashes the operational router, then it crashes the WIDS as well.

14.3.1.2 Overlay

In an overlay system, an entirely new monitoring network is deployed alongside the existing infrastructure. A WIDS constructed in this fashion will attempt to collect a majority of wireless traffic passing to the AP (access point) under protection directly from the wireless medium. It is not necessary to directly replicate every aspect of the network. Depending on the geography of the area, it may be possible to have one device collect information for many APs. Some positives of this system are the following:

- Equipment diversity
- Multiple source monitoring
- No network performance impact
- Larger resources for monitoring system
- No self DoS

This implementation prioritizes the operational network performance above WIDS performance but requires additional work to plan and install. Given that another entirely separate network is deployed, this can significantly increase the amount of work for security staff. There is also the potential for interference between the operational network and WIDS WiFi channels. Drawbacks include the following:

- Generally larger deployment cost overall
- Slower response and notification times
- Only monitors network traffic
- Increases network administration required
- Potential privacy issues in collecting unintended data

14.3.2   Host, Distributed, and Mobile Architectures

14.3.2.1   Host

Implementation of a host architecture ensures that all components of the IDS remain within the same physical hardware and do not rely on communication between other hosts. This allows intrusion detection within the host itself but not necessarily outside of it [12]. Communication to and from the host can be studied, but there is little or no information sharing between hosts and no means of corroborating data. Attacks that target multiple hosts (such as port scans) cannot be detected.

There are some system-level metrics that can only be gathered by monitoring on the host itself, such as system calls or many specification signatures. It also guarantees that only the host itself is compromised through any attack or compromise of the IDS itself.

Advantages	Disadvantages
• Unique detection metrics	• Expecting poor/no inter-host communications
• Only consumes host resources	• No distributed attack detection
	• Poor network/protocol detection
	• Attacks on host compromise IDS
	• No overlay available

14.3.2.2   Distributed

Distributed systems can operate at many different levels throughout the network hierarchy, in switches, routers, hosts, etc. [13]. Concentrating monitors within network equipment focuses on communication between hosts and alleviates some of the problems of host monitoring; no processing impact on the hosts, observing network events, and isolating monitoring station from host compromise.

There are drawbacks with this system. Because each host on a system may be different, the data for a network monitor can appear conflicting. The volume of data to process can grow exponentially as a deployment increases in size. Also, data that is encrypted will pass through uninspected by the equipment. Any network that utilizes a large number of protocols or applications can confuse or confound a distributed WIDS and the processing required to alleviate this problem can be prohibitive.

Advantages	Disadvantages
• Can detect network/protocol attacks	• Can struggle with disparate data
• Removes burden from users	• Loads network communication infrastructure
• Redundancy possible	
• Scales well	

14.3.2.3 Mobile Agents

Mobile agents cooperatively assist with intrusion detection in a dynamic environment [14]. While the previous systems rely on different placement and communication methods between stationary agents, in a mobile environment the agents themselves can move. Agents can be given specific roles within the network, for example, a monitor agent, analysis agent, retrieval agent, result agent, executive agent and manager agent [15].

Agents allow several independent and intelligent processes to cooperate in securing the network. While this allows distributed computation, asynchronous operation, and an updatable modular structure, there are questions of efficiency and security. The benefit to this approach is that, instead of duplicating agents over every monitoring point, you may instead create a smaller number of agents, which can transfer themselves through the network to provide coverage. These agents can be coordinated by a command structure to investigate suspicious activities. In theory, this should reduce network traffic, add redundancy to the system, and allow more efficient and directed response to intrusions.

There are some problems with this approach [16], such as the following:

- Expensive to design
- Difficult to quantify performance improvements
- Difficult to develop, test, and debug
- Poor security and control
- Can be brainwashed
- Cannot keep secrets
- Lacks necessary infrastructure support

14.4 DATA COLLECTION

Once the attacks that are of primary concern to a WIDS are chosen and the available network locations and resources available have been identified, a decision must be made on what data to collect. Attacks may be occurring within the architecture, but if the correct data is not collected from these locations, all subsequent stages in WIDS design can be compromised. The choice of incorrect metrics can restrict the options for detection algorithms, correlation techniques, and response mechanisms (Figure 14.4).

FIGURE 14.4 Data collection within WIDS categorization.

Unfortunately, at present, there is no standard for selecting, measuring, or tracking metrics. This leads to conflicting measuring approaches and conflicting research outcomes in some instances. As a result, there has been a trend in more recent publications toward identifying and classifying the features or metrics that are optimal [17]. Optimizing and prioritizing metrics is an important goal for WIDS research because it is possible for multiple attacks to be detectable via tracking a single metric while some attacks may require multiple metrics before they can be reliably detected. Optimal selection can reduce false positives, reduce false negatives, and improve root causing of alerts.

14.4.1 DATA COLLECTION METHODS

An important aspect of data collection is the *method* of collecting data. For WIDS research, one means of addressing this problem is the identification of appropriate data sets. It is not uncommon for research papers to generate their own data set; however, this presents problems in comparing data sets and the results based on them [18]. Selecting a suitable data source is an important factor in ensuring that the results drawn from experiments are accurate and relevant. This topic is dealt with in greater depth elsewhere in this book (Chapter 17).

14.4.2 METRIC CATEGORIES

It is not the case that the more metrics monitored, the more secure the system. Some metrics are more useful than others in detecting attacks, and irrelevant metrics may confound the detection system or human response [19]. Sources of metrics can come from all layers of the communication stack, any protocols that operate over the network and, potentially, the information from any system or process in operation. This creates a problem for optimal selection because many metrics may not be available or practical for tracking, depending on the environment the WIDS has been deployed in. Hence, metric possibilities are generally restricted to the most common protocols and network behavior to attempt to create solutions that are likely to work on many different systems installed in many different locations. Common metrics that are used in a WIDS can be separated into four categories:

- System log files
- System calls
- SNMP
- Network packets

14.4.2.1 System Logs

System or audit logs are sets of events created by the OS (operating system) for performing tasks and thus can only be tracked from within host systems [20]. Logs usually represent a list of the running processes on the machine and past activity on the machine. These are typically used with anomaly detection techniques to build applications policy.

The drawback with these logs is that each OS will create, store, and represent them differently, and there is no common format for intrusion detection. Work [21] proposes a specific language to define the meaning of intrusion events. These logs have an associated security risk as well because any attacker that can gain access may well be able to discover more information about the victim than if the monitor was not present.

14.4.2.2 System Calls

System calls are used for tracking illegitimate behavior of a program installed on a protected system. Should a program act maliciously or anomalously, it must communicate with the operating system. However, this means that the communication can be different across each OS. The process of determining these calls for the huge library of common programs in use is non-trivial and so tends to be performed only for critical programs. It is also possible to subvert the detection scheme in use by wrapping an attack within legitimate system calls [22].

14.4.2.3 SNMP

The SNMP (simple network management protocol) allows for various status updates between devices within a network and is routinely used for remote administration of network performance. It has been suggested that combining this information with an intrusion detection system can aid with detection effectiveness [23].

The TCP, IP, and ICMP data [24] are combined with system configuration, network traffic, control, and error statistics from the MIB (SNMP knowledge base). In an experiment in which the detection levels were set to 30%, the results indicate that most attacks can be detected to within a 95% success rate with less than a 1% false positive rate.

14.4.2.4 Network Traffic

Analyzing frame data passing through the network can provide information about the security of the network users and the network infrastructure. However, there are restrictions and challenges with inspecting this data in some cases. Due to privacy limitations, much of the data from the network traffic payload may not be accessible in all cases [18]. Hence, information from protocol headers is the primary source of this network traffic information. This can cause problems for overlay WIDS, which may then only be able to rely on WiFi management frames for detection purposes [11]. Network traffic is the primary metric source for WIDS, so a more in-depth analysis of the metrics available is considered here.

14.4.3 Network Metrics in Research

Many common metrics for IDSs are resident in the network (OSI Layer 3) and transport (OSI Layer 4) layers. As these protocols operate principally the same on wired and wireless installations, this theoretically allows conclusions to be applied to both. This is generally not tested however. Use of metrics at the physical (OSI Layer 1) and data link (OSI Layer 2) layers would deviate significantly for wired and wireless IDSs. Unfortunately, there are few metric investigations that investigate metrics for WIDS [19,25] and fewer at lower layers for WIDS [26]. Some examples of relevant metric selection investigations are outlined below.

Qu et al. [27] utilized a distance method for establishing how far a metric must deviate from its expected value before it can be considered anomalous. The metrics under consideration include the rate of outgoing TCP SYN packets, total number of outgoing UDP packets, ARP request rate, memory usage, and CPU utilization taken every second. No information on the levels or success of these metrics is given.

Chebrolu et al. [28] identified 12 attributes as key attack detection metrics. The exact relationship between each variable and their detection performance is not given. The metrics are the following:

• Service type	• Service count
• Source	• Srv_rerror
• Destination	• Srv_diff_host_rate
• Logged in	• Dst_host_count
• Packet count	• Dst_host_srv_count
• Error rate	• Dst_host_diff_srv_rate

Lu and Traore [29] detected DDoS attacks using the ratio of incoming IP traffic to outgoing IP traffic. An outlier removal strategy is employed using a Gaussian mixture model and an expectation maximum algorithm. Using this system, the response time was approximately 35 seconds for selected flood attacks.

Zargar and Kabiri [19] determined that certain metrics are better at detecting particular attacks. Key results include the following:

- SYN flags and stream index were most indicative of a DoS.
- Fragmentation commands best indicated a "user to root" attack.
- Distinction between "remote to local" attacks and normal traffic can be determined by a threshold.
- FIN flags and PUSH flags determine a port scan.

Milliken et al. [26] identified challenges and proposed means for detecting flooding DoS attacks using WiFi management frames in an overlay detection network. The work ascertains that an additional packet reception timeout metric is specifically required by an overlay network in order to function effectively.

14.5 INTRUSION DETECTION

Once the priority attacks have been identified, architecture and resources allocated, and data collection points established, the method of detecting intrusions must be chosen. This detection process is usually the most processing intensive as it requires operating potentially sophisticated algorithms over large volumes of data. Should the detection algorithm determine that an attack has occurred, then the alert is passed upward to subsequent stages for correlation and evaluation (Figure 14.5).

Detection algorithm testing and development is the most intensely researched field of the stages in WIDS operation outlined here. Nonetheless, it is heavily reliant on the three stages that precede it. If the data fed to the algorithm is incorrect, then poor performance is guaranteed. However there is little research to date that investigates the performance of an algorithm depending on the quality of the data provided [26].

The main objective of this stage is to differentiate normal traffic from potentially intrusive traffic. There are two major assumptions often used at this stage:

1. Attack traffic is inherently different from normal traffic.
2. Normal traffic is more prevalent than attack traffic.

Particularly in modern governmental and large-scale commercial systems at risk from APT (advanced persistent threat), the second assumption is becoming less applicable. Nonetheless, for the majority of systems, it holds true.

Development of an intrusion detection algorithm can be separated into two distinct fields:

- Detection methods
- Machine learning

| Threat | Architect | Collect | Detect | Correlate | Evaluate |

FIGURE 14.5 Detection algorithms within WIDS categorization.

Choice of detection method concerns the means of identifying attack signatures from changes in the chosen metrics. This directly addresses the goal of identifying attack traffic among legitimate traffic. Machine learning approaches the issue of teaching a machine to make these decisions. With the large volume of traffic passing through WIDSs, it is impractical to have a human observe and identify all the trends; computer automation must be employed.

14.5.1 DETECTION METHODS

Choice of detection method is the first component of a WIDS with decision-making intelligence. All previous stages have primarily relied on the work of experienced humans to make decisions. Detection techniques are one of the chief sources of false positives in the system, and the method employed can make a large difference to the eventual WIDS performance. The goal is to strike an effective balance between detection rate and the rate of false positives.

Typically, detection methods employed to differentiate legitimate and malicious traffic can be separated into one of four categories:

- *Anomaly detection*: Generates an idea of the normal traffic characteristics by observing normal network operation and detecting any deviations from this; i.e., *anything outside this expected norm is an intrusion*.
- *Misuse/signature detection*: Establishes a list of rules that should be not violated or known operations that represent attack heuristics; i.e., *anything that matches this pattern is an intrusion*.
- *Specification detection*: Categorizes all the normal and illegal operations of processes and determines which of the two the current activity represents. This lies between anomaly and misuse detection on the spectrum; i.e., *specific processes that perform non-allowed actions are intrusions*.
- *Hybrid detection*: Combines the best parts of any two of these approaches and uses them to offset the drawbacks of other areas. Much research into detection is concerned with how to get combinations of anomaly, misuse, or specification detection to work together effectively.

14.5.1.1 Anomaly Detection

Anomaly detection aims to establish a model for the normal operation of the network. Comparing current traffic to expectedly normal limits should mean that any anomalies will indicate intrusion or suspicious activity. This principle works under the assumption that abnormal traffic is distinct from normal traffic and that it is less common.

If the assumptions hold then, in general, this technique is capable of identifying novel attacks because even zero-day attacks should deviate from the expected norm. As with any system however this is an approximation of real life, represented by a finite number of attributes, so the model will always be limited. This limitation can lead to false positives (new traffic that is legitimate) or false negatives (attacks newly disguised as legitimate traffic).

A graphical representation of the typical operation of an anomaly detection algorithm is given in Figure 14.6. Note that the detection structure is made up of the profile, decisions, and responses. Profiles are necessary for each of the networks under protection, so if there are multiple devices or users, then the volume of profile data grows. The decision determining if traffic is statistically deviant is a comparison between incoming traffic and this profile. The attack decision allows for the profile to be adaptable and dynamic; however it may not be employed in all systems. The response level will be passed upward to a correlation engine before evaluation. Two important features that impact the success of this system are the quality of the profile generated and the "statistically deviant" decision technique employed.

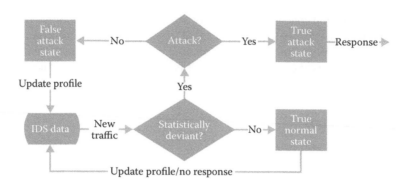

FIGURE 14.6   Anomaly detection process flow.

14.5.1.2   Misuse/Signature Detection

Misuse detection aims to identify intrusions by matching traffic to specific strings of known attack patterns. This is in contrast with anomaly detection, which tries to identify everything that *does not* fall within its bounds. Signature detection is the same process as misuse except that the patterns are defined by a human expert rather than computer learning. The technique has proven very effective at detecting known attacks and can give a good root cause explanation for the alert it generates.

Because signatures must be developed from known attacks, this detection method is entirely unable to identify novel intrusions. Furthermore, developing these patterns is a difficult and time-consuming process, whether done by hand or by machine and will always be limited by the inability to perfectly replicate real life, which contributes to false positives in the same fashion as anomaly detection. Patterns tend to be developed from historical attack data, which means that the attacks themselves are used less regularly, which causes the rules to become dated. The approach is also defeated by attacks that use a series of steps that could be innocuous in isolation but in a structured way can be used to compromise the system.

A graphical representation of the typical operation of a misuse/signature detection algorithm is given in Figure 14.7. One of the key influences on the performance, similar to profile generation in anomaly detection, is the generation and quality of the rule set. There are challenges around rules covering multiple occurrences and overlapping [30] because rules are added sequentially, not iteratively. This is not aided by the lack of a standard form and the format of IDS rules across systems [30] advocates an algorithm for determining rule clashes. These clashes can be both between rules or within one rule itself and be based on redundancy, verbosity, inefficiency, duplication, etc.

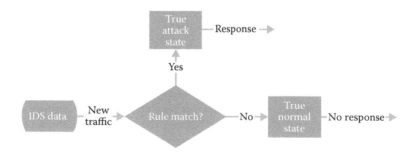

FIGURE 14.7   Rule/misuse detection process flow.

14.5.1.3 Specification Detection

Specification approaches occupy the middle ground between misuse and anomaly detection. They aim to create a system behavioral specification under the assumption that a legitimate and well-behaved system will only operate within these bounds, and any movement outside this can be considered an intrusion. This is functionally different from anomaly detection as it identifies a list of activities a system *may not do*, rather than identifying *uncommon* activities. It is functionally different from misuse/ signature detection as it identifies what a system *may do*, rather than only identifying what it *may not*.

The limitations of the specification are created through expert knowledge rather than machine learning, which suffers from many of the same challenges from previous approaches, particularly ensuring completeness. Specification detection should be able to detect both known and novel attack approaches; however, it suffers in terms of workload because creating these specifications for the large amount of common programs in use today is certainly not a trivial task. Even in instances in which a machine can generate some specifications, they still need to be verified by a human expert at some stage of the process. Some investigations into the feasibility of this system have been performed [31], in particular by [32] in WLANs.

14.5.1.4 Hybrid

Due to the benefits and drawbacks of each of these systems, it is clear that a combination (usually misuse and anomaly) would provide improved detection results, for example, allowing anomaly detection to handle unknown events while misuse detection identifies known attack signatures [33]. Such an approach should decrease the level of false positives if a sufficient method of managing conflicting decisions from multiple detection approaches can be properly managed. Some approaches have also married two anomaly detection engines together in order to try to balance the false positive rate of one against the other. A graphical representation of the typical operation of a hybrid detection algorithm is given in Figure 14.8.

14.5.2 MACHINE LEARNING

One of the major challenges in creating an effective intrusion detection algorithm is the difficulty of developing appropriate rules, profiles, or specifications. These attributes need to be both specific

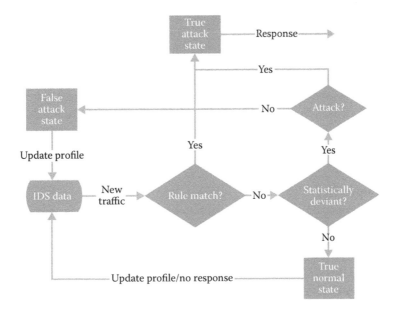

FIGURE 14.8 Hybrid process flow.

enough to identify attacks amongst normal traffic and general enough to apply in many different scenarios, locations, and network environments.

Relying on a human to design detection characteristics is highly reliant on the particular knowledge and beliefs of the human and can vary considerably. Machine learning is an area of research that aims to alleviate this problem either partially or entirely by providing the algorithm with a composition of training data. This data should be based on real-life traffic in that it should be primarily real traffic but can have specific attack instances added in to bias detection ability. Within machine learning for IDS, the machine can be taught to detect attacks within this data in any one of three ways:

- Supervised
- Unsupervised
- Semi-supervised

14.5.2.1　Supervised

Supervised machine learning relies on a human element to train the learning process of the machine so that it can determine which metrics indicate an attack and which indicate normal traffic. In supervised learning, the entirety of the data is labeled as either normal or attack data by a human. The machine uses this data to form thresholds, clusters, states, or relationships for generation of a set or rules or profiles [34].

The benefit of this approach is that it allows the machine to make connections that may be too sophisticated for a human to identify or which a human may erroneously omit. This approach also allows for constant, automatic updating of the detection parameters as more traffic travels through the network. Drawbacks include the remaining need for a human expert to identify the positive and negative traffic, which is a non-trivial task. Each expert may label data differently or suboptimally. The training data set is furthermore unlikely to be able to cover all possible eventualities of the system.

14.5.2.2　Unsupervised

Unsupervised learning relies heavily on the assumption that normal network traffic is appreciatively distinct from and more plentiful than abnormal traffic, and so a machine should be able to distinguish between the two without human guidance. A further assumption is that any large, frequent groups of calls or state transitions are likely to be normal rather than abnormal. If both of these assertions hold true, then a larger, unlabeled training set can be used.

This system does not require human guidance and can theoretically detect novel attacks, rather than being restricted to those attacks that a human is aware of and able to label [35]. It is also more likely to generate comprehensive rules or profiles that cover many eventualities. The drawbacks of this system are numerous. First, the rules and profiles generated may be too complicated for a human to interpret easily. This can make it challenging to provide root causes for detection alerts, which makes attribution and response recommendations more difficult. It also cannot account for traffic or nuances from the real world that a human may contribute.

14.5.2.3　Semi-Supervised

Semi-supervised learning occupies a midway point between supervised and unsupervised learning. In this approach, only the conclusively known or a subset of conclusively known [36] traffic is labeled by a human. This reduces the labeling burden on the human and does not require labeling of complex or distributed attacks, which can be time consuming. This allows the system to create parameters for suspicious or attack activities and can potentially differentiate between different attacks rather than normal and abnormal. Nonetheless, identification of conclusively good traffic is still a difficult task for a human to carry out correctly. Identifying "anomalous" rather than attack traffic has been discussed [37].

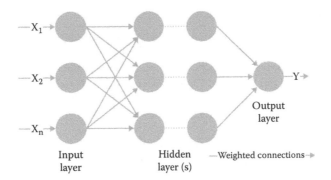

FIGURE 14.9 Multi-layer perceptron.

14.5.3 Machine Learning Techniques

A large number of techniques have been suggested for machine learning in intrusion detection; some of the more prominent methods are outlined here.

14.5.3.1 Neural Networks

Neural networks consist of interconnected nodes, or neurons, which are used for information processing based on the weighted connections between the nodes. The system can adapt the weighting of the node connections depending on incoming data. It is often demonstrated as a MLP (multi-layer perceptron) as seen in Figure 14.9.

In intrusion detection, the connections between nodes represent probable chances of transitions. The weighting of nodes is trained into establishing what a profile should be for the given system. The neural network is then able to identify behavior outside of this normal bound. As the system operates, the accuracy of the node weightings should increase and be more reactive to detection of abnormal values.

While this approach is well used in intrusion detection [38], it does suffer from the potential to allow anomalous behavior to be classified as legitimate, and attack root causing and attribution are not always clear. Operation and training of neural networks tends to be expensive [28].

14.5.3.2 Self-Organizing Maps

The SOM (self-organizing map) is a neural network model that maps multi-dimensional relationships between parameters into a two dimensional map used to analyze and visualize attack/security topography as described in [33].

Each model is formed of neurons (i) in a lattice or grid, in which each neuron has a number of associated n parameters (weight, reference, codebook, etc.). Adjacent neurons form a neighborhood for (i). A neighborhood function determines how closely related (i) is to its neighbors with the more neighbors giving a more accurate result/generalization.

The key advantage of SOM is the formation of clusters, which helps to reduce the input space into representative features. Hence, the underlying structure is maintained while the dimensionality of the space is reduced. There are some drawbacks, however. For example, SOM uses a fixed architecture in terms of number and arrangement of nodes, which has to be defined before training. For largely unknown input data characteristics, it is challenging to determine the network architecture that yields optimal results. Also, the topology of the input space has to match the topology of the output space that is to be represented. However, in real-world data sets, the output must be defined before learning can begin even though the input dimensions may not yet be known [39].

14.5.3.3 Bayesian Systems

Bayesian networks model probabilistic relationships between variables of interest and are very similar to neural networks. Here, connections represent conditional dependencies, and nodes that are not connected to each other represent variables that are conditionally independent, regularly described as a DAG (directed acyclic graph) [28] as in Figure 14.10. In a DAG, each node represents a domain variable, and each edge between nodes indicates a dependency, usually based on probabilities. Thus the probability of the event occurring is based on the evidence for the event based on the parent nodes (the posterior probability).

If these probabilities are calculated for all states, then an idea of the condition of the system as a whole can be established. However, this theory is based on previously observed distributions for each state and relies on the potentially unreasonable condition that states are independent. The major benefit of Bayesian approaches over the likes of neural networks and decision trees [40] is that they can closely represent the inter-dependent relationships among data attributes. It is also possible to add decision nodes to extend the system into decision analysis. These networks are fast, efficient, adaptive, offer good generalizations, and are quickly trained.

14.5.3.4 Markov Model

Markov chains generate a series of state transitions, which, if violated, flag intrusions. This technique regards events as state variables in a process. An event is considered anomalous if it occurs out of sequence or with a low probability of connection with its previous state [41]. In a first-order Markov chain, the next state depends only on the current state as in Figure 14.11. There are also higher-order Markov chains, in which the probability of the next state depends on some fixed number of previous states [42]. The training stage can evaluate the states in terms of internal movements or, in a hidden Markov model, on the outputs of the system. These are commonly used in IDSs and perform well against behavioral deviations.

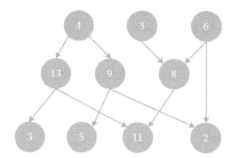

FIGURE 14.10   Directed acyclic graph.

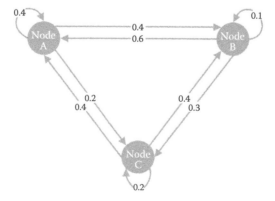

FIGURE 14.11   First-order Markov chain.

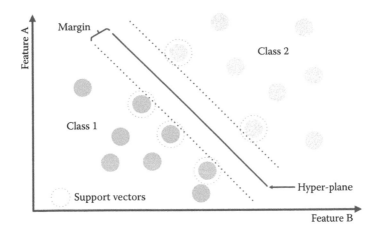

FIGURE 14.12 Support vector machine example.

14.5.3.5 Support Vector Machines

SVMs (support vector machines) create hyper-plane delimitations based on distances between points, creating maximum segments of classification [43]. The SVM finds the optimal separating plane between members and non-members of a class in a feature space. The margin, as indicated in Figure 14.12, represents the level to which the hyper-plane has managed to separate the classes, which should be maximal. However, SVM is a purely binary system and will only identify the divisions between two groups. It requires a small data sample for training and is not sensitive to the dimension of data. This approach has been shown to be effective for intrusion detection although it is more resource intensive and requires more training time.

Yu et al. [44] propose that a two-tier SVM implementation can provide the best results. The first stage categorizes the traffic into normal and abnormal, and the second stage utilizes a multi-stage SVM to identify the different attacks that are taking place, creating a hierarchy of SVMs.

14.6 ALERT CORRELATION

Once the detection algorithm has analyzed the metrics that have been provided, it generates detection alerts based on the belief that an intrusion has occurred. In a reasonably large WIDS installation, there may be multiple intrusion detection components deployed. A large number of detectors can generate a large number of alerts, potentially based on the same event. Therefore the generated alerts can be complementary, contradictory, true, false, or incomplete. Each of the alerts may also have different priorities or response time constraints. Correlating these alerts can help identify attacks, reduce unimportant events, and improve evaluation and response activities (Figure 14.13).

The ability of a correlation engine to correctly group alerts is directly related to the quality, accuracy, and completeness of data generated at the detection level and at subsequent stages that have contributed to detection performance. The most important difference between the alert correlation and intrusion detection stages is that while detection is concerned with separating "good" traffic from "bad" traffic (a divisive process), correlation is concerned with bringing those alerts with similar features together (a cohesive process). The authors in [45] observe a reduction in alert

Threat	Architect	Collect	Detect	Correlate	Evaluate

FIGURE 14.13 Correlation method within WIDS categorization.

volumes, using a correlation process in the range of 50%–99% over thousands of alerts. Generally, the steps of alert correlation can be divided into three categories:

- Pre-processing
- Correlation
- Post-processing

14.6.1 PRE-PROCESSING

The pre-process step converts alerts from various sources into a normalized format and combines multiple alerts into a single alert, removing duplicates and significantly reducing the amount of time processing and evaluation require.

14.6.1.1 Normalization

This step converts alerts into a generic format and reduces the number of alerts to be correlated. One method for normalizing this data into a useful standard is the IDMEF (intrusion detection message exchange framework). The framework requires alerts to conform to nine different attributes:

• Analyzer	• Detection time	• Target
• Create time	• Analyzer time	• Assessment
• Classification	• Source	• Additional data

14.6.1.2 Data Reduction

Reducing the data in the pre-processing stage removes redundant alerts from the processing chain. This speeds up the system, makes it more accurate and reduces the load on the human or automated response system [46]. Alerts may be

- *Aggregated*—Duplicate alerts coming from the same sensor or from different sensors. Aggregation characteristics include timestamp, source IP, destination IP, port(s), user name, process name, attack class, and sensor ID.
- *Filtered*—Removing low interest alert classes and known false alerts. These alerts are normally predefined by administrators.

Investigations in [47] advocate the use of run length encoding (RLE) to reduce alerts specifically from alert flooding attacks against a WIDS. Invoking RLE during high alert volume instances can greatly cut down on overload on the system. Only specific timing data is sacrificed.

14.6.2 CORRELATION TECHNIQUES

Correlation utilizes techniques such as feature similarity, known scenarios, prerequisite and consequence, to establish logical connections between alerts or to identify attacks that occur in stages. As the complexity and volume of attacks increases, the ability of a human or automated response system to derive meaning and context from these alerts decreases. Thus reliance on raw alert data is becoming less and less reasonable in a practical context [48].

14.6.2.1 Feature Similarity

Feature similarity clusters alert based on similarity in parameters, such as source IP, port number, target IP, etc., but cannot determine causal relationships between alerts. Links can be established for parameters, such as frequency of alerts and the number of links or associations between alerts.

For the feature similarity approach in [48], the features for the correlation engine to scrutinize included the following:

- Similarity between source IP
- Similarity between target IP
- Similarity in target port numbers
- Similarity between target IP and subsequent source IP
- Backward correlation
- Frequency of alert correlation

14.6.2.2   Known Attack Scenario

Known attack scenarios are coded using either expert rules or machine learned training rules. This uncovers the causal relationship between alerts but can only detect known intrusions. It fundamentally operates on states and transitions and attempts to identify patterns. Features in use in this approach include the following:

- Alert type (time and duplication)
- Time between alerts
- Similarity of consecutive bit of destination IP
- Similarity of consecutive bit of source IP
- Similarity of consecutive bit of last destination IP vs. new source IP

As is noted in [49] it does not necessarily follow that identified scenarios are actually intrusions. The resulting scenarios give watching administrators a better representation of the actions of the network and the ability to make more informed decisions. By grouping them into scenarios, it is hoped that false alerts will be more readily identified, and the false alert rate will drop.

Each time a new alert is produced, the likelihood that it belongs to an existing scenario is calculated. If it is unique, then a new scenario is constructed. Training on human sanitized data is needed to learn the appropriate probability measures.

14.6.2.3   Prerequisite/Consequence

The principle of this approach is that alerts do not occur in isolation; there is very often a pattern or trail of alerts from attack beginning to execution [50]. Recognizing early signs of attack can help to prevent the more damaging later stages from occurring. Combinations of alerts are generally formed with "fact, precondition, consequence" triplets in which fact is the attribute name, and precondition and consequence are logical combinations of events. The drawbacks with this approach are that it cannot detect unknown attacks, and even for known attacks, the future steps may be unclear or too numerous.

In [51], the authors implement techniques to cope with variations in attack strategy and a method of measuring the similarity between attack signatures. DAGs are automatically extracted from correlated alerts by first aggregating intrusion alerts that belong to the same step of a sequence of attacks and then extracting the constraints between the attack steps. Error-tolerant graph isomorphism is used to establish whether generated graphs are unique, similar, or subsets of each other. Using a distance calculation between graphs, the minimum number of edits necessary to change one DAG into another is the similarity measurement metric. While this approach can be computationally expensive if the graphs are large, the authors assume that in reality attack graphs will be small.

14.6.3   Post-Processing

The post-process step is used as a feedback mechanism to improve the performance of pre-processing and correlation, ranking, and prioritizing processed alerts. There may also be an intention recognition function, with which the system infers the end goal of any successful attack, informing early warning systems and potentially stopping future intrusions from escalating. The post-processing stage of the correlation engine also allows the generation of a historical database of alerts and signatures that can increase the effectiveness of the system.

14.6.3.1 Alert Prioritization

The purpose of alert prioritization is to classify alerts based on their severity and take appropriate actions for dealing with each alert class. Usually this operates as a means of finally assessing security incidents and ranking them in terms of known or expected damage.

In [52], alert prioritization is performed using two parameters: (a) The degree to which an alert is targeting a critical asset or resource, and (b) the amount of interest the user has registered for this class of security alert. Now the high priority incidents are identified for the environment within the organization within five grades from low priority to high priority. The final rank for any incident is the merging of the likelihood value and priority estimation.

14.6.3.2 Intention Recognition

Intention recognition is the process of inferring the goals of an intruder by observing their actions. This step aims to provide early warning capability and allow automatic response as well as preventing intrusions from escalating [53]. Offline data is inspected to allow a link between actions and intrusions to be determined. Intention recognition has also been considered for unique attacks in WLANs [54].

There are some issues that need to be overcome before proper intention recognition can be implemented in a network security situation [55]. The first of these issues is the tendency for attackers to try to cover their tracks. A malicious source can aim to take evasive action or masquerade in order to avoid discovery. This makes identification and root causing problematic. Second, there are practical limitations on the information sources:

- Holes in IDS coverage/unobserved actions
- Partial ordering of attack approaches
- Multiple attacker goals/effects
- Multiple hypotheses for attack intent in any situation

The plan recognition system proposed in the paper creates hierarchical options for an attacker, who is assumed to have an attack plan and does not just launch arbitrary attacks. Recognizing the plans of a hostile adversary requires implications and deductions rather than binary certainty. Due to this fact, it is difficult to recognize attacks that have long time scales. In order to compensate for unobserved events, the system may generate possibilities based on the observed actions.

14.7 EVALUATION

The final stage of the WIDS hierarchy defined here is evaluation. At this stage, decisions need to be made either by a human or an automated response system about the severity, likelihood, and impact of the alerts that are generated. It is important for the system to be able to readily identify the presence of a specific attack occurring at a specific time and the reasons for this alert in order to best inform any response or audit mechanism. Each of the planning decisions from previous steps directly contributes to the success of the outcome of the WIDS at this point; the selection of correct threats, architecture choices, metric and data collection identification, attack detection algorithm development, and intelligent correlation methods are employed (Figure 14.14).

Evaluation in the context of a WIDS covers two topics:

- Evaluation of WIDS–generated alerts
- Evaluation of the performance of the WIDS

Threat	Architect	Collect	Detect	Correlate	Evaluate

FIGURE 14.14 Evaluation method within WIDS categorization.

14.7.1 Evaluation of WIDS Alerts

The key components for administrators or automated response systems are the following:

- The volume of alerts
- The confidence in the validity of alerts
- The ability to interpret alerts in a meaningful way

It has been mentioned in [56] that these human factors of intrusion detection are more important in industry than the technology challenges, although they are interrelated. The goal at the evaluation stage for a WIDS is to reduce the amount of data displayed to the administrator, to display it in a meaningful way, and to make sure the administrator has confidence in the output presented. The success of a human administrator in evaluating the probability of an attack is based on the following information:

- False positives
- False negatives
- Visualization
- Clarity of response action

14.7.1.1 False Positives

A false positive occurs when the attack detection algorithm identifies traffic as suspicious and/or malicious but that later turns out to be legitimate. This eventuality is the greatest source of frustration for users and designers of WIDSs and reduction of false positives is a critical goal.

If an alert requires further investigation to ensure it is a true positive, then the resolution response time suffers, potentially allowing the attack to perpetuate before confirmation. Conversely, if the WIDS is deemed trustworthy and an immediate response is carried out, then the reaction could conceivably cause more harm than the false alert itself. Hence, reduction of false positives can be dependent on a trade off again between response speed and thoroughness.

Some sources [57] identify the presence and volume of false positives as a critical stumbling block of WIDSs. Intolerance of this level of WIDS false positives has led to the development of intrusion prevention systems (IPS) as an alternative. While there is much improvement required, it is important to remember that most security systems create false positives, but it is how they are dealt with that determines the success of the system.

14.7.1.2 False Negatives

A false negative occurs when an intrusion is not detected by the system or is detected by the system but flagged as legitimate. The problem of false negatives is another issue for WIDSs although, generally, reduction in false negatives can be achieved by lowering threshold limits or by reducing the precision of detection rules. Unfortunately, this tactic is likely to drastically increase the level of false positives.

14.7.1.3 Visualization

Due to the complex interactions between metrics or network components, the root causing and visualization of alerts can be problematic. For alerts and recommendations passed on to automated detection systems, this area is of little concern other than for potential human auditing. However, visualization of attack behavior and consequences is critical for any human observer in order to be able to make reasonable judgments about appropriate response.

Visualization techniques can be used to illustrate and characterize trends, events of interest, and incidents. This reduces the possibility of improperly interpreting the output of the WIDS and carrying out a potentially damaging, incorrect remediation activity. Intelligent visualization techniques represented in a timely, succinct, and meaningful format have the capability to aid the identification of and mitigation against false positives and false negatives.

Some open-source initiatives that provide IDS visualization include the following:

- *Graphviz*: Allows flowcharts and connected graphs to be automatically generated from simple text files.
- *EtherApe*: Graphical network analyzer for UNIX that displays the direction and volume of network traffic between hosts.
- *Netgrok*: A java implementation of a network analyzer that visually organizes network layout and data.

The focus of intrusive event visualization is largely related to graphic representation of traffic [61], topologies [59], decisions [60], and relationships in network activity. Demonstrating the performance of the WIDS in terms of detection performance is a method of visualization that is often overlooked and can include the following:

- *Accuracy*—In terms of percentage of detection, percentage of failure, and number of false positives.
- *Precision*—Number of predicted intrusions that were intrusions.
- *Recall*—Percentage of real intrusions covered by the system. This is quite difficult to gauge.
- *ROC curves*—ROCs (receiver operating characteristic) are detection visualization graphs that demonstrate the performance of a WIDS based on the link between false positives and true positives.
- *Timely response*—Display of the latency of alerting to an intrusion occurrence and/or speed of automated or human response.
- *Cost*—Calculating the cost associated with fighting an intrusion vs. the cost of the intrusion actually happening [61].

14.7.1.4 Response

At the top of the hierarchy, decisions need to be made about the severity, likelihood, and impact of the alerts that are generated as well as the response. Once an administrator can trust the alerts generated by a WIDS and can visualize the effect this alert is having on the network, the next step is identifying an appropriate response.

For interventions by humans, the choice of response is typically dependent on experience, and so responses can vary from person to person. This occurs due to the lack of comprehensive, effective response tactics to remediate many network attacks. Generation of these response tactics is a difficult task as serious consideration has to be put toward ensuring the response is proportionate and cost effective and does not cause more problems than the attack, such as a self DoS [61].

Recognition of this challenge has encouraged the development of IRSs (intrusion response systems), which are dealt with in greater detail elsewhere in this book. An IRS automates the human response behavior at the top level of a WIDS. Hence, many of the same issues with human response remain but with a technology rather than a human interpretation solution. This approach has many benefits, such as increase in response time, direct attribution of remediation to input data, and transfer of security responsibilities.

Implementation of an automated response strategy requires explicit trust in the performance of a WIDS and the tuning of attack detection parameters. In some cases, only those events that are classified with a high probability are dealt with by automated systems with uncertain events escalated to a human invigilator. In effect, this approach reduces the burden on human interpretation without removing it entirely. The same challenge remains in how to assist a human in making difficult security decisions.

14.7.2 EVALUATION OF WIDS PERFORMANCE

There is no simple or standardized method of verifying the performance of a WIDS against benchmarks or a method of comparing WIDSs to each other [62]. There are no open standards for testing or any public, comprehensive test suites available. Hence, assessing the performance of WIDSs proposed by academia or commercial enterprises is difficult. Scarfone and Mell [10] advocate that any evaluation should be based on the following factors:

- Configuration ability and ease
- Burden load detection system requires
- Dependence on positioning
- Processing power of detection machines

Although testing of research systems has been carried out, it was criticized [63] as suffering from only being a simulation with no real world tests and difficult tuning. Challenges that arise from trying to test a WIDS effectively include the following [10]:

- No standard, open methodology
- Need for system to be tested in real-world environments
- There are no testing suites available
- Lack of lab environment test resources
- No configuration equivalence between WIDSs

Some notable example of WIDS evaluation are demonstrated by NSS Labs* [7,9]. NSS Labs are a commercial organization that has produced reports analyzing the performance of various security products, one of which is WIDS. The most recent test on this area is from 2001 [64], however, with more modern investigations focusing on IPSs (intrusion preventing systems). Furthermore, many of the reports require subscriptions or payment for access. In [7], a confusion matrix is constructed to allow the relative coverage areas of WIDSs to be compared using attributes, such as prosecution, confirmation, identification, recognition, and detection. In [9], another confusion matrix is developed, which purports to be able to differentiate WIDSs based on their attack performance using target and attack type although this is only proposed and not proven.

Nonetheless, for academic research purposes, the statement in [14] that *"Exhaustive quantitative performance evaluations of currents IDSs in real-world environments do not exist"* unfortunately still holds true.

14.8 SUMMARY

This chapter has categorized the typical operation of a common WIDS into six sections: threat identification, architecture considerations, data collection, detection strategy, correlation method, and evaluation. These six categories are relevant for any IDS although the focus in the descriptions has concentrated on wireless IDSs.

---

* http://www.nsslabs.com/.

Discussion of the major attributes of each of these categories has demonstrated that the choice of IDS characteristics can influence the performance of subsequent stages. The field of "detection strategy" is the area of greatest current output in research; however, each of the remaining areas is either directly affected by or directly influences this stage in the process. Consequently, more work is needed to ensure that the data and recommendations produced by one stage are appropriate and meaningful for subsequent stages and, crucially, have easily evaluable and root causing components.

Maintaining a credible link between an indication of an attack occurring and comprehensible evaluation for a human administrator or automated response system should be the primary objective throughout the entire process. Future research should take into account the interrelationship between the stages and not solely consider them in isolation. Poor choices in the design of lower stages in the WIDS process can impact on the outcome of the entire system, leading to cascading suboptimal performance.

AUTHOR'S BIOGRAPHY

Jonny Milliken is a post-doctoral researcher at the Queen's University Belfast (QUB), Belfast, UK. He was awarded an MEng (first class) from QUB in 2009 with a specialization in WiFi intrusion detection systems, and he holds CAPM and LCGI qualifications. He graduated from QUB in December 2012 with a PhD investigating WiFi intrusion detection strategies for public and open access WLANs. Jonny's research interests include WiFi and cyber security, WiFi malware, testbed development, disaster response methods, and national infrastructure security, and his current work examines applications of WiFi for emergency search and rescue scenarios. He is also a member of IEEE and the IET and is involved with the IAESTE and ERASMUS programs in Northern Ireland.

REFERENCES

1. Hansman, S. and Hunt, R., A taxonomy of network and computer attacks, *Computers & Security*, vol. 24, pp. 31–43, Feb 2005.
2. Lough, D., A taxonomy of computer attacks with applications to wireless networks, PhD Dissertation, Virginia Polytechnic Institute, Blacksburg, Virginia, 2001.
3. Kumar, S., Classification and detection of computer intrusions, PhD Dissertation, Dept. Elec. Eng., Purdue University, West Lafayette, Indiana, 1995.
4. Straub, Jr., D.W. and Widom, C., Deviancy by bits and bytes: Computer abusers and control measures, in *Proc. of the 2nd IFIP International Conference on Computer Security*, pp. 431–441, Toronto, Canada, 1984.
5. Simmons, C. et al., AVOIDIT: A cyber attack taxonomy, University of Memphis, Tennessee, August 2009.
6. Killourhy, K.S. et al., A defence-centric taxonomy based on attack manifestations, in *Proc. of the International Conference on Dependable Systems and Networks*, Florence, Italy, 2004.
7. Tucker, C.J. et al., A new taxonomy for comparing intrusion detection systems, *Journal of Internet Research*, vol. 17, pp. 88–96, 2007.
8. Harrison, K. and White, G., A taxonomy of cyber events affecting communities, in *Proc. of the 44th Hawaii International Conference on System Sciences*, Hawaii, USA, 2011.
9. Milliken, J. and Marshall, A., The threat victim table: A security prioritisation framework for diverse network topographies, in *Proc. of the 2010 International Conf. on Security and Cryptography (SECRYPT '10)*, Piraeus, Greece, pp. 1–6, 2010.
10. Scarfone, K.A. and Mell, P.M., Guide to intrusion detection and prevention systems (IDPS), *National Institute of Science and Technology*, 2007.
11. Milliken, J. and Marshall, A., Design and analysis of an independent, layer 2, open-access WiFi monitoring infrastructure in the wild, in *Proc. of the 2012 International Conf. on Wireless Networks (ICWN '12)*, Las Vegas, USA, 2012.
12. Molina, J. and Cukier, M., Evaluating attack resiliency for host intrusion detection systems, *Journal of Information Assurance and Security*, vol. 4, pp. 1–9, 2009.
13. Verwoerd, T. and Hunt, R., Intrusion detection techniques and approaches, *Journal of Computer Communications*, vol. 25, pp. 1356–1365, 2002.

14. Helmer, G. et al., Lightweight agents for intrusion detection, *Journal of Systems & Software*, vol. 67, pp. 109–122, Aug 2003.

15. Dayong, Y.M.Z. et al., P2P distributed intrusion detections by using mobile agents, in *Proc. of the Seventh IEEE/ACIS International Conference on Computer and Information Science (ICIS '08)*, Paris, France, 2008.

16. Vigna, G., Mobile agents: Ten reasons for failure, in *Proc. of the IEEE International Conference on Mobile Data Management*, California, USA, 2004.

17. El-Khatib, K., Impact of feature reduction on the efficiency of wireless intrusion detection systems, *IEEE Transactions on Parallel and Distributed Systems*, vol. 21, pp. 1143–1149, Aug 2010.

18. Afansyev, M. et al., Usage patterns in an urban WiFi network, *Journal of IEEE/AM Transactions on Networking (TON)*, vol. 18, pp. 1359–1372, Oct 2010.

19. Zargar, P.B. and Kabiri, G.R.A., Category-based selection of effective parameters for intrusion detection, *International Journal of Computer Science and Network Security*, vol. 9, Sept 2009.

20. Ying, L. et al., The design and implementation of host-based intrusion detection system, in *Proc. of the Third International Symposium on Intelligent Information Technology and Security Informatics (IITSI '10)*, Jinggangshan, China, 2010.

21. Flack, C. and Atallah, M.J., Better logging through formality, in *Proc. of the Third International Workshop on Recent Advances in Intrusion Detection (RAID '00)*, Toulouse, France, 2000.

22. Mutz, D. et al., Anomalous system call detection, *ACM Transactions on Information and System Security (TISSEC)*, vol. 9, pp. 61–93, 2006.

23. Sangmee, P. et al., Anomaly detection using new MIB traffic parameters based on profile, in *Proc. of the 8th International Conference on Computing Technology and Information Management (ICCM '12)*, Berlin, Germany, 2012.

24. Qin, X. et al., Integrating intrusion detection and network management, in *Proc. of the IEEE/IFIP Network Operations and Management Symposium (NOMS '02)*, Florence, Italy, 2002.

25. Fragkiadakis, A.G. et al., Anomaly-based intrusion detection of jamming attacks, local versus collaborative detection, *Journal of Wireless Communications and Mobile Computing*, vol. 13, 2013.

26. Milliken, J. et al., The effect of probe interval estimation on attack detection performance of a WLAN independent intrusion detection system, in *Proc. of the IET International Conf. on Wireless Communications and Applications (ICWCA '12)*, Kuala Lumpur, Malaysia, 2012.

27. Qu, G. et al., Abnormality metrics to detect and protect against network attacks, in *Proc. of the IEEE/ACS International Conference on Pervasive Services (ICPS '04)*, Beirut, Lebanon, 2004.

28. Chebrolu, S. et al., Feature deduction and ensemble design of intrusion detection systems, *Journal of Computers & Security*, vol. 24, pp. 295–307, June 2005.

29. Lu, W. and Traore, I., An unsupervised approach for detecting DDoS attacks based on traffic-based metrics, in *Proc. of the IEEE Pacific Rim Conference on Communications, Computers and Signal Processing (PACRIM '05)*, Victoria, Canada, 2005.

30. Stakhanova, N. et al., Classification and discovery of rule misconfigurations in intrusion detection and response devices, in *Proc. of the 2009 World Congress on Privacy, Security, Trust and the Management of e-Business (CONGRESS '09)*, New Brunswick, Canada, 2009.

31. Stakhanova, N. et al., On the symbiosis of specification-based and anomaly-based detection, *Journal of Computers and Security*, vol. 29, pp. 253–268, 2010.

32. Gill, R. et al., Specification-based intrusion detection in WLANs, in *Proc. of the 22nd Annual Computer Security Applications Conference (ACSAC '06)*, Miami, USA, 2006.

33. Depren, O. et al., An intelligent intrusion detection system for anomaly and misuse detection in computer networks, *Journal of Expert Systems with Applications*, vol. 29, pp. 713–722, Nov 2005.

34. Gharibian, F. and Ghorbani, A.A., Comparative study of supervised machine learning techniques for intrusion detection, in *Proc. of the Fifth Annual Conference on Communication Networks and Services Research (CNSR '07)*, New Brunswick, Canada, 2007.

35. Hu, W. et al., Unsupervised active learning based on hierarchical graph-theoretic clustering, *IEEE Transactions on Systems Man and Cybernetics*, vol. 39, pp. 1147–1161, Oct 2009.

36. Mahajan, V.S. and Verma, B., Implementation of network traffic classifier using semi supervised machine learning approach, in *Proc. of the 2012 Nirma University International Conference on Engineering (NUiCONE '12)*, Ahmedabad, India, 2012.

37. Dasgupta, D. and Majumdar, N., A comparison of negative and positive selection algorithms in novel pattern detection, in *Proc. of the IEEE International Conference on Systems, Man, and Cybernetics*, Nashville, USA, 2000.

38. Liu, G. and Wang, X., An integrated intrusion detection system by using multiple neural networks, in *Proc. of the IEEE Conference on Cybernetics and Intelligent Systems (CIS '08)*, London, 2008.

39. Qiang, X. et al., A survey of some classic self-organizing maps with incremental learning, in *Proc. of the 2nd International Conference on Signal Processing Systems (ICSPS '10)*, Dalian, China, 2010.

40. Abbes, T. et al., Protocol analysis in intrusion detection using decision tree, in *Proc. of the International Conference on Information Technology: Coding and Computing (ITCC '04)*, Las Vegas, USA 2004.

41. Lee, D.-H. et al., Multi-stage intrusion detection system using hidden markov model algorithm, in *Proc. of the International Conference on Information Science and Security (ICISS '08)*, Hyderabad, India, 2008.

42. Huang, L. and Stamp, M., Masquerade detection using profile hidden markov models, *Journal of Computers & Security*, vol. 30, pp. 732–747, Nov 2011.

43. Zhou, H. et al., Application of support vector machine and genetic algorithm to network intrusion detection, in *Proc. of the International Conference on Wireless Communications, Networking and Mobile Computing (WiCOM '07)*, Shanghai, China, 2007.

44. Yu, J. et al., Traffic flooding attack detection with SNMP MIB using SVM, *Journal of Computer Communications*, vol. 31, pp. 4212–4219, Nov 2008.

45. Valeur, F. et al., A comprehensive approach to intrusion detection alert correlation, *IEEE Transactions on Dependable and Secure Computing*, vol. 1, pp. 146–169, 2004.

46. Sadoddin, R. and Ghorbani, A.A., Alert correlation survey: Framework and techniques, in *Proc. of the International Conference on Privacy, Security and Trust (PST '06)*, Ontario, Canada, 2006.

47. Tedesco, G. and Aickelin, U., Adaptive alert throttling for intrusion detection systems, *Journal of Intelligent Information Systems*, 2003.

48. Zhu, B. and Ghorbani, A.A., Alert correlation for extracting attack strategies, *International Journal of Network Security*, vol. 3, pp. 244–258, 2006.

49. Dain, O., and Cunningham, R., Fusing a heterogeneous alert stream into scenarios, *ACM Computer and Communications Security*, vol. 6, pp. 103–122, 2002.

50. Ning, P. et al., Constructing attack scenarios through correlation of intrusion alerts, in *Proc. of the 9th ACM Conference on Computer and Communications Security (CCS '02)*, Washington, D.C., USA, 2002.

51. Ning, P. and Xu, D., Learning attack strategies from intrusion alerts, in *Proc. of the 10th ACM Conference on Computer and Communications Security (CCS '03)*, Washington, D.C., USA, 2002.

52. Fong, M. et al., A mission-impact-based approach to INFOSEC alarm correlation, in *Proc. of the Conference on Recent Advances in Intrusion Detection (RAID '02)*, Zurich, Switzerland, 2002.

53. Chintabathina, S. et al., Plan recognition in intrusion detection systems using logic programming, in *IEEE Conference on Technologies for Homeland Security (HST '12)*, Massachusetts, USA, 2012.

54. Chen, G. et al., An intelligent WLAN intrusion prevention system based on signature detection and plan recognition, in *Proc. of the Second International Conference on Future Networks (ICFN '10)*, Sanya, China, 2010.

55. Geib, C.W. and Goldman, R.P., Plan recognition in intrusion detection systems, *Proc. of the DARPA Information Survivability Conference and Exposition II (DISCEX '01)*, California, USA, 2001.

56. Ibrahim, T. et al., Assessing the challenges of intrusion detection systems, in *Proc. of the 7th Annual Security Conference*, Las Vegas, USA, 2008.

57. Gartner, Gartner information security hype cycle declares intrusion detection systems a market failure, 2003.

58. Corchado, E. and Herrero, A., Neural visualization of network traffic data for intrusion detection, *Applied Soft Computing*, vol. 11, pp. 2042–2056, 2011.

59. Yang, L. et al., Alerts analysis and visualization in network-based intrusion detection systems, in *Proc. of the IEEE Second International Conference on Social Computing (SocialCom '10)*, Minnesota, USA, 2010.

60. Horn, C. and D'Amico, A., Visual analysis of goal-directed network defense decisions, in *Proc. of the 8th International Symposium on Visualization for Cyber Security (VIZSEC '11)*, Pennsylvania, USA, 2011.

61. Stakhanova, N. et al., On evaluation of response cost for intrusion response systems, in *Proc. of the Conference on Recent Advances in Intrusion Detection (RAID '08)*, Massachusetts, USA, 2008.

62. Wilkinson, M., Intrusion detection FAQ: How to evaluate network intrusion detection systems? SANS Institute, 2001.

63. Kumar, S. and Spafford, E.H., A pattern matching model for misuse intrusion detection, in *Proc. of the 17th National Computer Security Conference*, Maryland, USA, 1995.

64. NSS Labs, Intrusion detection systems: Group test (edition 2), Technical Report, NSS Labs, Cambridgeshire, England, 2001.

15 Cross Layer–Based Intrusion Detection Techniques in Wireless Networks
A Survey

Subir Halder and Amrita Ghosal

CONTENTS

15.1 INTRODUCTION

Wireless communication has been fast emerging as an important research paradigm, and its utility in several application areas is also gaining momentum. It is being implemented in various interesting application areas, such as battlefield surveillance, traffic monitoring, health care, environment monitoring, etc. [1]. Day-to-day experiments are being conducted for testing the feasibility of wireless networks in several new upcoming areas. Wireless networks make use of the unguarded wireless medium for communication that is largely responsible for making security one of the prime factors of importance in such networks. One of the prime networking requirements is the layered protocol architecture. Although layered architectures in wired networks have performed quite well, their use in wireless networks is still a debatable issue. This is because these networks are generally resource-constrained, and therefore, the concept of cross-layer architectures being used here is becoming quite popular. So cross-layer methodology came into the picture involving more than one layer and exploiting the dependence between protocol layers (Figure 15.1) instead of independent working of layers in layered networks.

Researchers working in the wireless network platform have always tried to use lightweight security schemes that are robust enough to handle the attacks faced by these networks. An IDS is one such area, use of which is gaining fast momentum in sensor networks. An IDS is defined as a system that tries to detect and alert attempted intrusions into a system or a network [2]. Intrusion detection is a set of actions that discover, analyze, and report unauthorized and damaging activities. A block diagram representing a basic IDS [3,4] is shown in Figure 15.2. It can be seen from Figure 15.2 that

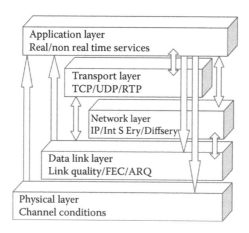

FIGURE 15.1 Dependencies among the protocol layers.

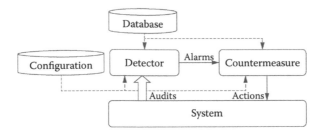

FIGURE 15.2 Block diagram of basic intrusion detection system.

the IDS receives audit information from the system it is protecting. There are several inputs that include a database containing presently known attacks, the current configuration of the system, and audit information that describe the events as they are happening in the system. When the detector has access to all the required data, it decides which information is important and deduces the possibility of normal actions that can be considered as indications of intrusions. Here, an IDS is used with the aim of detecting any breach in confidentiality and integrity and reduced availability of resources.

Coupled with cross-layer techniques [5], cross layer–based intrusion detection designs in wireless networks are coming up as a promising research area. Cross-layer design techniques are adopted for achieving optimization in network operation involving two or more layers whose parameters can be modified. Cross layering is preferred over a layered technique as it provides efficient routing, reduced energy consumption, and optimal scheduling. Therefore, all these factors make cross layer–based intrusion detection a viable design option for wireless networks from the perspective of securing such networks.

15.1.1 Limitations of Single Layer–Based Intrusion Detection

In the recent past, several new approaches have been proposed for enhancing the security of wireless networks including ad-hoc networks, mobile ad-hoc networks (MANETs), wireless sensor networks (WSNs), vehicular ad-hoc networks (VANETs), wireless local area networks (WLANs), and mobile cloud by use of intrusion detection. In these proposed works, every layer consists of a dedicated intrusion detection technique for detecting intruders. In such a dedicated intrusion detection technique, each layer has several limitations. Here we have examined, similar to [6], the limitations of such current approaches in terms of detecting intrusions in the wireless network.

(a) *Likelihood of attack on multiple layers*: Wireless networks are subject to adversarial attacks of various natures. These attacks are not targeted at a particular layer. For example, a denial of service (DoS) attack that prohibits channel access to legitimate users can manifest itself in several malicious ways at different layers. So it is quite evident that no single layer solution is adequate for detecting all possible attacks in wireless networks. Hence, it is more convincing that security solutions should span across all layers wherein each layer may contribute in the malicious detection process.

(b) *Redundant detection mechanism*: Several works have been done on detecting intruders in wireless networks. The proposed detection techniques mainly work on a particular layer for detecting threats associated with that layer. Although detection at every layer can mitigate the attacks and provide better defense, such designs may not be affordable in dynamic and resource-constrained wireless networks. This is because providing a separate detection mechanism at every layer can introduce redundant detection and result in increased power and resource consumption. Instead of independent detections at each layer, joint intrusion detection by different layers might be more effective in detecting attacks.

(c) *Lack of adaptive detection*: An efficient IDS is evaluated by its accuracy and reliability. In a mobile environment, due to the dynamics of channel and network conditions, detection systems encounter the challenge of distinguishing an attack from network irregularities that occur due to genuine reasons. This results in an increase in false positives rates. Following a layered approach for detecting intrusions, an actual network anomaly could be misunderstood as an attack of adversarial nature. By forcing layer interactions, intrusion detection systems (IDSs) can obtain information about the network behavior from other layers to make a more informed decision at the detection layer. This reinforces the argument that protocol layers need to interact and exchange parameters for building a robust detection system.

15.1.2 MOTIVATION

Security is a major area of concern in wireless networks due to their high susceptibility and exposure to different types of attacks. It is difficult to handle the security issues in wireless networks because of unreliable wireless links, frequent change in network topology, and an absence of a centralized system. Attacks in wireless networks can take place in more than one layer, and this issue has led to research in the multi-layer security solutions for such networks. A security mechanism designated for one layer cannot protect the other layers. So solutions are needed for providing detection mechanisms in all layers of the network. But these are not feasible to a great extent in resource-constrained wireless networks. Also, independent security solutions at different layers can result in conflicting actions leading to performance degradation. So the need is ensuring joint addressing of security and network reliability in all the protocol layers through cross-layer techniques. Cross-layer security mechanisms have also been found to be effective in protecting the wireless networks from attacks [7]. Also cross-layer security mechanisms perform well as compared to traditional approaches. This can be done through proper interaction and coordination among different protocol layers for developing a robust IDS suitable for wireless networks. Adopting cross-layer intrusion approach facilitates collaborative detection that results in effective fault diagnosis and reduced false alarms [8]. All these have motivated us to take up this chapter.

15.1.3 CHAPTER ORGANIZATION

This chapter has been organized as follows: Section 15.2, presents a layer-based classification of wireless network security threats and their defense solutions. Section 15.3 provides some important design requirements that must be supported by an ideal cross layer–based IDS for detecting a significant percentage of intrusions. Section 15.4 addresses the issue of appropriate architectures for cross layer–based IDS and examines various design restrictions and their feasibility in order to build an efficient, reliable IDS. There are certain parameters that interact among the protocol layers for enhancing the detection of malicious intrusions in wireless networks. The impact of such parameters on network security along with the advantages and limitations of cross layer–based IDS are discussed in Section 15.5. Section 15.6 provides existing cross layer–based IDS along with detailed descriptions of wireless networks, including ad-hoc networks, MANETs, WSNs, VANETs, WLANs, and mobile cloud. Section 15.7 deals with performance issues, and Section 15.8 talks about open issues in cross layer–based IDS. Finally, Section 15.9 concludes this chapter.

15.2 ATTACKS IN WIRELESS NETWORKS AND COUNTERMEASURES

Wireless networks are vulnerable to security attacks due to the broadcast nature of the transmission medium. They have an additional vulnerability because nodes are often placed in a hostile or dangerous environment where they are not physically protected. For a large-scale wireless network, it is impractical to monitor and protect each individual node from physical or logical attack. Attackers may devise different types of security threats to make the wireless system unstable. Here, in this section, we present a layer-based classification of wireless network security threats, and based on the capability of the attacker, appropriate defenses are proposed in the literature.

15.2.1 Attacks in Physical Layer

An attacker can attack the physical (PHY) layer in the form of getting physical access to the device with the objective of tampering with it. The information from the nodes can also be obtained by the adversary if it is not secured properly, which can be used further for launching different attacks. Some prevalent PHY-layer attacks in wireless networks are the following:

(a) *Jamming*: It is one form of DoS attack [9]. Here, the adversary attempts to disrupt the operation of the network by broadcasting a high-energy signal. This attack can be defended by using spread-spectrum techniques for radio communication.
(b) *Radio interference*: The adversary produces huge interference intermittently or persistently [10]. This can be handled with the use of symmetric key algorithms in which the disclosure of the keys is delayed by some time interval.
(c) *Tampering or destruction*: The attacker physically attacks the nodes for obtaining vital information, such as cryptographic keys, or other data in the nodes. This attack can be defended by tamper-proofing the node's physical package [11]. Whenever the nodes are accessed physically, they vaporize their memory contents preventing any leakage of information.

15.2.2 Attacks in Data Link/Medium Access Control Layer

Adversaries exploit the exponential back-off feature for launching attacks by sending data continuously in the medium. Also, they may send request to send (RTS)/clear to send (CTS) packets with a large amount of data for unlimited time, resulting in nodes waiting for an indefinite period of time. Attackers can also introduce errors on the medium by means of wireless interference. All these can be defended by limiting the data rates of nodes and also by use of time division multiple access (TDMA) in which a fixed time slot is allocated to every node for transmitting data. Some attacks that take place in the data link layer are given below:

(a) *Continuous channel access (exhaustion)*: In this attack, a malicious node disrupts the network communication by continuously requesting or transmitting over the channel leading to starvation for other nodes in the network with respect to channel access. One countermeasure of such an attack can be rate limiting using admission control mechanisms such that the network can ignore excessive requests, thus preventing the energy drain caused by repeated transmissions [10,11].
(b) *Collision*: This is very much similar to the continuous channel attack. A collision occurs when two nodes attempt to transmit on the same frequency simultaneously. Collisions result in changes in the data portion, causing a checksum mismatch at the receiving end. The packet is then discarded as invalid. A typical defense against collisions is the use of error-correcting code [10,11].
(c) *Unfairness*: This attack takes place on repeated application of exhaustion or collision-based medium access control (MAC) layer attacks or an abusive use of cooperative MAC–layer priority mechanisms. This kind of attack is a partial DoS attack, but results in marginal performance degradation. One major defense mechanism against such attacks is the use of small frames, so that any node occupies the channel for a smaller duration only [10,11].

(d) *Interrogation*: Here the attacker exhausts a node's resources by repeatedly sending RTS messages for receiving CTS responses from the targeted node under attack. To put a defense against such type of attacks, a node can limit itself in accepting connections from the same identity or use anti-replay protection and strong MAC–layer authentication [9,12].

15.2.3 ATTACKS IN NETWORK LAYER

The attacker in this layer can send a huge amount of packets containing false routes so as to over-flow the neighbors, resulting in routing tables containing fake data. This can be prevented by using packet leashes to the routing packet for restricting its transmission beyond some constraints. Some common attacks of the routing layer are the following:

(a) *Sinkhole*: In a sinkhole attack, the adversary tries to attract almost all the traffic towards the compromised node, creating a metaphorical sinkhole with the adversary at the center. Geo-routing protocols are known as one of the routing protocol classes that are resistant to sinkhole attacks. This is because the topology in such protocols is constructed using only localized information and traffic is routed through the physical location of the sink or base station, which makes it difficult to attract it anywhere else for creating a sinkhole [13–15].

(b) *Hello flood*: This attack exploits HELLO packets that are required in many protocols for the purpose of announcements. A node receiving such packets may assume that it is in the radio range of the sender. A laptop-class adversary can send this kind of packet to all nodes in the network so that they believe the compromised node is their neighbor. This causes a large number of nodes sending packets to this imaginary neighbor. Authentication is the key solution to such attacks [13–15].

(c) *Node capture*: It has been observed that even a single node capture can cause devastating network failure. It can happen if the attacker captures a node and is able to retrieve all the important information required for network operation. Using this information, the adversary disrupts the overall functioning of the network [14,15].

(d) *Selective forwarding*: In this type of attack, malicious nodes refuse to route certain messages and drop them. If they drop all the packets through them, then it is called a black hole attack. However, if they selectively forward the packets, then it is called selective forwarding. To overcome this, multi-path routing can be used in combination with random selection of paths to a destination [14,15].

(e) *Wormhole attack*: Here, an adversary tunnels messages received in one part of the network over a low latency link and replays them in another part of the network. This is usually done with the coordination of two adversary nodes in which the nodes try to understand their distance from each other by broadcasting packets along an out-of-bound channel available only to the attacker. To overcome this, the traffic is routed to the base station along a path that is always geographically shortest [14,15].

(f) *Spoofed, altered, or replayed routing information*: The most direct attack against a routing protocol in any network is to target the routing information itself while it is being exchanged between nodes. An attacker may spoof, alter, or replay routing information in order to disrupt traffic in the network. These disruptions include the creation of routing loops, attracting or repelling network traffic from select nodes, extending and shortening source routes, generating fake error messages, partitioning the network, and increasing end-to-end latency. A countermeasure against spoofing and alteration is to append a message authentication code after the message. Efficient encryption and authentication techniques can also defend spoofing attacks [15].

(g) *Misdirection*: This is a more active attack in which a malicious node present in the routing path can send the packets in the wrong direction through which the destination is unreachable. In place of sending the packets in correct direction, the attacker misdirects those towards one node, and thus this node may be victimized. If it is observed that a node's network link is getting flooded without any useful information, then the victim node can be scheduled into sleep mode for some time to overcome this [15].

15.2.4 Attacks in Transport Layer

The attacks taking place in this layer can be in the form of generation of false acknowledgment with large window size, acknowledging replay attacks, jamming acknowledgments, sequence number alterations, and connection request spoofing. Protocols such as transport layer security (TLS) or secure socket layer (SSL) can be used as the defense mechanisms against such attacks. Some general attacks in this layer are the following:

(a) *Flooding*: An attacker may repeatedly make new connection requests until the resources required by each connection are exhausted or reach a maximum limit. It produces severe resource constraints for legitimate nodes. One proposed solution to this problem is that each connecting client demonstrates its commitment to the connection by solving a puzzle. As a defense against this class of attack, a limit can be put on the number of connections from a particular node [14,15].

(b) *De-synchronization attacks*: In this attack, the adversary repeatedly forges messages to one or both end points, which request transmission of missed frames. Hence, these messages are again transmitted, and if the adversary maintains a proper timing, it can prevent the end points from exchanging any useful information. This will cause a considerable drainage of energy of legitimate nodes in the network in an endless synchronization-recovery protocol. A possible solution to this type of attack is authentication of all packets, including control fields communicated between nodes [14,15].

15.2.5 Attacks in Application Layer

This layer faces threats from much malicious software, such as viruses, worms, etc., as well as from insider nodes. Some attacks taking place in this layer are the following:

(a) *Overwhelm attack*: In this attack, the adversary attempts to overwhelm network nodes causing the network to forward large volumes of traffic to the base station. This attack consumes network bandwidth and drains node energy. This attack can be mitigated by carefully tuning sensors so that only the specifically desired stimulus, such as vehicular movement, triggers them as opposed to any movement. Rate-limiting and efficient data-aggregation algorithms can also reduce these attacks' effects [9].

(b) *Path-based DoS attack*: This involves injecting spurious or replayed packets into the network at leaf nodes. This attack can starve the network of legitimate traffic because it consumes resources on the path to the base station, thus preventing other nodes from sending data to the base station. Combining packet authentication and anti-replay protection prevents these attacks [9].

Various types of attacks on wireless networks at different layers and countermeasures that can be used to protect against these attacks as discussed above are summarized in Table 15.1.

TABLE 15.1

Summary of Attacks in Different Layers of Wireless Networks

Layers	Active Attacks	Passive Attacks		Solutions
Physical	Signal jamming, tampering			Spread-spectrum, priority messages, lower duty cycle, region mapping
Data Link	Exhaustion, unfairness, adversarial attack			Error correcting codes, small frames, rate limitation
Network	Wormhole, blackhole, byzantine, table overflow, cache poisoning, rushing attack	Location disclosure attack	Eavesdropping traffic analysis and monitoring	Secure routing protocols
Transport	De-synchronization attacks			Secure transport protocol
Application	Repudiation, malicious software			Intrusion detection systems, firewalls

15.3 DESIGN REQUIREMENTS FOR CROSS LAYER–BASED IDS

In this section, we have highlighted some important design requirements that any cross layer–based IDS must fulfill. There are two key design requirements for any cross layer–based IDS. They are effectiveness—how to make the cross layer–based IDS classify harmful and benign activity correctly and efficiently—how to run the cross layer–based IDS in a cost-effective manner as far as possible [5]. To be more specific, these two requirements, in essence, suggest that cross layer–based IDS should detect a substantial percentage of intrusions in the supervised system while keeping the false positive rates [16] at an acceptable level at a lower cost. It is expected that an ideal cross layer–based IDS is likely to support several of the following requirements:

15.3.1 Attack Detection Reliability

In order to build a reliable IDS, it is necessary to avoid misclassification of a non-malicious node as a malicious entity in the network. While measuring the efficiency of an IDS, the metric for attack detection reliability has immense impact on the performance of the IDS. In a cross layer–based IDS, attack detection reliability is primarily measured by calculating the false positive rates of the detection system. False positive rate is defined as the ratio of number of false alarms raised by the IDS to the total number of suspicious sources.

15.3.2 False Negative Ratio

In an IDS, it is desirable to prevent misclassifying intrusions and minimize false positives. It is also equally essential that the IDS must be capable of detecting any potential attacks accurately in the network. When the system circumvents an attack, it results in false negatives. Let ζ denote the total intrusion attacks in the network and γ be the true positive ratio denoting the number of attacks successfully detected by the IDS. Then the false negatives ratio Ω is defined as

$$\Omega = \frac{\zeta - \gamma}{\zeta}.$$

15.3.3 Detection Stability

The main challenge towards building a robust cross layer–based IDS is that the system must be consistent and uniform while detecting an intruder. Also, the cross layer–based IDS must act reliably under varying channel conditions and traffic loads. These external factors are primary causes for an increase in false positive ratio in a wireless environment.

15.3.4 Detection Capability

Most of the existing IDS techniques have considered misuse-based detection schemes wherein the IDS successfully detects known attacks using the attack signature patterns. However, in order to detect unknown attacks, anomaly-based intrusion detection schemes are preferred. Anomaly-based intrusion detection schemes detect attacks without use of any attack signatures, leading to higher false positives. The capability of the IDS is thus defined both in terms of the detection technique as well as its capacity to overcome failures.

15.3.5 Traffic Latency

The cross layer–based IDS must ensure that it does not incur any negative impact on the performance of the network due to its presence. Although the presence of cross layer–based IDS may introduce a certain amount of delay in the network traffic, the optimal operating point must be such that one can attain efficient detection with tolerable traffic latency.

15.3.6 Throughput

Throughput is another network performance metric that should be considered while designing cross layer–based IDS. During the intrusion detection process, the IDS must ensure that network capacity is not throttled. Also, the intrusion detection overhead must be kept at minimum possible extent. In distributed mobile environments, node mobility usually results in lower network throughput. Therefore, it is essential for the IDS to take the mobility factor also into consideration. Thus in varying network dynamic situations, a trade-off between performance and detection is essential for demand-driven and adaptive cross layer–based IDS.

15.4 ARCHITECTURE FOR CROSS LAYER–BASED IDS

In this section, we have investigated the suitability of cross-layer architectures for IDSs in wireless networks. As we are aware that cross-layer designs typically combine or extract information from two or more layers of the protocol stack, therefore, for creating a system, information can be shared either between adjacent layers or non-adjacent layers. Although there is no standard cross-layer architecture for intrusion detection, mostly the cross-layer detections are realized through direct interaction between the layers or through a structured method using a shared database [5]. In [8], authors have developed two generalized architectures for cross-layer IDS: One is based on direct per-layer interaction, and another is based on a shared database. Each of the developed architectures has merits and demerits. However, both the architectures yielded higher detection accuracy. We have described each of the architectures for cross-layer IDS along with their strengths and weaknesses in this section.

15.4.1 Direct per-Layer Interaction-Based Architecture

The design goal of direct per-layer interaction-based architecture is to improve malicious detection and better evaluation of malicious activity in the network. In this type of cross-layer IDS architecture, information is exchanged directly between two adjacent or non-adjacent layers of the protocol stack such that the layer adaptations result in improved end-to-end network performance. A schematic overview of the direct per-layer interaction-based architecture is given in Figure 15.3.

To achieve the design goal, every layer in the network protocol stack collects audit data by actively monitoring the channel. Whenever an anomaly is detected in a particular layer using its audit data information, it triggers or initiates detection at another layer. Such probe-based or event-based detection helps in confirming the malicious behavior of a node. For instance, a malicious packet drop in a network can be observed and detected through promiscuous network monitoring watchdog schemes. However, in wireless networks, packet drops can also occur due to poor channel quality, link contention, or network congestion. Hence, apart from relying on the network statistics from an individual layer, anyone can confirm the presence of this attack using the knowledge of current channel conditions from the lower layers.

Using such direct exchange of information between layers, IDS can detect intrusions with a higher confidence level. In [17], through simulation it has been shown that the designed architecture for cross layer–based IDS has improved the accuracy of intrusion detection. Also, it has been shown that the design architecture lowers the false positives. Although direct per layer–based architecture for cross-layer IDS has shown promising results in terms of detection efficiency, still there are certain shortcomings associated with these designs in terms of overall system optimizations. The architectural limitations of this design have been elaborated below.

(a) *Influences of detection protocol*: Direct interactions between the protocol layers in a cross-layer system might sometimes result in unintentional network consequences. For example, if the congestion information is used by the detection protocol in other layers to confirm malicious behavior, it leads to improved detection. But if a cross-layer network optimization design exists that chooses network routes according to the congested state of the network, then the exchange of detection information might lead to adverse routing protocol consequences.

The information passed through the network layer influences the routing protocols to choose less congested paths. Those chosen paths may either consist of longer hops or a higher percentage of malicious nodes. Therefore, the chosen paths have negative impact on the overall network performance.

(b) *Internal overhead*: Because the local intrusion detection mechanisms do not involve communication within a network, so it is free from any external overhead. However, communication among the layers through internal packets results in internal overhead of a node. The size of the overhead is proportional to the size of the audit data information collected through the internal packets. Availability of more information for sharing between the

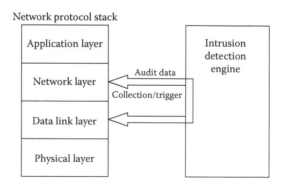

FIGURE 15.3   Direct per-layer interaction-based architecture for cross-layer IDS.

layers means efficient IDS with fewer detection errors but with high internal overhead. Thus, there exists a trade-off between obtaining lower false alarms at the cost of internal overhead.

(c) *Stability*: Another weakness of the direct per-layer interaction-based architecture is that it might result in system instability. Because detection information may be relayed back and forth among the layers, it may cause unnecessary loops in the system. Therefore, care should be taken to avoid such loops while adopting cross layer–based schemes.

(d) *Modularity*: Another disadvantage of detection using direct cross-layer designs is the loss of modularity in the protocol stack. Because detection approaches at different layers are no longer functionally independent, they impact each other and significantly affect the network optimizations. It is important to account for this architectural design weakness for developing robust cross-layer IDS in wireless networks.

Through appropriate modifications and enhancements in the developed framework and addressing the above limitations of cross layer–based designs, one can build stronger and successful architectures for cross layer–based IDS in wireless networks.

15.4.2 SHARED DATABASE-BASED ARCHITECTURE

This generalized architecture for cross-layer IDS is based on the shared database. In this architecture every layer of the protocol stack interacts with a common shared IDS server as shown in Figure 15.4. An interface, i.e., audit data collection module, is provided between the network elements at different layers and the cross-layer detection unit. An audit data collection module collects network information, intrusion alerts, and other such events from different layers at the IDS database for detecting network intrusion. Finally, the information collected from the various layers is correlated for obtaining accurate detection mechanisms.

The shared database-based architecture for cross-layer IDS is simpler and easier to manage due to significant difference between the protocol layers. The database unit possesses a local and global view of the network. An intelligent optimizing unit in the detection system ensures that the detection scheme can counter and adjust according to the varying threat levels in the network. This type of architecture is, in general, preferred to direct layer interactions, and it is free from the limitations associated with the direct per-layer interaction-based architecture. The reasons are as follows:

(a) *Modularity*: In the structural design of shared IDS, protocol interactions occur through a well-defined interface with a common database system. This ensures that the modularity of the network protocol stack is preserved to a certain extent. Instead of exposing the

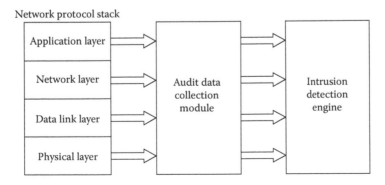

FIGURE 15.4 Shared database-based architecture for cross-layer IDS.

information across all layers, only the minimum necessary information is shared. Interface to the database thus enables parallel and independent evolution of the layers. As the protocol influences among the layers are kept at minimum, it improves the system efficiency.

(b) *Stability*: Because the layers of the protocol stack do not communicate directly with each other, and each layer interacts with a shared database, the system facilitates a controlled information transfer. As the database is responsible for coordinating detection information gathered across the layers, there is minimum possibility of loops created among the layers. This adds stability to the network.

(c) *Implementation complexity*: The shared database-based architecture has significant overhead in terms of updating parameter information obtained from all layers. However, compared to the direct per-layer interaction-based architecture, it has a lower implementation cost. It is because every layer in direct per-layer interaction-based architecture performs monitoring and triggering the network for intrusions. The shared database-based architecture, on the other hand, obtains the state information from the layers and triggers detection on a need basis.

An outline of the differences between the two cross-layer IDS architectures are given in Table 15.2. It can be concluded from Table 15.2 that the shared database-based architecture performs better in terms of higher system stability and lower implementation complexity. Although both the architectures provide good performances in terms of improving the detection accuracy, still there are significant differences in overall system optimization. Therefore, based on the requirements, one must select the appropriate cross-layer design for an IDS.

15.5 CONSTRAINS AND CHALLENGES FOR CROSS LAYER–BASED IDS DESIGN

Cross-layer designs typically combine or extract information from two or more layers of the protocol stack [8]. Cross-layer integration enables us to analyze the attack scenario in its entirety, and as a result, better performance in terms of both higher true positive and lower false positive rates [16] is achieved. The selection of correct combination of layers in the design of cross-layer IDS is very critical for detecting attacks targeted at or sourced from any layers rapidly. In this section, we describe major constraints and challenging parameters along with the advantages and limitations for cross layer–based IDS design.

15.5.1 PARAMETERS FOR CROSS LAYER–BASED IDS

Recent literature reveals a growing interest in exploring the cross-layer architecture and its rich parameter interactions among the protocol layers in wireless networks [6]. Although several

TABLE 15.2

Comparison of Two Cross-Layer IDS Architectures

Performance Metric		Architecture	
		Direct Per-Layer Interaction	Shared Database
Detection efficiency	Detection rate	High	High
	False positive	Very low	Low
Modularity		Low	Medium
Stability		Low	Medium
Protocol complexity		High	Low
Implementation complexity		High	Low
Resource consumption		Low	High

optimization opportunities are presented through layer interactions in varying network domains, the impact of such parameter exchanges on network security has not been analyzed. In this section, similar to [6], we explore some of the parameters that need to be considered while designing an efficient cross layer–based IDS in a distributed wireless network.

15.5.1.1 Channel Conditions

The wireless link between nodes in a mobile distributed network is susceptible to malicious attacks, such as eavesdropping, interference, and jamming. But these links are also vulnerable to wireless channel errors due to noise, fading, non-malicious interference, and poor link quality. Nodes may also malfunction resulting in network abnormalities. Due to such volatile characteristics, the wireless network performance may degrade to a significant extent. In such scenarios, the conventional IDSs may not be effective as they tend to overlook such genuine irregularities and misjudge the network behavior as a malicious attack.

In an effort toward building an efficient detection system, the current information about channel status may be beneficial in making the right decision. Typically, because lower layers can easily obtain the information about channel status, detection procedure at higher layers may utilize such data periodically from the lower PHY and MAC layers. Intrusion detection systems are bound to gain detection accuracy through such layer communications.

15.5.1.2 Carrier Sensing Time

At the PHY layer of the protocol stack, physical carrier sensing is used for determining the busy or idle state of a channel. This metric can be useful in estimating the channel utilization, defined as the amount of time the channel remains busy or idle around a node. When an attack, such as jamming, occurs, a measure of channel utilization from lower layers may indicate the occurrence of jamming in the channel. Navigation attacks at the MAC layer manipulate the network allocation vector field of a node, resulting in misuse and wastage of channel bandwidth. In such cases, periodic monitoring of channel utilization may be useful in detecting an idle channel for longer durations. Thus, exchange of information about physical carrier sensing time may assist in the detection process.

15.5.1.3 Channel Contention

Channel contention at the MAC layer measures the number of nodes contending for channel access. Collision occurs when more than one node attempts to reserve a channel for its use. Channel contention can be measured by monitoring the transmission in a wireless channel and the inter-frame spacing intervals. Knowledge of node positions in a radio range is also useful for determining the level of contention. When there are fewer nodes contending for the channel, if frequent collisions occur, an inconsistency in the network is observed. The real-time information about the channel contention status can thus facilitate collision detection at a node.

15.5.1.4 Retransmission Count

At the MAC layer of the protocol stack, control and data packets that are not acknowledged are retransmitted until a predefined retransmission threshold. The retransmission count is a useful metric that can be exchanged among the layers. This count is a MAC layer measure of the node's attempt of transmitting a packet to its next hop node. Detection of network layer attacks, such as packet drop, can be made more effective by obtaining the statistics of packet drop at the MAC layer. This information may also help in reducing frequent route updates at the network layer.

15.5.1.5 Congestion Level

Jamming and collision attacks occur in wireless networks due to simultaneous transmission of more than one node in a given radio range. However, often, a congested network with high traffic intensity might be the cause of packet collisions in the network. Network congestion level is a valuable measure of exchange between layers for understanding the erratic network behavior. This information may also help in eliminating any false conclusions about the network behavior, thus reducing false positive rates.

15.5.1.6 Power Consumption

Because mobile networks may be made of devices that are typically battery powered, power consumption is an important factor for consideration while designing network architectures. In order to conserve energy at critical conditions, certain nodes may demonstrate perceived selfish behavior, such as dropping forwarding packets. Few nodes may also appear to misbehave by not participating in routing process due to resource constraints. Detection at the network layer for packet drop attacks might incorrectly conclude such nodes as malicious and is harmful for the network. Accounting for a node's power statistics will substantially increase detection performance.

15.5.2 ADVANTAGES OF CROSS LAYER–BASED IDS

Cross-layer designs usually combine or extract information from two or more layers of the protocol stack. Information is shared either between adjacent layers or non-adjacent layers to create a system with an ease of adaptability. Existing literature reveals that cross-layer based IDS design leads to several advantages, and they are as follows:

- Several existing single layer–based IDSs have ensured mitigation of attacks and provided better defense against intruders. But such single layer–based IDSs may not be affordable in dynamic and resource-constrained wireless networks. This is because providing a separate detection mechanism at every layer can introduce redundant detection and result in increased power and resource consumption. Instead of independent detections at each layer, cross layer–based intrusion detection by different layers might be more effective in detecting attacks.
- In a mobile environment, due to the dynamics of channel and network conditions, an IDS faces the major challenge of distinguishing an attack from network irregularities. In presence of network irregularities, the false positive rates of the IDS increases. Following a single layered approach for detecting intrusions, an actual network anomaly could be misconstrued as an attack of an adversarial nature. By forcing cross-layer interactions, IDSs could obtain the information about the network behavior from other layers to make a more informed decision at the detection layer. Therefore, using this cross-layer interaction ultimately helps to build a robust as well as accurate and reliable IDS.
- The use of cross layer–based IDS for intrusion or malicious behavior detection has ensured improved probability of intrusion detection and maximized the detection accuracy.
- The use of cross layer–based IDS has also ensured performance optimization in terms of bandwidth, energy, and other resources.

15.5.3 LIMITATIONS OF CROSS LAYER–BASED IDS

Cross-layer methodologies are prone to certain boundaries and limitations according to the nature of their designs. It is possible that providing interfaces between the layers might sometimes lead to conflicting results in the network performance. In this section, we examine these limitations involved in adopting cross-layer design techniques.

(a) *Loss of modularity*: The success of the Internet today is primarily attributed to its open systems interconnection (OSI) protocol stack architecture. This layered architecture provides the abstraction and modularity to independently design protocols. With cross-layer interactions, however, the layering structure is broken, and the network design becomes complicated. Researchers lose the flexibility and capability of designing a particular protocol layer without impacting other layers.

(b) *Interactions and unintended consequences*: Cross-layer couplings enable information sharing and assist in network optimization. Creation of such interdependencies across protocol layers may inadvertently cause performance losses. For instance, an implementation change in the MAC protocol at the lower layer may affect the performance of a routing protocol at the network layer by creating paths with longer hops and delays. It is hence important for the designers to account for these layer interactions.

(c) *Adaptation loops*: Another significant challenge with information transfer between higher and lower layers is the potential creation of adaptation loops in the system. When an uncontrolled interaction occurs, each layer may become dependent on information from another layer leading to loops and causing system instability.

(d) *Chaos of unbridled cross-layer designs*: Because there are no independent layer modules in a cross-layer architecture, their implementation using network tools is a big challenge. Designers fear a software implementation of the cross-layer design might result in unstructured spaghetti-like code [7].

15.6 STATE-OF-THE-ART CROSS LAYER–BASED IDS

Cross layer-based intrusion detection techniques have been used in wireless networks in recent years. This section explores the use of intrusion detection in cross-layer by wireless networks including ad-hoc networks, MANETs, WSNs, VANETs, WLANs, and the mobile cloud. First the cross-layer exploiting IDS in ad-hoc networks and MANETs are described followed by their use in sensor networks, VANETs, WLANs, and the mobile cloud. Very limited work has been done on intrusion detection in cross layers for WSNs, VANETs, WLANs, and the mobile cloud. We have tried our level best to compile all the existing works on IDS–based cross-layering techniques in WSNs, VANETs, WLANs, and the mobile cloud.

15.6.1 Cross Layer–Based IDS in Wireless Networks

In this section, a brief description of each of the existing works in cross layer-based intrusion detection technique for wireless networks are presented.

Singh et al. [18] have proposed a cross layer–based intrusion detection technique for wireless networks. In the proposed technique, received signal strength (RSS) has been used for creating a dynamic profile for the communicating nodes. Along with RSS, authors have measured the time taken for the RTS–CTS handshake at the server for reliable passive attack (e.g., session hijacking attack) detection. Next, using these two parameters, i.e., RSS and time taken for the RTS–CTS handshake, authors have computed a combined weight value. Now, if the computed combined weight value is greater than a pre-computed threshold value, then those nodes are considered as attackers. Finally, through simulation, authors have shown that by adjusting the pre-computed threshold value and the weight constants, it is possible to reduce the false positive rate significantly. Also, they have shown that the proposed cross layer–based IDS attains a low misdetection ratio and false positive rate while increasing the packet delivery ratio.

Bansal et al. [19] have proposed a cross layer–based IDS architecture for wireless networks, especially for wireless mesh networks. The proposed architecture consists of two levels of intrusion detection as shown in Figure 15.5. First level intrusion detection monitors intrusions in a particular layer and shares the monitored information with other layers. Second level intrusion detection detects numerous intrusions in a layer using information collected from the first level. Finally, to confirm about the malicious nodes, the information obtained from various layers of the protocol stack are

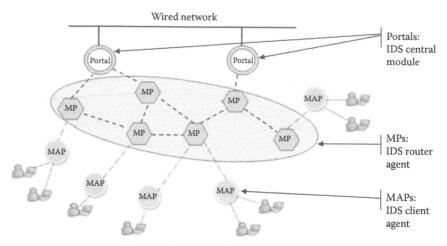

MP: Mesh point, MAP: Mesh access point

FIGURE 15.5 Two-level IDS architecture.

combined and analyzed. As the information is collected from different layers for detecting intrusion, therefore, the proposed architecture provides more accurate detection. Authors have claimed that their proposed cross layer–based IDS is efficient in detecting multi-layer internal attacks. Also the proposed cross layer–based IDS can detect low-intensity attacks and attack-switching behavior.

Chiang and Hu [20] have proposed a cross layer–based jamming detection system for wireless broadcast networks. The proposed system initially works by building an asymmetric system using a spread-spectrum technique. To be more specific, authors have used fast frequency hopping code division multiple access (FFH-CDMA) as a spread-spectrum technique for building an asymmetric system. The use of the FFH-CDMA technique is to divide the entire spectrum into a number of frequency bands, and each user is assigned a frequency hopping pattern. The user remains on any frequency band for one time slot, the duration of which is much shorter than the time it takes to send one bit, and changes frequencies according to its frequency hopping pattern. Based on this concept, each transmitter builds a balanced binary tree of randomly generated hopping patterns. The transmitter associates each legitimate receiver with a unique leaf in this binary tree and gives this receiver the hopping patterns corresponding to that leaf and all ancestors of that leaf in the tree. If there is no jamming in the network, a transmitter transmits the hopping pattern corresponding to the root of the tree, and it only can be decoded by a legitimate receiver. Now, if any jamming occurs on some hopping pattern, the transmitter removes those hopping patterns and adds hopping patterns corresponding to its two children. Here, in the proposed system, each receiver cooperates with the transmitter to detect any jamming in the network. Authors have claimed that the proposed system mitigates the jamming attack while allowing the transmitter to transmit on fewer codes than the number of users. Finally, through simulation, they have shown significant improvement of the proposed technique over naively transmitting on a single shared code for mitigating the jamming attack.

In another work [21], Chiang and Hu have proposed a cross layer–based jamming attack detection and mitigation system for wireless broadcast networks. The proposed system uses spread-spectrum as a part of modulation technique. To be more specific, fast-frequency-hopping code division multiple access (FFH-CDMA) and the direct-sequence code division multiple access (DS-CDMA) are used as a spread-spectrum technique for securing the communication. In the spread-spectrum technique, each user is assigned with a different set of spreading codes, and it changes over time. Now, in order to secure the spreading codes, authors have used a code tree scheme, which is similar to the binary key tree. In the initial phase of the proposed scheme, a transmitter transmits to all receivers on a single spreading code; specifically, it chooses the spreading code corresponding to the root of the tree. Transmissions on this spreading code can be decoded by any legitimate receiver if the code is not jammed. In order to ensure that every receiver can decode a packet while minimizing the number of spreading codes simultaneously used, the transmitter needs to transmit on a set of spreading codes such that any user can decode using exactly one spreading code in the set. To receive a message, each receiver simply decodes the signal using all the codes that it knows. Now, if any jamming occurs on some hopping pattern, the transmitter removes those hopping patterns and adds hopping patterns corresponding to its two children. Authors have shown that any system that relies on only using spreading code and no other physical factors to mitigate jamming must use at least $(j + 1)$ codes, where j is the number of jammers. Finally, authors have developed a technique called tree remerging to optimize the keying scheme so that a transmitter can group benign receivers together and let that group share one spreading code. To support the theoretical results, simulation has been performed and results shows that jamming can be effectively mitigated in a broadcast wireless system by the proposed system.

Kyriakopoulos et al. [22] have proposed a cross layer–based intrusion detection method for detecting a man-in-the-middle (MitM) attack in wireless networks. In the proposed method, authors have fused knowledge collected from multiple layers for making ultimate decisions about the attack. Authors have identified a number of metrics, e.g., received signal strength indication (RSSI), the transmission rate (or injection rate), and the time to live value (TTL), for improving the belief of whether an attack takes place or not. The beliefs from different metrics are fused with the Dempster–Shafer (D–S) technique with the ultimate goal of limiting false alarms. Finally, authors have performed testbed experiments and shown that cross-layer techniques and data fusion perform more efficiently in a variety of situations compared to conventional methods. Also the results show that the proposed cross layer–based intrusion detection method outperforms in terms of efficiency and accuracy than the single layer–based methods.

15.6.2 Cross Layer–Based IDS in Ad Hoc Networks and MANETs

A brief description of each of the existing works in ad-hoc networks and MANETs cross layer-based intrusion detection methods are given below.

In [23], Thamilarasu et al. have presented a decentralized IDS in cross layers for ad hoc networks. The IDS–based cross-layering mechanism is used for detecting the jamming attack in the network. The design incorporates mechanisms for differentiating the malicious jamming attack from actual network failures. The scheme has been implemented in two phases: phase I and phase II. Channel monitoring is performed at the MAC layer for detecting jamming in both the PHY and MAC layers. Detection of the attack is performed in phase I. If detection is confirmed in phase I, phase II detection is triggered using a cross-layer design technique for obtaining network congestion. This helps in distinguishing between an actual attack and normal network congestion. The IDS–based cross-layer design has been validated through simulation for showing the effectiveness of the model. Simulation results have proved that this scheme performs well with respect to accuracy of detection and lowering false positives.

Thamilarasu and Sridhar [24] have developed a scheme for detecting and mitigating DoS attacks, such as collision and packet drop attacks. A cross layer–based IDS referred to as CIDS is proposed by the authors for identifying the malicious nodes. A host-based IDS is considered that is present in every host and is responsible for monitoring its neighborhood for detection of any abnormalities. A cross-layer design framework is adopted that exchanges the detection information across the layers and triggers multiple levels of detection. This helps the IDS in making a more informed decision about the intrusion in the network. The reasons behind considering cross-layer design are to detect intrusion at multiple levels of the protocol layers and to exploit the information, such as energy and congestion, from one layer for accurate detection of intrusion in another layer. An intrusion detection mechanism is activated by triggering detection across the protocol layers. Two levels of intrusion detection are present here: level 1 detection and level 2 detection. Level-1 detection information is obtained from detecting DoS attacks in one layer and sharing that information with another layer. Level 2 detection is done by using information from other layers for multiple attack detection in one layer. Accuracy of detection is increased using this scheme as multiple detections are used. The rate of false positives is also lowered as the cross-layering design uses the knowledge of the network and node conditions for determining the misbehavior of any node.

Liu et al. in [25] have proposed a node-based IDS in cross layers for ad hoc networks. Information from the MAC and network layers is considered for creating a profile containing the normal behavior of normal nodes. For anomaly detection, a rule-based data mining technique is adapted. The IDS is effective in detecting any attack and localizes the attack zone within one perimeter. The IDS designed consists of four components: data collection module, profile module, detection module, and decision module. The data collection module is responsible for collecting the network activities within a network. The profile module has two subsystems: a pre-processor and a profiler. In the pre-processor, audit data is transformed for the profiling process. In the profiler, a rule-based data mining technique is employed along with a priori algorithm that is used for finding the association rules from audit data. In the detection module, anomaly detection is used for detecting any deviation from normal working. The test data profiles are compared with the expected normal profiles. A threshold level is considered, and if any testing result is below the threshold, it is considered as an anomaly. The false positive rate is reduced through the decision module of the IDS in which the intelligence gathered from neighbor nodes is used for making a collective decision and from a Bayesian network for evaluating multiple attack sources. The decision module also performs the task of triggering an alert, which is, at first, a local alert followed by a global alert used for warning the neighboring nodes. This work focuses on traffic-related attacks, such as resource consumption, flooding, deprivation attacks, and black hole attacks. Simulation results show the effectiveness of this work in detection of such attacks with low false positive rates.

Similar to the previous related work, in this work [26], Shrestha et al. have proposed a cross layer–based intrusion detection mechanism for identifying the malicious nodes in MANETs and various DoS attacks using the information available from the different protocol layers for better detection accuracy. The proposed cross layer–based IDS architecture is shown in Figure 15.6. Cooperative anomaly intrusion detection along with data mining techniques have been used here. The benefit of using a data mining technique improves the overall efficiency and effectiveness of the nodes. The clustering algorithm for this scheme uses fixed width clustering for detection efficiency. Also, the IDS employs a cross-layering technique for proper interaction between the network layers. An association module has been used for associating the OSI protocol stack and IDS module so as

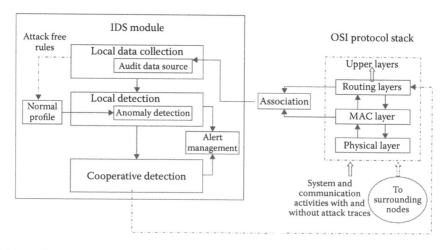

FIGURE 15.6 Cross-layer IDS architecture based on data mining technique in MANETs.

to lessen the overhead during data collection. The routing protocol and MAC protocol layers are chosen for detection of routing attacks. Clustering-based intrusion detection is adopted here as it is capable of detecting new attacks. Simulation has been performed using the OPNET simulator, and results prove the efficacy of this scheme.

In this paper [27], authors have proposed an IDS for detecting malicious packet dropping behavior in MANETs. Here, mobility aspects are considered using a heuristic that takes into consideration the forwarding process operation at the nodes. Also, using this heuristic approach, a significant improvement of the system's detection performance is achieved as false positive rates are low. The heuristic uses fundamental features of the network and MAC layers and is responsible for detecting malicious dropping actions against those resulting from legitimate movement of nodes. In this work, the ad hoc on demand distance vector (AODV) routing protocol is considered. Every node keeps track of its neighbor nodes (those with which it can communicate directly) by listening to HELLO messages broadcast at regular intervals by each node. The effectiveness of the proposed cross layer–based IDS is evaluated using two parameters: true positive rate and false positive rate.

In [28], the authors have proposed a cross layer–based IDS with an objective of detecting DoS attacks in ad hoc networks. The authors mainly focus on DoS attacks that propagate from MAC to routing layer resulting in disruption of important routes. They have presented many traffic patterns that can be followed by the attacker node for launching DoS attacks. The attacks considered are those that follow low rate traffic patterns. The attack detection is done using extended finite state machines (EFSM), and the IDS used has the capability of generating traffic patterns and checking the validity of communication patterns.

Authors in [29] have focused their work primarily on studying the feasibility of routing attack detection in MANETs using different IDS schemes. Also, they have studied the possibility of cross-layer IDS in MANETs for overcoming the problem faced by such networks with respect to minimal infrastructure, security threats, etc. The results of both cross-layer IDS and single-layer IDS were compared, and cross-layer IDS was found to perform much better than single-layer IDS. The cross-layer IDS architecture used in this work is decentralized in nature. The routing protocol used here is the optimum link-state routing (OLSR) protocol. Two types of attacks prevalent in such networks, namely sinking and spoofing, are detected in this work using the linear discriminant analysis (LDA) [30] classification technique.

In [31], the authors proposed an autonomous host-based IDS for detecting malicious behavior by the sink in cross-layer architecture. The reason for choosing cross-layer architecture is for maximizing the detection accuracy. A learning approach and adaptation to new attacks in the network are considered here. Support vector machine (SVM) and Fisher discriminant analysis (FDA) are used in a combined manner for achieving better accuracy of SVM and speed of FDA. The proposed IDS preprocesses the training data for reducing the computational overhead incurred by SVM. A number of features in the training data are also reduced using predefined association functions. The data reduction techniques employed here have made it possible for SVM to be implementable in ad hoc networks. Several experiments were performed considering different network conditions and the behavior of malicious nodes using metrics, such as mobility, traffic density, etc. Based on the experimental results, it can be inferred that this scheme outperforms other existing cross-layer IDS schemes.

15.6.3 Cross Layer–Based IDS in WSNs

Recently, a number of solutions for detecting intrusion have been proposed specifically for WSNs. Most of these intrusion detection solutions are concerned with attacks on one protocol layer. Such single-layered intrusion detection mechanisms are inadequate in providing security for WSNs, so cross layer–based intrusion detection mechanisms are needed to improve the security performance. In this section, we have described state-of-the art cross layer–based IDSs developed by various authors in WSNs.

Hortos [32] has proposed a cross layer–based IDS for detecting various intrusion attacks in WSNs. Here, security attributes are set up initially. Quantified trust levels at and among nodes are obtained by collecting data during network operation based on certain metrics, e.g., energy usage, reliability, route availability, and end-to-end quality-of-service. Next, statistical pattern recognition algorithms, which provide best network global performance, are applied on the data collected during network operation. In the proposed cross layer–based IDS, a set of mobile (software) agents are distributed among the nodes, which execute statistical pattern recognition algorithms by moving among the layers. The benefits of using mobile agents are that they significantly reduce communication overhead formed due to security mechanisms and the latency in network response. Also, the use of a mobile agent increases the fault tolerance in the network against intrusion. Because the mobile agents can behave like an ant colony, therefore, the author has considered that mobile agents perform ant colony optimization routines and other evolutionary algorithms on the data collected during network operation for detecting and responding to denial-of-service attacks. Finally, simulation has been performed for validating the proposed cross layer–based IDS and to show that it successfully detects few intrusion attacks, including black hole, flooding, and Sybil attack.

In another work, Hortos [33] has proposed a cross layer–based distributed intrusion detection and identification system for WSNs. Within the proposed system, swarm intelligence and unsupervised and supervised algorithms have been developed for providing the capability of processing large amounts of observed data to detect and recognize various intrusion attacks. The proposed system uses a two-stage processing procedure as shown in Figure 15.7 for detecting intrusion and identifying attack types. In the first stage, a model is built using an unsupervised clustering algorithm. This is done for detecting anomalies using a feature set formed from key parameters from the layers including PHY layer, MAC layer, network layer, transport layer, presentation layer, and application layer. In the second stage, supervised learning is applied on the detected results from the first stage for determining the intrusion type. As supervised learning is similar to traditional supervised classification approaches in which, in addition to patterns of normal behavior, profiles of known intrusion attacks are available for a priori training data, therefore, it can easily determine the intrusion type. In order to minimize movement of large amounts of audit-log data and locate routines closer to that data, the author has used a set of mobile software agents. Performance of the proposed two-stage cross layer–based IDS is evaluated through simulation considering black hole, flooding, and Sybil attacks. Results shows that the proposed two-stage cross layer–based IDS is more robust over the existing single-layer IDS.

In both of the above systems [32,33], the author has ensured a minimized communication overhead, but still there is significant computational overhead. Computational overhead can be reduced by using cooperative intrusion detection techniques.

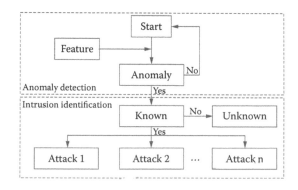

FIGURE 15.7 Structure of cross layer–based two-stage intrusion detection/identification procedures.

In [34], Hortos has proposed a cross layer–based intrusion detection approach for WSNs by combining multiple bio-inspired or evolutionary computational methods. The author has initially studied several bio-inspired or evolutionary computational methods for the functions of a single protocol layer in WSNs. For example, swarm intelligence in the form of ant colony optimization (ACO) has been used for detecting intrusions in the network layer while genetic algorithms (GAs) have been used for detecting an intrusion in the PHY layer. Similarly, anti-phase synchronization has been used for detecting intrusion in the MAC layer while artificial immune systems (AISs) have been considered for detecting intrusion in the application and presentation layers. Based on the outcomes of the studies, the author has proposed a cross layer–based intrusion detection scheme embedding GAs, anti-phase synchronization, ACO, and a trust model based on quantized data reputation at the PHY, MAC, network, and application layers, respectively. Finally, through simulation, it has been shown that the synergies among the bio-inspired or evolutionary methods of the proposed cross layer–based intrusion detection technique improve the overall performance of detecting intrusion in WSNs over that of a single computational method.

Boubiche and Bilami [35] use the concept of cross-layer interaction for detecting different types of attacks on several layers of the OSI model for WSNs. Here the MAC layer uses the cross-layer information from the network and PHY layers for detecting possible intrusions. Once intrusion is detected, actions such as dropping a packet, flagging a neighbor, etc., can be taken. This topology divides the network into several clusters and selects as the cluster head (CH) node that which has the greatest energy reserves in the cluster. The basic idea of this IDS is to detect intruders when they attempt to communicate with the network nodes. After receiving RTS packets of the intruder nodes by the targeted node, the detection system checks if it is one of the neighbors in the routing path (by consulting the routing table at the network layer). In addition, the authenticity of the intruder node will be checked by measuring the RSSI of the received packet (at the PHY layer). By using the routing information at the MAC layer, each sensor node can previously know the source of packets that will be received. Thus, any node trying to communicate (receive RTS or CTS packet) with the sensor nodes is immediately detected as an intruder if it is not included in the routing path. All network nodes can detect the intruders and the probability of detection augments gradually with the expansion of the number of attacked nodes and the decreasing of the collusion amount. Authors have proposed an agent-based cross-layer architecture, i.e., a cross-layer intrusion detection agent (CLIDA) as shown in Figure 15.8. The CLIDA agent is the entity through which the layers and applications communicate. It includes essentially two parts: the interaction interface and the cross-layer data module. The interaction interface facilitates the contact between the layers and application on one hand and the CLIDA agent on the other hand. The interaction interface takes as its main objective the management of sub-interfaces that provide access to the layers. Each sub-interface describes methods for reading and writing to facilitate the manipulation of parameters of the corresponding protocol. Via these methods is made the collection and/or updating data (e.g., the value of the calculated RSSI, routing tables, etc.).

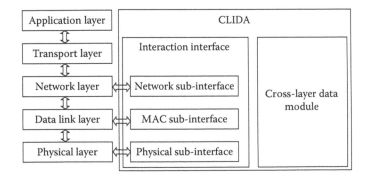

FIGURE 15.8 Agent-based cross-layer intrusion detection architecture.

The cross-layer data module represents data in a special way to make them quickly accessible by all layer protocols. Data provided by this module are the basis for any cross-layer adaptation and optimization. The module is also responsible for maintaining up-to-date data through cross-layer interaction interfaces.

In [36], Hortos has proposed a two-stage cross-layer intrusion detection identification technique for WSNs. The proposed technique considers a two-stage processing procedure in order to detect intruders similar to [33]. However, in the present work, the author has considered a different set of bio-inspired algorithms in each stage compared to the previous work. In the first stage, a bio-inspired, cross-layer neural-network (NN) algorithm is developed, based on the bio-inspired routines used at the PHY, MAC, network, and application/presentation layers. The second stage is based on reputation-based versions of a SVM and a K nearest neighbor (KNN) routine. Similar to [33], here also the algorithm is implemented via a system of mobile software agents. Through quantitative analysis, authors have shown that the proposed two-stage cross-layer intrusion detection identification technique can reduce complexity, distribute storage utilization, and respond robustly to a variability in sensor data compared to the previous work [33].

15.6.4   Cross Layer–Based Security Techniques in VANETs

After exploring the security techniques proposed in VANETs to our best possible extent, we came across a very limited number of papers that deal with cross layer–based IDS for providing security. For this reason, we were bound to include papers dealing with either cross-layer security mechanisms or solely IDS techniques in VANETs in this section.

Leinmüller et al. [37] have presented a modular cross-layer intrusion detection approach for enhancing security in VANETs. This scheme uses context information from systems, such as global positioning system (GPS), radar, or sensors, to evaluate the plausibility of information received via the network. The main issue is combining events on different layers and from different entities for detecting intrusion. In every node, different modules are responsible for collecting audit data on different layers. A local decision module continuously receives audit data. After that, it analyzes them with the aid of additional information, available from other non-network devices, such as GPS, sensors, and radar. Besides the central decision module, the different modules are a monitoring module for the network and routing layer, a context information module, an application evaluation module, an action module, and a module for communication with IDSs on other nodes. The monitoring module is responsible for collecting data on communication within the node's communication range. The current neighboring nodes' position data can be verified by active probing messages or GPS and sensor data from the context information module in order to help to identify abnormal or malicious node behavior. On the application layer, the received warning messages are first evaluated by the application evaluation module, which uses knowledge from applications in combination with sensor data provided by the context information module. This approach is neither purely based on anomaly-based detection nor on signature-based detection. The scheme has been effective in detecting the intrusions occurring in the network.

Singh and Sharma [38] have introduced a technique using an IDS for detecting wormhole attacks in VANETs. This is done by implementing a modular cross-layer IDS. There are various modules that are used for collecting audit data in different layers. A local decision module and a central decision module are used for detection purposes. In the application layer, the received warning messages are first evaluated by the application evaluation module, which uses knowledge from applications, in combination with sensor data provided by the context information module. The effectiveness of the IDS is tested by simulation using true positive and true negative values.

Biswas and Misic [39] have proposed a cross-layer approach for anonymous authentication and verification for WAVE-based VANETs. It provides vehicular message authentication as well as an efficient prioritized verification strategy for periodic road safety messages. The main objective of this work is preserving the privacy of messages as well as conditional authentication for signing and verifying vehicular safety application messages. A variant of enhanced distributed channel access (EDCA) is developed for this purpose. The probability of successful delivery of message broadcasts is dependent on two factors: WAVE's EDCA traffic class and traffic load. This enables the receiver for scaling the message verification rates. If traffic is dense, message verification is done by chronologically ordering them according to their relevance. As this approach is an identity-based signature approach, the common geographical area information of signing vehicles is taken as the signer's identity. Also a cross-layer message verification scheme verifies messages based on their MAC traffic class and traffic intensity so that it can be ensured that during rush hour congestion important messages are not overlooked by the verifier. Security analysis and performance evaluation of this scheme justifies the authentication and verification approach used in WAVE-enabled vehicular communication.

15.6.5 Cross Layer–Based Security Techniques in WLANs

Similar to the reason cited in Section 15.6.4, in this section, also we have described security-related works in WLANs related to either cross layer, intrusion detection, or both.

Gill et al. [40] have proposed an approach for constructing an IDS for infrastructure WLANs using a specification-based approach. The proposed IDS implements both attack detection and policy compliance monitoring. The benefit of using a specification-based approach, unlike observing and learning correct behavior during a training phase, represent a promising direction for improving the utility of anomaly-based IDSs and reducing their false positive or false negative rate. The specification used by the system comprises a state transition model and set of constraints. The correct model of behavior used by the proposed IDS is formed from a specification that is derived by combining a model of the underlying protocol state machines with the constraints imposed by the security policy of the system. Authors have evaluated the accuracy and sensitivity of the proposed IDS and shown that the IDS is capable of passively detecting all known attacks and is effective in monitoring for policy compliance. Also, authors have shown through experiments that the technique, when combined with the use of indices of suspicion, is able to detect all intrusions with a minimal number of false positives (i.e., the technique is accurate) and no attacks went undetected (i.e., the technique is sufficiently sensitive).

Tian et al. [41] have presented two anomaly intrusion detection methods in WLAN. One method is based on a hidden Markov model (HMM) whereas another one is based on adaptive resonance theory (ART). The ART method uses a learning algorithm to build a model for normal behavior and anomalous behavior. The main characters of these two methods are that they do not need expert knowledge and can efficiently detect intruders in real time. Authors have performed experiments for measuring the performance of the proposed two methods. The results show that the methods can find DoS attacks immediately and detect new intruders with low false alarm rates. However, the main drawback of both the proposed methods is that some parameters must be known a priori, such as probability matrices for HMM and threshold value for ART for efficient intrusion detection.

Kaur [42] proposed a cross layer–based intrusion detection strategy for WLANs under inconsistent miss detection ratio. The proposed strategy uses RSS as a parameter of the PHY layer and another parameter, RTS–CTS handshake time of the MAC layer, for detecting intruders. At first, RSS value is computed by the base station from the omni-directional antenna at the mobile station. Second, in the MAC layer, RTS–CTS handshake time is computed by the base station. Based on these two values, the server computes a threshold value (D_{thr}) for that session. In each subsequent session, the server also computes threshold value (D_{th}) based on the present RSS and RTS–CTS time and compares between D_{thr} and D_{th}. For a mobile station, if computed D_{th} is more than D_{thr} then that mobile station is designated as an attacker. Through simulation, authors have shown that the use of cross-layer information for detecting intruders effectively reduces the false positive rate in the proposed strategy.

15.6.6 CROSS LAYER–BASED SECURITY TECHNIQUES IN MOBILE CLOUD

As the mobile cloud is a very emerging topic, we could find no work dealing with its security based on cross-layer intrusion detection techniques. Therefore, we have illustrated those works that provide security in the mobile cloud using either cross-layer or intrusion-detection techniques.

Dastjerdi et al. [43] have proposed scalable, flexible, and cost-effective methods for detecting intrusion for cloud applications using mobile agents regardless of their locations. This method aims for protecting virtual machines (VMs) that are outside the organization. A mobile agent collects evidence of an attack from all the attacked VMs for further analysis and auditing. This approach is used for detecting intrusion in VMs migrated outside the organization. However, it produces more network load, if numbers of VMs are attached to mobile agent increases. The advantages of the proposed approach include achieving higher scalability; overcoming network latency; reducing network load and, consequently, lower operational cost; executing asynchronously and autonomously; adopting dynamically; operating in heterogeneous environments of clouds; and having robust and fault-tolerant behavior. The main components are IDS control center (IDS CC), agency, application-specific static agent detectors, and specialized investigative mobile agent.

Static agents are responsible for generating an alert whenever they detect suspicious activities, then saving those activities' information in a log file and send alerts ID to the IDS control center. Alerting the console in the IDS control center analyzes the coming information and compares and matches with intrusion patterns in the IDS CC database. It raises an alarm if intrusion is detected. The IDS control center saves the information received from investigative mobile agents into its database. Experimental results show that a scheme is efficient enough for increasing the performance of the IDS.

Vieira et al. [44] have proposed a hybrid IDS architecture for the cloud environment. Here, each node of the cloud contains IDS, which provides interaction among service offered, IDS service, and storage service. IDS service comprises two components: the analyzer and alert system. The event auditor captures data from several resources such as system logs. The IDS service is used for detecting intrusion on the basis of the data received from an event auditor by using a behavior-based technique or knowledge-based technique. The knowledge-based technique is used for detecting known attacks whereas the behavior-based technique is used for detecting unknown attacks. For detecting unknown attacks, an artificial neural network (ANN) is used in this approach. When any attack or intrusion is detected, an alert system informs the other nodes. So this approach is efficient for detecting known attacks by using a knowledge base as well as unknown attacks by applying feed forward ANN. Results show that the false positive and false negative alarm rate is very low when large numbers of training samples of intrusion attacks are applied for the behavior analysis method. The limitation of this approach is that it cannot detect any insider intrusions that are running on VMs.

Houmansadr et al. [45] have presented a cloud-based intrusion detection and response engine pertaining to smartphones. The proposed engine is responsible for taking suitable actions in case any misbehavior is detected and performs certain mechanisms for thwarting the attack. The main objectives of this work are 1) transparent operation to the users, 2) light resource requirement, and 3) real-time accurate intrusion detection and response. The proposed framework is based on a practical scenario in which smartphones cannot have heavyweight anti-malware software, but protecting them from attacks is necessary. The proposed framework emulates the actual smartphone device in a virtual machine in the cloud using a proxy that replicates the incoming traffic to the devices and forwards the traffic to the emulation platform. The real-time emulation makes it possible for the emulated environment in performing run-time, in-depth detection analysis. The proposed solution requires limited bandwidth. Also, if misbehavior is detected, the intrusion system decides the best countermeasure actions and sends it to a non-intrusive software agent in the device, which is in charge of carrying out the received actions.

15.7 SUMMARY ON CROSS LAYER–BASED IDS FOR WIRELESS NETWORK

The focus of our discussion in this section is on the evaluation of cross layer–based IDS design. The ability to detect intrusions in the network in terms of accuracy and reliability would determine the effectiveness of a particular cross layer–based IDS design. But in the presence of intruders, a significant amount of errors in the false positive ratio is bound to creep in. So there is need for qualitative evaluation of the cross layer–based IDS design.

15.7.1 RELIABILITY OF IDS

In order to evaluate the reliability of a cross layer–based IDS, most of the existing works has considered the false positive ratio as a measuring metric. For a reliable cross-layer IDS, it is necessary to obtain lower false positives during the detection process. It has been seen in several literatures that reliability of a system is highly affected by the several realistic parameters.

For example, several cross layer–based detection mechanisms have been proposed to detect a packet drop attack at the network layer. In a packet drop attack, a malicious node drops the packet it receives and does not forward the packet intended for the destination node. Now, in wireless networks, a packet drop in the network can occur due to poor link quality (multi-path, fading, and interference) as well as due to congested network traffic apart from malicious reasons. Therefore, while building reliable IDS, aforementioned realistic parameters need to be considered.

Authors in [6] have incorporated the information about congestion from the MAC layer and channel conditions from the PHY layer to detect the malicious packet drop at the network layer. Results show the reliability of the system increases compared to the system that did not incorporate such realistic parameters.

15.7.2 COMPUTATIONAL OVERHEAD

As energy efficiency is critical to wireless networks, especially for ad hoc networks and WSNs, it is necessary to consider the computational costs of the intrusion detection process in the evaluation of cross layer–based IDS design. In ad hoc networks and WSNs, nonlinear machine learning techniques, such as SVM, are infeasible due to the computational complexity induced by the large size of training data. Furthermore, as the cross-layer approach forms a bigger feature set, the high complexity incurred has made combining cross-layer schemes and nonlinear machine learning techniques infeasible [31]. In such case, to reduce the overhead, only a sample of the original associated and filtered training data can be used for training.

As far as computational overhead related to the cross-layer IDS architecture is concerned, there exists a trade-off between the lower false alarms and the computational overhead. Because direct per-layer interaction-based cross-layer IDS architecture does not involve communication within a network, so it is free from any external overhead. However, communication among the layers through internal packets results in increased internal computational overhead of a node. Moreover, availability of more information for sharing between the layers means fewer detection errors. Shared database-based cross-layer IDS architecture, on the other hand, has significant computation overhead in terms of updating parameter information obtained from all layers. However, compared the direct per-layer interaction-based architecture, it has a lower implementation cost.

15.7.3 THROUGHPUT

It is desirable from an IDS that during the intrusion detection process, the IDS must ensure not to throttle the throughput. However, it has been shown that all cross-layer designs can only improve throughput by a constant factor—which may still be very important—but they cannot result in any unbounded improvements even in networks with large numbers of nodes [7].

In distributed mobile environments, node mobility usually results in lower network throughput. Therefore, it is essential while designing a cross-layer IDS to take the mobility factor into consideration. Thus, in varying network dynamics situation, a trade-off between throughput and detection is essential for demand-driven and adaptive cross layer–based IDS.

15.8   OPEN ISSUES

There has been extensive research on cross-layer IDS; however, there are some important open issues especially relevant to wireless networks, including wireless mesh networks, ad hoc networks, and wireless sensor networks that either remain unresolved or not explored extensively. This section provides an insight into the research areas of cross-layer IDS for wireless networks in which very little has been done to date. Areas in which further improvements can be done are also described briefly.

(a) *Network throughput*: Improving malicious detection and better evaluation of malicious activity in the network has been addressed in the study of cross layer–based IDS for wireless network. The problem of maximizing network throughput of the cross-layer IDS process deserves further attention. As in Section 15.4.1, we have discussed that cross-layer IDS may degrade the network performance as it has significant impact on the routing protocol. Therefore, co-existence of various cross-layer optimizations is coming up as a prospective area of future research.

(b) *Reduction of design redundancy*: To detect anomalies due to intrusions in WSNs, the operations of each protocol layer reveal different facets of malicious behavior. The PHY layer improves information confidentiality through (physical) encoding. The MAC layer (along with the presentation layer) and network layer deal with the encryption of data frame and routing information. The application layer focuses on key management and exchanges that provide security support for encryption and decryption of the lower layers. Each layer's characteristics should be examined in depth in the cross-layer design to trade-off security protection and network performance and to reduce any redundancies found.

(c) *Performance optimization*: One of the main problems with the existing cross layer–based IDS is the lack of interoperability between various cross-layer optimization goals. In order to build a reliable and efficient network, it is necessary to optimize different goals simultaneously while improving interoperability between various cross layers. Therefore, addressing the joint optimization issues for cross layer–based IDS design to build an efficient network is an open research problem.

(d) *Standardized detection framework*: To improve the accuracy of detecting malicious intrusions, it is very much essential to develop a standardized detection framework for wireless networks. To achieve this goal, at first, we must explore the possibility of adopting a different cross-layer architecture. What should the boundaries be between modules? Should we stick to the architectures as discussed in Section 15.4, or should we look at completely new boundaries? Addressing these challenges requires greater synergy between the performance viewpoint and implementation concerns than is seen in the literature today.

15.9   CONCLUSIONS

Cross layer–based IDSs are being extensively used in the wireless domain for thwarting attacks prevalent in such networks. IDSs have coupled the advantages of cross-layer techniques for designing security mechanisms. This chapter envisages the different cross-layer IDS techniques that are developed in wireless networks, such as ad hoc networks, MANETs, WSNs, WLANs, VANETs, and mobile cloud. A brief overview of cross-layer IDS followed by its various requirements is also described here. A detailed description of the different advantages and disadvantages of cross-layer IDS is also given. Throughout this chapter, we have tried to cover all aspects related to cross-layer IDS.

Finally the paper concludes highlighting the important research areas that hold potential for future works and how improvisation can be brought about in these areas has also been discussed in this work.

AUTHORS' BIOGRAPHIES

Subir Halder is currently assistant professor in the Department of Computer Science and Engineering at Dr. B. C. Roy Engineering College, Durgapur, under West Bengal University of Technology, India. He received a BTech degree in electronics and communication engineering and a MTech degree in computer science and engineering from Kalyani Government Engineering College, Kalyani, India, in 2003 and 2006, respectively. He is currently pursuing a PhD in the Department of Computer Science and Technology, Bengal Engineering and Science University. His current research interests include network modeling and analysis, performance evaluation and optimization, wireless ad hoc and sensor networks. He has published research works in reputed conference proceedings and journals in his field. He has been a technical program committee member of many international conferences in his field. He is a member of ACM.

Amrita Ghosal is presently assistant professor in the Department of Computer Science and Engineering, Dr. B. C. Roy Engineering College, Durgapur, India. She received a BTech in electronics and communication engineering from Asansol Engineering College, and a MTech in computer science and engineering from Kalyani Government Engineering College, Kalyani, India, in 2003 and 2006, respectively. She is currently pursuing a PhD in the Department of Computer Science and Technology, Bengal Engineering and Science University. Her current area of research is wireless sensor networks. Her main areas of interest include different attacks and security in wireless sensor networks. She has published research works in reputed conference proceedings and journals in her field. She has been a technical program committee member of many international conferences and reviewer of journals such as *Wireless Personal Communication*, *Wireless Networks* in her field. She is a member of CRSI.

REFERENCES

1. Halder, S., Ghosal, A., DasBit, S. 2011. A pre-determined node deployment strategy to prolong network lifetime in WSN. *Computer Communication* 34: 1294–1306.
2. Heady, R., Lsugar, G., Servilla, M., Maccabe, A. 1990. The architecture of a network level intrusion detection system. In *Technical Report*, Computer Science Department, University of New Mexico.
3. Beyah, R. A., Holloway, M. C., Copeland, J. A. 2002. Invisible Trojan: An architecture, implementation and detection method. In *Proc. of 45th Midwest Symposium on Circuits and Systems* 3: 500–504.
4. Debar, H., Dacier, M., Wespi, A. 1999. Towards a taxonomy of intrusion-detection systems. *Computer Networks* 31: 805–822.
5. Srivastava, V., Motani, M. 2005. Cross-layer design: A survey and the road ahead. *IEEE Communications Magazine* 43: 112–119.
6. Thamilarasu, G., Sridhar, R. 2007. Toward building a multi-level robust intrusion detection architecture for distributed mobile networks. In *Proc. 27th Int'l Conf. on Distributed Computing Systems Workshops*, pp. 1–5.

7. Kawadia, V., Kumar, P. R. 2005. A cautionary perspective on cross layer design. *IEEE Wireless Communication* 12: 3–11.
8. Thamilarasu, G., Sridhar, R. 2007. Exploring cross-layer techniques for security: Challenges and opportunities in wireless networks. In *Proc. of Int'l Conf. Military Communications*, pp. 1–6.
9. Raymond, D. R., Midkiff, S. F. 2008. Denial of service in wireless sensor network: Attacks and defenses. *IEEE Pervasive Computing* 7: 74–81.
10. Saxena, M. 2001. Security in wireless sensor networks: A layer based classification. In *Technical Report*, Purdue University, CERIAS TR 2007-04.
11. Wang, Y., Attebury, G., Ramamurthy, B. 2006. A survey of security issues in wireless sensor networks. *IEEE Communications Surveys & Tutorials* 8: 2–23.
12. Sarma, H. K. D., Kar, A. 2006. Security threats in wireless sensor networks. In *Proc of 40th Int'l Carnahan Conf. Security Technology*, pp. 243–251.
13. Djenouri, D., Khelladi, L., Badache, N. 2005. A survey of security issues in mobile ad hoc and sensor networks. *IEEE Communications Surveys & Tutorials* 7: 2–28.
14. Zia, T., Zomaya, A. 2006. Security issues in wireless sensor networks. In *Proc. Int'l Conf. on Systems and Networks Communications*, pp. 40.
15. Pathan, A. S. K., Lee, H. W., Hong, C. S. 2006. Security in wireless sensor networks: Issues and challenges. In *Proc. of Int'l Conf. Advanced Communication Technology*, pp. 1043–1048.
16. Zhang, Y., Lee, W., Huang, Y. A. 2003. Intrusion detection techniques for mobile wireless networks. *Wireless Networks* 9: 545–556.
17. Thamilarasu, G., Balasubramanian, A., Mishra, S., Sridhar, R. 2005. A cross-layer based intrusion detection approach for wireless ad hoc networks. In *Proc. of Int'l Conf. on Mobile Adhoc and Sensor Systems Conference*, pp. 855–861.
18. Singh, J., Kaur, L., Gupta, S. 2012. A cross-layer based intrusion detection technique for wireless networks. *Int'l Arab Journal of Information Technology* 9: 201–207.
19. Bansal, D., Sofat, S., Kumar, P. 2011. Distributed cross layer approach for detecting multilayer attacks in wireless multi-hop networks. In *Proc. of Int'l Symposium on Computers & Informatics*, pp. 692–698.
20. Chiang, J. T., Hu, Y.-C. 2007. Cross-layer jamming detection and mitigation in wireless broadcast networks. In *Proc. of 13th ACM Int'l Conf. on Mobile Computing and Networking*, pp. 346–349.
21. Chiang, J. T., Hu, Y.-C. 2011. Cross-layer jamming detection and mitigation in wireless broadcast networks. *IEEE/ACM Trans. Networking* 19: 286–298.
22. Kyriakopoulos, K. G., Aparicio-Navarro, F. J., Parish, D. J. 2011. Fusing multi-layer metrics for detecting security attacks in 802.11 networks. In *Wireless Telecommunications Symposium*, pp. 1–6.
23. Thamilarasu, G., Mishra, S., Sridhar, R. 2006. A cross-layer approach to detect jamming attacks in wireless ad hoc networks. In *Proc. of Int'l Conf. on Military Communications*, pp. 753–759.
24. Thamilarasu, G., Sridhar, R. 2009. CIDS: Cross-layer intrusion detection system for mobile ad hoc networks. *Int'l Journal of Mobile Network Design and Innovation* 3: 10–20.
25. Liu, Y., Li, Y., Man, H. 2006. A distributed cross-layer intrusion detection system for ad hoc networks. *Annals of Telecommunications* 61: 357–378.
26. Shrestha, R., Han, K. H., Choi, D. Y., Han, S. J. 2010. A novel cross layer intrusion detection system in MANET. In *Proc. 24th Int. Conf. on Advanced Information Networking and Applications*, pp. 647–657.
27. Casado, L. S., Fernández, G. M., Teodoro, P. G. 2012. An efficient cross-layer approach for malicious packet dropping detection in MANETs. In *Proc. of 11th Int'l Conf. on Trust, Security and Privacy in Computing and Communications*, pp. 231–238.
28. Radosavac, S., Benammar, N., Baras, J. S. 2004. Cross-layer attacks in wireless ad hoc networks. In *Proc. of Conf. on Information Sciences and Systems*, pp. 1266–1271.
29. Felix, C. J. J., Das, A., Seet, B. C., Lee, B. S. 2007. Cross layer versus single layer approaches for intrusion detection in MANET. In *Proc. of Int'l Conference on Networks*, pp. 194–199.
30. Duda, R. O., Hart, P. E., Stork, D. G. 2000. *Pattern Classification*. Wiley Inter-Science Publication.
31. Joseph, J. F. C., Lee, B. S., Das, A., Seet, B. C. 2011. Cross-layer detection of sinking behavior in wireless ad hoc networks using SVM and FDA. *IEEE Trans. on Dependable and Secure Computing* 8: 233–245.
32. Hortos, H. S. 2007. Cross-layer design for intrusion detection and data security in wireless ad hoc sensor networks. In *Proc. of Next-Generation Communication and Sensor Networks*, SPIE 6773.
33. Hortos, H. S. 2009. Unsupervised algorithms for intrusion detection and identification in wireless ad hoc sensor networks. In *Proc. of Intelligent Sensing, Situation Management, Impact Assessment, and Cyber-Sensing*, SPIE 7352.

34. Hortos, H. S. 2011. Combined bio-inspired/evolutionary computational methods in cross-layer protocol optimization for wireless ad hoc sensor networks. In *Proc. of Evolutionary and Bio-Inspired Computation: Theory and Applications*, SPIE 8059.

35. Boubiche, D. E., Bilami, A. 2012. Cross layer intrusion detection system for wireless sensor network. *Int'l Journal of Network Security & Its Applications* 4: 35–52.

36. Hortos, H. S. 2012. Bio-inspired, cross-layer protocol design for intrusion detection and identification in wireless sensor networks. In *Proc. of 7th Workshop on Security in Communication Networks*, pp. 1030–1037.

37. Leinmüller, T., Held, A., Schäfer, G., Wolisz, A. 2004. Intrusion detection in VANETs. In *Proc. of 12th IEEE Int'l Conf. on Network Protocols (ICNP 2004) Student Poster Session*, pp. 1–2.

38. Singh, J., Sharma, N. 2012. Wormhole attack detection by using intrusion detection system in VANET. *Int'l Journal of Computer Networks and Wireless Communications* 2: 638–642.

39. Biswas, S., Misic, J. 2013. Cross-layer approach to privacy-preserving authentication in WAVE-enabled VANETs. *IEEE Trans. on Vehicular Technology* 1–1.

40. Gill, R., Smith, J., Clark, A. 2006. Specification-based intrusion detection in WLANs. In *Proc. of 22nd Annual Computer Security Applications Conference*, pp. 141–152.

41. Tian, D., Li, Q., Chen, S. 2008. Anomaly intrusion detection methods for wireless LAN. In *Proc. of Int'l Conf. on Natural Computation*, pp. 179–182.

42. Kaur, R. 2011. Cross layer based miss detection ratio under variable rate for intrusion detection in WLAN. *Int'l Journal of Computer Engineering Research* 2: 75–81.

43. Dastjerdi, A. V., Bakar, K. A., Tabatabaei, S. G. H. 2009. Distributed intrusion detection in clouds using mobile agent. In *Proc. of Third International Conference on Advanced Engineering Computing and Applications in Sciences*, pp. 175–180.

44. Vieira, K., Schulter, A., Westphall, C. B., Westphall, C. M. 2010. Intrusion detection for grid and cloud computing. *IEEE IT Professional Magazine* 12: 38–43.

45. Houmansadr, A., Zonouz, S. A., Berthier, R. 2011. A cloud-based intrusion detection and response system for mobile phones. In *Proc. of IEEE/IFIP 41st Int'l Conf. on Dependable Systems and Networks Workshops (DSN-W)*, pp. 31–32.

16 Intrusion Detection System Architecture for Wireless Sensor Network

Mohammad Saiful Islam Mamun

CONTENTS

16.1 INTRODUCTION

There has been a lot of research done on preventing or defending WSNs from attackers and intruders, but very limited work has been done for detection purposes. It will be difficult for the network administrator to be aware of intrusions. There are some intrusion detection systems that are proposed or designed for wireless ad hoc networks. Most of them work on distributed environments, which means they work on individual nodes independently and try to detect intrusion by studying abnormalities in their neighbors' behavior. Thus, they require the nodes to consume more of their processing power, battery backup, and storage space, which makes IDSs more expensive or unfeasible for most of the applications. Some of the IDSs use mobile agents in distributed environments [8]. Mobile agents support sensor mobility and intelligent routing of intrusion data throughout the network, eliminate network dependency of specific nodes. But this mechanism still is not popular for IDSs due to mobile agents' architectural inherited security vulnerability and heavy weight. Some of the IDSs are attack-specific, which make them concentrated to one type of attack [1]. Some of them use a centralized framework, which make an IDS capable of exploiting a personal computer's high processing power, huge storage capabilities, and unlimited battery backup [21]. Most of the IDSs are targeted to the routing layer only [7,21], but it can be enhanced to detect different types of attacks at other networking layers as well. Most of the architectures are based on anomaly detection

[2,18], which examines the statistical analysis of activities of nodes for detection. Most of the IDS techniques utilize system log files, network traffic, or packets in the network to gather information for intrusion detection. Some detect only intrusion, and some do more, such as acquiring more information, e.g., type of attacks, locations of the intruder, etc. There are many intrusion detection systems in the literature. Self-organized criticality and stochastic learning–based IDSs [2], IDSs for clustering-based sensor networks [3], a non-cooperative game approach [4], and decentralized IDSs [5] are distinguished among them. *Group-based* or *clustering-based* approaches [23,26] in which the whole network is divided into subgroups depending on having some common attributes, such as a sensor ID, close proximity, and sensor remaining power. A *semantic-based* [24] IDS builds a security ontology that represents the formal semantics for intrusion detection. A *game theoretic* or *payoff* [25,28] framework helps to decide the probability of starting IDS service in each cluster head node using a game theoretic model. *The traffic analysis* [29] method analyzes the neighbor behavior and selected parameters, e.g., number of received packets in a given period, used to detect anomalous behavior and inter-arrival time of packets. A *fuzzy neural network*–based [27] intrusion detection system takes advantage of fuzzy theory and neural networks for intrusion detection. In [31], authors survey different anomaly detection techniques and classify the techniques based on what type of background knowledge of the underlying data is available.

16.2   EXISTING CHALLENGES

Existing intrusion detection systems are not adequate to protect WSNs from inside and outside attackers. None of them are complete, e.g., most of the approaches offer clustering techniques without mentioning how they will be formed and how will they behave with the rest of the system. Most of the existing IDSs deal with wired architecture except for their wireless counterparts. The architecture of WSNs is even more sophisticated than ad hoc wireless architecture. So an IDS is needed with the capability of detecting inside and outside, known and unknown attacks with a low false alarm rate. Existing IDS architectures that are specifically designed for sensor networks are suffering from a lack of resources, e.g., high processing power, huge storage capabilities, unlimited battery backup, etc.

16.3   WIRELESS SENSOR NETWORKS: AN OVERVIEW

According to NIST (National Institute of Standards and Technology), "*a wireless ad hoc sensor network consists of a number of sensors spread across a geographical area*" [8]. The term *sensor network* refers to a system that is a combination of sensors and actuators with some general-purpose computing elements. A sensor network can have hundreds or even thousands of sensors and mobile or fixed locations and be deployed to control or monitor [7].

   A wireless sensor network comprises sensor nodes to sense data from their ambience and passes it on to a centralized controlling and data collecting identity called a *base station*. Typically, base stations are powerful devices with a large storage capacity to store incoming data. They generally provide gateway functionality to another network or an access point for human interface [21]. A base station may have an unlimited power supply and high bandwidth links for communicating with other base stations. In contrast, wireless sensor nodes are constrained to use low power, low bandwidth, and short-range links.

16.4   SECURITY THREATS AND ISSUES

Various security issues and threats that are considered for wireless ad hoc networks can be applied to WSNs. This is recited in some previous research. But the security mechanism used for wireless ad hoc networks cannot be deployed directly for WSNs because of their architectural inequality. First, in ad hoc networks, every node is usually held and managed by a human user whereas, in

TABLE 16.1
Threats and Attacks in WSN

Attacks	Brief Description
Attack on information in transit	Information that is to be sent can be modified, altered, replayed, spoofed, or vanished by an attacker
Hello flood	An attacker with high radio range sends more Hello packets to announce themselves to a large number of nodes in the large network, persuading themselves as a neighbor
Sybil attack	Fake multiple identities to attack on data integrity and accessibility
Wormhole attack	Transmit information between two WSN nodes in secret
Network partition attack	Threats to accessibility although there is a path between the nodes
Black hole attack	The attacker absorbs all the messages
Sink hole attack	Similar to black hole. Exception: the attacker advertises wrong routing information
Selective forwarding	The attacker forwards messages on the basis of some pre-selected criterion
Simple broadcast flooding	The attacker floods the network with broadcast messages
Simple target flooding	The attacker tries to flood through some specific nodes
False identity broadcast flooding	Similar to simple broadcast flooding except the attacker deceives with wrong source ID
False identity target flooding	Similar to simple target flooding except the attacker deceives with wrong source ID
Misdirection attack	The attacker misdirects the incoming packets to a distant node

sensor networks, all the nodes are independent, and communication is controlled by the base station. Second, computing resources and batteries are more constrained in sensor nodes than in ad hoc nodes. Third, the purpose of sensor networks is very specific, e.g., measuring the physical information (such as temperature, sound, etc.). Fourth, node density in sensor networks is higher than in ad hoc networks [10]. Architectural aspects of WSN make the security mechanism more prosperous as the base station could be used intelligently.

According to the basic need, security attacks in WSN can be categorized:

- DoS, DDoS attacks, which affect network *availability*
- Eavesdropping, sniffing, which can threaten *confidentiality*
- Man-in-the-middle attacks, which can affect packet *integrity*
- Signal jamming, which affects *communication*

There has been much research work done in the area of significant security problems. Here, a summary of existing well-known threats are discussed (Table 16.1).

16.5   IDS ARCHITECTURE

According to the *Network Security Bible*, *"Intrusion detection and response is the task of monitoring systems for evidence of intrusions or inappropriate usage and responding to this evidence"* [22]. The basic idea of IDS is to observe users as well as program activities inside the system via an auditing mechanism.

Depending on the data collection mechanism, IDSs can be classified into two categories: a *host-based IDS* monitors log files (applications, operating systems, etc.) and then compares them with logs of present signatures of known attacks from internal database. *A network-based IDS* works in different way. It monitors packets within communication and inspects suspicious packet information.

Depending on how attacks are detected, IDS architecture can be categorized into three types: *A signature-based IDS,* which monitors an occurrence of signatures or behaviors that are matched with known attacks to detect an intrusion. This technique may exhibit a low false positive rate but is not good for detecting previously unknown attacks. *An anomaly-based IDS* defines a profile of normal behavior and classifies any deviation from that profile as an intrusion. The normal profile of system behavior is updated as the system learns the behavior. This type of system can detect unknown attacks, but it exhibits a high false positive rate. In [11], another type of intrusion detection has been introduced. *A specification-based IDS* defines a protocol or a program's correct operations. Intrusion is indicated according to those constraints. This type of IDS may detect unknown attacks while showing a low false positive rate. In this chapter, we follow a *security architecture–* based IDS that is used for self-organizing mobile wireless sensor networks. Security architecture for a WSN consists of five layers of the open source interaction (OSI) model: physical, data link, network, transport, and application layers in which different layers are vulnerable to different potential attacks, such as the physical layer for sniffing, jamming attacks; the application layer for replay packets; the data link layer for integration, collision, rushing, DoS, and exhaustion attacks; and the network layer for sinkhole, wormhole, Sybil, and Hello attacks (Figure 16.1).

In [30], the authors present a modular intrusion detection system (IDS) architecture as a framework for WSN and discuss practical implementation issues regarding several attack types and their corresponding countermeasure approaches. Each module corresponds to one of the countermeasures that enable the administrator to monitor the network status. Alarms triggered by the detection modules are processed and visualized by the server for immediate intrusion response.

The basic IDS architecture in [30] consists of local detection modules built in the sensor nodes that forward IDS messages via wireless radio to the central IDS server through intermediate gateways. Each IDS message is assigned a unique identification according to the type of triggering in order to distinguish different modules and message types. Gateways summarize the received messages according to the essential parts of the server, i.e., message identifier, originator address, payload, etc. Local detection modules in sensor nodes are separated into periodic and event-based triggering. Based on the originator and payload messages, the server maps and displays the alarm/ status accordingly. Finally, the server processes and visualizes messages according to the type (Figure 16.2).

A generic architecture of an IDS for WSN using danger theory immune-inspired techniques has been proposed in [33] in order to identify a distributed DoS attack. The logical architecture of the WSN consists of several sensor nodes and a base station while a WSN IDS consists of several components, such as an intrusion detection manager, monitoring environment, context manager, decision manager, parameters base, storage, and countermeasures (Figure 16.3).

In [34], an integrated IDS is proposed for a cluster-based WSN, which consists of three individual IDSs: an intelligent hybrid IDS for the base station or the sink, a hybrid IDS (HIDS) for the cluster head, and a misuse IDS for the sensor node in order to raise the detection rate and lower the

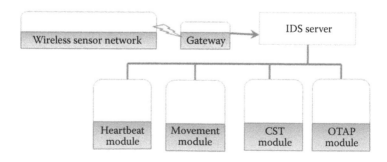

FIGURE 16.1 Basic IDS architecture (proposed by Rajasegarar et al. [30]).

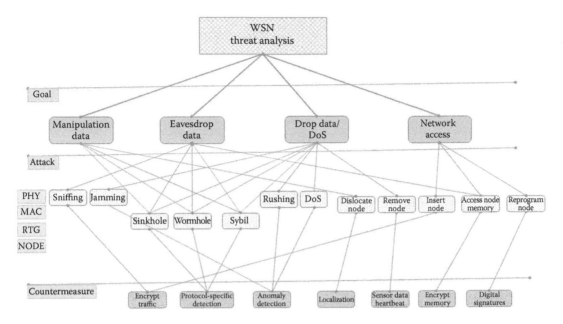

FIGURE 16.2 Threat analyses and their countermeasures. (Adopted from Rajasegarar, S. et al., *IEEE Wireless Communications*, 15, 34–40, 2008.)

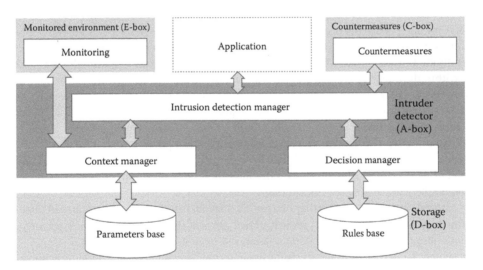

FIGURE 16.3 Logical architecture for IDS. (Adopted from Salmon, H. M. et al., *International Journal of Wireless Information Networks*, 20, 39–66, 2013.)

false positive rate through misuse detection and anomaly detection. There is a feedback mechanism between the base station and cluster heads while HIDS will be retrained for the new type of attacks (Figure 16.4).

In [11], wireless ad hoc network architecture is defined into three basic categories, which can be adjusted to IDS in WSN architecture.

Stand alone: Each node acts as an independent IDS and detects attacks for itself only without sharing any information with another IDS node of the system and does not even cooperate with other systems. So all intrusion detection decisions are based on information available to the individual

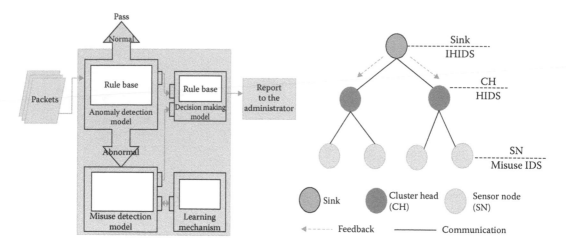

FIGURE 16.4   System architecture of integrated hybrid IDS. (Adopted from Wang, S.-S. et al., *Expert Systems with Applications*, 38, 15234–15243, 2011.)

node. Its effect is too limited. This architecture is best suited in an environment where all the nodes are capable of running an IDS [11].

Distributed and cooperative: Although each node runs its own IDS, finally they collaborate to form a global IDS. This architecture is more suitable for flat wireless sensor networks, in which a global IDS is initiated due to the occurrence of inconclusive intrusions detected by an individual node.

Hierarchical: This architecture has been proposed for a multilayered wireless network. Here, the network is divided into a cluster with cluster heads. A cluster head acts like a small base station for the nodes within the cluster. It also aggregates information from the member nodes about malicious activities. A cluster head detects attacks as member nodes could potentially reroute, modify, or drop a packet in transmission. At the same time, all cluster heads can cooperate with the central base station to form a global IDS.

To build an effective IDS model, several considerations take place:

First of all, detection tasks: How will they be separated? Local agent or global agent. Whether local or global agent, an IDS needs to consider how these agents would analyze the threats. And what would be the right sources of information?

A *local agent* detects the vulnerability of a node's internal information. It is supposed to be active 100% of the time to ensure maximum security. Here physical/logical integrity, measurement integrity, protocol integrity, and neighborhood are analyzed from nodes' status.

Global agent: To detect an anomaly from the external information of a node to achieve 100% coverage of a sensor network. Here, the main challenges are balancing tasks and network coverage. In case of a hierarchical network, the cluster head (CH) controls its section of the network. The CH is a part of global network. In case of a flat network, the spontaneous watchdogs concept is applied. Here, the premise is "For every packet circulating in the network, there are a set of nodes that are able to receive both that packet and the relayed packet by the next hop."

The second consideration is sharing information between agents. Information between agents can be transmitted through cryptography, voting mechanisms, or trust depending on the network's resource constraint.

The third consideration is how to notify users. Generally, users are behind base stations. So different algorithms can be used to notify the base station. E.G.U. Tesla uses a secure broadcast algorithm.

There are different techniques for IDS in wireless sensor network (WSN). Here, we represent some existing IDS models for WSN (Table 16.2).

TABLE 16.2
Comparative Study on Existing IDS

Name of the Intrusion Detection System	Data Collection Mechanism	Detection Technique	Handled Attacks	Network Architecture
Hybrid IDS for wireless sensor network [6]	Network based	Anomaly based	Selective forwarding, sink hole, Hello flood, and wormhole attacks	Hierarchical
Decentralized IDS in WSN [5]	Network based	Anomaly based	Repetition, message delay, blackhole, wormhole, data alteration, jamming, message negligence, and selective forwarding	Distributed
Intrusion detection in routing attacks in sensor network [1]	Host based	Anomaly based	DoS, active sinkhole attacks, and passive sinkhole	Distributed
Sensor network automated intrusion detection system (SNAIDS) [9]	Host based	Signature based	Duplicate nodes, flooding, blackhole, sink hole attack, selective forwarding, misdirection	Distributed
Self-organized critically and stochastic learning–based IDS for WSN [2]	Host based	Anomaly based	There is no guideline in this IDS model of which attacks it can resist and which cannot	Distributed

16.6 OUR MODEL

In this chapter, we propose a new model for IDS, which concentrates on saving the power of sensor nodes by distributing the responsibility of intrusion detection to three layer nodes with the help of a policy-based network management system. The model uses a hierarchical overlay design (HOD). We divided each area of sensor nodes into a hexagonal region (like GSM cells). Sensor nodes in each of the hexagonal areas are monitored by a cluster node. Each cluster node is then monitored by a regional node. In turn, regional nodes will be controlled and monitored by the base station (Figure 16.5).

This HOD–based IDS combines two approaches of intrusion detection mechanisms (signature and anomaly) together to fight against existing threats. Signatures of well-known attacks are propagated from the base station to the leaf-level node for detection. A signature repository at each layer is

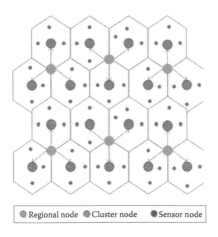
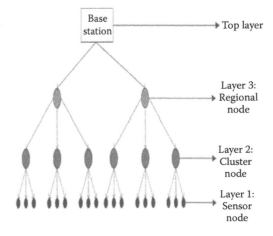

FIGURE 16.5 Hierarchical overlay design.

updated as new forms of attacks are found in the system. As intermediate agents are activated with predefined rules of system behavior, anomaly detection can take part from the deviated behavior of predefined specification. Thus a proposed IDS can identify known as well as unknown attacks.

16.6.1 Detection Entities

Sensor nodes have two types of functionality: sensing and routing. Each of the sensor nodes will sense the environment and exchange data in between sensor nodes and cluster nodes. As sensor nodes have many resource constraints, in this model, there is no IDS module installed in the leaf-level sensor nodes.

A *cluster node* plays as a monitor node for the sensor nodes. One cluster node is assigned for each of the hexagonal areas. It will receive the data from the sensor nodes, analyze and aggregate the information, and send it to the regional node. It is more powerful than sensor nodes and has intrusion detection capability built into it.

A *regional node* will monitor and receive the data from neighboring cluster heads and send the combined alarm to the upper layer base station. It is also a monitor node like the cluster nodes with all the IDS functionalities. It makes the sensor network more scalable. If thousands of sensor nodes are available at the leaf level, then the whole area will be split into several regions.

The base station is the topmost part of the architecture empowered with human support. It will receive the information from the regional nodes and distribute the information to the users based on their demand.

16.6.2 Policy-Based IDS

Policy implies a predefined action pattern that is repeated by an entity whenever certain conditions occur [13]. The architectural components of the policy framework include a policy enforcement point (PEP), a policy decision point (PDP), and a policy repository. The policy rules stored in the policy repository are used by the PDP to define rules or to show results. The PDP translates or interprets the available data to a device-dependent format and configures the relevant PEPs. The PEP executes the logical entities that are decided by PDP [12]. These capabilities provide powerful functions to configure the network as well as to re-configure the system as necessary to response to network conditions with automation. In a large WSN in which hierarchical network management is followed can be realized by policy mechanism to achieve survivability, scalability, and autonomy simultaneously. So in case of failure, the system enables one component to take over the management role of another component. One of the major architectural advantages of a hierarchical structure is that any node can take over the functionality of another node dynamically to ensure survivability. A flexible agent structure ensures dynamic insertion of new management functionality.

Hierarchical network management integrates the advantage of two (central and distributed) management models [14] and uses intermediate nodes (regional and cluster) to distribute the detection tasks. Each intermediate manager has its own domain called the regional or cluster agent, which collects and processes information from its domain and passes the required information to the upper layer manager for further steps. All the intermediate nodes are also used to distribute command/data/message from the upper layer manager to nodes within its domain. It should be noted that there is no direct communication between the intermediate members. Except for the leaf-level sensor nodes, all the nodes in the higher level are configured with higher energy and storage.

To achieve a policy-based management for IDS, the proposed architecture features several components that evaluate policies: a base policy decision point (BPDP), a number of policy decision modules (PDMs), and a policy enforcement point (PEP).

The base policy decision point (BPDP) is the controlling component of the architecture. It implements policies or intrusion rules generated by the intrusion detection tool (IDT) from receiving events, evaluating anomaly conditions, and applying new rules, algorithms, threshold values, etc. IDT supports creation, deletion, modification, and examination of the agent's configurations and policies. It can add new entities, e.g., a new signature of intrusion, modify or delete existing entities in RPA and LPA.

Policy decision modules (PDMs) are components that implement sophisticated algorithms in relevant domains. LPAs and RPAs act as PDMs. An LPA manages the sensor nodes, which are more powerful than sensor nodes. LPAs perform local policy-controlled configuration, filtering, monitoring, and reporting, which reduces management bandwidth and computational overhead from leaf-level sensor nodes to improve network performance and intrusion detection efficiency. An RPA can manage multiple LPAs. At the peak, BPDP manages and controls all the RPAs.

Policy enforcement points (PEP) are low-level sensor nodes.

Policies are disseminated from the BPDP to RPA to LPA as they are propagated from PDP to LPA. The policy agents described above help IDSs by reacting to network status changes globally or locally. It helps the network to be reconfigured automatically to deal with fault and performance degradation according to intrusion response.

16.6.3 STRUCTURE OF INTRUSION DETECTION AGENT (IDA)

The hierarchical architecture of policy management for WSN is shown in Figure 16.6. It is comprised of several hierarchical layers containing intrusion detection agents (IDAs) at each layer. They are the base policy decision point (BPDP), the regional policy agent (RPA), the local policy agent (LPA), and sensor nodes (SN).

An IDA consists of the following components: preprocessor, signature processor, anomaly processor, and post processor. The functionalities are described as follows (Figure 16.7).

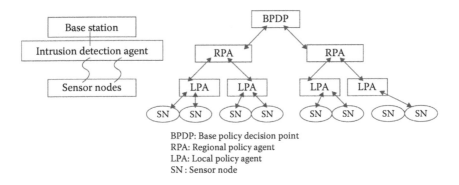

BPDP: Base policy decision point
RPA: Regional policy agent
LPA: Local policy agent
SN : Sensor node

FIGURE 16.6 Hierarchical architecture of IDS policy management.

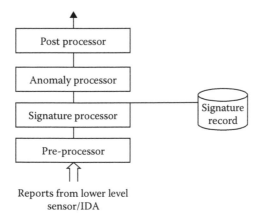

FIGURE 16.7 Intrusion detection agent structure.

The *pre-processor* either collects the network traffic of the leaf-level sensor when it acts as an LPA or it receives reports from a lower layer IDA. Collected sensor traffic data is then abstracted to a set of variables called a stimulus vector to make the network status understandable to the higher layer processor of the agent.

The *signature processor* maintains a reference model or database called the *signature record* of the typical known unauthorized malicious threats and high-risk activities and compares the reports from the *pre-processor* against the known attack signatures. If a match is not found, then misuse intrusion is supposed to be detected, and the signature processor passes the relevant data to the next higher layer for further processing.

The *anomaly processor* analyzes the vector from the *pre-processor* to detect an anomaly in network traffic. Usually, a statistical method or artificial intelligence is used in order to detect this kind of attack. A profile of normal activity, which is propagated from the base station is stored in the database. If the activities arrived from the pre-processor deviate from the normal profile in a statistically significant way or exceed some particular threshold value, attacks are noticed. Intrusion detection rules are basically policies that define the standard of access mechanism and uses of sensor nodes. Here, the database acts as a policy information base (PIB) or policy repository.

A *post processor* prepares and sends reports for the higher layer agent or base station. It can be used to display the agent status through a user interface.

16.6.4 SELECTION OF IDS NODE

Activating every node as an IDS wastes energy. So minimization of the number of nodes to run intrusion detection is necessary. In [15], three strategies are mentioned, involving selection of the intrusion detection node.

The *core defense* selects an IDS node around a center point of a subset of the network. It is assumed that no intruder can break into the central station in any cluster. This type of model defends from the most inner part then retaliates to the outer area.

The *boundary defense* selects a node along the boundary perimeter of the cluster. It provides defense on the intruder attack from breaking into the cluster from the outside area of the network.

A *distributed defense* has an agent node selection algorithm, which follows voting algorithm from [16] in this model. The node selection procedure follows the tree hierarchy.

Our model follows a *core defense* strategy in which a cluster head is the center point to defend intruders. In the core defense strategy, the ratio of alerted nodes and the total number of nodes in the network drops; this makes energy consumption very low, which make it more economical in their use of energy as it shows the least number of broadcast messages in case of attack. It has a strong defense in the inner network. Here, the IDS needs to wait for the intruder to reach the core area [16], which is one of the drawbacks of this strategy as nodes can be captured without notice.

16.6.5 IDS MECHANISM IN SENSOR NODES

Intrusions could be detected at multiple layers in sensor nodes (physical, link, network, and application layers).

In the *physical layer,* jamming is the primary physical layer attack. Identifying a jamming attack can be done by the received signal strength indicator (RSSI) [17,18], the average time required to sense an idle channel (carrier sense time), and the packet delivery ratio (PDR). In case of a wireless medium, received signal strength has relationship with the distance between nodes. Node tampering and destruction are another physical layer attack that can be prevented by placing nodes in a secured place. During the initialization process, the cluster node's LPA will store the RSSI value for the communication between the cluster node to the leaf-level sensor nodes and sensor to sensor node. Later, at the time of monitoring, an anomaly processor in the LPA will monitor whether the received value is unexpected. If yes, it will feedback RPA by generating an appropriate alarm (Figure 16.8).

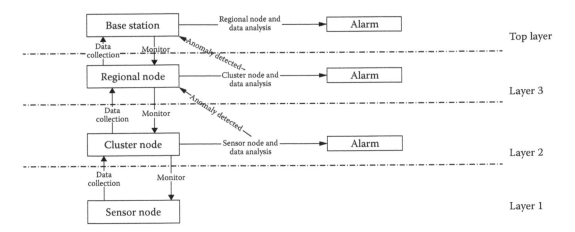

FIGURE 16.8   IDS mechanism.

Link layer attacks are collision, denial of sleep, and packet replay, etc. Here SMAC and time division multiple access (TDMA) can be used to detect the anomaly. *TDMA* [18] is a digital transmission process in which each cluster node will assign different time slots for different sensor nodes in its region. During this slot, every sensor node has access to the radio frequency channel without interference. If any attacker sends a packet using a source address of any node, e.g., A, but that slot is not allocated to A, then LPA's anomaly processor can easily detect that intrusion. *S-MAC* [18] protocol is used to assign a wake up and sleep time for the sensor nodes. As the sensor has limited power, S-MAC can be implemented for the energy conservation. If any packet is received from a source, e.g., A, in its sleeping period, then the LPA can easily detect the inconsistency.

In the *network layer,* route tracing is used to detect whether the packet really comes from the best route. If the packet comes to the destination via a different path rather than the desired path, then the anomaly processor can detect a possible intrusion according to predefined rules.

The *application layer* uses three level watchdogs. They are in the base station, regional node, and cluster node. Sensor nodes will be monitored by an upper layer watchdog cluster node, and cluster nodes will be monitored by a regional node watchdog, and finally the top level watchdog base station will monitor the regional nodes. So, if any one node is compromised by the attacker, then the higher layer watchdog can easily detect the attack and generate alarm.

16.7   INTRUSION RESPONSE

There are differences between intrusion detection and intrusion prevention. If a system has intrusion prevention, it is assumed that intrusion detection is built in. IDSs are designed to welcome an intrusion to get into the system whereas an intrusion prevention system (IPS) actually attempts to prevent access to the system from the very beginning. An IPS operates similarly to an IDS with one critical difference: An "IPS can block the attack itself; while an IDS sits outside the line of traffic and observes, an IPS sits directly in line of network traffic. Any traffic the IPS identifies as malicious is prevented from entering the network [19]." Therefore, in case of IDS, *intrusion response* should be the right title for recovery.

There are two different approaches for intrusion response: a hot response or policy-based response [20]. A *hot response* reacts by launching local action on the target machine to the end process or on the target network component to block traffic, e.g., kill any process, reset the connection, etc. It does not prevent the occurrence of the attack in the future. On the other hand, a *policy-based response* works on a more general scope. It considers the threats reported in the alert and the constraints and objectives of the information system of the network. It modifies or creates new rules in the policy repository to prevent an attack in the future. In our proposed IDS, the base station's policy decision point and other policy decision modules take part in the response mechanism together. The BPDP and PDM take part in the response mechanism. Intrusion can be detected either in the cluster node or regional node. Finally, base stations can be involved anytime if the network administrator wants to do so or to update the signature database or policy stored in an intermediate agent. Intrusions are detected automatically according to the policy implemented by BPDP. Reaction is also automatic, but an administrator may redesign the architecture according to requirements.

In [21], a novel intrusion detection and response system is implemented. We have applied their idea in our response mechanism with some modification. Our IDS system puts each sensor node into one of five classes: *fresh, member, unstable, suspect,* or *malicious.* We have a local policy agent, a regional policy agent, and finally, a base policy decision point to make decisions about the sensor node's class placement. A route guard mechanism uses a *Pathrating* algorithm to keep any node within these five classes [21]. In our model, we have a policy or rules defined in the base station's BPDP to select any node to be within these five classes as shown in Figure 16.4. When a new node is arrived, it will be classified as *fresh.* For a pre-selected period of time, this new node will be in the *fresh* state. By this time, the LPA will check whether this node is misbehaving or not. In this period, the node is permitted to forward or receive packets from another sensor node but not its own generated packet. After a particular time, its classification will be changed to *member* automatically if no misbehave is detected. Otherwise, the node's classification will be changed to the *suspect* state. In the *member* state, nodes are allowed to create, send, receive, or forward packets. At this time, *member* nodes are monitored by a watchdog at LPA in the cluster node. If the node misbehaves, its state will be changed to *unstable* for a short span of time. During the *unstable* state, nodes are permitted to send and receive packets except their own packets. In this state, the node will be kept under close observation of the LPA. If it behaves well, then it will be transferred to the *member* state. A node in the *unstable* state will be converted to the *suspect* state in two cases: Either the node was in the *unstable* state and interchanged its state within the *member* and *unstable* states for a particular amount of time (threshold values defined in LPA) within a predefined period or the node was misbehaving for a long time (threshold value). The LPA's post processor sends a "danger alert" to the RPA whenever a *suspect* node is encountered. The suspected node is completely isolated from the network. It is not allowed to send, receive, or forward packets and is temporarily banned for a short time. Any packets received from suspected node are simply discarded. After a certain period of time, the node is reconnected and is monitored closely for an extensive period of time by the intrusion detection agent in all three layers. If watchdogs report well, then the node status will be changed to *unstable.* However, if it continues misbehaving, then it will be labeled as *malicious.* After declaring any node *malicious,* that node is permanently banned from this network. To ensure that this *malicious* node will never try to reconnect, its MAC address or any unique ID will be added to the *signature record database* of the LPA (Figure 16.9).

Survivability is one of the major factors that are predicted from every system. We consider base stations to be failure free. But the regional nodes or cluster nodes may be unreachable due to failure or battery exhaustion. So in case of failures or any physical damage of the regional nodes or cluster nodes, control of those nodes should be taken over by another stable node. So in our proposed architecture, if any regional node fails, then its control is shifted to the neighbor regional node dynamically.

Therefore, control of the cluster nodes and sensor nodes belonging to that regional node will be shifted automatically to the neighbor node. In the same way, if any cluster node fails, then control of that cluster node will be transferred to the neighbor cluster node.

So in the proposed architecture, if any LPA is unreachable due to failure or battery exhaustion of cluster nodes, a neighbor LPA will take charge of the leaf-level sensor nodes that were in the area of the fault cluster node. In the same way, due to a regional node's failure, a neighbor regional node's RPA will take over the functionality of all the cluster node's LPA and sensor nodes belonged to the faulty regional node dynamically (Figure 16.10).

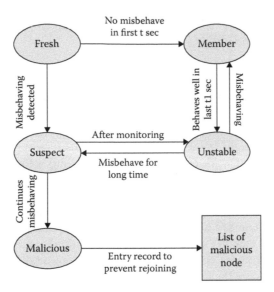

FIGURE 16.9 Operation of intrusion response.

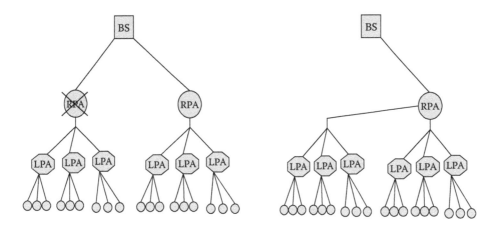

FIGURE 16.10 Regional node's failure.

As we mentioned before, cluster nodes or regional nodes have number direct communications between them. So how will a cluster node or regional node determine the failure of its neighbor? Actually, in the proposed architecture, the base station has direct or indirect connections with all its leaf nodes. The base station has direct connection with the regional node. So if any regional node fails, the base station can identify the problem and select one of its neighbor nodes dynamically according to some predefined rule in the BPDP. Then the BPDP needs to supply the policy, rules, or signatures of the failed node to the selected new neighbor regional node. In the same way, if any cluster node fails, then a neighbor cluster node will not be informed about its failure. So in this case, the regional node will take the necessary action of selecting a suitable neighbor cluster node. Here, policy, rules, or signatures of the failed cluster node will be supplied by the BPDP through the relevant RPA. So the RPA has the only responsibility to select an appropriate neighbor LPA of the unreachable LPA. The rest of the work belongs to the BPDP of the base station. As the base station is a much more powerful node with large storage, all the signatures, anomaly detection rules, or policies are stored primarily as a backup in the base station. This back-up system increases the reliability of the whole network system.

16.8 CONCLUSION

WSNs are prone to intrusions and security threats. In this chapter, we propose a novel architecture of an IDS for an ad hoc sensor network based on hierarchical overlay design. We propose a response mechanism also according to the proposed architecture. Our design of an IDS improves on other related designs in the way it distributes the total task of detecting intrusion. Our model decouples the total work of intrusion detection into a four-level hierarchy, which results in a highly energy-saving structure. Each monitor needs to monitor only a few nodes within its range and thus needs not spend much power for it. Due to the hierarchical model, the detection system works in a very structured way and can detect any intrusion effectively. As a whole, every area is commanded by one cluster head, so the detection is really fast, and the alarm is rippled to the base station via the region head, enabling it to take proper action. In this chapter, we consider cluster nodes or regional nodes to be more powerful than ordinary sensor nodes. Although it will increase the total cost of network setup, to enhance reliability, efficiency, and effectiveness of IDS for a large geographical area where thousands of sensor nodes take place, the cost is tolerable.

A policy-based mechanism is a powerful approach to automating network management. The management system for intrusion detection and the response system described in this chapter show that a well-structured reduction in management traffic can be achievable by policy management. This policy-based architecture upgrades adaptability and re-configurability of a network management system that has a good practical research value for a large geographically distributed network environment.

The IDS in a wireless sensor network is an important topic for the research area. Still, there are no proper IDSs in the WSN field. Many previously proposed systems were based on a three-layer architecture. But we introduced a four-layer overlay hierarchical design to improve the detection process, and we brought the GSM cell concept. We also introduced the hierarchical watchdog concept. The top layer base station, cluster node, and regional node are three hierarchical watchdogs. Our report proposes IDSs in multiple layers to make our system architecture robust.

16.9 FUTURE WORK

This chapter provides a first-cut solution to four-layer hierarchical policy-based intrusion detection systems for WSNs. So there is much room for further research in this area. The proposed IDS system is highly extensible in that as new attacks or attack patterns are identified, new detection algorithms can be incorporated into the policy. In this chapter, we actually focus on the general idea of architectural design for IDSs and how a policy management system can be aggregated to the system. But extensive work needs to be done to define detection and response policy as well.

However, the present model can be extended by exploring the secure communication between the base station, regional node, and cluster node by providing an election procedure to select the cluster and regional node, by implementing a risk assessment system in the manager stations to improve the reaction capability of IDS. In this chapter, we actually focus on the general idea of architectural design for IDS and how a policy management system can be aggregated to the system. But extensive work needs to be done to define detection and response policy as well. The current efficiency of an IDS needs to be verified in terms of resources and policy so that improvements of its future version(s) are possible. Further study is required to determine an IDSs scalability. To the best of our knowledge, its scalability highly correlates with the scalability of the WSN application and the policy management in use.

AUTHOR'S BIOGRAPHY

Mohammad Saiful Islam Mamun is a researcher at the Information Security Lab, School of Information Science, Japan Advanced Institute of Science and Technology (JAIST), Japan. He received a BSc (Hons) degree in computer science and engineering from the University of Dhaka, Bangladesh, and a MS degree in information and communication system security from the Royal Institute of Technology (KTH), Sweden, in 2005 and 2008, respectively. He worked as a lecturer at Stamford University Bangladesh from 2008 to 2011. His primary research interests include applied cryptography, security protocols, integrity, and authenticity in vehicular ad hoc networks (VANETs) and RFID.

REFERENCES

1. C. Loo, M. Y. Ng, C. Leckie, and M. Palaniswami, Intrusion detection for routing attacks in sensor networks, *International Journal of Distributed Sensor Networks*, vol. 2, December 2006, pp. 313–332, DOI: 10.1080/15501320600692044.
2. S. Doumit and D. P. Agrawal, Self-organized criticality & stochastic learning based intrusion detection system for wireless sensor network, *MILCOM 2003—IEEE Military Communications Conference*, vol. 22, pp. 609–614, 2003.
3. C.-C. Su, K.-M. Chang, Y.-H. Kuo, and M.-F. Horng, The new intrusion prevention and detection approaches for clustering-based sensor networks, in *2005 IEEE Wireless Communications and Networking Conference, WCNC 2005: Broadband Wireless for the Masses—Ready for Take-Off*, March 13–17, 2005.
4. A. Agah, S. Das, K. Basu, and M. Asadi, Intrusion detection in sensor networks: A non-cooperative game approach, in *3rd IEEE International Symposium on Network Computing and Applications, (NCA 2004)*, Boston, MA, August 2004, pp. 343–346.
5. A. da Silva, M. Martins, B. Rocha, A. Loureiro, L. Ruiz, and H. Wong, Decentralized intrusion detection in wireless sensor networks, *Proceedings of the 1st ACM International Workshop on Quality of Service & Security in Wireless and Mobile Networks*, 2005.
6. O. T. H. Hai, F. Khan, and E.-N. Huh, Hybrid intrusion detection system for wireless sensor network, in *Computational Science and Its Application 2007*, LNCS 4706, Part II, pp. 383–396, 2007. Springer-Verlag. Berlin 2007.
7. C. Karlof and D. Wagner, Secure routing in wireless sensor networks: Attacks and countermeasures, in *Proceedings of the 1st IEEE International Workshop on Sensor Network Protocols and Applications* (Anchorage, AK, May 11, 2003).
8. National Institute of Standards and Technology, Wireless ad hoc sensor networks, http://w3.antd.nist.gov/wahn_ssn.shtml, retrieved 12th January, 2008.
9. S. Gupta, Automatic detection of DOS routing attach in wireless sensor network, MS thesis, Department of Computer Science University of Houston, December 2006.
10. R. Roman, J. Zhou, and J. Lopez, Applying intrusion detection systems to wireless sensor networks, *Consumer Communications and Networking Conference, 2006. CCNC 2006. 3rd IEEE*, January 8–10, 2006, vol. 1, pp. 640–644.
11. P. Bruth and C. Ko, Challenges in intrusion detection for wireless ad hoc networks, in *Application and the Internet Workshops, 2003 Symposium on*, pp. 368–373, 2003.
12. R. Chadha, G. Lapiotis, S. Wright, Policy-based networking, IEEE Network special issue, March/April 2002, vol. 16, guest editors.
13. L. B. Ruiz, J. M. Nogueira, and A. A. F. Loureiro, MANNA: A management architecture for wireless sensor networks, *IEEE Communications Magazine*, 2003.
14. W. Chen, N. Jain, and S. Singh, ANMP: Ad hoc network management protocol, *IEEE Journal on Selected Areas in Communications*, vol. 17, pp. 1506–1531, August 1999.
15. P. Techateerawat and A. Jennings, Energy efficiency of intrusion detection systems in wireless sensor networks, *Proceedings of the 2006 IEEE/WIC/ACM International Conference on Web Intelligence and Intelligent Agent Technology (WI-IAT 2006 Workshops) (WI-IATW '06)* 0-7695-2749-3/06.
16. O. Kachirski and R. Guha, Intrusion detection using mobile agents in wireless ad hoc networks, *Proceedings of the IEEE Workshop on Knowledge Media Networking*, pp. 153–158, 2002.
17. D. R. Raymond and S. F. Midkiff, Denial-of-service in wireless sensor networks: Attacks and defenses, *IEEE Pervasive Computing*, vol. 7, pp. 74–81, 2008.

18. V. Bhuse and A. Gupta, Anomaly intrusion detection in wireless sensor network, *Journal of High Speed Networks*, vol. 15, pp. 33–51, January 2006.

19. B. Bhargava and W. Wang, *Visualization of Wormholes in Sensor Networks*, New York: ACM Press, 2004.

20. P. Albers et al., Security in ad hoc networks: A general intrusion detection architecture enhancing trust based approaches, *1st Int'l. Wksp. Wireless Info. Sys.*, Ciudad Real, Spain, April 3–6, 2002.

21. L. Zhou and Z. J. Haas, Securing ad hoc networks, *IEEE Network*, vol. 13, November–December 1999, pp. 24–30, January, 2008.

22. Y. F. Zhang, and W. Lee, Intrusion detection in wireless ad hoc networks, *The 6th Annual International Conference on Mobile Computing and Networking*, Boston, MA, August 2000, pp. 275–283.

23. G. Li, J. He, and Y. Fu, A group-based intrusion detection scheme in wireless sensor networks, *The 3rd International Conference on Grid and Pervasive Computing—Workshops*, 2008.

24. Y. Mao, A semantic-based intrusion detection framework for wireless sensor network, *Networked Computing (INC), 2010 6th International Conference on, IEEE*, 2010.

25. R. Dong et al., Intrusion detection system based on payoff matrix for wireless sensor networks, *Genetic and Evolutionary Computing, 2009. WGEC '09, 3rd International Conference on, IEEE*, 2009.

26. S. V. Patel, K. Pandey, and V. R. Rathod, Decentralised clustered and hash based intrusion detection system for wireless sensor networks, *Wireless Communication and Sensor Networks, 2008. WCSN 2008. Fourth International Conference on, IEEE*, 2008.

27. J. Tian and M. Gao, Intelligent community intrusion detection system based on wireless sensor network and fuzzy neural network, *ISECS International Colloquium on Computing, Communication, Control, and Management*, 2009.

28. Y. Ma, H. Cao, and J. Ma, The intrusion detection method based on game theory in wireless sensor network, *Ubi-Media Computing, 2008 First IEEE International Conference on, IEEE*, 2008.

29. Y. Ponomarchuk and D.-W. Seo, Intrusion detection based on traffic analysis in wireless sensor networks, *Wireless and Optical Communications Conference (WOCC), 2010 19th Annual IEEE*, 2010.

30. N. Aschenbruck et al., A security architecture and modular intrusion detection system for WSNs, *Networked Sensing Systems (INSS), 2012 Ninth International Conference on, IEEE*, 2012.

31. S. Rajasegarar, C. Leckie, and M. Palaniswami, Anomaly detection in wireless sensor networks, *IEEE Wireless Communications*, vol. 15, pp. 34–40, 2008.

32. H. M. Salmon et al., Intrusion detection system for wireless sensor networks using danger theory immune-inspired techniques, *International Journal of Wireless Information Networks*, vol. 20, pp. 39–66, 2013.

33. M. Zamani et al., A DDoS-aware IDS model based on danger theory and mobile agents, *Proceedings of the 2009 International Conference on Computational Intelligence and Security*, vol. 1, 2009.

34. S.-S. Wang et al., An integrated intrusion detection system for cluster-based wireless sensor networks, *Expert Systems with Applications*, vol. 38, pp. 15234–15243, 2011.

17 Unique Challenges in WiFi Intrusion Detection

Jonny Milliken

CONTENTS

17.1 WIFI SECURITY

WLAN networks are increasingly common in public, private, and commercial environments. As proliferation of these networks increases, the opportunity for exploitation of their vulnerabilities also increases. Perpetration of attacks on WLAN networks is increasingly frequent in real-life environments. The 2012 Verizon Breach Report [1] summarizes cyber-security breaches reported to the national security agencies of Australia, the Netherlands, Ireland, the United Kingdom, and the United States of America. This report estimates that 174 million compromised records were stolen through cyber attacks in 2011. These attacks represent a global problem as shown by the distribution of attack locations reported in Figure 17.1. In the same report, it is estimated that 81% of attacks incorporated some form of hacking, and 69% contained malware.

The UK insurance group CPP has produced a white paper [2], which specifically deals with the threat and danger of attacks on WiFi. The report states that, *"Wireless device users ... should think about what they may be forfeiting by continuing to utilise wireless network technology without thinking about their online security."* This was backed up by the actions of an ethical hacker who was hired to carry out wireless attacks on public WiFi hotspots in September 2010 in six cities across the UK. Findings remark the majority of users mistakenly think their networks are secure, all in spite of well-known examples of WiFi insecurity. This false assumption of security is also exposed when 20% of respondents admit to having logged onto unsecured wireless networks without permission. Reasons for this included the following:

- Because it was available
- Because it was convenient
- Because it was easy to do
- Because they were having access problems of their own
- By accident

The CPP investigation also uncovered that one in six wireless users say they regularly use public networks. When directly investigating public, open-access networks, the report uncovered that passwords and usernames could be gathered from these networks at a rate of more than 350 per hour in a typical town center. Furthermore, when a rogue access point was deployed at the same location,

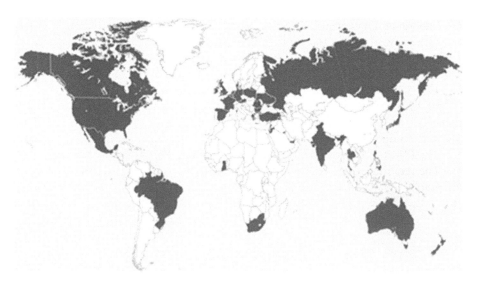

FIGURE 17.1 Countries in which a successful cyber security breach was recorded (in black) for 2011. (From Verizon 2012 data breach investigations report. With permission.)

more than 200 users unsuspectingly connected, putting themselves at risk from fraudsters. This is particularly dangerous given that more than 60% of respondents use these networks for online banking and shopping, potentially exposing their identity and credit card information to malicious hackers.

These threats in WiFi networks are an area of increasing concern for businesses as well as the public. The virus company Symantec has released commentaries [3] on how municipal WiFi offers threats to businesses through employees using these networks ahead of corporate options and thus potentially revealing internal information to hackers through a back door. One of the largest and most expensive examples of WiFi attacks on businesses was carried out against TJX, a large American department store, in 2007. The attackers carried out their attack while sitting in a car nearby the head office and pointing a directional antenna at the building. Within a short time frame, sufficient packets were collected to allow bypass of the WEP security on the internal company WiFi. Once this access was achieved, the attackers then set up a back door into the system and employed a home PC to harvest nearly 46 million credit card details from the database.

17.2 ATTACKS SPECIFIC TO WIFI NETWORKS

WiFi fundamentally differs from the Ethernet at the physical (layer 1) and medium access (layer 2) OSI layers. The shift from a wired medium to an openly contended wireless medium mandated that significant changes needed to be implemented. These changes expose WiFi-connected machines to unique attacks. This means that WIDS have a unique 802.11 threat burden, which is additional to that of their wired counterparts.

The basic catalogue of WiFi attacks can be distilled into three rudimentary attack types: DoS (denial of service), encryption bypass, and AP (access point) masquerading. Each of these attacks allows the hacker a different level of control over the network: control of the access medium, control of data confidentiality, or control over network access.

17.2.1 WiFi DENIAL OF SERVICE (DoS)

The vulnerabilities that allow DoS attacks in wireless networks come from two sources. The first is the trust placed in the fidelity of source MAC addresses. MAC addresses are expected to be unique identifiers used to distinguish one device from another; however, there is no mechanism for validating these addresses. An attacker can spoof the address of any client.

The second vulnerability is the lack of authentication on deauthentication frames. This means that any attacker armed with knowledge of a client's MAC address can deauthenticate the client by sending forged deauthentication frames known as a DeAuth attack as shown in Figure 17.2 and discussed in [4]. Although the client will soon attempt to reconnect, if the attack is continued, then the victim remains disconnected indefinitely.

It is possible to perform the same attack using disassociation frames; however, due to the single rather than double state retraction (see Figure 17.3) there is less work and time required by the victim to reconnect. This requires more effort for the attacker to maintain a loss of connection.

While this situation deals with a DoS attack on a single client, there is the possibility of using the same method to broadcast the attack to all users connected to the AP. The principle is the same, except that only the AP MAC address is needed. The attacker forges a frame seemingly to have come from the broadcast address of the AP, telling all clients that they have been disconnected.

A second DoS attack category for WLANs is the frame flood attack. The goal of this attack is to overload the victim AP with frames (usually either probe or association). This ensures that either no more clients can connect or overloading of the AP processor causes it to crash. The key difference between the two DoS methods is that the deauthentication attack exploits the authentication state machine (Figure 17.3) while the flooding attack exploits the limited resources available for APs.

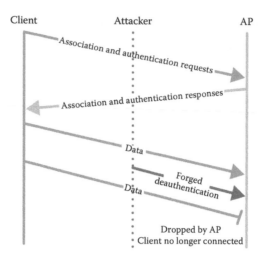

FIGURE 17.2 Deauthentication DoS attack.

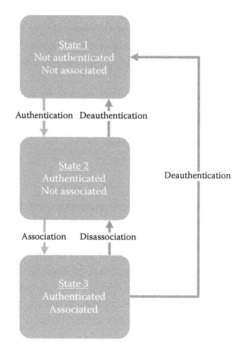

FIGURE 17.3 802.11 authentication state machine.

Now that the method of perpetrating these attacks is clear, why would an attacker wish to carry out such an attack? There can be many motives for a DoS attack:

- Nuisance
- Attacking adjacent networks
- Forcing a re-authentication to capture a client authentication handshake
- Tricking a client to re-authenticate to a masquerading AP
- Tricking a client to re-authenticate for a MITM (man-in-the-middle) attack
- Buffer overflow attack
- Blanket spamming the network to perform other attacks

17.2.1.1 Deauthentication Attack Detection

Current approaches to DeAuth DoS attacks have attempted to develop algorithms to detect these attacks [5,6]. The effectiveness of these algorithms is highly dependent on the data which is being used to fuel them [7]. As a result there has been a trend in more recent publications toward identifying and classifying the features or metrics that are optimal for DeAuth DoS detection [7,8]. It has been shown from these investigations that there are subsets of features that are optimal for attack detection. In some cases, using a reduced feature set can improve detection performance as there are less confounding factors or noise for an algorithm to filter [9].

Much of the work on feature selection has concentrated on the effects seen in the application and network layer [5,8]. Work in [7] has identified a set of features that are applicable to WiFi because layer 2 is an area of limited investigation in current research. What is lacking from each of these works is information on the parameters or bounds of these metrics. Some research has prioritized the features under consideration, but there is no identification of what values the metrics or features would undertake to detect an attack [7–9].

Underpinning the importance of parameter bound selection for DoS metrics is the appreciation of the effect that thresholds and windowing factors can have on performance [5]. The effect of thresholds is investigated in [10], showing that the choice of the value for this parameter must be both dynamic and considered unique for each deployment. Windowing refers to the selection of data under consideration of an algorithm, usually determined as the number of packets in a given time frame. The effect of varying this window is considered to influence the outcome of a detection algorithm [5,11]; however, it is not always taken into account in WLAN experiments as demonstrated by [6,8,12].

The effect of varying the parameter bounds in these values on detection outcome has been investigated in higher layers. If threshold values and metric parameters are set too high, then valid detections can be missed, and if they are set too low, then a larger number of false alerts can be generated, which obfuscates the real security concerns [10]. The same effect is observed for windowing, if the window of data under consideration is too small, then larger attack chains may be missed, and too large a window size wastes computational resources and can obfuscate attacks in a large pool of normal data [13].

17.2.1.2 Flooding DoS Attack Detection

Probe and association flooding attacks are considered trivial to carry out [14,15] but are much more difficult to detect as high levels of these frames can be legitimately present in a congested environment. The effect of increased levels of authentication or probe requests has been experimentally shown in [15] and [16] to have an impact on network performance, which is attributed to the overwhelming consumption of AP resources. Association request floods are equally effective as many practical 802.11 implementations are flawed and allow the AP to respond to these requests without having first gone through authentication [14].

Despite the danger that these attacks pose, the authors in [16] lament the scarcity of studies to investigate the impact and propose solutions to DoS flooding attacks. In order to address this deficit, the authors suggest several mitigation techniques for a VoIP application but consider them to be insufficient in practice. MAC address filtering can mitigate the effects; however, this does not scale as the whitelist grows. Furthermore, it is only appropriate for SOHO (single office/home office) environments because enterprise and open access deployments can have legitimately large number of unknown MAC addresses connecting to the AP. Another suggested defense technique employs a threshold for accepted requests, estimated at five per second. However, this threshold is acknowledged as having to vary with time as traffic loads increase, which poses similar problems as alluded to above.

Threshold and feature selection remains a problem for flooding attacks as observed in [17], in which a subset of features is determined as relevant for attack detection but the values of which are not developed. Work in [18] has established that threshold selection is an integral part of detection, which is sometimes overlooked due to the time and effort required to tune the correct values. Even in cases where this is done, the first step is for a human to arbitrarily guess the correct level and then tune based on traffic. Nonetheless, these factors are not always taken into consideration in flooding investigations as observed in [19].

Factors that impact on the performance of a DoS attack are listed in [12] as attack duration, attack rate, and average processing time for a frame. Research carried out in [12,14,15], however, suggests that these are not the only relevant factors in causing a DoS condition; parameters set within the AP can contribute too. In [15], it has been proposed that the main vulnerability actually lies in unacknowledged frame retransmission, which causes memory buffer exhaustion and freezes AP functionality. An AP requires a certain amount of memory and computing time to store and retransmit frames that have not been replied to, and if the limit of frames scheduled for retry is reached, then other received frames can be discarded, and the AP can hang.

If the AP retry limit is set too high, then many packets can be held in the buffer and make the AP more likely to fall victim to a flooding attack. In both [14,15], it is remarked that this retry limit is difficult to set via software or even at the firmware level. To compound this threat, the retry level has been observed as having different sizes for different frame types handled by a given AP and between different APs [15].

Even if a DoS condition is not caused, the response time for an AP can be affected by the size of this limit. This decreases the efficiency of the AP by increasing response time by up to 60%–80% versus the base value as seen in [15] for PRF (probe request flood), ASRF (association request flood), and ARF (authentication request flood). If an AP is also loaded with a high level of legitimate traffic processing requirements, the rate of frames required in order to cause resource exhaustion drops, making the attack more easy to perform and difficult to detect. Research carried out in [12] observed that as few as three requests generated 21 responses from a real AP, consuming more resources than would be expected. Thus, the practical environment for DoS flooding does not necessarily follow the strict 802.11 protocol in all cases.

17.2.2 WiFi Encryption Bypass (WEP & WPA/2)

Data transmitted over a WiFi connection is available to all devices within reception range, regardless of the intended recipient. Encryption is a critical requirement for WLANs to protect the confidentiality of the data in transit. This encryption is not without flaws however and detection of attempts at bypassing this protection is an important factor for any WIDS.

17.2.2.1 Encryption Attacks (WEP)

The WEP (wired equivalent privacy) security standard was ratified in September 1999 by the IEEE and was designed to emulate wired security over a wireless network. However, it was quickly discovered by the end of 2001 that this privacy system has serious structural flaws, for example,

- Poor key management and size
- The IV (initialization vector) is too small
- The checksum is insufficient
- Weak use of the RC4 stream cipher
- Authentication messages can be forged

The major flaw of the WEP encryption algorithm is the reliance on the RC4 stream cipher, IVs for secure encryption, and the linear CRC checksum for reliability [20]. The function of the stream cipher is to expand a short key into an infinite pseudo-random key stream before transmission, and the checksum ensures that the total bits received are the same as those sent. To begin with, the WEP algorithm forms the RC4 traffic key by concatenating the passkey with the IV. This cipher is then

XOR-ed with the plaintext to create the cipher text and sent across the medium. Upon reception of the cipher text at the destination, the algorithm XOR's the cipher text again (using the same cipher) to retrieve the original plaintext. This system is diagrammatically shown in Figure 17.4.

The purpose of the IV in this method is to prevent repetition of the RC4 key so that each packet has a different encryption key. However, because the size is only 24 bits, it is statistically likely that this IV will repeat over a relatively short space of time. The RC4 cipher has also been shown to favor some "weak" keys, in which the correlation between the key and the output is higher than tolerable [21].

WEP security can be bypassed using free, open source software and widely available processes [22]. There are different methods of perpetrating the attack. Of these attacks, the FMS (Fluhrer, Mantin, Shamir) and PTW (Pyshkin, Tews, Weinmann) are the most prominent and well known.

17.2.2.1.1 FMS

The RC4 algorithm uses the previous byte value in determining the calculation of each subsequent byte in the stream, which was meant to keep the encryption changing. Under a set of conditional values, it is possible for the FMS attack to compute the likely value of each subsequent part of the key based on the constantly incoming stream of encrypted packets. As the packets are changing and the value is never certain, each possible key value is given one "vote" every time it occurs with the most polled value given priority in final key guessing. After a certain number of packets, the correct value will statistically rise to the top and so on for the rest of the key.

Unfortunately, because this is a statistical attack, around 4–5 million packets are required for a 50% success rate. However, this was the first attack to show the vulnerabilities in the WEP attack and has since been improved.

17.2.2.1.2 PTW

While the FMS attack only used a small subset of packets, the PTW advanced this by discovering a correlation that did not require other conditions to be met, and thus every packet could be used—not just weak ones. Furthermore, a relationship was discovered between not only the next byte but on subsequent bytes. Thus the attack has the facility to guess multiple proceeding bytes rather than each one in turn, making the voting system much faster.

This attack only needs 35,000–40,000 packets for a 50% probability of success. This could allow key derivation within 60 s on a busy network. The number of packets required has since been further decreased through various tweaks.

17.2.2.2 Encryption Attacks (WPA/2)

Once the flaws in WEP were exposed, an upgrade was quickly released, known as WPA (Wi-Fi protected access). This certification algorithm was built upon the WEP security system as a precursor to the release of a much more secure system (WPA2). The biggest improvement was the addition of TKIP (temporal key integrity protocol), which has since been devalued [22]. This implements a key

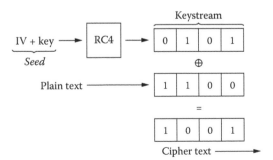

FIGURE 17.4 WEP RC4 cipher. (From Wikipedia, Author M. Handley released under CC-BY-SA license.)

mixing function that combines the root key with the IV before passing on to RC4, instigates a sequence counter to protect against replay attacks, and replaces CRC with a MIC (message integrity check).

Both the WPA and modern WPA2 systems (as part of 802.11i) operate a "four-way handshake" between AP and client. This is performed at the beginning of a client session or on the first access request to the network. As seen in Figure 17.5, an AP sends a nonce value to the client (STA), which can be used to construct the PTK (pairwise transient key). The client then responds with a nonce and the MIC (message integrity code). If the AP constructs the correct PTK from this data, then the STA has correctly hashed the key and is allowed access. If authentication is successful, then a GTK (group temporal key) is sent to the client. Once a client leaves the network or after a set timeframe, the GTK is retransmitted to all registered clients. This is much more secure because the master key is never used.

It has been shown however that the shared key can still be established from this handshake by forcing and listening to a re-authentication of a legitimate user. This will allow DoS attacks on the network.

17.2.2.2.1 802.11i & WPA2

802.11i is an amendment to the original 802.11 specification, which deals specifically with the security issues raised by the depreciation of the WEP security algorithm. Note that the four-way handshake mentioned previously is a part of this security improvement although it was applied to both WPA and WPA2.

All of the enhancements of this standard were implemented in the WPA2 algorithm. WPA2 is the most up to date wireless security and certification method and is considered a fully secure system. The 802.11i upgrade from WPA comes from the implementation of an AES algorithm called CCMP (counter mode CBC MAC protocol) to replace the compromised TKIP protocol.

AES (advanced encryption standard) is the cipher used in replacement of RC4 and is much more secure as it is a block cipher, operating on blocks 128MB long. CCMP is the security protocol used by AES and computes the MIC value. The total encryption system is much more complex than WEP but makes it much more difficult to break. Nonetheless, this system can also still be bypassed using a brute force or dictionary attack with a weak passkey.

Despite these improvements made to WPA/WPA2, it is still vulnerable to a dictionary attack. A dictionary attack is a cryptographic attack on a cipher in which a series of possible guesses are made against the passkey in an attempt to gain access. This attack works under the assumption that the user has chosen a dictionary-based word, name, place, etc. as the passkey, possibly with an additional numeric digit. A wordlist is used to encapsulate all the possibilities to fuel the attack.

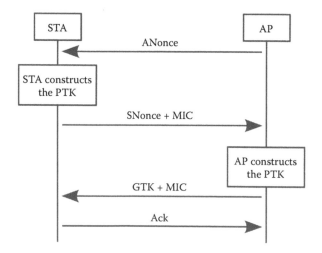

FIGURE 17.5 WPA four-way handshake. (From Wikipedia, Author Mikm released under public license.)

WPA/WPA2 is also susceptible to a brute force attack. This attempts to break the encryption by guessing *all possible* key combinations, aiming to guess the correct sequence. With most systems this can take an exceptional length of time. As an example, a seven-character password made up of any variation of ASCII characters would take five years to break with a computer that can test 500,000 passwords per second.* Thus, it is not considered a significant threat because most password-based systems are technically vulnerable to the attack.

The final vulnerability for WPA2 system is the "Hole 196" attack although it requires the attacker to already have access to the network, i.e., they must already be an authorized user. This insider may inject spoofed GTK encrypted packets, which allows them to obtain and decrypt data from other authorized users.

17.2.3 AP MASQUERADING

Although encryption will attempt to ensure that the connection from a client to an AP is secure, there is no facility to guarantee that the AP itself is legitimate. There is a real danger in modern networks from the threat of AP masquerading. This attack occurs when another device appears, trying to mimic the credentials of an existing AP. This is usually with the intention of having a client connect and then viewing their data as it passes through the malicious AP. Three types of common masquerading APs are outlined here.

17.2.3.1 Rogue AP

A succinct taxonomy of rogue APs is proposed in [23] in which each attack is categorized into one of four classes. These classes are the following:

- Improperly configured AP
- Unauthorized AP
- Phishing AP
- Compromised AP

An *improperly configured AP* is one which suffers from misconfiguration of security settings, which then allows an unauthorized user to gain access to an otherwise legitimate AP. Attacks leveraging poor configuration options are recognized as a major threat in WLANs in practice [10].

Unauthorized APs are defined as physical devices deployed and illegally connected to the network under threat. This creates an additional wireless hardware presence in the vicinity for attackers to use to gain access to a LAN.

A *phishing AP* is set up by a malicious entity outside of the network it wishes to attack, advertising itself as a trustworthy AP and enticing legitimate users to connect. Once a client has erroneously connected to this device, the controller of the phishing AP can harvest credentials and data.

The final type of rogue AP is a *compromised AP*, which the authors in [23] identify as a device that has had the WEP or WPA encryption bypassed using a piece of software. This allows access for an illegal user but with "legitimate" traffic through a legitimate device.

Research into detecting these attacks is currently lacking [24] although they are considered a more technically difficult but growing threat [25]. It is even estimated that as many as 20% of all enterprise locations already have a rogue AP connected to their systems and hence are particularly at risk from these attacks [24,26]. Users of WLANs in public environments are also considered vulnerable [27].

General solutions to these attack types in layer 2 are outlined, but not proven, in [23] as implementing AP probing and tracking location information for duplicate MAC addresses. These methods are insufficient as AP probing may simply identify networks that are legitimate nearby APs

---

* http://www.lastbit.com/pswcalc.asp

from the general public or other enterprises. Tracking duplicate MAC information also assumes there are no reflections or mobility issues within the environment, which can cause late or uncommon frame reception values, leading to false positives.

One of the most common measures of identity in WLAN systems in modern research is the RSSI (received signal strength indicator) of packets. The authors in [28,29] suggest that using a distributed set of sensors sufficient RSSI information can be gathered to provide identification to combat rogue APs.

There is disagreement on the usefulness of RSSIs in practical environments. The authors in [26,29] conclude that use of a RSSI as a WLAN location indicator is flawed as multipath effects and AP specific processing of RSSI frame values severely impact results and make them unreliable. Furthermore, in [30] it is suggested that attackers, knowing RSSI is used as a detection metric, can alter their transmission power in frequent intervals in order to defeat the detection algorithm. Thus the usefulness of RSSI as a metric for absolute identification in rogue APs is uncertain.

The future for detection in rogue APs is alluded to in [31] as devising *"irrefutable device identification through traffic characteristics."* This identifies the key problem as that of attributing traffic as being transmitted from a specific source. An identity-based detection system may be able to foil DoS attacks too [14].

17.2.3.2 Soft AP

A soft AP differs from a rogue AP in implementation rather than features. It is implied that a rogue AP is based in hardware, and a soft AP is a device that would otherwise be considered a client, a laptop or desktop for example, that begins to act like an AP.

Soft APs should be easier to spot given that in most cases the MAC address, power level, and location should be identical before and after the launch of the attack. However, if a new MAC address is forged by the soft AP, then there may be no way of distinguishing it from all other access points on the network side. In terms of resolution, a soft AP may also be much more difficult to find because it will not be a physical router as one might expect.

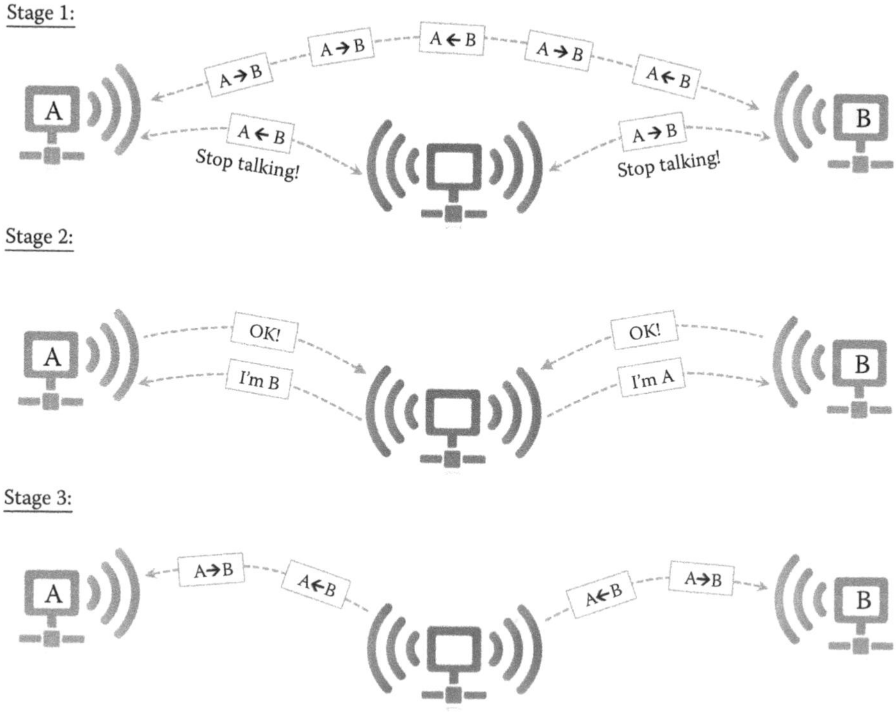

FIGURE 17.6 Man-in-the-middle attack.

17.2.3.3 MITM

A MITM (man-in-the-middle) attack begins with one of either a rogue or soft AP and attempts to have a client connect before routing the traffic back to the original AP through the attacker, shown in Figure 17.6. The attacker can then monitor all the actions of the client and uncover passwords, personal or banking details, or redirect traffic. This is most commonly performed in WiFi networks through an ARP (address resolution protocol) poisoning attack. ARP poisoning operates by sending faked ARP packets to the AP and the client with the aim of poisoning each node into believing that the attacker is the other device within the network.

17.3 THE EFFECT OF DEPLOYMENT ARCHITECTURE ON WIDS PERFORMANCE

Due to the additional challenges in moderating the use of a wireless medium, deployment of a WIDS in different locations or integration with different devices can have an impact on the WiFi traffic available for detection purposes. To give a trivial example, Windows Network Manager asks the user to define each access point it uses as home, at work, or in the open, and changes the security settings accordingly. Choosing the correct architecture for a WIDS is of particular importance to the performance of the system although this is very rarely addressed in research work.

Typically, WIDS deployments tend to be static and cannot be easily manipulated once set up, so it is important that sufficient planning is carried out at installation. Although there are many different ways that a WIDS could conceivably be constructed, it is important to develop broad categories to reduce the problem complexity. For the purposes of this chapter, three distinct network topographies are considered: home, enterprise, and open access (public).

In general there are four attributes that differentiate these three categories from each other:

- Access knowledge
- User behavior
- Equipment
- Threats

17.3.1 HOME NETWORK

Home networks are found in a variety of home environments. There are wide variations on this theme:

- A family network with a single desktop, mobile laptop, and no guests
- A tech savvy network with a stationary laptop, one games console, a media center and guests
- A HMO with many mobile laptops, many games consoles, and guests
- Any combination of the three

Nonetheless, due to the nature of the network and the circumstances of the location, there are still some factors in common across the majority of examples.

In general, a home network will consist of an enclosed environment without easy physical or network access. This assumes the home is secured from intruders and there is security enabled on the system, whether that security is WEP, WPA/WPA2, MAC filtering, etc. No person may enter the location or gain access to the network without the knowledge of the administrators.

There will likely be multiple administrators as each user will have a responsibility for security. Although most systems will have a head administrator who handles technical issues, all users have access to passwords and network resources without being overseen by others. The number of users is generally fixed and is unlikely to vary except for very minimal guests who will connect to the same network as normal clients.

Each of these users and guests will use the network up to its maximum capacity, i.e., for streaming video, downloading large files, or playing online games. Thus, while the amount of clients may be small, the network usage will be high with unpredictable peaks. With few users and high usage per user, if any one client connects or disconnects, then the entire traffic will be shifted dramatically and may often be unstable (Table 17.1).

Aside from exceptional circumstances, there is likely to be one routing AP for all users and so only one channel to consider. While there may be adjacent channel usage and nearby APs, they are not under the remit of the administrators and only contribute noise and interference. This single AP will likely only have to cover the home area, which may be over many floors.

The risks to the network will typically only come from one side of the physical divide—the outside. Those users inside the network have little vested interest in attacking the security or destroying the connection of the network because they all have total rights and access. Users on the outside may wish to either utilize the connection or simply nuisance DoS the users. There may be some confidential data going through the network, such as bank/social networking or personal details, and so attacks of this kind could be damaging if not considered in the network security.

Due to the low user count, low coverage area, and the requirement of monitoring only the single channel of the home AP, the most successful placement of a WIDS would most likely be in the access point itself. This would provide maximum security for all users while freeing them all from the burden of guaranteeing it. In a system in which the administrator terminal cannot guarantee attendance onsite (or constant operation), the only constant in the equation, the AP, must bear the burden. While this will impact on the throughput of the router, the trade-off between performance and security may well be beneficial.

17.3.2 Enterprise Network

Enterprise networks tend to have a quicker response time in terms of security because the data that can move through them is more sensitive and usually pertains to the actions of the business. Yet as businesses can be highly diverse so are their network security needs. A typical enterprise network could be defined as

- A large corporation with one network over many sites, in many countries, and with thousands of employees with different access privileges

TABLE 17.1
Home Network Topography Characteristics

	Characteristic	Home Network
Access knowledge	Physical	Always
	Network	Always
User behavior	Number	Low (1–5)
	Data usage	High and unstable
	Number of admins	All users
Equipment	Coverage area	Low
	# APs/# channels	1/1
Threats	Confidential data?	Some
	From outside network	Rogue AP/DoS
	From inside network	None

- A medium-sized enterprise with a single IT department and many employees on one site
- A small business with general access to all employees and a single member as an IT specialist

Any enterprise regulates who comes and goes from the building, but this is not necessarily true of the network access. Although there are often security policies in effect, there are ways of attaining wireless and wired access to the network outside of the administrative department's knowledge. This can stretch from BYOD (bring your own device) to setup of a rogue AP. Thus physical, but not necessarily network, access is mandated.

There will only be a finite amount of administrators of the wireless system, so in many instances, employees may be motivated to evade policy or security on the network. This limits the amount of staff who are employed to oversee the network and can create access issues. Many staff may accidently break security protocol without knowledge of the consequences.

The number of users in this situation is usually fixed or at least can vary predictably as does the entrance of guests. It is not uncommon to have a guest network set up in larger businesses so that invitees can avail of Internet resources without gaining access to company documents and files. The traffic that these users and guests generate can be high but is also predictable. High bandwidth applications, such as video conferencing, may be employed, and there will quite likely be a background of http activity (Table 17.2).

Typically, the location will require multiple APs to service all the users over a larger coverage area, and a WIDS may include dedicated sensors to remove any processing from enterprise machines. In order to facilitate these multiple APs, channel planning must be done to combat interference between devices. Usually, 802.11b/g/n channels, for example, are deployed in triplets with this same three channels re-used over changing locations.

Finally, there is quite likely to be a significant amount of confidential and important data flowing through this network. The risks to this data may come from both inside and outside of the physical barriers and inside and outside of the network so vigilance is necessary. Attacks from the inside are most likely to be innocent rogue or mis-configured APs although these can be very dangerous in providing access to confidential data by external sources.

External specific attacks may include attempting to bypass data encryption or setup of a rogue AP in order to gain access to an employee's data. While DoS attacks are dangerous under any circumstance, in this instance, they may be less of a priority due to the potentially distributed nature of the network.

TABLE 17.2
Enterprise Network Topography Characteristics

	Characteristic	Enterprise Network
Access knowledge	Physical	Always
	Network	Sometimes
User behavior	Number	High (10+)
	Data usage	High and stable
	Number of admins	Low
Equipment	Coverage area	High
	# APs/# channels	x/≈3
Threats	Confidential data?	Yes
	From outside network	Encryption bypass
	From inside network	Rogue AP

Due to the possibly large coverage area that may expand over many channels, a distributed series of detectors is likely to be the best WIDS solution to an enterprise problem. Because multiple frequencies may be used, it would be prudent for detectors to channel hop rather than embedding the solution in a static AP.

Each of the distributed nodes will likely feed the data back to a controller or multiple controllers who can monitor any suspicious activity in the network as well as receive alerts. In this solution, the administrator can take responsibility for the security of the entire system over a large area from a single terminal.

17.3.3 OPEN ACCESS NETWORK

Open access networks tend to be deployed in areas of high public attendance, such as airports, shopping malls, or cafes, and, to some extent, represent a small portion of wireless network coverage compared to the other two categories. For the purposes of this classification, open access means that anyone *can* access the network, and it is not restricted to set users, whether the access is paid or free.

Typical open access networks share two key characteristics:

- Open right to access for all
- Usually installed and available in a public place

First, it is clear that there are no physical or network access controls for administrators. Any client can connect whether or not they reside within a physical boundary and are not restricted through encryption or filtering.

The number of users may be highly variable and may use any traffic pattern although the general use is not typically high. Clients do not tend to play online games or hold video conferences. Generally, the traffic usage is much lower and unstable dependent on specific users of the network at any given instance.

In a commercial atmosphere, there is likely to only be one AP or possibly two, depending on size and demand and so one channel per device. The coverage area is likely to be small and manageable although it could stretch over several floors in some cases. In most businesses that provide this service, there will be a computer on site that could act as a point for security administration.

Confidential data should be kept to a minimum by any responsible user in this environment although this cannot be ensured. There is a significant risk of attack from both inside and outside the network although the severity of this threat is proportional to how well users adhere to a low confidential data policy. Because there is no backbone structure to the network other than Internet access, there should not be any files or documents to protect on the network itself.

In this environment, the main attack threat would be from rogue APs. It would be trivial to set up a false AP and have naive users accidentally connect to what would appear to be a legitimate open access network. Further threats come from client DoS attacks by other users, possibly hoping to gain a better connection by disconnecting other clients. Because there is unlikely to be encryption employed, a WEP/WPA/WPA2 attack does not apply (Table 17.3).

Due to the small coverage area of the network and the reliance on only one or two APs, the best WIDS solution to an open access topography would be a single administrator on an onsite computer who relies on data being fed back from detectors embedded in operational APs. Because the number of channels is limited, only these channels need to be monitored. However, there is a case to have the administrator computer channel hop on non-AP channels to try and alert to rogue APs. As the traffic demands and expectation of service are lower, the AP should be able to handle the extra workload without heavily compromising on throughput.

TABLE 17.3
Open Access Topography Characteristics

	Characteristic	Open Access Network
Access knowledge	Physical	No
	Network	No
User behavior	Volume	Variable
	Data usage	Low and unstable
	Number of admins	Low
Equipment	Coverage area	Small
	# APs/# channels	1–2/1–2
Threats	Confidential data?	No
	From outside network	Rogue AP
	From inside network	Soft AP, DoS

17.3.4 Summary

A comparison of each of the networks is given in Table 17.4. It is unlikely that any network will adhere entirely to the definitions, but the table can be used as a guide. For example, if a network takes five characteristics from home, three characteristics from enterprise, and two from open access, then the threats to each network can be scaled and prioritized. Regarding threat identification for WIDS purposes, each category places a different emphasis on the likely attacks and the relationship to the rest of the network, focused on those aspects that are under greatest threat.

17.3.4.1 The Importance of Live Data in WiFi Research

Although there has been research in establishing techniques for detecting attacks against WiFi networks, none has yet produced a comprehensive solution. One of the reasons for this is the difficulty in obtaining real-world data to work with in security assessments [32]. The majority of data used for validation is contrived or unverified either through use of synthetic network traffic modeling, laboratory testbed approximations, or protected data [33]. This has led to a significant disparity between research conclusions and their practical application to real networks [32].

Importantly, while WiFi data collection systems have been deployed in previous research endeavors, none have given sufficient information to be able to replicate and verify the collection systems, and

TABLE 17.4
Network Topography Comparison

	Characteristic	Home	Enterprise	Open
Access knowledge	Physical	Always	Always	No
	Network	Always	Sometimes	No
User behavior	Number	Low (1–5)	High (10+)	Variable
	Data usage	High and unstable	High and stable	Low and unstable
	Number of admins	All users	Medium	Low
Equipment	Coverage area	Low	High	Low
	# APs/# channels	1/1	x/≈3	1–2/1–2
Threats	Confidential data?	Some	Yes	No
	From outside network	Rogue AP/C & B DoS	Encryption hack	Rogue AP
	From inside network	None	Rogue AP	Rogue AP, C DoS

hence the data derived from them. Therefore, it is impossible to determine the effect of the method-ology used for data collection on the accuracy of the results drawn from the collected traffic. There are opportunities however for leveraging data collected from live networks to provide information on how attacks are carried out in practice that could aid the practical application of WiFi research.

A more flexible and effective method of obtaining research data may be to establish standardized methods of collection, rather than standardizing the data itself. This requires research into the best means of developing the equipment and structure of such systems so that they remain applicable and deployable in multiple environments. A system derived from these criteria can continue to generate new insights as user behavior and traffic evolves.

17.4   RESEARCH DATA SET CATEGORIZATION

One of the most important aspects of generating accurate, reliable, and replicable results in research is ensuring that the data on which conclusions are based is sound. For WLAN experiments, one means of addressing this problem is the identification of appropriate data sets. It is not uncommon for research papers to generate their own data set; however, this presents problems in comparing data sets and the results based on them [34]. Selecting a suitable data source is an important factor in ensuring that the results drawn from experiments are accurate and relevant.

Data sets in research generally fall into the following four categories:

* Baseline data
* Simulations
* Traffic generators
* Live network data

17.4.1   BASELINE DATA SETS

Baseline data has been produced specifically for the purposes of acting as a comparison between algorithms. Since the emergence of intrusion detection, many different baseline data sets have been produced.

Some examples of these data sets in intrusion detection include Lincoln Labs (2000) and DARPA (2002). DARPA is known as the standard, albeit imperfect, data set for intrusion detection experi-ments [13]. This data was produced by the US government by simulating background traffic and adding attacks. The suitability of the data set for research purposes has been extensively criticized [35], primarily because the data has not been validated or analyzed to see how similar it is to real-life traffic [36,37]. Furthermore, the DARPA data set is totally unsuitable for research in WLANs because the data was all collected over a LAN network [34].

17.4.2   SIMULATIONS

Simulations are a common approach to WLAN analysis and testing; however, it has been shown that Internet traffic is very difficult to simulate correctly [36] even when using protocol modeling tools, such as ns-3. This is in part due to the fact that many real-life networks do not precisely follow established protocols and have been shown to be composed of malformed or fragmented packets [36] and protocol errors [38].

17.4.3   LABORATORY GENERATED DATA SETS

Another approach is to generate a data set in a laboratory setting, using real equipment but manu-facturing traffic either manually or using traffic generators. Many of the same issues are found in traffic generating software as in simulation packages [37,39].

17.4.4 LIVE NETWORK DATA COLLECTION

Very little detailed information on live network data and its collection is available in research publications [41] even though the subject is of great interest. In many cases, this data is collected on the wired side of the network even though it does not reflect the nuances of WLAN operation [41] as it neglects all layer 2 WiFi information. In order to capture this influence, wireless-side collection is necessary [12,42].

Use of real-life data has produced many new insights into traffic [48], especially given that hostile agents are likely to try novel attack methods, which can only be observed through live data [49]. The lack of data sets collected in this fashion can be attributed to the fear of violating user privacy as well as the perceived difficulty in collecting and sanitizing the information [33].

A summary of the positive and negative attributes of each of these data sources is presented in Table 17.5. The negative aspects of live data are logistics problems, rather than issues with the data itself. Nonetheless, the lack of research publications utilizing live data for WLAN assessments is demonstrated in Table 17.6, in which a selection of relevant papers has been assessed. Of this list, only four of 21 publications (19%) underpin their results with live data with the vast majority preferring traffic generators employed in a custom testbed.

17.4.5 LIVE DATA FOR WLAN RESEARCH

The structure and operation of a collection system can have an impact on the validity and usefulness of the data itself [48]; this includes issues such as topology, deployment, loading, and focus [13,40,50]. Table 17.7 outlines the current data collection methods undertaken by relevant references. In this table, the source of the data, whether or not data collection is passive, and the documentation associated with the work are presented. Each of these factors plays a role in the reliability of data in WLAN research.

As seen from Table 17.7, there are subsets of live data. Some authors generate their own "live data" using laboratory testbeds although these approaches have already been dealt with previously. This is the most common approach observed (12/19). In many cases, these testbeds are deployed with a narrow research goal such that the data set and the collection system outlined are unsuitable for wider application by different researchers [40]. Generally, the network architecture, complexity, and capabilities are unspecified, and no comprehensive recommendations for design and documentation appear to exist [37].

To assist researchers in generating results based on good testbed design and practice, the authors in [51] established a configurable, replicable testbed for various research purposes. However, this

TABLE 17.5

Summary of the Positive and Negative Attributes of Traffic Sources

Source	Positives	Negatives
Baseline	• Was once based on real life networks	• No network response to injected traffic/activity • Usually proprietary
Simulations	• Scalable • Easy to implement new traffic activities	• Too rigid, not sufficiently close to imperfection of real life devices • Does not reflect real WLAN usage
Traffic generators	• Easily set up • Can make quick changes	• Based entirely on researcher best guess of what traffic looks like • Does not reflect real WLAN usage
Live networks	• Represents current usage of networks in practice • May contain novel attacks	• Logistically difficult to collect • Permission/privacy issues

TABLE 17.6

Data Set Usage and Experimental Setup in WLAN Research

Author(s)	Data Set	Experimental Setup
D'Amico et al. [43]	Traffic generators	Testbed
El-Khatib [7]	Traffic generators	Testbed
Singh et al. [6]	ns-2	Simulation
Haddadi and Sarram [34]	DARPA	Campus
Afansyev et al. [33]	Live data (LAN)	Live data (LAN)
Sarkar and Sowerby [39]	Simulation	Simulation
Bauer et al. [44]	Traffic generators	Campus
Deshpande et al. [42]	Traffic generators	Testbed
Tao et al. [28]	Traffic generators	Testbed
Schulman et al. [38]	Live data (WLAN)	Campus
Rachedi and Benslimane [45]	Traffic generators	Testbed
Bernaschi et al. [15]	Traffic generators	Testbed
Fayssal et al. [17]	Traffic generators	Testbed
Liu and Yu [16]	Traffic generators	Testbed
Karrer et al. [40]	Live data (WLAN)	Testbed
Shetty et al. [46]	ns-2	Simulation
Mahajan et al. [41]	Live data (WLAN)	Conference
Faria and Cheriton [29]	Traffic generators	Testbed
Gill et al. [18]	Traffic generators	Testbed
Franklin et al. [11]	Traffic generators	Testbed
Na et al. [47]	Live data (WLAN)	Live data (WLAN)

is achieved through a web portal, which researchers can use to submit scripts to run on an existing testbed. Thus, it creates a research bottleneck and restricts researcher autonomy over experimental processes. In [40], the authors lament the lack of semi-productive testbeds, in which real users utilize the network and research can be performed on the traffic as desired. If such a system was designed and documented, then the best practices could be replicated in multiple locations as required.

The next common collection method for live data from Table 17.7 is campus and engineering conference data (4/19). This data is valuable as an example of a user base which is technically competent; however, it is not necessarily reflective of general trends in public, enterprise, or home use. Campus networks, in particular, only represent the network usage habits of students and university staff. Because researchers who carry out these data collection methods are members of the universities in question, often it is a condition that only those researchers may use the data. In some cases, universities have even refused their own researchers access to this data [37].

Conference networks suffer from the same narrow user base issues as campus initiatives but have additional drawbacks. Conference networks are small snapshots, the conditions of which are almost impossible to replicate as they occur on an annual basis and often in different locations each year. Were conference WLAN data collected and released for use as a general rule, then this diversity would be of great use to researchers. However, presently this is not the case, and the data suffers from a time lapse, becoming less and less relevant to modern networks as the years pass. A more reliable source of modern, live network data is required.

The three remaining publications in Table 17.7 have produced data collection systems that have been deployed in a live environment and collect live network data. Each of these works has particular issues that render their data imperfect for WLAN specific experiments. In [40], the data collected excludes all layer 2 frames, and in [47], the data is harvested at the LAN side of a WLAN network. By discarding these factors in WLAN data collection, both works have removed the primary factor that defines WLAN and thus impairs the viability of the data sets for WLAN–specific research.

TABLE 17.7
Experimental Setup in WLAN Research

Author(s)	Data	Access Required	Equipment List	Layout Diagram
Yildiz et al. [51]	Lab testbed	✓	✓	✗
Haddadi and Sarram [34]	Campus	✓	✗	✗
Liu et al. [12]	Lab testbed	✓	✓	✗
Tao et al. [28]	Lab testbed	✓	✓	✓
Rachedi and Benslimane [45]	Lab testbed	Unknown	✓	✗
Stone-Gross et al. [52]	Conference	✓	✗	✓
Deshpande et al. [42]	Lab testbed	✗	✓	✗
Ma et al. [26]	Campus	✗	✓	✗
Karrer et al.[a] [40]	Live	✓	✓	✓
Bianchi et al. [53]	Lab testbed	✗	✓	✗
Fayssal et al. [17]	Lab testbed	✗	✗	✗
Watkins et al. [54]	Lab testbed	✓	✓	✓
Liu and Yu [16]	Lab testbed	✓	✓	✗
Gill et al. [18]	Lab testbed	✗	✓	✗
Bahl et al.[b] [55]	Live	✓	✓	✓
Franklin et al. [11]	Lab testbed	✗	✓	✓
Yamasaki et al. [56]	Lab testbed	✓	✗	✓
Na et al.[c] [47]	Live	✓	✓	✗
Dokas et al. [57]	Campus	✓	✗	✗

[a] Does not capture layer 2 traffic.
[b] Custom testing tools employed.
[c] Data collected on LAN side, not WLAN.

In [55], the data collected includes WLAN layer 2 information; however, the data is not collected passively, which raises concerns about the network performance impact. The authors also tailor their layout very specifically to a business deployment, where they utilize a dense array of desktop machines to act as sensors. This facility is unlikely to be available in all but the largest corporations.

17.4.5.1 Data Collection Methods

The third column in Table 17.7 identifies which publications utilize passive or intrusive data collection. Intrusive data collection is performed either in-line or is resident within the device that is to be monitored. Thus, the monitoring activities performed by this approach can impact on the data that is collected [58]. This effect was quantified in [59] in which the open source data collection software TCPDUMP, running on a WLAN AP, was seen to consume 38% of the CPU resources. An effect this large clearly impacts on the ability of the AP to process frames and handle clients. This influences the traffic produced by the device in normal operation, and thus the traffic cannot be considered truly realistic and reflective of the network in question when observed in this fashion, quite similar to the Heisenberg principle. In publications in which the criteria for a data collection system is considered [9,32,58,60], minimizing the influence (particularly regarding processor overhead) on the network traffic is a key principle in all cases.

The alternative to invasive monitoring is passive monitoring, in which data is collected without influencing the network. This is usually achieved through deploying additional monitoring devices within the vicinity of the WLAN device. This approach has further benefits [60], including isolating the monitoring station from the influence of host compromise. The major drawbacks of this collection tactic are that it cannot be used to monitor cryptographically protected data and that the data streams seen by both the monitor and the sensor may not be identical. To fill these gaps in knowledge, some assumptions or inferences from the network data may need to be made [13,61]. Thus, decision between the two approaches is a judgment call between fidelity and completeness of the data sets. In the majority of publications (12/18) in Table 17.7, the tactic used is to invasively monitor traffic.

Columns 4 and 5 in Table 17.7 identify the works that publish equipment lists for experiments and provide layouts of equipment used to generate data for their results. In data collection in particular, both of these issues are important as they directly impact on the ability of other researchers to replicate the systems used. Replication is important for two reasons,

1. Allowing researchers to copy existing systems rather than reinventing the wheel
2. Allowing researchers to recreate the conditions of experimentation in order to replicate and validate results

Scientific advances rely on reproducibility of results so that they can be independently validated and compared [36]. Evasion of this condition of replication is often found in engineering as espoused in [62] and shown by the data in Table 17.7 in which only a minority (5/19) provide this information.

Lack of information in publications is not the only barrier to replication; reliance on unavailable tools and software is also a barrier. In [42], a custom packet-capture software was written; in [18,55], custom testing tools were developed; and in [17], custom hardware was designed to facilitate testing. These additional factors in publications can impede replication. Often the reasons for this are simply that collection systems are designed to be used once and not in multiple locations or at multiple times [62]. In order for this case to be reversed, then research systems need to be designed and deployed with replication and reuse as criteria. Testing in multiple environments helps to validate the consistency and robustness of results [11]; however, this is very rarely undertaken in WLAN publications.

17.4.5.2   Impact of Testing Environment

It has been established that the location in which an AP resides can have an effect on the performance of that device, hence testing in multiple network locations is important for ensuring the fidelity and reliability of results [48]. In particular, seasonality and time are two factors that affect the results of an experiment [5]. It has also been observed that wireless networks have non-stationary traffic characteristics [64]. This effect is a negative attribute for training data, for example, where it is considered only a snapshot of an environment and may not be accurate as time goes on. Thus it has to be repeated to be made relevant for each new deployment [28].

Another factor that can impact on the relevance of data collection and the results from it is the lack of diversity in testing environments. Many campus and conference networks are the chosen sites for monitoring deployments; however, other locations have been tested in both academia and industry. Both [28,55] investigate using data collected from business environments. In [17], the authors argue that the reliance on academic data sets in research is matched by the bias of industry data collection solutions toward enterprises. Other networking environments have been excluded from investigation, such as home networks, espoused in [63]. Only through actively gathering information in new areas can inferences about their operation and security be garnered [50]. In public facing environments for example, deployments must also consider aesthetics because the equipment will have to blend in with existing facades [64].

17.4.5.3   Privacy

One of the largest barriers to utilizing real-life data is the concern of safeguarding user privacy. Internet traffic, specifically the data portions of packets, contains identifying information, which may be used to link the data back to the original user. This is also possible using IP addresses of users because some users can hold static IPs. Even when dynamic IP addressing is employed by ISPs (Internet service provider), this is no guarantee that the address is going to vary consistently.

In mesh networks, it has been shown that community contributors to the mesh can be very apprehensive about sharing traffic and personal data with each other. The authors in [59] investigate and establish that users may be more amenable to accepting packet header inspection but are averse to deep packet inspection. In [65], the authors propose a cooperative intrusion detection system but identify one of the major barriers as the lack of trust between owners. Thus, in enterprise situations, owner privacy must also be taken into consideration as in a cooperative system they are considered highly unlikely to be willing to share data about systems or policy.

One solution to the issue of privacy of data is to restrict the collected information to layer 2 management frame data [64]. This information has been shown to be useful for detecting WLAN attacks [61] but does not contain user identifiable or private data and is broadcast in plain text.

17.5 SUMMARY

WiFi networks are progressively being deployed in public, enterprise, and open access environments to provide greater accessibility for users. WiFi fundamentally differs from Ethernet at the physical (layer 1) and medium access (layer 2) layers. This means that WIDS have additional challenges, unique to 802.11 networks, which are not present for their wired counterparts. This chapter has investigated three of these challenges:

17.5.1 Attacks Specific to WiFi Networks

The catalogue of unique WiFi attacks has been distilled into three rudimentary 802.11 attack types: denial of service, encryption bypass and AP masquerading. Each of these attacks allows the attacker a different level of control over the network; control of the access medium, control of data confidentiality, or control over network access. This chapter has described the current capabilities and research for these three attack categories.

17.5.2 The Effect of Deployment Architecture on WIDS Performance

Due to the additional challenges in moderating the use of a wireless medium, deployment of a WIDS in different locations can have an impact on the WiFi traffic available for detection purposes. Choosing the correct architecture for a WIDS is of particular importance to the performance of the system although this is very rarely broached in research work. Although there are many different ways that a WIDS could conceivably be constructed, for the purposes of this chapter, three network topographies have been developed: home, enterprise, and open access (public). A comparison of these topographies has demonstrated that WIDS deployment environments can be separated by four characteristics: access knowledge, user behavior, equipment, and security threats.

17.5.3 The Importance of Live Data in WiFi Research

One of the most important aspects of generating accurate, reliable, and replicable results in research is ensuring that conclusions are based on sound data sources. Data sources in research generally fall into the following four categories: baseline, simulations, traffic generation, and live networks. This chapter has outlined some of the characteristics, positives, and drawbacks of each data source. The chapter concludes by advocating that collection of WLAN data from live network environments is a challenging endeavor, but one which presents many opportunities for future WiFi security research.

AUTHOR'S BIOGRAPHY

Jonny Milliken is a post-doctoral researcher at the Queen's University Belfast (QUB), Belfast, UK. He was awarded an MEng (1st class) from QUB in 2009 with a specialization in WiFi intrusion detection systems and holds CAPM and LCGI qualifications. He graduated from QUB in December 2012 with a PhD investigating WiFi intrusion detection strategies for public and open access WLANs. Jonny's research interests include WiFi and cyber security, WiFi malware, testbed development, disaster response methods, and national infrastructure security while his current work examines applications of WiFi for emergency search and rescue scenarios. He is also a member of IEEE and the IET and is involved with the IAESTE and ERASMUS programs in Northern Ireland.

REFERENCES

1. Baker, W. et al., Verizon 2012 data breach investigations report, Verizon, New York, USA, 2012.
2. CPP, UK wireless network hijacking, A CPP white paper. Available at: http://blog.cpp.co.uk/files/uploads/cpp-research/UK_Wireless_Network_Hijacking_2010.pdf, 2010, [Accessed on Sept. 9, 2011].
3. Hernacki, B., Muni Wi-Fi security. Available at: http://www.symantec.com/connect/blogs/muni-wi-fi-security, 2009, [accessed Sept. 2012].
4. Bellardo, J. and Savage, S., 802.11 denial-of-service attacks: Real vulnerabilities and practical solutions, in *Proc. of the 12th Conference on USENIX Security Symposium (SSYM '03)*, Washington, DC, USA, 2003.
5. Siris, V.A. and Papagalou, F., Application of anomaly detection algorithms for detecting SYN flooding attacks, *Journal of Computer Communications*, vol. 29, pp. 1433–1442, May 2009.
6. Singh, J. et al., A MAC layer based defence architecture for reduction-in-quality (RoQ) attacks in wireless LAN, *International Journal of Computer Science and Information Security (IJCSIS)*, vol. 7, pp. 284–291, Jan. 2010.
7. El-Khatib, K., Impact of feature reduction on the efficiency of wireless intrusion detection systems, *IEEE Transactions on Parallel and Distributed Systems*, vol. 21, pp. 1143–1149, Aug. 2010.
8. Zargar, P.B. and Kabiri, G.R.A., Category-based selection of effective parameters for intrusion detection, *International Journal of Computer Science and Network Security*, vol. 9, Sept. 2009.
9. Chebrolu, S. et al., Feature deduction and ensemble design of intrusion detection systems, *Journal of Computers & Security*, vol. 24, pp. 295–307, June 2005.
10. Ghosh, A.K. et al., Learning program behaviour profiles for intrusion detection, in *Proc. of the 1st Conf. on Workshop on Intrusion Detection and Network Monitoring (ID '99)*, Santa Clara, USA, 1999.
11. Franklin, J. et al., Passive data link layer 802.11 wireless device driver fingerprinting, in *Proc. of the 15th USENIX Security Symposium,* Vancouver, Canada, pp. 1–12, 2006.
12. Liu, C. et al., Empirical studies and queuing modelling of denial of service attacks against 802.11 WLANs, in *Proc. of the 2010 IEEE International Symposium on a World of Wireless Mobile and Multimedia Networks (WoWMoM '10)*, Montreal, Canada, pp. 1–9, 2010.
13. Valeur, F. et al., A comprehensive approach to intrusion detection alert correlation, *IEEE Transactions on Dependable and Secure Computing*, vol. 1, pp. 146–169, 2004.
14. Bicakci, K. and Tavli, B., Denial of service attacks and countermeasures in IEEE 802.11 wireless networks, *Journal of Computer Standards & Interfaces*, vol. 31, pp. 931–941, Sept. 2009.
15. Bernaschi, M. et al., Access points vulnerabilities to DoS attacks in 802.11 networks, *Journal of Wireless Networks*, vol. 14, pp. 159–169, March 2008.
16. Liu, C. and Yu, J., A solution to WLAN authentication and association DoS attacks, *International Journal of Computer Science (IAENG)*, vol. 34, pp. 7–14, 2007.
17. Fayssal, S. et al., Anomaly-based behaviour analysis of wireless network security, in *Proc. on the Fourth International Conf. on Mobile and Ubiquitous Systems: Networking & Services (MobiQuitous '07)*, Philadelphia, USA, pp. 1–8, 2007.
18. Gill, R. et al., Experiences in passively detecting session hijacking attacks in IEEE 802.11 networks, in *Proc. of the 2006 Australasian Workshop on Grid Computing and e-Research (ACSW '06)*, Hobart, Tasmania, pp. 221–230, 2006.
19. Hussain, A. et al., A framework for classifying denial of service attacks, in *Proc. of the 2003 Conf. on Applications, Technologies, Architectures, and Protocols for Computer Communications (SIGCOMM '03)*, Karlsruhe, Germany, pp. 99–110, 2003.

20. Borisov, N. et al., Intercepting mobile communications: The insecurity of 802.11, in *Proc. of the 7th International Conference on Mobile Computing and Networking (MOBICOM '01)*, Rome, Italy, 2001.

21. Fluhrer, S. et al., Weaknesses in the key scheduling algorithm of RC4, in *Proc. of the 8th International Workshop on Selected Areas in Cryptography (SAC '01)*, Las Vegas, USA, 2001.

22. Tews, E. and Beck, M., Practical attacks against WEP and WPA, in *Proc. of the 2nd ACM Conference on Wireless Network Security (WiSec '09)*, Zurich, Switzerland, 2009.

23. Ma, L. et al., RAP: Protecting commodity WiFi networks from rogue access points, in *Proc. of the Fourth International Conf. on Heterogeneous Networking for Quality, Reliability, Security and Robustness & Workshops (QSHINE '07)*, Vancouver, Canada, 2007.

24. Shivaraj, G. et al., A hidden Markov model based approach to detect rogue access points, in *Proc. of the IEEE Military Conf. (MILCOM)*, San Diego, USA, pp. 1–7, 2008.

25. Percoco, N.J., Trustwave global security report 2010, Trustwave, Chicago, USA, 2010.

26. Ma, L. et al., A hybrid rogue access point protection framework for commodity WiFi networks, in *Proc. of the IEEE 27th International Conf. on Computer Communications (INFOCOM '08)*, Phoenix, USA, pp. 1220–1228, 2008.

27. Nikbakhsh, S. et al., A novel approach for rogue access point detection on the client-side, in *Proc. of the 26th International Conf. on Advanced Information Networking and Applications Workshops (WAINA)*, Fukuoka, Japan, pp. 684–687, 2012.

28. Tao, Z. et al., X-mode: A real time approach of discriminating WiFi networking impersonators, in *Proc. of the 2008 4th International Conf. on Next Generation Web Services Practices (NWESP '08)*, Washington, DC, USA, pp. 151–158, 2008.

29. Faria, D.B. and Cheriton, D.R., Detecting identity-based attacks in wireless networks using signalprints, in *Proc. of the 5th ACM Workshop on Wireless Security (WiSe '06)*, Evanston, USA, pp. 43–52, 2006.

30. Nagarajan, V. et al., Using power hoping to counter MAC spoofing attacks in WLAN, in *Proc. of the 7th IEEE Consumer Communications and Networking Conf. (CCNC '10)*, Las Vegas, USA, pp. 1–5, 2010.

31. Beyah, R. and Venkataraman, A., Rogue access point detection: Challenges, solutions and future directions, *IEEE Journal of Security & Privacy*, vol. 9, pp. 56–61, Oct. 2011.

32. Ibrahim, T. et al., Assessing the challenges of intrusion detection systems, in *Proc. of the 7th Annual Security Conf.*, Las Vegas, USA, 2008.

33. Afansyev, M. et al., Usage patterns in an urban WiFi network, *Journal of IEEE/AM Transactions on Networking (TON)*, vol. 18, pp. 1359–1372, Oct. 2010.

34. Haddadi, F. and Sarram, M.A., Wireless intrusion detection system using lightweight agents, in *Proc. of the 2010 Second International Conf. on Computer and Network Technology (ICCNT '10)*, Bangkok, Thailand, pp. 84–87, 2010.

35. Garcia–Teodoro, P. et al., Anomaly-based network intrusion detection: Techniques, systems and challenges, *Journal of Computers & Security*, vol. 28, pp. 18–28, Feb.–Mar. 2009.

36. Mahoney, M.V. and Chan, P.K., An analysis of the 1999 DARPA/Lincoln Laboratory evaluation data for network anomaly detection, in *Proc. of the Sixth International Symposium on Recent Advances in Intrusion Detection (RAID '03)*, Pittsburgh, USA, pp. 220–237, 2003.

37. Athanasiades, N. et al., Intrusion detection testing and benchmarking methodologies, in *Proc. of the First IEEE International Workshop on Information Assurance (IWIA '03)*, Darmstadt, Germany, pp. 63–72, 2003.

38. Schulman, A. et al., On the fidelity of 802.11 packet traces, in *Proc. of the 9th International Conf. on Passive and Active Network Measurement (PAM '08)*, Cleveland, USA, pp. 132–141, 2008.

39. Sarkar, N.I. and Sowerby, K.W., The effect of traffic distribution and transport protocol on WLAN performance, in *Proc. of the 2009 Australasian Telecommunications Networks and Applications Conf. (ATNAC '09)*, Canberra, Australia, pp. 1–6, 2009.

40. Karrer, P. et al., MagNets: Experiences from deploying a joint research-operational next-generation wireless access network testbed, in *Proc. of the 3rd International Conf. on Testbeds and Research Infrastructure for the Development of Networks and Communities (TRIDENTCOM '07)*, Orlando, USA, pp. 1–10, 2007.

41. Mahajan, R. et al., Analysing the MAC-level behaviour of wireless networks in the wild, in *Proc. of the 2006 Conf. on Applications, Technologies, Architectures, and Protocols for Computer Communications (SIGCOMM '06)*, Pisa, Italy, pp. 75–86, 2006.

42. Deshpande, U. et al., Refocusing in 802.11 wireless measurement, in *Proc. of the 9th International Conf. on Passive and Active Network Measurement (PAM '08)*, Cleveland, USA, pp. 142–151, 2008.

43. D'Amico, A. et al., Integrating physical and cyber security resources to detect wireless threats to critical infrastructure, in *Proc. of the 2011 IEEE International Conf. on Technologies for Homeland Security (HST '11)*, Waltham, USA, pp. 494–500, 2011.

44. Bauer, K. et al., Physical layer attacks on unlinkability in wireless LANs, in *Proc. of the 9th International Symposium on Privacy Enhancing Technologies (PETS '09)*, Miami, USA, pp. 108–127, 2009.

45. Rachedi, A. and Benslimane, A., Smart attacks based on control packet vulnerabilities with IEEE 802.11 MAC, in *Proc. of the International Wireless Communications and Mobile Computing Conf. (IWCMC '08)*, Crete, Greece, pp. 588–592, 2008.

46. Shetty, S. et al., Rogue access point detection by analysing networking traffic characteristics, in *Proc. of the IEEE Military Conf. (MILCOM)*, Orlando, USA, pp. 1–7, 2007.

47. Na, C. et al., Hotspot traffic statistics and throughput models for several applications, in *Proc. of the IEEE Global Telecommunications Conf. (GLOBECOM '04)*, Dallas, USA, pp. 3257–3263, 2004.

48. Portoles-Comeras, M. et al., Techniques for improving the accuracy of 802.11 WLAN-based networking experimentation, *EURASIP Journal on Wireless Communications and Networking–Special Issue on Simulators and Experimental Testbeds Design and Development for Wireless Networks*, vol. 2010, pp. 26–37, 2010.

49. Geib, C.W. and Goldman, R.P., Plan recognition in intrusion detection systems, in *Proc. of the DARPA Information Survivability Conf. & Exposition, (DISCEX '01)*, Anaheim, USA, pp. 46–55, 2001.

50. Milliken, J. and Marshall, A., The threat victim table: A security prioritisation framework for diverse network topographies, in *Proc. of the 2010 International Conf. on Security and Cryptography (SECRYPT '10)*, Piraeus, Greece, pp. 1–6, 2010.

51. Yildiz, M. et al., User centric wireless testbed, in *Proc. of the 7th International Conf. on Testbeds and Research Infrastructures for the Development of Networks and Communities (TRIDENTCOM '11)*, Shanghai, China, pp. 75–87, 2011.

52. Stone-Gross, B. et al., Malware in 802.11 wireless networks, in *Proc. of the 9th International Conf. on Passive and Active Network Measurement (PAM '08)*, Cleveland, USA, pp. 222–231, 2008.

53. Bianchi, G. et al., Experimental assessment of the backoff behaviour of commercial IEEE 802.11b network cards, in *Proc. of the 26th IEEE International Conf. on Computer Communications (INFOCOM '07)*, Anchorage, USA, pp. 1181–1189, 2007.

54. Watkins, L. et al., A passive approach to rogue access point detection, in *Proc. of the IEEE Global Telecommunications Conf. 2007 (GLOBECOM '07)*, Washington DC, USA, pp. 355–360, 2007.

55. Bahl, P. et al., Enhancing the security of corporate Wi-Fi networks using DAIR, in *Proc. of the 4th International Conf. on Mobile Systems, Applications and Services (MobiSys '06)*, Uppsala, Sweden, pp. 1–14, 2006.

56. Yamasaki, R. et al., TDOA location system for IEEE 802.11b WLAN, in *Proc. of the IEEE Wireless Communications and Networking Conf. (WCNC '05)*, New Orleans, USA, pp. 2338–2342, 2005.

57. Dokas, P. et al., Data mining for network intrusion detection, in *Proc. of the NSF Workshop on Next Generation Data Mining*, Baltimore, USA, 2002.

58. Balasubramaniyan, J.S. et al., An architecture for intrusion detection using autonomous agents, in *Proc. of the 14th Annual Computer Security Applications Conf. (ACSAC '98)*, Scottsdale, USA, pp. 13–24, 1998.

59. Makaroff, D. et al., Intrusion detection systems for community mesh networks, in *Proc. of the 5th IEEE International Conf. on Mobile Ad Hoc and Sensor Systems (MASS '08)*, Atlanta, USA, pp. 610–616, 2008.

60. Verwoerd, D.T. and Hunt, R., Intrusion detection techniques and approaches, *Journal of Computer Communications*, vol. 25, pp. 1356–1365, 2002.

61. Milliken, J. et al., The effect of probe interval estimation on attack detection performance of a WLAN independent intrusion detection system, in *Proc. of the IET International Conf. on Wireless Communications and Applications (ICWCA '12)*, Kuala Lumpur, Malaysia, 2012.

62. Joujon, G. et al., A portal to support rigorous experimental methodology in networking research, in *Proc. of the 7th International Conf. on Testbeds and Research Infrastructures for the Development of Networks and Communities (TRIDENTCOM '11)*, Shanghai, China, pp. 223–238, 2011.

63. Edwards, W.K. et al., Advancing the state of home networking. *Journal of Communications*, vol. 54, pp. 62–71, June 2011.

64. Milliken, J. and Marshall, A., Design and analysis of an independent, layer 2, open-access WiFi monitoring infrastructure in the wild, in *Proc. of the 2012 International Conf. on Wireless Networks (ICWN '12)*, Las Vegas, USA, 2012.

65. Frincke, D. et al., A framework for cooperative intrusion detection, in *Proc. of the 21st NIST-NCSC National Information Systems Security Conf.*, Arlington, USA, 2008.

18 Intrusion Detection Systems for (Wireless) Automation Systems

Jana Krimmling and Peter Langendörfer

CONTENTS

18.1 AUTOMATION SYSTEMS

This section first introduces automation systems in general and then describes why automation systems are traditionally insecure by regarding the history of automation systems. The security mechanisms applied in traditional automation systems are weak if found at all. As long as automation systems have existed as isolated islands, they were reasonably well protected because physical access to the systems was needed to launch an attack. Recently, more and more automation systems are connected via the Internet to centralized control centers and also wireless networks are becoming more common in the automation world. In particular, the integration of wireless components leads to new attack risks due to the exposition of data beyond the visible borders of plants. Standard PC hardware and Ethernet are now used in automation systems. Those widely used technologies also have their own but well known vulnerabilities which make automation systems to better targets for possible malware and hacker attacks.

The most common security issues and their reasons are detailed in this section by regarding the structure and conditions in automation systems compared to normal IT networks. Threats to automation systems include unauthorized access through Internet connections, virus attacks, accidental misuse, hacker attacks, espionage, and so on. We explain widely used attack entry points for attacks on automation systems and important information security goals that have to be achieved in automation systems to secure them. Most people believe that they are not attacked by anyone. To show that the danger is real the last section focuses on known documented attacks on automation systems and their consequences.

18.1.1   INTRODUCTION TO AUTOMATION SYSTEMS

An automation system is used to control industrial processes, such as the production of chemicals or medicines or production lines, for example, for car or sweets production. They are also used in critical infrastructures for water processing or energy generation that may be widely spread infrastructures, such as water supply systems or energy grids, or localized infrastructures, such as bio gas or atomic plants. Automation systems collect measurement values to monitor the progress of the production process and to control it by driving different actuators, switches, or valves automatically or in a predefined order.

Such systems consist, in general, of several sensors (S) and actuators (A), control units, human-machine interfaces, computers, and maybe other devices. An industrial network (fieldbus) connects the sensors and actuators to these devices and to the process control system (PCS). The structure of an automation system is shown in Figure 18.1. All process parameters that are needed to control an industrial process are obtained using the sensors that deliver their values to a control unit. In most cases, the control unit is a programmable logic controller (PLC). The PLC is a device that was programmed to control equipment, such as pumps, valves, robots, and so on, to automatically intervene in the industrial process by predefined rules. Depending on the sensor values, the control unit automatically switches valves on or off, changes pump speeds or movements of robots, or does anything else to influence the process in such a way that the process matches its predefined parameters. The control unit additionally sends the current process information to the process control system and receives commands from it.

Automation systems can be regarded as event systems. The state of an automation system is represented by the operation of the automation devices, and thus, it is influenced by the state of the controlled technical process or production line. Changes to the state of an automation system may be triggered by changed measurement values, commands, or alarms. An attack, which can be a malicious command or a changed sensor value or something else, can also cause state changes and, therefore, accidentally trigger events.

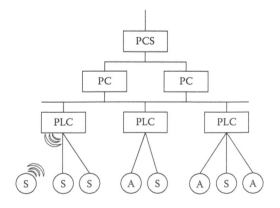

FIGURE 18.1   Structure of an automation system.

Occurring events may be identified and arranged in different event groups that help correlate them. Assuming that all events can be derived from a "global event," one can define different event groups, such as "structure change," "state change," or "behavior change," as shown in Figure 18.2. A "structure change" can be any change of the structure of the automation system, such as bringing in or removing a component or changing the configuration or parameters of a device or module. The "state change" event may be a change in the operation state of a device or the fieldbus. That can be any transition from run to stop, clear, memory reset, or the breakdown of a device or module. As an example, the control unit may communicate a state change with the broadcast of a global announcement message if the bus changes its state between normal operation, bus failure, sum failure, and also when timing problems occur. That means packets get lost, collide on the bus, or do not meet the timing requirements. "Behavior change" events may be triggered when the communication between a control unit and devices changes in an unusual way. Examples can be corrupted or malicious packets on the bus, a packet that contains an unspecified sensor value or command, or a sequence of commands in an unexpected order or time interval. Malicious packets can, for example, have wrong content, a wrong size, or be sent at the wrong time or too often. The detection of events is important as is their temporal occurrence.

Some events can already be derived from the alarm messages that are created by the devices. Such predefined alarms are triggered if an unwanted state was detected by the device. To correlate these events, they have to contain substantial information about the concerned device, such as device number, name or address, triggering module, specified value, current value, and so on. That also depends on the manufacturer of the automation device because special customized alarms can be implemented apart from using the predefined standard alarms.

A proper intrusion detection system (IDS) has to identify and correlate all events that occur in an automation system and to separate them from events that are accidentally or intentionally triggered by attacks. In order to detect attacks, an event correlation has to be implemented within the intrusion detection system. In comparison to other networks, the behavior of automation systems is more predictable due to existing rules that have been already implemented on the control units. Fortunately, there is no heavy load change in standard automation systems compared to normal IT networks because the devices are mostly polled by the control unit at specified time intervals. This means, apart from systems startups in which a lot of asynchronous traffic is created, the load in normal operation is nearly constant. Mostly synchronous traffic is produced that uses request/response sequences in a fixed time interval. The number of devices on the bus will also not change during operation apart from possibly hot-plugged devices.

The difficulty is to distinguish between valid events, such as changed measurement values, commands, or alarms, and malicious events, such as invalid process parameters, wrong commands that disturb the process or damage equipment, and false or missing alarms. Depending on the order and time of the occurrence of malicious events and their origin, an IDS can be programmed to distinguish between valid and malicious events (accidental faults, malware, or attacks).

18.1.1.1 History of the Development of Automation Systems

To understand why security functions have not been implemented in traditional fieldbuses, one has to consider the history of the development of automation systems. The first automation systems were highly customer-specific, and the circuits were directly connected to each other and to the sensors and actuators in parallel. Later, the analog parallel connections between devices were replaced by serial digital communication that highly reduced the cost and maintenance effort for the connections and improved the robustness against electrical disturbances. This allowed systems to spread over wide areas, such as found in power grids or water supply systems today. At no time, information security functions were considered necessary because all systems were closed, highly proprietary, and very difficult to operate.

Ethernet-based industrial networks are used for a few years, and automation systems are gradually connected to an increasing number of different other networks to speed up the information

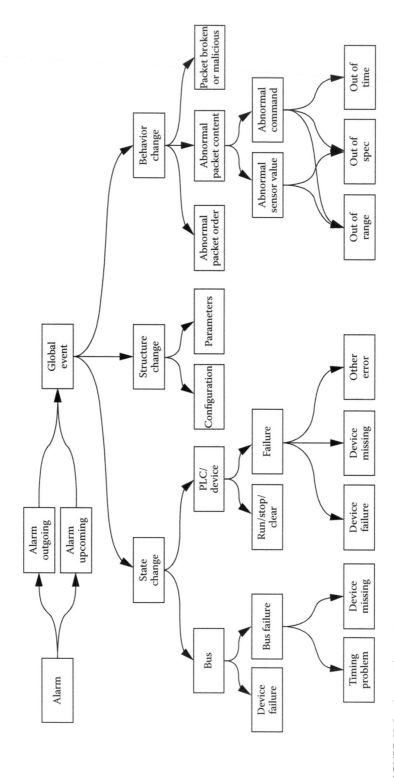

FIGURE 18.2 Automation system events.

flow and to optimize operation procedures. Industrial Ethernet supports a number of information security features and provides other improvements. It is now possible to change parameters and settings of devices from central control sites through the network that unfortunately also enables remote attacks. Standard PC hardware and software is increasingly used in automation systems and raises their attractiveness to attackers. Together with Ethernet-based communication networks, they offer high flexibility but also bring in widely spread or well-known vulnerabilities. WLAN access points and wireless sensor networks find their way into automation systems and add an additional number of new vulnerabilities. Because the air is a shared medium, every bit sent through the air may also reach people behind the factory borders. Hence, the automation network is theoretically accessible for everyone in the close proximity. In consequence, more and more automation systems are exposed to malware or hacker attacks.

To protect automation systems from other networks, gateways and firewalls are installed. A number of incidents that occurred in recent years show that this security measure is not sufficient. The majority of automation systems still operate with traditional industrial networks without even basic security features. This particularly affects widely distributed systems while the number of attacks on automation systems grows each day. An attack can have serious consequences for people and the environment. Because the networks, in general, get larger, the number of interconnections between them is also increasing and sometimes unknown. That is a common source for unauthorized access.

18.1.1.2 Security Goals in Automation Systems

To cover security measures means to achieve important information security goals within automation systems. The three main information security goals in IT systems are integrity, confidentiality, and availability. In contrast to normal IT systems, the requirements for automation systems are often safety, reliability, and availability. At a first glance, these goals seem completely opposing except from availability. On closer consideration, information security can affect safety. That puts the information security goals on a par with safety and leads to five main security goals for automation systems: integrity, confidentiality, safety, reliability, and availability.

To ensure integrity and confidentiality, at least the following security mechanisms have to be applied: encryption of data, integrity check for packets, authentication of the communicating partners, and authorization management. Even without consideration of the three last points, the secure and fast encryption of data is possible but already challenging. A lot of industrial networks still do not support any encryption mechanisms.

18.1.2 Security Issues in Automation Networks

Automation systems differ from normal IT networks in their structure, communication mechanisms, and operation, in particular, traditional non-IP based systems, such as Profibus or Modbus. Most automation systems operate by using continuously repeated request and response sequences that are triggered by the control units. At a first glance, it seems to be difficult to manipulate or attack an automation system. The system's behavior depends on the control units that have to be reprogrammed with a new firmware to change it. That also means if an attacker wants to change an automation system's behavior, he has to find a way to reprogram the firmware of a control unit without the awareness of the user. However, the Stuxnet worm attack showed that this is possible. In fact, automation systems are vulnerable against attacks that do not require a firmware reprogramming. That can be achieved by blocking SCADA traffic to the control units or by disturbing automation equipment in another way, for example, by sending commands to them that bypass the control units. Reasons why this may be possible can be poor security management or old hardware and software that are used within the automation system.

Security is an economic factor, most notably in small businesses or local critical infrastructures. Their operators often have little to no security knowledge and are not aware of possible attacks and, therefore, do not involve any security experts or advisors. Information security is, in a lot of cases, not regarded as very important but expensive and sometimes completely unnecessary for automation systems. Even in large companies, the existing security mechanisms can often be improved by well thought out security management. In addition, the network logging is often poor, and backup strategies are missing. Hence, belated analyses of attacks are difficult or impossible. The correction of these issues or even the awareness of an existing problem can already improve the overall system security.

It is a matter of common knowledge that a system is as secure as its weakest point. That may be a gateway or firewall, a PC within the office network, a wireless access point, a programmable logic controller (PLC) that provides services through an integrated web server or another device within the network. A gateway or firewall is frequently exposed to attacks through the Internet and also is a single point of failure. The whole network that is secured by the gateway or firewall is completely insecure if these devices are bypassed by an attacker. This might be achieved by a DNS attack or stealing or guessing access credentials. There are often no additional physical or social security measures taken apart from firewalls and gateways. However, firewalls also do not protect against infections by other routes, such as wireless access points or dial-up modem connections. The attack on the sewage works in Queensland in the year 2000 was, for example, executed wirelessly. And in 2003, the Slammer worm bypassed the installed firewall of a nuclear plant in Ohio, USA, by using a T1 line to infect the internal network. These incidents are discussed among other attacks in Section 18.1.4.

Over time, a lot of the used automation devices evolve to weak parts of the network. They are not exchanged because of their long lifetime that lasts up to 30 years and for economic reasons. A large number of existing installations of industrial automation systems therefore suffer from a lack of up-to-date information security functions. Examples can be quickly found in traditional automation networks that mostly have no or few authorization, encryption, and authentication features today. Nearly all systems lack secure key exchange protocols and automatic key management. This also includes newer devices because key exchange and key management protocols were defined as optional instead of mandatory in existing automation standards.

Unfortunately, it is not possible to always resolve all security issues. There will almost always be still a lack of security features left for the automation network because of the long lifetime of the devices. By the growing number of different attacks, it is just a matter of time when an automation system is attacked. An intrusion detection system helps to detect attacks inside the network that were not covered by other security mechanisms. A preceding risk analysis is at least useful for critical infrastructures. Many companies also demand a cross-network security mechanism that reaches beyond the borders of the control network and includes the control units. An intrusion detection system that is adapted to the requirements of automation systems can also fill that gap. Section 18.2 introduces intrusion detection systems for automation systems in detail.

18.1.3 ATTACK ENTRY POINTS

Ethernet connections to the office network or the Internet are common entry points for attacks on automation systems, but they are not the only source of infections. Further sources of infections are wireless systems, VPN connections, telecommunication networks, dial-up modems, and more. A summary of different infection ways can be found in [1]. As already mentioned, the attack on the sewage works in Queensland was, for example, executed over a wireless access point. In fact the Slammer worm attacked various plants through different connections [1]. The worm infected its victims at least by using a T1 line that was connected to a contractor's network, a VPN connection, a laptop, and a dial-up modem.

VPN connections for the remote access to devices can also cause security issues. Newer security approaches use smart cards with a security token to additionally protect such devices against unauthorized external access. However many attacks, including accidental attacks by potential misuse, are triggered in-house.

Devices that offer web services can, for example, represent serious additional attack points. A number of programmable logic controllers (PLC) are online accessible and provide services and information about connected equipment using web services. Tests of Parker and Pollet [2] have shown that it is possible to access some of the web interfaces via Google or other search engines although they should not even be findable. These interfaces are sources for possible attacks because some of them are not protected by a password, the password is very weak, or the password can be easily found by a simple search routine in the internal network of the company or the vendors.

Parker and Pollet [2] have found web interfaces of automation equipment, for example, a transformer running an electricity substation, that were online accessible and very poorly protected. In this way, attackers can easily obtain information about parts of an automation system's structure, the control device, and the connected equipment. If they discover the address of the control device in the automation network, they can start serious attacks by sending commands to it that disturb or destroy the connected equipment.

18.1.4 KNOWN ATTACKS AND CONSEQUENCES

The white paper on industrial automation [3] comprehensively describes weaknesses of traditional and IP-based industrial networks and how to disturb them. Boyer [4] also shows security issues in smart grids. In the end, a lot of security incidents result from weak passwords and poor data protection. Common threats and vulnerabilities and known incidents are documented in the Guide to Industrial Control Systems (ICS) Security [5] and by other authors [6] that help researchers to develop security measures. The majority of attacks are not made public by the affected companies for fear of a loss of reputation. However, this prevents the proposal of solutions by researchers. Some well-known examples of attacks on automation systems are discussed below.

The *Stuxnet worm* was designed to disturb Iran's nuclear program [7]. In 2009, it was found attacking a nuclear enrichment facility in Natanz, a nuclear plant in Bushehr and, according to (maybe unreliable) reports, a plant in Hormozgan in 2012. By the attack on the nuclear enrichment facility in Natanz, Iran, Stuxnet destroyed the centrifuges that were installed there for the uranium enrichment. The worm started a man-in-the-middle attack on the uranium centrifuges by sending destructive commands to the frequency converters for the centrifuges and information with wrong conditions indicating that the centrifuges are working correctly to the SCADA PCs. Thus, the centrifuges seemed to be working correctly to the process control system but instead were throttled and accelerated to not produce any enriched uranium until the mechanical destruction of the centrifuges.

The *Slammer worm* was one of the fastest spreading worms ever found. In 2003, Slammer attacked various plants through different connections [1]; among them was a T1 line, a VPN connection, a laptop, and a dial-up modem. By the attack on the nuclear plant in Ohio, USA, the worm spread from a contractor's network through the T1 line to the internal network of the plant. The infection slowed down the internal network and caused a crash of the safety system. A redundant analog safety system was fortunately not affected by the Slammer worm.

The *sewage spill* in Queensland, Australia, was caused in 2000 by an attacker [6]. He hacked into the system using an insecure wireless network and caused a spill of a huge amount of sewage into a river and a park by switching pumps on and off and disabling alarms.

In summary, it can be said that the protection of automation systems should be carried out in three stages. First, basic physical and organizational security measures have to be made, such as firewalls, multi-level network design, setup of security zones, proper security management, and setting up a DMZ. Second, software-based security measures should be taken, such as the elimination of vulnerabilities, software updates, or hardening devices. And, at least for critical infrastructures, the installation of a monitoring system in form of an intrusion detection system is useful.

18.2 INTRUSION DETECTION SYSTEMS

Automation systems are essential for our modern society because they are used for all kinds of production and process control and in critical infrastructures that are essential supply systems. A malfunction of automation systems can have serious consequences for their environment in case of a critical infrastructure for huge parts of the society. As learned from the example incidents discussed in the past sections, it is evident that information security directly influences safety. The mentioned incidents showed that it is possible to attack plants even if they are protected by state-of-the-art security mechanisms just by finding an unknown or unguarded attack entry point. At least for critical infrastructures or for the protection of valuable assets, it is useful to install an additional intrusion detection system (IDS) to detect attacks that were not covered by other security mechanisms.

This section introduces intrusion detection systems (IDS) for the protection of automation systems and wireless sensor networks that are more and more becoming part of automation systems. Wireless devices are increasingly used to save costs for wiring in automation networks and to benefit from the flexibility they provide. Wireless sensor networks consist of several distributed sensors that communicate wirelessly and act autonomously. Their number can reach from a few to hundreds. Thus, they can help to create even more distributed automation systems in the future with reduced fieldbus traffic and more distributed and autonomously acting computing power and intelligence. It is just a matter of time that large wireless sensor networks are widely used in automation systems. For the moment they still suffer from energy problems and real-time requirements.

Due to the different requirements on IDS in automation systems and WSN compared to normal IT networks, existing intrusion detection solutions cannot be used without adaptions. In many cases, the design of a new IDS solution is necessary. Because automation systems and wireless sensor networks are highly specialized to their task, the implementation of intrusion detection systems can be challenging. Therefore, the first part of the section gives an overview about existing intrusion detection methods. IDS design requirements and limits are discussed regarding automation systems and wireless sensor networks in the middle of the section. Information on the design of intrusion detection systems in special regard to wireless sensor networks is presented in the last part. The section closes with a discussion on novel approaches toward IDS solutions.

18.2.1 IDS IN AUTOMATION SYSTEMS

Intrusion detection systems for automation systems are necessary, but they are challenging with regard to many aspects. There are several IDS products available for Ethernet-based communication, for example from Cisco, Symantec, McAfee, Juniper, ISS, or Fortinet. As mentioned in the last section, the operation of automation systems, however, differs from that of normal IT networks. Known IT security mechanisms cannot be applied in the fieldbus area without major adaptions. In contrast to normal IT systems, the applications in automation systems are time critical. Continuous processes require constant availability of data. The information flow has to be fast with low response times; failures and reboots have to be avoided. This guarantees safety, availability, and the protection of equipment (PLCs, machines, products) at all times. Because the lifetime of automation devices is by a factor of three to five higher (approximately 20 years) than that of normal IT systems (three to five years), a lot of traditional non-IP based fieldbuses are still in use, but most available IDS products were designed to run on IP-based protocols.

Wireless sensor networks are increasingly integrated into automation systems. Available standard IDS products are not applicable to WSNs either due to hardware limitations. Wireless sensor nodes are low power devices with limited energy resources. The structure of WSN is also completely different to automation systems. Wireless sensor networks consist of loosely coupled sensor nodes with unreliable radio links whereas automation systems are coupled by a highly reliable and fast industrial network. Both are compared in Table 18.1. Existing intrusion detection solutions for WSNs are mostly developed for a specific protocol, such as AODV or OLSR that makes them hard to reuse for other systems. Therefore intrusion detection is still not very common in such networks.

As it is hard to find IDS solutions that support the fieldbus area of automation systems or wireless sensor networks in general, it is even worse to find an IDS solution that can support both. Automation systems and wireless sensor networks are quite different in their behavior at a first

TABLE 18.1

Common Network Properties

Type of Network	Availability	Speed	Latency
IT network	High	High	Middle
Industrial network	Very high	Middle	Low
Wireless sensor network	Low	Low	High

glance. It is, however, possible to design customized IDS solutions by paying attention to a possible later use with integrated wireless sensor networks. Currently available microcontrollers that are used in automation devices and WSNs have enough computing power to run at least simple customized intrusion detection systems. A solution is proposed in Section 18.2.3. It can be assumed that the computing power increases and the energy consumption of microcontrollers further decreases with upcoming new technologies. This allows more complex intrusion detection systems, but more research is needed for advanced intrusion detection solutions.

Known IDS solutions are still restricted to areas outside of the sensor level although distributed IDS solutions that also involve the sensors and actuators would be beneficial. A distributed IDS in automation systems would, for example, directly allow the verification of entered and performed commands. Moreover, it would be well prepared for future use with wireless sensor networks. Because automation systems can be regarded as distributed event systems, they share this important property with wireless sensor networks. This knowledge can be used for the design of an IDS solution that supports both structures at the same time.

18.2.1.1 IDS Preconditions

As mentioned in Section 18.1.1, the control units inside automation systems continuously gather process information using sensors and control the industrial process by driving actuators after following predefined rules. The control units can only work in the way intended if the following requirements are fulfilled:

1. The process operation is sufficiently understood.
2. All predefined rules and process parameters sufficiently characterize the process operation.
3. The control program of the control unit (PLC) was correctly implemented and matches the predefined rules and process parameters in every case.
4. Connected sensors and actuators deliver correct and accurate values to the PLC.
5. All connected sensors and actuators behave as expected by the programmer of the PLC (according to the specification).
6. Values and commands to and from the PLC are not changed on their way between sensors, PLC, and actuators.
7. The values and commands are delivered fast enough to control the process (the reaction time of the automation system has to be shorter than the reaction time of the controlled process).

If any of the above requirements is not satisfied, the process can possibly not be controlled in the way intended. Each of the above stated points needs highly specialized knowledge about the industrial process, automation system, and IT infrastructure. In fact, only point 1 cannot be influenced by external threats. The following lines give an overview of possible threats to the mentioned points, indicating the point by repeating its number:

2. Malware changes predefined process parameters to disturb the industrial process.
3. The control unit is reprogrammed with a malicious firmware.
4. A sensor or actuator is infected with a malware and now delivers incorrect values.

5. Malicious devices do not behave as expected.
6. A malicious device changes sensor values or commands.
7. Malware disturbs the internal network.

In fact, the Stuxnet attack on the uranium enrichment facility in Natanz, Iran, let four of those mentioned threats occur. Although difficult to achieve, Stuxnet changed the PLC programming software WinCC to produce malicious PLC firmware and program it to PLCs (3) that controlled the uranium centrifuges. This caused a man-in-the-middle attack on the centrifuges by changing the control commands to them (6). The centrifuges and the PLC did not behave as expected (5). Stuxnet changed the predefined rotation speed of the uranium centrifuges (2).

The problem with those kinds of attacks is that an intrusion detection system for automation systems is able to detect the changed behavior of devices by observing changed sensor values, control commands, or unusual access attempts depending on the network structure and the implementation of the IDS, but it cannot detect if a device was infected nor if an attack is currently going on. The conclusion that a device was infected by malicious software or an attack occurs still has to come from the user of the IDS.

For the IDS, it does not have to matter if the devices are connected by wire or wireless to each other because wireless sensor networks become part of automation systems. The intrusion detection system has to work precisely to detect any malicious devices because a single captured device may be sufficient to seriously attack the network, and it is possible to attack only selected devices. IDS solutions that reach beyond the borders of automation systems could help to detect single attacked devices more precisely.

18.2.1.2 Requirements for IDS in Automation Systems

IT networks, in general, face a variety of internal and external threats. An IDS for Ethernet-based communication needs to be at least fast enough to handle large amounts of network traffic. Because a lot of different protocols and services are in use, an IDS needs to be flexible and should deal with changing behavior of devices. The kind of traffic created within the network depends on the behavior of users, routing algorithms, load balancing, and other factors.

In contrary, automation systems have to be protected properly over the long lifetime of the devices. IDS for automation systems should not influence the operation of process devices and pay attention to safety considerations. To support the integration of wireless sensor networks, an IDS has to tolerate unreliable connections that are typical for those loosely coupled networks. Unreliable wireless links between the sensor nodes cause varying speed rates and latencies. Therefore, single wireless sensor nodes or wireless network parts may be only temporarily available in the automation network. That makes the existence of self-healing mechanisms necessary and leads to alternating communication paths within a wireless sensor network. Future applications of WSN may also include more mobile nodes or changing behavior of nodes that has to be considered for the design of IDS. For the integration of WSNs into automation networks, it is demanded by customers to connect the IDS to the existing visualization and process control system if possible. This may be achieved by exchanging data using OPC interfaces or by implementing the IDS or parts of the IDS as a field device.

As described in [8], it is expected that future third-generation automation systems have a more open system structure, use open protocols, and are linked much more to other networks, in particular to the Internet. This leads to more service- or event-based architectures with real distributed intelligence [9] and increased computing power of field devices. It can be expected that wireless sensor networks then can themselves process and provide information about the current process that enables even more distributed automation structures. Future intrusion detection systems also have to consider possibly mobile field devices or sensor nodes. Apart from unreliable radio links to mobile devices, it can be assumed that these devices work cooperatively due to increased computing power and accelerated wireless technologies.

18.2.2   STATE-OF-THE-ART INTRUSION DETECTION SYSTEMS

Different system models for IDS are available; the oldest is the host-based intrusion detection method. There, an IDS is installed on a host that analyzes the internal state and behavior of a system. This includes the resource access of programs, traffic targeted to the system, or states of specific data in the memory of the system.

The whole network traffic is scanned using network intrusion detection systems. Network intrusion detection systems analyze the network traffic to find unauthorized or malicious activities in the network. In most cases, this is done by a device or computer that is placed in a central position of the network or, in the case of an intrusion prevention system, near the firewall. Therefore, most existing IDS solutions are centralized approaches. This means that devices cannot evaluate correct behavior by themselves. Therefore, current centralized IDS solutions that just scan the network traffic for attacks may be insufficient.

A combination of both methods may be useful and is partly used today but depends on the application. If each device in an automation system or WSN is additionally equipped with a small IDS, decentralized approaches are possible that enable every device to decide independently if it is attacked or not. In this case, the IDS then needs some knowledge about the application of the device to prevent attacks. An application-layer IDS, such as AppSensor [10] is a good starting point for those IDS implementations. In the next step, distributed IDS components could be designed as cooperating objects that communicate about collective security goals and detected malicious contents.

18.2.2.1   IDS Detection Methods

The ideal intrusion detection system has a detection rate of 100% for attacks and does not create false alarms. In reality, all IDSs are dependent on the used detection method in each case and, therefore, produce more or less false alarms and may not be able to detect all attacks. The most used detection mechanism for current intrusion detection systems is the rule-based or signature-based detection, but there is an increasing number of anomaly-based (behavior-based) detection mechanisms [11].

A *rule-based* intrusion detection system uses known signatures (or patterns) to detect malware or attack schemes by predefined rules or filters. The network traffic is continuously scanned to find matching signatures. These are known temporal occurrences of packets and specific traffic data of already analyzed malware or attack schemes. A rule-based IDS continuously needs rule or signature updates. A lot of currently available IDS solutions for Ethernet-based communication use a rule-based IDS. Predefined signature sets and rules are continuously created by the vendors. Common free IDS products for Ethernet-based communication are, for example, Snort [12], Bro [13], OSSEC [14], or Samhain [15]. Commercial products are available from Cisco, Symantec, and other companies.

Rule-based IDSs work well against known attacks with low false-alarm rates. They also create a higher false-negative output for new attacks (attack not detected) because they cannot detect new attacks as long as their signature is not similar to known ones. This is due to the fact that the signatures set is never really up to date because new incidents or malware first has to be analyzed by the vendor or community to create new signatures. The IDS needs to be frequently updated to be prepared against the latest attacks and malware.

One of the most famous rule-based IDS for Ethernet communication is SNORT because it is powerful and available for free. Snort and similar IDSs sniff the whole network traffic using the promiscuous mode of a network device and compares it with characteristic patterns of known attacks. SNORT can be used to prevent attacks by blocking network traffic according to fixed rules (intrusion prevention). SNORT is platform independent, but the existing signatures cannot be applied to traditional fieldbuses and WSN without adaptions because the used protocols for WSNs and traditional fieldbuses differ a lot from the IP-based solutions. SNORT and its relatives also need a certain amount of computing power and memory to store the signatures. The more signatures are added, the more memory is needed. The detection speed also may decrease the more signatures have to be compared. That memory and computing speed are usually not available in small field devices and on wireless sensor nodes because these devices have low computing power. This disqualifies SNORT and similar IDS for applications in wireless sensor networks (WSNs) and small field devices. The distribution of the signatures would increase the energy consumption of wireless sensor nodes as well as the traffic in WSNs. In general, the amount of data transferred in WSNs is low compared to the size of a signature set for a standard IDS for IT networks.

Currently, available IDSs for WSNs mostly use other rule-based approaches [16] to detect attacks. Some use an initial learning phase to train the devices in the network for correct IDS behavior; sometimes the final decision is taken by a central station. Devices that do not behave as expected are considered as malicious and are excluded from the routing. For all current approaches, correct behavior is what is considered to be correct by other devices. The reliability of such assumptions can be increased by exchanging and evaluating them among communicating devices.

New IDS products for Ethernet communication are on the market that combine stateful packet inspection, rule-based analysis and statistical detection methods. However, there is nothing like this available on the market for WSNs.

There is a huge number of different *anomaly-based* intrusion detection methods, such as statistics-based anomaly detection, cognition-based methods, machine learning-based techniques, and other methods that are comprehensively surveyed in [11]. An anomaly-based intrusion detection system continuously analyzes the network traffic using a model that describes normal network traffic to detect unusual behavior. Incoming traffic is compared to the model that can be created using historical traffic data to find deviations in the packet flow or kind of data. The behavior model is either preset or needs to be learned during an initial adaption phase after the installation of the IDS. Anomaly detection does not need predefined rules or signatures because it can adapt to changing network behavior. Therefore it is able to detect new attacks without updates. This reduces the permanent effort for rule or signature updates.

Anomaly detection seems to be pretty well suited for IDS in automation systems because their behavior is known a priori. This means the detection of deviations of the predefined behavior is easy to do and produces almost no false positives. Any change indicates something bad; if it is not an attack, an unexpected alarm message caused the IDS to fire, which means there is a critical situation anyway.

18.2.2.2 IDS Limitations

Because an IDS continuously scans the whole network traffic it is always possible to overload it with a huge amount of packets or invalid packets. The IDS has to be fast enough to scan the network traffic, or packets will be dropped. Therefore, all intrusion detection systems are vulnerable against DOS attacks or packet insertion. Attack techniques on IDS are surveyed in [17] regarding insertion and evasion techniques.

Although the amount of corrupted packets in industrial networks should be low, they constantly occur and create traffic noise on the network. Common bit error rates in wired networks are around 10^{-12} to 10^{-15}, which means one out of 10^{12} to 10^{15} bits is erroneous. In wireless networks, the bit error rate is 10^3 to 10^6 higher, which causes significantly increased traffic noise. Other corrupted packets are, for example, created by software bugs. Traffic noise can raise the false alarm rate of an IDS.

The behavior description (rule set, signature set, or behavior model) that is needed for the operation of an IDS cannot be 100% accurate as it is based on either insufficient knowledge about possible attacks or incomplete historical data. Due to this non-ideal behavior description and influences, such as traffic noise, the number of attacks may be significantly lower than the false alarm rate.

18.2.3 IDS Design for Automation Systems

There are three main problems when adding intrusion detection systems to existing automation systems. First, most devices use a closed firmware. For most of them, it is impossible to add any IDS software components. Second, many automation devices have limited hardware resources and are not designed to run additional IDS software components without affecting their real-time capabilities. That restricts the simple implementation of IDS by adding software components on existing devices of the automation network. It is therefore necessary to create a network intrusion detection system by adding several hardware components to the network.

Because the network structure of large automation systems may be nested in hierarchical layers with different industrial network protocols, this can quickly become a complicated task. The designed IDS may consist of components that are distributed over protocol borders. This means that the IDS implementation for every used protocol may be slightly different according to the connected devices, but in any case, the hardware interface will differ a lot. For the creation of a distributed IDS, these components need to communicate with each other over protocol borders. Although there is sometimes a gateway functionality for automation systems available, most industrial communication protocols are not designed to support such systems. Therefore, an extra parallel network may be needed for the distributed IDS. Platform independent communication mechanisms, such as MessagePack [18], are available to quickly implement communication between components by providing a fixed interface.

Additionally, safety and reliability requirements have to be considered so that the IDS must not disturb the existing devices. As mentioned, the integration of wireless devices and WSN brings unreliable connections into the automation network that can cause continuous behavior changes of those networks parts.

18.2.3.1 Limitations for IDS in WSN

Energy consumption is the main problem in wireless sensor networks because most devices are battery-powered and therefore low power devices. This influences the whole design of a wireless sensor node: the available computing power, the range of the radio, and the reliability of the radio. Further factors depending on that are fluctuations of the radio range and latency, availability of services, and support of state-of-the-art security mechanisms. A lot of effort is made to save energy within wireless sensor networks by using sleep modes and reducing the availability of services as often as it is possible. This also means that the processor and radio should only wake up if packets are incoming that are intended for the receiver.

The main requirement of intrusion detection systems is, in contrast, that scans of the whole network traffic are continuously accomplished. It is hard to accomplish constantly reliable scans in WSNs in which the radio and processor shall sleep most of the time, the wireless network connection is not even reliable enough, and packet routes are changing over time. To compensate for this issue, the detection algorithms of the IDS and the management of the sleep modes have to be more intelligent. Also, the processor of the wireless sensor nodes has to be powerful enough to deal with its task as a sensor device with the running IDS and also with the incoming network traffic. This, in turn, depends on the number of neighbors in the wireless sensor network and also from the speed or polling frequency of the used communication protocol. For automation systems, most traffic is cyclic and, therefore, at least somewhat predictable for the implementation of the sleep management. Any optimizations on the sleep time also highly depend on the clock drift between the wireless sensor nodes. If the clock drift cannot be compensated, the sleep times have to be shorter, or more packets between sensor nodes will get lost because some radios may be still or again in sleep mode. This, in turn, consumes more energy. Some low duty cycle protocols for WSN have been developed [19,20].

Another problem in wireless networks is the vulnerability to disturbances on the wireless channel. Because the air is a shared medium, only one device can send data through the air at a specific point in time or the data will interfere with the data sent by other devices and be destroyed. This is true for a certain radius around the device because the transmission power decreases rapidly with increasing distance. Disturbances can be caused by objects that move or are located within the radio channel, weather conditions, other wireless devices [21] that operate on the same channel or by attackers that deliberately provoke them, also called jamming. By using jamming, an attacker can immediately disturb the operation of wireless devices because the radio channel is at least partly blocked. This affects the reliability of the network and can therefore cause serious control problems if SCADA traffic is blocked or delayed. Jamming detection is a complicated task even if the jamming characteristic is known. Different mathematical models (random, reactive, periodic, constant) were evaluated for jamming detection [22,23], but some of them need so much computing power that they cannot be usefully applied on wireless sensor nodes. Among the available countermeasures are many packet-based metrics and metrics that rely on signal strength measurements. A lot of these metrics perform poorly or are not suitable for low power devices without adaptions. A well working lightweight jamming detection component using RSSI was introduced in [24].

18.2.3.2 IDS Design Using Additional Hardware

Due to closed firmware, an intrusion detection system can, in most cases, only be installed to an existing automation system by placing a number of additional hardware components into the automation structure as shown in Figure 18.3. They listen to the traffic on the automation network and gather information according to the behavior of the connected devices. Depending on the gathered information, the IDS components can decide if there is traffic that was caused by an attack or if they deliver the information to a central component that evaluates it further. If malicious traffic was found, the IDS can trigger alarms to the process control system.

18.2.3.3 IDS Design Using Software Components

Because most WSNs do not have a closed firmware, it is possible to simply add IDS software components to WSNs. To cope with the unreliable connections and temporarily available sensor nodes, it is demanded to place an IDS component at every node or at least on all central nodes. With this amount of IDS components, it is possible to implement distributed IDS out of cooperating components to increase the detection rate and to reduce the false alarm rate.

Available small expert systems can be used to create a simple custom intrusion detection system. These are systems that make decisions based on logic (and, or, not, equal, lower, greater, ...) and arithmetic operations (+, −, *, /) and preset rules. The expert system then returns the Boolean values true and false. The rules are used to create a behavior model for the IDS. This is an easy way to create an IDS that does not need an initial training phase but is able to learn because the rule set can be either predefined but also changed during the operation of the expert system. It is not difficult to create a predefined rule set for the expert system due to the mostly predetermined behavior of automation systems in comparison to normal IT networks.

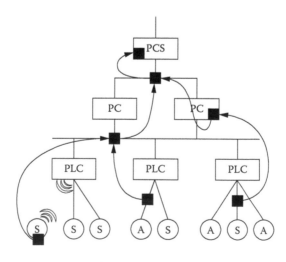

FIGURE 18.3 Automation system equipped with IDS components (black rectangles).

One challenge hereby is the implementation of secure communication between the IDS components. There has been some research on cryptographic methods for low power devices recently. Secure methods, such as elliptic curves cryptography and AES, can be implemented on current devices and should be used.

18.2.3.4 Design Choices

The design of IDS for automation systems is complicated, and there are several different methods the IDS can use to detect attacks. First, the system model of the IDS system should be defined. As mentioned in Section 18.2.2, there are host-based and network-based approaches that can be combined to create a more effective IDS. The choice of the detection method may be the most difficult one. Even if most intrusion detection solutions use rule-based methods, there are lots of anomaly-based detection methods that were evaluated [11], most noteworthy the statistical- and cognition-based detection methods. The choice of the detection method determines the necessity of frequent updates and the possibility to detect zero day attacks. A simple solution for a cognition-based method that can be used in automation systems that contain WSNs was presented above. This solution can be implemented on devices with low computing power and memory and does not need an initial training phase.

18.2.4 Novel Approaches toward IDS

Although the most available IDSs use rule-based methods, anomaly detection is used for some time. Czejdo [25] gives a good general overview of detection mechanisms. A comprehensive survey about existing anomaly-based intrusion detection techniques can be found in [11]. Additionally, a number of interesting recently found methods are presented below.

The approach of Czejdo [25] is a system for the extraction of anomalies that uses a learning feedback loop. Security data records are created from existing firewall logs. Thereby, event models are created from the logs that contain information about source, destination, time of request, and kind of request. The events are collected in tables and aggregated to summarized event tables in a hierarchical way in different levels and layers of aggregation. These levels are then searched for anomalies. The security data records are periodically updated with new events. This process is promising and can, with adjustments, be applied to automation systems. The adaptation could use a simpler model for automation systems because the temporal sequence of packets is more preordained.

Cárdenas [26] mathematically modeled a control system as a linear system and shows that attacks can always be detected if a behavioral description is available. Input and output behavior of the devices is compared with the help of the formulas. Amin [27,28] uses physical process data and presents a linearized shallow water partial differential equation (PDE) system. This calculates the flow of water in sewer systems that are usual for water utilities in order to derive vulnerabilities from it for possible attacks. The system was tested on a channel system in southern France. This approach shows that it is possible to derive vulnerabilities from the system behavior. This is a promising preventive measure to improve the overall security of a system if the approach can generally be transferred to all automation systems. The two approaches help to better understand and describe the behavior of automation systems.

Haack [29] describes an adaptive cyber-defense architecture based on swarm intelligence, agents, and humans in a hierarchical framework. The software agents control the swarm and form an interface for feedback by the human. They act autonomously, but the human can intervene at any time. A prototype of the system was built in an agent simulation framework written in JAVA. In automation systems, humans are yet involved in the feedback process because they control the HMI, process control, or visualization system. Unfortunately, this approach cannot be applied directly to automation systems because it consists entirely of software agents that cannot be integrated into the field level of most existing automation systems due to mostly closed firmware.

Fovino [30] analyzed the security state of a power plant in order to find possible improvements. Several attacks (DoS attacks, virus, theft of password credentials) are descripted, and their impact on the power plant is shown. Fovino claims that the communication protocol of a SCADA system is the core of the control system that is often unprotected and therefore vulnerable to attacks by malware that is exploiting the system's weaknesses. In [31], Fovino proposes a state-based filtering system for SCADA protocols. It is based on a firewall to detect complex attacks that uses an internal system model of the SCADA system. The architecture is explained with reference to the Modbus and DNP3 protocol.

18.3   OPEN PROBLEMS

A comprehensive overview about the design of IDSs for automation systems was given in the last section. This section summarizes all the open problems that could not be covered in detail throughout the last section or are, in general, open issues.

There are two main design issues concerning automation systems that complicate the implementation of intrusion detection systems. One problem is that most available control units have closed firmware and therefore cannot be equipped with additional IDS software modules, which implies the placement of hardware components within the automation system. The other problem is that many different protocols exist for automation systems, and therefore, no standard IDS solutions exist that can be used for a large number of automation systems. This may change in the future because Ethernet-based industrial networks become more and more common. That offers a single basis for all implementations.

The IDS design for a WSN suffers from a large number of open issues. First, the used devices within a WSN are mostly low power devices that restrict the use of complex behavior models for IDS implementations. Improved detection methods for low power IDS systems are needed and, in particular, description methods for behavior models and methods show how to quickly and easily create behavior models. Unreliable connections between sensor nodes cause varying connection speeds, high latency, and latency jitters between wireless sensor nodes. In addition, these devices can be easily disturbed by other wireless devices and by jamming attacks. Few solutions that provide acceptable jamming detection algorithms and countermeasures for low power devices have been proposed yet. Because of all the above-mentioned issues, IDS systems for WSN are still not very common.

18.4   SUMMARY

This chapter introduced readers to automation systems in general and their security weaknesses and presented famous attacks on automation systems that have become known. Because the number of attacks on an automation system increases daily, additional security mechanisms, such as intrusion detection systems, are needed for automation systems, in particular for critical infrastructures. Wireless systems and wireless sensor networks become familiar in automation systems and bring new vulnerabilities into these systems. Therefore, intrusion detection systems for automation systems were introduced with special regard to wireless sensor networks. Their requirements and limitations were discussed in detail. Intrusion detection systems that were designed for IT networks are not applicable to wireless sensor networks due to hardware limitations. Only a few IDSs for WSNs are available, but these are not adaptable for use within automation systems. Thus, in most cases, IDSs for automation systems have to be developed from scratch. Design choices for IDSs were presented as starting points for building new IDSs for automation systems, and a solution for an IDS that supports a WSN within automation systems was proposed.

AUTHORS' BIOGRAPHIES

Jana Krimmling received her diploma in information technology in 2008 and is now working on her doctoral thesis. Since 2009, she has been working in the sensor networks and mobile middleware group at the System Design department of the IHP in Frankfurt (Oder). Her research interests include wireless sensor networks, cyber physical systems, and automation systems. In the RealFlex project, she worked on the development of intelligent real-time capable wireless sensor nodes for the integration into automation systems for process and factory control. In the recently finished ESCI project, she worked on a distributed reactive security platform for automation systems.

Peter Langendörfer holds a diploma and a doctorate degree in computer science. Since 2000, he has been with the IHP in Frankfurt (Oder). There, he leads the sensor networks and mobile middleware group. Since 2012, he has been the chair for security in pervasive systems at the Technical University of Cottbus. He has published more than 100 refereed technical articles, filed 10 patents in the security/privacy area, and worked as guest editor for many renowned journals, e.g., *Wireless Communications and Mobile Computing* (Wiley). He has chaired international conferences, such as WWIC, and has served in many TPCS, for example, at Globecom, VTC, ICC, and SECON. His research interests include wireless sensor networks and cyber physical systems, especially privacy and security issues.

REFERENCES

1. Byres, E., Leversage, D., and Kube, N., Security incidents and trends in the SCADA and process industries. 2007.
2. Mills, E., Researchers warn of SCADA equipment discoverable via Google, 2011: http://news.cnet.com/8301-27080_3-20087201-245/researchers-warn-of-scada-equipment-discoverable-via-google/.
3. Sundell, M., Kuivalainen, J., Mäkelä, J., Gervais, A., Orava, J., and Hyppönen, M.H., Whitepaper on industrial automation security in fieldbus and field device level. 2011.
4. Boyer, W.F. and McBride, S.A., *Study of Security Attributes of Smart Grid Systems–Current Cyber Security Issues.* Idaho National Laboratory, USDOE, Under Contract DE-AC07-05ID14517. 2009.
5. Stouffer, K., Falco, J., and Scarfone, K., *Guide to Industrial Control Systems (ICS) Security.* 2011.
6. Slay, J. and Miller, M., Lessons learned from the Maroochy water breach. *Critical Infrastructure Protection*, 2007: 73–82.
7. Langner, R., Stuxnet: Dissecting a cyberwarfare weapon. *Security and Privacy, IEEE*, 2011: 9(3), 49-51.
8. Karnouskos, S. and Colombo, A.W., *Architecting the Next Generation of Service-Based SCADA/DCS System of Systems*, 2011: 359–364.
9. Marron, P.J. et al., *The Emerging Domain of Cooperating Objects*, 2011: Springer.
10. OWASP AppSensor Project [Application Layer Intrusion Detection System]. Available from: http://www.owasp.org/index.php/OWASP_AppSensor_Project.
11. Jyothsna, V. and Prasad, R., A review of anomaly-based intrusion detection systems. *International Journal of Computer Applications*, 2011: 28(7).
12. Sourcefire. SNORT. Available from: http://www.snort.org/.
13. The Bro Project. Bro network security monitor. Available from: http://www.bro.org/.
14. OSSEC intrusion detection system. Available from: http://www.ossec.net/.
15. Samhain intrusion detection system. Available from: http://www.la-samhna.de/samhain/.
16. da Silva, A.P.R. et al., Decentralized intrusion detection in wireless sensor networks. In *Proceedings of the 1st ACM International Workshop on Quality of Service & Security in Wireless and Mobile Networks.* 2005. ACM.
17. Ptacek, T.H. and Newsham, T.N., Insertion, evasion, and denial of service: Eluding network intrusion detection. 1998. DTIC Document.
18. Furuhashi, S., MessagePack binary serialization format. Available from: http://msgpack.org/.
19. El-Hoiydi, A. and Decotignie, J.-D., WiseMAC: An ultra low power MAC protocol for multi-hop wireless sensor networks, in *Algorithmic Aspects of Wireless Sensor Networks.* 2004, Springer. pp. 18–31.
20. Demirkol, I., Ersoy, C., and Alagoz, F., MAC protocols for wireless sensor networks: A survey. *Communications Magazine, IEEE*, 2006: 44, 115–121.
21. Lee, J.-S., Su, Y.-W., and Shen, C.-C., A comparative study of wireless protocols: Bluetooth, UWB, ZigBee, and Wi-Fi. In *Industrial Electronics Society, 2007. IECON 2007. 33rd Annual Conference of the IEEE.* 2007. IEEE.
22. Xu, W. et al., The feasibility of launching and detecting jamming attacks in wireless networks. In *Proceedings of the 6th ACM International Symposium on Mobile Ad Hoc Networking and Computing.* 2005. ACM.

23. Fragkiadakis, A.G., Siris, V.A., and Petroulakis, N., Anomaly-based intrusion detection algorithms for wireless networks, in *Wired/Wireless Internet Communications*. 2010, Springer. pp. 192–203.

24. Langendörfer, P., Ortmann, S., and Kornemann, S., Demonstrating self-contained on-node counter measures for various jamming attacks in wireless sensor networks. *SIGMOBILE Mob. Comput. Commun. Rev.*, 2011: 15, 39–40.

25. Czejdo, B.D. et al., Network intrusion detection visualization using aggregations in a cyber security data warehouse. *Int. J. Communications, Network System Sciences*, 2012: 5, 593–602.

26. Cárdenas, A.A., Amin, S., and Sastry, S., Research challenges for the security of control systems. In *Proceedings of the 3rd Conference on Hot Topics in Security*. 2008, USENIX Association.

27. Amin, S. et al., Stealthy deception attacks on water SCADA systems. In *Proceedings of the 13th ACM International Conference on Hybrid Systems: Computation and Control*. 2010, ACM.

28. Amin, S. et al., Cyber security of water SCADA systems: (I) Analysis and experimentation of stealthy deception attacks. *IEEE Transactions on Control Systems Technology*, 2012: 20.

29. Haack, J.N. et al., Mixed-initiative cyber security: Putting humans in the right loop. In *The First International Workshop on Mixed-Initiative Multiagent Systems (MIMS) at AAMAS*. 2009.

30. Fovino, I.N. et al., Cyber security assessment of a power plant. *Electric Power Systems Research*, 2011: 81, 518–526.

31. Fovino, I.N. et al., Critical state-based filtering system for securing SCADA network protocols. *IEEE Transactions on Industrial Electronics*, 2012: 59, 3943–3950.

19 An Innovative Approach of Blending Security Features in Energy-Efficient Routing for a Crowded Network of Wireless Sensors

Al-Sakib Khan Pathan and Tarem Ahmed

CONTENTS

19.1 INTRODUCTION

Wireless sensor networks (WSN) are emerging as both an important new tier in the IT (information technology) ecosystem and a rich domain of active research involving hardware and system design, networking, distributed algorithms, programming models, data management, security, and social factors [1,2]. The basic idea of a sensor network is to disperse tiny sensing devices over a specific target area. These devices are capable of sensing certain changes of incidents or parameters and of communicating with other devices. WSNs could be very useful for providing support for some specific purposes, such as target tracking, surveillance, environmental monitoring, etc. Today's sensors can monitor temperature, pressure, humidity, soil makeup, vehicular movement, noise levels, lighting conditions, the presence or absence of certain kinds of objects or substances, mechanical stress levels on attached objects, and other properties. As such types of networks are composed of resource-constrained tiny sensor nodes, many research works have tried to focus on efficient use of the available resources of the sensors. Energy is, in fact, one of the most critical factors that play a great role to define the duration of an active and operable network. Energy efficiency is often very crucial in these sorts of networks as the power sources of the inexpensive sensors are (in most of the cases) not replaceable after deployment. If any intermediate node between any two communicating nodes runs out of battery power, the link between the end nodes is eventually broken. So any protocol should ensure a competent way of utilizing the energies of the sensors so that a fair connectivity of the network could be ensured throughout its operation time. Energy efficiency is also very necessary to maximize the lifetime of the network.

Security, on the other hand, is another critical issue, especially for ensuring the legitimacy of transmitted readings from the sensors to the base station [3,4]. It is anticipated that, in most application domains, sensor networks constitute an information source that is a mission critical system component and, thus, require commensurate security protection. If an adversary can thwart the work of the network by perturbing the information produced, stopping production, or pilfering information, then the usefulness of sensor networks is drastically curtailed. Thus, it should be made sure that the messages from the sensors in action are authentic and reach the base station without any fabrication or modification. As a strong property of security, authenticity of the messages is often considered as the most crucial.

The task of securing wireless sensor networks is, however, complicated, considering the fact that the sensors are mass-produced anonymous devices with a severely limited energy budget and, initially, with no knowledge of their locations in the deployment environment (in general cases). The architectural aspect of wireless sensor networks could make the employment of a security scheme a little bit easier as the base stations or the centralized entities could be used extensively in this case. Nevertheless, the major challenge is induced by the constraint of resources of the tiny sensors. In many cases, sensors are expected to be deployed arbitrarily in the enemy territory (especially in a military reconnaissance scenario) or over dangerous or hazardous areas. Therefore, even if the base station (or sink) resides in the friendly and safe area, the sensor nodes need to be protected from being compromised. At least, it should be made sure that the reports that reach the base station are authentic and are not corrupted on the way of transmission.

In this chapter, we deal with the challenge of energy efficiency and secure routing in wireless sensor networks in a highly dense deployment scenario. We propose a secure energy-efficient routing protocol (SERP) [23], which aims at minimizing the wasteful energy consumption by energy-efficient structuring of the network and then securing the data transmissions from the sensors to the base station using a one-way hash chain and shared secret keys. SERP selects a minimum number of forwarding nodes in the network. It provides a good level of confidentiality and authenticity of the reports sent from the source sensors to the base station.

The major contributions of this chapter are the following:

1. Energy and distance-based efficient structuring of the network, which helps for maximizing the lifetime of the network.
2. Providing data transmission security in wireless sensor networks. Here, we have mainly focused on data authenticity and confidentiality during their transmissions from the source sensors to the base station. There is also an optional key refreshment mechanism in our scheme, which could be applied based on the application at hand to provide data freshness.
3. Detailed analysis and simulation results of our proposed protocol.
4. Overview of security in WSN along with discussion on the impact of different network structures on the security in WSN.

The rest of the chapter is organized as follows: Section 19.2 presents an overview of the threats and attacks against WSNs, Section 19.3 presents the literature review and motivation of this work, Section 19.4 presents our assumptions and preliminaries, Section 19.5 describes our protocol in detail, simulation results and analysis are presented in Section 19.6, and Section 19.7 discusses the possible inclusion of intrusion detection systems (IDSs) based on the network structure and use of SERP as the routing protocol. Finally, Section 19.8 concludes the chapter delineating the achievements from this work with future research directions.

19.2   WSN SECURITY AND THREATS AND ATTACKS AGAINST WSN AT A GLANCE

There are mainly three angles of looking at the security in wireless sensor networks. These angles could cover all the security requirements and issues that we should consider. Figure 19.1 shows a diagram explaining these aspects.

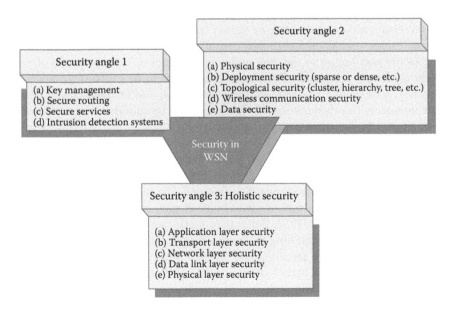

FIGURE 19.1   Three angles of looking at security in wireless sensor networks.

19.2.1 WSN Security Viewing Angle 1

The first angle is based on the mechanism used to deal with security in WSNs. These mechanisms include (a) key management, (b) security routing, (c) secure services, and (d) intrusion detection systems.

19.2.2 WSN Security Viewing Angle 2

The second angle could be based on where the security is employed. This angle includes the following:

(a) Physical security, that is, the physical protection of the sensors in a network, tamper-proof methods, self-destruction method if cracked by attacker, shielding and camouflaging of sensors, etc.

(b) Deployment security, which is dependent on whether the network is sparsely deployed or densely deployed. A densely deployed sensor network may have redundancy in a small area, which could find out alternative ways to protect the traffic flow if attacked by attackers in one way or other. Also, based on the deployment types or the method of deployment of sensors, the security measures may need different types of prior works. If the network is uniformly distributed, the security schemes may be installed uniformly among nodes; again a random deployment may require installing security components in key nodes in the network that cover the entire network.

(c) Topological security: Based on the network structure or network formation, the security could be different. There are mainly three types of network structures: cluster, tree, and hierarchy. In a cluster structure, there is a cluster head in each cluster and some subordinate nodes under the cluster head. In this formation, instead of installing security schemes in each node, cluster heads could be the most suitable entities. This is because of the reason that the cluster heads collect data from the other subordinate nodes and process those before forwarding it toward the base station. If cluster heads with higher computing and energy resources are used in a network, the task becomes easier as they can take the load of processing and forwarding secure packets. If the network formation is tree-based, the nodes have parent-child relationships among themselves from the leaf toward the sink node or vice versa. In such a case, each individual node may include security measures, and along a path in a tree, the packets could be checked before forwarding to the next hop or to the sink node or base station. The third type of network formation is hierarchy, in which there are several hierarchical levels of the nodes in the network. Say, for example, in one level, there are several clusters with cluster heads and subordinate nodes. The cluster heads of this level could be considered as the subordinate nodes in another bigger scale cluster (another level), which might have a higher power cluster head, and it could be repeated for several levels. A well scalable and large WSN with some strategically positioned high power nodes with higher transmission ranges could have such a structure. So such a network formation needs security measures in a different way than the other two types of formations. The thematic diagrams of all these types of network formations are shown later in the chapter when discussing these in relation to our work (see Section 19.7). Other than these categories, there might be hybrid topology in the network, combining different network formation styles, for example, a network with partly a cluster structure and partly a tree-based structure. So it becomes crucial where the security schemes should be installed so that the network security is ensured up to the expected level.

(d) Wireless communication security: Due to the nature of wireless communications, a WSN is always vulnerable. The wireless medium is of an open nature, hence the signaling and reception mechanisms must be secured in the best way possible. An attack such as jamming [25], for example, could disrupt the natural wireless transmissions within the network.

(e) The last category is the data security, which includes the encryption and decryption of data packets, efficient packet authentication techniques, hop-by-hop checking, and so on.

19.2.3 WSN SECURITY VIEWING ANGLE 3

The third angle is the holistic security. This brings forward the concept of layer-wise security in such type of network. Based on the very well known OSI (open systems interconnection) reference model, we could think about ensuring security in each layer. Especially for wireless sensor networks, five layers are relevant: application layer, transport layer, network layer, link layer, and physical layer. Lack of security in any of these levels weakens the overall security of the network. A full working solution in which different mechanisms could work in cooperation is still an open area of research, which would take a huge effort to develop. After knowing all these views and angles of security in a WSN, in the subsequent section, we will explore the major types of threats and attacks against such type of network.

There are several well-known and a few less well-known security attacks that exist in wireless sensor networks. In this section, we discuss these security attacks in brief. Almost all of the attacks described below focus on the limitations of routing protocols in WSNs. However, some unknown attacks that are launched considering other security constraints of the network are presented as well. Table 19.1 introduces a brief summary of well-known and less known (or less studied) security attacks and their characteristics in terms of attack behaviors and techniques.

TABLE 19.1
Security Attacks in WSNs

Well Known		Less Known (or Less Studied)	
Name	**Characteristics**	**Name**	**Characteristics**
DoS attacks in different layers [25–27]	Flooding, jamming, misdirection	Bogus message during reprogramming [28]	Unsecure reprogramming process with bogus messages
Sinkhole/blackhole [29–32]	Shortest path, drop the packets	External stimuli [33]	Use external physical stimuli to create a large number of packets
Selective forwarding [3,34–37]	Selectively drop the packets	Homing [33]	Hamper the normal functioning of cluster heads
The node replication [38,39]	Add extra node to the network with the same cryptographic secrets	Neglect and greed [40]	Deny transmission of legitimate packets and give higher priority to own packets
HELLO flood [41]	Flood with HELLO packets	Unfairness [40]	Unfair resource allocation on MAC protocols
Wormhole [42–45]	Offer less number of hops and less delay, which is fake		
Sybil [36,46–48]	A malicious node pretends to be more than one node		

19.2.4 DENIAL OF SERVICE (DoS) ATTACKS

We consider any type of intentional activity that can disrupt, subvert, or even destroy the network as a denial of service (DoS) attack.

Basically, DoS attacks can be categorized into three types:

- Consumption of scarce, limited, or non-renewable resources
- Destruction or alteration of configuration information
- Physical destruction or alteration of network resources

These types of DoS attacks are the most significant for WSNs as the sensors in the network suffer from the lack of limited resources. Also, DoSs can be categorized according to the layers of the network architecture. An attacker can use different tools at different layers to stop proper functioning of the entire network or some sensor nodes. Even though it has been said that it is too difficult to know whether any particular DoS situation is caused intentionally or unintentionally, there are some detection methods that exist to thwart each type of DoS attack [72]. In general terms, DoS means any situation that prevents providing proper service that is expected from the network and "DoS attack" means any deliberate activity by an entity (or some) that causes DoS (denial of service) in the network.

Jamming and tampering attacks that exist in the physical layer of WSNs are also considered as kinds of DoS attacks. Jamming is the deliberate interference with radio reception to deny a target's use of a communication channel. Due to their unpredictable nature, WSNs are very vulnerable to "radio channel jamming"–based DoS attack [26]. Tampering is actually any type of physical attack on sensors in the network. They might be physical damage or replacing the sensors, parts of computational or sensitive hardware; one can even extract cryptographic keys to gain unrestricted access to higher communication layers. These types of attacks cannot be defended by some system or base station; only accurate and effective designer of the network can handle it.

19.2.5 SINKHOLE OR BLACK HOLE ATTACKS

In this attack, a malicious node acts as a black hole [22] to pull in all the traffic in the network. The attacker listens to the route requests and then replies to the target node informing that it has the shortest path to the base station. A victim node is enticed to select it as a forwarder for its packets. Once the malicious node is able to put itself between the base station and the sensor node, it is able to do whatever it wants (drop packets, change the content, etc.) with the packets that pass through it. This type of attack can be very harmful for sensor nodes that are deployed considerably far from the base station. We have to keep in mind that black hole and sinkhole attacks are basically the same attacks by definition. Some recent works have addressed this attack, and possible IDSs have been proposed in [19,30–32].

19.2.6 SELECTIVE FORWARDING

Multi-hop networks like WSNs rely on a significant assumption that all nodes in the network will faithfully forward the received messages to the base station (BS). In these attacks, a malicious node acts as a normal node by forwarding only certain messages but selectively drops sensitive packets, which are hard to detect by the system. The specific form of this attack is the sinkhole or black hole attack with which a node might drop all messages it receives. As possible solutions to detect this type of attack, some secure routing algorithms and IDSs using different techniques have been proposed [3,34,35,37].

19.2.7 THE NODE REPLICATION ATTACKS

Due to the resource constraints of sensor nodes and often unattended environment of a WSN, an attacker can easily capture the nodes and analyze and replicate them. In this attack, an attacker attempts to add one or more nodes in a network that use the same cryptographic secrets as any other legitimate node in that network. This kind of attack may have severe consequences such as corruption of data by an adversary or even disconnection of some critical parts of the network. Some centralized detection schemes with one point of failure, neighborhood voting protocols with the lack of detecting distributed node replications, and some successful distributed detection techniques have been proposed [38,39].

19.2.8 HELLO Flood Attacks

This attack uses HELLO packets as a tool for convincing the sensors in the network. Many of the routing protocols require broadcasting of HELLO packets to discover the neighbors. An attacker uses this assumption as a weapon to attract the sensor nodes. A node that receives such a packet may assume that it is within normal radio range of the sender node. Hence, an attacker with a large radio range and enough processing power can send HELLO packets to a large number of sensor nodes by flooding the entire network. Thus, the sensor nodes could be persuaded that the adversary is their neighbor. Possible solutions to detect this type of attacks could be the use of bidirectional verification of links before using them, secure multipath routing, and use of multiple base stations [41].

19.2.9 Wormhole Attacks

In this attack, an attacker records the packets at one location in the network and tunnels those to another location. Wormhole attack is another significant and serious threat to WSNs because this is possible even if the attacker has not compromised any node and even if all communications provide authenticity and confidentiality. Attackers offer less number of hops and less delay than other normal routing paths, which leads to attract the sensor nodes to send data through them. While forwarding packets, the attackers can arbitrarily drop sensitive packets. In a recent work, Sharif and Leckie propose three types of wormhole attacks, namely energy depleting wormhole attack (EDWA), indirect wormhole attack (IBA), and targeted energy depleting wormhole attack (TEDWA) [42]. Also, IDS using connectivity information to detect the wormhole attacks has been proposed [44]. Other work proposes a wormhole detection technique using directional antennas, which is, in most of the cases, infeasible for sensor networks due to their limited resources.

19.2.10 Sybil Attacks

In some applications, the sensor might need to work collaboratively to accomplish a certain task; hence, management policy of the network can use distribution of subtasks or redundancy of information. In this case, a malicious node can pretend to be more than one node at the same time using the identities of other legitimate nodes. An attacker tries to degrade the integrity of data, level of security, routing mechanism, data aggregation, and even misbehavior detection techniques. As possible countermeasures, we can use a logically centralized authority (base station or cluster head) in the network. Some recent IDSs could be found in [36,47–49]. Newsome et al. [46] proposed a taxonomy of Sybil attacks in WSNs based on three orthogonal dimensions.

19.2.11 Other Security Attacks in WSNs

There are a few less known (or commonly unknown or less studied) security threats that exist in WSNs. These attacks mostly concentrate on service availability (i.e., DoS) of the networks in different layers. We briefly describe them in the following paragraphs.

Bogus message during reprogramming: This attack could be launched in the application layer if a WSN application allows reprogramming of the network. Reprogramming of the network may be needed for scope selection, encoding-decoding, completion validation, code acquisition, or for network management purposes [28]. If the reprogramming process is not secure enough, the attackers can effectively cut off a portion of the network by using bogus messages.

External stimuli: A possible attack against WSNs in the application layer could be launched by using some external physical stimuli. The attacker uses the external stimuli to stimulate the nodes with a huge number of events to be sent directly to the base station. However, this attack is not effective when packets are sent with predefined regular intervals. The possible solution might be using an IDS that detects attackers in the network if a particular region creates a large number of packets within a short period of time [33].

Homing: Depending on WSN application, some nodes (e.g., cluster heads) are given special responsibilities, such as managing keys, maintaining a local group, etc. The adversaries try to handle and eavesdrop on the activities of those leader nodes. In this attack, the attackers hamper the normal functioning of leader nodes within a WSN application [33].

Neglect and greed: If a sensor node drops packets or denies transmitting legitimate packets or if a node is very greedy to give undue priority to its own messages, then it could be considered as a neglecting node. The protocols that are based on dynamic source routing (DSR) are the most vulnerable to this type of attack [40].

Unfairness: This attack is a weaker form of DoS attack in the link layer. This attack could degrade service for real-time MAC protocols by using unfair resource allocations. In fact, providing fairness in WSNs is often viewed as a separate research issue [40].

So far, we have discussed various types of security threats in WSNs. These attacks can be tackled by using some successful and efficient countermeasures that will be discussed later. Most of the research works basically rely on some statistical assumptions and simulation results. At the time of the implementation of those mechanisms in real environments, they might face plenty of difficulties due to the unpredictable nature of wireless sensor networks.

19.3 LITERATURE REVIEW

We have talked about the major threats and attacks to investigate the grounds of our work a bit. It is, in reality, impossible to tackle all the attacks with a single routing protocol or a single mechanism of any kind (unless different parts of the mechanism work in different layers to cover all the security needs, or different mechanisms work in collaboration to secure the entire network). However, what we can do is the security measures could be blended within the routing mechanism as a first line of defense. Then, on top of that, other security mechanisms could work to deal with specific network-related problems and issues. Hence, the intent of this chapter is to introduce to the readers such a scheme that could give some innovative idea of blending security measures within a routing strategy. There are a few prior works that motivate us to devise our mechanism. Although none of them is directly related to our proposed solution, the underlying principles are sometimes similar to some of them.

Çam et al. [5] propose an energy-efficient security protocol for wireless sensor networks by using symmetric key cryptography and their NOVSF (non-blocking orthogonal variable spreading factor) code-hopping technique. They consider a hierarchical architecture of the network in which data are routed from sensor nodes to the base station through cluster heads. The basic idea of their protocol is to implement two algorithms in the sensor nodes and in the base station, which the sensor nodes and the base station would follow at the time of data transmission and reception. To ensure a better level of security, they introduced the NOVSF technique, which basically scrambles the data blocks using a multiplexer in the system while transmitting data from the sensor nodes. Their scheme is secure and energy efficient, considering the fact that it increases the level of security during data transmission using the NOVSF technique without utilizing any additional power. However, this scrambling technique increases the complexity of tasks for the base station as it has to aggregate and reorder the incoming data blocks correctly. To address the issue of energy-efficient data aggregation with secure data transmission, an ESPDA (energy-efficient secure pattern-based data aggregation) protocol [6] is proposed. In contrast to the conventional data aggregation protocols, ESPDA avoids the transmission of redundant data from the sensor nodes to the cluster head. To make the data transmission and aggregation more secure, a cluster head is not required to decrypt or encrypt the data received from the sensor nodes. On the whole, though, it [5] is an energy-efficient secure protocol; it increases the processing burden of the base station and to support the associated ESPDA scheme, it requires more energy, which literally ruins the gains of the original scheme.

Ye et al. [7] propose a statistical en-route filtering (SEF) scheme to detect and drop false reports during the forwarding process. In their scheme, a report is forwarded only if it contains the message authentication codes (MACs) generated by multiple nodes by using keys from different partitions in a global key pool. According to their findings, SEF can drop up to 70% of bogus reports injected by a compromised node within five hops and reduce energy consumption by 65% or more in many cases.

Zhu et al. [8] propose the interleaved, hop-by-hop authentication scheme that detects false reports through interleaved authentication. Their scheme guarantees that the base station can detect a false report when no more than t nodes are compromised, where t is a security threshold. In addition, their scheme guarantees that t colluding compromised sensors can deceive at most B noncompromised nodes to forward false data they inject, where B is $O(t^2)$ in the worst case. They also propose a variant of this scheme, which guarantees $B = 0$ and which works for a small t.

Motivated by [8], Lee and Cho [9] propose an enhanced interleaved authentication scheme called the key inheritance-based filtering that prevents forwarding of false reports. In their scheme, the keys of each node used in the message authentication consist of the node's own key and the keys inherited from its upstream nodes. Every authenticated report contains the combination of the message authentication codes generated by using the keys of the consecutive nodes in a path from the base station to a terminal node. Other than these works, [10–12] focus only on energy efficiency in a wireless sensor network and the works like [3,4,13] deal with the security measures for routing in WSN.

After analyzing all these works, we design our protocol in which we create a tree structure in the network, based on the energy levels and distances (from the base station) of the sensor nodes. Along with the energy-efficient structuring of the network, we initialize an efficient security scheme down the paths of the tree to ensure secure data transmission in the network. Security is in fact a vast area of research, but our focus of this work is to address secure data transmission from the source sensors to the base station along with energy-efficient structuring and operation of the network. We develop our protocol in a way in which false injection of data cannot deceive the base station or, more specifically, cannot reach the base station. We emphasize the authenticity of sensor readings so that, before transmitting each packet, the forwarding nodes can detect the irregularities with a minimum effort and thus drop unnecessary or flawed packets. By stopping the false packets traveling a long distance along the created paths in the network, our mechanism helps for greater energy efficiency as the intermediate nodes are thus saved from extra transmissions. For employing the entire protocol, we develop it in a way that before starting its operation for secure data transmission, the network is formed in an energy-efficient way. Periodic restructuring of the network is proposed to keep a balance among the nodes to dissipate energies in nearly equal proportion. Our goal here is to achieve maximum lifetime of the network with secure data transmission from any source sensor to the base station.

19.4 ASSUMPTIONS AND PRELIMINARIES

19.4.1 SENSOR DEPLOYMENT AND NETWORK MODEL

We consider a wireless sensor network with densely deployed sensing devices. The deployment could be made by aerial or vehicular scattering or by physical installation. We assume that, initially, all the nodes and the base station in the network have the same transmission range (say r). Like µTESLA [24], our protocol requires that the base station and nodes are loosely time synchronized, and each node knows an upper bound on the maximum synchronization error. The base station has enough energy to support the network's operations for its full lifetime. The sensors deployed in the network have the computational, memory, communication, and power resources such as the current generation of sensor nodes (e.g., MICA2 motes [14]). Once the sensors are deployed over the target area, they remain relatively static in their respective positions. That means the nodes do not move with respect to their neighbor. The transmissions of each node are isotropic (i.e., in all directions) so that each message sent is a local broadcast within the transmission range of the node. The link between any pair of nodes in the network is bidirectional, that is, if a node n_i gets a node n_j within its transmission range (i.e., one hop), n_j also gets n_i as its one-hop neighbor.

An accurate model for the energy consumption per bit at the physical layer is given by

$$E = E_{elec}^{trans} + \beta d^\alpha + E_{elec}^{recv} \tag{19.1}$$

where E_{elec}^{trans} is the distance-independent amount of energy consumed by the transmitter electronics (PLLs, VCOs, bias currents) and digital processing, E_{elec}^{recv} is the energy utilized by receiver electronics, and βd^α accounts for the radiated power necessary to transmit over a distance d between source and destination. As in [15,16] we assume that

$$E_{elec}^{trans} = E_{elec}^{recv} = E_{elec} \tag{19.2}$$

So overall energy consumption between source and destination within one hop can be calculated using

$$E = 2.E_{elec} + \beta d^\alpha \tag{19.3}$$

Broadly speaking, hierarchical routing protocols use control packets for topology construction phase. For a particular node i, control packet transmission cost can be calculated by

$$C_i^{ctrl}(r) = \left[L_{ctrl} \times \beta r^\alpha + (nbr_i(r)+1) \times L_{ctrl} \times L_E \right]\frac{1}{T} \tag{19.4}$$

where, α is the path loss exponent ($2 < \alpha < 5$), β is a constant [joule/bit.m²], r is the transmission range, L_{ctrl} is the length of control packet in bits, nbr_i is the average number of neighbors of node i for range r, L_E is the energy needed by the transceiver circuitry to transmit or receive a packet, and T is the time period between two consecutive restructurings of the network.

For a particular path p, data communication cost from source i to the base station can be represented as

$$C_i^{data}(p) = \left[\sum_{i=1, j=2}^{N} (nfrd_p(d_i)+1) \times L_{data} \times \beta d_{i,j}^\alpha + (nbr_p(d_i)+1) \times L_{data} \right] \times L_E \tag{19.5}$$

Here, N is the total number of nodes in the network, $i,j \in 0, 1, 2, ..., N$ is the node index, p is the path associated for data transmission from source i to sink, d_i is the transmission range set by node i, $d_{i,j}$ is the distance between the node i and j, $nfrd_p(d_i)$ indicates the number of forwarding nodes for a path p and range d, $nbr_p(d_i)$ indicates the number of neighboring nodes for a path p and range d, L_{data} is the length of data packets in bits, and, finally, α and β are same as the previous equation. Total communication cost for sending a data packet from source i is

$$C_i^{total}(p) = \sum_{i=1}^{N} \left[C_i^{ctrl}(r) \right] + C_i^{data}(p) \tag{19.6}$$

The observations from the above equation are the following:

- Wasteful (due to idle listening, overhearing, etc.) energy consumption increases as the number of redundant forwarder increases.
- Wasteful energy consumption increases as the number of idle nodes increases.
- Energy consumption increases exponentially as the distance between nodes increases.
- Frequency of control packet transmission is proportional to the energy consumption.

To reduce energy consumption, the following things could be done:

- Reducing the number of forwarding nodes (not hampering the level of connectivity and the reliability of the network)
- Putting a certain portion of the nodes in sleep mode to reduce idle mode energy consumption
- Employing adaptive transmission range according to the distance from the forwarder node to save energy
- Fixing the network restructuring frequency to ensure balanced energy consumption

19.4.2 BASIC TERMS AND DEFINITIONS

We consider three states of the nodes in our protocol during its operation:

Non-forwarding—Nodes keep their radio transceivers "off" but continue to sense the events in their sensing ranges using sensing circuitry. Sensing of any event turns on the radio of a non-forwarding node.

Forwarding—Both the transceiver and sensing circuits remain "on" in this state.

Active—During the tree construction and OHC initialization phase (later described in Section 19.4.1), all nodes remain in the active state. In the active state, both the sensing and radio circuitries of the sensors remain "on." Basically, there is no major difference between forwarding and the active state. We term these two states to differentiate the two phases in our protocol (explained later).

Active State Time. Let v be a node and $N_1(v)$ be the number of one-hop neighbors of v for a particular transmission range r (r is same for all nodes in the network, including the sink). Let T_{rtt} be the round trip time for data propagation between the longest distant pair within one-hop neighbors. Then, the active state time for node v is given by the equation

$$T_{active} = T_{rtt} \times N_1(v)$$

In our protocol, within the time T_{active}, a node could be able to determine whether it should participate in the tree as a forwarding node or not.

One-Way Hash Chain (OHC). To ensure security for data transmissions from the sensors to the base station, we use pre-stored shared secret keys and a one-way hash chain. A one-way hash chain [17] is a sequence of numbers generated by one-way function F that has the property that for a given x, it is easy to compute $y = F(x)$. However, given F and y, it is computationally infeasible to determine x, such that $x = F^{-1}(y)$. A one-way hash chain (OHC) is a sequence of numbers $K_n, K_{n-1}, ..., K_0$, such that, $\forall i : 0 \leq i < n, K_i = F(K_{i+1})$. To generate an OHC, first a random number K_r is selected as the seed, and then F is applied successively on K_r to generate other numbers in the sequence. In the next section, we describe in detail how the shared secret keys are used with OHC in our protocol to provide data transmission security.

It should be noted here that in this chapter we have used the terms *base station* and *sink* interchangeably.

19.4.3 SECURITY ASSUMPTIONS AND THREAT MODEL

The base station could not be compromised in any way. We assume that no node could be compromised by any adversary while creating the tree structure in the network (i.e., the first phase of our scheme). This particular assumption is necessary to protect the network from being wrongly structured or to prevent the inclusion of any rouge entity in the network. In this case, we are mainly assuming that compromising a node with physical capture is not possible. Also some other attacks, such as jamming, could hamper proper relaying of the control messages. We assume that, at least in the tree structuring process, any physical capture or jamming attack is not done by any adversary. In fact, such types of initial attacks (for example, HELLO Flood attack [3]) could be another topic for research. In this chapter, our focus is to secure the data transmissions from the source sensors to the base station, and addressing jamming or physical capture are beyond the scope of this work. Initially, each node is equally trusted by the base station.

Each node in the network has a unique shared secret key with the base station. These keys are pre-stored into the sensors' memories so that, after deployment, the sensors could use the keys to encrypt data while sending it to the base station. The base station keeps an index of the IDs of the sensors and the corresponding shared secret keys. Due to the use of wireless communications, the nodes in the network are vulnerable to various kinds of attacks. We assume that an adversary could try to eavesdrop on all traffic, inject false packets, and replay older packets. If, in any case, a node is compromised, it could be a full compromise in which all the information stored in that particular sensor are exposed to the adversary or could be a partial compromise, that is, partial information is exposed.

19.5 SECURE ENERGY-EFFICIENT ROUTING PROTOCOL (SERP)

19.5.1 TREE CONSTRUCTION AND OHC INITIALIZATION PHASE

We consider distances and residual energies of the nodes to construct a sink rooted tree (SRT) in the network. At the time of the tree construction, all nodes keep their radio transceivers "on" to verify whether it should remain active as a forwarding node or not. A timer parameter is defined to ensure each node's active participation in this process for a specific period of time. Each node is prioritized for transmission according to its residual energy and distance from the sink.

Now, according to our assumption, all the sensors and the base station have shared secret keys that are pre-stored before deployment of the network. So when the sensors are deployed in the target area randomly, each sensor contains a shared secret key with the base station, which could be used to provide confidentiality of the reports. However, to provide authenticity of the transmitted data, all the intermediate nodes between any source node and the base station must be initialized with the basic one-way hash chain number. Let us suppose the initial OHC number is $I_{OHC} = HS_0$.

To initiate the first phase of network structuring and OHC number initialization, the base station B generates a control packet containing HS_0, a MAC (message authentication code) for the control packet using the key K_i along with some other parameters. Here, K_i is the number in the key chain corresponding to time slot t_i. The format of the control packet is

$$bcm: B|sid|ren|dist|fid|HS_0|MAC_{K_i}(B|sid|ren|dist|fid|HS_0)$$

where, *sid* indicates the sender's ID, *ren* is the remaining energy of the sender, *dist* is the calculated cumulative distance to reach the sink using forwarding node(s), and *fid* is the ID of the upstream node (i.e., immediate parent or immediate forwarding node) selected by the current node for forwarding data toward the sink. The sink node initiates *bcm* with sender ID *B*, and the values of *sid*, *ren*, *dist*, and *fid* as −1 as, according to our assumption, the base station has unlimited energy compared to the energies of the sensors in the network, and in this case, no forwarding node is needed to reach itself.

When the BS transmits *bcm*, at first, its one-hop neighbors get the message. Receiving the message, each node in the one-hop neighborhood of the base station first calculates its distance (i.e., *dist*) from the base station based on the received signal strength, stores the value of HS_0 and sets *B* as its forwarder node (the ultimate destination is the base station). Now, each of these nodes transmits the message again within its own one-hop neighborhood (i.e., local broadcast). In this case, the *sid* is set to its own ID, *ren* is its own residual energy, and the MAC part is kept the same as the base station message, *bcm*. To ensure prioritization of the transmission of control messages, each node waits for a threshold time before each further transmission. Waiting time of a node before further transmission is defined by

$$T_{wait} = \{D_s/E_r\} \times R \tag{19.7}$$

where D_s is the cumulative distance between the sink and the node, E_r is the residual energy of the node, and R is a constant that is needed to normalize the value of T_{wait}. As with the course of time, the sensors lose their energy levels, and the value of the ratio of distance and residual energy increases; we need to normalize this value. In our case, R is the ratio of the node's initial energy and transmission range.

Each node receiving the control messages from one or more upstream neighboring nodes first calculates the distance of each sender based on the received signal strength, then calculates the cumulative distances up to the sink via different possible forwarders (i.e., the upstream senders), stores the ID and residual energy information of each sender, and stores HS_0 from the message sent by the first sender. To choose its forwarder node, it compares the values of the distance and energy ratios (D_s/E_r) of the neighboring upstream nodes and chooses the node with the least value of the ratio as its forwarder node. It then senses the channel, and if the channel is idle, it waits for T_{wait} time and then retransmits the message containing its own status information and with its chosen forwarder node ID as its *fid*. As the selected upstream node could also get the message (as the link between any two nodes is bidirectional), it sets itself as a forwarding node for this transmitting node. This process continues, and eventually a tree structure is created in the network in which each node has a forwarder node on the way to reach the base station and possibly one or more downstream nodes that can send data to it destined to the base station. Here, the value of T_{wait} depends mainly on the values of E_r and D_s. In fact, these values are used to set the priority of the nodes to be selected as forwarding nodes.

To authenticate HS_0, *B* releases the key K_i in time slot t_{i+d}. Here, *d* is the delay parameter for the time slot, which could be set depending on the application at hand. It indicates after how many time slots the key for time slot *i* should be released. On receiving this key, a node can verify the integrity and source authentication of HS_0. Thus, along each path, the initial OHC number is initialized. It is to be noted that *bcm* won't bring any attack against the network even if the nodes on the other side of the network don't receive K_i at t_{i+d}. Because the messages that are MACed by K_i are supposed to be sent out at time slot *t*, an adversary cannot launch any attacks with K_i when it gets K_i at t_{i+d}. Within the time T_{active}, a node that does not get any message from any of its neighbors that it should be a forwarding node, sets itself as a non-forwarding node. Figure 19.2 shows the sample input and output networks.

19.5.2 Network Operation and Secure Data Transmission Phase

We construct the sink rooted tree (SRT) based on the energy levels and distances of the nodes. After the tree is constructed within the network, all nodes are either in forwarding or non-forwarding

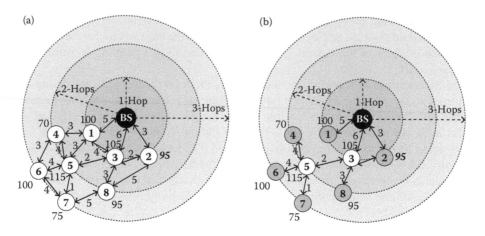

FIGURE 19.2 A portion of an example network (a) before execution of the first phase. All the white nodes are in active status (b) after execution of the first phase. The gray nodes are in non-forwarding status while the other two nodes are in forwarding status. We have shown the N-hop ($N = 1, 2, 3, \ldots$) neighbors of the sink on the circumference of the same circle regardless of their actual calculated distances from the sink.

states. Nodes with the non-forwarding state turn off their radio transceivers while keeping the sensing circuitry "on." On the other hand, forwarding nodes keep both radio and sensing circuitry "on." All nodes try to sense any change of parameters (such as temperature, pressure, magnetism, etc. based on the duty assigned to the nodes) within their vicinities, and upon detecting any event, the non-forwarding nodes turn their radios on and transmit data toward the base station via their selected forwarding nodes.

To send the data securely to the sink, each source node n_s maintains a unique one-way hash chain, HS: $< HS_n, HS_{n-1}, \ldots, HS_1, HS_0 >$. When a source node n_s sends a report to the sink using the path created in the sink-rooted tree (for example, a path is $n_s \rightarrow \ldots \rightarrow n_{m-1} \rightarrow n_m \rightarrow B$), it encrypts the packet with its shared secret key with the base station, including its own ID and an OHC sequence number from HS in the packet. It attaches HS_1 for the first packet, HS_2 for the second packet, and so on. To validate an OHC number, each intermediate node $n_1, \ldots, n_m$ maintains a verifier I_{n_s} for each source node n_s. Initially, I_{n_s} for a particular source node is set to HS_0. When n_s sends the ith packet, it includes HS_i with the packet.

When any intermediate node n_k receives this packet, it verifies whether $I_{n_s} = F(HS_i)$ or not. If so, n_k validates the packet, it forwards it to the next intermediate node, and sets I_{n_s} to HS_i. In general, n_k can choose to apply the verification test iteratively up to a fixed number w times, checking at each step whether, $I_{n_s} = F(F \ldots (F(HS_i)))$. If the packet is not validated after the verification process has been performed w times, n_k simply drops the packet. By performing the verification process w times, up to a sequence of w packet losses can be tolerated, and the value of w depends on the average packet loss rate of the network. An intermediate node need not decrypt the packet; rather it can check the authenticity of the packet before forwarding to its immediate forwarder. Figure 19.3 illustrates these.

In Figure 19.3a, the source node n_s sends the first packet to the base station with the OHC value HS_1. The content of the packet is encrypted with the secret key that it shares with the base station. Getting the packet, the base station performs the authenticity check by verifying the hash chain number and gets the report by decrypting it with the shared key for that particular source node. Figure 19.3b shows a scenario in which the packet P_2 could not reach the base station for some reason. In spite of that, the OHC verification is not hampered as for the next packet the third intermediate node performs the hash verification twice (Figure 19.3c). Here, at the very first attempt, it cannot get the value of HS_1 in the verification process, but in the second iteration, it verifies it as a valid packet from the source n_s. In fact, in this case, the intermediate node can

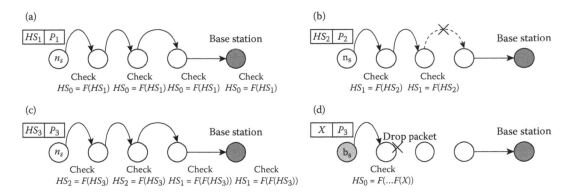

FIGURE 19.3 (a) Authenticated packet delivery to the base station using the OHC numbers, (b) an example scenario in which the packet could not reach the base station, (c) but it cannot affect the OHC verification technique, (d) a bogus packet with a false *HS* value is dropped by an intermediate node.

perform the hash number verification w times, and w is an application-dependent parameter. In Figure 19.3d an adversary tries to send a bogus packet with a false hash chain number, and it is detected in the next upstream node. Eventually, such a bogus packet fails to pass the authentication check and is dropped in the very next hop. This feature saves energy of the network as such falsely injected packets cannot travel through the network for more than one hop. After the tree construction, at the time of data transmission, each node could dynamically set its transmission range according to the distance of the parent or immediate forwarding node. If the distance of the forwarding node is less than the initially used transmission range for tree construction, the node decreases the range by decreasing the transmission energy. This feature gives the flexibility in our protocol to dynamically set the transmission ranges, and thus it helps for conserving network-wide energy.

The first phase is executed after every T time, and T is an application-dependent parameter. T depends on the event generation rate as well as on the load of the network. Each node participating in tree construction should have at least a certain level of energy.

19.5.3 Optional Key Refreshment

To provide data freshness and to increase the level of security, our scheme has an optional key refreshment mechanism. In this case, the base station periodically broadcasts a new session key to the sensors in the network. The format for this message is

$$B|K_s| \, \mathrm{MAC}_{K_j}(B|K_s)$$

where K_j is the number in the key chain number corresponding to time slot t_j. To authenticate K_s, like the OHC initialization phase, B releases the key K_j in time slot t_{j+d}. On receiving this key, the nodes can verify the integrity and source authentication of K_s. Then each node gets the new key by performing an X-OR (exclusive OR) operation with its old shared key. This method could also be utilized for refreshing the keys of a specific number of nodes. In that case, the base station could simply send the K_s to the specific node by encrypting it with its previous shared secret key. Upon receiving the new key, the node can perform the X-OR operation and could use the newly derived key for subsequent data transmissions.

Changing encryption keys from time to time has an advantage as it guarantees data freshness in the network. Moreover, it helps to maintain confidentiality of the transmitted data by preventing the use of the same secret key at all the times.

19.5.4 Repairing a Broken Path and OHC Re-Initialization

If, in any case, any node between the source node and the base station fails, it could make one or more paths useless. Eventually, in such a case, all the downstream nodes along that particular path get disconnected from the base station. To repair such a broken path, we use the stored upstream knowledge of the sensors. We know that, in the first phase, each downstream node stores the IDs of the one-hop upstream senders of the control message. So this knowledge could be used for repairing the path quickly.

Let us illustrate it with an example. Say, in Figure 19.2b, node 5 is somehow damaged or failed to continue (Figure 19.4a). So the nodes 4, 6, and 7 get disconnected from the base station. This failure could first be detected by the one-hop neighbors of node 5 in the tree, i.e., nodes 4, 6, 7, and node 3. In the first phase, as node 4 got a message from node 1, which tried to become its forwarder, node 4 could use that knowledge to repair the path. So node 4 first does a local broadcast of an error message that it has lost its previous forwarder and sets node 1 as its forwarder. Accordingly, node 1 gets a forwarding status. If there were more senders who had sent control messages to node 4 at the time of tree construction, node 4 would have chosen the node with the least distance and energy ratio as recorded earlier. We know that in the first phase, each node stores the information about its neighbors who try to become its forwarder. If node 4 is required to send any packet as a source node, it could simply send it using the OHC number in the sequence, HS_{k+1}, which is next to its last-used OHC number, HS_k. For node 1, node 4 is a new source, so it could save its HS value in I_4. The subsequent transmissions from node 4 are verified by node 1 based on this initial knowledge. There are other two stranded nodes in our example, node 6 and node 7. In the similar fashion, these nodes use their stored knowledge. The structure of the new path after broken path recovery is shown in Figure 19.4b.

As we are considering a highly dense deployment scenario, we think that, in most of the cases, a node might initially get two or more upstream senders who would try to be its forwarder. This procedure works fine as long as no more than w packets are lost on the way from any source node (after a path is broken due to a node failure). If, within the time of repairing the path, more than w packets are lost from a particular source, the OHC chain along that path breaks down. In fact, this is the worst case in which all the downstream nodes along the path become invalid to the base station and their sent data are discarded on the way to reach the base station. To overcome this problem, the entire OHC initialization phase (the first phase of our protocol) could be made periodic (after an certain interval, which is an application-dependent parameter). Determining the best possible time interval for re-initialization of the first phase is kept as our future work.

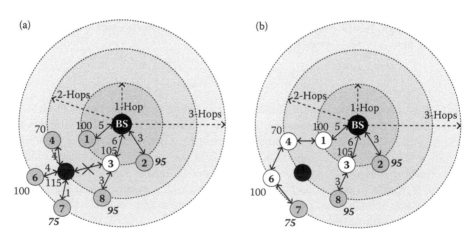

FIGURE 19.4 (a) Node 5 failed; (b) repairing a broken path. White nodes are in forwarding status, and gray nodes are in non-forwarding status.

19.6 SIMULATION RESULTS AND PERFORMANCE ANALYSIS

19.6.1 SIMULATION

To understand the performance of our proposed protocol, we simulated the network in NS-2 [18] with 50 to 300 nodes uniformly distributed in a 100 m × 100 m square sensor field. The transmission range of each sensor node was set to 25 m. Each node was provided with 2 Joule of initial energy. Transmitter and receiver electronics were set to dissipate 50 nJ/bit.m². The data packet length was set to 2 KB. The sink or base station was located at (150, 150) coordinate. We varied the number of sources from 1 to 7, and the data generation interval was randomly chosen. Initially, tree construction time was set to 10 seconds. As our protocol creates a hierarchical structure in the network, we compared our protocol with two other hierarchical energy-aware routing protocols LEACH [10] and EAD [11]. All the simulation parameters are shown in Table 19.2.

After the construction of the sink rooted tree, some of the nodes are selected as the forwarding nodes. The size of the set of forwarding nodes indicates at least how many nodes are needed to stay awake for data transmission. A small set of forwarding nodes is desirable for minimizing the routing overhead. The smaller the size of the set of forwarders, the better the energy efficiency is for the network as more nodes could be in the non-forwarding status. Figure 19.5a shows the percentage of forwarding nodes among the total number of nodes in LEACH, EAD, and our protocol. Now, an interesting feature to note for the Figure 19.5a is that as the number of nodes in the network grows, the percentage of cluster heads decreases slightly for LEACH because more nodes become associated with a single cluster head in the network. For the reason of dense deployment, relatively more nodes are covered by a cluster head. Thus, the percentage of cluster heads (forwarding nodes) becomes slightly lower than the suggested percentage of cluster heads as the number of nodes increases in the network.

Figure 19.5b shows the energy dissipation given a number of source nodes. Less energy dissipation eventually helps for increasing the lifetime of the network. The relative gain of our proposed scheme compared to LEACH and EAD increases with the increase of number of sources. More sources issue more data to be transmitted. In case of LEACH, each transmission requires one hop to reach the cluster head and one hop to reach to the sink. In case of EAD, multiple hops are required to reach to the sink. As wireless transmission power varies depending on distance, for the same packet size, LEACH requires much higher energy for transmission. EAD requires less energy than that of LEACH as it uses multiple hops (hence, less transmission range). As our algorithm uses adaptive transmission range, the amount of energy consumption is much less than LEACH and EAD, considering the same packet size.

TABLE 19.2
Simulation Parameters

Simulation time	1300 s
Simulation area	100 × 100 m²
Total number of nodes	50 ~ 300
Initial energy	2 J
Transmit/receive electronics (L_E)	50 nJ/bit/m²
Transmission power	5.85 e – 5 watt
Receive signal threshold	3.152 e – 20 watt
Sleep mode energy	0
Number of sources	1 ~ 7
Offered load	4 ~ 6 pkts. per s (pps)
Transmission range	25 m
Packet size	2048 bytes

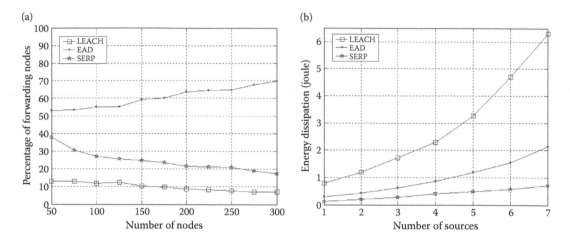

FIGURE 19.5 (a) Percentage of forwarding nodes in total number of nodes in the network, (b) energy dissipation for different number of sources in LEACH, EAD, and SERP.

Figure 19.6a and 19.6b present the number of *alive* nodes versus simulation time with 50 and 100 nodes. Our proposed scheme generates a fewer number of forwarding nodes compared to EAD. As a result, the energy dissipation is much less than that of EAD as there are less nodes participating actively in the network operation phase. Also adaptive transmission range saves more energy for the same packet size. Single hop transmission, the main drawback of LEACH, leads to huge energy consumption for data transmission. Our experimental results show that our algorithm achieves better lifetime compared to LEACH and EAD.

19.6.2 Storage Requirement for One-Way Hash Chain

The method of generating and storing a long OHC in a sensor node is a little difficult. Naive algorithms require either too much memory to store every OHC number or too much time to compute the next OHC number. None of these algorithms are practical on resource-constrained sensor nodes. Recently, some efficient OHC generation algorithms for resource-constrained platforms have been proposed [19–21]. Among these algorithms, the fractal graph traversal algorithm [19] could perform

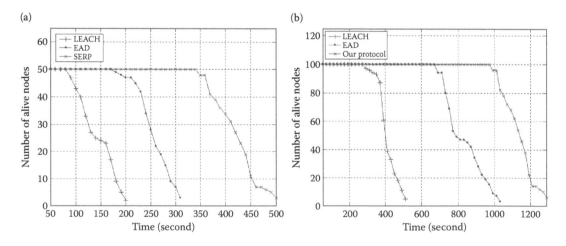

FIGURE 19.6 Number of alive nodes versus time for (a) 50 nodes and (b) 100 nodes.

well on the traditional sensor nodes. This algorithm stores only some of the intermediate numbers, called pebbles, of an OHC, and uses them to compute other numbers. If the size of an OHC is n (there are total n numbers in this OHC), the algorithm performs approximately $\frac{1}{2}\log_2 n$ one-way function operations to compute the next OHC number and requires a little more than $\log_2 n$ units of memory to save pebbles.

The length of an OHC that is needed for a source node is also an important factor. The typical length is between 2^{11} to 2^{22}. If the length of an OHC is 2^{22}, and a node uses one OHC number per second, it will take more than a month to exhaust all numbers from this chain. Figure 19.7a shows the storage requirements for storing pebbles for different lengths of an OHC. This includes a skipjack-based one-way function and OHC generation based on [19]. We see that a node needs about 930 bytes to maintain an OHC of length 2^{22}. This includes a 256-byte lookup table for skipjack, which can be shared with other applications. Other than this, each node has to store only a few IDs and neighbor information of its one-hop neighbors. Overall, the memory requirement for our scheme could be well afforded with today's sensor nodes.

19.6.3 Security Analysis

We analyze the security of our scheme with respect to two design goals: the ability of the base station to detect a false report and the ability of the nodes en route to filter or detect false reports.

19.6.3.1 Base Station Detection

In our scheme, whenever the base station receives a report from any sensor, it first checks the ID of the sensor, checks the authenticity of the report by verifying the one-way hash chain number for that particular source, looks for the corresponding shared secret key, and decrypts the packet. The base station could not be compromised in any way. So it is in fact the final entity that could confirm the authenticity, confidentiality, and integrity of the transmitted reports. Our security scheme is designed in a way that, any bogus report cannot reach the base station; rather it would be detected and dropped by the intermediate nodes. However, if, somehow, a bogus packet is sent directly to the base station, it would certainly be discarded by it for the failure of the authentication check. If in any application, the optional key refreshment mechanism is employed, once the time slot of releasing the new session key is over, the base station first tries to decrypt the incoming packets from any particular source with the X-ORed new key for that node. In case it produces a garbage result, the base station tries with the previous shared secret key with that node (the previous key could easily be obtained again

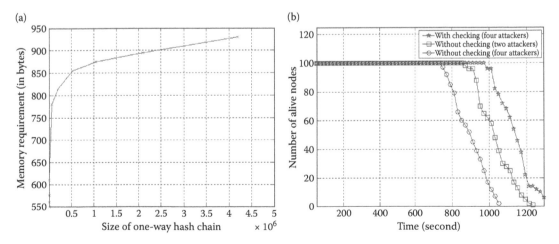

FIGURE 19.7 (a) Memory requirement for OHC generation; (b) Number of alive nodes versus time for two cases: without packet authentication and with packet authentication (2 ~ 4 attackers generating bogus packets).

by X-ORing the most recent session key with the newly computed key for that node). This case might happen when somehow some node cannot get the new session key released by the base station.

19.6.3.2 Detection by the Intermediate Nodes

Two types of attempts from the adversaries are considered:

Outsider Attack: In this case, as shown in Figure 19.3d, if an outsider node generates a packet with a fake OHC number, the authentication must be failed in the very next node in the path, and as a result, this packet would never be forwarded even to the node that is only two hops away from it. Simple verification of the OHC number prohibits the forwarding of such bogus packets.

Insider Attack: If a legitimate node along any path is compromised, the attacker could grab the OHC sequence and the shared secret key with the base station. However, it should be noted that, to use the OHC numbers successfully, the adversary should also know the last OHC number used by that particular node to send the packet to the base station. If it gets the last-used OHC number, then it could use this for sending false packets successfully. Otherwise, any arbitrary use of the OHC number from that source might not be forwarded by the next intermediate node because of authentication failure. Now, in case of a node that is fully compromised, that is, if the adversary obtains all the required information, it actually gets the status of a legitimate node in the network. This fully compromised node could be used to generate false reports with valid authentication numbers. To prevent such type of malicious adversary, there are several factors that come into play to detect the abnormal behavior of the node. In our scheme, the base station considers a report legitimate if it is reported by at least δ number of source nodes in the network, where δ is an application-dependent parameter. So the different or modified reports from a single source cannot convince the base station about any event. Also the base station could notice the amount of packets generated by a particular source. These are basically a part of an intrusion detection system (IDS) implemented in the base station. The detailed description of the IDS is beyond the scope of this work.

The worst case scenario occurs if more than δ number of nodes in a particular region in the network are somehow compromised. This sort of collaborative and large-scale attack is handled by the periodic restructuring of the whole network. Finding an optimal value of the time interval for periodic restructuring is kept as our future works.

In Figure 19.7b, we show the number of alive nodes versus simulation time considering the packet authenticity checking method and without checking. We considered two to four attackers in addition to the number of actual source nodes. The graph shows that if the detection method is absent, the nodes lose energy rapidly, which causes a shorter network lifetime. The result is plotted for total of 100 nodes in the network. In this experiment, four to 16 packets per second (pps) were generated by the attackers to drain energy of the nodes. When the packet authentication method is employed, the nodes can detect false packets, and by dropping those other intermediate nodes, are relieved from the burden of forwarding false reports.

As a whole, the efficiency of our protocol is increased with the number of false packets transmitted by the attackers. The more false packets that are tried to be sent by the adversaries, the more gain we have as those packets cannot travel a long distance toward the base station and thus save the network from consuming unnecessary energy by extra forwarding or transmission. This is, in fact, very helpful for the longer lifetime of the network in a heavy flooding attack in which the attackers try to inject a huge number of false packets into the network data flow.

19.7 DISCUSSION ON IMPLEMENTING AN IDS WITH SERP

As we noted earlier, the description of a complete IDS is beyond the scope of this chapter. However, in this section, we briefly discuss the implementation of an IDS alongside SERP, considering different WSN structures. Depending on the network structure used, the location of the employed IDS could be different, which could also affect various parameters in the network. The objective of putting this section is to link up some IDS techniques that could be considered for a network in which SERP is used as the routing protocol. While SERP provides partial protection by providing authentication of packets and minimizing the energy drain, any IDS in particular locations of the network could give the rest of the protection that the network needs for its overall security.

WSN is a highly application-dependent network. Hence, network structures vastly differ depending on the application types. We have discussed the major structures in the introductory section in a more detailed way. However, in this part, for the convenience of the readers, we are recapping the gist of the previously noted information to relate IDS with current discussion:

- *Tree based*—In this structure, the base station plays the role of the main parent node (i.e., root), and sensor nodes take the roles of leaf nodes or intermediate nodes. The one-hop neighbor nodes of the base station can become parent nodes for the second hop neighbor nodes, and this method continues to cover the entire network in this fashion.
- *Cluster based*—In this scenario, the network is divided into clusters with the main base station. Every cluster has its own selected cluster head (CH), which is the medium between cluster members and the base station. In addition, cluster heads are often allowed to communicate among themselves for some specific purposes.
- *Hierarchical*—The network is organized into a tree-like structure with several different types of clusters in it. This structure may have several layers representing parent-child type relationships (at least thematically). Note that this is different than a hybrid model in which a portion of the network is cluster based while some other portion is tree based and some other portion may be of hierarchical structure or combination of all.

Figure 19.8 illustrates these network structures with possible IDS locations at which IDSs can function in a perfect and efficient manner. For instance, in a tree-based structure, it would be perfect if the

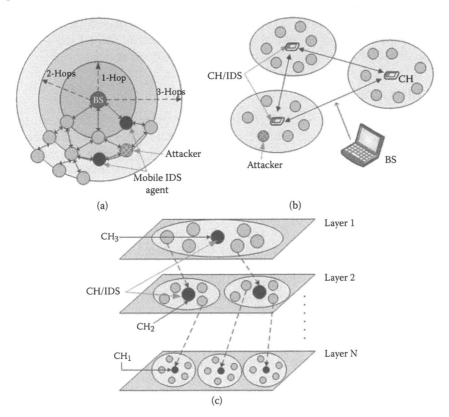

FIGURE 19.8 Three types of network structures with possible IDS locations. (a) Tree-based, (b) Cluster-based, and (c) Hierarchial.

IDS could have several mobile agents in leaf nodes and a global agent in parent node (i.e., base station). This helps the IDS to detect attacks with higher accuracy at the same time maintaining less resource [50].

Furthermore, we believe that it would be very efficient to have one IDS agent for a group of sensor nodes (i.e., installed on a cluster head) in cluster-based network structures. Assuming that cluster heads are slightly more powerful devices than their cluster members, we can implement powerful IDS modules on them (which may not be efficient on typical sensor nodes).

It might be a challenging problem to select the perfect IDS locations for hierarchical structure, which includes both tree-based and cluster-based network structures (thematically). Hence, we advise using a combination of mobile agents between layers and static agents in cluster heads.

19.8   CONCLUSIONS AND FUTURE EXPECTATIONS

In this chapter, we considered a dense deployment scenario of WSNs and have proposed an energy-aware routing protocol that ensures data transmission security for the network. According to our design goals, our protocol structures the network in an energy-efficient way; the base station or the intermediate nodes can detect the presence of falsely injected data, and the network is robust enough to node failures. In this work, in case of security, we have mainly considered the delivery of authenticated and encrypted data from the sensors to the base station. To cover various aspects of security in WSN, alongside presenting our protocol, we offered a comprehensive discussion on the features of security that could be considered for such type of network. Also, we offered a discussion on the usage of an intrusion detection system alongside our proposed mechanism to ensure a complete security architecture for an implemented wireless sensor network with maximum security features maintaining the requirement of energy efficiency.

Other security schemes could be built upon our scheme to protect the network from other types of attacks, if any. In fact, there is a lot of scope to extend the work further. As an example, it could be an interesting topic to find out an optimal value of the time interval for periodic restructuring of the network, so that the maximum longevity of the network could be ensured.

AUTHORS' BIOGRAPHIES

Al-Sakib Khan Pathan received a PhD degree in computer engineering in 2009 from Kyung Hee University, South Korea. He received a BSc degree in computer science and information technology from Islamic University of Technology (IUT), Bangladesh, in 2003. He is currently an assistant professor in the Computer Science Department at International Islamic University Malaysia (IIUM), Malaysia. Until June 2010, he served as an assistant professor in the Computer Science and Engineering Department at BRAC University, Bangladesh. Prior to holding this position, he worked as a researcher at Networking Lab, Kyung Hee University, South Korea, until August 2009. His research interests include wireless sensor networks, network security, and e-services technologies. He is a recipient of several awards/best paper awards and has several publications in these areas. He has served as a chair, organizing committee member, and technical program committee member in numerous international conferences/workshops such as HPCS, ICA3PP, IWCMC, VTC, HPCC, IDCS, etc. He is currently serving as the editor-in-chief of *IJIDS*, an area editor of *IJCNIS*, editor of *IJCSE, Inderscience*, associate editor of *IASTED/ACTA Press IJCA and CCS*, guest editor of some special issues of top-ranked journals, and editor/author of nine books. He also serves as a referee of some renowned journals. He is a member of Institute of Electrical and Electronics Engineers (IEEE), USA; IEEE Communications Society, USA; IEEE ComSoc Bangladesh Chapter, and several other international professional organizations.

Tarem Ahmed was born in Dhaka, Bangladesh. He received a bachelor's degree with a double major in physics and economics from Middlebury College, Middlebury, VT, USA, in 1999 and a master's degree in electrical engineering from the University of Pennsylvania, Philadelphia, PA, USA, in 2000. After serving in industry as an ASIC design engineer in the Silicon Valley area of CA, USA, he has held research positions at the Department of Electrical and Computer Engineering at McGill University, Montreal, QC, Canada, and the Computer Engineering and Networks Laboratory at the Swiss Federal Institute of Technology (ETH), Zurich, Switzerland. He is presently affiliated with the department of computer science at the International Islamic University Malaysia, Kuala Lumpur, Malaysia, and the Department of Electrical and Electronic Engineering at BRAC University in his native city of Dhaka, Bangladesh.

REFERENCES

1. Akyildiz, I. F., Su, W., Sankarasubramaniam, Y., and Cayirci, E. Wireless sensor networks: A survey. *Computer Networks*, 38 (2002), 393–422.
2. Dai, S., Jing, X., and Li, L. Research and analysis on routing protocols for wireless sensor networks. In *Proceedings of the ICCCS*, Volume 1 (May 27–30, 2005), pp. 407–411.
3. Karlof, C. and Wagner, D. Secure routing in wireless sensor networks: Attacks and countermeasures. *Ad Hoc Network Journal, SI on Sensor Network Applications and Protocols*, (September 2003), 293–315.
4. Pathan, A.-S. K., Lee, H.-W., and Hong, C. S. Security in wireless sensor networks: Issues and challenges. In *Proc. of IEEE ICACT '06*, Vol. II, Phoenix Park, Korea, (February 20–22, 2006), pp. 1043–1048.
5. Çam, H., Özdemir, S., Muthuavinashiappan, D., and Nair, P. Energy efficient security protocol for wireless sensor networks. In *IEEE 58th VTC 2003 Fall*, 2003, 5 (October 6–9, 2003), pp. 2981–2984.
6. Çam, H., Özdemir, S., Nair, P., Muthuavinashiappan, D., and Sanli, H. O. Energy-efficient secure pattern based data aggregation for wireless sensor networks. *Com. Commun.*, 29, I.4, (2006), 446–455.
7. Ye, F., Luo, H., Lu, S., and Zhang, L. Statistical en-route filtering of injected false data in sensor networks. *IEEE Journal on Selected Areas in Communications*, 23(4), (April 2005), 839–850.
8. Zhu, S., Setia, S., Jajodia, S., and Ning, P. An interleaved hop-by-hop authentication scheme for filtering of injected false data in sensor networks. *Proceedings of S&P*, (2004), 259–271.
9. Lee, H. Y. and Cho, T. H. Key inheritance-based false data filtering scheme in wireless sensor networks. *Lecture Notes in Computer Science, LNCS 4317*, Springer-Verlag, (2006), pp. 116–127.
10. Heinzelman, W. R., Chandrakasan, A., and Balakrishnan, H. Energy-efficient communication protocol for wireless microsensor networks. In *Proc. of the 33rd HICSS* (2000), pp. 3005–3014.
11. Azzedine, B., Xiuzhen, C., and Joseph, L. Energy-aware data-centric routing in microsensor networks. In *Proceedings of the 8th MSWiM 03*, San Diego (2003), pp. 42–49.
12. Hyunh, T. T. and Hong, C. S. An energy* delay efficient multi-hop routing scheme for wireless sensor networks. *IEICE Trans. on Information and Systems*, E89-D(5) (May 2006), pp. 1654–1661.
13. Yin, C., Huang, S., Su, P., and Gao, C. Secure routing for large-scale wireless sensor networks. In *Proceedings of IEEE ICCT 2003*, 2 (April 9–11, 2003), pp. 1282–1286.
14. Xbow Sensor Networks, Available at: http://www.xbow.com/
15. Hass, Z. J. Design methodologies for adaptive and multimedia networks. *IEEE Communications Magazine*, 39(11), (November 2001), pp. 106–107.
16. Heinzelman, W. B., Chandrakasan, A. P., and Balakrishnan, H. An application-specific protocol architecture for wireless microsensor networks. *IEEE Trans. Wire. Commun.*, 1(4) (2002), 660–670.
17. Lamport, L. Constructing digital signatures from one-way function. Tech. report SRI-CSL-98, 1979.
18. The Network Simulator–ns-2, http://www.isi.edu/nsnam/ns/
19. Coppersmith, D. and Jakobsson, M. Almost optimal hash sequence traversal. In *6th International Financial Cryptography 2002*, Bermuda (March 2002).
20. Jakobsson, M. Fractal hash sequence representation and traversal. In *2002 IEEE International Symposium on Information Theory*, Switzerland (July 2002).
21. Sella, Y. On the computation-storage trade-offs of hash chain traversal. In *7th International Financial Cryptography Conference*, Guadeloupe (January 2003).
22. Ee, C. T. and Bajcsy, R. Congestion control and fairness for many-to-one routing in sensor networks. In *Proceedings of ACM SenSys '04*, (2004), pp. 148–161.
23. Pathan, A.-S. K. and Hong, C. S. A secure energy-efficient routing protocol for WSN. In *ISPA 2007, LNCS 4742*, Springer-Verlag (2007), pp. 407–418.
24. Perrig, A., Szewczyk, R., Tygar, J. D., Wen, V., and Culler, D. E. SPINS: Security protocols for sensor networks. *Wireless Networks*, 8 (2002), pp. 521–534.
25. Xu, W., Trappe, W., Zhang, Y., and Wood, T. The feasibility of launching and detecting jamming attacks in wireless networks. In *Proc. 6th ACM Int'l. Symp. Mobile Ad Hoc Networking and Computing (MobiHoc, 05)*, Urbana-Champaign, IL (May 2005).

26. Cagalj, M., Capkun, S., and Hubaux, J.-P. Wormhole-based anti jamming techniques in sensor networks. *IEEE Transactions on Mobile Computing*, 6(1) (2007), 100–114.

27. Chen, H., Han, P., Zhou, X., and Gao, C. Lightweight anomaly intrusion detection in wireless sensor networks, PAISI (2007), *LNCS,* 4430, 105–116.

28. Wang, Q., Zhu, Y., and Cheng, L. Reprogramming wireless sensor networks: Challenges and approaches. *IEEE Network*, (May 2006) 48–55.

29. Pathan, A.-S. K., Lee, H.-W., and Hong, C. S. Security in wireless sensor networks: Issues and challenges. In *Proceedings of the 8th International Conference on Advanced Communication Technology (IEEE ICACT 2006)*, Volume II, February 20–22, Phoenix Park, Korea (2006), 1043–1048.

30. Krontiris, I., Dimitriou, T., Giannetsos, T., and Mpasoukos, M. Intrusion detection of sinkhole attacks in wireless sensor networks. *LNCS*, 4837 (2008), 150–161.

31. Krontiris, I., Dimitriou, T., Giannetsos, T., and Mpasoukos, M. Intrusion detection of sinkhole attacks in wireless sensor networks. In *3rd International Workshop on Algorithmic Aspects of Wireless Sensor Networks (AlgoSensors, 07)*, Wroclaw, Poland (2007).

32. Ngai, E. C. H., Liu, J., and Lyu, M. R. An efficient intruder detection algorithm against sinkhole attacks in wireless sensor networks. *Computer Commun.*, 30 (2007), 2353–2364.

33. Raymond, D. R. and Midkiff, S. F. Denial of service in wireless sensor network: Attacks and defenses. *IEEE Pervasive Computing*, 7(1) (March 2008), 74–81.

34. Kaplantzis, S., Shilton, A., Mani, N., Kaplantzis, Y. A. S., Shilton, A., Mani, N., and Sekercioglu, Y. A. Detecting selective forwarding attacks in wireless sensor networks using support vector machines. In *33rd Conf. of Intelligent Sensors Sensor Networks and Information Processing*, Melbourne, Australia (2007), pp. 335–340.

35. Hai, T. H. and Huh, E. N. Detecting selective forwarding attacks in wireless sensor networks using two-hops neighbor knowledge. In *Proc. of the 2008 Seventh IEEE International Symposium on Network Computing and Applications*, (2008), pp. 325–331.

36. Demirbas, M. and Song, Y. An RSSI-based scheme for Sybil attack detection in wireless sensor networks. In *Proc of IEEE WoWMoM*, (2006), pp. 564–570.

37. Loo, C. E., Ng, M. Y., Leckie, C., and Palaniswami, M. Intrusion detection for routing attacks in sensor networks. *International Journal of Distributed Sensor Networks*, 2(4), (2006), 313–332.

38. Zhou, J., Das, T. K., and Lopez, J. An asynchronous node replication attack in wireless sensor networks. In *Proceedings of the IFIP TC 11 23rd International Information Security Conference*, 278, Boston, Springer (2008), pp. 125–139.

39. Parno, B., Perrig, A., and Gligor, V. Distributed detection of node replication attack in sensor networks. *IEEE S&P* (2005).

40. Wang, Y., Attebury, G., and Ramamurthy, B. A survey of security issues in wireless sensor networks. *IEEE Communications Surveys and Tutorials*, 8(2), 2006.

41. Hamid, M. A., Mamun-Or-Rashid, M., and Hong, C. S. Routing security in sensor network: HELLO flood attack and defense. In *Proc. of IEEE ICNEWS 2006*, Dhaka, Bangladesh (January 2–4, 2006), pp. 77–81.

42. Sharif, W. and Leckie, C. New variants of wormhole attacks for sensor networks. In *Proc. of the Australian Telecommunication Networks and Applications Conference* (2006), pp. 26–30.

43. Hu, C. Y. and Perrig, A. Wormhole attacks in wireless networks. *IEEE Journal on Selected Areas in Communications*, 24(2) (2006), 370–380.

44. Maheshwari, R., Gao, J., and Das, S. R. Detecting wormhole attacks in wireless sensor networks using connectivity information. In *Proc. of INFOCOM* (2007), pp. 107–115.

45. Graaf, R. D., Hegazy, I., Horton, J., and Safavi-Naini, R. Distributed detection of wormhole attacks in wireless sensor networks, Ad Hoc Networks. *LNCS*, 28(1) (2010), 208–223.

46. Newsome, J., Shi, E., Song, D., and Perrig, A. The Sybil attack in sensor networks: Analysis and defense. In *Proc. of ACM IPSN '04* (2004), pp. 259–268.

47. Mukhopadhyay, D. and Saha, I. Location verification based defense against Sybil attack in sensor networks, ICDCN 2006. *LNCS*, 4308 (2006), 509–521.

48. Chen, R. C., Haung, Y. F., and Hsieh, C. F. Ranger intrusion detection system for wireless sensor networks with Sybil attack based on ontology, *AIC '10* (2010).

49. Pathan, A.-S. K. *Security of Self-Organizing Networks: MANET, WSN, WMN, VANET.*, Auerbach Publications, CRC Press (2010).

50. Roman, R., Zhou, J., and Lopez, J. Applying intrusion detection systems to wireless sensor networks. *Consumer Communications and Networking Conference*, 1 (2006), 640–644.

Index

Page numbers followed by f and t indicate figures and tables, respectively.

Milton Keynes UK
Ingram Content Group UK Ltd.
UKHW051929141024
449569UK00027B/1418